A History of Russia
Volume II: since 1855

Walter G. Moss

Department of History and Philosophy
Eastern Michigan University

ronto

McGraw-Hill Higher Education

A Division of The McGraw·Hill Companies

A History of Russia, Volume II since 1855

A History of Russia, Volume II since 1855 by Walter G. Moss. Copyright © 1997 by the McGraw-Hill Companies, Inc. Reprinted with permission of the publisher.

3 4 5 6 7 8 9 0   QSR QSR   0 9 8 7 6 5 4 3

ISBN 0-07-283914-7

Editor: Mike Hemmer
Production Editor: Jennifer Pickel
Printer/Binder: Quebecor World

A History of Russia

Volume II: Since 1855

About the Author

WALTER G. MOSS is a professor at Eastern Michigan University, where he has taught history since 1970. He was born in Cincinnati, where he attended Xavier University. After service as an officer in the U.S. Army, he enrolled at Georgetown University, where he earned his Ph.D. and wrote a dissertation on Vladimir Soloviev's polemics with Russian nationalists. He is the author of articles and numerous book reviews on Russian history, literature, and philosophy. He is also one of four authors of *The Twentieth Century: A Brief Global History*, now being prepared by McGraw-Hill for its 5th edition; co-author of *Growing Old* (Pocket Books, 1975); and the editor of *Humanistic Perspectives on Aging* (University of Michigan Institute of Gerontology, 1976). Between 1978 and 1995, he visited the former Soviet Union and Russia on ten occasions. Professor Moss has received grants from the National Endowment for the Humanities and served as a panelist for its Public Programs Division. He can be reached at His_Moss@Online.emich.edu, or at WWW.mhcollege.com

To Nancy

Contents

Part II
RUSSIA AND THE SOVIET UNION, 1917–1991

8. The 1917 Revolutions

9. Anti-Bolshevism, Civil War, and Allied Intervention

10. The Years of the New Economic Policy, 1921–1927

List of Maps

Preface

The completion of this two-volume text has been made possible by the contributions of numerous people. My former professors at Georgetown University, especially Cyril Toumanoff, Olgerd Sherbowitz-Wetzor, Frank Fadner, and John Songster, helped prepare me to teach Russian history and contributed to my enthusiasm for it. For three decades my students have stimulated my desire to make it more intelligible to them. In numerous trips to the former Soviet Union, I learned much from the many Russians and other Soviet citizens with whom I spoke. My indebtedness to U.S. and other scholars is only hinted at by the many references to them or their works that are scattered throughout this text. More than most works of scholarship, a textbook depends on the primary research of hundreds of others. Among U.S. scholars, special thanks are due to the reviewers of this text, who provided many helpful suggestions and criticisms: Alan Ball, Marquette University; Charles E. Clark, University of Wisconsin-Stevens Point; Patricia Herlihy, Brown University; Hugh D. Hudson, Jr., Georgia State University; Robert E. Jones, University of Massachusetts, Amherst; Richard D. Lewis, St. Cloud State University; Gary Marker, State University of New York at Stony Brook; Thomas S. Noonan, University of Minnesota; and Ted Uldricks, University of North Carolina-Asheville.

At Eastern Michigan University, my colleague Leonas Sabaliunas has been kind enough to read and comment on many of my chapters, and his special concern with Lithuania has stimulated my own interest in nationalities that were once part of the Russian Empire or Soviet Union. Another colleague, James McDonald, has shared his knowledge of Russian geography with me, and David Geherin has furnished assistance on the correct use of the English language; Dick Goff, George Kline, and James Waltz were also helpful in various ways. Ira Wheatley and Margot Duley helped provide three semesters' release from teaching responsibilities so that I could complete this text, and Nancy Snyder and her secretarial staff constantly provided any secretarial assistance I requested. Brandon Laird and Charles Zwinak read many chapters and offered me the perspective of intelligent students of Russian history. Other students who assisted me with bibliographical and other help were Rick Czarnota, Judy Hannah, Andy Rowland, and Julie Thomas.

Among colleagues at other universities, I am grateful to Helen Graves and Paulis Lazda for their support. At McGraw-Hill, Chris Rogers first suggested that I write a Russian history text, and subsequently Niels Aaboe, David Follmer, Pamela Gordon, Leslye Jackson, and Amy Mack provided additional editorial support. David Lindroth produced the maps in the text. Nancy Dyer, Natalia Yamrom, and Elsa Peterson have provided assistance with illustrations and permissions, and Peg Markow and her assistants with copyediting and proofreading.

My greatest debt, I owe to my wife, Nancy. Not only has she shared many trips to Russia with me and put up with the many tribulations of having a spouse work on a text for seven years, but her own interest in Russian women and health care has helped broaden my knowledge of these subjects. Likewise, my understanding of law and architecture has been broadened by the interests of our daughter, Jenny, and our sons, Tom and Dan, in one or another of these subjects.

The spellings of Russian names used in this text are based on the Library of Congress system, though I have made a few alterations in the interest of making Russian names more accessible to U.S. students. I use "i" instead of "ii" for appropriate first name endings (thus Dmitri not Dmitrii), "y" instead of "ii" for appropriate last name endings (Kandinsky not Kandinskii), and "Yu" and "Ya" instead of "Iu" and "Ia" at the beginning of appropriate words (Yuri not Iuri). Familiar names such as Tchaikovsky and Yeltsin are rendered in keeping with the spellings to which we have become accustomed, and the names of émigré writers are generally spelled as they spell them in their Western publications (thus Aksyonov not Aksenov). The spelling of non-Russian individual names or geographical areas while subject to or within the boundaries of Kievan Rus, Muscovy, the Russian Empire, or the USSR are rendered according to their Russian spelling prior to the breakup of the USSR in 1991. Thus, Belorussia and Belorussians, not Belarus and Belarusians until after 1991. When dating internal Russian events that occurred before March 1917, I use the "Old Style" (O.S.) dates of the Julian calendar (by 1917, it was thirteen days behind the Gregorian calendar used in the West). International events, such as the diplomatic developments leading to World War I, are rendered according to the Gregorian calendar.

Walter G. Moss

A Note to Students

This second volume of a two-volume history of Russia deals with modern Russian history, including its Soviet period. This modern era, however, must be seen within the context of a much longer historical development. Therefore, the topics that received special attention in the first volume continue to be emphasized here: (1) the struggle for and against political authority, including autocracy and dictatorship; (2) the expansion and contraction of Russia and its dealings with other nationalities and foreign powers; and (3) the life and culture of the Russian people. In addition, this second volume also stresses topics such as industrial modernization, which are more unique to the modern age.

While keeping these topics in the forefront, this volume (like Volume 1) also reflects the realization of what Marc Raeff has referred to as the "messiness of history." Although we need generalizations to make sense of history, not all important historical facts fit into neat categories.

The history of Russia involves a complex ethnic mosaic. By 1900, after centuries of expansion, the Russian Empire encompassed greater than 100 different nationalities. The story of that expansion—and later contraction—and Russia's dealings with these nationalities is a most important part of Russian history. Throughout both volumes of this text, however, the primary focus is on Russia; it barely touches on any distinct aspects of the social and cultural lives of Ukrainians, Georgians, Armenians, or other nationalities that were once a part of the Russian Empire or Soviet Union. Students desiring to know more about these nationalities and nations should turn to some of the excellent histories about them that are available. (See the section on nationalities and peoples in the General Bibliography at the end of this volume.)

The great Russian novelist Leo Tolstoy once criticized the historian Sergei Soloviev for concentrating too much on just the Russian government and neglecting those who "made the brocades, broadcloth, clothes, and damask cloth which the tsars and nobles flaunted, who trapped the black foxes and sables that were given to ambassadors, who mined the gold and iron, who raised the horses, cattle, and sheep, who constructed the houses, palaces, and churches, and who transported goods." In this history text, such everyday life is not ignored. Special attention is paid to the lives of women, children, and families; the material culture of the people (their food and drink, their health and housing); and their legal and illegal dealings with the state, including their crimes and the punishments they suffered.

CHAPTER 1

Russia: Geography, Peoples, and Premodern Developments

As German troops discovered in late 1941, when fierce winter weather hindered them from taking Moscow, geography affects history. Although Russia's geography helped defeat the forces of Hitler, it has also made life more difficult for Russians than for people located in less harsh lands.

The amount of territory controlled by Russian and Soviet governments has varied considerably throughout Russian history (see Map 1.1), but the enormous size of Russia throughout most of its history has made centralized rule more difficult than in smaller countries. In 1533, after substantial expansion but before moving into Siberia, the Russian government ruled over 2.8 million square kilometers. At the height of the Russian Empire, around 1900, the empire contained eight times as much territory (22.4 million square kilometers). Although the new Soviet government ruled over slightly less land in the period between the two world wars, victory in World War II enabled the USSR to become as large as the Russian Empire had once been. Following the collapse of the USSR at the end of 1991, Russia was left with 17.1 million square kilometers, or 76 percent of the former Soviet Union.

Although smaller than the former USSR, Russia remains the largest country in the world and is about 1.8 times the size of the United States. From east to west, it extends about 10,000 kilometers (more than 6,000 miles) and traverses eleven time zones. From north to south, it spans more than 4,000 kilometers (or about 2,500 miles). Alaska, which once belonged to Russia and today is separated from Siberia only by the narrow Bering Straight, is closer to much of eastern Siberia than is Moscow. Even Seattle is closer to the Russian city of Magadan, which became famous as part of Stalin's labor camp system, than is the Russian capital.

THE LAND: PHYSICAL FEATURES, CLIMATE, AND RESOURCES

Russia can be divided into European and Asiatic Russia, with the Ural Mountains being the dividing line. Although the Russian Empire and the USSR con-

1

Growth of Russia 1533–1900

█████ Russia (Muscovy) in 1533   ▭▭▭ Russian Empire in 1900

Union of Soviet Socialist Republics in 1930

▨▨▨ Russian Empire in 1900   ▭▭▭ Soviet Union in 1930

MAP 1.1A, B

Union of Soviet Socialist Republics in 1950

| Soviet Union in 1930 | Soviet Union in 1950 | ---------- Republic boundaries |

Russia in 1993

——— Boundary of the Soviet Union in 1950   ○ Capitals of U.S.S.R. successor states

MAP 1.1C, D

tained additional Asiatic territories, Asiatic Russia today can be thought of as synonymous with Siberia (this definition of Siberia includes Russia's Far Eastern Provinces, which are sometimes dealt with separately).

European Russia is primarily a large plain, as is western Siberia, which extends from the Urals to the Enisei River. The Urals are not high, reaching only a little over 6,000 feet at their highest point. East of the Enisei River, the Siberian terrain becomes more hilly, and east of the Lena River stretching to the Pacific Ocean are various mountain ranges. Other mountain ranges exist in south-central and eastern Siberia, and the Caucasus Mountains are along Russia's southern border between the Black and Caspian seas.

Russia possesses many large rivers and lakes, and for centuries the waterways provided the best means of transportation. The longest rivers are in Siberia: the Lena, the Irtysh, and the Ob. The Enisei is fifth in size, behind the Volga River, European Russia's (and Europe's) largest river and almost as long as the American Mississippi. Most of the main Siberian rivers flow south to north and empty into the Arctic Ocean. The Irtysh flows through Kazakhstan before entering Siberia and empties into the Ob. The Amur River, which forms part of the Chinese-Russian border before turning northward and entering into the Pacific Ocean, is an exception and flows mainly west to east.

Although not as long as the greatest Siberian rivers, several of Russia's European rivers, such as the Dnieper and Volga, have played a greater historical role. In European Russia, most of the major rivers also flow northward, such as the Northern Dvina and Pechora, or southward, such as the Volga and Don. As in Siberia, many tributaries are located on an east-west axis. Several important rivers have their headwaters southeast of the city of Novgorod in the Valdai Hills. Here in heights of only about 1,000 feet above sea level, lakes and marshes give birth to the Volga, the Western Dvina, and the Dnieper. West of these Valdai Hills, some 50 to 100 miles, are the Lovat and Volkhov Rivers, divided by Lake Ilmen. By way of connecting rivers and portages (and, later in history, canals), the Lovat-Volkhov waterway and the three bigger rivers (the Volga, the Western Dvina, and the Dnieper) have provided water routes between the Baltic and the Black and Caspian seas.

Often, however, Russia was cut off from access to these seas. Its desire to obtain access, especially to the Baltic and Black seas, and then play a larger maritime role became significant in Russian foreign policy. Despite the breakup of the Soviet Union, Russia still has coastline on both seas, although not as much as earlier. The Western Dvina and Dnieper rivers, for example, now empty into sea waters outside Russian borders. Although its vast Arctic and Pacific ocean coastlines (the latter first reached in the seventeenth century) have been less significant in Russia's historical development, they have become more important in recent centuries.

Although lakes are especially numerous in the European northwestern part of the country, the greatest lake (in Russia or the world) in terms of water volume is Siberia's Lake Baikal. Despite being called a "sea," the Caspian, which Russia shares with several other former Soviet republics and Iran, is actually the world's largest lake if measured by surface area.

Russia's extreme northern location, comparable to Alaska's and Canada's,

FIGURE 1.1 Lake Baikal and a small settlement on its western shore.

has combined with other factors to make Russia's climate harsh. Average January temperatures in some parts of northeastern Siberia are between –50°F and –60°F; these areas can also experience hot, but short, summers. Further south and west, temperatures are less extreme, but winters are still long and summers short. Average January temperatures in Novosibirsk hover around 0°F and in Moscow are about +14°F, only about 7°F below Chicago's.

Russia's rainfall pattern is also less than ideal. Precipitation is heaviest in the northwest and diminishes as one moves southeast. In many parts of the country, including the Moscow area, rain tends to be less plentiful in the spring and early summer, when it would most help crops, and instead falls more heavily in the late summer. Taken together, Russia's northern location and unfavorable rainfall patterns have adversely affected Russian agriculture, which, in turn, has affected many other aspects of Russian life from the people's diet to state revenues.

Not counting transitional areas, Russia can be divided into four main vegetation zones: From north to south, they are the tundra, taiga, mixed forest, and steppe (see Map 1.2). The tundra region is a treeless one where much of the ground beneath the surface remains permanently frozen year-round. Permafrost also extends south into much of the taiga forest zone. This is an area primarily of coniferous trees such as the pine. Next comes the smaller mixed forest belt of both coniferous and leaf-bearing trees. This area is much more densely populated than the taiga and contains many of Russia's larger cities including Moscow. Taken together, Russia's two forest areas equal almost one-quarter of the world's total forest lands. South of the mixed forest is a steppe or

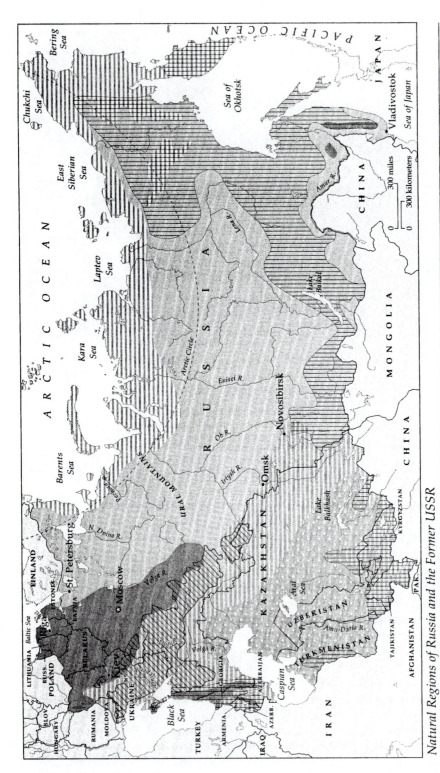

Natural Regions of Russia and the Former USSR

MAP 1.2

	Tundra		Mixed forest		Steppe		Desert		Mountain regions		Black Earth region

6

prairie zone that originally contained few trees. In pre-Russian and early Russian history, the steppe was a dangerous area from which numerous nomadic groups, including the Mongols, threatened the Slavic peoples residing in the northern forest areas.

A Central Asian desert zone that existed in the Soviet Union and the Russian Empire at its height is no longer under Russian control.

Russia's most fertile soils lie in a black-earth belt that can be found in the transitional area between the mixed forest and steppe and in the steppe itself. Because the transitional area receives more rain during appropriate times, it is the more productive agricultural area.

Further north, the soils of the mixed forest zone are not as favorable but have been farmed throughout much of Russian history. In early Russian history, peasants used the "slash-and-burn" technique of clearing lands by cutting trees and burning the stumps (the ashes making good fertilizer) before farming.

Although nature has been rather harsh to Russia in some regards, it has been generous in other areas. Besides its great timber resources, it has possessed abundant wildlife, including many valuable fur-bearing animals. It is a world leader in the possession of mineral resources, including mineral fuels. Among its abundant resources are coal, petroleum, natural gas, iron and iron alloys, copper, diamonds, gold, silver, lead, zinc, mercury, asbestos, potassium, magnesium, salt deposits, phosphate ores, sulfur, and limestone. Aluminum is about the only major mineral resource that Russia lacks. Of course, large quantities of many of these materials are in areas of Russia, especially Siberia, that have not always been part of the Russian state, and harsh climactic conditions have often made extraction costly and difficult.

GEOGRAPHY'S IMPACT ON COLONIZATION AND NATIONAL IDENTITY

The great Russian historian Vasili Kliuchevsky (1841–1911) believed that the history of his country was one of colonization, and there is little doubt that Russia's geographic conditions helped stimulate its colonization and expansion. Among other reasons, the Russians expanded to acquire better agricultural lands, Siberian furs, and access to warm-water ports.

This colonization was also encouraged by few natural barriers; an excellent artery of rivers; and fluid, poorly defined frontiers. Such porous frontiers could be a danger and a source of contention as well as an opportunity. They contributed to the heavy emphasis on the military throughout most of Russian history. Russia today, like the USSR before it, borders on more nations than any other country in the world.

Colonization led to the absorption of many non-Russian peoples and the creation of a multinational empire. Ruling over so many non-Russians affected both Russian domestic and foreign policies. The difficulties of ruling over so many differing peoples helped lead to the collapse of the USSR in 1991.

The Eurasian location of Russia—part European, part Asian—has been another geographic feature that has had a significant impact on Russian history and culture. During the nineteenth century, Russian Slavophiles and Westernizers debated whether Russia was culturally part of Europe or not. Later on, the émigrés from the Russian Empire who founded "Eurasianism" in 1920 emphasized the importance of a Eurasian location. Just a few years earlier, the great Russian poet Alexander Blok had foreshadowed their doctrine in his poem "The Scythians." There he depicted Russians as between Europe and Asia, but also wrote: "Yes, we are Scythians! Yes, we are Asians."

Today, in the confusion following the collapse of the Soviet Union, Russians are once again vigorously debating their national identity and relationship to the West.

THE PEOPLES

The Russians (or Great Russians) are part of the large number of Slavic peoples who reside from the Adriatic Sea to the Russian Far East. By the thirteenth century, the Russians had emerged as a distinct ethnic group as a result of East Slavs in the north of Russia intermingling with Finnish peoples of the area.

Some Finnish tribes, however, such as the Komi, the Mordva, and the Mari, although subject to various pressures throughout Russian history, maintained their separate identities. (Komi, Mari, and Mordovian Autonomous Republics exist in present-day Russia, although the native peoples are outnumbered in each by Great Russians.)

As the Russian state expanded in medieval and modern times, more than 100 other nationalities were brought under Russian control. Among them were the peoples of modern-day Ukraine and Belarus, Siberia, part of the Baltic area, the Caucasus, and Central Asia. In the Russian Empire's census of 1897 (which excluded Finland), those who listed their native language as Russian composed only 44.3 percent of the population. Using language as a rough guide to ethnicity, Ukrainians made up 17.8 percent, Poles 6.3 percent, and Belorussians 4.7 percent. Among the non-Slavic population, the many Turkic peoples, primarily in Central Asia and the Caucasus, together composed 10.8 percent. Jews were 4 percent, and other nationalities (including Armenians, Georgians, Latvians, Lithuanians, and Finnish peoples) each composed a smaller percentage.

At the time of the breakup of the Soviet Union in December 1991, the Russians were just a bare majority in the USSR. In the new post-Soviet Russia, however, the Great Russians in 1992 made up more than 80 percent of the total population of almost 150 million people. Although Tatars and Ukrainians were the only other nationalities possessing more than 1 percent of the total, more than 100 national groups still existed within Russian borders. Conversely, the 25 million Russians residing in other former Soviet republics almost equaled the number of non-Russians still inside Russian borders.

ANCIENT RUS TO 1855: A SUMMARY OF MAJOR HISTORICAL DEVELOPMENTS

By 1853, when the Crimean War began, Russia was recognized as one of Europe's major powers. Yet, as the Crimean War made clear, Russia had not pro-

FIGURE 1.2. Peoples of the Russian Empire from an early nineteenth-century engraving.
(From Robert Wallace and the Editors of Time-Life Books, Rise of Russia. *Time Inc., New York, 1967, p. 132.)*

gressed industrially in the preceding half-century as rapidly as some of its chief rivals, especially Great Britain. Although easily more than sixty times the size of the British Isles, the Russian Empire in 1855 possessed only about two and a half times the population, and about five Russian babies died in infancy for every three in Britain. Although half of the British people were already living in urban districts, and more than half of them could read and write, nine out of ten Russian subjects still lived in rural areas, and nineteen out of twenty were illiterate. The backward nature of Russian agriculture, along with its climate and growing conditions, meant that it took the work of about three peasants just to produce what one Englishman could. Despite Russia's much greater size, its railway tracks covered only about one-tenth the distance of British ones, and its production of such a vital modern industrial resource as pig iron suffered even more in comparison.

Russia also suffered from less tangible drawbacks. For example, the state discouraged social initiative, and Russia lacked a civil society—that is, a social sphere standing between the government and the family or individual, in which people can freely interact and create their own independent organizations. Partly because of state dominance, Russian commercial and civil law was poorly developed. The most characteristic features of the Russian Empire in 1855 were autocracy,[1] serfdom, and the many nationalities Russian expansion had brought into the empire.

No one knows for sure when the East Slavs first moved into the European lands they dominate today. The closeness of various Slavic languages has led some historians to suggest a common homeland for all Slavs—north of the Carpathian Mountains—and then a split, by the seventh century A.D., into Southern, Western, and Eastern Slavic groups. From the Eastern Slavs would eventually emerge the Russians, Ukrainians, and Belorussians.

For thousands of years before the appearance of the Eastern Slavs, a series of nomadic steppe peoples had roamed across areas of modern southern Russia as well as Ukraine. Most of them were Asiatic, including the Cimmerians, Scythians, Huns, Avars, Türks, Bulgars, and Khazars. Some, such as the Khazars, eventually became more settled. By the ninth century A.D., the Khazars had established a great trading and tribute-collecting network radiating out from their capital on the lower Volga River and including some of the East Slavic tribes.

Kievan Rus (860–1240)

In Kievan Rus, Great Russians as well as Ukrainians and Belorussians were not yet a distinct nationality. The Rus chronicles divide the East Slavs only by tribes, about a dozen of them at the dawn of Kievan Rus. Thus, along with Ukrainians and Belorussians, the Russians share a common early history.

Before the extensive Slavic colonization of northern Rus, a process that continued throughout the Kievan Rus period, the area was settled primarily by Finno-Ugric peoples. By the mid-ninth century, another group was present in future Rus territories—Scandinavian Vikings similar to those who burst upon other parts of Europe in this era. The name *Rus* appears to have been first applied to these Vikings (or Varangians) before finally being used in its wider sense. Like many southern steppe peoples, these "nomads of the sea" were raiders and traders. They eventually played an important role in organizing the multiethnic trading and tribute-gathering elite that founded and furnished the political leadership for Kievan Rus.

This leadership, although headed by a single Riurikid dynasty (Riurik being its legendary founder), was never able to achieve the degree of political power later realized by grand princes and tsars in Muscovite Russia. In Kievan Rus, political authority was much more divided and fragmented: There were about a dozen principalities, and in them were noble and town councils which to varying degrees shared powers with the ruling prince of each principality.

Just as no autocracy existed in Kievan Rus, another characteristic of late Muscovite Russia did not exist—serfdom. In Kievan Rus, peasants were freer, not yet enserfed by noble masters. Yet, as the period went on, princes rewarded more

---

[1]There has been some scholarly controversy as to whether the word "autocracy" is the best translation of the Russian *samoderzhavie*. Yet, if we take it to mean the *legally* unlimited authority of a ruler, it still remains the best word to describe the Russian tsarist system, at least before 1906. Of course, from a practical standpoint, any ruler, whether a tsar or dictator, could rule only with the help of others, whether they be called a ruling elite or some other name.

and more of their followers with lands, including some that peasant groups had formerly considered their own. From the beginning of the tribute-collecting Riurikid dynasty, the Riurikids and the elite who supported them exploited the common people, thus beginning a long tradition of state and elite exploitation.

Another characteristic of Kievan Rus was its thriving urban life. Close to 300 towns existed in it, and Kiev was one of the largest cities in Eastern Europe.

At the end of the tenth century, Kievan Rus's Prince Vladimir mandated Christianity for the Rus. It offered the promise of giving greater cultural unity to a diverse group of peoples. Although it faced considerable resistance and gained ground only slowly in the countryside, it quickly began to transform urban life and urban culture. It would become the first of several important cultural changes in Rus-Russian history that a governing urban elite would attempt to impose on its mostly rural subjects.

Christianity and the Byzantine and South Slavic influences that accompanied it played the central role in stimulating the creation of a Rus high culture, which produced literary and artistic works of considerable merit.

Leading churchmen attempted to further the Christian unity of Kievan Rus, but during the twelfth and early thirteenth century, they witnessed increasing centrifugal tendencies. Princes and principalities warred against each other, and new centers arose to challenge Kiev's leadership. Three of these were the principalities of Vladimir-Suzdal in the northeast; Volhynia-Galicia in the southwest; and Novgorod, where the prince's powers were strictly limited, in the north. At the same time, local princes were increasingly subdividing their principalities among their sons, who often engaged in fratricidal conflicts with one another and refused to unite against foreign foes. Thus, by late 1237, when the Asiatic Mongols (or Tatars) began their onslaught on Kievan Rus, its disintegration was already well underway.

Before the Mongol invasion, the Rus battled and made treaties with various states and peoples. Conflicts were frequent, partly because of poorly defined boundaries. Among the most prominent of Rus neighbors were the Byzantine Empire, the Poles, the Bulgars of Bulgaria and the Volga, and several nomadic warrior peoples of the southern steppe or prairie. The Mongols were the last of the steppe peoples to confront Kievan Rus, and by 1240 their fierce attacks brought an end to it.

Mongols and the Rise of Moscow (1240–1533)

For more than a century after the Mongol invasion, the Mongols remained overlords over most of the old Rus territories. Within decades after the Mongols' sweeping victories, however, the Lithuanians began chipping away at their westernmost Rus conquests and adding them to their own. By 1380, Lithuania and Poland had already annexed most of the Belorussian and Ukrainian parts of old Rus. In that same year, the Muscovite prince Dmitri Donskoi won an important victory over the Mongols. Although Mongol control was not completely overthrown for another century, Dmitri's victory symbolized both the beginning of the erosion of Mongol subjugation and the rise of Moscow and the Russians (Great Russians).

Before the Muscovite state could completely throw off the Mongol yoke and form a united and independent Russia, it had to overcome the divisive legacy of princely conflicts and defeat such rivals as Tver and the Republic of Novgorod. Princely discord stemmed in part from the problems of political succession. Both before and after the Mongol conquest, princely holdings had been getting smaller as princes divided up their lands among their sons. With time and smaller landholdings, distinctions between being a private land-holder and a public ruler began to disappear. So prominent did this tendency become that some historians have called the period from the late Kievan era to the late fifteenth–early sixteenth century "the appanage period"—appanage designating one of these many princely landholdings.

By the ascension of the infant Ivan IV in 1533, Moscow had already over-come most of the Russian divisiveness fostered by the princes' subdividing of their lands. Even by 1450, the grand prince of Moscow ruled over some 430,000 square kilometers; by 1533, after annexing Tver and the vast Novgorodian lands, Moscow controlled 2.8 million square kilometers, or about five times the size of modern France. Most instrumental in this expansion was the Muscovite ruler Ivan III (the Great), who ruled from 1462 to 1505.

Not only had the Muscovite princes united the Russians by 1533, but also they had begun to snip away at Polish-Lithuanian holdings in Ukraine and Belorussia.

By 1533, Moscow symbolized a new political center as well as a new Russian civilization. Although Moscow's ruling elite remained just as concerned with economic gain as the Rus elite had been—perhaps even more so—Muscovy was more rural, more authoritarian, more centralized, and more hierarchical than Kievan Rus had been. Its peasants and townspeople were less free. Part of this was the price Muscovy had to pay to possess a military strong enough to deal with its enemies and expand at the rate it did. Its culture was primarily shaped by Orthodox religious beliefs, which now permeated deeper into the Russian countryside and soul. By holding itself up as the guardian of these beliefs, the Muscovite government strengthened its own control over the country.

Muscovy and Its Expansion (1533–1689)

In 1547, Ivan IV (the Terrible) was the first Muscovite ruler to be crowned tsar (from the Latin *Caesar*, meaning emperor) and eventually became a tyrant. He also stressed that he was an autocrat, by which he meant a ruler whose powers were unlimited. From 1547 until Peter the Great overthrew his half-sister Sophia in 1689, Muscovite autocracy had many ups and downs but ended up stronger.

Ivan the Terrible's policies weakened Russia and helped lead to a period of great chaos, the Time of Troubles (1598–1613), in which for a while no tsar ruled. In 1613, a *zemskii sobor* (land council) established Mikhail Romanov on the throne, thus beginning the Romanov dynasty's rule of more than three centuries. Although the *zemskii sobor* continued in existence, as the century progressed it was summoned together less frequently, and by 1689 this consultative body had ceased to exist.

No other institution or group willing and able to resist actively and successfully Muscovite autocracy existed. For their own reasons, the ruling elite supported the autocratic system: Although it left tsarist authority legally unchecked, the system provided the elite with administrative and military positions and enabled them to share in the fruits of power. The Orthodox Church, which also helped strengthen Muscovite autocracy, suffered a major schism in 1666–1667. This split deprived Orthodoxy of many of its most ardent former believers and helped prevent it from successfully resisting further tsarist demands upon it.

Although the government's ambitions often exceeded its still limited capacities, state and elite control over the common people increased during this period. One reason for the landowners' acceptance of autocracy was the tsar's willingness to prevent peasants from ever leaving their masters' service. This restriction was finalized by the 1649 Law Code, and it thereby completed the enserfment of the Muscovite peasantry.

By 1689, commoners were overwhelmingly serfs, and their goals and desires were often far different than those of the government. Although the peasants resisted serfdom by flight and other methods and sometimes broke into open rebellion, they envisioned no real alternative to the autocratic order, only petitions to the tsar or a mixture of tsarist pretenders and anarchy. In 1670–1671, the colorful pretender Cossack Stenka Razin and his followers—Cossacks, peasants, non-Russian tribesman, and other malcontents—stormed up the Volga, taking one town after another. More disciplined and better armed government troops, however, soon ended the rebellion and the lives of many rebels, including Razin.

Although autocracy was strengthened, serfdom finalized, and state power increased, Muscovy's territorial expansion was even more striking. By 1689, Russia was five to six times as large as in 1533 and had reached the Pacific Ocean and acquired Kiev and Polish Ukrainian territory east of the Dnieper. Thus, in 160 years, it *added* territory slightly larger than the present fifty United States and Mexico combined.

The achievement of such expansion as well as the defense of Russia's ill-defined borders required substantial military forces and expenditures. Much of the preoccupation of the government was over economic and military needs, which, in turn, had a major impact on molding a hierarchical social order that was bequeathed to future generations.

The government's needs, plus the seeking and then gaining of Ukrainian territory during the reign of Alexis (1645–1676), helped to foster Western and other outside influences in Muscovy. But these new influences conflicted with the old belief that Moscow was the true center of the Christian world, and this conflict helped bring about the church schism of 1666–1667.

Early Imperial Russian (1689–1855)

This era begins with the rule of Peter I (the Great), who, before his death in 1725, had Russia declared an empire and himself an emperor. He also traveled to Western Europe, forced some westernizing ways upon his people, and established a new capital, the more westernized St. Petersburg.

During this period, autocracy and serfdom continued to flourish. Following the example of Peter the Great, his successors generally presented themselves as "reforming tsars" desiring to rule Russia in an enlightened manner. Their reforms, however, were not intended to weaken autocracy; rather they were to be manifestations of an enlightened absolutism that would strengthen Russia. The period's last tsar-emperor, Nicholas I, staunchly defended autocracy as one of Russia's main pillars.

To help them rule, Russia's emperors depended on the nobility. One of the era's greatest rulers, Catherine II (the Great), issued a Charter of the Nobility in 1785, enhancing the nobles' privileged status. Earlier, Peter the Great had attempted to broaden access to the nobility so that talented nonnobles could more easily obtain noble status. But throughout most of this period, as earlier, a small number of aristocratic clans dominated Russia's ruling class. During the early nineteenth century, however, growing state needs for talented military and civilian personnel steadily increased the influence of those outside the aristocratic families.

By 1855, the nobility made up about 1.5 percent of the population and had become more diverse than ever. Many of them were non-Russians, and most nobles had never been wealthy. By midcentury, a significant minority of high-ranking noble bureaucrats were not gentry[2] serfowners and did not especially identify with their fellow nobles who owned estates worked by serf labor.

Although tsarist powers remained legally unlimited throughout this period, there were practical limits. The Russian Empire was simply too large and the number of faithful government officials too small for tsarist decrees ever to be complied with to the extent the rulers desired. In Russia's provincial towns and villages, the everyday lives of nobles, townspeople, and peasants were determined more by tradition and inertia than by any new laws.

Furthermore, tsars who overstepped the bounds of what the noble elite considered legitimate autocratic behavior could be overthrown, as both Peter III, husband of Catherine the Great, and her son Paul tragically discovered. To prevent such coups, most tsars remained mindful of noble interests. Such concern helps explain why no tsar of the era attempted to dismantle serfdom.

Despite opposition to specific tsarist policies and another great rebellion along the Volga (the Pugachev rebellion of 1773–1774), the only notable challenges to the autocratic concept itself were a feeble aristocratic effort in 1730 and a failed conspiracy of 1825. Other opposition to autocracy was limited to the isolated voices of a small number of intellectuals, beginning in the late eighteenth century.

As autocracy and serfdom continued, so too did Russian expansion. Peter the Great gained Baltic lands, including most of modern-day Estonia and Latvia, and made Russia a Baltic power. His successors, especially Catherine the Great (1762–1796) and her grandson Alexander I (1801–1825), added many new territories. By 1855, the empire included Finland in the north; most of the Caucasus in the south; and Lithuania, Belorussia, Bessarabia, and most of Poland and Ukraine in the west. Further east, Russia expanded into Kazakhstan and in the northeast onto the North American continent.

The government gradually integrated its outlying regions more firmly with its Russian center. Catherine the Great centralized primarily because of her con-

[2]The term *gentry* is used in the text as a synonym for the landowning nobility.

cern for orderliness and efficiency. Nicholas I shared such concerns. By his time, however, nationalism had become a greater force, and his emphasis on Russian nationalism and Russian Orthodoxy helped fuel his centralizing policies.

Many of Russia's territorial gains resulted from wars. Peter the Great was almost constantly at war, Catherine the Great fought two wars against the Ottoman Turks, Alexander I withstood and defeated the great Napoleonic challenge, and Nicholas I died in the midst of the Crimean War. Unfortunately for Nicholas and his successor, Alexander II, this war was less successful than most earlier ones: Russia lost not only a half-million lives, but by the Treaty of Paris in 1856, it recognized the loss of southern Bessarabia (to Moldavia) and gave up the right to have warships in the Black Sea.

During the Early Imperial Period, Western influences became much stronger in Russia, but also helped produce a nationalistic reaction. While not abandoning a selective use of Western symbols and methods, Nicholas I reflected the age of nationalism in which he lived by placing more emphasis on Russian traditions. During his reign, a group of intellectuals known as Slavophiles criticized Peter the Great for his westernizing policies and for creating a cultural gap between a small westernized elite and the Russian masses, who remained committed to Russian traditions. The Slavophiles were answered by another group labeled the Westernizers, who defended Peter's westernizing ways and criticized traditional Russia, including its Orthodox-based culture. By the early 1840s, the two sides were waging a full-scale debate over Russia's relationship to the West.

Legacies of the Past: Russia on the Eve of the Modern Age

By 1855, Russia was still an autocracy, and five of every six inhabitants in European Russia (excluding the Kingdom of Poland and the Grand Duchy of Finland) were still peasants. Among these peasants, almost half of them were serfs, with most of the others being state peasants who had no noble master over them.

Although there were legal, cultural, and ethnic differences between Russian serfdom and U.S. slavery, serf and slave conditions were similar in many ways. In practice, Russian serfowners could treat their serfs almost as they wished, with serfs having no legal recourse to defend themselves. For them, the noble master was the law.

Most serfs farmed portions of their owner's land. In exchange for the right to farm some estate strips for themselves, serfs paid their landowners in primarily one of two ways, *barshchina* (obligatory work) or *obrok* (payment). By the late eighteenth century, three days work for the master on land from which he received the produce was the general *barshchina* practice, but landowners sometimes demanded more labor, leaving serfs little time to farm the strips they were allotted for their own use.

By 1855, most serfs and other peasants, especially in the Great Russian portion of the empire, worked in repartitional communes that periodically redistributed strips of land in different fields to each peasant household. On noble estates, these strips were the legal property of the estate owner, who allowed the commune to allocate them in exchange for *barshchina* or *obrok*. Serf-owners or their stewards generally dealt with the communes and not with individual serfs, and the heads of households in a commune elected their own communal officials. How many strips were assigned to each household depended on various criteria, for example, a household's size, its labor strength, or its number of men. However it was done, peasants generally did not farm consolidated plots but harvested their crops from scattered strips.

In addition to the commune, the village was central to peasant life. Villages varied in size from a few households to many hundreds. Larger villages usually had a church of their own, plus other buildings such as a tavern. Each village was most often represented by a single commune, but one commune sometimes represented more than one village or just a portion of one, with one or more other communes representing the other villagers.

One curious aspect of the *obrok* system was that it enabled serfs, if they obtained their master's permission, to leave his estate and work somewhere else—as long as they kept sending back *obrok* money. This explains the high percentage of *obrok*-paying serfs in many Russian cities. Besides serfs under *barshchina* or *obrok*, there was still another category—house serfs, serving in such positions as butlers, carpenters, cooks, nannies, seamstresses, scribes, shepherds, and stablemen.

Although autocracy and serfdom were characteristic of the Russian Empire as a whole, the country's vast expanses and multinational character allowed for some exceptions. In Siberia, for example, serfdom was all but nonexistent; after gaining Finland and new Polish lands, Alexander I forbade the extension of serfdom to them and granted them more political autonomy than the rest of the empire. A Polish revolt of 1830, however, led Nicholas I to curtail Polish autonomy.

Along with autocracy and Orthodoxy, nationality was a third key word in the ideology of Nicholas I and his supporters. It meant an emphasis on the Russian nationality, most of whose members were Orthodox believers. The problem of ruling a multinational empire in an age of rising ethnic nationalism was a legacy inherited by Nicholas's successors.

One reason for linking autocracy, Orthodoxy, and the Russian nationality was that they were supposed to reinforce each other and the stability of the tsarist system and patriarchal social order. In such an order, women and children had few rights, and the law discriminated between social estates, especially favoring the nobility.

The government recognized the need for moral persuasion to convince the masses to accept tsarist authority and social inequalities. The more that religious beliefs and other values could hold the empire and society together, the less it would be necessary to resort to force. But whether an ideology stressing autocracy, Orthodoxy, and the Russian nationality helped or hindered bringing the empire's many peoples together is another question.

Thus, as the Russian Empire stood on the threshold of the modern age, it brought with it its legacies from the past—a multinational, autocratic, patriarchal system, characterized by serfdom, the lack of a civil society, and a history of elite exploitation of the common people. Justifying this system was an ideology that seemed poorly prepared to meet the challenges ahead.

Yet within the country, there was also great potential. Its vast size and resources, along with the abilities of its many peoples, held out the promise of better days ahead. So too did some enlightened bureaucrats; for despite Nicholas I's generally conservative policies, he had furthered the careers of a small number of them. After the Crimean defeat, they were eager to help Russia meet the challenges of the modern era.

SUGGESTED SOURCES

Geography and Peoples*

BATER, JAMES H. *The Soviet Scene: A Geographical Perspective*. London, 1989.

BATER, JAMES H., and R. A. FRENCH, eds. *Studies in Russian Historical Geography*. 2 vols. London, 1983.

CHANNON, JOHN, with ROBERT HUDSON. *The Penguin Historical Atlas of Russia*. New York, 1995.

COLE, J. P. *Geography of the Soviet Union*. London, 1984.

FORSYTH, JAMES. *A History of the Peoples of Siberia: Russia's North Asian Colony, 1581–1990*. Cambridge, England, 1992.

GILBERT, MARTIN. *Atlas of Russian History*. 2d ed. New York, 1993.

KAISER, ROBERT J. *The Geography of Nationalism in Russia and the USSR*. Princeton, 1994.

KOZLOV, VIKTOR. *The Peoples of the Soviet Union*. Bloomington, 1988.

LYDOLPH, PAUL E. *Geography of the USSR*. 5th ed. Elkhart Lake, Wis., 1990.

NAHAYLO, BOHDAN, and VICTOR SWOBODA. *Soviet Disunion: A History of the Nationalities Problem in the USSR*. New York, 1990.

PARKER, W. H. *An Historical Geography of Russia*. Chicago, 1969.

SMITH, GRAHAM, ed. *The Nationalities Question in the Soviet Union*. London, 1990.

WIECZYNSKI, JOSEPH L. *The Russian Frontier: The Impact of Borderlands Upon the Course of Early Russian History*. Charlottesville, 1976.

WIXMAN, RONALD. *The Peoples of the USSR: An Ethnographic Handbook*. Armonk, N.Y., 1984.

History to 1855

BALZER, MARJORIE MANDELSTAM, ed. *Russian Traditional Culture: Religion, Gender, and Customary Law*. Armonk, N.Y., 1992.

BILLINGTON, JAMES H. *The Icon and the Axe: An Interpretive History of Russian Culture*. New York, 1970.

BLACKWELL, WILLIAM L. *The Beginnings of Russian Industrialization, 1800–1860*. Princeton, 1968.

BLUM, JEROME. *Lord and Peasant in Russia, from the Ninth to the Nineteenth Century*. Princeton, 1961.

BRUMFIELD, WILLIAM. *A History of Russian Architecture*. Cambridge, England, 1993.

CHERNIAVSKY, MICHAEL. *Tsar and People: Studies in Russian Myths*. New York, 1969.

CLEMENTS, BARBARA EVANS, BARBARA ALPERN ENGEL, and CHRISTINE D. WOROBEC, eds. *Russia's Women: Accommodation, Resistance, Transformation*. Berkeley, 1991.

CRUMMEY, ROBERT O. *The Formation of Muscovy, 1304–1613*. London, 1987.

*See also the General Bibliography at the back of the text for works dealing with specific non-Russian peoples.

DUKES, PAUL. *The Making of Russian Absolutism, 1613–1801.* 2d ed. London, 1990.

FENNELL, JOHN. *The Crisis of Medieval Russia, 1200–1304.* London, 1983.

HALPERIN, CHARLES J. *Russia and the Golden Horde: The Mongol Impact on Medieval Russian History.* Bloomington, 1985.

HELLIE, RICHARD. *Slavery in Russia, 1450–1725.* Chicago, 1982.

KAISER, DANIEL H., and GARY MARKER, eds. *Reinterpreting Russian History: Readings, 860–1860s.* New York, 1994.

KLYUCHEVSKY (KLIUCHEVSKY), V. O. *Course of Russian History.* 5 vols. New York, 1960.

KOLCHIN, PETER. *Unfree Labor: American Slavery and Russian Serfdom.* Cambridge, Mass., 1987.

KOLLMANN, NANCY SHIELDS. *Kinship and Politics: The Making of the Muscovite Political System, 1345–1547.* Stanford, 1987.

LEDONNE, JOHN P. *Absolutism and Ruling Class: The Formation of the Russian Political Order, 1700–1825.* New York, 1991.

LINCOLN, W. BRUCE. *The Conquest of a Continent: Siberia and the Russians.* New York, 1994.

———. *In the Vanguard of Reform: Russia's Enlightened Bureaucrats. 1825–1861.* DeKalb, Ill., 1982.

———. *The Romanovs: Autocrats of All the Russias.* New York, 1981.

MOSS, WALTER G. *A History of Russia: To 1917.* Vol. I. New York, 1997.

PASZKIEWICZ, HENRYK. *The Making of the Russian Nation.* Chicago, 1963.

PIPES, RICHARD. *Russia under the Old Regime.* New York, 1974.

PRITSAK, OMELJAN. *The Origin of Rus'.* Cambridge, Mass., 1981.

RAEFF, MARC. *Understanding Imperial Russia: State and Society in the Old Regime.* New York, 1984.

RAGSDALE, HUGH, ed. *Imperial Russian Foreign Policy.* Cambridge, England, 1993.

RANSEL, DAVID L., ed. *The Family in Imperial Russia: New Lines of Historical Research.* Urbana, Ill., 1978.

RIASANOVSKY, NICHOLAS V. *A Parting of Ways: Government and the Educated Public in Russia, 1801–1855.* Oxford, 1976.

———. *Russia and the West in the Teaching of the Slavophiles: A Study of Romantic Ideology.* Gloucester, Mass., 1965.

RIEBER, ALFRED J. "Persistent Factors in Russian Foreign Policy." In *Imperial Russian Foreign Policy,* ed. Hugh Ragsdale. Cambridge, England, 1993 (offers some good insights on geography's impact on foreign policy).

RYWKIN, MICHAEL, ed. *Russian Colonial Expansion to 1917.* London, 1988.

SAUNDERS, DAVID. *Russia in the Age of Reaction and Reform, 1801–1881.* London, 1992.

SAWYER, P. H. *The Age of the Vikings.* London, 1962.

SMITH, R. E. F., and DAVID CHRISTIAN. *Bread and Salt: A Social and Economic History of Food and Drink in Russia.* Cambridge, England, 1984.

SUBTELNY, OREST. *Ukraine: A History.* 2d ed. Toronto, 1994.

TERRAS, VICTOR, ed. *Handbook of Russian Literature.* New Haven, 1985.

TREADGOLD, DONALD W. *The West in Russia and China.* Boulder, 1985.

VERNADSKY, GEORGE, and MICHAEL KARPOVICH. *A History of Russia.* 5 vols. New Haven, 1943–1968. (Goes up to 1682.)

WARE, TIMOTHY. *The Orthodox Church.* New ed. London, 1993.

WIECZYNSKI, JOSEPH L., ed. *The Modern Encyclopedia of Russian and Soviet History.* 58 vols. to date. Gulf Breeze, FL, 1976–. A source of great value.

WORTMAN, RICHARD. *Scenarios of Power: Myth and Ceremony in Russian Monarchy.* Vol. I: *From Peter the Great to the Death of Nicholas I.* Princeton, 1995.

YANOV, ALEXANDER. *The Origins of Autocracy: Ivan the Terrible in Russian History.* Berkeley, 1981.

PART ONE

Late Imperial Russia, 1855–1917

Late Imperial Russia calls to mind the tsarist symbol, the two-headed eagle, for like it, Russia in this era looked in two different directions. One face stared backward toward the old autocratic and patriarchal order, and the other peered forward into a future whose exact outlines could not be discerned.

The period began and ended with Russia at war—first the Crimean War and later World War I. The Crimean

The tsarist symbol, the two-headed eagle, over the St. Peter's Gate, Sts. Peter and Paul Fortress, St. Petersburg.

19

defeat forced the tsarist government to look forward and accelerate economic modernization, for if it did not, it would eventually cease to be a Great Power. This realization helped spur the Great Reforms of Alexander II's reign (1855–1881), the most important of which was the emancipation of the serfs in 1861. It also spurred an acceleration of railway building and manufacturing. Other signs of modernization were significant increases in the number of industrial workers and professionals and in urbanization, life expectancy, and literacy.

Yet, if one face of tsarist policy looked forward, another looked nostalgically backward. The era was not only one of reforms, but also of counterreforms. The policies of the last two Russian emperors reflected an ideology similar to that of Alexander II's father, Nicholas I, with its emphasis on Orthodoxy, autocracy, and the Russian nationality. Like Nicholas I, the last two Romanov rulers as well as the reforming Alexander II hoped to maintain autocracy. All three of Nicholas I's successors felt uncomfortable dealing with the new elements strengthened by modernization, for example, the growing cities, industrial workers, professionals, and proliferating private organizations.

Nicholas II especially liked to think of himself as following in the old-fashioned tsarist tradition—his favorite tsar was the Muscovite ruler Alexei (father of Peter the Great). In his own mind, he was the tsar-*batiushka* (the affectionate father) of the peasant masses. Although he believed in the myth of the benevolent tsar and (like his predecessors) relied

upon ceremonies, symbols, and the Russian Orthodox Church to reinforce it and his God-ordained right to rule over his people, the myth itself was losing its hold over the masses. In this disintegrating process, events during 1905 and World War I were especially important.

Another element of traditional Russia, the nobility, became more diverse during this era. A decreasing percentage remained agricultural landowners. The majority of nobles lived by other means, such as government service, business activities, or professional occupations. Some, such as Vladimir Lenin, whose father had earned hereditary noble status, even became full-time revolutionaries.

The government's attitude toward the landed nobles reflected its basic dilemma. On the one hand, the desire to modernize led it sometimes to act contrary to their needs, for example, in emancipating the serfs. On the other hand, the desire to maintain autocracy and social stability inclined the tsars, especially Alexander III and Nicholas II, to rely upon these nobles as a bedrock of tradition.

For their part, the landed nobles also faced a dilemma. They resented their declining influence and St. Petersburg's modernizing bureaucrats such as Sergei Witte, who served under both Alexander III and Nicholas II. To gain more power, many of them were willing to curtail that of the tsar. At the same time, they were dependent on tsarist authority to help maintain their social position, a fact that the events of 1917 made all too clear.

The tragedy of Late Imperial Russia was that the old and the new were not harmoniously blended. Given the

Romanov rulers' desire to maintain autocracy, it is difficult to see how such a blending could have occurred, even if the last emperors had been more effective autocrats. Although Nicholas II agreed in 1905 to the creation of an elected legislative body, he did it in the midst of a revolt and under duress. Although four legislative Dumas met from 1906 to 1917, Nicholas never gave up the belief that he was still an autocrat and that he could take away rights he had once granted, whether to a Duma or any other body.

Besides tsarist policy and the condition of the nobility, other aspects of Russian political, economic, social, religious, and cultural life manifested the tension between old traditions and new ways. Like many other aspects of Russian life, modernization trends were only partly because of government initiatives. Moreover, the government's impact outside the capital remained limited by its relatively small number of civil servants. Whatever its causes, however, modernization contributed to the increase of political opposition across a broad spectrum of Russian society.

So too did Russia's unsuccessful wars. After gaining enough territory in Asia during this era to more than offset the sale of Alaska in 1867, Russian expansion halted in 1904–1905, when Russia was defeated in the Russo-Japanese War. The Russian Empire even shrank a bit when it was forced to cede Southern Sakhalin to Japan.

While the failures of the war against Japan helped spark the 1905 revolt and force concessions from the autocracy, the failures of World War I helped lead to its overthrow in early 1917. The tensions of the latter war, along with Marxist propaganda regarding class conflict, also heightened resentment and opposition to the upper classes. Eight months after the fall of the Romanov dynasty, they were toppled from the heights of the social pyramid by the Marxist Bolsheviks, who came to power and launched a new era.

CHAPTER 2

Alexander II, Reformism, and Radicalism

Alexander II was the "tsar liberator," the ruler who finally freed the serfs in 1861. He also instituted other important reforms, especially in local government, the judiciary, and the military. Mindful of Russian weaknesses displayed during the Crimean War and faced with serious economic problems, he hoped the reforms would strengthen Russia without weakening autocracy. Fulfilling such a combined goal, however, was an almost impossible task, even if Alexander II had been a stronger and more visionary leader than he was.

Although the reforms helped modernize Russia, the climate that bred them also fostered discontentment and discord. Reactionaries, conservatives, liberals, radicals, and government officials battled against each other and among themselves. In a famous dream sequence in his novel *Crime and Punishment*, Dostoevsky wrote apropos of this period: "All were in a state of unrest and did not understand one another. Each thought that he alone possessed the truth." Alexander's reign ended tragically when he was assassinated in 1881 and his reactionary son, Alexander III, came to the throne.

ALEXANDER II: THE MAN AND HIS TIMES

When he came to the throne, Alexander II was thirty-six. Although his father, Nicholas I, had attempted to educate and train him for his future responsibilities, the new tsar was not a man who relished his work except perhaps when reviewing his troops. Although fairly intelligent, he did not possess an agile, curious mind, and as tsarevich his thinking had seemed little different than his father's. As tsar, during Russia's Golden Age of Literature, he displayed more interest in hunting and whist (an early form of bridge) than he ever did in the writings of Dostoevsky, Tolstoy, or Turgenev. He did, however, possess some humane sentiments and once told the writer Turgenev that his *Sportsman's Sketches*, with its sympathetic treatment of the peasants, had influenced his decision to free the serfs.

23

Although Alexander's boyhood tutors had noted that he was easily discouraged by difficulties, he did, like most of the Romanovs, have a high sense of duty. This sense of obligation, coupled with the demands of the time, helped energize him to carry out the bulk of his reforms during the first decade of his reign. After that, however, his energy waned. By the end of his reign, he was a tragic figure, criticized by much of the educated public and hunted by assassins. His tragedy and Russia's was that he possessed no clear ideas, no grand vision, on how to reconcile his basic conservative instincts with the modernizing demands of the second half of the nineteenth century. Without such a vision, he seemed irresolute and weak to many contemporaries—at times a reformer, at others, an opponent of reform. The judgment of the Moscow historian, professor, and occasional tutor to Alexander's children, Sergei Soloviev, is harsher than some but still valid: "Fate did not send [Alexander II] a Richelieu or a Bismarck; but the point is that he was incapable of using a Richelieu or a Bismarck; he possessed pretensions and the fear of a weak man to seem weak."

Yet, despite his personal flaws, circumstances propelled Alexander II toward enacting the "Great Reforms." After the Crimean War ended in early 1856, the country's main problem was its economic and social backwardness. Indeed, it had been a major cause of Russia's loss to its enemies. In 1856, for example, the Slavophile Yuri Samarin wrote:

> We were defeated [in the Crimean War] not by the external forces of the Western alliance but by our own internal weakness. . . . Now, when Europe welcomes the peace and rest desired for so long we must deal with what we have neglected. . . . At the head of the contemporary domestic questions which must be dealt with, the problem of serfdom stands as a threat to the future and an obstacle in the present to significant improvement in any way.[1]

EMANCIPATION OF THE SERFS

Causes and Background

The Crimean defeat called into question not only Russia's military prowess, overestimated since the defeat of Napoleon four decades earlier, but also economic traditions that were thought to affect it adversely. Thus, any economic factor that stood in the way of increasing Russia's overall strength was now examined with a new urgency. Many thought, like Samarin, that serfdom was a major impediment to a whole range of economic as well as social improvements.

Nikolai Miliutin, who participated in bringing about the reform, believed that it was necessary to end serfdom to increase agricultural productivity and thereby increase the capital required for industrialization. His friend the legal

---

[1]Martin McCauley and Peter Waldron, eds., *The Emergence of the Modern Russian State, 1855–81* (Totowa, N.J., 1988), pp. 99–100.

historian and westernizer Constantine Kavelin, who had good connections with reform-minded relatives of the tsar, maintained that serfdom was the chief cause of poverty in Russia. Although historians have debated to what extent serfdom retarded economic development, what is crucial is that Alexander II and important figures such as Samarin, Nikolai Miliutin, and Kavelin believed that ending serfdom would strengthen the Russian economy and thereby the country as a whole.

In 1856, General Dmitri Miliutin, the brother of Nikolai, composed a memorandum on army reform in which he indicated the necessity of reducing the size of Russia's traditionally large and costly standing army and creating instead a large trained reserve. He pointed out, however, that this could be done only if serfdom were first eliminated. The historian Alfred Rieber has plausibly argued that Miliutin's thinking, and military considerations in general, strongly influenced the tsar's decision to emancipate the serfs. In 1861, Alexander II made Dmitri Miliutin his minister of war.

Also related to Russia's strength was its great-power status. Larisa Zakharova has written that its loss and diplomatic isolation were the ruling elite's chief fears emanating from the Crimean defeat. These fears, along with a desire to create a more positive view of Russia abroad, helped propel Alexander and his officials toward ending serfdom.

Another cause was the increase in peasant disturbances in recent decades and the fear of massive rebellions in the future. In early 1856, Alexander II told a group of Moscow nobles: "It is better to begin to abolish serfdom from above than to wait until it begins to abolish itself from below." Although Alexander might have alluded to the possibility of dangers "from below" partly to scare Russia's serfowners into working with him to abolish serfdom, he also took the threat seriously himself.

Two additional factors helping to bring an end to serfdom were public opinion and enlightened bureaucrats. Although most serfowners were opposed to losing their serfs, and some land along with them, most leading opinion makers, from the influential radical émigré editor Alexander Herzen to the conservative publicist M. P. Pogodin, were for emancipation.

From 1857 to 1861, reforming officials such as the tsar's brother, Grand Duke Constantine, and Nikolai Miliutin, deputy minister of interior, were instrumental in preparing for the emancipation of the serfs. The Interior Ministry pressured Lithuanian and then other nobles to establish gentry committees to draft proposals for freeing the serfs. Although most lords wished to free their peasants without providing them land, Alexander II made it clear by the end of 1858 that some gentry land would have to be made available to former serfs.

In the capital, a Main Committee directed the work of the newly established provincial gentry committees, whose various reports were considered by Editing Commissions established in 1859. It was in these commissions, soon combined into one, that Nikolai Miliutin was especially influential in drafting the emancipation legislation of 1861.

FIGURE 2.1. The Kremlin's Grand Palace and churches, Moscow. In August 1856, with the Crimean War now over, Alexander's official coronation took place in the Kremlin.

Emancipation Statutes

On February 19, 1861, Alexander II signed the legislation into law. The government did not issue Alexander's emancipation manifesto and have it read in the churches until two weeks later—after the annual pre-Lenten carnival-week drinking had come to an end and the populace was, it was hoped, in a sober Lenten mood. The new law was a political compromise between the interests of the nobles and those of the peasants and their supporters, and the government was unsure of the response of either side.

The nearly 400 pages of statutes and annexes that made up the new law were terribly complex, but the emancipation provisions can be summed up as follows: (1) "the right of bondage" over serfs was "abolished forever" (except in some outlying areas of the empire such as the Caucasus, where separate emancipation legislation came later); (2) new arrangements regarding gentry-peasant relations and landholding were to be worked out in stages during the next few decades; (3) peasants who had previously farmed gentry land, as opposed to household serfs, were eventually to receive land, the exact amount to be determined by a combination of negotiation, government maximum and minimum norms for each province, and the use of mediators; (4) most of this new land was to go to peasant communes, not directly to individual peasants; (5) landowners were to be compensated for their loss of lands by a combination of government notes and peasant payments; and (6) peasants, unless they chose a free and minuscule "beggars' allotment," were obligated to repay the government with annual redemption payments spread over a 49-year period.

This legislation applied only to the country's serfs—about 40 percent of the total population and slightly less than half of all peasants. By the end of 1866, however, the government had promulgated further legislation to bring the status of other peasants more into line with that of the freed serfs. In general, all these peasants were still treated as a separate class: They were judged on the basis of common law, the powers of the communes and households over individual peasants were strengthened, and peasants continued to pay a head tax from which the nobles were exempt.

Reaction of the Peasants and Analysis

As was to be expected, the reaction to the emancipation manifesto was mixed. Many of the emancipated serfs were confused about the complex new statutes and disbelieving or disappointed when told they would have to make payments (for half a century) for land they received. Many peasants believed that

FIGURE 2.2. Serfs on a Moscow noble's estate hear the provisions of Alexander's emancipation decree.
(*Novosti Press Agency.*)

the fault lie with evil officials and nobles who were frustrating the tsar's real intentions. They thought that as soon as he overcame these troublemakers, new, more favorable, legislation would be forthcoming. Before the year was over, nobles reported more than 1,000 disturbances, most of which required troops to quell. In the summer of 1861, Alexander felt it necessary to admonish a delegation of peasants: "There will be no emancipation except the one I have granted you. Obey the law and the statutes! Work and toil! Obey the authorities and noble landowners!"

Collectively the former serfs received less land than their pre-emancipation allotments. More than one-fourth of them received allotments insufficient to maintain their households—former serfs of Polish landowners, especially after the Polish rebellion of 1863, and imperial and state peasants came off better. Overall the noble serfowners kept roughly two-fifths of their lands, whereas the ex-serfs, greatly outnumbering them, received the rest. And the

---

Peasant Opinions on the Emancipation

The following selection is from D. M. Wallace, *Russia* (New York, 1877), pp. 500–501. This is from the first edition of the Englishman's first-hand observations and reflections. This selection offers valuable insights not only into the peasants' reaction to the emancipation, but also into their general mentality. Ellipses are mine.

It might be reasonably supposed that the serfs received with boundless gratitude and delight the Manifesto. . . . In reality the Manifesto created among the peasantry a feeling of disappointment rather than delight. To understand this strange fact we must endeavor to place ourselves at the peasant's point of view.

In the first place it must be remarked that all vague, rhetorical phrases about free labor, human dignity, national progress, and the like, which may readily produce among educated men a certain amount of temporary enthusiasm, fall on the ears of the Russian peasant like drops of rain on a granite rock. The fashionable rhetoric of philosophical liberalism is as incomprehensible to him as the flowery circumlocutionary style of an

Oriental scribe would be to a keen city merchant. The idea of liberty in the abstract and the mention of rights which lie beyond the sphere of his ordinary everyday life awaken no enthusiasm in his breast. And for mere names he has a profound indifference. What matters it to him that he is officially called, not a "serf," but a "free village inhabitant," if the change in official terminology is not accompanied by some immediate material advantage? What he wants is a house to live in, food to eat, and raiment wherewithal to be clothed. . . . If, therefore, the Government would make a law by which his share of the Communal land would be increased, or his share of the Communal burdens diminished, he would in return willingly consent to be therein designated by the most ugly name that learned ingenuity could devise. Thus the sentimental considerations which had such an important influence on the educated classes had no hold whatever on the mind of the peasants. They looked at the question exclusively from two points of view—that of historical right and that of material advantage—and from both of these the Emancipation Law seemed to offer no satisfactory solution of the question.

peasants eventually paid more for their land than it was worth and received land less suitable than that retained by the owners.

On a more positive note, the ending of the serfs' personal bondage to serf-owners was an important step forward, and relatively little bloodshed resulted from the emancipation. Finally, in assessing the settlement, the practical difficulties and realities of the economic and political situation should be noted. The tsar feared to force a more equitable settlement upon a resentful gentry that made up the backbone of the country's elite.

ADDITIONAL REFORMS

Although censorship remained in place, Alexander II eased up on some of its restrictions—during the first seven years of his reign, the number of Russian periodicals increased about eightfold. Furthermore, Alexander II's government enacted measures to improve state financing, allowed more freedom to the empire's universities, expanded educational opportunities, and enacted other minor reforms. Three other major reforms in addition to emancipating the serfs dealt with local government, the judiciary, and the military.

Zemstvo Reform

The zemstvo (or local government) reform was enacted in early 1864 to help fill the void left by the collapse of the gentry's control over their serfs. As with the emancipation legislation, it did not immediately apply to all areas of the empire; Belorussia and western Ukrainian provinces, for example, were not allowed to establish zemstvo institutions until 1911, and the tsars never permitted them in Siberia. Nevertheless, by the end of Alexander II's reign there were zemstvo institutions in thirty-four of the country's fifty European provinces and in more than 300 districts within these provinces.

District assemblies were elected by three separate electorates: private rural landowners, peasants, and industrial property owners and merchants. These assemblies, which varied in size but averaged almost forty delegates per assembly, met annually for no longer than ten days. Gentry representatives slightly outnumbered those from the vast peasantry, and together the two estates made up about 80 percent of district assembly representatives.

One of the main jobs of a district assembly was the election to a three-year term of a district board of three to six members. This board operated year-round, overseeing the work of the zemstvos. Another job of a district assembly was the election of delegates, again for a three-year term, to participate in an annual provincial assembly, which, in turn, elected a provincial executive board. For a variety of reasons, including the gentry's greater education, leisure, and wealth—zemstvo assembly and board service was not remunerated—the gentry furnished a clear majority of the members of zemstvo boards and an even greater majority of provincial assembly representatives.

To carry out their work, boards hired administrative staff and specialists.

The latter included teachers, physicians and other medical personnel, veterinarians, agronomists, and statisticians. In areas such as primary education, the zemstvos made a major difference. By the end of Alexander's reign, they were involved in the running of some 18,000 primary schools in European Russia—twenty-five years earlier, there had been only 8,000 in the whole empire. Professional medical and veterinary services often became available to peasants for the first time. The insane, paupers, and orphans also received meaningful assistance from zemstvo workers. By organizing fire brigades and other measures, the zemstvos helped peasants deal with village fires, in addition to offering them fire insurance.

Although the zemstvos were primarily known for these services, the central government required additional functions from them: They had to assist in recruiting and housing troops, maintaining local roads, and operating the postal system. Local taxes were the main source of zemstvo revenues, although they were limited to a small amount compared with central government taxation. Despite the uplifting work of the zemstvos, peasants often blamed them for problems and complained of the additional burden of zemstvo taxes. In Chekhov's story "The Peasants," he writes: "The zemstvo was blamed for everything—for the arrears, the unjust exactions, the failure of the crops."

In 1870, many of the zemstvo principles were copied when the government established town councils (dumas) in the cities. The delegates were selected by three electorates divided by wealth. Again, improvements, especially in education, were soon evident. In St. Petersburg, for example, spending on municipal schools increased tenfold during the last ten years of Alexander II's reign.

Judicial Reform

In late 1864, the judicial reform became law after several years of strenuous effort. It replaced the old arbitrary, backlogged (over 3 million undecided cases before the courts in 1842), corrupt, and despotic judicial system with one based largely on Western principles. As with the previous two "Great Reforms," however, it was not applied immediately in all parts of the empire. Some of its provisions, for example, trial by jury, were not introduced at all in Belorussia, parts of Ukraine, Poland, and the Caucasus.

Where it was applied fully, the following principles came into effect: (1) the creation of two separate court systems—for major civil or criminal cases, there were regular courts, and for minor cases, there were courts presided over by a Justice of the Peace, elected by a zemstvo or city duma; (2) rights to appeal under either system to higher courts; (3) the independence of the judiciary from administrative interference and the appointment of judges for life except when removed for moral misconduct; (4) trial by jury for serious criminal cases unless considered crimes against the state; (5) the right to a lawyer; (6) the open publicity of court proceedings; (7) the use of oral testimony and pleadings—as opposed to the use of exclusively written evidence as under the old system; and (8) the establishment of a professional bar.

In addition to the new courts, separate military, ecclesiastical, and peasant courts continued to exist. Because the country's peasants made up about four-fifths of the population, their *volost* courts were especially significant. Following the emancipation, the government reconstituted these courts, which had previously existed for state peasants. In each *volost* (an administrative unit generally containing several village communes), peasants now elected from among themselves their own judges. These judges dealt with minor peasant criminal offenses and most civil disputes involving only peasants. They could impose small fines, imprisonment for short periods, and even sentence a peasant to be flogged with a rod for up to twenty blows. Their decisions were to be based upon customary practices, as opposed to written law.

Although the Russian official Nikitenko complained in his diary that the new laws failed to generate widespread discussion or enthusiasm, the new judicial profession that it created did prove popular with university students. By the end of the 1860s, more than half of them were majoring in law.

Military Reform

The fourth major reform, that of the military, was actually a series of reforms culminating in the Universal Military Service Statute of 1874. The driving force behind them was Dmitri Miliutin, who for two decades (1861–1881) served as Alexander II's war minister.

The motivation for reform was the clear necessity of modernizing Russia's military and in a manner as economically efficient as possible. The country's many conquered territories, its continuing expansion, its extensive borders, and its great-power ambitions all seemed to necessitate a strong military. But rubles to finance improvements were scarce. By 1863, the military was already soaking up about one-third of the state's budget.

Therefore, influenced by both military and economic considerations, Miliutin attempted to create a more efficient, streamlined army. To accomplish this, he reorganized the army structure and improved the training and education of both officers and enlisted men. The pre–Crimean War army had emphasized parade ground maneuvers and ignored such basics as target practice. Miliutin rectified this and had recruits taught the basics of reading and writing. Moreover, he set out to improve morale by abolishing the worst abuses of the old military justice system, for example, running the gauntlet, whereby soldiers sometimes died from thousands of blows. Because of rapidly changing armaments and high costs, rearming the military with the latest weapons was more difficult, but Miliutin made some progress even in this area.

One of his greatest desires was to create a large, efficiently trained reserve and to reduce the length of service in the regular army. By the 1870s, he thought that such a reduction would bring about savings, which could be used for further expansion of the railways—from 1855 through 1870, there had already been about a tenfold increase in the country's railway track. The success of the Prussians in using their railways to mobilize troops during the Franco-Prussian War of 1870–1871 seemed to strengthen his case, and in 1874 he won a major victory with the enactment of the Universal Military Service Statute.

Its provisions reduced to six years the maximum period of required active service—at the beginning of Alexander II's reign, fifteen or more years was the norm. After a six-year stint, the new law required nine more in the reserves and five in the militia. Lesser amounts of time, however, were usually served. Reductions could be achieved for volunteering or for educational attainment; university graduates, for example, had to serve only six months. Another major change was that now men of all estates could be drafted upon reaching the age of twenty if their names were selected in a draft lottery. Previously the upper classes had been exempt, and pre-reform enlisted men had come almost entirely from the peasants, often from those considered minor criminals or at least troublemakers.

As with the emancipation of the serfs, some nobles fought this reform, especially the stipulation making young noblemen liable to the draft. Alexander II stated, however, that military service was a task that should be "equally sacred" for all.

AUTOCRACY AND ITS OPPONENTS

Although willing to grant sweeping reforms, Alexander II was unwilling to limit his autocratic powers. In 1865, he reacted forcefully to an assembly of Moscow nobles who urged him to create an elected General Assembly to discuss state needs. He dissolved the noble assembly and responded with a document that stated:

> The right of initiative . . . belongs exclusively to ME, and is indissolubly bound to the autocratic power entrusted to ME by GOD. . . . No one is called to take upon himself before ME petitions about the general welfare and needs of the state. Such departures from the order established by existing legislation can only hinder me in the execution of MY aims.[2]

At about the same time, he privately stated that he would sign a constitution if he were convinced that it was good for Russia, but that he knew that the result would only be Russia's disintegration.

Moderate Reformism and Radicalism, 1855–1865

The great Russian writer Leo Tolstoy later described the year 1856 in this way: "Everyone tried to discover still new questions, everyone tried to resolve them; people wrote, read, and spoke about projects; everyone wished to correct, destroy, and change things, and all Russians, as if a single person, found themselves in an indescribable state of enthusiasm." Although ideas and projects

---

[2]As quoted in Terence Emmons, *The Russian Landed Gentry and the Peasant Emancipation of 1861* (London, 1968), p. 411. Although Alexander II resisted legal limits on his autocratic powers, the Great Reforms and other changes helped weaken his actual controls. See Alfred R. Rieber, "Interest-Group Politics in the Era of the Great Reforms," in *Russia's Great Reforms, 1855–1861*, eds. Ben Eklof, John Bushnell, and Larissa Zakharova (Bloomington, 1994), pp. 79–80.

were plentiful in the first decade of Alexander II's reign, moderate reformers and radicals were the chief proponents of change.

In 1856, the historian Boris Chicherin wrote: "Liberalism! This is the slogan of every educated and sober-minded person in Russia. This is the banner which can unite about it people of all spheres, all estates, all inclinations." Liberalism, he thought, would also cure Russia of its social ills and enable it to take its rightful place among the nations of the world. In this one word, he wrote, lies "all the future of Russia." Chicherin identified liberalism with various freedoms, including freedom from serfdom, and with due process of law and openness (*glasnost*) regarding government activities and legal procedures.

But the hopes of Chicherin and other liberals were soon smashed on the rocks of Russian reality. Rather than becoming a rallying flag, liberalism increasingly became a target of scorn. Its failure was crucial for the future of Russia.

In the West, liberalism had been supported by a strong middle class and by those wishing to reduce monarchical and governmental powers. In Russia, the middle class was weak, and its businessmen were not especially liberal. In addition, men such as Chicherin and the Miliutin brothers wanted a reforming monarch but did not wish to weaken his powers. In fact, they wanted a strong monarch who would stand above class interests and champion progressive policies in the interest of the entire empire. Thus, as paradoxical as it might seem, Constantine Kavelin (Chicherin's fellow reformer and former professor) wrote about the "complete necessity of retaining the unlimited power of the sovereign, basing it on the widest possible local freedom."

These liberal "statists" soon came into conflict with another group of moderate reformers. They were gentry liberals, whose appetites for political participation had been whetted by involvement in the provincial assemblies set up to discuss emancipation. Already in the late 1850s and early 1860s, most liberal statists had opposed gentry requests for more extensive participation in formulating public policy. Although ideas such as convening an elected national assembly might seem to be liberal, the liberal statists feared such an assembly would be dominated by the gentry and their own narrow interests.

The split between liberal statists and liberal gentry was one reason why a Western-style liberalism was not more successful in Russia. Although the liberal statists correctly feared gentry bias, they failed to perceive adequately the inherent unlikeliness of any lasting marriage between an unlimited monarchy and reform.

If the two liberal groups could not be held together, it was even more unlikely that the radical Alexander Herzen, then publishing in London, would long cooperate with divided reformers. But this founder of Russian agrarian socialism, who had left Russia in 1847, temporarily toned down his radicalism, hoping to encourage reform. His periodical, *The Bell,* was smuggled into Russia and became essential reading for many liberals and radicals. Each of its few thousand copies passed through countless hands, even those of members of the royal family. It alone delivered news and opinions not subject to censorship. Among its Russian contributors were not only radicals, but also some government officials writing anonymously—for example, Nikolai Miliutin.

From 1857 until 1862, Herzen continued to exert a major influence on Russian public opinion. Although many educated people disagreed with him, not many chose to ignore him. Visiting him in London became a must for Russian intellectuals traveling to Europe, including the writers Tolstoy, Turgenev, and Dostoevsky.

If moderates such as Turgenev tried to restrain Herzen's more militant tendencies, radicals such as Herzen's co-editor Nikolai Ogarev and the fiery Mikhail Bakunin encouraged such leanings. After being imprisoned and exiled for more than a dozen years, Bakunin escaped from Siberia and arrived in London at the end of 1861 eager for revolutionary action. Alluding to his penchant for believing revolution ever imminent, Herzen later wrote that he always "mistook the second month of pregnancy for the ninth."

The influence of Ogarev and Bakunin contributed to Herzen's stepped-up criticism of the government and his increasing support of radical ventures. At the end of 1861, he charged that the government consisted of "riffraff, swindlers, robbers, and whores." In 1862, he aided in the formation of a revolutionary organization called "Land and Liberty." One of the causes supported by this organization was Polish independence. When a full-scale Polish rebellion broke out in January 1863, Herzen supported it in *The Bell*. (For the Polish rebellion, see Chapter 4.) As a result of this support, his popularity and that of his journal plummeted in Russia.

The Polish revolt was the culmination of several years of rising radicalism in the Russian Empire. Student demonstrations led to the closing of St. Petersburg University in 1861, and when mysterious fires broke out in the capital in 1862, many people blamed them on radical students. Blood-thirsty pamphlets such as one entitled "Young Russia" increased the alarm. It called for revolution, for socialism, for the abolition of marriage and the family; and if the defenders of the imperial party resisted, it proclaimed: "We will kill [them] in the streets . . . in their houses, in the narrow lanes of towns, in the broad avenues of cities, in the hamlets and villages."

As a result of Turgenev's controversial novel *Fathers and Sons* (1862), a new word was popularized that some soon applied to such radical beliefs. The term was *nihilism*, and nihilists thought that nothing (*nihil*), including family, society, or religion, should be accepted that was not based on Reason. Many nihilists were noteworthy for their utter contempt for traditional authorities and for their unconventional behavior and appearance (for example, long hair for men or short hair for women).

Although there is some debate as to whether Nikolai Chernyshevsky and Nikolai Dobroliubov should be considered nihilists, they are usually linked with the nihilist Dmitri Pisarev as the most important of the new radical thinkers. All three men were journalists. Pisarev was the son of a landowner, and Chernyshevsky and Dobroliubov were the sons of priests and members of the *raznochintsy*—a term applied to those who did not fit into any other legal estate.

All three men thought that progress lay in following the path of Reason, science, philosophic materialism, and an enlightened utilitarianism, or "rational egoism," which saw no real conflict between the true good of the individual and that of society. All three also preached the necessity of emancipating women.

Chernyshevsky and Dobroliubov generally believed that the liberals' concern for "rights" and participation in government was not nearly as important to the peasant masses as was climbing out of poverty and stopping a situation whereby "one class sucks another's blood." As the radical Belinsky had earlier put it: "The people need potatoes, but not a constitution in the least."

Pisarev's writings were less political than those of Chernyshevsky and Dobroliubov, who were not only champions of the peasant masses, but also of socialism. Although Chernyshevsky's view of the peasants was in general sober and realistic, the younger Dobroliubov tended more toward idealizing them.

Alarmed by the growing radicalism, the government arrested both Chernyshevsky and Pisarev in mid-1862. Chernyshevsky's two-year imprisonment in the capital's infamous Sts. Peter and Paul Fortress, his subsequent trial, and his nineteen-year exile to Siberia—all based on flimsy and fabricated evidence—were glaring examples of the injustice of the pre-reform legal system. Pisarev's treatment was less scandalous but still harsh; he was jailed for four and a half years for trying to have an illegal article printed. Amazingly, both men were allowed to write while in prison and have some of their works printed legally. While in prison, Chernyshevsky wrote his most famous work, *What Is To Be Done?* (see Chapter 7).

Yet it was the Russian nationalistic reaction to the Polish rebellion of 1863–1864, rather than the earlier arrests of Chernyshevsky and Pisarev, that was most important in slowing, at least temporarily, the growth of radicalism. In the new climate, flirting with radicalism became less popular.

Liberalism was another casualty of the reawakened Russian nationalism and one that did not bounce back as quickly. The nationalist reaction ripped apart any tattered hopes of rallying public opinion around a liberal banner. Just as many liberals in Germany in the 1860s opted for the nationalist policies of Bismarck over their own earlier liberal principles, so too in Russia some liberals became more nationalistic and less liberal as a result of the emotions generated by the conflict with the Poles.

Reformism and Radicalism, 1866–1881

During the last fifteen years of Alexander II's reign, reformism from below made little headway. As the judicial and zemstvo reforms were gradually implemented, many lawyers and zemstvo workers, including physicians and teachers, supported further reforms. So too did several journals, such as *The Messenger of Europe*. Yet, having already implemented most of his major reforms, Alexander II was disinclined to go much further. In fact, after an assassination attempt on him in 1866, a period of reaction set in.

The would-be assassin, Dmitri Karakozov (subsequently hanged), had been influenced by the ideas of a cousin who headed a revolutionary group in Moscow called "Organization." A small cell within it, labeled "Hell," advocated terrorist methods and talked of freeing Chernyshevsky from Siberian exile. Before trying to shoot the tsar, Karakozov composed a manifesto which stated that the tsar was the greatest enemy of the "simple people" and that he enabled the rich to continue exploiting them.

Although Karakozov was acting on his own and the "Organization" that influenced him had only about fifty members, the attempted assassination led to a major government shake-up. The most prominent new appointments, both conservatives, were Dmitri Tolstoi as minister of education and General Peter Shuvalov as head of the Third Section (secret police). Shuvalov often represented the interests of wealthy landowners, and he soon became the second most powerful man in Russia. He remained as head of the Third Section until 1874, when he became ambassador to England. In the eyes of War Minister Miliutin, Shuvalov overemphasized the dangers facing Alexander and was primarily responsible for impeding new reforms.

After Karakozov's arrest, the next big revolutionary case stemmed from a murder committed in 1869 by the revolutionary Sergei Nechaev. After a trip to Switzerland, where he had impressed Bakunin and Ogarev, Nechaev returned to Russia and, with some accomplices, murdered a young revolutionary named Ivanov, who had refused to subordinate himself to Nechaev. Whether there were other causes is not certain. The subsequent publicity given to the murder helped to discredit Nechaev and some of his more unsavory and authoritarian beliefs and tactics—many of these were spelled out in *The Revolutionary Catechism*, a pamphlet he had prepared with the help of Bakunin.

The populist radical movement of the 1870s emerged partly in reaction to Nechaev's methods. One of its first groups, the "Chaikovsky Circle," was opposed to having a single leader and thought of itself as a group of friends working together for their own improvement and for the good of the people. At first, the group confined itself primarily to distributing radical literature to various parts of the country and to teaching and propagandizing among city workers and peasants.

The two strongest influences on these young populists were Bakunin and Peter Lavrov. By the beginning of the 1870s, Bakunin had completed the development of his anarchistic philosophy. He believed that any centralized government was incompatible with human liberty and that the state and religion were humankind's two greatest enemies.

Bakunin's ideal, similar to that of Herzen's, was a system of free federated communes. In contrast to Herzen, who by his death in 1870 had foreseen that a revolution of blood would have to be maintained by blood, Bakunin wanted violent revolution. He encouraged young Russians to become brigand-rebels among the peasant masses. Whereas Herzen admired the Russian peasants primarily for their socialistic and democratic tendencies, Bakunin also saw in them potential rebels. Like those who had joined the Razin and Pugachev rebellions of earlier centuries, Russia's peasants, he thought, were just waiting for an opportune time to rebel.

Peter Lavrov was a more moderate man than Bakunin. Like Bakunin, he was from the wealthy gentry and escaped from Russian exile and settled in Western Europe. From there, he continued to influence young Russian radicals. Both before and after his 1870 escape, he stressed the *debt* of the educated and privileged minority to the masses, a debt they owed because their privileges, including education, had come at the expense of the peasants, who had been exploited for centuries. Although he desired an agrarian socialist society, he emphasized patient educational and propagandistic work among the peasants, rather than trying to incite them to any premature upheaval.

The influence of both Bakunin and Lavrov was especially evident in 1874. That spring and summer, more than 1,000 radicals went into the countryside to work among the masses, to repay their debt to the people. Depending upon the varied inclinations of the radicals, "work" took on various forms: for example, carpentry or cobbling, giving smallpox inoculations, teaching literacy, propagandizing, and fomenting revolution. Many also believed that there was much they themselves could learn from the peasants.

But centuries of oppression had made the peasants naturally wary and cautious. Although they did not generally denounce the radicals to the authorities, they realized that being too receptive to these outsiders might get them in serious trouble. In addition, the mental gap between the peasants and newcomers was often great. And the local gentry and others were often not as reluctant as the peasants to report them to the police. Before the year was out, more than 700 of these populists were arrested.

As a result of the failure of this spontaneous, poorly organized movement, radicals began to emphasize more organization and in 1876 formed a new "Land and Liberty" group. In 1879, however, this group split in two.

It did so primarily because of differences over the use of terrorism. One of the new groups, the Black Repartition, opposed emphasizing it, believing it would distract them from further work among the masses. The other group, the People's Will, thought such tactics were now necessary.

Even before 1879, as the radicals saw their friends arrested, some of them turned to violent methods out of frustration and to facilitate escapes. A forerunner of things to come was the famous case of Vera Zasulich. Because she had heard that General Trepov, the military governor of St. Petersburg, had ordered the flogging of a prisoner, she walked into his office one day in 1878, pulled a revolver out of her muff, and shot him.

Another motivation for now stressing terrorism was the fear of some radicals that capitalism was rapidly developing in Russia and that it would increase the misery of the people. Members of the People's Will blamed the government for being "the greatest capitalist force in the country" and for excessively taxing the peasants to pay for this development. They thought that their best hope of reversing the situation was to overthrow the tsarist government and work toward the establishment of a socialist society. They hoped that terror, especially the assassination of Alexander II, would demoralize the government and awaken the masses to the realization that the government could indeed be overthrown.

Meanwhile, dissatisfaction with the tsarist government had increased. Passions unleashed in the 1876–1877 crusade to help the South Slavs in their battle against the Ottoman Turks were further inflamed by a Russo-Turkish War of 1877–1878 (see Chapter 4). But the eventual peace settlement agreed upon at the 1878 Congress of Berlin left many nationalists critical of the government. And the liberal zemstvo assembly of the province of Tver passed a resolution noting that the tsar had helped the Bulgarians establish a liberal constitutional order, which included an elected assembly. The Tver assembly hoped, fruitlessly as it turned out, that Alexander would see fit to grant his own people a similar benefit.

Alexander's personal life was also a source of dissatisfaction to many in royal circles. Some were privately critical of his treatment of his wife Maria and his continuing relationship with the young Catherine Dolgorukova, with whom he maintained a second family. Constantine Pobedonostsev, the chief advisor to Tsarevich Alexander, referred privately to Alexander II as a "pitiful and unfortunate man" whose will was exhausted and who wanted "only the pleasures of the belly" [sic].[3] Only six weeks after the Empress Maria's death in mid-1880, Alexander married his mistress of fifteen years in a morganatic marriage.

By this time, he was being hunted in earnest by the People's Will, who had already organized a couple of failed assassination attempts. The first had blown up an imperial train but not the one the tsar was on, and the second had killed eleven people in his Winter Palace. After the second explosion, wild rumors spread around the city. The tsar's brother, referring to the terrorists, lamented in his diary: "We do not see, do not know, do not have the slightest idea of their numbers."

To deal with the increase of terrorism after the Russo-Turkish War, Alexander resorted to more authoritarian measures and curtailed some of the previous freedoms of the zemstvos, educational institutions, and the press. Following the explosion in the Winter Palace in early 1880, he appointed a Supreme Administrative Commission. Its head was General Loris-Melikov, who became extremely powerful. Although the commission remained in place only for several months, Loris-Melikov retained his power by then becoming minister of interior.

Loris-Melikov allied himself with Alexander's more progressive ministers, such as Dmitri Miliutin, and combated the influence of more reactionary ministers, such as Dmitri Tolstoi, who was both minister of education and procurator of the Holy Synod. Loris-Melikov also pursued a two-pronged policy of trying to fight terrorism more effectively, while gaining public support for the government. To accomplish the latter, he lessened government restraints on the zemstvos and press and even recommended going one big step further. In early 1881, he presented a plan that provided for the creation of several commissions that would make legislative recommendations in the areas of finance and administration to the tsar's advisory State Council. Moreover, some of the delegates of the commissions would be elected, as would fifteen others who would sit with the State Council to consider the recommendations.

Although this project was a long way from granting an elected national assembly or a constitution to his country, Alexander II expressed fears after approving it that he was "going along the road toward a constitution."

---

[3]As quoted in Robert F. Byrnes, *Pobedonostsev: His Life and Thought* (Bloomington, 1968), pp. 143–144.

FIGURE 2.3. The Church of the Resurrection of the Savior on the Blood, St. Petersburg, 1883–1907, architect A. Parland, was built on the spot where Alexander II was assassinated near the Catherine Canal.

As it turned out, however, the road he went down later that day, March 1, 1881, was the road to his death. Directed by the diminutive Sophia Perovskaia, daughter of a former civilian governor of the capital, People's Will assassins finally killed him. After a first home-made bomb rocked his carriage and mortally wounded a few people, Alexander got out of his carriage but was then hit by another bomb, thrown by another assassin. It knocked him to the ground and ripped his legs apart. Bleeding profusely, he was rushed to the Winter Palace, but his life could not be saved. Later that same afternoon, the reign of the "tsar liberator" came to an inglorious end.

*SUGGESTED SOURCES**

ALMENDINGEN, E. M. *The Emperor Alexander II: A Study.* London, 1962.
BERGMAN, JAY. *Vera Zasulich: A Biography.* Stanford, 1983.
BROIDO, VERA. *Apostles Into Terrorists: Women and the Revolutionary Movement in the Russia of Alexander II.* New York, 1977.
BROWER, DANIEL R. *Training the Nihilists: Education and Radicalism in Tsarist Russia.* Ithaca, N.Y., 1975.

*See also books cited in footnotes.

CARR, E. H. *Michael Bakunin.* New York, 1961.

———. *The Romantic Exiles: A Nineteenth Century Portrait Gallery.* Boston, 1961.

CHERNYSHEVSKY, N. G. *What Is to Be Done? Tales about New People.* New York, 1961.

EMMONS, TERENCE, ed. *Emancipation of the Russian Serfs.* New York, 1970.

EMMONS, TERENCE, and WAYNE S. VUCINICH, eds. *The Zemstvo in Russia: An Experiment in Local Self-Government.* Cambridge, England, 1982.

ENGEL, BARBARA ALPERN, and CLIFFORD N. ROSENTHAL, EDS. *Five Sisters: Women against the Tsar.* New York, 1975.

FIELD, DANIEL. *The End of Serfdom: Nobility and Bureaucracy in Russia, 1855–1861.* Cambridge, Mass., 1976.

———. *Rebels in the Name of the Tsar.* Boston, 1976.

FOOTMAN, DAVID. *The Alexander Conspiracy: A Life of A. I. Zhelyabov.* LaSalle, Ill., 1974.

GLEASON, ABBOTT. *Young Russia: The Genesis of Russian Radicalism in the 1860s.* New York, 1980.

HAMBURG, GARY M. *Boris Chicherin and Early Russian Liberalism, 1828–1866.* Stanford, 1992.

HARDY, DEBORAH. *Land and Freedom: The Origins of Russian Terrorism.* New York, 1987.

HERZEN, ALEXANDER. *My Past and Thoughts.* 4 vols. London, 1968.

KROPOTKIN, PETER. *Memoirs of a Revolutionist.* New York, 1971.

LINCOLN, W. BRUCE. *The Great Reforms: Autocracy, Bureaucracy, and the Politics of Change in Imperial Russia.* Dekalb, Ill., 1990.

MENDEL, ARTHUR P. *Michael Bakunin: Roots of Apocalypse.* New York, 1981.

MILLER, FORRESTT A. *Dimitrii Miliutin and the Reform Era in Russia.* Nashville, 1968.

MOSSE, W. E. *Alexander II and the Modernization of Russia.* Rev. ed. New York, 1962.

NIKITENKO, ALEKSANDR. *The Diary of a Russian Censor,* abridged, ed. and trans. Helen Saltz Jacobson. Amherst, Mass., 1975.

ORLOVSKY, DANIEL T. *The Limits of Reform: The Ministry of Internal Affairs in Imperial Russia, 1802–1881.* Cambridge, Mass., 1981.

PEREIRA, N. G. O. *Tsar-Liberator: Alexander II of Russia, 1818–1881.* Newtonville, Mass., 1983.

POMPER, PHILIP. *Sergei Nechaev.* New Brunswick, N.J., 1979.

RIEBER, ALFRED J. "Alexander II: A Revisionist View," *JMH*[†] 43 (March 1971): 42–58.

———, ED. *The Politics of Autocracy: Letters of Alexander II to Prince A. I. Bariatinskii, 1857–1864.* Paris, 1966.

SAUNDERS, DAVID. *Russia in the Age of Reaction and Reform, 1801–1881.* London, 1992. Chs. 8–11.

SCHAPIRO, LEONARD. *Rationalism and Nationalism in Russian Nineteenth-Century Political Thought.* New Haven, 1967.

ULAM, ADAM B. *In the Name of the People: Prophets and Conspirators in Prerevolutionary Russia.* New York, 1977.

VENTURI, FRANCO. *Roots of Revolution: A History of the Populist and Socialist Movements in Nineteenth Century Russia.* New York, 1966.

WCISLO, FRANCIS WILLIAM. *Reforming Rural Russia: State, Local Society, and National Politics, 1855–1914.* Princeton, 1990.

WORTMAN, RICHARD. *The Development of a Russian Legal Consciousness.* Chicago, 1976.

ZAIONCHKOVSKII, PETER A. *The Abolition of Serfdom in Russia.* Gulf Breeze, Fla., 1978.

†See General Bibliography at the back of the text for a list of journal abbreviations.

————. *The Russian Autocracy in Crises, 1878–1882*. Gulf Breeze, Fla., 1979.

ZAKHAROVA, L. G. "Alexander II," *RSH* 32 (Winter 1993–94): 57–88. Reprinted in *EER*, pp. 295–333.

————. "Autocracy and the Abolition of Serfdom in Russia, 1856–1861," *SSH* 26 (Fall 1987). (The whole issue is devoted to this work except for the useful introduction of the editor and translator of it, Gary M. Hamburg.)

CHAPTER 3

Reactionary Politics, Economic Modernization, and Political Opposition, 1881–1905

In the quarter century after the death of Alexander II, tsarist domestic policy combined reactionary policies designed to safeguard the autocratic order with modernizing economic measures intended to strengthen Russia in the world. Yet the two aspects were difficult to harmonize and frequently undercut each other. Modernization, for example, greatly increased the number of educated people, but by 1905 opposition to Nicholas II's autocracy was widespread among them and took primarily two forms: socialist and liberal.

ALEXANDER III AND POBEDONOSTSEV: THE AUTOCRAT AND HIS CHIEF ADVISER

Just a few days after his thirty-sixth birthday, Alexander III succeeded his assassinated father. He was a bearded, herculean man who liked to entertain the friends of his twelve-year-old son Nicholas by twisting iron pokers into knots. In a train wreck in 1888, he protected his wife and children by holding up a collapsing dining car roof. His approach to ruling was similar. By the strength of his will and crown, he tried to prevent the collapse of the autocratic political order and showed no more mercy to its opponents than he did to iron pokers.

The new tsar was honest, dutiful, and forthright. He was also often ungracious and could be blunt to the point of rudeness. Once at a state dinner, after the Austrian ambassador had mentioned the possibility of mobilizing a few army corps because of Balkan differences with Russia, the tsar bent a fork into a knot and pitched it toward him, saying: "That is what I am going to do to your two or three army corps."[1]

Alexander III's straightforward, unswerving approach to problems was made simpler by his lack of intellectual discernment, curiosity, or flexibility. Yet, unfortunately for him and Russia, the country required a ruler with just

[1]Aleksandr Mikhailovich, Grand Duke of Russia, *Once a Grand Duke* (New York, 1932), pp. 66–67.

such intellectual qualities as well as a strong will. Only such a ruler stood much of a chance of successfully overseeing Russia's modernization, while maintaining stability and order.

The chief adviser to the new tsar was Constantine Pobedonostsev, a tall, thin, humorless man. He was the grandson of a priest and considered himself fortunate to have graduated from the noble-dominated Imperial School of Jurisprudence. In addition to other positions, he had been the chief tutor and guide of Alexander since 1865. Although as tsar Alexander sometimes took competing advice from other advisers, his policies most often mirrored Pobedonostsev's ideas, which coincided with the tsar's basic instincts.

Pobedonostsev spelled out his ideas most clearly in 1896 in *Moskovskii Sbornik*, a book published in England two years later with the title *Reflections of a Russian Statesman*. His view of the human condition was pessimistic. ("From the day that man first fell falsehood has ruled the world.") He divided men into two groups: a small intellectual aristocracy and the vulgar "herd," incapable of higher thinking. Because he believed that humans were by nature sinful and the masses ignorant, and because of Russia's historical development, he thought that autocracy was the only form of government for it.

He stated that parliamentary bodies were "one of the greatest illustrations of human delusion." Universal suffrage is "a fatal error, and one of the most remarkable in the history of mankind." The press, the organ of public opinion, "is one of the falsest institutions of our time." Also, "faith in abstract principles is the prevailing error of our time." Parliaments, democracy, the press, and rationalism, like the ideas of human perfectibility and secular progress, led to discontentment and misery. So too, he thought, did education beyond one's needs.

Because the natural, organic development of a nation was important to Pobedonostsev, he was more tolerant of parliamentarism in England, where it had slowly evolved, than he was of it in other countries where it was not an organic growth. He thought it had no place in Russia, however, and Western imports such as liberalism, legalism, and religious tolerance did not belong there either. He believed the Orthodox Russians should dominate the empire.

Pobedonostsev took his religion most seriously and from 1880 until 1905 served as the procurator of the Holy Synod. He believed that the true religion and faith were the only hope for sinful humanity, but happiness was to come primarily in heaven, not on earth.

The Orthodox Church was not only to help Russians save their souls and get to heaven, but also it was "to inspire the people with respect for the law and for power." Orthodoxy was to be the moral glue that bound people to their Orthodox tsar. For the non-Orthodox of the empire (counting Old Believers and sectarians, probably more than a third of the population), Pobedonostsev could offer no effective "moral glue," only coercion.

REACTIONARY POLICIES OF ALEXANDER III

Although the oppression of ethnic and religious minorities was one characteristic of Alexander III's reign (see Chapter 4), his first task was to deal with his father's assassins and other members of the People's Will. A panel of government-appointed officials, acting as both judges and jury, condemned six individuals, including two women, to be hanged. After it was discovered that one of the women was pregnant, her sentence was changed to life imprisonment. The other woman was the noble-born Sophia Perovskaia, who had directed the assassination.

Before the sentences could be carried out, two prominent individuals appealed to the tsar to act like a true Christian monarch and forgo applying capital punishment. One was the famous novelist Leo Tolstoy; the other was the philosopher and religious thinker Vladimir Soloviev, whose father, the University of Moscow's Sergei Soloviev, had once tutored Alexander III in history. Upon hearing of the appeals, Pobedonostsev wrote to the tsar, advising him not to heed the requests of those possessing "weak minds and hearts." The tsar did not. Despite one of the condemned twice hitting the scaffold floor before being strung up for a third try—shades of the Decembrists' slipshod hangings in 1826—all five were hanged on April 3, 1881.

FIGURE 3.1. The hanging of Alexander II's assassins on Semenovskii Square, St. Petersburg, April 3, 1881.
(From Ian Grey, The Horizon History of Russia, *American Heritage Publishing Company, New York, 1970, p. 287, New York Public Library.)*

In the next several months the new tsar made it clear that he intended to rule with an iron hand. Siding with Pobedonostsev, who (according to Dmitri Miliutin) called the Great Reforms of Alexander II a "criminal mistake," the tsar rejected Loris-Melikov's earlier plan for the establishment of advisory commissions and issued a manifesto affirming the necessity of maintaining absolute power. Upset at this course of events, Loris-Melikov, Miliutin (who thought Pobedonostsev a "fanatic-reactionary"), and a few other reform-minded ministers resigned.

In August, in an effort to root out revolutionaries still at large, the tsar approved a "Regulation on Measures for the Safety of the State and the Protection of Public Order." Strictly speaking, it was not a "law," arrived at by normal bureaucratic procedure (through the Council of State), but an emergency ordinance. Although applying to only some provinces and supposedly lasting only three years, these "temporary regulations" were gradually extended and continued to exist for more than three decades. They squelched the hopes of reformers who wished to see Russia build upon Alexander II's judicial reforms and become a country in which the due process of law was a recognized right of citizens.

The "temporary regulations" recognized two types of emergencies and permitted governors to bypass regular courts and laws. Under varying conditions, they could fine, imprison for three months or less, turn over to military courts, or banish from their province any suspected person. They could also prohibit meetings and gatherings, including those of zemstvos, shut down factories or schools, suppress newspapers, and fire certain officials.

Throughout his reign, Alexander III attempted to strengthen the state's control over society. The University Statute of 1884 curtailed university autonomy. From 1889 to 1892, the government cut back on rights of peasants and local governing bodies. Most significant of Alexander's "counterreforms" was the creation of land captains in 1889. By 1895, there were about 2,000 of them. These government-appointed noblemen received sweeping administrative and judicial powers over the peasants. Each land captain was responsible for overseeing part of a district's peasants, their elected peasant officials, and institutions such as the village and canton (*volost*) assemblies and cantonal courts. He could overturn assembly decisions and suspend peasant officials and cantonal court rulings. He could even fine or briefly jail such officials. He also became a judge in civil and minor criminal cases involving peasants beyond the cantonal court level, replacing for them the elected Justices of the Peace created by the 1864 judicial reform.

In 1890, a new law strengthened the government's powers over the zemstvos. It stipulated that henceforth zemstvo heads had to be confirmed by the minister of interior and zemstvo boards and employees by their provincial governor. The latter also received new powers, including that of appointing the peasant members of the district zemstvos from lists of candidates submitted by canton assemblies. Not only did peasants lose their previous right of electing delegates to the district zemstvos, but also they saw their proportion of delegates decline to less than one-third of the total delegates in district assemblies.

Conversely, noble representation in them increased, and the 1889–1890 changes are sometimes taken as a sign that Alexander III wished to rely more on the nobles as a bulwark of the regime. Thomas Pearson's study of the autocracy's local government policies in this era indicates, however, that the 1889–1890 changes polarized and alienated the nobles. Although the policies were intended to strengthen Ministry-of-Interior control while making local government more efficient, St. Petersburg also hoped they would gain it more provincial support. It proved an illusory hope, as peasants as well as nobles became more disillusioned with the government.

In 1892, town councils, officials, and voters experienced the government's heavy hand. A new law stipulated the government confirmation of elected officials, regulated the number of council meetings, and, by increasing property qualifications, shrunk the electorate. For example, the already small number of eligible voters in St. Petersburg and Moscow was reduced by more than 60 percent. This meant that in the two cities combined, less than 1 percent of the total population could now vote.

Other measures also reflected the government's distrust of the masses. In 1887, for example, the government increased gymnasium fees in the hope of keeping lower-class children out of the gymnasiums.

POLICIES OF ECONOMIC MODERNIZATION, 1881–1903

Although reactionary measures were one aspect of tsarist policy, economic modernization, which had begun earlier but accelerated most rapidly in the century's final two decades, was another. Not all government economic policies contributed to modernization, however, and it occurred for many reasons in addition to governmental actions.

The government pursued modernization chiefly by investing or encouraging investment in railways, mining, and manufacturing. This policy necessitated building up capital for investment, which, in turn, spurred other increases: in tax revenues, the balance of payments, the gold reserve, and foreign loans.

Alexander III's first of three finance ministers was N. K. Bunge. He inherited a national budget drained by heavy military expenditures and servicing a high foreign debt. To build up Russia's gold reserve, he set out to improve its balance of payments by raising import tariffs. By thus boosting the prices of foreign products, Bunge aided competing Russian industries. He also reorganized the railway system, which in 1880 was overwhelmingly in private hands, and increased the state's role in constructing and operating new lines. Believing that Russia's tax policy placed an unrealistic burden on the peasants and that it had to be overhauled if the Russian economy was to be healthy, he reduced peasants' taxes, even eliminating the long-standing soul tax. Although careful not to drive capital out of Russia, he introduced new taxes that affected mainly the upper classes, for example, on inheritance, profits, and savings. Finally, he oversaw the establishment of a factory inspectorate and peasant and noble land banks to provide loans.

Compared to the policies of his two successors, Bunge's initiatives were fairly moderate, but they did not generate enough income to enable the government to balance its budget or reduce its foreign debt. He resigned in 1886.

Alexander III's second finance minister (1887–1892) was I. A. Vyshnegradsky. As with Bunge, not all his policies were directly motivated by the modernizing impulse, but collectively they did move Russia further down that road. To balance Russia's budget, increase gold reserves, and produce a healthy trade surplus, he increased indirect taxes and exports, especially grain, and upped import tariffs to higher levels than those of any other power.

These policies contributed to both positive and negative results. The most devastating of the latter was the famine of 1891–1892. Increases in indirect taxes on basic goods, along with other government measures, led the peasants to sell more grain, leaving them little surplus if an emergency arose. Vyshnegradsky's statement of 1887 that "we may undereat, but we will export" now took on a grim reality. The resulting famine and the public outcry it created forced him to resign. (For more on this famine, see Chapter 6.)

His successor from 1892 to 1903 was one of the most dynamic ministers of late imperial Russia, Sergei Witte, a man who came to symbolize Russia's modernization drive. After studying mathematics at Novorossiisk University in

FIGURE 3.2. Peasants depicted taking thatch from their roof to feed their animals during the famine of 1891–1892.
(From Otto Hoetzsch, The Evolution of Russia. *Harcourt, Brace & World, New York, 1966, #137, p. 161. © Thames & Hudson of London.)*

MAP 3.1

Odessa, he began a successful career in railway administration. By the time he became minister of finance, he had gained a reputation for his practical business sense, his hard-working habits, and his passionate belief in the necessity of rapid Russian industrialization.

To achieve it, he continued and expanded some of his predecessors' policies regarding high import tariffs, indirect taxes (on such items as sugar, matches, tobacco, and kerosene), and the maintenance of a favorable trade balance. Although grain exports had to be reduced in 1891 and 1892, by 1894 they accounted for more than 50 percent of the value of all Russian exports. During his eleven years in office, the state's annual revenue doubled. To facilitate foreign loans and make the ruble convertible, in 1897 he put Russia on the Gold Standard. Not only foreign loans, but also foreign investment rose quickly while he was in office, and he estimated that in 1900 about half of all industrial and commercial capital was of foreign origin.

The results of all these financial moves were impressive. Partly because of them, government investment in industrial modernization increased significantly, as did industrial production, which more than doubled in the 1890s. Especially notable was the growth of iron and petroleum production and of railways. As the government's railway head and then minister of finance, Witte oversaw the building of most of the Trans-Siberian Railway, begun in 1891 and almost completed by the time he left office in 1903.

But Witte's policies also had negative consequences. For almost a century, the dominant view was that his policies—along with those of Vyshnegradsky before him—led to an extended agrarian or peasant crisis. Some recent research, however, has challenged this view. Yet there still seems little doubt that at least sectors of the peasant economy and parts of the country (for example, the central black-soil provinces) suffered increased economic hardship, that government financial policies had something to do with it, and that many of Witte's contemporaries believed his policies were helping to cause an agrarian crisis.

His policies certainly helped accelerate changes, such as the rapid growth of industrial workers, and helped fuel the rising manifestations of public discontent. The landed nobility were critical of him, and in the late 1890s, industrial and student strikes became more prevalent. In 1902, peasant disturbances broke out in the provinces of Kharkov and Poltava. Other sectors of the public were also becoming more restive.

Partly to further industrialization and keep foreign loans (primarily French) and investments coming, Witte advocated an easing of government repression. This displeased many of Nicholas II's more reactionary ministers and advisers, especially his minister of interior, V. K. Plehve, who blamed much of the increased dissatisfaction in the country on Witte. Witte's standing was further undercut by an economic depression that began around 1900. Finally, in 1903, Nicholas replaced him as finance minister. Although the tsar appointed him chairman of the Council of Ministers, the council seldom met, and the position was largely honorific.

NICHOLAS II AND THE POLITICS OF REACTION, 1894–1904

When Alexander III died unexpectedly of nephritis in October 1894, his oldest son, Nicholas, was only twenty-six. His reaction to his father's death is described by Grand Duke Alexander Mikhailovich (then twenty-eight) to whom Nicholas addressed the following words:

> What is going to happen to me, to you, to Xenia, to Alix, to mother, to all of Russia? I am not prepared to be a Czar. I never wanted to become one. I know nothing of the business of ruling. I have no idea of even how to talk to the ministers. Will you help me, Sandro?[2]

These words revealed much of Nicholas's character. Much shorter and thinner than Alexander III, he was also much less confident and outspoken. Although adoring and in awe of his father, he was closer to his solicitous mother, Maria, who had been born a Danish princess. He grew up surrounded by his parents, his large extended family of relatives, and a faithful array of servants and tutors. Partly as a result of the terrorism that brought the terrible death of his grandfather, Alexander II (which he had witnessed as a twelve-year-old boy), Nicholas was raised in a sheltered environment.

Whatever the complex reasons, he grew up a dutiful son, showing few signs of rebellion or independence. As his later life made clear, he was often fatalistic, resigned to suffering what he felt was inescapable—a feeling reinforced by the fact that he was born on St. Job the Sufferer's day. After he became tsar, observers commented on his politeness and charm, but they often failed to discern the personality behind these external appearances. He was cautious and suspicious and could be stubborn, but he hated confrontation. He also hated complexity and lacked the intellectual stamina, although not the intelligence, to work through complex problems. Like most of the Romanovs, however, he possessed a high sense of duty and believed in autocracy. Moreover, his mother had emphasized to him how important it was to display the correct imperial behavior. So he did his best, but he probably spoke from the depths of his soul when he said he never wanted to become tsar.

If one looks at his course of studies and the positions he held as tsarevich, it seems, at first glance, that he was adequately prepared to be tsar, but a deeper look reveals serious deficiencies. He became proficient in French, German, and English; studied history, geography, math, science, religion, drawing, music, and military matters; and was tutored by Pobedonostsev in law and by Bunge in economics and finance. Yet, except for history and especially military matters, he displayed little enthusiasm for learning. The pattern was similar in the positions the young tsarevich assumed after reaching adulthood. Only military duties, and not very taxing ones at that, elicited much sustained enthusiasm from him. His sheltered upbringing, coupled with the belief that Alexander III (only forty-nine at the time of his death) still had many years to rule, further contributed to his unpreparedness for the awesome task of becoming autocrat of the Russian Empire.

One reason for the tsarevich's interest in the military was his preference for the outdoors. He enjoyed pastimes such as riding, hunting, skating, and sledding and chores such as chopping wood. He also enjoyed other pleasures common among young officers. For several years in the early 1890s, he had an af-

[2]Ibid., pp. 168–169.

fair with a young ballerina, while simultaneously hoping that a marriage could be arranged between him and Princess Alix (later Alexandra) of Hesse-Darmstadt. Not only did he spend much time at the ballet, but also he enjoyed the theater and the operas of such composers as Glinka, Musorgsky, and Tchaikovsky.

Joining Nicholas at his father's deathbed was Princess Alix, who by then had agreed to give up her Protestant faith and convert to Orthodoxy to marry Nicholas. Although four years younger than he and in a foreign country, she did not hesitate to advise the tsarevich to be firm, show his own mind, and demand the respect due to him from his father's doctors and others. This was typical of the advice this tall, proud woman often gave him after their marriage, which occurred a month after Alexander III's death.

At first, Nicholas II maintained most of his father's officials, including Pobedonostsev as procurator of the Holy Synod and Witte as finance minister. Even though Pobedonostsev's influence on Alexander III had waned somewhat in the final years of his reign, it was reportedly Pobedonostsev who advised Nicholas in January 1895 to object to zemstvo hopes for a greater political role. At a reception of zemstvo delegates and others who had come to congratulate the new tsar, Nicholas referred to wishes of zemstvo government participation as "senseless dreams." He stated his intention to maintain "the principle of autocracy just as firmly and unshakably" as had his father. Not possessing his father's iron will, however, and in the face of rising opposition, this was easier said than done.

Also exercising influence on the tsar were his uncles, especially his father's brother Grand Duke Sergei, governor-general of Moscow. He was primarily responsible for planning the traditional coronation distribution of presents to commoners and for choosing the site, a large field full of ditches, where this would occur. Some of the large crowd who rushed forward on that May morning in 1896 fell in the ditches and were trampled on by others. Estimates of the number of dead varied from hundreds to thousands. Although some advised Nicholas to display his sympathy for the dead and cancel further festivities, Sergei and his brothers argued against canceling anything. The attendance of Nicholas and Alexandra at a ball that night left a bad impression on many, and Nicholas missed an important opportunity to display his concern for the common people.

Once Nicholas settled into the routine of trying to run the empire, he found the task difficult and often distasteful. Although influenced by his own beliefs and personality, his work life reflected primarily traditional autocratic practices. It consisted of innumerable meetings with individual ministers and others who reported on and received his instructions on everything from promotions to divorce applications. Sensing that he was a much weaker man than his father, ministers and relatives competed to win his backing for various causes, schemes, and ideas.[3] He had to read many reports and correspondence, and,

---

[3]Tuomo Polvinen in his *Imperial Borderland: Bobrikov and the Attempted Russification of Finland, 1898–1904* (Durham, N.C., 1995), pp. 269–271, quotes numerous primary sources to indicate this competition for Nicholas's favor during his first decade of rule and how it contributed to the perception that a firm autocratic hand was lacking.

FIGURE 3.3. Nicholas II and family early in the century.
(UPI/Bettmann Newsphotos.)

unwilling to trust a private secretary, he personally wrote out his own letters. There were also the countless formal and ceremonial appearances, military reviews and parades, and social gatherings that a tsar was expected to attend.

His main solace in such a world was his family, especially his wife and children, four girls and a boy, all born between 1895 and 1904. Alexandra grew increasingly weary of the social aspects of being an empress and never mixed comfortably in Russian high society.

Nicholas's domestic policies in the first decade of his rule followed the pattern set by his father: a continuation and extension of the "temporary regulations," further restrictions on local government, more Russification and persecution of ethnic and religious minorities, and support of Witte's industrialization program. Although never personally close to Witte, he recognized his ability and therefore retained him as finance minister until 1903.

Yet there was one important way in which Nicholas was not able to imitate his father, and that was in dealing with opposition to his autocratic regime.

PUBLIC OPINION AND POLITICAL OPPOSITION, 1881–1904

Nicholas's failures to squash political opposition as effectively as his father had done was not just a result of his being a weaker man. The modernizing needs of the country had increased the number of opponents to traditional autocratic practices, making repression more difficult.

In early 1905, the historian Paul Miliukov noted "the enormous growth of the politically conscious social elements that make public opinion in Russia." Among these elements were more professionals, artists and writers, men of business, government officials, and zemstvo workers. Especially notable was the growth of zemstvo employees, which by 1905 numbered about 70,000 individuals spread out over 358 districts. Although more than half of them were teachers, there were also zemstvo doctors; paramedics; midwives; veterinarians; pharmacists; insurance agents; statisticians; librarians; agronomists; and administrative, technical, and clerical personnel.

Earlier, in 1881, Alexander III had heard two voices giving him the same unsolicited advice to forgo inflicting capital punishment on his father's assassins. In the decades ahead, Leo Tolstoy and Vladimir Soloviev continued to criticize government policies, primarily from an ethical-religious perspective.

Tolstoy's specific criticisms of the government were many, ranging from its persecution of religious and ethnic minorities to its failures to deal adequately with famine needs in 1891–1892, a famine that Tolstoy personally did much to alleviate. In 1901 and 1902, he wrote to Nicholas II advising him on certain minimum steps he should take. But since the early 1880s, Tolstoy's ultimate desires had gone much further. He wanted to abolish centralized governments, which he believed acted in behalf of the upper classes, and he evolved a philosophy of nonviolent anarchism. His main methods for bringing an end to government were for people to refuse to pay taxes or serve the government in any manner, including military service.

Tolstoy especially irritated Pobedonostsev, still the procurator of the Holy Synod, by rejecting many basic Orthodox teachings and doctrines. In 1901, a Holy Synod edict all but excommunicated him for his heresies. If Tolstoy had not by then possessed such an imposing worldwide reputation, there is little doubt that the government would have dealt with him more severely.

The unconventional religious philosopher Vladimir Soloviev also irritated Pobedonostsev. He polemicized with Russian nationalists and criticized religious and ethnic persecution. An early ecumenical thinker, he was especially eloquent in his criticism of Russian antisemitism. Although primarily a philosopher, he was also a gifted poet. He possessed a utopian temperament and was not especially interested in political details. But to further such goals as religious toleration, he allied from the late 1880s until his death in 1900 with secular liberals and contributed to their most popular journal, *The Messenger of Europe.*

Yet despite Soloviev's strong philosophic and poetic influence (see Chapter 7) and the "Tolstoyan" followers of Tolstoy's ideas, most of educated society's political opposition was more secular. Although it was diverse, Miliukov was essentially correct in identifying its two chief currents as socialist and liberal.

Russian Socialism: The Populist Strain

From 1881 until the beginning of 1905, there were basically two types of Russian socialism. One was an eclectic homespun brand in the populist tradition, and the other was Marxist.

After the assassination of Alexander II, the Executive Committee of the populist People's Will printed thousands of copies of an open letter to Alexander III. The committee promised that their organization would disband if the new tsar agreed to certain conditions. These included an amnesty for all past political crimes and the calling of a freely elected constituent assembly to remodel Russia's government in accordance with the wishes of the people. If Alexander III failed to agree to their demands, they promised increased terrorism.

Arrests, however, helped prevent them from carrying out any extensive terrorism, and despite efforts of revolutionaries to keep the People's Will alive, it slowly withered and died. By 1887, when a group of St. Petersburg students attempting to assassinate Alexander III claimed to be part of the People's Will, no such organization still existed. There were only some individuals, like the older brother of Vladimir Ulianov (Lenin), who wished to follow in its tradition. For their plans and actions, which included preparing assassination bombs, Alexander Ulianov and some of his co-conspirators were arrested. Ulianov and four others were hanged.

Before his death, Alexander Ulianov had been troubled by the question of whether Russia had to undergo a capitalist era before inaugurating socialism. For decades to come, this issue remained vital to many Russian socialists, including Alexander's brother Vladimir.

Among other socialists concerned with this question were the legal populists. The government permitted them to publish "legally" because they advocated no political overthrow or major political reforms. A major figure in whose journals they often published was the populist writer and editor N. K. Mikhailovsky (1842–1904). Already at the end of the 1860s, he had written an article entitled "What Is Progress?" It spelled out his belief that progress was not the type of capitalist development and increasing division of labor that was occurring in the West. Rather it was whatever contributed to the fullest development of the individual personality and the full use of one's physical and mental capacities. Like most populists, Mikhailovsky stressed the importance of free will and rejected the belief that any historical laws predetermined Russia's future.

Two of the most important legal populists of the 1880s and 1890s were V. P. Vorontsov and N. F. Danielson. What both men wanted was to avoid a fully developed capitalism in Russia, a capitalism both men believed would only increase the suffering of the Russian masses. Indeed, they believed its early stages were already doing so. Instead, they desired a state-sponsored industrialization that would be carried out not for the profits of a minority, but for the good of the masses, including small producers and peasants.

The famine of 1891–1892 helped stimulate a revival of populist activists in the 1890s, especially in the black-earth provinces stretching from Ukraine to the Urals. Until 1901, there was no large populist party, only a small number of groups and individuals working in the populist tradition. In 1901, however, several of these groups came together to form the party of Socialist Revolutionaries (SRs).

The SRs main theoretician was Viktor Chrenov, who had organized a populist peasant group in the Tambov Province. In the populist tradition, the SR program emphasized a dislike of capitalism, the belief that Russia's future was not determined by any "historical laws," that it could follow its own unique path of development, and that the interests of small producers and peasants had to be safeguarded. Although the SRs were active in the cities and propagandized and recruited urban workers, SR leaders considered the peasants and their welfare their chief concerns. Peasant disorders in the Kharkov and Poltava provinces in 1902, including attacks on noble estates, strengthened the SRs' belief in the revolutionary potential of the peasants.

The SRs' immediate goals were raising the revolutionary consciousness of workers and peasants and undermining tsarist rule. Ending autocracy would allow the free will of the masses to be expressed, and SR leaders were confident the masses would favor socialism. Because some SRs strongly believed in the use of terrorism to help accomplish party goals, an autonomous "Combat Organization" was formed that was ultimately responsible for killing many officials. From 1902 to 1905, its members killed, among others, Grand Duke Sergei (Nicholas II's uncle) and two interior ministers, including the much hated V. K. Plehve.

After the collapse of autocracy, the SRs envisioned a transition period in which land would be socialized and farmed by individuals or collectives and capitalist practices gradually limited. While predicting a final socialist order, marked by collective cultivation and the socialization of industry, the SRs claimed they would not try to dictate future developments.

Many populists of this period, although not considered Marxists, were familiar with Karl Marx's ideas and admired him for his criticism of capitalism. Danielson had helped translate *Das Kapital* into an 1872 Russian edition. In this work, Marx had quoted British factory inspectors' reports to expose such evils as the exploitation of child labor. To take just one short example, Marx quoted a father who said: "'That boy of mine . . . when he was 7 years old I used to carry him on my back to and fro through the snow, and he used to have 16 hours [of work] a day . . . I have often knelt down to feed him as he stood by the machine, for he could not leave it or stop.'"

Russian Socialism: The Marxists

The "father of Russian Marxism," Georgi Plekhanov, was a former populist and leading member of the Black Repartition. By 1883 (the year of Marx's death), Plekhanov had come to believe that full-scale capitalism was inevitable in Russia. In that year, in Geneva, he and some other former populists, including Vera Zasulich, formed the first Russian Marxist organization, the Emancipation of Labor. For them, the essence of Marx's self-proclaimed scientific socialism was his theory of "the materialist conception of history," or "historical materialism."

Marx spelled out its essence most succinctly in 1859 in a preface to his *A Critique of Political Economy:*

In the social production which men carry on, they enter into definite relations that are indispensable and independent of their will; these relations of production correspond to a definite stage of development of their material productive forces. The sum total of these relations of production constitutes the economic structure of society—the real foundation, on which arises a legal and political superstructure and to which correspond definite forms of social consciousness. The mode of production in material life determines the general character of the social, political, and spiritual processes of life. It is not the consciousness of men that determines their existence, but, on the contrary, their social existence determines their consciousness. At a certain stage of their development the material forces of production in society come into conflict with the existing relations of production. . . . From forms of development of the forces of production these relations turn into fetters. Then comes the period of social revolution.

More specifically, Marx stated that such productive forces as technology, material resources, and labor determined economic relationships. The productive forces and economic relationships together made up the foundation (or base) of society and, in turn, determined—or at least conditioned—the *superstructure* of government, laws, religion, and culture used by the dominant class in any historical period to strengthen its position.

Productive forces, Marx declared, had evolved in the course of history—which he divided into five stages: primitive communism, slavery, feudalism, capitalism, and socialism\communism. The general pattern was that a new class supported productive forces that evolved out of the old society, and this new class came into conflict with the class that dominated the older relations of production and superstructure. The old dominant class, however, never relinquished its power without a struggle. Thus, class conflict was inevitable and would continue until the establishment of socialism\communism—although Marx often used the two terms interchangeably, he sometimes used *socialism* to indicate the transitional period between capitalism and communism, a practice later adopted in the Soviet Union.

Marx and his frequent collaborator, Friedrich Engels (1820–1895) had begun their famous *Communist Manifesto* with the sentence: "The history of all hitherto existing society is the history of class struggles." In his own era in Western Europe, Marx believed the capitalist class of merchants and industrialists had proved victorious over the old feudal landowning class. Just as inevitably, said Marx, the industrial working class or "proletariat" would associate itself with still newer productive forces, even then evolving out of capitalist society. This working class would clash with the capitalist class and would eventually overthrow it.

Following the overthrow of the capitalists, the proletariat would establish a "dictatorship of the proletariat." It would deal with any remaining class enemies, end private control over productive forces, and introduce a classless socialist society. Since the main role of the state had previously been to protect class interests, the dictatorship of the proletariat and all the machinery of government would then no longer be necessary. Thus, it would gradually wither away and be followed by a Communist age of equitable social relations, humanized labor, and increased leisure.

Although Marx himself was unclear on the subject, Plekhanov interpreted Marx's writings, as did many others, to mean that Russia had to go through a fully developed capitalist stage before it could reach socialism.[4] In contrast to most of the populists who, following Lavrov and Mikhailovsky, believed that free will created various future possibilities, Plekhanov emphasized deterministic laws of development that humankind could not avoid. In the Marxist tradition, he emphasized the importance of the proletariat rather than the peasants. And because he believed a capitalist era would have to precede a socialist one, he was willing to cooperate with liberals to bring an end to the tsarist regime.

While Plekhanov and the other founders of the Emancipation of Labor remained abroad, by 1896–1897 Marxist circles operated in numerous cities of the Russian Empire. Many of these circles recognized a debt to Plekhanov and his comrades in Switzerland. This was partly because of the Russian censors' willingness to allow works penned by Plekhanov (but under various pseudonyms) to be published in Russia—the government viewed theoretical Marxist works, which often attacked the Populists, as not especially dangerous.

Among those impressed by Plekhanov was Vladimir Ulianov or Lenin, who traveled to Switzerland and met with him in 1895. Lenin was born in the Volga town of Simbirsk in 1870, where his father was a school inspector and passionate believer in education. By the time of his father's death in 1886, his civil service rank was equivalent to that of a general and had earned him and his family hereditary noble status. After graduating at the top of his gymnasium class (shortly after his brother was executed), Lenin enrolled at the University of Kazan, where he was soon expelled for taking part in a demonstration. From 1888 to 1893 he read, studied, and discussed radical ideas, first in Kazan and then in the Samara Province. In 1891, authorities permitted him to take the law examination at St. Petersburg University, which he passed, and in 1893 he moved to the capital, supposedly to practice law.

It was there that he first became involved with leading young Russian Marxists such as Peter Struve and Yuli Martov and began encouraging industrial workers to strike for their rights. Arrested at the end of 1895, he spent the next several years in prison and Siberian exile.

Meanwhile, despite organizing a founding congress of the Russian Social Democratic Labor party (RSDLP) in Minsk in 1898, Marxists within Russia were already becoming divided. Plekhanov was especially troubled by what he perceived as Russian variations of the Marxist revisionism of the German Eduard Bernstein, who believed that some commonly held Marxist assumptions had proven false.

At the end of Book I of *Kapital*, Marx had written of the diminishing num-

---

[4]For more on Lenin's interpretation of this and other Marxist doctrines by the end of 1917, see Chapter 8.

ber of capitalists and the increasing misery and class consciousness of the masses that would precede and help trigger the final collapse of the capitalist system and the "expropriation of the [capitalist] expropriators." He also believed that this collapse would be brought about by the inability of the impoverished masses to purchase the growing number of goods turned out under advanced capitalism. But Bernstein argued that too much emphasis was placed on this one section of Marx's writings and that even it was open to different interpretations.

Regardless, however, of what Marx's true views were, Bernstein maintained that the facts were that the number of capitalists was increasing, that many workers now were better off, and that class conflict was decreasing. As a result of these developments and the growing political role that the proletariat was beginning to play in some countries, Bernstein argued that the dream of a Marxian socialist revolution was outdated and that workers were right to use trade unions and democratic and parliamentary means to improve their everyday lives and gradually evolve toward socialism.

Plekhanov believed that "Economism" was the Russian variant of these ideas, for Economism's adherents also emphasized, above all, the workers' economic struggle. To some extent, they were merely mirroring the priorities of the growing number of radical workers. In Siberian exile, where Lenin had completed *The Development of Capitalism in Russia* and married a fellow Marxist, Nadezhda Krupskaia, he was also troubled by Economism and other signs of Bernstein's influence in Russia. Like Plekhanov, Lenin was fearful that Bernstein's influence might lead Russian workers from revolutionary thoughts to a trade-union mentality.

Upon being released from Siberian exile in 1900, Lenin joined Plekhanov in Switzerland, and the two men plus Martov and three others began publishing a Marxist journal, *Iskra* (*The Spark*). In it they defended what they considered Marxist orthodoxy against revisionism—besides Economism, they also thought that the "Legal Marxism" of Struve and others was tainted with Bernsteinism.

By 1903, *Iskra,* smuggled into Russia, was having a strong influence on the growing Marxist (or Social Democratic) movement, and Economism was all but smashed. To unify the Social Democrats better, the *Iskra* editors prepared a second congress of the RSDLP. It was held in the summer of 1903 in Brussels and then, for better security, in London. Forty-three delegates represented twenty-six local groups, among them the Jewish Bund.[5]

By then, however, Lenin and Martov disagreed over the nature of the RSDLP. In *What Is To Be Done?*, published in 1902, Lenin stated: "We have said that *there could not have been* Social Democratic [i.e., Marxist] consciousness among the workers. It would have to be brought to them from without. The history of all countries shows that the working class, exclusively by its own effort, is able to develop only trade union consciousness."

Although Marx at times wrote of a leading role for Communist intellectu-

---

[5]On the Jewish Bund, see Chapter 4.

als, Lenin went much further in downplaying the role of the proletariat and increasing that of the revolutionary intelligentsia. He feared that if workers were left to their own devices, they would be co-opted by the capitalists and sell their potentially revolutionary souls for better working conditions and wages.

The battle between Lenin and Martov at the congress revolved around party membership and centralized control over the party. Lenin's basic mistrust of workers' instincts and his fear of revisionism prodded him to attempt to limit membership to active participants in party organizations. Martov wanted a more broad-based party, which would include not only full-time revolutionaries, but also less active supporters.

Lenin lost the vote on membership to Martov, but he won out over his rival when the congress agreed to stronger controls over the RSDLP by a reduced *Iskra* board including Lenin and Plekhanov (who had supported Lenin). At the congress, Lenin labeled his faction the Bolsheviks (the majority) and Martov's the Mensheviks (the minority). It was not immediately evident that the split and names would long continue after the congress ended, but they did. Plekhanov's support of Lenin, however, did not last long. Within months, Plekhanov was trying to reconcile the factions, and when his efforts failed, he increasingly blamed Lenin and charged him with trying to establish a "dictatorship over the proletariat."

Liberalism and Reformism

In the era of counterreforms, the meaning of liberalism continued to be as elusive as it had been under Alexander II. Historians still disagree on whether some men were *liberal* or not, and the term was not one that individuals frequently applied to themselves. Be that as it may, it is used here to characterize the chief nonsocialist opposition of Alexander III and Nicholas II.

The liberalism of the 1880s and early 1890s has often been referred to as a liberalism of "small deeds." Many reformers were connected with the zemstvos or city councils, as representatives, members of the boards, or hired employees. In their local work, they tried to improve the lot of peasants and urban residents through such means as improving education, sanitation, and health care.

At times, local leaders suggested additional steps. From late 1881 to mid-1883, Boris Chicherin, who in 1856 had called Russians to rally around the banner of liberalism, served as head of Moscow's municipal government. For giving a speech in which he called for "crowning" the zemstvo and municipal structure by establishing a national body, Alexander III forced him to give up his position.

Such government reactions and the counterreforms of Alexander III weakened the voices of moderate reform and ultimately turned many to more radical measures. The government's ineffective response to the famine of 1891–1892, followed by Nicholas II's signals that he intended to follow in his father's footsteps, further stimulated liberals to switch from "small deeds" to more radical demands.

After Nicholas had warned the zemstvos against "senseless dreams" in 1895, some liberals wrote an open letter to the tsar indicating the effect of his action:

> You challenged the zemstvos, and with them Russian society, and nothing remains for them now but to choose between progress and faithfulness to autocracy. Your speech has provoked a feeling of offense and depression; but the living social forces will soon recover from that feeling. Some of them will pass to a peaceful but systematic and conscious struggle for such scope of action as is necessary for them. Some others will be made more determined to fight the detestable regime by any means. You first began the struggle; and the struggle will come.

By 1900, even the "conservative liberal" Chicherin had despaired of autocratic government and was now calling for a "limited monarchy." In 1904, the emerging liberal leader Professor Paul Miliukov called Chicherin's proposed limitations "the minimum program of contemporary liberalism." Along with Miliukov, Peter Struve, a former Marxist, became another liberal leader more radical than most of the liberals of Chicherin's generation. Backed by zemstvo financial support, in 1902 Struve began editing abroad a new liberal Russian-

---

Chicherin's Call for a Limited Monarchy

In 1900, Boris Chicherin's *Russia on the Eve of the Twentieth Century* was published in the Russian original in Berlin. The present English language excerpt of it is taken from Paul Miliukov's *Russia and Its Crisis* (Chicago, 1906), pp. 329–330. Ellipsis marks are in the Miliukov text.

It is impossible to limit bureaucracy without limiting the power whose weapon it is, or—as more often happens—which itself serves as a weapon in the hand of bureaucracy. I mean the unlimited power of the monarch. As long as this exists, unlimited arbitrariness at the top will always generate like arbitrariness in the dependent spheres. Legal order can never be affirmed where everything depends on personal will, and where every person invested with power may put himself above the law, while sheltering himself behind an imperial order. If the regime of legality may be said to form

the most urgent need of the Russian society, we must conclude that this need can be satisfied only by the change of the unlimited monarchy into a limited. . . . It is necessary that the elective assembly should be invested with definite rights. A consultative assembly, whose decisions may or may not be followed, will always be swayed by the ruling bureaucracy, though it is just bureaucracy that must be limited. Only such an organ as would be entirely independent and possess a deciding voice in state affairs can counterbalance the officials surrounding the throne. Only such an assembly, possessing some rights, can limit the will of the monarch—which is the first condition of the legal order. As long as the monarch will not grow accustomed to the idea that his will is not almighty, that there exists a law independent of his will, and that he must defer to it, every hope to overrule the arbitrariness of the officials, every dream about "guaranties," are vain and futile.

language journal, *Liberation*. The following year, in Switzerland, he and 19 others founded the Union of Liberation.

The ideas of Miliukov, Struve, and others were spelled out in the program the new organization adopted in October 1904. Like Chicherin and Constantine Kavelin in 1856, the new leaders hoped to rally the nation around a liberal banner. Among other demands, including an eight-hour day and more land for peasants, this program called for elections to a Constituent Assembly. This would mean that the future government of Russia would be decided by elected delegates—for Russia a radical step indeed.

Meanwhile, zemstvo leaders, including some Union of Liberation members, prepared for a zemstvo congress to be held in St. Petersburg in November 1904. The assassination of Plehve in July and early setbacks in the Russo-Japanese War (see Chapter 4) had been followed by the appointment of a new reform-minded minister of interior, Prince P. D. Sviatopolk-Mirsky. He allowed the congress to proceed, as long as it met in private residences.

The results of the congress were a clear sign that the majority of zemstvo representatives were becoming more radical. Besides basic freedoms, equal rights, and expanded zemstvo rights, they recommended that elected representatives be empowered to legislate (and not just consult), control the budget, and determine the legality of administrative actions.

Following this early November congress, groups of students, businessmen, and others met to discuss the zemstvo recommendations. The Union of Liberation arranged for a series of banquets to discuss them. While some banquet gatherings supported the recommendations, others went further and called for a Constituent Assembly.

Mirsky realized that Nicholas II would never agree with the majority of the zemstvo congress but tried to convince him of the necessity of at least some reforms, including allowing elected representatives a consultative role in formulating legislation. The minister believed that 99 percent of educated opinion favored some sort of participation by elected individuals. Nicholas did sign a decree in December 1904 that promised a reduction of both censorship and the "emergency rule" begun in 1881, more religious toleration, and an expansion of zemstvo activities. After considerable wavering, however, he followed the advice of Witte, his uncle Sergei, and Pobedonostsev: He refused to go along with his minister of interior's suggestion for a consultative role for elected deputies. Thus, almost a quarter century after his grandfather Alexander II had agreed to allow some elected delegates to offer advice on new legislation, Nicholas II, like his father, refused such a concession.

SUGGESTED SOURCES*

ANAN'ICH, BORIS V., and RAFAIL SH. GAMELIN. "Nicholas II," *RSH* 34 (Winter 1995–96): 68–95. Reprinted in *EER*, pp. 370–402.
BARON, SAMUEL H. *Plekhanov: The Father of Russian Marxism.* Stanford, 1963.

*See also books cited in footnotes.

BASIL, JOHN D. "Konstantin Petrovich Pobedonostsev: An Argument for a Russian State Church," *CH* 64 (March 1995): 44–61.

BILLINGTON, JAMES H. *Mikhailovsky and Russian Populism.* New York, 1958.

BYRNES, ROBERT F. *Pobedonostsev, His Life and Thought.* Bloomington, 1968.

CHERMUKHA, VALENTINA G. "Alexander III," *RSH* 34 (Winter 1995–96): 39–67. Reprinted in *EER*, pp. 335–368.

DALY, JONATHAN W. "Emergency Legislation in Late Imperial Russia," *SR* 54 (Fall 1995): 602–629.

FERRO, MARC. *Nicholas II: The Last of the Tsars.* London, 1991.

GALAI, SHMUEL. *The Liberation Movement in Russia, 1900–1905.* Cambridge, England, 1973.

HAMBURG, GARY M. *Politics of the Russian Nobility, 1881–1905.* New Brunswick, N.J., 1984.

JUDGE, EDWARD H. *Plehve: Repression and Reform in Imperial Russia, 1902–1904.* Syracuse, 1983.

JUDGE, EDWARD H., and JAMES SIMMS, eds. *Modernization and Revolution: Dilemmas of Progress in Late Imperial Russia: Essays in Honor of Arthur P. Mendel.* New York, 1992.

LIEVEN, DOMINIC. *Nicholas II: Emperor of all the Russias.* London, 1993.

LINCOLN, W. BRUCE. *In War's Dark Shadow: The Russians Before the Great War.* New York, 1983.

MCLELLAN, DAVID. *Karl Marx.* New York, 1975.

MEYER, ALFRED G. *Leninism.* New York, 1957.

MILIUKOV, P. N. *Russia and Its Crisis.* Chicago, 1905.

NAIMARK, NORMAN M. *Terrorists and Social Democrats: The Russian Revolutionary Movement Under Alexander III.* Cambridge, Mass., 1983.

OFFORD, DEREK. *The Russian Revolutionary Movement in the 1880s.* Cambridge, England, 1986.

PEARL, DEBORAH L. "Marxism's Russian Centennial: Soviet Scholars and the Emancipation of Labor Group," *RR* 49 (April 1990): 189–198.

PEARSON, THOMAS S. *Russian Officialdom in Crisis: Autocracy and Local Self-Government, 1861–1900.* Cambridge, England, 1989.

PIPES, RICHARD. *Struve: Liberal on the Left, 1870–1905.* Cambridge, Mass., 1970.

POBEDONOSTSEV, KONSTANTIN P. *Reflections of a Russian Statesman.* Ann Arbor, 1965.

ROBBINS, RICHARD G. *The Tsar's Viceroys: Russian Provincial Governors in the Last Years of the Empire.* Ithaca, N.Y., 1987.

ROGGER, HANS. *Russia in the Age of Modernization and Revolution, 1881–1917.* London, 1983.

SERVICE, ROBERT. *Lenin: A Political Life.* Vol. I, *The Strength of Contradiction.* Bloomington, 1985.

SNOW, GEORGE E., ed. *The Years 1881–1894 in Russia—a Memorandum Found in the Papers of N. Kh. Bunge: A Translation and Commentary.* Philadelphia, 1981.

TIMBERLAKE, CHARLES E., ed. *Essays on Russian Liberalism.* Columbia, Mo., 1972.

ULAM, ADAM B. *The Bolsheviks: The Intellectual and Political History of the Triumph of Communism in Russia.* New York, 1965.

VERNER, ANDREW M. *The Crisis of Russian Autocracy: Nicholas II and the 1905 Revolution.* Princeton, 1990.

VOLKOGONOV, DMITRI. *Lenin: A New Biography.* New York, 1994.

VON LAUE, THEODORE. *Sergei Witte and the Industrialization of Russia.* New York, 1963.

WALICKI, ANDRZEJ. *The Controversy Over Capitalism: Studies in the Social Philosophy of the Russian Populists.* Oxford, 1969.

WHELAN, HEIDE W. *Alexander III and the State Council: Bureaucracy and Counter-Reform in Late Imperial Russia*. New Brunswick, N.J., 1982.

WILDMAN, ALLAN K. *The Making of a Workers' Revolution: Russian Social Democracy, 1891–1903*. Chicago, 1967.

WITTE, S. IU. *The Memoirs of Count Witte*. Armonk, N.Y., 1990.

ZAIONCHKOVSKII, PETER A. *The Russian Autocracy under Alexander III*. Gulf Breeze, Fla., 1976.

CHAPTER 4

Russian Imperial and Foreign Policy, 1856–1905

Tsarist policies toward the empire's minority nationalities reached their Russifying and reactionary pinnacle during this era. Because many nationalities (such as the Poles, Ukrainians, and Armenians) existed not only in Russia, but also in large numbers in neighboring countries and because of Russia's poorly defined southern and southeastern borders, nationality policies often overlapped with foreign affairs. Those who were "foreigners" one year might become part of the empire the next, as happened in certain Asian areas during this era. It is hardly surprising, therefore, that the government's Asiatic Department dealt with both imperial and foreign policies.

After the Crimean War (1853–1856), the Russian government attempted to maintain its empire and great-power status by modernizing its economy and avoiding costly wars with major European powers. It did not, however, forgo its perceived right to expand in Asia, which it did until checked by Japan in the Russo-Japanese War of 1904–1905. Also, it did not cease to believe that it had a special ethnic and religious relationship to the Balkans. This belief helped drag it into the Russo-Turkish War of 1877–1878. Although Russia's victories won it substantial gains in the Treaty of San Stefano, they were soon reduced by other European powers at the Congress of Berlin.

Although imperial and foreign policy goals during this half-century were generally consistent, the means of implementing them fluctuated. Such changes were due primarily to changing circumstances and to the difficulties of reconciling major goals with each other and determining the best means to achieve them. These uncertainties left the door open for different ministers and public voices to influence tsarist policies.

THE FAR EAST, THE CAUCASUS, CENTRAL ASIA, AND ALASKA, 1856–1895

Alexander II's policies regarding China, the Caucasus, and Central Asia manifested the long-held Russian conviction that it had a right to Asian expansion and to civilize "backward" peoples. Alexander's actions in these areas built upon those taken by his father, Nicholas I. They also reflected Russian desires to compensate for the loss of the Crimean War and to battle against any further English gains in Asia.

Alexander II's China policy was strongly influenced by the Amur River gains of the early 1850s made by the governor-general of Eastern Siberia, Nikolai Muraviev (later Muraviev-Amursky in honor of his acquisitions). Muraviev had argued that the Amur was needed to insure Russian control of Eastern Siberia and to subvert any possible British moves to control the mouth of the Amur. He also argued that Russian possession of the Amur would enable Russia to strengthen its control over the Kamchatka Peninsula, expand trade with China, and maintain its influence there.

Alexander II allowed Muraviev to continue strengthening Russia's position along the Amur and even to advance into the area east of the Ussuri River. At the same time that British and French troops and diplomats (along with U.S. diplomats) were trying to force concessions of their own from the Chinese emperor, Russia was able to win recognition of its territorial gains. By the Treaties of Aigun and Tientsin (both in 1858) and the Treaty of Peking (1860), Russia gained territories from China about the size of Germany and France combined. Although containing few inhabitants, these lands strengthened Russia's Pacific position, placing it on the Sea of Japan and giving it a border with Korea. On that sea and near that border, Russia founded, in 1860, Vladivostok (meaning Ruler of the East) (see Map 4.1).

Russia's other major gain in the Far East under Alexander II was the island of Sakhalin, over which Japan and Russia contested before finally coming to an agreement in 1875. By the Treaty of St. Petersburg, Japan recognized Russia's claim to the island in exchange for Russia's recognition of Japanese control over the Kurile Islands.

In 1859, Russian forces in the Caucasus defeated Chechen and other Moslem forces and captured Shamil, who for a quarter of a century had led the Moslem "holy war" against Russia. This broke the Moslem resistance in the eastern Caucasus. Russian forces were now able to concentrate on the Circassians in the northwest Caucasus. By 1864, Circassian opposition was crushed, and the Circassians were forced to move to other Russian territories or leave the country. Most of them, some 400,000, left for Turkey, but many never reached it because of the difficulties of the journey. More importantly to the Russian government, after more than a half century of repeated warfare, almost all of the Caucasus was finally under Russian control (see Map. 4.3).

The focus now shifted to Central Asia and its Moslem peoples. Russian military moves in this region were part of an ongoing rivalry with the British, who controlled India and frequently interfered in Afghanistan. British protests in 1863 against Russia's treatment of the rebelling Poles seemed to many Russians just another sign of British hostility toward Russia. Russian gains in Central Asia were one means of countering British strengths elsewhere and of forestalling any British attempts to move north from India.

From 1864 to 1885, Russian troops south of the Kazakh steppe conquered the khanates of Kokand, Khiva, and Bukhara and the Turkmen or Transcaspian

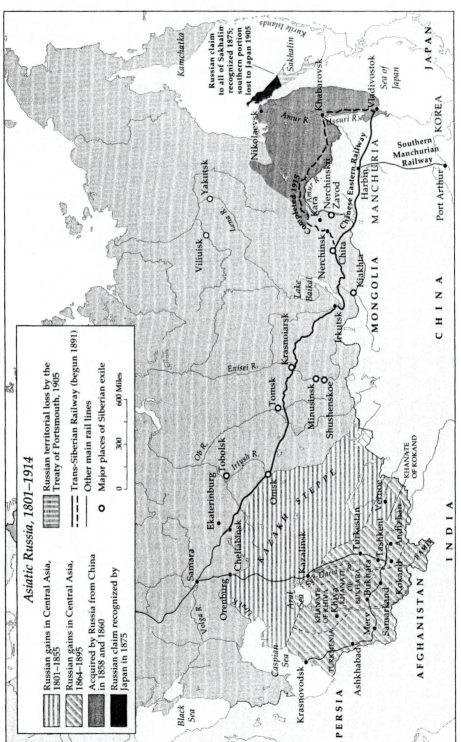

Asiatic Russia, 1801–1914

Russian gains in Central Asia, 1801–1855

Russian gains in Central Asia, 1864–1895

Acquired by Russia from China in 1858 and 1860

Russian claim recognized by Japan in 1875

Russian territorial loss by the Treaty of Portsmouth, 1905

Trans-Siberian Railway (begun 1891)

Other main rail lines

○ Major places of Siberian exile

0   300   600 Miles

Russian claim to all of Sakhalin recognized 1875; southern portion lost to Japan 1905

Kamchatka

Kurile Islands

Sakhalin

JAPAN

Sea of Japan

Khabarovsk

Vladivostok

Amur R.

Ussuri R.

Nikolaevsk

Amur R.

Kara

Completed 1915

Nerchinskii Zavod

Nerchinsk

Chita

Kiakhta

Chinese Eastern Railway

Harbin

MANCHURIA

KOREA

Southern Manchurian Railway

Port Arthur

CHINA

MONGOLIA

Yakutsk

Lena R.

Viliuisk

Lake Baikal

Irkutsk

Krasnoiarsk

Enisei R.

Tomsk

Minusinsk

Shushenskoe

Tobolsk

Ob R.

Irtysh R.

Ekaterinburg

Cheliabinsk

Omsk

KAZAKH STEPPE

KHANATE OF KOKAND

Turkestan

Vernoe

Andizhan

Tashkent

Kokand

Pamir

INDIA

Samara

Volga R.

Orenburg

Kazalinsk

Syr Darja R.

Aral Sea

KHANATE OF KHIVA

Khiva

Amu Darja R.

KHANATE OF BUKHARA

Bukhara

Samarkand

Mery

TURKMENIA

Ashkhabad

AFGHANISTAN

Krasnovodsk

Caspian Sea

PERSIA

Black Sea

MAP 4.1

66

region, east-southeast of the Caspian Sea and northeast of Persia. In 1884, Russia took over the city of Merv and the Merv region, and the following year Russian forces moved further south and engaged Afghan troops along the Afghan border.

For a while in the spring of 1885, it looked as if this latest Russian advance might lead to war with Great Britain. Not only were the British agitated over Russia's decades-long southern advance, but also they regarded Afghanistan as a buffer state to protect India. But the powers soon stepped back from the crisis and agreed to arbitrate the Russo-Afghan border. In 1895, Russia and Britain settled the disputed Pamir frontier, completing Russia's Central Asian expansion.

Although the Central Asian advances were partly motivated by Russia's rivalry with Great Britain, there were other factors at work. Some of these were explained by Foreign Minister Alexander Gorchakov in a memorandum intended to clarify Russia's policy to foreign powers.

A Justification for Russian Advances in Central Asia

The following selection is excerpted from Gorchakov's memorandum of November 1864, which was to be communicated to foreign governments. This excerpt was taken from Alexis Krausse, *Russia in Asia: A Record and a Study, 1558–1899* (London, 1899), pp. 224–225. A few spellings have been modernized.

The position of Russia in Central Asia is that of all civilized states which are brought into contact with half-savage nomad populations possessing no fixed social organization.

In such cases, the more civilized state is forced in the interest of the security of its frontier, and its commercial relations, to exercise a certain ascendancy over their turbulent and undesirable neighbors. Raids and acts of pillage must be put down. To do this, the tribes on the frontier must be reduced to a state of submission. This result once attained, these tribes take to more peaceful habits, but are in turn exposed to the attacks of the more distant tribes against whom the State is bound to protect them. Hence the necessity of distant, costly, and periodically recurring expeditions against an enemy whom his social organization makes it impossible to seize. If, the robbers

once punished, the expedition is withdrawn, the lesson is soon forgotten; its withdrawal is put down to weakness. It is a peculiarity of Asiatics to respect nothing but visible and palpable force. The moral force of reasoning has no hold on them.

In order to put a stop to this state of permanent disorder, fortified posts are established in the midst of these hostile tribes, and an influence is brought to bear upon them which reduces them by degrees to a state of submission. But other more distant tribes beyond this outer line come in turn to threaten the same dangers, and necessitate the same measures of repression. The state is thus forced to choose between two alternatives—either to give up this endless labor, and to abandon its frontier to perpetual disturbance, or to plunge deeper and deeper into barbarous countries, when the difficulties and expenses increase with every step in advance.

Such has been the fate of every country which has found itself in a similar position. The United States in America, France in Algeria, Holland in her colonies, England in India; all have been forced by imperious necessity into this onward march, where the greatest difficulty is to know where to stop.

MAP 4.2

Despite the justifications for advancing in Central Asia, the 1864 memorandum stated that Russia's advancement in Central Asia would be limited. When, in succeeding decades, Russia continued to advance far beyond the limits suggested by the memorandum, the cautious Gorchakov sometimes blamed it on adventurous generals who went beyond the orders of the tsar.

Although there was some truth to this excuse and Alexander II apparently

MAP 4.3

possessed no master plan to take all the lands gained in subsequent decades, both he and Alexander III supported cautious, piecemeal advancement. The tsars believed (correctly as it turned out) that such a policy could be pursued without leading to a war with Britain.

The memorandum's comparison of Russia's situation with that of Western powers reflected the belief that Russia's policies were consistent with those of other major countries. War Minister Dmitri Miliutin believed that Russia owed Great Britain no apology for its advancement, noting that the British did not consult the Russians before expanding their empire. But the advance in Central Asia was perhaps more comparable to the American white man's movement westward at the expense of Native Americans. Like Native Americans, the Moslems in Central Asia lost out to a better organized and united force that possessed superior military technology and moved steadily forward on contiguous territory. Only when the British, along with high southern mountain ranges, rose up to impede further advances did Russia's southern thrust come to an end.

Although hope of economic gain also enticed Russia southward, this aspiration was not a major factor. In fact, Minister of Finance Reutern warned about the costs of expansion and made every effort to keep them to a minimum.

Concern about state finances also influenced Russia's decision to sell Alaska to the United States in 1867. Although the new Asian territories gained in the Far East and Central Asia more than compensated for the amount of land lost by the sale of Alaska, it was still a large area to relinquish. By 1867, however, the Russian government considered it more of an economic liability than an asset, and it badly needed the $7.2 million the U.S. government was willing to pay. Besides, Alaska was all but impossible for Russia to defend, and Russia hoped its sale would help solidify good relations with the United States. Although today the price offered by U.S. Secretary of State William Seward seems ridiculously cheap—less than two cents an acre—some Americans thought Russia got the better of the deal and referred to it as "Seward's Folly" and to Alaska as "Seward's Icebox."

EUROPE, THE POLES, AND RUSSIA'S WESTERN NATIONALITIES, 1856–1875

From 1856 until 1870, the regaining of military rights in the Black Sea was an important goal of Russian diplomacy. Gorchakov's appointment as foreign minister in 1856 indicated how this end might be gained, for he was known to favor a rapprochement with France. Yet, despite improved Franco-Russian relations, France's Napoleon III failed to provide the diplomatic support Russia needed to overturn the hated Black Sea clauses. France's opposition to Russian actions during the Polish revolt of 1863–1864 further doused hopes for any Black Sea help from the French.

The full-scale rebellion that broke out in Warsaw in January 1863 was due to many reasons, including permanent Polish resentment against Russian control, rising Polish nationalism, and Alexander II's relaxation of the Russian reins on Poland. This easing fueled Polish expectations that exceeded the concessions Alexander II was willing to grant.

Because of Polish guerrilla tactics and the rebellion's spread to other western borderlands, it took more than a year for Russian forces to restore order. But restore it they did, and with a special vengeance in the Lithuanian area, where the governor-general, Mikhail Muraviev, became known as "the hangman of Vilna."

In Lithuania, Belorussia, Ukraine, and Kingdom of Poland (which now lost this special designation), the government instituted new Russification policies that went further than those of Nicholas I. They involved primarily the further Russification of the schools and government. For example, Russian now became the principal language of instruction in Poland's secondary schools. In the nine western provinces Catherine II had gained from Poland, a law of 1865 forbade people of Polish descent from acquiring further land except through inheritance. Catholicism was also subjected to new discriminations, and, in 1875, the government forced Catholic Unites in Poland to cease their separate existence and "reunite" with Russian Orthodoxy.

Yet for peasants in Poland and in the Lithuanian, Belorussian, and western Ukrainian provinces, some good did emerge from the revolt. To win them over to the Russian side, the government enacted more generous land provisions for emancipated peasants than it did for Russian peasants. Because so many lords in the western provinces were Polish or Polonized, the government had few qualms about demanding greater land sacrifices from them than from the Russian landowners.

Russification in Ukraine was stimulated not only by the Polish rebellion, but also by signs of growing Ukrainian nationalism among Ukrainian students and intellectuals. In 1863, Minister of Interior Peter Valuev prohibited educational, scholarly, and religious publications in the "Little Russian dialect"—he refused to admit that a separate Ukrainian language existed. In 1876, the government went further by prohibiting Ukrainian from being spoken on the stage or by teachers in the classroom. Furthermore, Ukrainian could not appear in any new or imported publications or in school libraries.

Other nationalities fared better, especially the Finns, who were permitted considerable autonomy. In 1863, in the midst of the Polish rebellion, Alexander II allowed the first Finnish Diet to meet since 1809 and continued thereafter to allow regular sessions of that legislative body. In the Baltic provinces, the Baltic Germans retained their privileged status throughout Alexander II's reign. But resentment of them grew in this nationalistic age, especially on the part of some Great Russian nationalists. In 1867, the use of the Russian language was required by imperial officials in the Baltic provinces, and ten years later Baltic towns were required to adopt Russian municipal institutions and the use of Russian in official activities.

Jewish life under Alexander II improved in some ways but in others foreshadowed the more oppressive conditions that would follow under Alexander III. The hated special draft of Jewish boys was ended in 1856, and more Jews were allowed opportunities outside the Jewish Pale of Settlement and Congress Poland (see Map 4.4). Nevertheless, in 1881 about 19 out of every 20 legally registered Jews continued to reside in these restricted areas. When new municipal rules were enacted in 1870, it was mandated that no more than one-third of any town council could be composed of Jews and that no Jew could serve as a mayor.

FIGURE 4.1. Statue of
Alexander II on Senate
Square, Helsinki. This
statue was erected in 1894
by the Finns and still
stands today, a tribute to
Alexander II's relatively
tolerant attitude to Finnish
autonomy.

In 1871, an anti-Jewish pogrom occurred in Odessa, a city about one-quarter Jewish. Eight people were killed, and hundreds of Jewish apartments and
shops were looted or vandalized. By the end of Alexander II's reign, Judeopho-
bia was on the rise. The writer Dostoevsky was just one of many individuals
who expressed his prejudices. In 1880, he wrote: "The Jew and the bank now
dominate everything: Europe and Enlightenment, the whole civilization and
socialism—especially socialism, for with its help the Jew will eradicate Christianity and destroy the Christian civilization."[1]

Meanwhile, internationally, France's strong objections to Russia's crushing
of the Polish rebellion, along with Prussia's support of Russian actions, led
Alexander II to move closer to Prussia. While Prussia's Wilhelm I (Alexander's
uncle) and his indispensable minister, Otto Von Bismarck, were fighting three

[1]Quoted in Hans Kohn, *Prophets and Peoples: Studies in Nineteenth Century Nationalism* (New York,
1961), p. 181, n. 27.

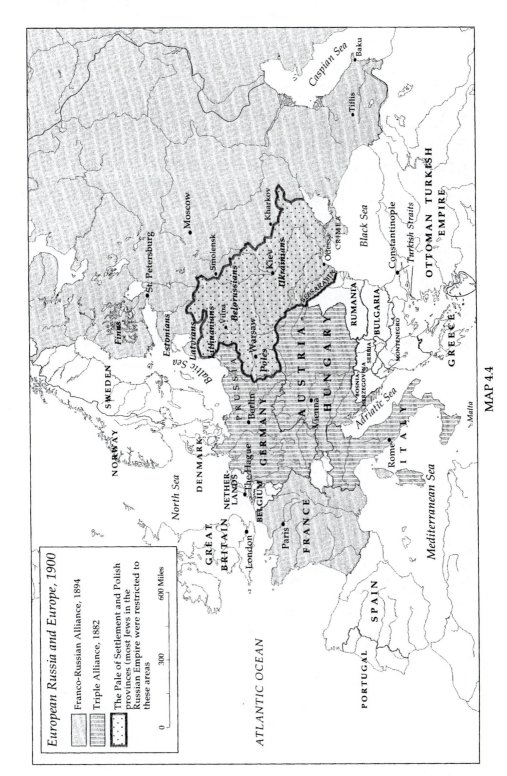

MAP 4.4

European Russia and Europe, 1900

Franco-Russian Alliance, 1894

Triple Alliance, 1882

The Pale of Settlement and Polish provinces (most Jews in the Russian Empire were restricted to these areas)

0   300   600 Miles

ATLANTIC OCEAN

PORTUGAL

SPAIN

Mediterranean Sea

FRANCE

Paris

London

GREAT BRITAIN

North Sea

NETHER-LANDS

BELGIUM

The Hague

DENMARK

NORWAY

SWEDEN

Finns

Baltic Sea

Estonians

Latvians

Lithuanians

Vilna

Belorussians

Warsaw

Poles

PRUSSIA

Berlin

GERMANY

Rome

ITALY

Adriatic Sea

AUSTRIA

HUNGARY

Vienna

BOSNIA-HERZEGOVINA

SERBIA

MONTENEGRO

RUMANIA

BULGARIA

BESSARABIA

Odessa

Kiev

Ukrainians

Kharkov

CRIMEA

Black Sea

Constantinople

Turkish Straits

OTTOMAN TURKISH EMPIRE

GREECE

Malta

St. Petersburg

Moscow

Smolensk

Caspian Sea

Baku

Tiflis

73

wars and uniting Germany between 1864 and 1871, Alexander II and Russia remained benevolently neutral. In 1870, Russia used the occasion of the Franco-Prussian War to abrogate the hated Black Sea demilitarization clauses of the Treaty of Paris—a move allowed to stand by an international conference in London the following year.

Russia therefore gained an immediate benefit from Prussia's wars and its own benevolent neutrality. After the tremendous German devastation of Russia in two twentieth-century wars, however, the question must at least be posed whether aiding the creation of a strong, united Germany was in Russia's long-term interest.

Once Prussia had defeated France in 1871, Bismarck worked to insure diplomatic arrangements that would enable the new Germany to keep its gains. Again, Alexander II was willing to cooperate. In 1873, Russia and Germany agreed to come to each other's aid, with an army of 200,000, if attacked by another European power. Later that year, Alexander II and Franz Joseph of Austria signed an agreement pledging consultation and cooperation in case of another power's aggression. The two agreements together created the Three Emperors' League, which was aimed at any major threat that would destabilize the three empires.

CRISIS IN THE BALKANS AND THE RUSSO-TURKISH WAR OF 1877–1878

Despite the Three Emperors' League, cooperation between Austria and Russia proved difficult. This was primarily because of Russo-Austrian competition in the Balkans, where rising Slavic national movements threatened to overthrow Turkish control. Both Austria and Russia had strong special interests in the area. Containing many Slavic nationalities itself, the Austro-Hungarian Empire feared that unchecked nationalism south of its borders would carry over into its own empire and act as a disintegrating force. Russian interest in the area stemmed primarily from Balkan domination by the Moslem Turks, Balkan linkage with the Black and Mediterranean seas, and Orthodox-Slavic Russia's traditional role as an intermediary for its Balkan co-religionists.

As Russian nationalism grew stronger during and after the Polish rebellion, so too did Russian panslavism. Its most ardent champions, including the historian M. P. Pogodin, dreamed of a Slavic union under Russian hegemony that would stretch from the Pacific to the Adriatic. For more than a decade before his death in 1875, Pogodin had been the president of the Slavonic Benevolent Committee, which reached the height of its influence in the late 1870s. By 1877, its Moscow committee and branches in St. Petersburg, Kiev, and Odessa possessed more than 1,000 members. They included the journalist and Slavophile Ivan Aksakov, who succeeded Pogodin as president; the influential editor Mikhail Katkov; the writer Dostoevsky; General (retired) R. A. Fadeev;

the botanist N. Danilevsky; and Russia's ambassador to Constantinople, N. P. Ignatiev. Fadeev's *Opinion on the Eastern Question* and Danilevsky's *Russia and Europe* both appeared in 1869 and called for Russia to battle her enemies and unite the Slavs.

In mid-1875, Herzegovina and then Bosnia revolted against Turkish rule. The following spring, Bulgaria joined them in revolt; and early in the summer of 1876, Serbia and Montenegro declared war on Turkey.

At first, Alexander II worked with other European rulers to deal with the crisis. The major powers, with the exception of Great Britain, agreed upon a program of land, tax, and religious reform in the Balkans that Turkey would administer under their watchful eyes. But British Prime Minister Disraeli distrusted Russian intentions and hoped to drive a wedge between the members of the Three Emperors' League. His attitude encouraged Turkish resistance to European diplomatic efforts.

Meanwhile, Russia's enthusiasm for the heroic struggle of its fellow Orthodox Slavs spread rapidly. The Slavonic Benevolent Committee and Orthodox Church leaders were in the forefront of relief efforts. The tsarina and the tsarevich also helped. Russian officers were allowed to take furloughs to serve as volunteers in the Serbian army. Other Russian volunteers also assisted the Serbs. The semiretired Russian General Cherniaev, called the "Lion of Tashkent" for his Central Asian conquest, soon became the head of the Serbian army. Leo Tolstoy, who was then writing *Anna Karenina* and who was unsympathetic with the mood of educated society, described it in his novel (as translated by Aylmer Maude).

> Among the people to whom he belonged, nothing was written or talked about at that time except the Serbian war. Everything that the idle crowd usually does to kill time, it now did for the benefit of the Slavs: balls, concerts, dinners, speeches, ladies' dresses, beer, restaurants—all bore witness to our sympathy with the Slavs. . . . The massacre of our co-religionists and brother Slavs evoked sympathy for the sufferers and indignation against their oppressors. And the heroism of the Serbs and Montenegrins, fighting for a great cause, aroused in the whole nation a desire to help their brothers not only with words but by deeds.

In Constantinople, still another force acted to encourage Russian assistance to the Slavs—Russia's ambassador to the Ottoman Empire, Nikolai Ignatiev. Apparently without tsarist authority, he encouraged the Serbs to believe they could count on Russian aid if they went to war with Turkey.

In the autumn of 1876, after the Serbs had suffered a series of defeats and the Turks were threatening Belgrade, Alexander sent an ultimatum to the Turks, demanding a truce. They agreed to a six-week armistice.

With his finance minister, M. K. Reutern, warning of the economic consequences of a war, Alexander continued to seek a diplomatic solution. He assured the British ambassador to Russia that British fears of Russian intentions regarding Constantinople and India were ludicrous. But Disraeli remained uncooperative, and Alexander remained under pressure from various quarters, including his wife Maria and his oldest son, the future Alexander III. After several more months of futile diplomatic efforts and fearful of alienating public opinion, Alexander II decided on war. In April 1877, after obtaining Austria's assurance of neutrality by assenting to a future Austrian occupation of Bosnia and Herzegovina, Russia declared war on Turkey.

Russia's educated public cheered the declaration. Many liberals and radicals supported the Slavs rebellions in the Balkans because they saw them as a struggle of freedom-fighters against Turkish tyranny. Others, such as Dostoevsky, thought that Russia was fighting for a sacred cause and that the war would help to unite Russia around the true Orthodox ideas it should be following.

Although Russian troops suffered some setbacks in Bulgaria and the Caucasus, they generally advanced, and in early 1878 Turkey agreed to an armistice. In March, the two powers signed a treaty at San Stefano, a little village occupied by Russian troops only about six miles from the walls of Constantinople.

Among others, Ignatiev and Dostoevsky had wanted Russia to seize Constantinople, but fear of English and Austro-Hungarian intervention restrained the tsar. British ships had already advanced to within a few miles of the Turkish capital, and Britain threatened war if Russia seized it.

The Treaty of San Stefano allowed Russia to regain southern Bessarabia (lost in the Crimean War); created a large autonomous Bulgaria with a sizable Aegean coastline; provided for Russian territorial gains in the Caucasus and a Turkish indemnity to Russia; recognized the independence of Serbia, Montenegro, and Rumania; stipulated territorial gains for Serbia and especially Montenegro; and mandated Turkish reforms in Bosnia and Herzegovina.

Russian nationalists and panslavists were generally happy with the treaty, although some thought it was the minimum Russia could accept. Austria and Britain were far from pleased, however, and exerted diplomatic pressure for modifications to it. Fearing war and its effects on an already strained Russian budget, Alexander II agreed to a peace congress in Berlin, where Bismarck was to act as an "honest broker."

The Congress of Berlin met in mid-1878. By the Treaty of Berlin, the enlarged Bulgaria that Russia hoped to dominate was greatly reduced in size; Austria-Hungary obtained the right to occupy Bosnia and Herzegovina and Britain to administer the island of Cyprus. In Asia Minor, Russia retained most of its gains at Turkey's expense. The powers also recognized Russia's right to annex southern Bessarabia.

Although territorial gains, an indemnity, expanded rights for the peoples of the Balkans, and a weakening of the Ottoman Turkish Empire remained as real accomplishments, Russians realized that the new treaty was a diplomatic setback and a blow to Russian pride. Although he felt helpless to prevent it, Alexander II considered it one of the darkest moments of his reign. Russian nationalists were especially upset. The panslav leader Ivan Aksakov openly criticized Russian actions in Berlin, a criticism that led to his exile in the country-side and the closing of the Moscow Slavonic committee.

EUROPEAN RELATIONS, 1881–1905

Although angered at Germany and Austria-Hungary for their part in the Berlin settlement of 1878, Alexander II once again pressed these two neighbors to renew the Three Emperors' League. This was after he received word that they had entered negotiations for a new treaty, which they soon signed in 1879. In this alliance, they promised to come to each other's aid if either were attacked by Russia. Later, in 1882, they would join with Italy to sign a a Triple Alliance, which stipulated that if one or two of the three signatories were attacked by two or more powers, the other member(s) of the alliance should render assistance. Alexander II feared diplomatic isolation, and the conservative monarchies of Germany and Austria-Hungary still seemed the best potential allies.

In 1879, however, Bismarck was in no hurry to renew the Three Emperors' League. It was not until mid-1881, after Alexander III had come to the throne, that a secret Three Emperors' Alliance was finally signed. Its most important clause stipulated benevolent neutrality in case any of the three powers became involved in a war with a fourth power. If that fourth power happened to be Turkey, the agreement became operative only if the three signatories first agreed on the results of a Turkish war. Other clauses reaffirmed recognition of the closure of the Straits to warships—Russia especially wished to keep British naval vessels out of the Black Sea—and addressed Russian and Austro-Hungarian interests in the Balkans, which were to come at the expense of Turkey. These clauses allowed for the eventual enlargement of Bulgaria (by the addition of Eastern Rumelia) and the Austro-Hungarian annexation (when opportune) of Bosnia and Herzegovina. The treaty was for three years and was renewed for another three in 1884.

The fact that the Three Emperors' Alliance called for neutrality, not military aid, is worth emphasizing because Russia's fragile economy necessitated avoiding war with any major power. To put its economic house in order and invest more in the basic industrial structure so important for modern war, Russia cut back on direct military spending in 1882. For more than two decades after that, Russia avoided any major conflict.

As a result of clumsy policies and practices, Russia lost the leverage it had possessed in Bulgaria, and Austrian and British influence in that country increased. Tensions between Russia and Austria-Hungary over Bulgaria helped prevent the renewal of the Three Emperors' Alliance when it expired in June 1887. Yet that same month Germany's Bismarck concluded a secret Reinsurance Treaty with Russia, binding for three years. He was mindful of France's desire to win back what it had lost in 1870–1871 and feared a Russo-French alliance. The Reinsurance Treaty stipulated neutrality if either country became involved in a war with a third power, but if Germany attacked France, or Russia attacked Austria, the neutrality clause would not apply. The treaty also declared that Germany recognized Russia's right to predominant influence in Bulgaria, once again reaffirmed the two powers' support of the closure of the Straits, and promised German "moral and diplomatic support" if Russia found it necessary to defend the entrance to the Black Sea against foreign warships.

German support regarding Bulgaria and the Black Sea had minimal practical effect and cost Bismarck little. Russia's predominant influence in Bulgaria was already disappearing, and the closure of the Straits had already been agreed to many times by the European powers.

Until the mid-1880s, Russo-German relations were buttressed by close economic cooperation. German capital, industrial goods, and technical expertise flowed into Russia, while Germany received large amounts of Russian grain. Already by 1887, however, a tariff conflict between the two powers was underway, as protectionism became more prominent in both countries. Toward the end of that same year, Germany seriously curtailed its loans to Russia. In 1890, two years after coming to the throne, the young Emperor Wilhelm II of Germany dismissed Bismarck and refused to renew the Reinsurance Treaty. The Russian government finally overcame its ideological scruples toward republican France and moved toward a Franco-Russian alliance.

Already in 1888 and 1889, republican France and autocratic Russia had begun to move closer. French bankers furnished loans, helping to fill the vacuum created by the tightening of German credit in 1887, and French officials agreed to furnish information about, and allow the purchase of, a new French rifle then being developed.

After Emperor Wilhelm's rebuff, Franco-Russian cooperation accelerated. In July 1891, Alexander III greeted a French naval squadron and its admiral at Kronstadt, the naval base guarding St. Petersburg. A Russian band played the "Marseillaise," the anthem of the French Revolution, while the autocratic Alexander III stood at attention. The following month, the two countries signed an agreement promising to consult if peace was endangered.

In 1892, the French presented the Russians with a draft military convention. After considerable changes and delays, it was ratified in January 1894 (N.S.). The heart of this Franco-Russian secret agreement was the mutual promise to assist each other, with all available forces, in case of a German attack on either country. German support for Italy against France or for Austria against Russia obligated the nonattacked ally (Russia or France) to fight Germany. The French were so pleased with the new treaty and Alexander III that in 1896, two years after his death, they began building the Alexander III bridge over the Seine River in Paris.

Yet the Russian government remained hopeful that war with Germany would not occur, and it continued attempting to improve relations with both Germany and Austria. In 1894, Russia and Germany signed a new tariff treaty, and during the next decade, Russia's trade with Germany exceeded that with any other country. In 1897, Russia and Austria agreed not to disturb the status quo in the Balkans.

Russia's desire for peace was partly motivated by its realization of its weak economic and military position at a time when world military spending and military technology were advancing rapidly. In 1898, this same realization helped prompt the Russian government to call for an international conference to limit armaments. Out of this Russian initiative, two peace conferences (in 1899 and 1907) eventually resulted, both held in The Hague. But in this militaristic era, there was little chance of any serious arms limitation agreement. All that the delegates could agree on were the rules of war and the establishment of an international (but not compulsory) court of arbitration.

NATIONALITIES, RUSSIFICATION, AND DISCRIMINATION, 1881–1905

By 1897, Great Russians were a minority in the Russian Empire, and together with the Ukrainians and Belorussians (both mainly Orthodox Slavs), they still constituted only about two-thirds of the empire's population.

Russification Policies

Despite some Russification of Russia's nine western provinces and the former Kingdom of Poland after the Polish revolt of 1863, Russification and discrimination against non-Russians did not reach their height until 1881–1905. Although in retrospect such policies seem foolish and counterproductive, there were many factors nudging the government in the direction it took.

Among European powers, Germany's growing strength after 1870 most impressed its neighbors. In minority areas, such as its Poland lands, it imposed Germanization by such measures as demanding the use of German in administration and schools. Austria-Hungary was weaker than Germany, and some Russian nationalists believed this was partly because of the Dual Monarchy's inability to impose a unifying nationality policy upon its peoples. Besides the German example, there was a growing fear of Germany, especially by the 1890s, and Russification measures were especially prevalent in border areas that could be threatened by Germany.

Other causes also stimulated Russification. Economic modernization sped up centralizing tendencies that were often accompanied by Russifying measures. In a more backward direction, Russification was part of the counter-reform mentality of the times, a reaction to the growing forces threatening autocracy and the empire's political stability. In some ways, this reaction hearkened back to the Official Nationality policies of Nicholas I. By the 1880s, however, nationalism in Russia and throughout Europe (as the philosopher V. Soloviev noted and decried) had taken on harsher tones. The new mood was evidenced by the increased popularity of Danilevsky's Europe-bashing *Russia and Europe*, which was published in new editions in 1888 and 1889.

Certainly one cause of the increased Russification of the 1881–1905 period was Pobedonostsev. As procurator of the Holy Synod and a tsarist adviser, he

FIGURE 4.2. Alexander Nevsky Cathedral, Reval (Tallinn), 1894–1900. The construction of this Orthodox Cathedral exemplified Pobedonostsev's policy of trying to strengthen Orthodox influence among the predominately Lutheran Estonians and Latvians.

pushed Russification policies along with ones designed to win converts to Orthodoxy and discourage other religions in the Russian Empire.

Pobedonostsev realized the danger of national movements to the unity of "composite states" such as Austria-Hungary and Russia. One reason he gave for rejecting parliamentary government was that in multinational states, a parliament became a forum for "racial hatred, both to the dominant race, to the sister races, and to the political institution which unites them all." Russian autocracy, he claimed, had "succeeded in evading or conciliating" racial or national "demands and outbreaks, not alone by means of force, but by the equalization of rights and relations under the unifying power."

The problem was that Pobedonostsev's "equalization of rights and relations" too often meant forcing Russian ways and the Russian language upon national minorities. Such standardization, which was often supported by other government bureaucrats and military leaders, including some co-opted non-Russians, was a far cry from equal rights. Although some ministers, such as Finance Minister Witte, opposed extreme Russification, thinking it counterproductive to stability and financial growth, their opinions on the subject had little impact.

Both government nationality policies and opposition to them, however, were quite complex and varied from one region to another. Pobedonostsev, for example, although generally pushing Russification, opposed some of the specific measures applied in Finland. And if non-Russians often suffered from Russification, the ethnic Russians—less urbanized, less literate, and with lower life expectancies than many of the non-Russian western nationalities—could hardly be considered a privileged people.

In many areas, the nationality issue was complicated by the presence of more than one non-Russian nationality. Russia's Jews, for example, resided mainly in the former Kingdom of Poland, Lithuania, Belorussia, Ukraine, and Bessarabia. The Baltic Germans were the dominant class in the Baltic region but were still a minority among native Latvians and Estonians. The Caucasus were a hodgepodge of nationalities. Armenians, for example, were outnumbered by the combined total of other nationalities in most of their own provinces, but Armenian merchants, traders, and artisans were important to the economic life of non-Armenian Caucasian cities such as Tiflis and Baku.

The presence of large numbers of Armenians, Poles, Ukrainians, and other non-Russian nationalities outside as well as inside the empire's borders further complicated Russia's nationality policies. So too did the overlapping of non-Orthodox faiths with non-Russian peoples. Powerful and influential Catholic and Lutheran voices abroad, for example, could not be completely ignored as Russia pursued its policies in its Polish and Baltic lands.

Despite these foreign voices, however, the Russification policies instituted by Alexander II in the western provinces and Poland continued, and his two successors went even further. For example, in 1885, the Russian government extended to Polish primary schools the use of Russian as the language of instruction for almost all subjects. As relations with Germany grew cooler, Russian anxieties about Baltic security increased and helped usher in the most extensive Russification policies the region had ever witnessed. The government enacted them in Estland, Livland, and Courland primarily between 1887 and 1894 and in Finland from 1899 to 1904.

Because of the previous tolerance of Finnish autonomy, the attempted Russification in Finland was especially significant. For five years, until his assassination in 1904, Governor-General N. I. Bobrikov administered a policy that curtailed the rights of the Finnish Diet, decreed Russian the official administrative language, and proclaimed a new conscription law that made Finns susceptible to being drafted directly into Russian units. The law also aimed at integrating the small (and previously separate) Finnish military into the Russian army. After these policies awakened massive resistance, Bobrikov, in 1903, suspended remaining traditional rights and assumed strengthened emergency powers.

In contrast to the Baltic area, there was little direct Russification in Central Asia and among the Turkic and Moslem peoples. Any large-scale Russification effort among these peoples would have been extremely expensive. Largely for this reason, the khanates of Bukhara and Khiva retained autonomy and responsibility for their own internal affairs, and even the directly annexed parts of Central Asia retained considerable control over local affairs.

Yet, aided by the growth of railways, Russian colonists migrated to cities like Tashkent and Samarkand and even to some rural Central Asian areas. This colonization facilitated the growth of Russian schools and other institutions in the region and offered some competition to native Moslem traditions.

Opposition Among the Nationalities

Opposition to Russian nationality policies was sometimes spurred by religious grievances. In 1898, a Moslem religious leader and his followers proclaimed a holy war against the Russians and marched on the Central Asian city of Andizhan, where they were defeated by Russian troops. After the Russian government confiscated Armenian Church property in 1903, Armenians launched a massive passive resistance campaign.

Opposition movements among the non-Russians were also fueled by more secular forces. Accompanying increased urbanization was the growth of socialist parties. Although some non-Russians, including Joseph Stalin, joined the Russian Social Democratic party (later split between Bolsheviks and Mensheviks), others joined more local national Marxist or socialist organizations. Among those formed between 1887 and 1904 were the Jewish Bund and socialist parties in Armenia, Georgia, Poland, Ukraine, Belorussia, Latvia, and Lithuania. An important issue to many of these parties was whether national or socioeconomic goals should receive a greater priority. This debate sometimes led to a split and the formation of new parties.

Organized political opposition, whether fueled by religious or secular ideas, developed more slowly among Russia's Moslem population. Nevertheless, the Crimean Tatar Ismail Bey Gasprinsky (1851–1914), an influential publicist and educator, advocated the development of a single Turkic language and furthered a sense of unity among Russia's Turkic Moslems.

National consciousness and participation in national opposition to Russification varied considerably. Among Poles, Finns, and Armenians, opposition was at times widespread. Among Ukrainians and Belorussians, overt opposition was more limited, involving primarily students and intellectuals. And some non-Russians among virtually all nationalities were willing to pay the price of Russification for the benefits they believed it brought them.

Jews

Russification and reactions to it do not tell the entire story of Russia's nationality policy. Russia's treatment of its Jewish population was less a question of Russification and more a case of exclusion.

After anti-Jewish pogroms broke out in Ukraine in spring 1881, the panslavist Ignatiev became minister of interior. He blamed the anti-Jewish violence (eventually some 20,000 Jewish homes were destroyed) on the Jews themselves. Like Dostoevsky earlier, he complained of Jewish monetary influence, and he thought the pogroms were a reaction to "Jewish exploitation."

Although scholars such as Rogger have challenged the traditional belief of strong government complicity in the pogroms of this period, there remains little doubt that Judeophobic attitudes were widespread in government and conservative nationalist circles, starting at the top with the era's last two tsars. Pobedonostsev was especially hostile to Jews. Although he knew it was unlikely, he hoped—in the words of his leading biographer—"one-third of the Jews would emigrate, one-third would be assimilated, and one-third would die out."[2] Such attitudes fertilized the soil out of which both pogroms and antisemitic measures germinated.

To curtail "Jewish exploitation" and thereby remove what he considered a main cause of the pogroms, Ignatiev prepared new "temporary regulations." By the May Laws of 1882, any new Jewish settlement in villages or rural purchase of property was prohibited, as was doing business on Sunday mornings or Christian holy days.

Other prohibitions and restrictions soon followed. Jews were limited to no more than 5 percent of army medical personnel. By a law of 1887, Jewish students could make up no more than 10 percent of the total secondary and higher school enrollments within the Pale of Settlement (the restricted western areas where the overwhelming majority of Russia's Jews resided); in St. Petersburg and Moscow, the limit was 3 percent and in other areas 5 percent. In 1889, Jews were excluded from practicing law without special ministerial permission; and in 1890 and 1892, they were denied voting rights in zemstvo and municipal elections. In 1886, many Jews were expelled from Kiev and in 1891 from Moscow.

The series of pogroms that began in 1881 finally sputtered to a halt in 1884. Another wave hit Russia from 1903 until 1906, accelerating in frequency with the Russo-Japanese War of 1904–1905 and the rebellion of 1905.

The 1903 pogrom in the Bessarabian city of Kishinev became infamous. Because Jews were overwhelmingly confined to an urban existence, Kishinev, like most cities in the Pale of Settlement, contained many Jews—about 50,000 or roughly one-third of the city's population. Enflamed by a local antisemitic paper that spread rumors that religious ritualistic needs had led Jews to kill a Christian boy, mobs attacked the city's Jews, killing about forty-seven of them, wounding hundreds of others, and burning or looting about 1,300 houses and shops.

The response of Jews to all this discrimination and violence (plus economic misery) varied, but it did drive some to revolutionary activities. The most significant Jewish radical group was the Jewish Bund (General Jewish Workers' party of Russia and Poland), founded in 1897 and containing some 25,000 members by 1903. Following the Kishinev pogrom, it urged resistance against pogroms and organized self-defense groups. Many other Jews became Bolsheviks, Mensheviks, or members of other radical groups.

As more Jews became revolutionaries, the Russian government overestimated and magnified their impact, contributing to further antisemitism.

[2]Robert F. Byrnes, *Pobedonostsev: His Life and Thought* (Bloomington, 1968), p. 207.

Among others, Nicholas II and Plehve believed that Jews were the head and heart of the revolutionary movement.

Although some Jews stayed and became radicals, many more left the country, helping fulfill at least one-third of Pobedonostsev's formula for solving the "Jewish Problem." By 1914, almost one-third of Russia's Jews (who had totaled roughly 5 million in 1897) had emigrated, mostly to the United States. The strong appeal of Zionism, which encouraged emigration to Palestine, was another manifestation of the same phenomenon.

Russian Advances in Asia and the Russo-Japanese War of 1904–1905

After it was humiliated by other European powers at the Congress of Berlin, Russia began focusing more attention on Asia. General M. D. Skobelev's victory over Turkmen forces at the fortress of Gok Tepe in January 1881 delighted panslavists such as Dostoevsky, who now believed Russia should concentrate, at least temporarily, on Asia. He suggested that because Europeans hated Russia, and Russia was part Asian, it should leave Europe to its own squabbles, while it expanded its civilizing influence and control in Asia.

In the next few decades, a number of scholars, publicists, statesmen, and military men echoed Dostoevsky. The focus gradually changed, however, from Central Asia to the Far East. Even Vladimir Soloviev, the philosopher, poet, and eloquent critic of Russian nationalism and antisemitism, wrote in the 1890s about the necessity of Russia advancing in East Asia.

Siberia and Russian Far Eastern Policies

In a report in late 1892, Witte argued that the completion of the Trans-Siberian Railway would greatly facilitate Russian trade with China. At the same time, it would allow Russia to operate a fleet in the Far East, which could dominate the area's Pacific coastline. To supply future Far Eastern Russian forces, whether on land or sea, was certainly one reason for proceeding with the difficult construction of what was to be the world's longest railway.

The laying of some 4,000 miles of track began simultaneously: westward from Vladivostok, and eastward from Miass in the Urals (about 60 miles west of Cheliabinsk). Tens of thousands of workers, including convicts and Chinese laborers, worked in often appalling conditions. Winter brought subzero temperatures and summer enough daylight for seventeen-hour workdays. To lay track across or through plains, mountains, marshes, and rivers, workers had to chop down millions of trees, transport countless tons of dirt, and cut through miles of rocks. The most daunting task was constructing bridges over Siberia's wide rivers, including the Irtysh, the Ob, and the Enisei, and completing the final mountainous link around the southern shore of Lake Baikal.

By the beginning of the Russo-Japanese War in early 1904, all but the Baikal link was completed, although most of the railway's eastern section, the Chinese Eastern Railway, cut across northern Manchuria. (Not until World War I would an all-Russian Trans-Siberian line link Vladivostok with European Russia.)

The Trans-Siberian greatly facilitated migration to Siberia. In the two decades before the start of World War I, some 3 million people moved to Siberia, which was about the same number of people living in all of Siberia around 1860.

Along with the Trans-Siberian construction, the Chinese-Japanese War of 1894–1895 stimulated more Russian involvement in the Far East. Alarmed by Japanese gains in the war, Witte led a campaign in 1895 to deny Japan the Manchurian Liaotung Peninsula, gained from China in the treaty ending the war.

In 1896, Witte won Chinese permission to have the Russian-run Chinese Eastern Railway constructed, a shorter and easier way of linking the cities of Chita and Vladivostok than completing the eastern Trans-Siberian on Russian territory. In 1898, in the midst of other great-power pressures on China, Russia wrenched from the hapless Chinese what it had denied Japan—the Liaotung Peninsula and, at its tip, the ice-free Port Arthur. Not only did Russia receive a lease to the peninsula, but also permission to build a railway branch (the Southern Manchurian Railway) linking the Chinese Eastern Railway at Harbin with Port Arthur.

These steps of 1898 went beyond Witte's more moderate approach to Chinese penetration, but Nicholas II had by now begun listening to more impa-

FIGURE 4.3. Railway Station at Krasnoiarsk. On the Trans-Siberian Line, the population of Krasnoiarsk almost tripled from 1897 (when Lenin spent five weeks of his Siberian exile there) to 1911.

tient and reckless advisers who fed his belief that Russia could dominate the Far East. During the next five years, Russia increased its forces in Manchuria, partly as a response to the Boxer Rebellion of 1900, and stepped up its challenge to Japan's hope to dominate Korea. Japan attempted to negotiate a compromise on Far Eastern spheres of influence but received little positive response from Russia. Nicholas II underestimated both Japanese determination and strength. He thought Russia could pursue its policies without risking war. Even if war came, his minister of interior, V. Plehve, apparently believed that such "a successful, little war" would help dampen revolutionary sentiments at home.

Russo-Japanese War of 1904–1905

In early February 1904, exasperated by Russian unwillingness to negotiate, the Japanese launched a surprise attack on the Russian squadron at Port Arthur. Although a few Russian ships were damaged, none sank. Nicholas II shrugged the attack off as a flea bite and was confident Russia would successfully end the war Japan had begun.

But the Japanese "flea" proved more than a match for the Russian bear. Japan profited from modernized military forces operating close to their home base and enthusiastically supported by the civilian population. In contrast, Russian Far Eastern forces were undermined by overconfidence, by poor governmental and military leadership, by insufficient weapons, by great distances from the Russian industrial heartland, and by quickly dissipating societal support for the war.

Symbolic of Russia's frustration was the fate of its Baltic Fleet, sent halfway around the world to link up with its ships at Port Arthur. After more than seven months at sea, during which time Port Arthur had surrendered to Japan, the Baltic Fleet was met by a Japanese fleet before it could reach safe harbor in Vladivostok. In May 1905, at the battle of Tsushima Straits, the Baltic Fleet was sunk, scattered, or forced to surrender. The loss shocked Russian society and contributed to growing discontent back home. Despite Russia's improving capacity to ship men and equipment to the Far East and its ability eventually to far outnumber Japanese forces, public opinion and financial considerations led it to seek peace.

U.S. President Theodore Roosevelt, not wishing either side to grow too strong, offered to host a peace conference at Portsmouth, New Hampshire. By the Treaty of Portsmouth (September 1905), Russia ceded to Japan the southern half of Sakhalin, its lease of Port Arthur and the rest of the Liaotung Peninsula, and the Southern Manchurian Railway. It also recognized Japan's paramount interests in Korea. Russia was permitted to retain control over the Chinese Eastern Railway and maintain predominant influence in northern Manchuria. Despite considerable pressure on Witte, who negotiated for Russia, he refused to go along with Japanese demands for monetary indemnity. Yet there was little doubt that Japan had won the war against one of Europe's major powers.

Besides its treaty losses, the war cost Russia billions of rubles and hundreds of thousands of dead and wounded. Rather than deflating revolutionary ardor, as Plehve had hoped, this "little war" helped spark it.

SUGGESTED SOURCES*

BECKER, SEYMOUR. *Russia's Protectorates in Central Asia: Bukhara and Khiva, 1865–1924.* Cambridge, Mass., 1968.

BOURNE, KENNETH, and D. CAMERON WATT, eds. *British Documents on Foreign Affairs: Reports and Papers from the Confidential Print.* Part I: *From the Mid-Nineteenth Century to the First World War.* Series A: *Russia, 1859–1914,* ed. Dominic Lieven. Frederick, Md., 1983.

CARRÈRE D'ENCAUSSE, HÉLÈNE. *Islam and the Russian Empire: Reform and Revolution in Central Asia.* London, 1988.

CLAY, CATHERINE B. "Russian Ethnographers in the Service of Empire, 1856–1862," *SR* 54 (Spring 1995): 45–61.

DOSTOEVSKY, F. M. *The Diary of a Writer.* New York, 1949.

FADNER, FRANK. *Seventy Years of Pan-Slavism in Russia: Karamzin to Danilevskii.* Washington, D.C., 1962.

GEYER, DIETRICH. *Russian Imperialism: The Interaction of Domestic and Foreign Policy 1860–1914.* Leamington Spa, N.Y., 1987.

HABERER, ERICH. *Jews and Revolution in Nineteenth-Century Russia.* Cambridge, England, 1995.

HOPKIRK, PETER. *The Great Game: The Struggle for Empire in Central Asia.* New York, 1992.

JUDGE, EDWARD H. *Easter in Kishinev: Anatomy of a Pogrom.* New York, 1992.

KAZEMZADEH, FIRUZ. *Russia and Britain in Persia, 1864–1914: A Study in Imperialism.* New Haven, 1968.

KENNAN, GEORGE F. *The Fateful Alliance: France, Russia, and the Coming of the First World War.* New York, 1984.

KLIER, JOHN DOYLE. *Imperial Russia's Jewish Question, 1855–1881.* Cambridge, England, 1995.

KLIER, JOHN, and SHLOMO LAMBROZA, eds. *Pogroms: Anti-Jewish Violence in Modern Russian History.* Cambridge, England, 1992.

LANGER, WILLIAM L. *European Alliances and Alignments, 1871–1890.* 2d ed. New York, 1964.

LESLIE R. F. *Reform and Insurrection in Russian Poland, 1856–1865.* London, 1963.

LONG, JAMES W. *From Privileged to Dispossessed: The Volga Germans, 1860–1917.* Lincoln, Nebr., 1988.

MACKENZIE, DAVID. *The Lion of Tashkent: The Career of General M. G. Cherniaev.* Athens, Ga., 1974.

———. *The Serbs and Russian Pan-Slavism, 1875–1878.* Ithaca, N.Y., 1967.

MARKS, STEVEN G. *Road to Power: The Trans-Siberian Railroad and the Colonization of Asian Russia, 1850–1917.* Ithaca, N.Y., 1991.

McDONALD, DAVID M. *United Government and Foreign Policy in Russia, 1900–1914.* Cambridge, Mass., 1992.

McNEAL, ROBERT H. *Tsar and Cossack, 1855–1914.* New York, 1987.

MOSSE, W. E. *The European Powers and the German Question, 1848–1871, with Special Reference to England and Russia.* Cambridge, England, 1958.

*See also books cited in footnotes.

PETROVICH, MICHAEL B. *The Emergence of Russian Panslavism, 1856–1870.* New York, 1956.

PIERCE, RICHARD A. *Russian Central Asia, 1867–1917: A Study in Colonial Rule.* Berkeley, 1960.

POLVINEN, TUOMO. *Imperial Borderland: Bobrikov and the Attempted Russification of Finland, 1898–1904.* Durham, 1995.

QUESTED, R. K. I. *The Expansion of Russia in East Asia, 1857–1860.* Kuala Lumpur, Malaysia, 1968.

RAGSDALE, HUGH, ed. *Imperial Russian Foreign Policy.* Cambridge, England, 1993.

ROGGER, HANS. *Jewish Policies and Right-Wing Politics in Imperial Russia.* Berkeley, 1986.

———. *Russia in the Age of Modernization and Revolution, 1881–1917.* London, 1983. Chs. 8–9.

SUMNER, B. H. *Russia and the Balkans, 1870–1880.* Oxford, 1937.

TAYLOR, A. J. P. *The Struggle for Mastery in Europe, 1848–1918.* Oxford, 1954.

THADEN, EDWARD C. *Conservative Nationalism in Nineteenth-Century Russia.* Seattle, 1964.

———, ed. *Russification in the Baltic Provinces and Finland, 1855–1914.* Princeton, 1981.

WESTWOOD, J. N. *Russia Against Japan, 1904–1905: A New Look at the Russo-Japanese War.* Albany, 1986.

WOOD, ALAN, ed. *The History of Siberia: From Russian Conquest to Revolution.* London, 1991.

CHAPTER 5

Revolution or Evolution? Politics and War, 1905–1917

In 1905, the largest general strike the world had ever witnessed forced Nicholas II to issue a manifesto promising fundamental reforms. The manifesto indicated that an elected Duma (or legislative council) would be created and be given power to approve or reject all laws.

The elections to the four Dumas that met between 1906 and 1917, especially to the last two, were far from democratic. From the beginning, the powers of the Duma were weak and had to be shared with a conservative State Council. Yet the Duma's existence could have led to Russia's gradual evolution from autocracy into a true constitutional monarchy with a parliamentary type of government. That it did not was due primarily to Nicholas II (and his wife, Alexandra), although there were also numerous other causes for this failure, including World War I. The war itself displayed Nicholas's lack of leadership as never before; by the end of 1916, his disillusioned subjects were on the verge of rebellion.

THE 1905 REVOLUTION: FROM BLOODY SUNDAY TO THE OCTOBER MANIFESTO

In the same month (December 1904 O.S.) that Nicholas II refused to appease a swelling opposition by allowing for elected deputies to advise the government, Port Arthur fell to the Japanese. This embarrassing defeat fueled still further opposition. By the beginning of the second week of January, more than 100,000 St. Petersburg workers were on strike. On Sunday, January 9, 1905, many of them, still believing in the old myth of the benevolent tsar, marched to his Winter Palace to present him with a petition.

Their leader was a priest in his mid-thirties, Father Georgi Gapon. Hoping to turn workers away from socialist influences, the government had allowed him to head a new organization called the St. Petersburg Assembly of Russian Factory and Mill Workers. Gapon, however, had ideas of his own.

Although the men, women, and children who marched toward the palace carried pictures of Nicholas II and Alexandra as well as icons, and Gapon's petition contained no direct criticism of his monarch, it was nevertheless a radical document. It mirrored both general political concerns and specific worker grievances. It criticized capitalists and bureaucrats for exploiting the people, and it called for a Constituent Assembly elected by universal suffrage. It also listed as indispensable full civil liberties; universal, state-financed education; equal legal treatment; the separation of church and state; an end to the Russo-Japanese War; the abolition of peasant redemption payments; the transfer of more land to the peasants; an eight-hour workday; and numerous other provisions, mainly empowering workers in their battle with employers.

The tsar never received the petitioners, for he was outside the city at his Tsarskoe Selo residence. But troops near the palace and on snowy avenues leading to it did greet them—with shots and swords. More than 100 men, women, and children were killed and hundreds of others wounded on this "Bloody Sunday."

The events of this day ignited still more opposition, both within the capital and in other areas such as the Volga city of Saratov. Bloody Sunday also undercut the common people's trust in the goodness of the tsar. As the year proceeded, and bad news kept arriving from the Far East, the turbulence increased. Students voted to boycott classes. Workers struck in cities around the

FIGURE 5.1. General Staff Building (1819–1829, architect C. Rossi) and Palace Square, St. Petersburg, looking down from the Winter Palace. Scene of bloodshed on Bloody Sunday.

empire. Nationalities voiced their grievances, formed new parties, and increasingly called for autonomy. Peasants began appropriating landowners' goods and sometimes burning their houses. Some military units mutinied—the most famous example (later immortalized in an Eisenstein film) being the June mutiny of the sailors aboard the battleship *Potemkin.*

In May, a Union of Unions, under the chairmanship of the Union of Liberation's Paul Miliukov, was formed of fourteen unions. They represented agronomists, clerks and bookkeepers, doctors, engineers, journalists, lawyers, pharmacists, professors, railway workers, teachers, veterinarians, zemstvo-constitutionalists, and two organizations dedicated to Jewish and women's emancipation. That same month, peasants met in Moscow and agreed to form a Peasants' Union that became a reality two months later. Although its main concern was obtaining more land for peasants, it also agreed with the Union of Unions on the necessity of convening a Constituent Assembly.

In the months from Bloody Sunday through the end of the summer of 1905, the response of an often perplexed Nicholas II was to make concessions he thought would not touch the autocratic core. He decreed greater religious toleration, curtailed some censorship and university restrictions, and made limited concessions to the nationalities—for example, rescinding the confiscation of Armenian Church property. In August, he finally issued a manifesto stipulating procedures for electing and convening what he had resisted before Bloody Sunday: an elected, yet purely consultative, assembly, the Duma.

Such measures, however, were no longer enough. Many groups were unhappy with the proposed unequal and discriminatory election procedures and with the limited role proposed for the Duma. Although some moderate liberals were willing to accept such a Duma as a first step, the Union of Unions recommended boycotting elections to it. Most socialist parties went even further. They called for a general strike that they hoped would lead to an armed revolt that would end monarchical rule.

Although the Bolsheviks, Mensheviks, and Social Revolutionaries by no means controlled the workers, their socialist ideas were now falling on increasingly receptive ears. Many workers perceived that their everyday economic and labor grievances could no longer be separated from larger political issues.

In September and October, a Moscow printers' strike spread to bakeries, factories, and railroad shops. Sympathy strikes were held in St. Petersburg. In early October, railway strikes spread from Moscow to other areas of the empire, shutting down the country's rail traffic and igniting the biggest general strike in history. It involved roughly 2 million people. Most of them were industrial and railway workers, but they were joined by many government employees and others, including actors, ballet dancers, doctors, lawyers, professors, shop clerks, stockbrokers, students, and teachers.

In St. Petersburg, where regular activities and electricity were suspended, workers and socialist intellectuals formed an organization to direct strike activities. In less than a week, it was calling itself the Soviet (or Council) of Workers' Deputies and had decided to publish its own newspaper, *Izvestiia.*

On October 17, the same day the Soviet adopted its official name, the tsar issued a manifesto. He was convinced by Witte and others that he had little

other choice. His manifesto directed his ministers to grant civil liberties and expand the electorate and rights for the already planned Duma. Previously excluded classes were now to participate in electing it, and thereafter no law was
to be issued without Duma confirmation. The manifesto also promised that
Duma members would be allowed to participate in overseeing the legality of
government actions. Although Nicholas II did not wish to admit it, the manifesto seemed to signal an end to autocratic rule.

CONTINUING DISORDERS AND DUMA PREPARATION

Although the tsar hoped his October Manifesto would end the turmoil, it did
not. Nor did the appointment of Witte as a prime minister with real powers,
including the right to replace ministers (such as Pobedonostsev) with ones
more to his liking. Although these steps mollified some moderates and ended
most strikes, the manifesto was also followed by a proliferation of soviets, ethnic and national disturbances (including anti-Jewish pogroms), and peasant
violence.

Following the example of the St. Petersburg Soviet, roughly fifty other soviets sprang up in the next few months. Overwhelmingly, they were in cities,
but several also appeared among peasants and soldiers.

The St. Petersburg Soviet itself continued to push demands such as an
eight-hour workday and the convening of a Constituent Assembly. And it took
upon itself certain governmental responsibilities, for example, decreeing freedom of the press, which it attempted to enforce by having printers refuse to
print censored papers.

The most dynamic force in the capital's soviet and an author of many of its
proclamations and appeals was Leon Trotsky. Born Lev Bronstein into a
Ukrainian Jewish family in 1879, he later was exiled to Siberia for revolutionary activity. After he escaped abroad, he impressed Lenin, who in early 1903
recommended him for inclusion on the editorial board of the journal *Iskra*. But
during and after the Russian Social Democratic Congress held later that year,
Trotsky sided with the Mensheviks in denouncing Lenin's plans for the party,
claiming they would lead to dictatorship.

On December 2, 1905, the St. Petersburg Soviet called upon people to withhold their taxes. The government responded by arresting and jailing about half
the more than 500 Soviet members, including Trotsky and most other Executive Committee members. Later in the month, it crushed a ten-day strike and
insurrection led by the Moscow Soviet and followed it up with severe reprisals, including immediate executions.

In late October 1905, Nicholas II wrote to his mother that "nine-tenths of
the troublemakers are Jews." Although he grossly exaggerated Jewish involvement, there were enough revolutionary Jews to make them convenient scapegoats and victims at a time of dissatisfaction and anxiety.

In Odessa, where Trotsky had earlier received most of his formal education, news of the October Manifesto was followed by a fierce pogrom that lasted several days. About one-third of Odessa's approximate half-million people were Jews. Some were involved in anti-tsarist demonstrations, which were countered by patriotic processions. In one of the latter, a boy carrying an icon was shot. Soon afterwards, mobs began attacking Jews, killing hundreds of them. Thousands more were victimized by beatings; rapes; and pillaging and destruction of their apartments, houses, and businesses.

Odessa's Jews were not alone in their suffering. In the two months following the October Manifesto, more than 500 other pogroms occurred, taking approximately another 2,000 Jewish lives and destroying additional Jewish property. Overwhelmingly, they occurred in other Pale of Settlement locations, including Kiev and Minsk.

Local officials, police, and soldiers sometimes encouraged the pogroms through either actions or inactions (such as standing aside while Jews were beaten). Although there is no evidence to support claims that the pogroms were directed by Witte's government—which was wary of any lawlessness—nevertheless, the antisemitic attitudes of Nicholas II and some of his ministers encouraged, at least inadvertently, such developments. Toward the end of October 1905, Nicholas II wrote that the pogroms were a case of "loyal people" attacking "bad people."

Proliferating right-wing antisemitic organizations and publications played a more direct role in the 1905 pogroms. Such groups, especially their more activist, violent followers, were often labeled "the Black Hundreds."

Strong national and ethnic feelings were also displayed among other groups. Shortly after the October Manifesto, Nicholas II attempted to appease the Finns by restoring rights he had earlier taken away. He was less willing, however, to accommodate other nationalities. In late November, he imposed martial law on Estonians and Latvians in response to their unrest and demands for greater autonomy and a reduction of Baltic German prominence. When rebellions continued in the region, the government dispatched fresh Russian troops to crush them.

Some of the Baltic rebels were peasants, and peasant disturbances increased dramatically after the October Manifesto. They were especially prevalent in the mainly black-earth, south-central region, including the provinces Chernigov, Poltava, Voronezh, Tambov, Penza, and Saratov. They reached their peak in November–December 1905 and again in June–July 1906 but continued into 1907. Even the termination of the hated emancipation redemption payments in 1905–1906 proved unable to stem the tide of peasant dissatisfaction.

Although the peasants looted, destroyed, and sometimes seized noble estates, they took almost no noble lives. Their aim was primarily to drive nobles and other nonpeasants off rural lands so that, by one way or another, they could obtain them. They hoped the government would grant them these lands and appealed to various sources, including the Peasant Union and new Duma, to help them realize their hope.

To restore order, both in the countryside and in scattered rebellious cities around the empire, Nicholas II sent in more punitive military expeditions similar to those sent to the Baltic region. Fortunately for him, Russia's troops generally remained loyal.

Meanwhile the government prepared new laws to carry out the changes indicated in the October Manifesto. In December, it spelled out election procedures for the new Duma. Although the exclusion of women and young people (those under twenty-five) was typical of the era, the denial of voting rights to some subgroups of commoners and the grossly disproportionate weight of peoples' vote was less common: One landowner's vote was to equal that of 15 peasants or 45 workers—believing that the peasants still revered their tsar, Nicholas trusted them more than urban workers.

In April 1906, the tsar accepted the resignation of Witte as prime minister. Although in moments of crisis Nicholas sometimes turned to strong and determined men reminiscent of his father, reactionary voices eventually convinced him that they were undermining his autocratic prerogatives, and he ceased offering them much support. Such was the case with Witte and later with Peter Stolypin.

On April 23, just one day after officially accepting the frustrated Witte's resignation, Nicholas made public "The Fundamental Laws." They were to provide the legal framework for the new era promised in the October Manifesto, but they also reflected Nicholas's desire to make as few concessions as possible. Although the laws stipulated that no new law could be passed without Duma approval, they also declared that the Emperor retained "supreme autocratic power." Because Nicholas viewed the Fundamental Laws and the Duma as favors he bestowed, he thought they could be revoked whenever he wished.

The powers granted to the new Duma were few. Although it could initiate new legislation, it was normally expected to react to proposed laws submitted to it. Although it could reject proposed laws, the tsar had the right to determine the length of annual Duma sessions and the interval between them, or to dissolve a Duma before its members served a normal five-year term, provided that he scheduled new elections. Between Duma sessions, he could (by the infamous Article 87) decree emergency laws that could continue in force for up to sixty days after a new session convened. Duma-passed legislation could not become law unless approved by the State Council, now transformed into an upper legislative house, and the tsar. The State Council was to be partly appointed by the tsar and partly elected, primarily by groups that insured upperclass, ethnic-Russian domination of the council. Only the tsar could review or revise the Fundamental Laws and exercise control over foreign policy and military affairs, including the decision to go to war.

Contrary to the statement in the October Manifesto, the Duma received no real powers in overseeing the legality of government measures. It could question ministers about the legality of their actions but could not force compliance.

Along with the State Council, the Duma was allowed to review the proposed annual state budget. But both houses were exempted from exercising any control over certain areas, including traditional Imperial Household expenses and most military spending and state debt payments. If a new state budget were not approved, the government could operate according to the previous year's budget.

THE FIRST TWO DUMAS, 1906 AND 1907

On April 27, 1906, four days after the promulgation of the Fundamental Laws, the first Duma gathered in St. Petersburg. During the next few months, its number and composition varied slightly but hovered near 500 members.

The left-liberal Constitutional Democrats (or Kadets) had the largest number of delegates (approximately 180). Founded in late 1905, its leader was Paul Miliukov, although he was not among its delegates. The government had charged him with violating censorship and disqualified him from running. More radical than the Kadets, especially on the land question, was a coalition of leftist factions, called the Trudoviks or Laborites. They possessed about 100 delegates, many of them peasants.

Other parties and factions had much smaller representation. Most radical leftists had boycotted the elections. To the right of the Kadets were the Octobrists (moderate liberals who had accepted the October Manifesto) and other smaller parties. Altogether they constituted about 45 delegates. The rest of the delegates were from national or religious minorities or had no clear affiliation. Many of the latter were peasants, and these and peasants in the other groupings composed about two-fifths of the total delegates.

From the beginning, it was clear that the tsar and his new prime minister, the loyal but undistinguished bureaucrat I. L. Goremykin, intended to prevent any meaningful power-sharing with the Duma. Conversely, Duma members were unsatisfied with the small role Nicholas II intended for them and insisted on expanded powers. They wanted ministers to be responsible to them, democratic suffrage, the abolition of the State Council, amnesty for political offenses, the rule of law, and land reform, including the confiscation of private lands over a certain maximum, for which compensation would be paid. Alarmed at such radical demands, especially regarding land transfers, Nicholas dissolved the Duma on July 8, 1906.

Fearful the police would prevent their further actions, Miliukov and about 200 delegates, mostly Kadets, retired to the Finnish city of Vyborg. There, most of them signed a manifesto calling on people to refuse paying taxes or providing military recruits until another Duma met. The manifesto had little effect except for getting the Duma members who had signed it arrested and barred from running in the next election.

The activities of the signatories were later criticized extensively by V. A. Maklakov, a Kadet lawyer who disagreed with his party's majority. Many later historians also faulted Miliukov and others for their impatience and unrealistic expectations in late 1905 and 1906. In his memoirs, Miliukov responded to such criticism by contending that if the Kadet party would have become as "moderate" as Maklakov and others desired, it would have lost authority, many followers, and become insignificant.

On the same day that Nicholas II dissolved the First Duma, he replaced

A Description of the First Duma

The following selection is from Bernard Pares, *Russia and Reform* (London, 1907), pp. 550–552. Pares spent much time in Russia, observing its life and institutions, and became England's first professor of Russian history. Ellipses are mine.

If the Duma did nothing else, it brought together for the first time representatives of every class and of every interest in Russia. It was of course far more Imperial than any other European Parliament. It would be difficult to imagine a more picturesque gathering. Each man wore the costume of his class. The country gentry of the Intelligents dressed very simply, but there were Russian priests with long beards and hair, a Roman Catholic bishop in skull-cap lined with red, finely accoutred Cossacks from the Caucasus, Bashkirs and Buryats in strange and tinselled Asiatic dress, Polish peasants in the brilliant and martial costumes of their people, and a whole mass of staid, bearded, and top-booted Russian peasants. Strangers easily obtained admittance; and amongst the most picturesque visitors were the so-called "walking deputies" who were sent by peasant constituents to look after their members, and others who had tramped for hundreds of miles to ask the Duma to settle their private disputes. Groups of members and non-members formed in the corridor to discuss without reticence any question of the moment. Small party conferences, sitting in the committee-rooms, seemed in no way disturbed by passing strangers. Milyukoff [Miliukov], in the simple dress of an English country gentleman, walked up and down the corridor receiving the suggestions of various party leaders, which seldom induced him to deviate a yard from the tactics upon which he had determined. One noticed that the Cadets as a body quite failed to get hold of the non-party members. These peasants, who would not sink their individuality in any party formula, expressed the most fresh and interesting opinions of all. . . . but Milyukoff was hardly ever to be seen talking to a non-party man. . . . The Duma was allowed to discuss the franchise, and it of course declared in favour of the well-known formula "universal, direct, equal, and secret." The debate on women's suffrage excited a lively interest. On this day the corridor was invaded by an active band of suffragettes, who evidently thought that they could give the necessary lessons to the non-party peasant. It was amusing to watch the peasants dealing with these young ladies. One very typical peasant admitted that it was most unfair that women should receive lower pay than men for similar work. "We will put that right for you," he said "let us get on our legs first, then we will give you some rights." But the young ladies wanted not to receive, but to take, and claimed that women ought to be sitting in the Duma. "Look here," said he, "I will tell you what: you go and marry! You will have a husband and children, and your husband will look after you altogether." "Look after, indeed!" said the young ladies; but the peasant would not promise anything more. Equally interesting was the attitude of the Non-party group towards the Jews: they spoke without any ill-will, but remarked: "Even without rights, the Jews are on the top of us."

Goremykin with his minister of interior, Peter Stolypin. Only months earlier, Stolypin, still in his early forties, had come to St. Petersburg, previously having served several years as a provincial governor.

His first task as prime minister was to restore order. Peasant disturbances

FIGURE 5.2. Tauride Palace, St. Petersburg, 1783–1789, architect I. Starov. Commissioned by Catherine II for Prince Potemkin, this building was where the Duma met.

had again risen sharply in June 1906. In the cities, SR Maximalists (members of the Combat Organization) and other revolutionaries often assassinated police and government officials. Stolypin claimed that in the eight months preceding June 1906, almost 300 Ministry of Interior officials and police had been killed. In August, a few SR Maximalists threw explosives into his own residence, injuring his two children and killing about thirty others, including the terrorists themselves.

Forceful man that he was and mindful of Nicholas II's impatience to end such terror, Stolypin used Article 87 to set up special new military courts to deal with civilians accused of antigovernment crimes. Within three days of a crime, a court was to meet and conclude its verdict. Proceedings were secret, and no defense lawyer was allowed. If execution was the verdict (as it was in about 1,000 cases over the next eight months), it was to occur within twenty-four hours. After the Second Duma convened in late February 1907, the special courts failed to gain Duma approval and thus expired in April. They had left an indelible impression, however—the ropes used to hang the condemned became known as "Stolypin's neckties"—and other military courts continued to sentence civilians to be executed. Altogether, from 1906 to 1909, many more Russians were executed than in the previous eighty years combined.

Stolypin also used other methods to counter violence and unrest in the country. Much of Russia continued to be ruled by martial law; while unrest and assassinations continued, so too did exiling and death sentences. Although rural unrest declined considerably in 1907, urban terrorism, while slowing somewhat, continued to be a major problem. From late 1905 until mid-May 1910, more than 6,000 officials and police were killed or wounded.

Elections to the Second Duma brought no comfort to Stolypin and Nicholas II: It was more radical than its predecessor and had no intention of cooperating with Stolypin's policies. The Bolsheviks, Mensheviks, and Socialist Revolutionaries had decided to participate in elections and together gained almost as many delegates as the Trudoviks (or Laborites). All these leftist delegates, including the Trudoviks, outnumbered the Kadets by more than two to one. The Kadets themselves were becoming more moderate and centrist. Deputies to the right of the Kadets also outnumbered them but more slightly. The antisemitic and far-right Union of the Russian People, which had more than 200 branches in the country, gained ten Duma seats.

Stolypin was no reactionary and believed law and order had to be accompanied by reforms. Like Bismarck earlier in Germany, he hoped to deflate leftist appeals by taking away some of their grievances. He proposed to the Duma land and tax reforms, advancement toward compulsory primary education, workers' insurance and the recognition of their right to unionize and strike, and the strengthening and extension of local government and the rule of law.

But cooperation was doomed primarily by one fundamental difference between Stolypin and a majority of the Duma delegates: land confiscation of nonpeasant lands to benefit the peasants. Nicholas II and Stolypin were firmly against confiscation; the socialists and Kadets were for it, although the Kadets on a more modest scale and with compensation for confiscated noble lands. In early June, three and a half months after it was convened, the Second Duma was dissolved.

STOLYPIN'S LAND POLICIES

In 1906, between the First and Second Dumas, Stolypin began a bold new agricultural policy, later furthered by legislation of 1910 and 1911. He made more state and crown lands available for peasant purchase, made Peasant Bank mortgages easier to obtain, and facilitated resettlement to areas such as Siberia where more land was available. He also freed peasants from some legal restrictions (for example, on domestic travel) that separated them from the rest of society. Most significantly, he empowered peasants to withdraw from the commune and obtain title to the strips of land they had previously farmed or, where possible, to a consolidated plot of equal land.

In 1905, a little more than three-fourths of peasant households in the country's European provinces farmed in communes; most of those who did not reside in Ukraine and other western areas. By 1916, approximately half of European Russian peasant households owned their land outside the communes, but only about one-tenth possessed consolidated plots, and most of these owners did not reside on their farmland but in nearby peasant villages.

Stolypin's measures were designed to create a strong class of individual peasant proprietors who would respect private property and support the government. In 1908, he stated that the government had staked its future "on the sober and strong" peasants, not the "drunken and the weak."

He knew that an agricultural transformation would take several peaceful decades of determined implementation. The outbreak of World War I in 1914, three years after his own assassination, deprived Russia of peace. Besides time and government determination, peasant attitudes toward Stolypin's policy were also crucial. Although some peasants took advantage of the new opportunities, many others did not. One thing they all agreed on, however, was that they needed more land.

THE THIRD AND FOURTH DUMAS, 1907–1914

The dissolution of the Second Duma was accompanied by a new electoral law that violated Nicholas's own Fundamental Laws. It strengthened the already weighty vote of large landowners and reduced that of most peasants, workers, and non-Russian nationalities. The failure of Duma peasant delegates to support tsarist policies had been especially disappointing to Nicholas II, a failure he blamed on outsiders who misled the peasants. The electoral changes meant that most future Duma delegates were elected by landowners who made up only about 1 percent of the population. As Stolypin said in 1908: "If you took an assembly which represented the majority . . . sane ideas would not prevail in it. . . . We want not professors but men with roots in the country, the local gentry, and such like."

Given the new electoral laws, the composition of the Third Duma, labeled the "Masters' Duma," is hardly surprising. Nobles outnumbered peasants by more than two to one, and there were ten times more Great Russians than all the other nationalities combined. The Octobrists became the largest party, with slightly more than one-third of the delegates. Other more conservative parties totaled an almost equal fraction. The remaining deputies were from parties to the left of the Octobrists, including the Kadets, and from the non-Russian nationalities and unaffiliated. The SRs had no deputies, having once again boycotted Duma elections.

The Third Duma opened on November 1, 1907. Its composition facilitated more cooperation with Stolypin and Nicholas II, and in its five-year term it initiated more than 200 pieces of legislation and voted on more than 2,500 bills introduced by the government.

The value of its work varied greatly. Besides backing Stolypin's agricultural policies, the Duma passed legislation designed to expand educational opportunities and literacy, provide workers' health insurance, and extend women's inheritance rights. Other acts helped bring zemstvos to new provinces (although discriminating against non-Russians in them) and restored justices of the peace, while concurrently reducing the powers of the land captains. The Duma passed additional legislation that never found its way into law, much of it never getting past the State Council, which was more conservative than Stolypin.

If at times progressive, at other times the Third Duma was more reactionary, especially when it came to nationality issues. Among other steps, it helped Stolypin roll back Finnish autonomy, restore and expand Russification measures in Poland, repress Ukrainian nationalism and desires for cultural autonomy, and increase colonization and Great Russian interests in Moslem areas of the empire.

Despite heightened cooperation with Stolypin, the Third Duma often differed with him as well as with the State Council. In early 1911, he managed to alienate the overwhelming majority of both houses, plus the tsar.

By late 1911, Nicholas II had lost confidence in Stolypin, and his effectiveness was waning. Rumors circulated that the tsar was about to replace him. A bullet saved him the trouble. At an intermission to a performance of *The Story of Tsar Saltan*, Stolypin was shot in a Kiev opera house and died several days later on September 5. Strangely enough, although such circumstances were by no means unique under Nicholas, the assassin had been a police informant who shot Stolypin to prove his loyalty to fellow revolutionaries.

Nicholas II replaced Stolypin with his finance minister, Vladimir Kokovtsov. Miliukov considered him a faithful servant of the tsar with a deserved

FIGURE 5.3. Opera House, Kiev, scene of Stolypin assassination in 1911.

reputation as an "honest bookkeeper." He remained in office until early 1914, when Goremykin, like an "old fur coat," was brought out once again to become prime minister.

The Fourth Duma, with a makeup as conservative as the Third, first met in November 1912. In the less than two years that remained before World War I, however, the Duma found it increasingly difficult to cooperate with tsarist policies that were becoming more rigid. Indicative of the Duma's sentiments was a resolution it passed in 1913, condemning the Ministry of Interior for its arbitrary actions, its "illegal acts," and its delay of reforms.

Minister of Interior N. A. Maklakov responded by asking Nicholas to warn the Duma to correct its ways and if it did not, to dissolve it. The tsar was prepared to go even further. He asked his ministers to consider a plan requiring the Duma to submit majority and minority reports to him for selection and confirmation—essentially turning the Duma into a consultative body. Although his Council of Ministers thought this was going too far, Nicholas's request indicates that he still opposed any real power-sharing.

Also indicative of the government's tone in 1913 was the Belis case. Spurred on by the antisemitic Union of the Russian People, the government brought a Jewish clerk (Belis) to trial for allegedly committing a ritual murder against a Christian boy. It thus furthered antisemitism and the myth that Jews committed such murders.

THE RADICAL OPPOSITION, 1907–1914

Following the turbulent 1905–1907 period, Stolypin's "necktie" and other measures helped weaken the radical opposition. Popular support of the major socialist parties declined. Factionalized and living mainly abroad, the socialist leaders looked at times like impractical, squabbling émigrés living on the fringes of reality. In 1911, the government found it necessary to exile only about one-quarter the number of political opponents exiled two years earlier.

During this period, criticism of the revolutionary intelligentsia, including the leaders of the socialist parties, reached new heights. For some time, right-wing groups had accused them of being too cosmopolitan, antireligious, and anti-Russian. Now the most famous criticism came from a group of leading intellectuals, most of them former Marxists, who had participated in the Union of Liberation. It appeared in a book of essays called *Vekhi* (*Landmarks*), which appeared in 1909, and was hotly debated for years afterward. The crux of their critique was that the intelligentsia had placed too much faith in political revolution, been too dogmatic, and failed to realize that the transformation of society depended first on the inner spiritual transformation of each individual.[1]

The *Vekhi* essays were symptomatic of an emphasis on idealism, religious

---

[1]Although debate has existed for more than a century on just who should be included in the category "intelligentsia," it was generally used to indicate critically thinking people who expressed the belief that Russia's sociopolitical order was unjust, especially to the lower classes.

thinking, and new cultural approaches that marked the period. The intellectual spirit of the times reflected more the influence of the poet and philosopher Vladimir Soloviev, who died in 1900, than it did Karl Marx or Mikhail Bakunin.

Yet the festering social and political problems of Russia left the door open for a resurgence of the radical Left. Workers and peasants remained more susceptible to socialist agitation than Solovievian ideas. A replay of 1905, this time with a different ending, remained a distinct possibility.

News that troops had killed some 200 unarmed strikers at the Siberian Lena goldfields in April 1912 helped spark a new wave of worker unrest. Strikes, which had declined considerably between 1907 and 1911, now increased dramatically. During the month following the killings, twice as many workers struck as had done so during the entire previous four years. The number kept increasing until it reached well over 1 million in the first half of 1914. Moreover, the increasing influence of the Bolsheviks on workers during the 1912–1914 period boded ill for those desiring stability.

RUSSIAN FOREIGN POLICY, 1906–1914

In November 1913, Octobrist leader Alexander Guchkov feared that the new labor militancy and, even more, the government's reactionary and incompetent policies were leading Russia to disaster. Russia's only hope, he thought, lie with those whose first desire was to see Russia remain a major power.

Such patriotic sentiments were typical of this period and not just in Russia. Thus, it is hardly surprising that maintaining great-power status (and the military might needed to guarantee it) was a goal the Russian government shared with much of educated Russian society, including most Duma members. Yet, given Russia's defeat in the war against Japan and its own internal conditions, maintaining such a status required great skill and leadership. Unfortunately for Russia, Nicholas II could not provide them.

Nicholas was wise enough, however, to realize the dangers of war before a major Russian rearmament program could be completed. In 1911, he declared that "it would be out of the question for us to face a war for five or six years." What he lacked were the skills to manage a cautious but forceful diplomacy, or at least to find someone who could. He was fatalistic and, although stubborn at times, rather weak-willed—during World War I, Alexandra wrote to him: "How I wish I could pour my will into your veins." These were not the most desirous qualities for a leader on the eve of World War I.

After a decade in office, Nicholas illustrated in July 1905 that he was still a babe in the diplomatic woods. His bullying cousin, Kaiser Wilhelm II of Germany, had little respect for him—once referring to Nicholas as "only fit to live in a country house and grow turnips." He personally persuaded Nicholas to sign a defensive alliance, the Treaty of Björkö, that shocked his foreign minister and Witte, who together discussed whether Nicholas had forgotten about the Franco-Russian treaty. Convinced by his ministers that he had made a mistake, Nicholas was forced to inform Wilhelm that the treaty they had just signed could not become operational without major changes. Wilhelm responded, "What is signed is signed!" But the treaty was dead.

In 1908, it was Foreign Minister Izvolsky's turn to be duped and then reverse himself. He agreed that Russia would look benevolently upon Austria's annexation of Bosnia-Herzegovina (consisting mainly of ethnic Serbs), which it had occupied since 1878. In exchange, Austria's foreign minister agreed to provide diplomatic support for Russian efforts to open up the Turkish Straits to Russian warships. It remains unclear what, if anything, was agreed to regarding when these activities might occur.

When Austria acted more quickly than Izvolsky thought it would, he was left unprepared. France and Great Britain were angered at the Austrian move and with Izvolsky's assistance in making it possible. Gaining further diplomatic support for his Straits' policy now proved impossible. Moreover, Serbian and Russian nationalists were incensed over the Austrian annexation, and Stolypin informed Izvolsky to oppose it, which he now did. Germany promised Austria its backing and bluntly demanded recognition of the annexation. Humiliated, but unwilling to risk the consequences suggested by Germany if it did not comply, Russia yielded. Neither Russia nor Serbia forgot the incident, and both became determined not to suffer such humiliation again.

Although France and Britain were angered at the course of events and left wondering at the reliability of Russia, the three countries had moved closer together in recent years. In 1904, Britain and France concluded an entente, or understanding, concerning North African spheres of influence. Kaiser Wilhelm's belligerence toward the entente and a continuing German naval buildup pushed Britain to improve its ties with France further. Britain also moved closer to France's ally, Russia. By the Anglo-Russian Entente of 1907, the two long-time rivals agreed over the status of Persia, Afghanistan, and Tibet. Most significantly, they agreed that Britain would have dominant influence over southeast Persia; Russia over northern Persia; and that a neutral zone would exist between the two other Persian spheres. The growing closeness of Russia, Britain, and France (the Triple Entente), however, only increased Germany's fear of encirclement and its determination to maintain its Austro-Hungarian alliance by vigorously supporting its ally.

The next major trouble in the Balkans came in 1912–1913. Warfare there involving Turks and Balkan nations chipped away more Turkish territory in Europe, nudged the Ottoman Empire closer to Germany and Austria-Hungary, and increased tensions and hostilities between Serbia and Austria-Hungary. Although Sergei Sazanov, who had replaced Izvolsky as foreign minister in 1910, attempted to prevent war, his vacillating policies inadvertently contributed to bringing it about.

Then, on June 28, 1914, a Bosnian of Serbian nationality assassinated Austrian Archduke Franz Ferdinand. Austria was convinced that the Serbian government was implicated but feared Russia would support Serbia in case of a conflict. Austria therefore sought and received German backing (the infamous "blank check") before it proceeded to send an ultimatum to Serbia on July 23. If fully complied with, the ultimatum would have guaranteed Austrian dominance over Serbia.

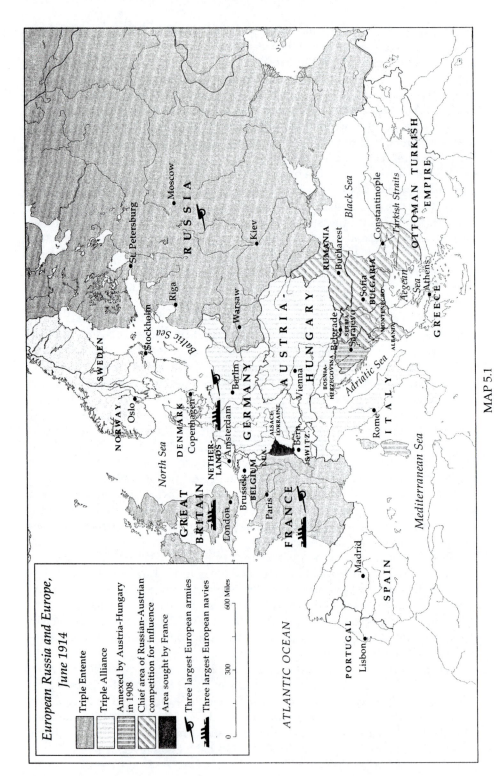

European Russia and Europe,
June 1914

Triple Entente

Triple Alliance

Annexed by Austria-Hungary
in 1908

Chief area of Russian-Austrian
competition for influence

Area sought by France

Three largest European armies

Three largest European navies

0   300   600 Miles

ATLANTIC OCEAN

PORTUGAL
Lisbon

SPAIN
Madrid

Mediterranean Sea

FRANCE
Paris

GREAT BRITAIN
London

NORTH Sea

NETHER-LANDS
Amsterdam

BELGIUM
Brussels

LUX.

ALSACE
LORRAINE

SWITZ.
Bern

GERMANY
Berlin

DENMARK
Copenhagen

Baltic Sea

SWEDEN
Stockholm

NORWAY
Oslo

ITALY
Rome

AUSTRIA-HUNGARY
Vienna

BOSNIA-HERZEGOVINA
Sarajevo

SERBIA
Belgrade

MONTENEGRO

ALBANIA

Adriatic Sea

RUMANIA
Bucharest

BULGARIA
Sofia

GREECE
Athens

Aegean Sea

Constantinople

Turkish Straits

OTTOMAN TURKISH EMPIRE

Black Sea

RUSSIA
Moscow

St. Petersburg

Riga

Warsaw

Kiev

MAP 5.1

Neither Serbia nor Russia could tolerate this. It would have ended Russian hopes for major Balkan influence and sealed Austrian supremacy in the area. After hearing of Austria's ultimatum, Sazanov declared: "That means a European war!" Although advising Serbia to proceed cautiously, on July 25 (N.S.), Russia approved preliminary military preparations, hoping to alarm Austria into a compromise or, failing that, to be ready to help Serbia. France backed Russia's stand.

Encouraged by Russian support, Serbia, although somewhat conciliatory, did not accept all the Austrian demands. On July 28, Austria declared war on Serbia and bombarded Belgrade, the Serbian capital.

After some indecisiveness about how to mobilize, on July 30 (N.S.), Russia ordered a general mobilization of its troops. France encouraged this action because it knew of the general thrust of Germany's Schlieffen Plan, which called for a fatal German blow against France before Russian mobilization would force Germany to divert more troops to its eastern front.

Because of Germany's plan, its response to Russia was no surprise. On July 31, after several warnings on previous days, it sent an ultimatum with a twelve-hour limit demanding that Russia end its war preparations along the German frontier. On August 1, having received no reply, Germany declared war on Russia. Two days later, certain that France was preparing to aid Russia, Germany declared war on France. It directed its attack through neutral Belgium, thereby alarming Britain, which declared war on Germany on August 4.

The responsibility of Russia and other powers in beginning World War I has been greatly debated. Certainly Russia played its part in the combustible nationalistic-militaristic-imperialistic climate of the era. And its decision to mobilize fully on July 30 was especially important. Along with the other powers, Russia valued security, prestige, influence, and allies more than peace.

Yet, shortly before he ordered full mobilization on July 30, Nicholas told one of his ministers that "everything possible must be done to save the peace. I will not become responsible for a monstrous slaughter." Nicholas made his fateful decision because he was assured by his generals that no partial mobilization plan existed to mobilize troops just against Austria-Hungary and not Germany. This fact reflected more the Russian government's ineptness and lack of flexibility than any lust for war.

Moreover, many historians have followed Fritz Fischer's lead in placing the primary blame for World War I on Germany. For example, Lieven has argued that even without the Russian general mobilization, war would have come and "the major immediate responsibility for the outbreak of the war rested unequivocally on the German government."[2]

TSARIST RUSSIA AND WORLD WAR I, 1914–1916

In Russia, as in most European countries, the beginning of World War I brought a lessening of political opposition and a patriotic rallying around the

---

[2]D. C. B. Lieven, *Russia and the Origins of the First World War* (New York, 1983), p. 151.

government. This was especially true among Great Russian urban dwellers. The strikes that had been surging for two years now ended. Symbolic of the new spirit was the crowd of close to a quarter-million that jammed the vast Palace Square on August 2 (N.S.). After Nicholas appeared on the Winter Palace balcony overlooking the square and swore he would make no peace while enemy troops remained on Russian soil, the crowd sang "God Save the Tsar" and the hymn "Lord, Save Thy People and Bless Thine Inheritance."

Russia began the war by rushing troops into East Prussia, a move critical to relieving German pressure on France. The campaign proved a disaster for Russian troops, who were defeated at the battles of Tannenberg (August 26–30) and Mansurian Lakes (September 6–15). In December, the Russians lost the Polish industrial city of Lodz to the Germans. Against Austria, the Russian army had been more successful, moving into Galicia and capturing its capital of Lemberg (Lvov or Lviv) in September (see Map 5.2). Overall, by the end of 1914, the war had cost Russia more than 1 million dead, wounded, or captured, plus hundreds of thousands of weapons.

During 1915, German and Austrian forces attacked over a broad area from the Baltic to the Rumanian frontier. By October 1915, they had captured Vilna (Vilnius), Pinsk, and Lemberg; Riga and Minsk were not far away. As Russia retreated, it practiced scorched-earth policies, attempting to leave as little as possible to the enemy, but also swelling the number of refugees into the millions. Some victories in the Caucasus against Turkey, which had entered the war in the fall of 1914, hardly compensated for huge losses in Russia's western provinces.

In the late spring of 1916, one of Russia's most able generals, A. A. Brusilov, launched an offensive against Austrian forces, pushing them back, inflicting many casualties. His success encouraged Rumania to join the war on the Entente side, but it also led Germany to divert troops to halt the Russian advance, which they did.

Meanwhile, Russian losses continued to mount. By the end of 1916, killed, wounded, missing, or captured numbered about 7 million. As losses steadily rose, morale just as steadily fell.

Even during the first year of war, many soldiers deserted. By the beginning of 1917, the number reached perhaps 1 million or more. As more new men replaced those killed or otherwise lost, discipline declined. In November 1916, Paul Miliukov, leader of the Progressive Bloc, which was formed in August 1915 and contained a majority of Duma deputies, surveyed the state of affairs at home and on the front and asked his fellow Duma members: "Is this stupidity, or is this treason?" At the front, rumors incorrectly favored the latter explanation.

There was also discontent brewing among minority nationalities. After the government attempted to draft a half-million Central Asians for labor service in mid-1916, scattered rebellions broke out in their region, resulting by year's end in thousands of Russian civilian and military deaths. Central Asian losses were much higher.

Although many Russian villagers were by now condemning the war, the greatest dissatisfaction was displayed in the cities, where population had in-

Russia in World War I

Russia's western border, 1914

✕ Major battle, 1914

Russia's allies in the Balkans and on the Eastern Front, by the end of 1916

Russia's enemies, by the end of 1915

The Eastern Front by October 1915 (little change over next 2 years)

Gains against Ottoman Turks by 1916

0   300   600 Miles

MAP 5.2

Labels on map:

ATLANTIC OCEAN
North Sea
GREAT BRITAIN
London
Paris
FRANCE
NETH.
BEL.
LUX.
Berlin
GERMANY
DENMARK
NORWAY
SWEDEN
Helsingfors
Gulf of Finland
Reval
Riga
Baltic Sea
No
Pskov
Vilna
Minsk
Pinsk
POLAND
Warsaw
Lodz
TANNENBERG, AUG. 1914
MASURIAN LAKES, SEPT. 1914
GALICIA
Lemburg (Lvov)
AUSTRIA-HUNGARY
ITALY
Malta
Mediterranean Sea
Belgrade
Sarajevo
SERBIA
MONTE-NEGRO
ALBANIA
GREECE
BULGARIA
RUMANIA
Constantinople
Turkish Straits
OTTOMAN TURKISH EMPIRE
Black Sea
Odessa
CRIMEA
Sea of Azov
Kars
Baku
Caspian Sea
Tsaritsyn
Don R.
Voronezh
Kharkov
Volga R.
Volga R.
Nizhnii Novgorod
Tver
Vologda
Archangel
Moscow
Tula
Smolensk
Mogilev
Rovno
Kiev
Brusilov Offense 1916
Dvinsk
Petrograd
Allies 1915-1916

107

creased by about one-fourth between 1914 and 1916. In Petrograd (no longer the German-sounding St. Petersburg), Moscow, and other cities, food and fuel grew more scarce and difficult to afford. Workers' pay failed to keep up with the soaring prices of basic needs. Not surprisingly, the lull in strike activity that greeted the war did not last long. In September 1915, there were 100,000 strikers in Russia; in October 1916, there were about 250,000 in Petrograd alone. In the Duma, many shared Miliukov's disgust. Police reports and memoirs from the period indicate that by the end of 1916, many in the capital thought revolution was just around the corner.

The military's poor showing was a major cause of discontentment. At first, it was primarily because of shortages of supplies and poor leadership—the priorities of Russia's prewar rearmament program overemphasized some items, such as battleships, at the expense of more vital needs. By the end of 1914, Russia was almost 2 million rifles short of what it needed to arm its 6.5 million men. For a while in 1915, the situation grew worse. Many men were forced into combat without rifles, unless or until they were able to pick them up from their fallen comrades. Not only rifles, but also machine guns, bullets, cartridges, artillery shells, motorized vehicles, uniforms and boots, telephone and telegraph equipment, airplane spare parts, and other supplies were all insufficient. What Russia did possess, including manpower, it could not get to the front as quickly as Germany. This was due largely to the greater distances Russian supplies needed to travel and because per square mile of territory, European Russia possessed less than one-tenth the railway of Germany. Yet by the spring-summer of 1916, dramatic domestic production increases and more supplies from its allies and the United States had helped surmount most of the supply problems.

The problem of poor leadership was more difficult to overcome, primarily because at the top of the pyramid stood Nicholas II. He was ultimately responsible for appointing and retaining so many inept military and civilian leaders. Time and again he ignored or refused good advice to get rid of poor leaders, while listening to poor advice to dismiss good ministers and generals.

Although already displaying this poor lack of judgment before August 1915, the problem worsened after that because Nicholas was absent from the capital. Despite the alarm it caused some of his ministers, he went to army headquarters in the Belorussian city of Mogilev to take command of his troops personally. Henceforth, he was increasingly influenced by his generals and the unlimited advice sent to him from his wife, Alexandra, who remained on the outskirts of Petrograd, at the nearby tsarist retreat of Tsarskoe Selo.

Even under normal circumstances, she was less capable than he of making good political judgments, but by now she had fallen under the sway of the notorious Grigori Rasputin. He was a self-proclaimed holy man of Siberian peasant background—he was also a great lecher and carouser, but Alexandra refused to believe it. His influence over her was due chiefly to his ability, apparently hypnotic, to alleviate the bleeding of her only son, the hemophiliac Alexei, an ability she attributed to Rasputin's closeness to God. His peasant background also appealed to the royal couple, who wished to believe they were still loved by the peasants. Alexandra's influence on Nicholas, and

Rasputin's on her, is illustrated in her letters to Nicholas and in his subsequent actions. Rasputin helped bring about the dismissal of some ministers and the appointment of others, a major criteria being whether or not they favored him.

One of his recommendations was Boris Sturmer. After Alexandra recommended him to replace Goremykin as prime minister, Nicholas appointed him in January 1916. The French ambassador, Maurice Paléologue, described Sturmer as: "worse than a mediocrity—a third rate intellect, mean spirit, low character, doubtful honesty, no experience, and no idea of state business. The most that can be said is that he has a rather pretty talent for cunning and flattery." Nicholas entrusted such a man not only with the office of prime minister, but also he served concurrently for part of 1916 as minister of interior and then foreign minister.

Sturmer failed to remain as close to Rasputin and Alexandra as they had hoped, so they backed the appointment of Alexander Protopovov as minister of interior. Appointed in September 1916, he proved to be a disastrous choice.

The "ministerial leapfrog" now at its height especially disgusted one of the Duma's right-wing leaders, the Union of Russian People's Vladimir Purishkevich. For it, he placed much of the blame on Rasputin and decided that the so-called holy man had to go before he brought down the monarchy itself. By now the most scandalous rumors were common, for example that Rasputin and Alexandra were lovers and that they were both working for the Germans. Rasputin's negative effect on the monarchy's image was perhaps more damaging than his actual influence. Purishkevich and Prince Felix Yusupov, one of Russia's richest men and related to the tsar by marriage, decided to kill Rasputin. The murder was to take place at Yusupov's palace along the Moika Canal.

On December 17, 1916, in one of history's most bizarre deaths, the two conspirators poisoned Rasputin, shot him several times, beat and kicked him, and finally tied up his body and disposed of it beneath icy waters. News of Rasputin's death brought joy to many in Petrograd and Moscow. Upon hearing it, an audience at the Imperial Theater in Moscow burst out in applause and demanded the singing of the national anthem.

CONCLUSION

Although the actual fall of the monarchy was still a few months away, the ground was well prepared by the end of 1916. Andrew Verner believes that Nicholas's negative attitude toward Duma cooperation and his failures to address properly the crisis of 1905–1906 were crucial. "Russian autocracy was doomed, or rather, had doomed itself. With the crisis of 1905–1906, its ultimate fate had been decided; the ten years remaining until 1917 were little more than a death rattle."[3] Other "pessimists" agree with Verner that developments be-

[3]Andrew M. Verner, *The Crisis of Russian Autocracy: Nicholas II and the 1905 Revolution* (Princeton, 1990), p. 6.

fore World War I made the monarchy's fall at least likely. Many emphasize long-range developments such as the incompatibility between economic modernization and autocracy, the gap between autocracy and educated society, or the government's continuing failure to address nationality and peasant concerns adequately. From such a perspective the influence of Rasputin, as Read insists, was more of a symptom than a cause of the monarchy's downfall.

Although not necessarily denying Nicholas's hostility to power-sharing, other historians have emphasized the progress Russia was making in the years 1906 through 1914. They point to indicators such as economic growth; Stolypin's agricultural reforms; and increases in education, participatory government, political patience, and civil rights. Despite the increased strikes of 1912–1914, these "optimists" believe that if the war had not intervened, Russia might have continued a gradual evolution toward a true constitutional monarchy.

Yet, even many "optimists" recognize that Nicholas II bore a heavy responsibility for Russia's failures and declining morale during the war. True, he inherited many of his problems, including an outmoded autocratic system and a country less economically developed than other European powers, but his own wartime failings were costly.

From the criticism of V. A. Maklakov and the *Vekhi* contributors to more recent criticism by Alexander Solzhenitsyn and Richard Pipes, the intelligentsia have also been faulted for their pre-1917 behavior. Pipes, for example, writes: "Had the Russian intelligentsia been politically more mature—more patient, that is, and more understanding of the mentality of the monarchic establishment—Russia might perhaps have succeeded in making an orderly transition from a semi-constitutional to a genuinely constitutional regime."[4]

Despite such criticism, Pipes by no means ignores the many failings of Nicholas II. In the final analysis—despite the increased sympathy displayed in post-Soviet Russia for this tragic tsar, this loving husband and father—Nicholas II was a poor ruler. As Lincoln's lengthy study of Russia during World War I illustrates again and again, the tsar himself was a major cause of his own, and the Romanov dynasty's, demise.

SUGGESTED SOURCES*

ASCHER, ABRAHAM. *The Revolution of 1905.* 2 vols. Stanford, 1988, 1992.

Battleship Potemkin. A 1925 film directed by Sergei Eisenstein. Available on videocassette.

BUSHNELL, JOHN. *Mutiny amid Repression: Russian Soldiers in the Revolution of 1905–1906.* Bloomington, 1985.

EDELMAN, ROBERT. *Gentry Politics on the Eve of the Russian Revolution: The Nationalist Party, 1907–1917.* New Brunswick, N.J., 1980.

---

[4]Richard Pipes, *The Russian Revolution* (New York, 1990), p. 156.
*See also books cited in footnotes.

————. *Proletarian Peasants: The Revolution of 1905 in Russia's Southwest.* Ithaca, N.Y., 1987.

EMMONS, TERENCE. *The Formation of Political Parties and the First National Elections in Russia.* Cambridge, Mass., 1983.

ENGELSTEIN, LAURA. *Moscow, 1905: Working-Class Organization and Political Conflict.* Stanford, 1982.

FERRO, MARC. *Nicholas II: The Last of the Tsars.* New York, 1991.

FULLER, WILLIAM C. *Civil-Military Conflict in Imperial Russia, 1881–1914.* Princeton, 1985.

GAPON, GEORGE. *The Story of My Life.* London, 1905.

GASSENSCHMIDT, CHRISTOPH. *Jewish Liberal Politics in Tsarist Russia, 1900–1914: The Modernization of Russian Jewry.* New York, 1995.

GATRELL, PETER. *Government, Industry, and Rearmament in Russia, 1900–1914: The Last Argument of Tsarism.* Cambridge, England, 1994.

GEIFMAN, ANNA. *Thou Shalt Kill: Revolutionary Terrorism in Russia, 1894–1917.* Princeton, 1993.

GURKO, VLADIMIR I. *Features and Figures of the Past: Government and Opinion in the Reign of Nicholas II.* Stanford, 1939.

HOSKING, GEOFFREY A. *The Russian Constitutional Experiment: Government and Duma, 1907–1914.* Cambridge, England, 1973.

KORROS, ALEXANDRA SHECKET. "Activist Politics in a Conservative Institution: The Formation of Factions in the Russian Imperial State Council, 1906–1907," *RR* 52 (January 1993): 1–19.

LIEVEN, D. C. B. *Nicholas II: Emperor of All the Russias.* London, 1993.

————. *Russia's Rulers under the Old Regime.* New Haven, 1989.

LINCOLN, W. Bruce. *Passage through Armageddon: The Russians in War and Revolution, 1914–1918.* New York, 1986.

MAKLAKOV, VASILII A. *The First State Duma: Contemporary Reminiscences.* Bloomington, 1964.

McDONALD, DAVID M. *United Government and Foreign Policy in Russia, 1900–1914.* Cambridge, Mass., 1992.

McKEAN, ROBERT B. *St. Petersburg between the Revolutions: Workers and Revolutionaries, June 1907–February 1917.* New Haven, 1990.

MELANCON, MICHAEL. *Stormy Petrels: The Socialist Revolutionaries in Russia's Labor Organizations, 1905–1914.* The Carl Beck Papers . . . , no. 703. Pittsburgh, 1988.

MILIUKOV, PAUL N. *Political Memoirs, 1905–1917.* Ann Arbor, 1967.

OLDENBURG, S. S. *Last Tsar: Nicholas II, His Reign and His Russia.* Vols. 2–4, Gulf Breeze, Fla., 1975–1978.

PALÉOLOGUE, MAURICE. *An Ambassador's Memoirs.* 3 vols. New York, 1972.

PARES, BERNARD. *The Fall of the Russian Monarchy: A Study of Evidence.* London, 1939.

PORTER, THOMAS, and WILLIAM GLEASON. "The Zemstvo and Public Initiative in Late Imperial Russia," *RH* 21 (Winter 1994): 419–437.

RADZINSKY, EDVARD. *The Last Tsar: The Life and Death of Nicholas II.* New York, 1992.

Rasputin. A 1985 film directed by Elem Klimov. Available on videocassette.

READ, CHRISTOPHER. *From Tsar to Soviets: The Russian People and Their Revolution, 1917–1921.* New York, 1996. Chs. 1 & 2.

————. *Religion, Revolution and the Russian Intelligentsia, 1900–1912: The Vekhi Debate and Its Intellectual Background.* London, 1979.

REICHMAN, HENRY. *Railwaymen and Revolution: Russia, 1905.* Berkeley, 1987.

SAZONOV, S. D. *Fateful Years, 1909–1916: The Reminiscences of Serge Sazonov.* New York, 1928.

SHANIN, TEODOR. *Russia, 1905–07: Revolution as a Moment of Truth.* New Haven, 1986.

SHATZ, MARSHALL, and JUDITH ZIMMERMAN, eds. *Signposts: A Collection of Articles on the Russian Intelligentsia.* Irvine, Calif., 1986.

SHOWALTER, DENNIS E. *Tannenberg: Clash of Empires.* Hamden, Conn., 1991.

SHULGIN, V. V. *The Years: Memoirs of a Member of the Russian Duma, 1906–1917.* New York, 1984.

STAVROU, THEOFANIS GEORGE, ed. *Russia under the Last Tsar.* Minneapolis, 1969.

STONE, NORMAN. *The Eastern Front, 1914–1917.* New York, 1975.

SURH, GERALD D. *1905 in St. Petersburg: Labor, Society, and Revolution.* Stanford, 1989.

SWAIN, GEOFFREY. *Russian Social Democracy and the Legal Labour Movement, 1906–1914.* London, 1983.

SZEFTEL, MARC. *The Russian Constitution of April 23, 1906: Political Institutions of the Duma Monarchy.* Brussels, 1976.

WARTH, ROBERT D. "Peter Arkad'evich Stolypin," *MERSH* 37: 152–156.

WEINBERG, ROBERT. *The Revolution of 1905 in Odessa: Blood on the Steps.* Bloomington, 1993.

WEISSMAN, NEIL B. *Reform in Tsarist Russia: The State Bureaucracy and Local Government, 1900–1914.* New Brunswick, N.J., 1981.

ZENKOVSKY, A. V. *Stolypin: Russia's Last Great Reformer.* Princeton, 1986.

CHAPTER 6

Economics and Society, 1855–1917

In the Late Imperial, period the Russian Empire remained overwhelmingly agrarian, but some dynamic changes occurred: its population, cities, industry, trade, and middle and urban working classes all grew significantly. In contrast, noble landholding decreased. Although some changes (such as Alexander II's reforms) stemmed from government policies, such policies were themselves affected by a global modernization trend. To remain a major power, Russia had to modernize.

Reaction to Russian modernization varied greatly, both then and later. Some applauded the growth of capitalism in Russia; others, such as the populists or Leo Tolstoy, believed it did not represent true progress. Some historians have emphasized statistics indicating Russia's rapid economic growth or the eventual decline in its high death rate; other scholars have stressed Russia's continuing lag behind the major Western powers.

Although officials and nobles supported some modernizing developments, they often resisted others that threatened to undermine autocracy or Russia's patriarchal social system. While perceiving the necessity of modernization, the tsars remained more comfortable with the old world of social estates, especially nobles and peasants, than they did with emerging classes and urban society. Thus, Russia's economic and social order entered World War I with one foot in the modern world, while the other remained imbedded in traditional Russia.

POPULATION, TOWNS, AND URBAN SOCIETY

From 1855 until 1913, the population of the Russian Empire increased from about 73 million to about 168 million. Although new territories were annexed, population growth was due more to other factors, especially a declining death rate and, despite some decline, a birth rate that remained much higher than Western Europe's. The most dramatic population growth occurred in areas of significant in-migration, for example, southern European Russia, Siberia, the Kingdom of Poland, and urban areas in general.

From 1856 until 1913, the urban population increased from about 10 percent to about 18 percent of the total population.[1] Based on Thomas Fedor's figures, from 1856 to 1910, St. Petersburg's population more than tripled and Moscow's more than quadrupled, bringing the capital to slightly more than 1.5 million people and Moscow to a little under that figure. Growth in the empire's third to fifth largest cities by 1910 was even more rapid, increasing more than fivefold in Warsaw and Odessa and more than eightfold in Kiev. Beneath these cities, Fedor lists eight others with more than 200,000 people by 1910. They included, in descending order of population: Lodz, Riga, Tiflis, Kharkov, Baku (which increased almost thirtyfold), Saratov, Ekaterinoslav, and Tashkent.

Although still considerably less urban by 1913 than Western Europe or the United States, Russian cities were large by world standards. Although smaller than Tokyo, both Moscow and St. Petersburg were much larger, for example, than any city in China or Latin America.

The cities grew faster than the countryside primarily because trade and manufacturing made more jobs available in them, and the growing transportation system, mainly railways, provided the means to reach them. By 1897, more than half of the inhabitants of large cities (those with over 50,000 people) were born elsewhere, mainly in the countryside. When seasonal or temporary work was completed, or disillusionment set in, peasants sometimes made their way back to their villages or headed for other cities. Daniel Brower has compared the empire's cities to "great revolving doors."[2]

The empire's major cities at the turn of the century were vibrant, dynamic places, teeming with different nationalities and social groups. (Smaller provincial towns, in contrast, often seemed boring and stagnant, at least to many intellectuals, such as the writer Chekhov.) In Warsaw and Odessa, Jews made up one-third of the population. In Riga, the Latvians made up about two-fifths of the population, as did the Germans and Russians combined. In the booming oil town of Baku, Russians were the largest nationality but were outnumbered by the combined total of Azerbaijani Turks and Armenians. In the Georgian city of Tiflis (later Tbilisi), Armenians made up almost two-fifths of the population. Although nationalities often lived side-by-side in harmony, pogroms and other ethnic conflicts sometimes occurred.

Even on St. Petersburg's fashionable Nevsky Prospect, where before World War I stood a Singer Sewing Machine building and an Equitable Life Insurance office, so many of the empire's nationalities were visible that one tourist called it "a valuable lesson in ethnography." In the capital one could see, for example, Moslems in white turbans; Hasidic Jews with earlocks hanging down beneath their skullcaps; Russian factory workers with peaked caps; bearded Russian

---

[1]As earlier, conditions of the time make almost all statistics merely rough approximations. Unless indicated otherwise, they are for the Russian Empire as a whole.

[2]"Urban Revolution in the Late Russian Empire," in *The City in Late Imperial Russia*, ed. Michael F. Hamm (Bloomington, 1986), p. 327.

peasants fresh from the countryside; kerchiefed women and more elegantly dressed ones with their hands enveloped in muffs; and uniformed officials, students, and military men.

Partly for the benefit of illiterates (still an urban majority in 1900), many shops displayed signs picturing what they carried, and street vendors and peddlers still hawked their goods on city streets. In the center of major cities, horse-drawn trams and gas lighting were just beginning to give way to electric trams and lighting. But horse-drawn sleighs and carriages still far outnumbered trams of any sort or automobiles, although by 1914 both St. Petersburg and Moscow offered motorized taxi service, and some cities had motor clubs.

While the rich shopped in the elite foreign and domestic shops on streets such as the capital's Nevsky Prospect, the poor were more likely to do their buying in areas such as that of Moscow's Khitrov market. Set in one of Russia's most infamous slums, it was surrounded by flophouses, penetrated by foul smells, and often enveloped in river mists.

While the rich lived in palaces or roomy, richly decorated apartments, the poor lived in factory dormitories, slums, or attics or basements of buildings whose other occupants were better off. As migrants streamed into the big cities and housing became more scarce, the practice of renting out small corners of rooms, often in basements, became increasingly common. By 1900, about one-sixth of Moscow's population lived in such corners. The conditions were similar in St. Petersburg. Cities, especially the largest, were beginning to make some progress in regards to water supply and sanitation. By 1900, roughly three-fourths of St. Petersburg's apartments possessed piped water, and about two-thirds had toilets.

During this era, the social profile of cities became more diversified. The government continued to classify people by social estate (*soslovie*). This classification, however, was becoming more cumbersome each year—industrial workers, for example, had no category of their own and were chiefly included in the peasant category. In Moscow, where many businesses were owned by those listed as "peasants," Leo Tolstoy discovered some nobles living in flophouses.

ENTREPRENEURS AND CIVIL SOCIETY

By 1914, Russia's small entrepreneurial elite numbered only a few thousand individuals. Yet, during this period, it became a more dynamic social force, both in behalf of its own interests and in relation to larger public issues. This elite came from different backgrounds, including the peasant, merchant, and noble estates; showcased its goods at major exhibitions; and organized regional and, less commonly, national meetings and organizations. The most public-spirited entrepreneurial families resided in Moscow. They had generally made a fortune in textiles and then branched out into other areas such as railways, mining, and banking. At first, they displayed their civic-mindedness primarily in the city's duma (council) and by patronizing the arts (see Chapter 7).

National political involvement came more slowly. Ethnic, religious, and re-

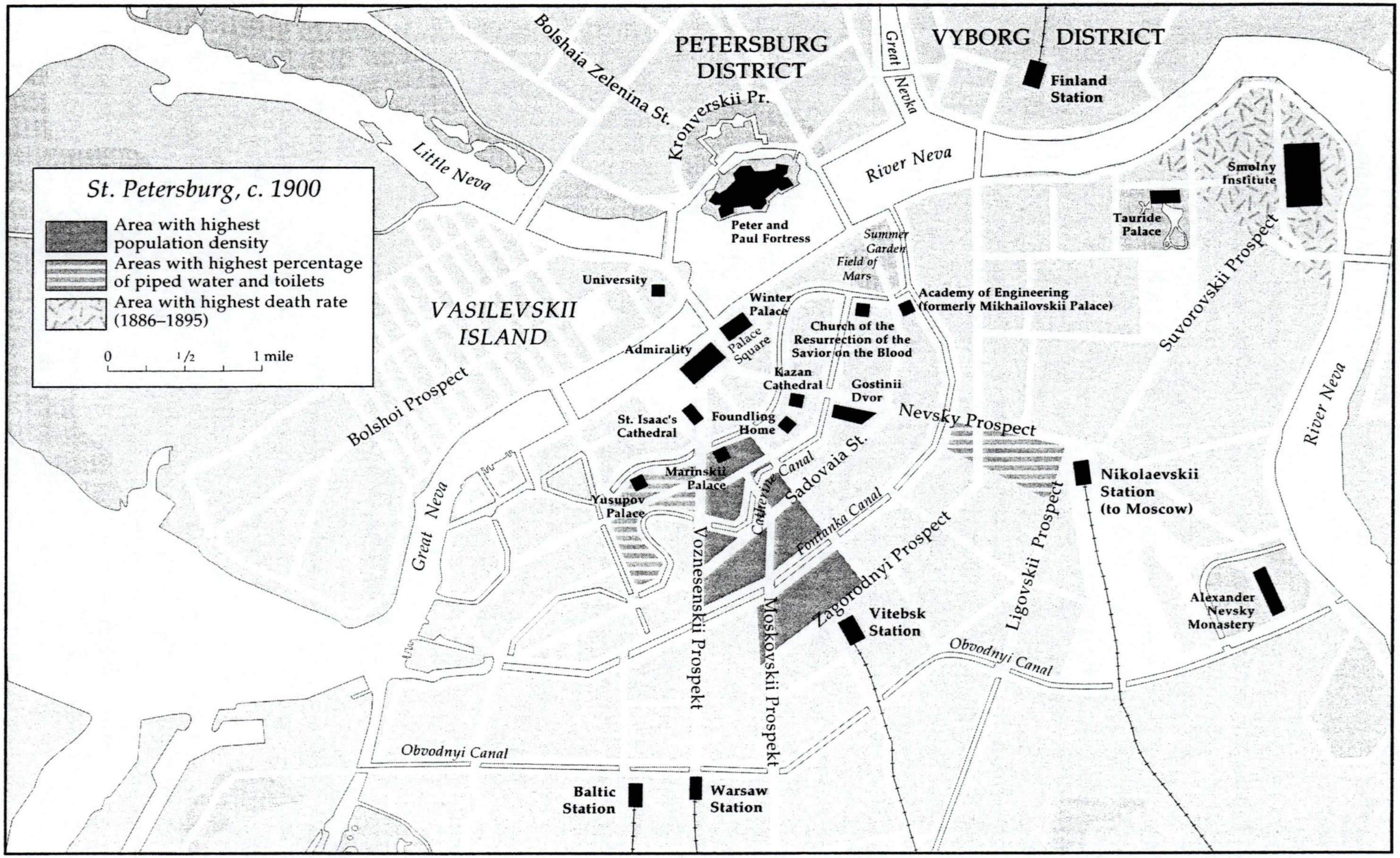

St. Petersburg, c. 1900

Area with highest population density

Areas with highest percentage of piped water and toilets

Area with highest death rate (1886–1895)

0   1/2   1 mile

VYBORG DISTRICT

PETERSBURG DISTRICT

VASILEVSKII ISLAND

River Neva

River Neva

Great Neva

Little Neva

Great Nevka

Kronverskii Pr.

Bolshaia Zelenina St.

Bolshoi Prospect

Obvodnyi Canal

Obvodnyi Canal

Zagorodnyi Prospect

Ligovskii Prospect

Suvorovskii Prospect

Nevsky Prospect

Moskovskii Prospect

Voznesenskii Prospect

Sadovaia St.

Ekaterininskii Canal

Fontanka Canal

Smolny Institute

Tauride Palace

Finland Station

Alexander Nevskii Monastery

Nikolaevskii Station (to Moscow)

Academy of Engineering (formerly Mikhailovskii Palace)

Summer Garden

Field of Mars

Church of the Resurrection of the Savior (on the Blood)

Gostinii Dvor

Kazan Cathedral

Foundling Home

Winter Palace

Palace Square

Admiralty

University

Peter and Paul Fortress

St. Isaac's Cathedral

Mariinskii Palace

Yusupov Palace

Vitebsk Station

Warsaw Station

Baltic Station

MAP 6.1

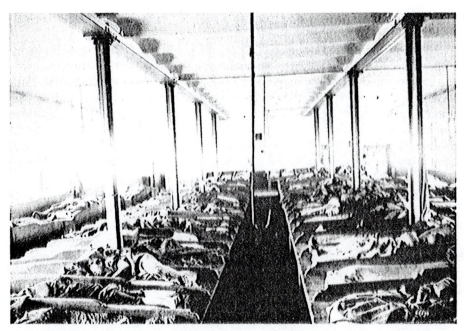

FIGURE 6.1. A workers' dormitory around the turn of the century, Trekhgornaia Textile Mill, Moscow.
(From Chloe Obolensky, The Russian Empire: A Portrait in Photographs. *Random House, New York, 1979, #292.)*

gional differences continued to divide business leaders, as did their differing social backgrounds, making it difficult for them to speak with one voice. Before 1904–1905, government actions were not threatening enough to spur more unity—the administration's tariff and tax policies and its contracts and guarantees were generally favorable to the business elite.

Intelligentsia hostility to capitalism and the bourgeoisie also hindered the major entrepreneurs from exercising more national political influence. Herzen's sentiment—"God save Russia from the bourgeoisie"—was shared by most intellectuals. Despite the Marxist belief that capitalism was a progressive stage on the way to socialism, both Marx and many of the Russian Marxists were contemptuous toward the capitalists. Most liberals also were unsympathetic to them. Historian and Kadet party leader Paul Miliukov warned industrialists in 1905–1906 that he did not wish his newly formed party to be sullied by narrow class interests. In 1906, Leo Tolstoy, neither a socialist nor a liberal, referred to the bourgeoisie as "a class of people living idly on others' labor."

Despite these impediments to a more dynamic national role, the outbreak of political opposition in 1904–1907 spurred industrialists and financiers to greater political activity. In early 1906, for example, business leaders formed a Council of Representatives of Industry and Trade to represent their interests.

During the next decade, the council often objected to the government's competition with private enterprise and its interference in business.

Between 1906 and 1916, there was one major attempt to create a strong entrepreneurial-led political party. The most dynamic force behind this effort was the Moscow manufacturer, banker, and publisher Paul Riabushinsky. His family belonged to the schismatic Old Believer religious community, and he was initially sympathetic to the Octobrists, whose principal leader, Alexander Guchkov, was a fellow Moscow industrialist also from an Old Believer background. Along with some other industrialists, however, Riabushinsky soon became disenchanted with the Octobrists, believing them too accommodating to the government.

In 1912, Riabushinsky and some like-minded liberal Moscow industrialists formed the Progressive party. His publications and party activities indicate that Riabushinsky was a nationalist who harbored panslavist dreams but criticized St. Petersburg bureaucrats. He advocated freedom of thought, religious belief, and legal safeguards. He and his like-minded colleagues thought of themselves as forward-looking capitalists who had the practical knowledge and energy to lead Russia into a more democratic, enlightened, and prosperous future.

Although the Progressive party had fewer delegates in the Fourth Duma than the Octobrists or Kadets, they became an important moderate voice in that body. They were a vital part of the Duma's Progressive Bloc, formed in 1915. That same year, Riabushinsky called for the creation of a War Industries Committee (WIC) to help supply the military. Nicholas II permitted its creation, and Alexander Guchkov became its chairman and the industrialist V. I. Konovalov, Riabushinsky's close political ally, its vice-chairman. Riabushinsky became chairman of its Moscow District branch.

Many of the civic activities of Riabushinsky and other progressive entrepreneurs reflected the growth of an embryonic civil society—a social sphere standing between the government and the family or individual, in which people could freely interact and create their own independent organizations. Its rapid evolution before World War I was closely connected with the growth of urban life. Joseph Bradley has noted that Moscow's 1912 City Directory "listed more than six-hundred societies, organizations, clubs, and associations, covering a wide range of charitable, technical, literary, sporting, artistic, educational, and learned activities."[3] Such organizations were essential for the development of an autonomous civil society and for the growth of middle-class values.

Yet any continued development of the public sphere (and the respect for law and pluralism that was linked to it) was threatened by two major fissures that grew wider during World War I. One was between the tsar's government and educated society, the other between educated society and the urban and rural masses. Like some others in educated society, Riabushinsky and his publications attempted to lessen both these gaps. But the revolutionary earthquake

[3]"Voluntary Associations, Civic Culture, and *Obshchestvennost'* in Moscow," in *Between Tsar and People: Educated Society and the Quest for Public Identity in Late Imperial Russia*, eds. Edith Clowes, Samuel Kassow, and James L. West (Princeton, 1991), pp. 136–137.

of 1917 toppled both the liberal aspirations of urban leaders such as Riabushin-sky and the autonomous civil society that had been slowly developing.

ECONOMIC GROWTH

The increase of entrepreneurial influence by 1917 reflected the rapid growth of Russian industry and trade during the half-century before World War I. This growth was especially evident in the 1890s and again from 1909 to 1913. In 1913, 14 times as much pig iron and 120 times as much coal was being pro-duced as in 1860. In this same period, 44 times more railway track came into existence. The textile industry also accelerated its already rapid growth of the early nineteenth century. By 1913, it and the metal-machine industry were the largest employers of factory workers, with the former being dominant in Moscow and the latter in St. Petersburg. Overall, Russian factory and handi-craft production increased at least tenfold from 1860 to 1913.

The reasons for this rapid development include Russia's significant popula-tion growth, which led to greater demand and a larger work force. State policies and practices both hampered and helped industrial growth. Largely as a result of government actions and inactions, the number of Russian corporations in ex-istence by 1913 trailed far behind that of other European powers. By emancipat-ing the serfs and spurring railway construction, however, the government helped stimulate the economy. Western Europe's example and the growing real-ization of the connection of industrial might and military power prompted the state to take additional steps, including encouraging foreign investment.

On the eve of World War I, about one-third of the capital of Russian com-panies was owned by foreigners, primarily the French, British, and Germans. Foreign capitalists were especially prominent in the oil industry, which the Nobel brothers helped launch in Baku during the 1870s. Along with two U.S. Corporations, International Harvester and Singer Sewing Machine, Nobel Brothers Petroleum was still by 1914 one of the largest businesses operating in Russia. Foreigners also figured prominently in Russian mining and metallurgy. In 1869, the Welshman John Hughes received a government concession to pro-duce coal, iron, and rails in the Donets Basin. The Lena goldfields, site of the 1912 tragedy that killed strikers and helped reenergize Russian labor militancy, were owned by a British firm.

The prominence of foreign capitalists in Russia, plus that of capitalists of minority nationalities such as Armenians, Germans, Jews, and Poles, led many Russians to think of capitalism as foreign to Russia's traditions. From the Late Imperial period into the 1990s, as Thomas Owen has pointed out, Russian anti-capitalism has frequently been heightened by Russian xenophobia.

Among Russian workers who labored in foreign-owned factories was fu-ture Soviet leader Nikita Khrushchev, who, in 1908, came to Yuzovka (a city of almost 50,000 named after John Hughes). By this time the area had become a vital part of Ukraine's quickly developing heavy industry. Along with the Krivoi Rog area west of it, the Donets Basin by 1914 had overtaken the Urals as

Russia's leading metallurgical center. Besides these areas and the St. Petersburg and Moscow provinces, the former Kingdom of Poland and the Baltic area, especially Riga, were other important industrial regions (see Map 6.2). In general, Russian industry was more concentrated than in other major countries.

Despite Russia's impressive industrial growth, in 1913 it still ranked behind the leading Western countries. By then, it produced only about one-eighteenth the coal, one-thirteenth the electricity, and one-seventh the steel produced by U.S. industry. Although Russia's total industrial output by 1913 trailed only that of the United States, Germany, Britain, and France, on a per-capita basis it also ranked behind several other countries, including Belgium and Sweden. Per mile of land, even countries such as Serbia and Bulgaria had more railway track.

Although growing more slowly than its industry, Russia's domestic trade also expanded. Wholesale and retail sales, for example, more than tripled between 1885 and 1913. Trade fairs continued to be important and grew in number, but they generated a decreasing percentage of total trading volume. Regular trading establishments remained primarily small scale—in 1912, small stores, chiefly family owned and operated, and market stalls made up more than 80 percent of the total. Haggling and bargaining over prices remained customary, especially outside the more modern and fashionable stores and shops.

Foreign trade grew faster than domestic commerce and by 1913 constituted just a little over 4 percent of world trade. Most of it continued to be transported in and out of Russia in foreign ships. Government policies generally insured that the value of exports (still mainly food products and raw materials) exceeded imports (still chiefly industrial and luxury goods).

Yet within this broad continuity, there were some new variations. Wheat, eggs, butter, sugar, and petroleum all became more important export goods, as did industrial products sent to Asia. Among imports, machines and machine tools became more significant; and in 1913, almost five times as much cotton was imported as the yearly average in the late 1860s. Because of the textile industry's need for cotton, imports would have been much greater had it not been for a sharp increase in the supply of domestic cotton, primarily from the new Central Asian regions.

Perhaps more importantly, Germany replaced Great Britain as Russia's leading trading partner. By 1913, it furnished almost half of Russia's imports and more than one-third of its exports; this prewar reliance on German trade was an additional reason for Russia's supply problems during World War I.

As important as industry and trade were, agriculture remained the backbone of the Russian economy and continued to employ most of the empire's workforce. An expansion of sown areas and improved per-acre yields helped agricultural output outdistance population growth and provide more agricultural produce, whether for export or domestic consumption. Nevertheless, agriculture grew much less rapidly than industry, lessening the rate of overall economic growth.

According to Paul Gregory's figures, Russian national income in 1913 was about quadruple what it had been in 1861, although on a per-capita basis it had less than doubled. By 1913, Gregory estimates that Russia's per capita national income was roughly one-tenth the U.S. figure, one-fifth the United Kingdom's, and less than two-fifths Germany's or France's. Overall the gap between Russian per capita income and that of the major Western powers increased from 1861 to 1913.

Yet, despite some bad years and economic zigzags, consumption levels and living standards gradually improved. There were sharp regional variations, however. In the last few decades of the era, the central Russian provinces seemed to suffer more economic want than peripheral areas such as the Baltic provinces, Siberia, and Russian Poland.

A much greater disparity existed among social groups, whether living in the cities or countryside. The municipal statute of 1870 divided voting rights and direct taxpayers into three categories. The top group was the smallest and richest and had to pay the most taxes, which might be many thousand times more than the kopecks paid by some of the poorest members of the third and largest group. Yet few urban dwellers owned or made enough even to be included in the third group. In Moscow during the 1870s and 1880s, all three groups constituted less than 1 percent of the city's population.

INDUSTRIAL AND URBAN WORKERS

According to the 1897 census, slightly more than half of Russia's manufacturing laborers worked outside the empire's cities. Inside them, they composed only one-fourth of the urban workforce, and many of them were artisans not factory workers. In 1902, Moscow shops, stores, and the lodging and restaurant business combined to employ tens of thousands more people than did the factories. Domestics and transportation workers (such as those working on docks and railways and driving horse-cabs) were another significant grouping. In the decade after 1902, Moscow's office and sales clerks, teachers, bookkeepers, and cashiers grew at a faster rate than its factory workers.

Yet, although urban factory workers remained greatly outnumbered by all the other laborers in the cities, they still increased rapidly in the final decades of this era, especially in the larger cities. In St. Petersburg by 1902, one of four hired employees worked in a factory; in Moscow, about one in five worked in factories. Compared to other industrialized countries such as the United States or Germany, a higher percentage of factory laborers worked in large factories employing more than 1,000 workers. During crisis years such as 1905 and 1917, such concentrations proved significant.

Before labor legislation of the 1880s and 1890s, both factory workers and artisans often worked more than twelve hours a day. Women and children, many under ten years old, worked for less wages than men. At the workplace, working conditions were usually unsafe; workers were often fined, paid late, and sometimes forced to buy food at inflated prices from company stores. Workers had no rights and were forbidden to form unions. Whether they lived inside or outside factory dormitories, they were crowded together and had to contend with the twin scourges of urban inflation and fear of being fired.

Beginning in the 1880s, legislation, although often evaded, gradually improved conditions, more in the factories than among artisans. An 1882 law pro-

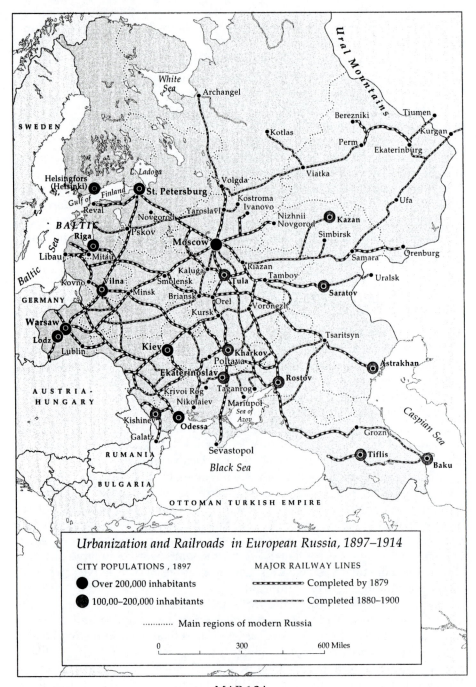

Urbanization and Railroads in European Russia, 1897–1914

CITY POPULATIONS , 1897

● Over 200,000 inhabitants

● 100,00–200,000 inhabitants

MAJOR RAILWAY LINES

▭▭▭▭▭ Completed by 1879

▭▭▭▭▭ Completed 1880–1900

.... Main regions of modern Russia

0   300   600 Miles

MAP 6.2A

Industry and Agriculture in European Russia, 1897–1914

- Leading mining- metallurgical areas
- Other major industrial areas
- Major petroleum areas
- Major sugar beet production
- Major commercial grain farming
- Major grain farming, but primarily for local use

·········· Main regions of European Russia

0   300   600 Miles

MAP 6.2B

hibited factories from hiring children under twelve or from employing those aged twelve to fifteen more than eight hours a day. By the end of the century, factory inspectors, who began operating in the 1880s, attempted to enforce other new legislation that limited the factory workday to 11.5 hours (ten hours on Saturdays) and prohibited or limited mining and night work for women and adolescents.

By mid-1914, factory workers, still less than 2 percent of the empire's population, had made additional gains. Most now toiled only about ten hours a day, six days a week (except for the forty-some religious and other holidays). A sickness and accident law of 1912 provided some pay while off the job. (Nonfactory workers were less fortunate; for example, many of Kiev's bakers still worked nineteen hours a day.) Factory workers also won wage gains, although inflation and inadequate statistics make it difficult to compute any changes in purchasing power. The proliferation of workers' consumer cooperatives did, however, help make some items more affordable.

A fundamental gain was the right to unionize, which the government finally granted in 1906. In the revolutionary year of 1905, 165 unions sprang up in St. Petersburg and Moscow. Although some had been crushed by early 1906, 137 unions in the two cities received legal status in the fifteen months after a law of March 1906 made this possible. From mid-1907 until the Lena goldfield shooting of April 1912, the government and employers reacted against the developing unions and took successful steps to reduce them. Even the prewar resurgence of union activity following the Lena massacre failed to bring the number of unions and union members close to the totals of 1906–1907.

World War I further reduced earlier gains. Employers lengthened workdays but cut back on safety regulations and protections for women and adolescent workers. As urban inflation increased faster than wages, many workers discovered they had to work longer to buy less.

All these generalizations, however, just hint at the workers' broad diversification. Besides regional, gender, age, ethnic, and rural-urban distinctions, workers differed in regard to education, skills, and experience. Such differences also affected wages. St. Petersburg's metal workers, for example, were overwhelmingly male and 90 percent literate by 1913, and they averaged almost twice the income of textile workers, among whom women and illiterates were more common.

NOBLES AND RURAL PEASANTS

As in earlier times, great economic diversity also continued to exist among the nobles. The extent of economic differences among the peasantry was hotly debated by Lenin and the Populists in the 1890s and still remains murky.

Nobles

In 1897, nobles made up about 1.5 percent of the empire's population, with about two-thirds being hereditary nobles. About half the nobility was non-Russian, with the Polish nobles alone accounting for slightly more than one-quarter the total. Some nobles remained wealthy and influential. In 1905, 155 nobles possessed more than a 135,000 acres each, with the wealthiest possessing more than a half-million acres. But most nobles did not make their living from the land. Indeed, by 1905, a majority of even the hereditary nobility no longer owned an estate. Although some nobles became wealthy by other means, most did not.

Seymour Becker has correctly warned against overstating the nobles' decline and emphasized that many of them left the land for better opportunities elsewhere. Nevertheless, many nobles (such as the fictional Madame Ranevskaia in Chekhov's 1904 play *The Cherry Orchard*) were forced to sell their land because of their improvident ways. By 1905, the nobility of European Russia (exclusive of Finland, Poland, and the Caucasus) had sold roughly two-fifths of the land it had held after the 1861 emancipation. This left nobles with less than one-sixth of the total public and private land (arable and nonarable) in European Russia; the peasants, communally or individually, by then owned almost three times as much land as did the nobles. The peasant disturbances of 1905–1907 prodded more nobles to sell their land. By 1914, they possessed only about half the land they had kept after the 1861 settlement, and the peasants now possessed more than four times as much as the nobles and rented some of the rest. The challenge to noble preeminence was not limited to landholding. As never before, individuals from other social groups chipped away at their dominance of the officer corps, high officialdom, and the universities.

A major difficulty for noble landowners was adjusting to postemancipation developments. Although a minority of them modernized their estates, most made little changes except for relying on hired or sharecropping labor instead of serfs. Hans Rogger has noted that in 1911 there were only 166 tractors being used in all of European Russia, whereas in the United States there were then 14,000 in use. A worldwide decline in grain prices during the 1880s and 1890s, partly because of increased American productivity, also hurt most noble landowners.

Considering military needs and other pressures to industrialize, the government did what it could to arrest the nobles' decline. A manifesto of 1885, drawn up by Pobedonostsev, stressed the desirability of maintaining the nobles' leading position and announced the creation of a state-funded Nobles' Land Bank to help them retain and operate their estates successfully. By early 1904, the Nobles' Bank had lent out more than 700 million rubles, almost twice the amount loaned out by the Peasants' Land Bank (created in 1883) and on cheaper terms. Other government actions, such as the changed Duma electoral laws of 1907, also favored the nobility.

Despite the mutual dependence of the government and nobility on each other, conflicts occurred. They resulted partly from the diversity of the nobility. Many nobles were among the professionals and zemstvo spokesmen who pushed for changes the government considered too radical. Other nobles, especially landowning ones, opposed many of Witte's policies that they considered unsympathetic to their needs—in his memoirs, Witte refers to the majority of the nobility as a group of "degenerates," attempting to gain privileges at the expense of the common people.

Frightened by the rural disturbances of 1905–1906, many landholding nobles agreed on the need for law and order and the preservation of noble rights. In 1906, some large landowners formed a group known as the United Nobility to represent their interests. Despite their advocacy of law and order and the breakup of peasant communes, the organization criticized Stolypin whenever it believed he was not sufficiently heeding its needs. And despite its support for tsarist autocracy, it joined with many other groups in late 1916 and criticized the tsar's disastrous policies.

Yet, even in the 1906–1916 period, the nobility as a whole was too diverse in nationality, occupations, wealth, and political views to unify. The United Nobility represented primarily the interests of Great Russian large landowners and was hostile to "alien" elements; in the Duma, noble deputies joined different parties and factions.

Rural Peasants

In Anton Chekhov's short story "The Peasants" (1897), he depicts a three-generational peasant family of thirteen living in one heated room. It was dark, dirty, and filled with flies. As with most peasant huts, it contained a large stove of clay or brick, the top of which was a favorite sleeping spot. Although the average family according to the census of 1897 contained only 6.3 members and was probably not a three-generational one, the peasant housing conditions described by Chekhov were otherwise fairly typical of those that had prevailed for several centuries.

Considerable continuity in peasant life, however, coexisted with accelerating changes. The emancipation of the serfs in 1861 ended the major difference among peasants—that between serfs and state peasants. As trade, industrialization, and urbanization accelerated and rural population growth increased the demand for farmland, more peasants moved into nonagricultural occupations. Whether engaged in such work temporarily or permanently, part-time or full-time, in the city or in the countryside, most of these workers officially continued to be classified as part of the peasant estate. Yet despite some peasant departures from farming, by 1913 seven out of ten working Russians were still primarily farming peasants.

Although the emancipation legislation attempted to modify the old communal structure, it did not wish to destroy it, and most peasants continued to operate within its confines. Many different types of communes remained, and new ones were sometimes created. Although most village communes were engaged in agriculture, there were also some made up primarily of artisans or other types of workers. Some communes represented one village, others more than one, and still others only part of one. Some periodically redivided the land, others part of it, and still others none at all. Regional variations existed, and changes occurred over time.

Most typical in central Russia was the small or medium-sized repartitional agricultural commune that represented a single village. As described by Boris Mironov, such a commune (in the 1860s and 1870s) contained anywhere from four to eighty households and mediated between the outside world, especially the state, and individual peasant. The commune (including its assembly and elected officials) regulated land distribution; exercised legal, administrative, and police powers; and helped coordinate cultivation and the religious, cultural, educational, and social aspects of village life.

Despite many pressures on the communes, especially Stolypin's attempt to break them up, they survived and even grew stronger in the turmoil of 1917. Although often blamed for the backwardness of Russian agriculture, the communes were much more flexible, pragmatic, and adaptable than most outsiders realized and provided a basic security in a fast-changing world.

The adherence of many peasants to the commune did not preclude their taking a strong interest in improving their own household's position. Household attempts to gain either more communal or noncommunal lands were ongoing, and some peasants found ways to prosper within the communal structure. The influence of wealthier peasants within the communes was strong, and many such peasants were firmly opposed to their breakup.

The mention of wealthy peasants leads to two related questions: How did the peasants as a whole fare between 1861 and 1916? To what extent did economic diversification among the peasants increase?

The evidence and range of opinions on peasant welfare are mixed. The traditional historical view stressed the economic decline of the peasantry, especially from the 1860s until 1905. The decline was attributed primarily to the reduction of land held by the average peasant household. The emancipation settlement provided ex-serfs with smaller allotments on average than they had earlier farmed, and the rapid rise of rural population thereafter further decreased the size of the average household allotment. Although resettlement and new peasant land purchases occurred, they were believed insufficient to compensate for the increased pressure that population growth placed upon the limited lands available. The perceived deterioration of the peasants' condition was made worse in the 1880s and 1890s by an increase in Russia's chief form of taxation—indirect taxes on items such as sugar, tea, kerosene, matches, tobacco, and vodka.

This picture of growing peasant misery, however, has been challenged by more recent and convincing revisionist views (such as those of Gregory, Gatrell, and Hoch). These views indicate that the rural peasantry *as a whole* shared in the overall increase in Russian living standards from 1861 to 1913. The revisionist perspective maintains that the traditional view had too often concentrated on specific regions and years, rather than considering the entire empire and the era as a whole. The older view had also underestimated the importance of peasant families' nonfarm income (some of it sent from family members in the cities).

Significant differences also exist on the second question mentioned previously: To what extent did economic diversification among the peasants increase? In his *Development of Capitalism in Russia* (1899), Lenin stated that the percentage of rich and poor peasants was increasing at the expense of middle-level peasants, and many historians later accepted this view.

Certainly differences existed in peasant wealth, measured by such criteria as landholding and the possession of animals and farm machinery. Although some peasant households possessed no land and worked for others or pos-

FIGURE 6.2. Women dressed in traditional peasant costumes standing outside the large cabin of a prosperous late-nineteenth-century peasant, the Suzdal Outdoor Museum of Wooden Architecture and Peasant Life.

sessed just a few acres, other peasant households possessed more than 100 acres, sometimes considerably more.

Such differences, however, were neither notably increasing nor permanent. They were often correlated to household size and went up or down as it changed over a family's life cycle. Generally the more adult male workers per household, the greater the landholdings and the total household wealth. After a detailed review for the years 1880–1905, Heinz-Dietrich Lowe found: "In central Russia (black soil and non-black soil regions) and down the Volga, there were practically no trends to a greater differentiation of peasant society."[4] A number of other studies also indicate that Lenin overestimated differentiation increases. That economic differences did not increase rapidly was partly due to the communes. Although not preventing peasant economic differentiation, they did help to restrain it.

[4]"Differentiation in Russian Peasant Society: Causes and Trends, 1880–1905," in *Land Commune and Peasant Community in Russia: Communal Forms in Imperial and Early Soviet Society,* ed. Roger Bartlett (New York, 1990), p. 191.

FOOD AND DRINKING; FAMINE AND DISEASES

People's eating habits during this era remained much the same as earlier. Grain, especially in the form of bread, continued to provide most of the calories for most of the population. The most significant change was probably the increase in the consumption of potatoes, tea, and sugar. The use of samovars spread increasingly to the villages, often becoming one of a household's most prized possessions. Foreign visitors commented on the masses' practice of drinking tea through a piece of sugar held in the mouth.

Both statistical and anecdotal evidence make it clear that alcoholism increased during this era. One reason for this was an increase in modern drinking habits. As David Christian has pointed out, increased urbanization and wage work stimulated more regular drinking, especially on weekends and in the taverns, which were overwhelmingly male domains. In St. Petersburg and Moscow, many workers by the turn of the century reported for work on Mondays hung over from weekend drinking and then spent part of such "Blue Mondays" drinking more.[5] At the same time, especially in the villages, traditional drinking customs, which stressed communal and festive drinking and in which women participated more fully, also continued.

As always, governmental alcohol policies continued to influence vodka consumption. In 1858 and 1859, the increasing vodka prices charged by liquor dealers were countered by mass vodka boycotts and attacks on taverns in many areas of European Russia. Partly as a result of these disturbances, in 1863 the government opened up the production and sale of alcohol and ended the old "farming-out" method, by which it had sold these liquor rights to selected entrepreneurs (tax farmers). At the same time, it introduced an excise tax, which in subsequent years more than made up for government revenues lost by ending the old system. At first, the changeover led, at least in Great Russia, to a decrease in vodka prices and an increase in consumption.

Despite subsequent increases in the excise taxes levied by the government, alcoholism showed few signs of abating. According to Minister of Finance Witte, Alexander III wished to decrease alcohol consumption and backed a plan of Witte's that established an Imperial Vodka Monopoly. It was enacted in 1894 and gradually applied throughout the empire. Once again, however, both alcohol consumption and resulting government revenues increased.

Despite the government's continuing reliance on liquor revenues—about 30 percent of total revenues from 1905 to 1913—the government was not completely two-faced in dealing with the alcohol problem. It continued to hope that it could maintain its alcohol revenues by encouraging people to spread their drinking out and thereby engage in less binge drinking. Drunkenness might thereby be decreased without decreasing alcohol revenues. As part of its effort to deal with increased drunkenness, the government offered some encouragement and support to a temperance movement, which sputtered along

---

[5]For an excellent treatment of workers' drinking habits (and other material conditions) outside the two major cities, see Theodore H. Friedgut, *Iuzovka and Revolution*, Vol. 1, *Life and Work in Russia's Donbass, 1869–1924* (Princeton, 1989).

for a while and then became a conspicuous phenomenon beginning in the 1890s.

Later the Duma studied ways to reduce government dependence on vodka revenues. But the Ministry of Finance remained unsympathetic to any attempts to reduce this reliable source of income. World War I, however, accomplished what peacetime could not—prohibition. The selling of vodka was first curtailed during the mobilization of troops, and in August 1914 prohibition was decreed for the duration of the war.

Besides war, Russia also suffered in this era from the traditional scourges of hunger and famine. Drought and poor environmental policies and practices—including deforestation (especially stimulated by railway development), overploughing, and overgrazing—contributed to frequent food shortages. After a severe drought in 1891, such shortages produced a major famine in the Central Black-Earth and Volga regions in 1891–1892. (See Chapter 3 for how government economic policies helped bring it about.)

In confronting it, peasants turned to their traditional method of dealing with grain shortages: They made "hunger bread," stretching out their grain by adding such ingredients as acorns, bark, leaves, straw, and weeds to it before baking. Often unable to feed their animals, they sold many of them.

Although at first attempting to downplay the crisis and prevent too much private involvement, the government did temporarily suspend grain exports and begin its own massive relief efforts. Working largely through local officials, including the land captains and those of the zemstvos, it dispersed grain to millions of Russians. Private and foreign assistance, especially from the United States, also helped meet the crisis. Writers such as Vladimir Soloviev and Leo Tolstoy helped awaken public opinion, with Tolstoy taking an especially active role including the establishment of food kitchens.

No reliable figures are available as to how many deaths the famine caused. As was often the case, many people died prematurely as a result of reduced resistance to diseases. In 1892, typhus and cholera epidemics struck the famine-stricken provinces especially hard, and the death rate in these provinces was higher than normal.

Despite Russia's gradually declining death rate in the Late Imperial period, by 1913 it was still much higher than Western Europe's and roughly 40 percent higher than Japan's. Infant and child mortality rates remained especially high. Among the European Russian Orthodox population at the end of the 1890s, more than one-fourth of the infants died before their first birthday. Between 1907 and 1911, the European Russian death rate in the same age group was about twice as high as those born in England and France.

Although susceptibility to diseases varied from towns to villages, the frequent movement back and forth between them by peasants looking for work helped spread infectious diseases in both areas. The alarming spread of syphilis to the villages by returning peasants was just one example. Besides cholera, typhus, and syphilis, other diseases that killed significant numbers were consumption and pneumonia (the two leading killers in St. Petersburg around 1900), diphtheria, dysentery, influenza, malaria, measles, scarlet fever, and smallpox. In the countryside, many Russians also died painful deaths from eating contaminated grain.

WOMEN AND FAMILY LIFE

In 1912, women's inheritance rights were extended, and in 1914 marital separation was made easier, but overall Russian women made few legal gains before 1917.

Throughout this era, the "woman question" was intertwined with that of radicalism, reform, or reaction. Radicals tended to be most sympathetic with female equality, whereas reactionaries resisted proposals for equalizing women's rights. Following Chernyshevsky's lead, most women radicals concluded that female equality depended upon the overthrow of the existing system and made that their first priority. By the 1870s, about 20 to 25 percent of the active revolutionaries were women.

After feminists founded the All-Russian Union for Women's Equality in 1905 and began pushing for female suffrage, they discovered that many liberals were hesitant to commit fully to their cause. Although more supportive than some liberals, Paul Miliukov, head of the Kadet party, attempted at times to soften proposals of his wife Anna, who was active in the women's union.

As with political opposition generally, feminist political activity was strong between 1905 and 1907 but then ebbed in the more reactionary period that followed it. Nevertheless, although unable to obtain many goals such as suffrage, by 1914 women had still made substantial educational and professional gains (see Chapter 7).

Most of these advances affected upper-class and middle-class women, but lower-class women, both in the villages and in the towns, also made gains. Some peasant women used the new township courts to obtain justice, especially in property disputes with their in-laws. And peasant women often were responsible for three-generational family breakups. Considering the unfavorable position of the daughters-in-law within these large peasant households, it is hardly surprising that, despite the economic risks involved, many of them preferred to go off with their husbands and establish their own nuclear families.

As more husbands went to the cities in search of work, wives assumed more tasks traditionally performed by their spouses. In addition, in the decades immediately following the emancipation of the serfs, more village women, especially in Russia's Central Industrial Region, engaged in domestic production for markets outside their village. Working in their own huts or in village workshops or small factories, they supplemented their family income by working at such tasks as weaving, knitting stockings and gloves, gluing cigarette tubes, and unwinding cotton. Often they worked for merchants who provided materials and disposed of the products of their labor. They also worked for manufacturers who put out work to village women and children because they could pay them less than regular factory workers.

By the end of the nineteenth century, however, this labor started to be undercut by new factory machinery, and more village women moved to the cities in search of income. Before World War I, most of them who found work did so as domestic servants, but a growing number became factory or shop workers. In St. Petersburg's textile industry, women workers increased from 57 percent of the total in 1900 to 68 percent in 1913. In food processing, they went from 33 percent to 47 percent in the same period. Generally, women entered into the lower-paying, less skilled jobs and were less likely to become unionized.

As cities grew and more peasant women entered them, prostitution increased. The government used special police and urban medical-police committees to ferret out, medically inspect, and license prostitutes. But unregistered prostitutes continued to outnumber "yellow-ticketed" ones—a registered prostitute had to exchange her internal passport for a "yellow ticket," which more sharply restricted her movements. Poverty was a major cause of girls and women entering the profession.[6] Feminists and others debated how to end, or at least reduce, prostitution and founded philanthropic organizations such as the Russian Society for the Protection of Women, established in 1900. Despite vigorous lobbying, however, reformers were unable to stem the growth of prostitution. Most radicals believed the only solution to the problem was the overthrow of tsarist autocracy.

Despite the small percentage of women in labor unions, women workers gradually became more radical. In 1913, socialist women in Russia observed International Women's Day for the first time. A prime mover in encouraging this participation and an advocate of socialism as the only valid response to the woman question was Alexandra Kollontai, herself of noble background. Lenin's wife, Nadezhda Krupskaia, who authored the pamphlet *The Woman Worker* (1900), and Inessa Armand, another Marxist close to Lenin, were two other women who helped launch a working-women's movement in Russia. They established an underground journal, also called *The Woman Worker*, which appeared in seven issues in the first half of 1914.

Although World War I brought great hardships to Russian women, many of whose husbands were called to military service, it also brought new opportunities. As in other participating countries, women now sometimes served in occupations that previously had been closed to them, making it harder to maintain stereotypical beliefs about women's proper roles in the country's economic and social structure.

Most of the changes affecting women also affected family life in general. Changes came most slowly in the countryside, where the patriarchal order remained least affected by modern developments and thinking. Even in rural areas, however, education and urban influences were making dents in the old system. Particularly after 1905, signs of youthful hostility to authority, espe-

---

[6]A concise summary of prostitution and the intrusive medical police, especially in St. Petersburg, is presented in Barbara Alpern Engel, *Between the Fields and the City: Women, Work, and Family in Russia, 1861–1914* (New York, 1994), pp. 166–197. A more exhaustive study can be found in Laurie Bernstein, *Sonia's Daughters: Prostitutes and Their Regulation in Imperial Russia* (Berkeley, 1995).

cially in the form of rural hooliganism, alarmed many defenders of traditional society.

In the cities, challenges to old family ways came earlier and more forcefully. The radical pamphlet *To the Younger Generation* (1861) called upon the young to overthrow the old order. It was distributed by M. I. Mikhailov, a young poet and essayist, who a few years earlier had begun the first major press discussion of the woman question by advocating female equality. Turgenev's novel *Fathers and Sons* (1862) mirrored the new generational conflict and stimulated discussion about it. From the 1860s until 1917, urban youth were the chief followers of radical ideas, including those that challenged traditional patriarchal authority.

Besides radical challenges, other forces were also eroding traditional family life. As peasants flocked in growing numbers into the cities, housing space became increasingly scarce. Many married couples were even forced to live separately. Housing scarcity was one reason why many male peasants left their wives and children back in the villages. This shortage also helps explain why more permanent town-dwellers married later and had fewer children than did villagers. Family life was further changed by the increasing number of unmarried peasant women who went to the cities. If they eventually married, they usually did so later than village women.

Partly because of the growing number of single women entering the cities, more illegitimate children were born. Only around the turn of the century did the trend begin to level off and finally go down—an increasing use of birth control, especially abortion (which was illegal), being perhaps one explanation. The number of children left at the foundling homes of St. Petersburg and Moscow displayed a similar pattern, although a tightening of admission procedures at the beginning of the 1890s had a more dramatic immediate effect in finally reducing admissions.

Although urban youth of all classes had better educational opportunities than villagers, poor children raised in the cities led a difficult life. Both parents often worked long hours outside their miserable lodgings, and children were often left with little or no supervision. Furthermore, children themselves often began working at a young age. Although labor laws of the 1880s and 1890s reduced exploitation of child labor, by the early 1900s most artisan, sales, and service apprenticeships still began before, or shortly after, children had reached their teens.

As these young apprentices put in their long work days—fourteen to sixteen hours were still common for nonfactory workers—they soon became exposed to adult ways, including drinking and smoking. As young workers learned new skills, earned money, and spent most of their time away from home, they had more opportunity to develop independently than did youth raised in village families, whose values were often reinforced by village institutions such as the commune.

The overall decline in marriage, birth, and death rates, which was especially notable in European Russia during the last two prewar decades, affected and reflected rural as well as urban developments. But female peasants who remained in their villages generally continued to marry young and give birth to many children. In 1897, the mean age that women first married in the Russian areas of European Russia (rural and urban) was 20.4, and peasant women seem to have averaged around a half dozen births or so, although this varied from province to province.

Changes in family life concerned many Russian writers, Dostoevsky and Tolstoy being two who lamented a decline in family values. The most sweeping proposals for changes in family life came from socialists such as Lenin, Krupskaia, and Kollontai, who were only able to put some of their ideas into practice after 1917.

LEGAL DEVELOPMENTS

The Late Imperial period was one of important legal developments, including the Judicial Reform of 1864 (see Chapter 2). By 1914, almost 19,000 registered attorneys and assistant attorneys existed. The number of civil cases heard by district courts increased faster than population growth, with about 300,000 cases being submitted in 1914.

According to Walicki "the main concern of Russia's liberal thinkers was

FIGURE 6.3. The 1881 trial of the assassins of Alexander II. In this trial, government-appointed officials acted as both judges and jury.
(From Ronald Hingley, Nihilists: Russian Radicals and Revolutionaries in the Reign of Alexander II. *Weidenfeld & Nicolson, London, 1967, p. 110.)*

the problem of the rule of law."[7] A growing number of professionals, entrepreneurs, and even some reform-minded officials desired to transform the empire into a state in which the rulers as well as the ruled would be bound by the country's laws (a *Rechtsstadt*, to borrow the German term). In 1905, for example, industrialists from the Ural area stated that only under such conditions could business life adequately develop. The traditionalist officials dominant under Alexander III and Nicholas II, however, viewed law primarily as an instrument to help maintain government control, not as a guarantor of individual or corporate rights.

Russian rule under the last three Romanovs was characterized by concessions, usually under pressure, to the rule of law and then "takebacks" when the pressure eased or threats to the autocratic order seemed too great. Alexander III's long-lasting "temporary regulations" of 1881 (see Chapter 3) were just the most egregious circumvention of the spirit of the 1864 legal reform.

The political turmoil surrounding 1905 produced new concessions. In the October Manifesto of 1905, the government appeared ready to meet some demands for the rule of law and the expansion of civil liberties. The manifesto promised to grant the population "the unalterable foundations of civic freedom based on the principles of real personal inviolability, freedom of conscience, speech, assembly, and association." During subsequent months, the government took some steps to fulfill this commitment by issuing new laws on matters such as censorship and freedom of assembly and association. But the Fundamental Laws of April 1906 indicated that Nicholas did not intend to fulfill all the promises of the October Manifesto. During the next decade, the tsar along with the conservative State Council blocked most measures that would have fully implemented the rights promised in late 1905. The electoral law of 1907, guaranteeing more conservative Dumas than the first two, was perhaps the best example of "takebacks" during the Duma era.

In 1907, the perceptive Bernard Pares stated that "the Government has, in principle, capitulated to the principle of law, but has, in practice, so multiplied the exceptions that they altogether swamp the principle. Thus it has not yet been possible for the ordinary Russian to have any confidence in the principle of law as protecting him from arbitrary and exceptional chastisement."

As the legal profession expanded, along with legal journals and societies, so too did debates about legal approaches. Many members of the Russian intelligentsia, including Russian Marxists and Tolstoy, disparaged law, considering it an instrument of the state and of class domination. Intellectuals who emphasized the importance of law for securing individual freedoms and rights were in the minority.

Although the Third Section was abolished in 1880, its Corps of Gendarmes continued under the jurisdiction of the Ministry of Interior, which also oversaw other antisubversive sections such as the Okhrana. The latter often recruited agents to infiltrate revolutionary organizations. In pursuing its tasks, the political police did not hesitate to violate basic civil rights. Even members

---

[7]Andrzej Walicki, *Legal Philosophies of Russian Liberalism.* (New York, 1987), p. 1.

Policing the Russian Empire in the 1880s

The following selection is from George Kennan, "The Russian Police," *The Century Illustrated Monthly Magazine* 37 (April 1889): 890–891. Kennan spent considerable time in Russia and later wrote the two-volume work *Siberia and the Exile System.* To keep the selection short, I have abbreviated the list of required "permissions" that Kennan mentions, indicating these omissions and others by ellipses.

Matters that in other countries are left to the discretion of the individual citizen, or to the judgment of a small group of citizens, are regulated in Russia by the Minister of the Interior through the imperial police. If you are a Russian, and wish to establish a newspaper, you must ask the permission of the Minister of the Interior. If you wish to open a Sunday-School, or any other sort of school . . . you must ask the permission of the Minister of Public Instruction. If you wish to give a concert or to get up tableaux for the benefit of an orphan asylum, you must ask permission of the nearest representative of the Minister of the Interior, then submit your programme of exercises to a censor for approval or revision, and finally hand over the proceeds of the entertainment to the police, to be embezzled or given to the orphan asylum, as it may happen. If you wish to sell newspapers on the street, you must get permission, be registered in the books of the police, and wear a numbered brass plate as big as a saucer around your neck. If you wish to open a drug-store, a printing-office, a photograph-gallery, or a book-store, you must get permission. If you are a photographer and desire to change the location of your place of business, you must

get permission. If you are a student and go to a public library to consult Lyell's "Principles of Geology" or Spencer's "Social Statics," you will find that you cannot even look at such dangerous and incendiary volumes without special permission. . . . If you are a peasant and wish to build a bath-house on your premises, you must get permission. If you wish to thresh out your grain in the evening by candlelight, you must get permission or bribe the police. If you wish to go more than fifteen miles away from your home, you must get permission. . . . In short, you cannot live, move, or have your being in the Russian Empire without permission.

The police, with the Minister of the Interior at their head, control, by means of passports, the movements of all the inhabitants of the Empire; they keep thousands of suspects constantly under surveillance; they ascertain and certify to the courts the liabilities of bankrupts; they conduct pawnbrokers' sales of unredeemed pledges; they give certificates of identity to pensioners and all other persons who need them; they superintend repairs of roads and bridges; they exercise supervision over all theatrical performances, concerts, tableaux, theater programmes, posters, and street advertisements; they collect statistics, enforce sanitary regulations, make searches and seizures in private houses, read the correspondence of suspects, take charge of the bodies of persons found dead, "admonish" church members who neglect too long to partake of the Holy Communion, and enforce obedience to thousands of multifarious orders and regulations intended to promote the welfare of the people or to insure the safety of the state.

of the nobility complained of having their mail opened by police officials, and the practice did not cease after 1905.

Although new laws eliminated or reduced some of the harshest corporeal punishments, the number of exiles sent to Siberia increased. By 1898, more than 300,000 exiles were living in Siberia. Only about 1 percent could be considered political exiles, and almost half the total exiles had been legally sent there by their communities. One could be exiled to Siberia as a convict, necessitating imprisonment or hard labor, or as exile-deportee. The convicts in Siberia, such as those described in Dostoevsky's *House of the Dead* or Chekhov's *Sakhalin Island*, were much worse off than those simply exiled. Lenin, for example, spent a comparatively comfortable three years in exile in southern Siberia, where he was free to live in a peasant cottage and spend his days, indoors or outdoors, much as he wished. During the Communist era, such an exile would have seemed more like a vacation to the millions who found themselves exiled to Siberia under Stalin.

With some justification, tsarist Russia's critics sometimes called it a "police state." Yet the ratio of its police to citizens remained far smaller, especially in small towns and rural areas, than in more liberal and democratic countries such as France and England. Because of this shortage, the state did a poor job protecting its citizens.

From about 1900 to 1914, the problem of hooliganism—the term was borrowed from England—was continually reported on and debated. It was believed to be rising and spreading from towns into the countryside. It most often implied brazen, insulting, disrespectful behavior, especially toward authority or "respectable" people. At times, it went beyond verbal assaults, cursing, and lewd suggestions and involved violent actions such as window breaking, assaults, muggings, rape, and murder. The problem seemed especially acute in the Great Russian areas of the empire.

Despite efforts to increase the number of policemen, especially in major urban areas, the perception in villages and towns alike by the early twentieth century was that crime was on the rise. Policemen and officials were thought to be either unwilling or unable to do much to protect the common people. One problem was that the police spent a disproportionate amount of time on victimless crimes and security measures. Hans Rogger cites figures for St. Petersburg that indicate that of the 115,000 people detained by the police in 1896, more than half were for passport violations, beggary, and "idleness." Furthermore, low police salaries contributed to police corruption, and hatred of the police was common among workers.

In the villages, the peasants' customs dominated their legal dealings. Most legal matters were settled outside of court or according to "customary law" in courts on the village and canton (*volost*) levels. Out-of-court methods for solving disputes included arbitration, compromise, swearing oaths, and casting lots. Community-decided punishments, part of the peasants' world of *samosud* (self-adjudication or taking the law into one's own hands) included requiring an individual to treat the village to vodka, expulsion from the village, beatings, shaming rituals, and worse. Although villagers might punish petty thievery with a mild punishment, they were not as tolerant with horse thieves, especially habitual ones, who might be subjected to maiming that would permanently mark them or to gruesome tortures and murder.

Such violent acts were contrary to statutory law, but the peasants believed that statutory law and the official courts were too lenient with horse thieves. In this respect and in others, the peasants and the authorities' views of law often differed. The peasants were more concerned with what they considered justice than with obeying any outside-imposed law. They had little ability or desire to apply abstract principles to specific cases. Their main concern was the practical one of maintaining their own security, interests, and way of life. Such an act as stealing wood from a state or noble's forest was considered laudable, permissible, or no more than a minor offense by most peasants.

In the battle that sometimes ensued between state law and peasant "justice," the state was often at a disadvantage because of its paucity of police and police officials in the countryside. As earlier in Russian history, a gap continued to exist between the government's desires and its abilities to control the population.

SUGGESTED SOURCES*

BATER, JAMES H. *St. Petersburg: Industrialization and Change.* Montreal, 1976.

BECKER, SEYMOUR. *Nobility and Privilege in Late Imperial Russia.* DeKalb, Ill., 1985.

BONNELL, VICTORIA E. *Roots of Rebellion: Workers' Politics and Organizations in St. Petersburg and Moscow, 1900–1914.* Berkeley, 1983.

BRADLEY, JOSEPH. *Muzhik and Muscovite: Urbanization in Late Imperial Russia.* Berkeley, 1985.

BROWER, DANIEL R. *The Russian City between Tradition and Modernity, 1850–1900.* Berkeley, 1990.

CHEKHOV, ANTON. "The Peasants." In *Great Stories by Chekhov,* ed. David H. Greene. New York, 1959.

CHRISTIAN, DAVID. *"Living Water": Vodka and Russian Society on the Eve of Emancipation.* New York, 1990.

CLEMENTS, BARBARA EVANS, BARBARA ALPERN ENGEL, and CHRISTINE D. WOROBEC, EDS. *Russia's Women: Accommodation, Resistance, Transformation.* Berkeley, 1991. Pt. II.

CONROY, MARY SCHAEFFER. *In Health and in Sickness: Pharmacy, Pharmacists, and the Pharmaceutical Industry in Late Imperial, Early Soviet Russia.* Boulder, 1994.

CRISP, OLGA, and LINDA EDMONDSON, eds. *Civil Rights in Imperial Russia.* New York, 1989.

EDMONDSON, LINDA H. *Feminism in Russia, 1900–17.* Stanford, 1984.

ENGELSTEIN, LAURA. "Combined Underdevelopment: Discipline and the Law in Imperial and Soviet Russia," *AHR* 98 (April 1993): 338–352.

FARNSWORTH, BEATRICE, and LYNNE VIOLA, eds. *Russian Peasant Women.* New York, 1992. Pt. I.

FEDOR, THOMAS S. *Patterns of Urban Growth in the Russian Empire during the Nineteenth Century.* Chicago, 1975.

*See also books cited in footnotes.

FITZPATRICK, ANNE L. *The Great Russian Fair: Nizhnii Novgorod, 1840–90*. New York, 1990.

FREEZE, GREGORY L. *From Supplication to Revolution: A Documentary Social History of Imperial Russia*. New York, 1988. Pts. 2–3.

———, ed. "The Soslovie (Estate) Paradigm and Russian Social History," *AHR* 91 (February 1986): 11–36.

FRIEDEN, NANCY. *Russian Physicians in an Era of Reform and Revolution, 1856–1905*. Princeton, 1981.

FRIEDGUT, THEODORE H. *Iuzovka and Revolution*. 2 vols. Princeton, 1989–1994.

FRIERSON, CATHY A. *Peasant Icons: Representations of Rural People in Late Nineteenth Century Russia*. New York, 1993.

———, ed. *Aleksandr Nikolaevich Englegardt's Letters from the Country, 1872–1887*. New York, 1993.

GATRELL, PETER. *The Tsarist Economy, 1850–1917*. New York, 1986.

GEYER, DIETRICH. *Russian Imperialism: The Interaction of Domestic and Foreign Policy 1860–1914*. Leamington Spa, N.Y., 1987.

GLICKMAN, ROSE L. *Russian Factory Women: Workplace and Society, 1880–1914*. Berkeley, 1984.

GREGORY, PAUL R. *Before Command: An Economic History of Russia from Emancipation to the First Five-Year Plan*. Princeton, 1994.

HAIMSON, LEOPOLD. "The Problem of Social Stability in Urban Russia, 1905–1917," *SR* 23 (December 1964): 619–642; 24 (March 1965): 1–22; Discussion. 24 (March 1965): 23–46.

HAMM, MICHAEL F., *The City in Late Imperial Russia*. Bloomington, 1986.

HOCH, STEVEN L. "Russian Peasant Standard of Living," *SR* 53 (Spring 1994): 41–75.

HOGAN, HEATHER. *Forging Revolution: Metalworkers, Managers, and the State in St. Petersburg, 1890–1914*. Bloomington, 1993.

HUTCHINSON, JOHN F. *Politics and Public Health in Revolutionary Russia, 1890–1918*. Baltimore, 1990.

JOHNSON, ROBERT E. *Peasant and Proletarian: The Working Class of Moscow in the Late Nineteenth Century*. New Brunswick, N.J., 1979.

KINGSTON-MANN, ESTHER, and TIMOTHY MIXTER, eds. *Peasant Economy, Culture, and Politics of European Russia, 1800–1921*. Princeton, 1990.

LINDENMEYR, ADELE. *Voluntary Associations and the Russian Aristocracy: The Case of Private Charity*. The Carl Beck Papers . . . , no. 807. Pittsburgh, 1990.

MACEY, DAVID, A. J. *Government and Peasant in Russia, 1861–1906: The Prehistory of the Stolypin Reforms*. DeKalb, Ill., 1987.

MANNING, ROBERTA. *The Crisis of the Old Order in Russia: Gentry and Government*. Princeton, 1982.

McCAFRAY, SUSAN P. *The Politics of Industrialization in Tsarist Russia: The Association of Southern Coal and Steel Producers, 1874–1914*. DeKalb, Ill., 1996.

McKAY, JOHN P. *Pioneers for Profit: Foreign Entrepreneurship and Russian Industrialization, 1885–1913*. Chicago, 1970.

MIRONOV, BORIS. "The Russian Peasant Commune after the Reforms of the 1860s," *SR* 44 (Fall 1985): 438–467.

NEUBERGER, JOAN. *Hooliganism: Crime, Culture, and Power in St. Petersburg, 1900–1914*. Berkeley, 1993.

OWEN, THOMAS C. *Capitalism and Politics in Russia: A Social History of the Moscow Merchants, 1855–1905*. Cambridge, England, 1981.

———. *Russian Corporate Capitalism from Peter the Great to Perestroika*. New York, 1995. Chs. 3 & 5.

PARES, BERNARD. *Russia and Reform*. New York, 1907.

PLAGGENBORG, S. "Tax Policy and the Question of Peasant Poverty in Tsarist Russia, 1881–1905," *CMR* 36 (1995): 53–69.

RANSEL, DAVID L. *Mothers of Misery: Child Abandonment in Russia*. Princeton, 1988.

RIEBER, ALFRED J. *Merchants and Entrepreneurs in Imperial Russia*. Chapel Hill, 1982.

ROBINSON, GEROID T. *Rural Russia under the Old Regime: A History of the Land-Lord-Peasant World and a Prologue to the Peasant Revolution of 1917*. New York, 1932.

ROGGER, HANS. *Russia in the Age of Modernization and Revolution, 1881–1917*. London, 1983. Chs. 5–6.

ROOSEVELT, PRISCILLA. *Life on the Russian Country Estate: A Social and Cultural History*. New Haven, 1995.

RUCKMAN, JO ANN. *The Moscow Business Elite: A Social and Cultural Portrait of Two Generations, 1840–1905*. DeKalb, Ill., 1984.

SEMYONOVA, TIAN-SHANSKAIA, OLGA. *Village Life in Late Tsarist Russia*. Bloomington, 1993.

STITES, RICHARD. *The Women's Liberation Movement in Russia: Feminism, Nihilism, and Bolshevism, 1860–1930*. Princeton, 1978.

THURSTON, ROBERT W. *Liberal City, Conservative State: Moscow and Russia's Urban Crisis, 1906–1914*. New York, 1987.

TOLSTOY, LEO. "On the Moscow Census." In *The Complete Works of Count Tolstoy*. Vol. 17. New York, 1968.

TROYAT, HENRI. *Daily Life in Russia Under the Last Tsar*. London, 1961.

VUCINICH, WAYNE S., ed. *The Peasant in Nineteenth-Century Russia*. Stanford, 1968.

WAGNER, WILLIAM C. *Marriage, Property, and Law in Late Imperial Russia*. New York, 1994.

WALLACE, DONALD MACKENZIE. *Russia on the Eve of War and Revolution*. New York, 1961.

WITTE, S. IU. *The Memoirs of Count Witte*. Armonk, N.Y., 1990.

WOROBEC, CHRISTINE. *Peasant Russia: Family and Community in the Post-Emancipation Period*. Princeton, 1991.

WYNN, CHARTERS. *Workers, Strikes, and Pogroms: The Donbass-Dnepr Bend in Late Imperial Russia, 1870–1905*. Princeton, 1992.

YANEY, GEORGE. *The Urge to Mobilize: Agrarian Reform in Russia, 1861–1930*. Urbana, Ill., 1985.

ZELNIK, REGINALD E. *Labor and Society in Tsarist Russia; the Factory Workers of St. Petersburg, 1855–1870*. Stanford, 1971.

ZUCKERMAN, FREDERICK S. *The Tsarist Police in Russian Society, 1880–1917*. Washington Square, N.Y., 1996.

CHAPTER 7

Religion and Culture, 1855–1917

In the Late Imperial period, the Russian government continued to rule over religious organizations and education. It also exercised censorship over literature and other cultural spheres. Yet government controls were increasingly being resented and challenged, and the state's own modernizing needs seemed to demand less authoritarian approaches, especially in education, which expanded rapidly in this era. In the face of such challenges, government policy oscillated between reform and reaction. The former was most evident under Alexander II and then again between 1905 and 1917; the latter coincided almost exactly with Pobedonostsev's tenure as procurator of the Holy Synod from 1880 to 1905.

In the realm of high culture, this was Russia's greatest era, first producing a Golden Age for the Russian novel and a little later a more diffuse Silver Age of the arts. The names of writers, painters, and composers, including Turgenev, Dostoevsky, Tolstoy, Chekhov, Kandinsky, Chagall, Musorgsky, Tchaikovsky, Scriabin, and Stravinsky, eventually became familiar to people around the world.

The works of these and other artists often reflected similar concerns, such as Russia's past and its uniqueness or kinship with the West. In the late nineteenth century, realism predominated in the arts, and many works dealt with the common people. During Russia's Silver Age, which coincided with the reign of Nicholas II (1894–1917) and was a great age for poetry, many artists became more concerned with their own fulfillment. They experimented with a multiplicity of styles and often dealt with topics such as religion, mysticism, sexuality, demonology, and humanity's transformation or collapse.

As cities, technology, and education expanded, high culture became more diffused; popular culture, especially in the cities, more modern; and the lines between high culture and popular culture more blurred. Yet the gap between Russia's elites and the urban and rural lower classes was not closed and in some ways even widened. During the reigns of Alexander III and Nicholas II, most writers, painters, and composers displayed less concern than under Alexander II with awakening sympathy for "the people" (narod).

RUSSIAN ORTHODOXY AND THE STATE

Despite the restoration of certain powers to the hierarchy of the Holy Synod in the late 1850s, it and the church in general remained strongly subject to state control. Although the tsar and his government did not interfere in questions of church dogma and ritual, he did sometimes personally decide which clergyman to appoint to a high position or make "suggestions" with which the Holy Synod complied. And the government still expected Orthodox clergymen to help act as its ears and voice. If they heard of a crime against the state, even in the privacy of confession, they were supposed to report it. They were also to encourage obedience to government decrees and to preach the sinfulness of disobeying the tsar's will.

Not only did the state depend on the Orthodox Church, but also the church depended on the state, for both income and support against other religions.

By the mid-1890s, Pobedonostsev, the Synod's lay procurator from 1880 to 1905, had tightened most restraints over the hierarchy that had been loosened in the late 1850s. Some churchmen complained that he and other lay officials of the Synod really governed church affairs.

The church, however, was not immune to changes in Russia under Nicholas II. Bishops, priests, and laypersons became increasingly dissatisfied with state control over the church. Although some clergy supported the reactionary "Black Hundreds," Father Gapon was just one of many priests who sympathized with liberal or even radical political ideas in 1905.

After the 1905 revolt subsided, the government tried to suppress dissenting church voices, and the Synod urged the clergy to support the forces and parties of "order." But even among Synod members and other members of the church hierarchy, there was unhappiness with the state's failure to back what they considered reasonable reforms. The reputed influence of Rasputin, the self-proclaimed holy man, over church appointments and other matters was a final insult that upset many churchmen. When in the midst of the March 1917 revolution, the Holy Synod's procurator, N. P. Raev, sought from the Synod a proclamation supporting the monarchy, it refused.

Although this era witnessed some efforts to improve overall church conditions, by 1917 little headway had been made. Most of a series of church reforms in the late 1860s ultimately did little good. Writing about the end of this era, Gregory Freeze concluded that "despite strong and continuing interest, despite dozens of committees and commissions, despite the clamor of public opinion, reform left the Church little better—if not worse—than it was in 1825."[1] Most priests remained poor and financially dependent on their parishioners; ecclesiastical education remained inadequate; many priests were poorly trained (in 1904, only about two-thirds of the priests had even received

[1]*The Parish Clergy in Nineteenth Century Russia: Crisis, Reform, Counter-Reform* (Princeton, 1983), p. 459.

FIGURE 7.1. The most imposing church opened while Pobedonostsev was the procurator of the Holy Synod was the massive Cathedral of Christ the Savior in Moscow, which opened in 1883 after more than four decades of construction (architect K. Ton). (*From Jim Harter,* Images of World Architecture: A Definitive Volume of 2000 Copyright-free Images. Bonanza Books, New York, 1990, p. 431, #1.)

a seminary degree); and most parishioners remained ignorant of fundamental doctrines.

Despite Pobedonostsev's efforts to increase the number of priests and parishes, by 1904 the ratio of both to Orthodox believers had lessened, especially in rapidly growing areas. Around 1900, for example, Odessa's quarter-million Orthodox believers had only five parish churches.

THE NON-ORTHODOX AND OTHER CHALLENGES TO TRADITIONAL ORTHODOXY

The government's policy toward the one-third of its people who were non-Orthodox was consistent in its goal—to buttress state security—but oscillated in its means. At times, the government concluded that repression of the non-Orthodox stirred discontentment and was counterproductive. At other times, especially during most of Pobedonostsev's years as procurator of the Holy Synod, the state tightened its restraints and increased its discrimination against the non-Orthodox. Discrimination against Lutherans, Catholics, Jews, and Moslems was often part of the larger Russification policies that coincided with Pobedonostsev's years in office.

A law of 1883 recognized the right of schismatics (Old Believers) and sectarians (except the Skoptsy) to practice their beliefs in their houses of prayer or private homes. It prohibited them, however, most types of public display allowed to the Orthodox. It also forbade them from building new churches or proselytizing among the Orthodox faithful, who were forbidden to convert to other religions. During the next few decades, Pobedonostsev worked hard to insure that schismatic and sectarian rights remained strictly limited, and sometimes he initiated new repressions.

One group that saw its rights curtailed was that of the Stundists, a Baptist-like movement that had developed rapidly in southern Russia during the late nineteenth century. Although in 1883 the Stundists obtained the same rights as most other sects, in 1894, Pobedonostsev, alarmed at their spreading influence, persuaded the government to declare them "especially dangerous." Among the rights they lost was that of meeting together for prayer.

Several years later, persecution of the Dukhobors, most of whom advocated nonviolence, reached such a level that the great writer Leo Tolstoy began a campaign to find a home for them outside the Russian Empire. By 1900, thousands of them had been allowed to emigrate to Canada.

The increase of political agitation that marked the early twentieth century and led to the 1905 revolt pressured the government into issuing several edicts promising to respect religious toleration. Especially notable was one of April 1905 that specifically called for removing restrictions on the Old Believers— these schismatics greatly outnumbered the sectarians, and Curtiss has estimated that there were more than 17 million Old Believers in the empire by 1897. That same 1905 edict allowed Orthodox believers to convert legally to other Christian faiths or even, under certain circumstances, to certain non-Christian ones. During the next two years, more than 300,000 individuals took advantage of this new right. To implement greater toleration, the Stolypin government in late 1906–early 1907 prepared more than a dozen bills. Yet, because of the temporary waning of the revolutionary threat and the opposition of Orthodox Church leaders and conservative voices in such forums as the State Council, these bills did not become law.

During the final prewar decade, the threat of increased competition from non-Orthodox faiths was only one of many challenges facing the Orthodox Church. The increasing urbanization and modernization of society placed strains upon an institution not known for its ability to adapt to new ways. Churchmen lamented a decrease in the religiosity of the masses, both in the towns and in the villages—the revolving traffic of peasants from villages to cities and then often back again made it difficult to prevent secular urban influences from affecting village life.

A different type of challenge was presented by many intellectuals who had renounced atheism and adopted a more religious, although often not traditionally Orthodox, viewpoint. In literature and other arts, in societies and journals, the new interest in the spiritual was evident. Although a few outstanding intellectuals, such as Sergei Bulgakov (1871–1927), eventually became Orthodox priests, the religious thought of the prewar decade was diverse, free-thinking, and hardly within the Orthodox mainstream. The religious ideas of the ecumenical Vladimir Soloviev, often contrary to those of Pobedonostsev, were the chief influence on intellectuals who embraced the new spiritual interests. Many of these same intellectuals were also influenced by the ideas of Tolstoy and Germany's Friedrich Nietzsche (1844–1900), both radical critics of traditional Christianity.

EDUCATION AND SCHOLARSHIP

During the Late Imperial era, educational opportunities increased significantly, especially in its final decades. By 1914, just over half the empire's children aged eight to eleven were enrolled in primary schools, with the percentage being closer to 60 percent in European Russia. By then, there were roughly eighteen times as many pupils in the empire's primary and secondary schools as there had been in 1856, and the combined university and higher institute enrollments displayed growth just as impressive.

Because Russia existed in a competitive world, this growth must be placed in a comparative perspective. On the eve of World War I, England, France, Germany, the United States, and Japan all enrolled three times or more as high a percentage of their overall population in primary and secondary schools. Most of Russia's students, residing in the countryside, never completed more than two or three years of schooling.

Educational growth was affected by elite and popular attitudes toward it. Peasants increasingly came to appreciate the possible benefits of literacy for their children. Before the 1890s, most of the initiative for obtaining literacy, either in school or outside, came from the peasants themselves. Yet, they generally had little interest or incentive in seeing their children obtain more than a few years of education.

Meanwhile, the government seemed more interested in controlling education than in greatly expanding it. After a brief liberal phase during Alexander II's first decade of rule, ministers of education such as D. A. Tolstoi (1866–1880) and I. D. Delianov (1882–1897) retightened government controls. In 1871, believing that the study of Latin, Greek, and mathematics helped instill discipline, while posing less danger than most other subjects, Tolstoi increased the class time devoted to them in the classical gymnasiums. He did not believe, however, such gymnasiums were for everyone: He encouraged ambitious students from the lower estates to attend the more vocational and technical gymnasiums (the *realschulen*). After becoming minister of interior in 1882, Tolstoi worked with Delianov to bring about the University Statute of 1884, which ended the university autonomy granted in 1863. The government took the occasion to remind professors that their teaching must be patriotic and serve state interests.

Harboring a great mistrust of secular teachers and professors, Pobedonost-sev took additional steps to strengthen government control over education. Thanks largely to his efforts, a statute of 1884 authorized the establishment of a new system of parish schools under the jurisdiction of the Holy Synod. During the next two decades, these primary schools multiplied swiftly, jumping from 5,517 in 1884 to 44,421 in 1903. Their purpose, as stated in 1884, was "to strengthen the Orthodox faith and Christian morality among the people and to impart useful elementary knowledge."[2] Given Pobedonostsev's view of the church's role in buttressing state power, there is little doubt that he intended the parish schools to foster loyalty to the regime.

By the 1890s, elites, both within and outside the government, realized that widespread education was important for Russia's development. In the twenty-five years before 1914, zemstvo and central-government spending for educa-tion increased sharply. By 1907–1908, the Ministry of Education was introduc-ing bills before the Duma calling for the gradual establishment of universal primary education.

Yet educational development after 1890 continued to be hampered by gov-ernment fears. Frequent student strikes, beginning in 1899, exacerbated its dis-trust of the universities. Although the 1905 revolution forced some govern-

[2]As quoted in Robert F. Byrnes, *Pobedonostsev, His Life and Thought* (Bloomingson, 1968), p. 278.

FIGURE 7.2. A Siberian church school from circa 1900, with an icon in the corner and a portrait of Nicholas II in the front, at the outdoor Museum of Wooden Architecture near Irkutsk.

ment concessions, soon afterwards, under Stolypin, the state increased its efforts to insure university loyalty.

Its new measures heightened tensions, leading to new strikes, the expulsion of thousands of students, and the resignation of some professors. In 1912, Nicholas refused to establish any new universities—not counting Helsinki University and one private Moscow university, there were only ten universities in the empire (two more were approved in 1916). The government's fears of university radicalism was one reason that it continued to establish more higher technical institutes than universities. One scholar has concluded that by 1914 "relations between the Russian government and the professoriate were worse than at any time since the reign of Nicholas I."[3]

The students at a majority of the universities had their choice of four departments: history and philology, law, medicine, and natural sciences and mathematics. Law and medicine were generally the most popular choices, and history and philology was chosen least.

By the turn of the century, most university students came from the middle strata of Russian life, with many of their fathers being employed in urban occupations and government service. Few of them came from peasant or blue-collar families. Yet most students were dependent on student aid, work, or both to make their way through the universities. Subsidized dining halls helped, but few dormitories were available, and students generally lived in poor rented quarters. They were often harassed by university inspectors, who attempted to insure students' political reliability and compliance with the many rules of student conduct, which included properly wearing student uniforms.

Until the beginning of World War I, women were not allowed to enroll as regular students in the universities and even then only in small numbers. In 1876, the government permitted the establishment of separate "women's higher courses" in St. Petersburg, Moscow, Kiev, and Kazan, but at the end of the reactionary 1880s, the latter three were closed. Before 1905, only Moscow was allowed (in 1900) to reestablish such women's courses. After the 1905 revolution, other university towns were permitted to establish them, and women were also allowed to audit courses in the regular universities.

Concurrently, new advanced technical schools for women, such as the St. Petersburg Women's Technical Institute, were opened. Before 1905, some women had attended medical schools abroad or been trained at home (a women's medical school had first appeared in St. Petersburg during the 1870s), and by 1911 there were some 1500 women doctors. After 1905, opportunities to pursue advanced studies in preparation for other professions such as architecture, engineering, and law began opening up to women. Between 1900–1901 and 1913–1914, the number of women enrolled in higher educational institutions of all types increased about fifteenfold to almost 40,000.

At other educational levels, female opportunities also increased. Whereas in 1850 only about one-tenth of all primary school students were girls, by 1911

[3]Samuel D. Kassow, *Students, Professors, and the State in Tsarist Russia* (Berkeley, 1989), p. 40.

the percentage had reached one-third. By then, women already composed more than 60 percent of all village teachers and a much higher percentage of St. Petersburg and Moscow primary school teachers.

Both within and outside the higher educational institutions, scientists, engineers, and scholars made important contributions. In chemistry, Dmitri Mendeleev (1834–1907) presented his groundbreaking Periodic Table. In physics, P. N. Lebedev (1863–1912) measured the pressure of light, and A. S. Popov (1859–1905) demonstrated—before Marconi's patent application—that messages could be transmitted by electromagnetic waves. N. E. Zhukovsky (1847–1921) and K. E. Tsiolkovsky (1857–1935) made pioneering discoveries in aviation, with Tsiolkovsky's early contributions to rocketry being especially significant. The physiologist I. P. Pavlov (1849–1936) was awarded a Nobel Prize in 1904 for his work on digestion, and he later gained world fame for his experiments with dogs, which demonstrated the workings of conditioned reflexes.

Several important scholars did much of their work abroad. Sophia Kovalevskaia (1850–1891) studied in Germany and later became a professor of mathematics at the University of Stockholm. Her work on motion won her recognition from the Academy of Paris in 1888. Two years later, the biologist and bacteriologist I. I. Mechnikov (1845–1916) joined Paris's Pasteur Institute and in 1895 became its director. In 1908, he was a co-recipient of the Nobel Prize for Physiology and Medicine.

The Late Imperial era also provided a rich harvest in the social sciences (especially history) and philosophy. From 1851 to 1879, despite his teaching and administrative duties at Moscow University, Sergei Soloviev (1820–1879) completed each year a new volume of his *History of Russia from Ancient Times.* His pupil Vasili Kliuchevsky (1841–1911) became renowned for his graceful style, both in lecturing and writing, and his five-volume *Course in Russian History* made an indelible impression on many future historians of Russia, both within and outside the country's borders. Other historians of note included S. F. Platonov (1860–1933), who did valuable work on the Time of Troubles; Paul Miliukov, the Kadet leader; and several Ukrainian historians, especially M. I. Kostomarov (1817–1885) and M. S. Hrushevsky (1866–1934).

The empire's most important philosopher was Vladimir Soloviev (1853–1900), the son of the historian. He studied and wrote on Western philosophy and developed his own original philosophic ideas. His *The Justification of the Good* (1895) was Russia's most important work in ethical philosophy and also offered an impressive philosophy of law.

LITERATURE

The Late Imperial age was Russia's greatest literary era. First came the Golden Age of the Russian novel, which basically coincided with the reign of Alexander II. Then a little later, during the reign of Nicholas II, literature shared a Silver Age with the other arts. Bridging the two ages was Russia's great short-story writer and dramatist Anton Chekhov.

Turgenev, Dostoevsky, and Tolstoy

The three greatest novelists of the Golden Age were Ivan Turgenev (1818–1883), Fedor Dostoevsky (1821–1881), and Leo Tolstoy (1828–1910). Turgenev and Tolstoy were from wealthy noble landowning families; Dostoevsky grew up in more modest surroundings in Moscow. Although their literary styles differed in many ways, all three writers were primarily realists in an age of literary realism.

Turgenev first received wide acclaim for his *Sportsman's Sketches*. The sketches began appearing in 1847 and were published in book form in 1852. By depicting serfs sympathetically, the sketches contributed to the growing dissatisfaction with the evils of serfdom.

Turgenev's most famous novel, which created a storm in Russia when it first appeared in 1862, was *Fathers and Sons*. Literary critics and others debated the meaning and significance of its central character, the nihilist Bazarov, and whether Turgenev had depicted him too harshly or sympathetically. Other Turgenev novels include *Rudin, A Nest of the Gentry, On the Eve, Smoke,* and *Virgin Soil*.

In his novels, he often dealt with contemporary social issues. He was a liberal westernizer, spent much time in Western Europe, and was the first Russian writer to gain a widespread European following, even receiving an honorary degree from Oxford University in 1879. His characters sometimes reflect his own views, but he prided himself on his objectivity and claimed that above all he was trying to portray life realistically.

Turgenev was also the author of several plays and many pieces of short fiction. His best play was *A Month in the Country*, written in 1850 but first produced in 1872. Compared to his novels, Turgenev's many shorter works tend to be more personal, poetic, and romantic, some even dealing with fantastic, otherworldly types of occurrences. His strong lyrical gift is more evident in his shorter fiction, as are his personal feelings: He looked back nostalgically at young love (he never married), lamented his own aging, and expressed a great fear of death.

Whether writing novels or stories, Turgenev's prose was characterized by brevity and clarity. All six of his novels together fall far short of the length of Tolstoy's *War and Peace*. In contrast to Dostoevsky and Tolstoy, Turgenev did not generally tell the reader a great deal about the inner life of his characters but revealed their feelings primarily through their words and actions.

Dostoevsky's life and works were both filled with more turbulence than Turgenev's. Although he received early acclaim for his first novel, *Poor Folk*, published in 1846, his involvement in the Petrashevsky Circle led to his arrest in 1849, followed by a decade of imprisonment and exile. While in a Siberian prison, he experienced a strong religious reawakening and became convinced that Russian intellectuals like himself must be spiritually reunited with the common people and their Orthodox religious beliefs.

In 1866, Dostoevsky published *Crime and Punishment*, the first of his four major novels—the other three being *The Idiot* (1868), *The Possessed* (1872), and *The Brothers Karamazov* (1880). In *Crime and Punishment*, he attempted to demonstrate the bankruptcy of nihilism and radical thinking, which he blamed primarily on Western influences. In *The Possessed*, which reflected his alarm at the behavior of nihilists such as Sergei Nechaev, Dostoevsky suggested that westernized liberals such as Turgenev helped create a climate conducive to the growth of radicalism.

His criticism of Western influences and his Russian nationalism were sometimes accompanied by ugly prejudices, including antisemitism. At other times, as in his "Pushkin Speech" of 1880 or in *The Brothers Karamazov*, Dostoevsky spoke or wrote of universal reconciliation, establishing the Kingdom of God on earth, and displaying brotherly love toward Western Europe.

Religious themes were important to him. He believed that free will often led to sin and suffering, but that such freedom was priceless and that from suffering, both humility and redemption could flow. He intended Prince Myshkin, the hero of *The Idiot*, to be a Christ-like figure, possessing great humility. In *The Brothers Karamazov*, Alyosha Karamazov and the monk Zosima reflect some of Dostoevsky's own religious thinking.

Although Dostoevsky's reputation rests primarily on his four great novels, he also authored many other works, including other novels, short stories, sketches, and journalistic essays. *The Adolescent* is sometimes included in the ranks of his major novels. *Winter Notes on Summer Impressions* contains reflections on his 1862 trip to Western Europe. *The House of the Dead* is a novel based on his own Siberian prison experiences. *Notes from the Underground* and its Underground Man defend "irrational" behavior in the name of freedom. *The Gambler* reflects Dostoevsky's own gambling addiction during the 1860s.

Dostoevsky's style is more dramatic and frenzied than Turgenev's. The clashes of his characters often flow from their differing ideas—he was a master of the novel of ideas. His realism, which at times is mixed with gothic romantic touches, is primarily a psychological realism, and he was especially insightful when delving into the depths of abnormal behavior. Many of his characters, such as Raskolnikov of *Crime and Punishment*, were split personalities. Raskolnikov's behavior is partly explained by his residence in St. Petersburg, and much more than Turgenev and Tolstoy, Dostoevsky's prose captures the heartbeat of the new urban environments emerging in Russia.

As with Turgenev and Dostoevsky, Tolstoy first made his literary mark while still in his twenties. His trilogy *Childhood, Boyhood,* and *Youth* and his *Sevastopol Sketches,* all based largely on his own experiences, won him early acclaim for his realism. Among other works, he wrote two masterpieces, *War and Peace* during the 1860s and *Anna Karenina* during the 1870s.

While writing *Anna Karenina*, Tolstoy began experiencing a spiritual crisis—a "middle-age crisis" it might be termed today. The acute realization that "the dragon of death" awaited everyone temporarily sapped life's enjoyments and led him to despair. Like Dostoevsky in prison two decades earlier, Tolstoy was "reborn" by the example of common Orthodox believers, only not convicts, but the peasants around him. And like Dostoevsky, Tolstoy retained a faith in the common people and their essential goodness until the end of his life.

In his last three decades, Tolstoy continued writing fiction as well as many nonfictional, often religious or didactic works. He also wrote several plays, the most famous being *The Power of Darkness*. During this period, he developed his own religious-political philosophy, one that attracted Tolstoyan followers and got him into trouble with both the Orthodox Church and the government (see Chapter 3). His religious beliefs infused much of his late fiction, but despite his frequent didacticism, he still wrote many excellent works. Stories such as *Master and Man* and *Hadji Murad* are among his finest, and even the novel *Resurrection*, which the critic Prince Mirsky thought an example of Tolstoy "at his worst," has its strong defenders.

Although the fictional characters of Turgenev and Dostoevsky often reflected the political-ideological struggles of their day, Tolstoy's characters were more concerned with eternal questions such as individual and family happiness and the meaning of life and death. At times, as in *War and Peace*, Tolstoy interrupts his narrative to discourse on topics such as war and history.

Tolstoy was a master at depicting and analyzing his characters. Although some of them reflect his own inner turmoil and search for life's meanings, others exist more in their own mental worlds. Anna Karenina, Natasha (in *War and Peace*), and the Moslem warrior Hadji Murad are just a few notable examples. Although his writings before his "crisis" are full of realistic detail, his latter works are more concise and sparse.

Chekhov, Gorky, and Other Writers

Besides Turgenev, Dostoevsky, and Tolstoy, Russia's Golden Age produced other fine novelists, including Ivan Goncharov, Nikolai Leskov, Alexei Pisemsky, and Mikhail Saltykov-Shchedrin. Although both Turgenev and Tolstoy wrote a few plays, the chief playwright of their day was Alexander Ostrovsky (1823–1886), who wrote close to fifty plays. Ostrovsky's plays reflected the literary realism of the era; were usually full of drama; and often displayed the vices of merchants, patriarchal fathers, and others.

The leading poets of this generation were Nikolai Nekrasov (1821–1877) and Afanasi Fet (1820–1892). The two men presented quite a contrast. Nekrasov, the radical editor and friend of Chernyshevsky and Dobroliubov, wrote realistic poetry reflecting his social concerns. The conservative Fet, who was known to register his disapproval at the liberalism of Moscow University by spitting out his carriage window when passing it, was a proponent of "art for art's sake" and wrote melodic love and nature poems. The leading poet of the succeeding generation was Vladimir Soloviev, the philosopher, religious thinker, and mystic, who died in 1900.

From the early 1880s until his death, Anton Chekhov (1860–1904) wrote the hundreds of stories and numerous plays that have gained him a worldwide reputation. Among his plays, *The Sea Gull, Uncle Vania, The Three Sisters,* and *The Cherry Orchard* are his most famous.

Chekhov gained early success writing humorous, often satirical, short stories, which have always been more appreciated in Russia than abroad. They made it unnecessary for him to earn a living as he had been trained to do, practicing medicine. A sadder atmosphere envelopes many of Chekhov's later works, partly because of his suspicion and eventual awareness that he had tuberculosis, but also because of the social conditions of Russia.

Chekhov considered himself a realistic writer, a chronicler of his times; and being a humane and decent man, he was saddened by the life around him. His works reflect the poor state of the peasants, the backwardness of provincial life, the inhumane treatment of convicts (as depicted in his book *Sakhalin Island*), the decline of the nobility, and the ineffectualness of intellectuals.

Chekhov's characters are often bored, unable to connect with others, and more willing to talk than act. Even Chekhov's dramas are short on dramatic action. His style depends more on creating an atmosphere, a mood, a "slice of life"—often sad but lyrical. In this respect and in the conciseness of his language and frequent use of symbols, Chekhov's plays and latter stories display a strong poetic sensibility.

Another writer of short stories and plays was Alexei Peshkov (1868–1936), who adopted the pen-name Maxim Gorky. He grew up in harsh conditions, and before he reached his teens he began earning his own living—these experiences were later described in some of his best writing, an autobiographical trilogy (*Childhood, In the World, My Universities*). His short stories earned him fame in the mid-1890s, and other stories, novels, and plays soon added to his reputation. His play *The Lower Depths* (1902), like Chekhov's greatest plays, was staged by the new Moscow Art Theater, under the direction of C. S. Stanislavsky, one of the pioneer directors of modern theater. In this play and in works such as the novel *Mother* (1907), Gorky's radical sympathies are clear—although frequently supporting Lenin, Gorky also had his differences with him. In 1905, he spent more than a month in the Sts. Peter and Paul Fortress for penning a protest against Bloody Sunday. About a year after public pressure helped free him, he left Russia and lived abroad until 1913, including part of 1906 in the United States.

Literature in the Silver Age

The Silver Age was characterized by experimentation and a wide variety of writings and literary camps, but also by a new cultural spirit. It veered away from realism toward neoromanticism and philosophical idealism. In literature, this change was most evident in the new poetry of "decadence" and "symbolism."

The Silver Age was a great age for poetry. So many talented poets began writing in this period that only a small number can be mentioned here. Constantine Balmont and Valeri Briusov were two pioneering poets of the time, and Alexander Blok and Andrei Bely, both born in 1880, were two of the Symbolist movement's greatest practitioners. Viacheslav Ivanov was another leading Symbolist. A slightly younger group of poets (all born between 1886 and 1893) who published at least some of their poetry before 1917 include Nikolai Gumilev, Anna Akhmatova, Boris Pasternak (who later wrote *Doctor Zhivago*), Osip Mandelstam, Marina Tsvetaeva, and Vladimir Maiakovsky.

A central influence on many of the poets was Vladimir Soloviev's mystical poetry, but they were also influenced by foreign works such as those of the

French Symbolist poets and Nietzsche. The experimentation and diversity that marked the poetry of the Silver Age emanated from the era's restless intellectual searching. Writers and other intellectuals sought fulfillment in religious and mystical truths and sensual delights or by helping "transform humanity," but they also feared apocalyptic catastrophe.

Although it was not a great age for the novel, Bely's *Petersburg* (1913) and Fedor Sologub's *The Petty Demon* (1907) were noteworthy. Like Bely, both Sologub and Ivan Bunin (1870–1953), another fine prose writer, were also poets of note. Bunin's short story, "The Gentleman from San Francisco" (1915), is perhaps his best-known piece of fiction. Some of Bunin's work was published by the Knowledge Publishing House, which resisted the dominant trend of the time by supporting realistic literature. Among some of the other first-rate short stories and longer fiction it published were works by Gorky, Leonid Andreev, and Alexander Kuprin.

ART AND ARCHITECTURE

Developments in painting paralleled those in literature: first an age of realism and later a reaction against it and an explosion of artistic experimentation. In 1863, fourteen art students at the St. Petersburg Academy of Arts protested its choice of a competition subject—the Feast of the Gods in Valhalla. They believed it irrelevant to their interests and those of society. Their aesthetic ideas owed a debt both to earlier pioneers of artistic realism, such as A. Venetsianov, and to new aesthetic theories, such as those of Chernyshevsky. Under the leadership of Ivan Kramskoi (1837–1887), they formed an "Association of Free Painters." In 1870, Kramskoi and others, including some who had not been among the original fourteen rebels, formed a new organization, The Society of Traveling Exhibitions. Its members, often called the "Wanderers," not only stressed artistic realism, but also the importance of taking art to the people. Some of them also hoped their paintings would contribute to social reforms.

Perhaps the most famous painting of the 1870s was "The Volga Boathaulers" (1870–1873). Its creator was Ilia Repin (1844–1930), the son of a state peasant, who joined the Wanderers later in the decade. It fit in well with the populist mood of of the 1870s, especially the going-to-the-people movement of 1874 (see Chapter 2). Like the writings of the Populist Lavrov or the poetry of Nekrasov (himself the subject of a sympathetic portrait by Kramskoi), Repin's canvas helped stimulate sympathy for the masses. Dostoevsky noted that it would awaken in those who saw it a realization of their debt to the people.

Beginning in the 1880s, many of the Wanderers were caught up in a wave of cultural nationalism, which was reflected in a new enthusiasm for Russian historical subjects. Repin painted such works as "Ivan the Terrible and His Son Ivan" and "The Zaporozhe Cossacks Writing a Letter to the Turkish Sultan." An even more prolific painter of historical canvases was Vasili I. Surikov. In 1881, he painted "The Morning of the Streltsy Execution" and in the next few decades followed it up with numerous other historical paintings, including

"Boyarynia Morozova" and "Stenka Razin." Both Repin and Surikov, like many other artists, benefited from the support of the Moscow merchant Savva Mamontov and his wife Elizabeth, who encouraged and supported the nationalist revival in the arts.

By the 1890s, new winds were blowing through the Russian art world. Mikhail Vrubel and his friend Valentin Serov, two more artists patronized by the Mamontovs, were transitional figures between the realistic art of the Wanderers and the new artists that emerged around the turn of the century. As compared to the Wanderers, the new artists were more open to foreign artistic influences and shared the Symbolist poets' reaction against realism. They were more concerned with a spiritual world that existed beyond earthly phenomena; with their own inner world; or with technical challenges relating to shapes, space, and color.

New journals such as *The World of Art* (1898–1904) helped stimulate the creation of Russia's new art. So too did the rich collections of Impressionist, Post-Impressionist, Matisse, and Picasso paintings gathered by some of Russia's Moscow merchant collectors. Still another stimulus was artists' travel and study abroad and, at home, the rediscovery of the beauty of old icons, just then being restored to their original brilliance.

Just as in poetry, so too in art, one movement after another appeared. Symbolism, Neo-Primitivism, Cubo-Futurism, Rayonism, Suprematism, and Constructivism were among the most prominent. Prolific painters such as Mikhail

FIGURE 7.3. The house of Stepan Riabushinsky, Moscow, 1900–1902, architect F. Shekhtel.

Larinov, Natalia Goncharova, and Kasimir Malevich often passed from one phase to another. Two of the most gifted younger artists at the close of this era were Vladimir Tatlin and Natalia Popova. Of the many Russian painters of the prewar period, probably the two best-known in the West are Vasili Kandinsky, one of the founders of modern abstract art, and Marc Chagall, whose modernist paintings often reflected Jewish life as well as his own rich imagination.

Although architecture displayed less creative dynamism than painting, the profession expanded rapidly, especially to meet new urban needs. Much of the new building was eclectic, but two styles are worth noting: the national-revival style and the "style moderne," which combined a decorative aestheticism with a rational-functionalist approach to new materials and technology. Late-nineteenth century examples of the national-revival style include St. Petersburg's Church of the Resurrection of the Savior on the Blood (see Figure 2.3), Moscow's History Museum, and its City Duma (later the Central Lenin Museum). The turn-of-the-century "style moderne" received support from Moscow merchant families such as the Riabushinskys. They commissioned Fedor Shekhtel, the era's most renowned architect, to design both houses and commercial buildings for them in this new style.

MUSIC

Thanks to composers such as Anton Rubinstein, Modest Musorgsky, Peter Tchaikovsky, Alexander Scriabin, and Igor Stravinsky, musical life was as vibrant as that of literature and painting. In St. Petersburg, Anton Rubinstein, a great pianist as well as a composer, founded the Russian Musical Society in 1859. In 1862, he became director of a recently opened school of music that was renamed the St. Petersburg Conservatory. His brother Nikolai followed his example in Moscow, establishing there both a branch of the Musical Society and a conservatory. Other branches and conservatories soon followed in other cities. For almost four decades, Anton Rubinstein remained the head of the St. Petersburg Conservatory, which trained many future composers, including Tchaikovsky, who later taught at the Moscow Conservatory.

Some composers found Rubinstein's musical approach too conservative and Western. The chief rebels were a group named "The Five" or "Mighty Bunch," which originated in the late 1850s–early 1860s. Their leader, and the only one who trained for a musical career, was Mili Balakirev. Alexander Borodin was a scientist, and the other three—Musorgsky, Nikolai Rimsky-Korsakov, and Caeser Cui—were all trained for military careers. Influenced by the music of Glinka and Alexander Dargomyzhsky as well as the intellectual currents of their own era, The Five espoused nationalism and realism in music.

Of The Five, Musorgsky was the most gifted. With great passion, he set out to depict Russian life, especially that of the common people. They are the true heroes of his two great operas set in Muscovite Russia, *Boris Godunov* and *Khovanshchina*.

If Musorgsky's passion for Russia's people and history, including their music and folklore, was unmatched, his interest in them was more common.

This can be seen in such operas as Borodin's *Prince Igor* and Rimsky-Korsakov's *Sadko*, *The Tsar's Bride*, and *The Golden Cockerel*.

The music of Tchaikovsky, both in technique and content, stands somewhere between that of Anton Rubinstein and The Five. Compositions such as his *Sixth Symphony*, his ballets *Swan Lake* and *Sleeping Beauty*, and his opera *Evgeni Onegin* are just a few of the many works that earned him international fame before his death in 1893.

During the Silver Age, the music of Alexander Scriabin reflected the strong mystical influences of Vladimir Soloviev. And Scriabin's compositions along with those of Igor Stravinsky displayed the Silver Age's passion for artistic experimentation. When Stravinsky's ballet *The Rite of Spring* premiered in Paris in 1913, its daring dissonance created an uproar that threatened to drown out the music.

DIAGILEV AND ARTISTIC CROSS-FERTILIZATION

Stravinsky's ballet was put on by Serge Diagilev and his Ballet Russes company, who a few years earlier had staged the composer's *The Firebird* and *Petrushka*. The efforts of Diagilev perhaps best exemplify an important tendency of the era—the intertwining and cross-fertilization of the arts.

Such intertwining was not new. To take one of many examples, Musorgsky was inspired by Repin's "The Volga Boathaulers" and wrote to the artist that he also wished to portray "the people" in his work. Realistic, populist, and nationalist tendencies swept through various art forms during the reigns of Alexander II and Alexander III.

But Diagilev's organizing energy on behalf of artistic interaction was unprecedented. This aim was one of the reasons why in 1898 he launched his new magazine, *The World of Art*. Its pages dealt with Russian and Western art, poetry, music, and religious ideas. Before taking his ballet company abroad, Diagilev had introduced Paris to the world of Russian painters and treated them to the music of Musorgsky, Borodin, Scriabin, Rimsky-Korsakov, and Rachmaninov. The last two composers accompanied him to Paris, where Rimsky-Korsakov conducted and Rachmaninov played the piano.

The Diagilev ballets featured not only great music, but also showcased the talents of leading choreographers and dancers, such as the famed Vaslav Nijinsky. And Diagilev employed leading artists such as Leon Bakst, Mikhail Larinov, and Natalia Goncharova to help design his sets and costumes.

POPULAR CULTURE

As urbanization, education, and literacy developed, so too did the diffusion of the fruits of high culture. Books, journals, newspapers, museums, learned societies, public lectures, performances, concerts, exhibitions, and films proliferated. The lines between elite and popular culture became increasingly blurry. For example, many of Chekhov's short stories appeared in popular humor magazines and in newspapers, and Tolstoy's short novel *The Kreutzer Sonata* (completed in 1889) appeared on the popular stage in 1911 and as a film in 1914.

The popularity of *The Kreutzer Sonata* in various forms and with various audiences was partly due to its treatment of sexuality. After the turn of the century, especially after 1905 and the reduction of censorship, popular culture (as well as high culture) increasingly dealt with sexual themes. The works of artists, poets, dancers, dramatists, filmmakers, philosophers and especially fiction writers reflected this concern. Andreev's short stories "In the Fog" and "The Abyss" (both 1902), Mikhail Artsybashev's novel *Sanine* (1907), Kuprin's novel *Yama* (1909–1915), and Anastasiia Verbitskaia's six-volume novel *The Keys to Happiness* (1910–1913) were some of the more popular works dealing with sex. Verbitskaia's novel, which also had a feminist following, was made into a film in 1913 and became Russia's most popular pre-1917 film.

Film houses began appearing around the turn of the century, and by 1913 there were almost 1500 of them throughout the country. Other forms of urban entertainment included opera, ballet, theater, the circus, the variety stage, cabarets, concerts, dance halls, fairs, and taverns. Amusement parks, which like films appealed to people of various classes, also sprung up in increasing numbers during this era and often offered many types of entertainment. In St. Petersburg's Arcadia (opened in 1881), for example, entertainments included opera, drama, comedy, vaudeville, band music, Gypsy ensembles, clowns, a tightrope walker, wild beasts, fireworks, balloon fights, reenactments of army and naval battles, and a roller coaster. Of course, how much urban entertainment was available varied greatly, especially depending on the size of any given city.

Organized sports, including spectator sports such as horse racing, cycling, and soccer, developed during this period and sometimes drew crowds into the tens of thousands in places like the Moscow Hippodrome. By 1914, forty-eight soccer teams competed in the two major city leagues of Moscow and St. Petersburg. Besides these athletes, other individuals organized teams or clubs for ice hockey, fencing, gymnastics, lawn tennis, skating, skiing, swimming, yachting, rowing, and other sports. Boxers, weightlifters, and wrestlers participated in circuses and at fairs and organized clubs for such "heavy athletics."

As can be imagined, most working-class people had little time or money to join sports clubs (even if permitted to) or to see spectator sports. After the 1905 revolt, however, some government officials and factory owners concluded that organized sports might channel workers' energies into more constructive pursuits than revolutionary activities. Thus, the number of workers' soccer teams increased, and in 1914 such teams were permitted for the first time to play against teams made up of middle-class or upper-class men. (Future Communist party head Nikita Khrushchev once claimed that he had been on a soccer team of the foreign-owned company he worked for in pre-1917 Yuzovka.)

Overall, organized sports in Russia reflected the country's social and political makeup. Workers participated much less and the government exercised more control over sports than in more democratic countries. In 1912, an office

A Best-Selling Novel of 1907

The following selection is from Michael Artzibashef [Mikhail Artsybashev], *Sanine*, trans. Percy Pinkerton (New York, 1914), pp. 99–100, 176–177. It reflected not only the prewar decade's fascination with sexual themes, even hinting at incest, but also stressed individual (whether male or female) freedom from traditional moral constraints, another popular theme of the decade. Some critics have charged it with being both a vulgarization of Dostoevsky's *Notes from the Underground* and Nietzschean ideas. The first passage expresses Sanine's philosophy, and the second the thoughts of his sister Lida after she has allowed herself to be seduced by a young cavalry officer. Ellipses, except the final ones, are mine.

"One thing I know," replied Sanine, "and that is, that I don't want my life to be a miserable one. Thus, before all things, one must satisfy one's natural desires. Desire is everything. When a man's desires cease, his life ceases, too, and if he kills his desires, then he kills himself."

A series of books which she had read had served to give her greater freedom of thought. As she believed, her conduct was not only natural but almost worthy of praise. She had brought harm to no one thereby, only providing herself and another with sensual enjoyment. Without such enjoyment there would be no youth, and life itself would be barren and desolate as a leafless tree in autumn.

The thought that her union with a man had not been sanctioned by the church seemed to her ridiculous. By the free mind of a man such claims had long been swept aside. She ought really to find joy in this new life, just as a flower on some bright morning rejoices at the touch of the pollen borne to it on the breeze. Yet she felt unutterably degraded, and baser than the basest. . . .

. . . She had had an intrigue. Very good. It was at her own wish. People would despise and humiliate her; what did it matter? Before her lay life, and sunshine, and the wide world; and, as for men, there were plenty to be had. Her mother would grieve. Well, that was her own affair. Lida had never known what her mother's youth had been, and after her death there would be no further supervision. They had met by chance on life's road, and had gone part of the way together. Was that any reason why they should mutually oppose each other?

Lida saw plainly that she would never have the same freedom which her brother possessed. That she had ever thought so was due to the influence of this calm, strong man whom she affectionately admired. Strange thoughts came to her, thoughts of an illicit nature.

"If he were not my brother, but a stranger! . . ." she said to herself, as she hastily strove to suppress the shameful and yet alluring suggestion.

headed by a general was established to supervise sporting activity in the Russian Empire.

The government also was involved in other aspects of popular culture. Well before the turn of the century, concern with lower-class drunkenness and other vices had energized government officials and private organizations to sponsor public readings and provide "People's Houses," where respectable and morally uplifting dramas were presented. By 1913, almost 150 such "houses" had been established throughout Russia. They also usually contained tea and reading rooms. Neither in number nor in popularity, however, could they come close to competing with the taverns, which remained the favorite haunt of the lower classes.

Some entertainments and pastimes were seasonal, such as sledding, ice-skating, sleighing parties, swimming, fishing, picnics, and mushroom-picking. The church calendar also continued to affect leisure activities. Baedeker's 1914 guidebook noted that the theater season lasted from "the end of August to the beginning of May" but also pointed out that theaters "closed on the eves of the chief church festivals, and also for several weeks in Lent." Just before Lent was carnival time, when special amusements were provided.

By the early twentieth century, reading material varied from that provided by "thick journals" and serious literature to that provided by the boulevard or penny press. Major national newspapers such as *Novoe Vremia* fell somewhere in the middle. The boulevard press was inexpensive and depended on advertising and large sales. To make money, boulevard newspapers such as the *Moskovskii Listok* (*The Moscow Sheet*) appealed to people's interest in crime, disasters, human interest stories, and exposés. To the degree possible under censorship, they sometimes defended the interests of the common people (most of their readers) against those who victimized them, such as dishonest merchants or officials.

Fiction produced by the boulevard press, like the new film industry that made use of it, was often melodramatic, with crime and sex being popular themes. The owner of *Moskovskii Listok*, Nikolai Pastukhov, was the author of the popular novel *The Bandit Churkin*, which his paper serialized and which served as the basis for a film and popular song. Some foreign works, including Sherlock Holmes stories and the science fiction of Jules Verne, were also popular.

As Jeffrey Brooks has noted, the overall impact of popular fiction was to nudge its readers closer to modern secular and cosmopolitan attitudes and to a greater desire for social mobility and individual freedom. Thus, popular fiction, as so many other modern trends, tended to undermine the old tsarist, religious, and patriarchal order.

A variety of songs as well as stories appealed to the expanding urban audience. The songs came from many sources, including professional songwriters, and often appeared in penny songbooks, on sheet music, and on phonograph records; they were sung in cafes, restaurants, and on stage. Some singers, male and female, became very popular, toured the country, and appeared in films. "Gypsy songs"—often neither composed nor sung by gypsies and laced with bittersweet longings—were among the most popular.

Foreign characters and settings frequently appeared in popular literature and films. Foreign imports such as the tango also left their mark on Russian urban popular culture—although hardly to the extent suggested by the title of the Russian film *Everyone Tangos in Russia*. World War I reduced foreign influences, and, especially in the early stages of the war, Russian popular culture mirrored wartime patriotism. Germany's Kaiser Wilhelm II, for example, was vilified in the press, on postcards, in cartoons, on the stage, and in films.

There was no absolute division between urban and rural popular cultures. Many urban workers were not long removed from village life and often returned to their native villages for varying periods of time. After leaving their villages, many workers continued to participate in customs such as collective fistfights and religious processions once they became urban laborers. When they visited their villages, they helped introduce villagers to aspects of more modern urban popular culture.

Yet village culture, like village life in general, continued to reflect much more of traditional Russia than did the rapidly expanding urban areas. The seasons and the church calendar largely determined village leisure patterns, just as they did village work life. Songs, dances, and games were major leisure pastimes, especially for young people. During the late fall and winter, they often gathered for evening parties, sometimes combining work with talk, stories, or other entertainment. Young women might gather together in a hut to spin or knit, and in some villages young men would be allowed to come by and join in the socializing.

Youth parties were part of village courting rituals. A church wedding provided a major occasion for celebration, as did a baptism. Thus, religious beliefs, sometimes intermingling pagan elements, intertwined with seasonal patterns and the family life cycle to provide much of the context for rural popular culture.

Yet by the early twentieth century, it also contained new elements, some of which Russia's elites found disturbing. Although peasants continued to dance traditional circle dances and sing traditional songs, they also began to dance newer dances, such as the polka, and sing newer songs. Many of these new songs expressed individualistic desires, hostility to the upper classes, disrespect for elders or Russian traditions, or desires for new ways or products. Peasant popular culture, like peasant life in general, was not as static as observers once thought. In the early twentieth century, the pace of change in peasant culture, as in the country as a whole, was quickening.

SUGGESTED SOURCES*

ALSTON, PATRICK L. *Education and the State in Tsarist Russia.* Stanford, 1969.

BENET, SULA, ed. *The Village of Viriatino: An Ethnographic Study of a Russian Village from Before the Revolution to the Present.* Garden City, N.Y., 1970.

BOWLT, JOHN E. *The Silver Age, Russian Art of the Early Twentieth Century and the "World of Art" Group.* Newtonville, Mass., 1979.

BROOKS, JEFFREY. *When Russia Learned to Read: Literacy and Popular Literature, 1861–1914.* Princeton, 1985.

BRUMFIELD, WILLIAM CRAFT. *A History of Russian Architecture.* Cambridge, England, 1993. Chs. 13–14.

CLOWES, EDITH, SAMUEL KASSOW, and JAMES L. WEST, eds. *Between Tsar and People: Educated Society and the Quest for Public Identity in Late Imperial Russia.* Princeton, 1991.

---

*See also books cited in footnotes. Many of the literary works mentioned in the text are available in English translations.

CRISP, OLGA, and LINDA EDMONDSON, eds. *Civil Rights in Imperial Russia*. New York, 1989.

CURTISS, JOHN S. *Church and State in Russia; the Last Years of the Empire, 1900–1917*. New York, 1940.

DUDGEON, RUTH. "The Forgotten Minority: Women Students in Imperial Russia, 1872–1917," *RH* 9 (1982): 1–26.

EKLOF, BEN. *Russian Peasant Schools: Officialdom, Village Culture, and Popular Pedagogy, 1861–1914*. Berkeley, 1986.

ENGELSTEIN, LAURA. *The Keys to Happiness: Sex and the Search for Modernity in Fin-de-Siècle Russia*. Ithaca, N.Y., 1992.

FRANK, JOSEPH. *Dostoevsky*. 4 vols. to date. Princeton, 1980–1995.

FRANK, STEPHEN P. "Simple Folk, Savage Customs? Youth, Sociability, and the Dynamics of Culture in Rural Russia, 1856–1914," *JSH* 25 (Summer 1992), 711–736.

FRANK, STEPHEN P., and MARK D. STEINBERG, eds. *Cultures in Flux: Lower-Class Values, Practices, and Resistance in Late Imperial Russia*. Princeton, 1994.

FRIERSON, CATHY A. *Peasant Icons: Representations of Rural People in Late Nineteenth Century Russia*. New York, 1993.

GILMAN, RICHARD. *Chekhov's Plays: An Opening into Eternity*. New Haven, 1995.

GRAY, CAMILLA. *The Russian Experiment in Art: 1863–1922*. New York, 1962.

HARE, RICHARD. *Portraits of Russian Personalities between Reform and Revolution*. London, 1959.

HINGLEY, RONALD. *Russian Writers and Society, 1825–1904*. New York, 1967.

JAHN, HUBERTUS F. *Patriotic Culture in Russia during World War I*. Ithaca, N.Y., 1995.

JOHANSON, CHRISTINE. *Women's Struggle for Higher Education in Russia, 1855–1900*. Montreal, 1987.

KOBLITZ, ANN HIBNER. *A Convergence of Lives: Sofia Kovalevskaia, Scientist, Writer, Revolutionary*. New Brunswick, N.J., 1993.

MCREYNOLDS, LOUISE. *The News under Russia's Old Regime: The Development of a Mass-Circulation Press*. Princeton, 1991.

MIRSKY, D. S. *A History of Russian Literature from Its Beginnings to 1900*. New York, 1958. Chs. 6–10.

MOSER, CHARLES A., ed. *The Cambridge History of Russian Literature*. Cambridge, England, 1989. Chs. 6–8.

PROFFER, CARL, and ELLENDEA PROFFER, eds. *The Silver Age of Russian Culture: An Anthology*. Ann Arbor, 1975.

READ, CHRISTOPHER. *Religion, Revolution and the Russian Intelligentsia, 1900–1912: The Vekhi Debate and Its Intellectual Background*. London, 1979.

RIORDAN, JAMES. *Sport in Soviet Society: Development of Sport and Physical Education in Russia and the USSR*. Cambridge, England, 1977.

ROSENTHAL, BERNICE GLATZER, and MARTHA BOHACHEVSKY-CHOMIAK, eds. *A Revolution of the Spirit: Crisis of Value in Russia, 1890–1924*. 2nd ed. New York, 1990.

RSH 31 (Winter 1992–1993). The whole issue is devoted to "Nightlife at the Turn of the Century."

RUANE, CHRISTINE. *Gender, Class, and the Professionalization of Russian City Teachers, 1860–1914*. Pittsburgh, 1994.

RUUD, CHARLES A. *Fighting Words: Imperial Censorship and the Russian Press, 1804–1906*. Toronto, 1982.

SCHAPIRO, LEONARD. *Turgenev, His Life and Times*. New York, 1978.

SEREGNY, SCOTT J. *Russian Teachers and Peasant Revolution: The Politics of Education in 1905*. Bloomington, 1989.

SIMMONS, ERNEST J. *Chekhov: A Biography*. Boston, 1962.

———. *Leo Tolstoy*. Boston, 1946.

SINEL, ALLEN. *The Classroom and the Chancellery: State Educational Reform in Russia under Count Dmitry Tolstoy.* Cambridge, Mass., 1973.

SLONIM, MARC. *From Chekhov to the Revolution: Russian Literature, 1900–1917.* New York, 1962.

SPENCER, CHARLES. *The World of Serge Diaghilev.* Chicago, 1974.

STITES, RICHARD. *Russian Popular Culture: Entertainment and Society since 1900.* Cambridge, England, 1992. Ch. 1.

VALKENIER, ELIZABETH. *Ilya Repin and the World of Russian Art.* New York, 1990.

———. *Russian Realist Art: The State and Society: The Peredvizhniki and Their Tradition.* Ann Arbor, 1977.

WEISS, PEG. *Kandinsky and Old Russia: The Artist as Ethnographer and Shaman.* New Haven, 1995.

YARMOLINSKY, AVRAHM. *Turgenev, the Man, His Art and His Age.* New York, 1959.

PART TWO

Russia and the Soviet Union, 1917–1991

In 1917, eight months after the collapse of the Romanov dynasty, a Marxist-Leninist government under Vladimir Lenin seized power in Petrograd. After several years of civil war, it ruled over most of the former Russian Empire. In many ways, the new state continued the centuries-old Russian imperial tradition.

Despite inaugurating a New Economic Policy (NEP) in 1921, which lessened Communist controls, the Soviet government did not cease repression. Joseph Stalin increased it after gradually emerging as the new Soviet leader following Lenin's death in 1924. In 1928, Stalin brought NEP to an end and began a "revolution from above." Tapping both the revolutionary enthusiasm of those tired of NEP's ideological compromises and the mundane career interests of party members, Stalin collectivized agriculture and established a command (or planned) economy.

By the early 1930s, Stalin's statist policies were crushing much of the earlier revolutionary utopianism. In various spheres from the economy to family policy and the treatment of women, revolutionary ideas were replaced by policies intended to strengthen Stalin's rule. Stalin killed many of the earlier ardent Communists, replacing them with younger, more career-minded party members.

Even more than its tsarist predecessor, the Communist party-government propagated certain ideas that strengthened its control over the population. For example, it exploited the masses' longtime resentment of the upper classes, and it taught that the party would have to lead the fight to overcome class enemies and "capitalist encirclement" before a golden age of Communist equality and justice could begin.

This vision of a golden age, of "paradise" on earth as Leon Trotsky

163

promised in 1918, inspired some Soviet citizens to religious-like enthusiasm for the new order. To further such allegiance and solidify the bond between the Soviet government and people, Soviet leaders created new rituals. Stalin, who had once studied to be a priest, created a cult of Lenin and later of himself, and Stalin and his successors attempted to capitalize on the deep emotions generated by the Soviet population's heroism and suffering during World War II. By words, rituals, and symbols, including innumerable war memorials, the party-government stressed its unity with the peoples of the USSR in overcoming the century's greatest threat to their existence.

These attempts to solidify support for the party-government were not necessarily cases of cynical party manipulation. Most party leaders genuinely believed in the superiority of the Communist system. One such believer was Nikita Khrushchev, the man who succeeded Stalin as party leader in 1953. In 1956, Khrushchev criticized Stalin for perverting Leninism and charged the dead dictator with various crimes—Stalin had indeed killed millions of innocent people. Khrushchev also freed millions from the forced-labor camps where Stalin had placed them.

Yet both Khrushchev and his more cautious successor, Leonid Brezhnev, party chief from 1964 to 1982, attempted to maintain party control over society. Despite some minor tinkering, the party also retained the command structure over the economy that Stalin had instituted: Businesses remained state-owned and the state,

Like countless streets and squares in the Soviet period, this square in Baku was named after Lenin, whose 37-foot statue was erected on it in front of the massive Government House.

This gigantic statue in Kiev is one of the many Soviet-era memorials to World War II. Brezhnev, who especially furthered the remembrance of the war, presided at the opening of the memorial in 1981.
(From Goff, Richard, et al. The Twentieth Century: A Brief Global History. *4th ed. New York, McGraw-Hill, 1994, p. 271.)*

not market demand, decided what goods were produced and in what quantities. In the late 1970s and early 1980s, the economy stagnated and was increasingly unable to meet consumers' rising expectations.

Soviet foreign policy reflected both Marxist-Leninist and traditional Russian geopolitical influences. As a result of its victories in World War II, the Soviet Union gained additional territory, so that after the war it equaled the approximate size of the Russian Empire before World War I. It also controlled a bloc of Eastern European countries that became Soviet satellites. For four decades stretching from the late 1940s on, it was engaged in a Cold War with the United States and other Western powers. Crises and confrontations alternated with periods of limited cooperation, but the underlying hostility remained.

Despite the party's attempt to control Soviet life, opposition to government policies never completely died out. This opposition took many forms, but sullen, though muted, noncooperation and low-risk violations of the law (such as minor black marketeering) were more common than the open dissent of the late 1960s and early 1970s.

After Mikhail Gorbachev came to power in 1985, he attempted to reduce hostility to the government and to recharge and restructure the Soviet economy and society. His challenge was similar to that faced by the last tsars: To remain a great power, the country needed to modernize its economy, yet such a modernization threatened to destabilize the existing political system. In a series of dramatic moves, Gorbachev loosened government controls over Soviet life. He also ended the Cold War, hoping such a step would free up money for investing in the civilian economy. He could not control the reform process he had started, however, partly because his approach abandoned the heavy reliance on state-coercion that had characterized the Soviet system from the beginning.

Sensing less risk, opponents to Gorbachev quickly multiplied. Some thought he was moving too fast, others not fast enough. In the non-Russian republics, calls for autonomy and then independence threatened to rip the USSR apart. Long-standing grievances over decades of party privileges and oppression now combined with growing impatience and dissatisfaction with Gorbachev's economic policies.

In 1990 and 1991, most people's standard of living declined. So too did the already sinking reputations of the Communist party and of Gorbachev, who served as both government and party head until resigning the latter position in late August 1991. Ethnic nationalism grew stronger, inspired by the overthrow of Communist leaders and Soviet hegemony in Eastern Europe. Within the Russian republic, Boris Yeltsin, who proclaimed a democratic approach, was elected president of the republic. In early December 1991, along with leaders from the Ukrainian and Belorussian republics, he declared the Soviet Union dissolved. On Christmas day, Gorbachev, now without a country to rule, resigned as Soviet president. The red hammer-and-sickle Soviet flag came down over the Kremlin, replaced by the white, blue, and red Russian flag. Thus ended the Soviet period of Russian history.

CHAPTER 8

The 1917 Revolutions

In 1917, two revolutions occurred in Russia. The first, in March, overthrew Tsar Nicholas II and established a Provisional Government. The second, in November,[1] brought the Bolsheviks (called Communists after March 1918) to power.

Even before the war, modernizing demands and economic, social, and cultural developments had eroded the foundations of the old autocratic order. World War I set off tremors that further weakened support for the ancient royal house, and Nicholas II lacked the strength, flexibility, and wisdom to maintain it in such perilous times.

After his fall, the Provisional Government's powers were restricted by the Petrograd Soviet, an institution representing workers, soldiers, and leftist intellectuals. The new government was crippled by its own efforts to continue the increasingly unpopular war it had inherited. Despite several changes in its composition and the eventual inclusion of Menshevik and Socialist Revolutionary deputies, the Provisional Government was unable to remain in power until a Constituent Assembly could decide on a new government. Even before elections for such an assembly could be held, the Bolsheviks, working through the Petrograd and other soviets, seized power.

The Bolshevik success was due to fortuitous circumstances, their own successful tactics and political platform, and the failures of the Provisional Government and the parties who participated in it. After returning from Switzerland in April 1917, the Bolshevik leader Lenin preached his own brand of Marxism, and the popularity of his party, despite an occasional setback, gradually increased. This heightened popularity owed a great deal to the Bolsheviks' slogans and promise of "Peace, Land, and Bread" and "All Power to the Soviets" and to their ability to capitalize on class antagonisms. The Bolsheviks also

---

[1]Although Russia retained the Old Style dates of the Julian calendar until 1918, the New Style dates of the Western Gregorian calendar (thirteen days ahead of the Old Style) henceforth are used in this text. Hence, the March and November (not February and October) revolutions.

benefited from the failure of the masses to understand that Lenin and his party were much less democratic than they claimed and that many of their true aims differed from those of the masses. Only in the years 1918–1921 did this become more evident. Meanwhile, by November 1917, the Bolsheviks and their Left Socialist Revolutionary allies were able to dominate the Second All-Russian Congress of Soviets, which gave its blessing to the Bolshevik takeover and a new government with Lenin at its head.

THE MARCH REVOLUTION AND THE FALL OF THE ROMANOVS

In the winter of 1916–1917, conditions worsened for Petrograd's lower classes. Their wages lagged further behind accelerating inflation, and especially harsh weather exacerbated fuel and food shortages. Many workers believed that the government and educated society were indifferent to their worsening fate, and some struck for higher wages.

On March 8, International Women's Day, women textile workers in Petrograd's Vyborg District joined those already on strike and poured into the streets demanding more bread. Other Petrograd workers soon joined them, and within two days more than 200,000 strikers brought everyday life to a standstill.

After being informed of mounting chaos in the capital, Nicholas II telegraphed from army staff headquarters at Mogilev that order should be restored. Fearful that the Duma also opposed him, he demanded its adjournment. The city's military commander then ordered police and troops to disperse demonstrators, firing upon them if necessary. But after some shooting, the key turning point occurred on March 11–12: Soldiers in one regiment after another refused to comply with orders and instead joined the demonstrators.

On March 12, two other important events occurred. Some members of the Duma, defying the tsar, formed a Provisional Committee in an attempt to help control events. And, fearing the committee's upper-class bias, socialists looked back to the example of 1905 and held an organizational meeting for a Petrograd Soviet of Workers' Deputies.

The following day Nicholas II attempted to return to his Tsarskoe Selo estate, near the capital, but hostile troops prevented this. Nicholas then decided to go to Pskov, where the Northern Front headquarters was located. He arrived there on March 14, and the following day he met with two representatives (A. Guchkov and V. Shulgin) of the Provisional Committee. By now it was considering itself a Provisional Government and empowered Guchkov and Shulgin to request Nicholas's abdication in favor of his son, Alexei. Such a move, it hoped, would stem the spreading anarchy and provide some continuity.

Meanwhile, Nicholas's generals had convinced him that the interests of Russia and its war effort demanded his abdication, and on March 15 he signed an abdication manifesto. It indicated, however, that the royal throne should pass to his brother Mikhail and not to the young (and hemophiliac) Alexei, whom the tsar feared would be separated from him.

Back in the capital, hostility to the monarchy continued to grow, and the two-headed eagle and other imperial symbols were ripped down. Fearful of growing opposition to any monarch and afraid that Mikhail would prove less popular than the young Alexei, the Provisional Government persuaded Mikhail to renounce the crown unless it was later offered to him by a Constituent Assembly. On March 17, the public was informed of the collapse of the Romanov Dynasty. After more than three centuries, it fell with surprising ease and relatively little bloodshed.

DUAL POWER

From mid-March to early November, two centers of power resided in the capital: the Provisional Government and the Petrograd Soviet. The new government consisted primarily of moderates with only one socialist in its cabinet, the minister of justice, Alexander Kerensky. Prince G. Lvov, a rich landowner

FIGURE 8.1.
Women demonstrate on Petrograd's Nevsky Prospect shortly after the establishment of a Provisional Government. Their banner reads "Comrade Workers and Soldiers, Support Our Demands."
(Sovfoto.)

and head of the Union of Zemstvos, became the new prime minister and minister of interior. Industrialist leaders of the War Industries Committees, formed to help the war effort, were well represented in the cabinet: Alexander Guchkov became minister of war; Alexander Konovalov, minister of trade and industry; and M. I. Tereshchenko, minister of finance. From the beginning, Prince Lvov exercised little leadership, and Foreign Minister Miliukov and Justice Minister Kerensky became the cabinet's most dominant personalities.

Although Miliukov represented the desires of many of his moderate cabinet colleagues to contain the revolution and keep it out of extremist hands, Kerensky adopted a much more militant posture. A radical lawyer who was born in the same Volga town (Simbirsk) as Lenin, Kerensky had earned a reputation as a fiery orator and Duma politician. He was the only cabinet member who was also a member of the Petrograd Soviet. In fact, Kerensky had played a leading role in the Soviet's formation and remained a member of the Executive Committee that led it. Composed primarily of socialist intellectuals, this committee had banned Soviet participation in the new *bourgeois* government, but Kerensky gained an exemption.

Both the Petrograd Soviet and its Executive Committee were fluid bodies, reflecting the spontaneity of the times and, so they believed, the will of the masses. The Soviet almost immediately became the Soviet of Workers' and Soldiers' Deputies, with military units joining factories and shops in choosing delegates to the Soviet. By the fourth week of March, it numbered some 3,000 deputies, more than two-thirds of them soldiers. At first, it met in the same Tauride Palace as did the Provisional Government, although the latter soon transferred its operations to the Marinskii Palace and later the Winter Palace, whereas the Soviet eventually moved to the Smolny Institute.

The Soviet's Executive Committee also expanded. It continued to be dominated by socialist intellectuals, mainly Mensheviks and Socialist Revolutionaries and mainly self-appointed or selected by their socialist party or faction. During April, it added some delegates elected from within the larger Petrograd Soviet and others from the many soviets that had sprung up outside the capital, especially in large cities and military units. The latter addition transformed the body into an All-Russian Executive Committee of an All-Russian Soviet of Workers' and Soldiers' Deputies. As the Executive Committee ballooned to more than seventy members, some of its day-to-day functions were assumed by a "bureau" of committee members.

Although the Soviet (including its Executive Committee) distrusted the "capitalist" Provisional Government and issued certain orders, its leaders did not wish to assume formal power. Some were influenced by the Marxist view of history, which held that a country could not initiate a socialist stage until it had first undergone a capitalist one. In their eyes, Russia had just overthrown a feudal order, and a lengthy capitalist period would have to ensue before the newly born capitalist government could be replaced by a socialist one. On a more practical level, as the socialist N. N. Sukhanov later explained, the far Left was then structurally too weak to rule a war-devastated Russia successfully or to lead the country to peace. He thought that any socialist attempt to seize power would lead to the crushing of the "democratic movement."

Yet while shunning the responsibilities of government, Soviet leaders were unwilling to grant the distrusted Provisional Government a free hand. On March 14–15, they won its agreement to abide by an eight-point program. It included an amnesty for political prisoners, abolishing the old police and provincial government system, full civil liberties (to be enjoyed by off-duty soldiers as well as other citizens), a promise not to send Petrograd's revolutionary military units to the front, and the speedy preparation of democratic elections to a Constituent Assembly, which was to decide Russia's future form of government.

Many of these points were ones that the new government's leadership was sympathetic to, but another initiative of Soviet leaders on March 14 caused more friction. This was the infamous Order Number One, which they issued to Petrograd soldiers. It reflected the Soviet's distrust of officers (suspected of having upper-class sympathies) and called on military units to elect sovietlike committees that would exercise control over all weapons. For political guidance, these committees were to look to the Petrograd Soviet, in which they would be represented and which reserved for itself the right to reverse any military orders of the Provisional Government.

The new minister of war, Guchkov, was dismayed by Order Number One, whose effects were soon felt throughout Russian military units. In late March, he complained that troops and real power were in the hands of the Petrograd Soviet and not the Provisional Government.

LENIN'S RETURN AND LENINISM

While the dramatic events of March 1917 were occurring, the Bolshevik leader, forty-six-year-old Vladimir Lenin, was still living in Switzerland. Because he considered World War I a capitalist-imperialist war that workers should not be fighting, German authorities, hoping he would spread that message in Russia, allowed him to cross Germany to return to his homeland. On the night of April 16, along with a number of other prominent Bolsheviks, he arrived at Petrograd's Finland Station.

Before his return, the Bolsheviks had not been in the forefront of revolutionary leadership. Although lower-rank Bolshevik activists had played some role in the March revolution, it contained many spontaneous elements, and the Menshevik and Socialist Revolutionary (SR) leaders were more prominent in the Petrograd Soviet than were any Bolsheviks. Besides Lenin and his fellow European exiles, several other prominent Bolsheviks, most notably Joseph Stalin and Lev Kamenev, were also in exile until they returned from Siberia about three weeks before Lenin's arrival.

Lenin was welcomed at the Finland Station by revolutionary music (the French "Marseillaise"), Bolshevik supporters, and the head of the Petrograd Soviet, the Georgian Menshevik Nikolai Chkheidze. Chkheidze expressed the hope that Lenin would cooperate with other socialists and help defend the revolution against internal and external threats. (Soviet leaders justified their support of the war effort by now seeing it as a defense of the revolution against

Germany and by persuading the Provisional Government to renounce any annexation intentions.) In speeches that night and the next day (April 17), Lenin proclaimed his own agenda. It opposed the Soviet's policy of "revolutionary defensist" support for the ongoing war and guarded support for the Provisional Government.

On April 17, Lenin also called for the establishment of a republic of Soviets of Workers', Agricultural Laborers', and Peasants' Deputies; "confiscation of all landed estates" and the nationalization of all lands; Soviet government control over banking, production, and distribution; and "abolition of the police, the army and the bureaucracy" coupled with the "arming of the whole people"; the changing of his party's name to the Communist party; and the creation of a new International of Marxist parties.

These "theses" reveal a further development of Lenin's Marxism. Besides his belief in party dominance by revolutionary intelligentsia like himself (see Chapter 3), Lenin by now had worked out additional modifications to Marx's ideas. The most important of these dealt with imperialism as the last stage of

---

Lenin's April Theses

Lenin's remarks of April 17, printed in the Bolshevik paper three days later, are referred to as his April Theses. Thesis 1 and part of 2 are excerpted here. They reveal well Lenin's hostility to capitalism and the bourgeoisie and his belief that World War I was motivated by capitalist interests. The excerpt is taken from V. I. Lenin, *Collected Works* (Moscow, 1964), Vol. XXIV, pp. 21–22.

1. In our attitude towards the war, which under the new government of Lvov and Co. unquestionably remains on Russia's part a predatory imperialist war owing to the capitalist nature of that government, not the slightest concession to "revolutionary defencism" is permissible.

The class-conscious proletariat can give its consent to a revolutionary war, which would really justify revolutionary defencism, only on condition: (a) that the power pass to the proletariat and the poorest sections of the peasants aligned with the proletariat; (b) that all annexations be renounced in deed and not in word; (c) that a complete break be effected in actual fact with all capitalist interests.

In view of the undoubted honesty of those broad sections of the mass believers in revolutionary defencism who accept the war only as a necessity, and not as a means of conquest, in view of the fact that they are being deceived by the bourgeoisie, it is necessary with particular thoroughness, persistence and patience to explain their error to them, to explain the inseparable connection existing between capital and the imperialist war, and to prove that without overthrowing capital *it is impossible* to end the war by a truly democratic peace, a peace not imposed by violence.

The most widespread campaign for this view must be organized in the army at the front.

Fraternisation.

2. The specific feature of the present situation in Russia is that the country is *passing* from the first stage of the revolution—which, owing to the insufficient class-consciousness and organisation of the proletariat, placed power in the hands of the bourgeoisie—to its *second* stage, which must place power in the hands of the proletariat and the poorest sections of the peasants.

capitalism, the role of the peasants, the nature of Russia's revolution and its relationship to worldwide revolution, and, finally, Russia's nationalities issue.

Lenin's modifications were strongly influenced by two facts: Global conditions had changed considerably since Marx's death in 1883, and the Russian Empire was more "backward" than the advanced capitalist countries that had been Marx's primary concern. Moreover, Lenin did not think of Marxism as cast-iron dogma but as a guide to action. His flexible approach was further aided by his enthusiasm for Marxian dialectics. This was the theory that history progresses through the conflict of a series of apparent opposites (thesis and antithesis) that are united in a higher synthesis, which, in turn, becomes a new thesis, which gives birth to a new antithesis, and so on throughout history—or at least until the final Communist stage is reached. Such a theory allowed considerable room for zigzagging through the political minefields of the day.

Imperialism: The Last Stage of Capitalism

Like Lenin's concept of the party, his thoughts on imperialism were partly a response, although somewhat belatedly, to Bernstein's revisionism (see Chapter 3). The basis of this German Marxist's ideas was the belief that the proletariat's condition was not deteriorating, and therefore revolution was unlikely. By 1915–1916, when Lenin wrote *Imperialism: The Highest Stage of Capitalism*, he was also ready to admit that the condition of the Western proletariat had not deteriorated as Marx had predicted. In Lenin's eyes, Marx was not wrong in predicting a cataclysmic collapse of capitalism; his timetable was just off. The tremendous development of imperialism since the death of Marx had extended the life of capitalism, but, Lenin thought, it would still die a violent death.

Relying on sources such as the Englishman John Hobson, Lenin argued that imperialism's spread brought great profits to the major imperialistic powers and enabled them "to bribe certain sections of the workers . . . and win them to the side of the bourgeoisie." Imperialism, however, the "monopoly stage of capitalism" as Lenin called it, carried within itself seeds of self-destruction: As imperialistic rivalries increased, so too would militarism, wars, and discontent among peoples. This was exactly what Lenin thought was occurring during World War I, a war he referred to as "a war between the biggest slave-holders for the maintenance and consolidation of slavery." From the ashes of this war, he believed, socialism could arise triumphant.

Revolutionary Role for Peasants

Another Leninist addition to Marxism was to expand greatly the revolutionary role of at least some peasants. Although Marx had acknowledged that Russian peasants might play a positive role, he generally distrusted peasants' conservative instincts and once wrote of peasants as "the class that represents barbarism within civilization." Focusing primarily on the capitalist countries of the West, Marx paid little attention to the peasants.

Lenin, however, was primarily concerned with the Russian Empire. In it, four out of five people were still peasants, and, by 1914, only one out of fifty subjects was a proletarian. By 1917, Lenin had concluded that under the firm guidance of the party, at least the poorer peasants could play a major revolutionary role, although not equal to the proletariat. By this time, Lenin had also begun to speak more of the needs of the "masses," or "poorest masses," rather than just those of the proletariat.

Two-Stage Revolution

In his April Theses, Lenin wrote of a two-stage Russian revolution. In the first, the bourgeoisie gained power; in the second, the proletariat and poor peasants were to take it from them. In a "Farewell Letter to Swiss Workers," written just before the April Theses, Lenin noted that the revolution in Russia could be "the *prologue* to the world socialist revolution."

Although Lenin has sometimes been accused of opportunistically adopting Trotsky's earlier idea of "permanent revolution," Neil Harding has convincingly argued otherwise. According to him, World War I transformed Lenin's thinking, and the stance he took in 1917 followed from this revised viewpoint. Although he had earlier accepted the classic Marxist belief that a substantial period of time would separate the bourgeois and proletarian revolutions, the war convinced him that "the epoch of capitalist imperialism is one of ripe and rotten-ripe capitalism which is about to collapse, and which is mature enough to make way for Socialism."

Because Lenin thought Russia was the weakest link in the capitalist-imperialist chain, he believed that the establishment in Russia of a dictatorship of the proletariat and poor peasants could be the spark for European socialist revolutions. Once such revolutions were successful in Europe, the new socialist governments there could assist the Russians in establishing the productive forces (such as technology) necessary to complete the economic foundation for establishing socialism in Russia.

As with many other Leninist modifications of Marx's thought, this one also had some basis in Marx's varied writings. Although Marx generally believed that decades would separate the capitalist and proletarian revolutions, on a few occasions he was tempted to believe that the two could occur back-to-back. For example, during the revolutionary days of 1848, he stated in *The Communist Manifesto* that "the bourgeois revolution in Germany will be but the prelude to an immediately following proletarian revolution." In a preface to a Russian edition of *The Communist Manifesto*, written shortly before his death, he wrote: "If the Russian Revolution becomes the signal for a proletarian revolution in the West, so that both complement each other, the present Russian common ownership of land may serve as the starting-point for a communist development."

Nationalities Issue

Lenin's concern with the multinational Russian Empire necessitated still another Marxist modification, that regarding the nationalities question. Marx had been quite critical of nationalism, viewing it as an impediment to the development of a supranational Communist civilization. In *The Communist Manifesto,* he and Engels wrote that "the workers have no country" and exhorted: "workers of all countries, unite!" Moreover, he had little understanding of the complex relations of the nationalities of Eastern Europe and Russia.

Before World War I, Lenin criticized Great Russian chauvinism. He and his party also publicly recognized the right of minority nationalities to self-determination, even to seceding from the Russian Empire. In November 1917, the new Bolshevik government would reiterate these rights in a "Declaration of the Rights of the Peoples of Russia."

There was, however, a catch. If the right of secession clashed with the rights of the proletariat, those of the proletariat were to come first. In addition, as earlier indicated, Lenin believed that his Bolshevik party spoke for the true interests of the workers and was in the best position to interpret them. Further, he believed that there should be only one Marxist party in the Russian Empire, and he had no sympathy for any autonomous Marxist nationality parties. The Bolsheviks were to be a strongly centralized supranational party looking out for the welfare and equal treatment of all nationalities.

In some notes written for a series of Swiss lectures in 1913, Lenin made it clear "that workers who place political unity with 'their own' [nation's] bourgeoisie above complete unity with the proletariat of all nations, are acting against their own interests, against the interests of socialism, and against the interests of democracy." In a pamphlet of the same year containing Bolshevik resolutions on the national question, it was stated that "the right of nations to self-determination . . . must under no circumstances be confused with the expediency of a given nation's secession. The Social-Democratic Party [now dominated by the Bolsheviks] must decide the latter question . . . in conformity with the interests of social development as a whole and with the interests of the proletarian class struggle for socialism."

Thus, the prospect, for example, of Ukrainians, including Ukrainian workers, being able to achieve independence if they wished was not good under any possible Bolshevik government. It would be unlikely that the Bolshevik leaders would regard it as being in the "interests of socialism."

Furthermore, Lenin was opposed to creating any loose federation of nationalities or any "cultural-national autonomy" that would retard the growth of a socialist "international culture." His Marxist views predisposed him to believe that the economics of the day was favorable to the creation of large centralized states that facilitated the growth of proletarian class consciousness. And before circumstances in 1917 forced him into making some concessions, he believed that transforming the Russian Empire into a federation of nationalities would be regressive. Thus, although genuinely opposed to Great Russian chauvinism and the unequal treatment of non-Russian nationalities, Lenin would be no real friend to non-Russian nationalists who desired their nations' separation from the new Soviet state he wished to create.

Although Lenin had supported secessionist movements that he thought would weaken tsarism, he hoped that when socialism was finally victorious in the empire, none of its former nations would choose to leave the new state.

With the granting of full equality to all of the nationalities, including the (theoretical) right of nations to secede, and with the gaining of economic benefits that a new socialist system would bring, Lenin apparently thought (or at least hoped) that no nation would wish to secede. In the meantime, his advocacy of a nation's right to secede could help strengthen the Bolshevik following among discontented nationalities, especially among those who did not examine too closely the Bolshevik's nationality statements.

DEEPENING OF THE REVOLUTION, MAY–SEPTEMBER

While Lenin did what he could to discredit the Provisional Government, the government also undermined its own effectiveness. In early May, Foreign Minister Miliukov angered Soviet leaders by sending out a note assuring Allied Powers that the Russian government shared their war aims and determination to fight until victory was achieved. It seemed contrary to the Soviet campaign for a nonimperialist peace and to the government's promise not to seek other nations' territories. It appeared as if Miliukov still intended to hold the Allies to their promise of rewarding Russia with Constantinople and the Turkish Straits.

The note triggered street demonstrations and, shortly thereafter, the resignation of Miliukov and War Minister Guchkov, followed (on May 18) by the formation of a new cabinet. This first Coalition Government included six socialist ministers. Prince Lvov remained as prime minister. Kerensky became minister of war. SR leader Victor Chernov became minister of agriculture. Two Mensheviks took over as minister of post and telegraph and as minister of labor.

Lenin opposed the new coalition just as he had the previous cabinet. But the First All-Russian Congress of Soviets, which convened for three weeks beginning on June 16, rejected Lenin's call for "All Power to the Soviets" and voted to support the new government. Although Lenin's slogan of "Peace, Land, and Bread" was beginning to win converts among workers and soldiers, the Mensheviks and SRs still continued to dominate the soviets. Delegates from these two parties together totaled about five times the number of Bolshevik delegates at the congress.

Yet by participating in successive coalition governments, which pursued unpopular policies and proved incapable of successful rule, the Mensheviks and SRs soon undermined their own popularity among the masses. The government's continued support of the war proved especially costly. In early July, Kerensky launched an unsuccessful offensive along the Austrian front. On July 16, soldiers of a Petrograd Machine Gun Regiment, fearful of being sent to the front, helped incite large demonstrations of soldiers and workers in the capital. The demonstrations swelled, reaching their peak on July 17. Demonstrators demanded that the Soviet take power, but the Menshevik and SR leaders, who still dominated its Executive Committee, refused. Although lower-ranking Bolsheviks were involved in the disturbances, Lenin and other top Bolsheviks were ambivalent about them, fearing they might backfire, and endorsed them only after they had already begun.

Bolshevik fears proved justified. After regaining control of the streets, the government made the Bolsheviks a convenient target for its countermeasures. It released documents allegedly demonstrating that the Bolsheviks received large sums from Germany and that Lenin was a German agent. Although the first charge was true, this did not make Lenin a "German agent." He was pursuing his own agenda, which sometimes coincided and sometimes contradicted that of Imperial Germany. Nevertheless, the charges damaged Bolshevik prestige and helped the government regain control of the streets, which they did on July 18. A disguised Lenin soon fled the capital, while many other Bolsheviks were arrested.

Just before the July demonstrations, four Kadet ministers had resigned from the government because socialists in the cabinet had agreed to Ukrainian demands for autonomy. This and other cabinet disagreements soon led to Prime Minister Lvov's resignation and, in late July, his replacement by Kerensky. In early August, Kerensky formed a new cabinet dominated by Mensheviks and SRs.

Even before the cabinet was formed, Kerensky had named General L. G. Kornilov, the son of a Siberian Cossack, as the new commander-in-chief of the army. Still in his late forties, Kornilov had earned a reputation as a brave and forceful leader. Contemptuous of the Soviet and of Lenin for harming the war effort, he now urged Kerensky to allow him to take strong measures to restore military discipline and put an end to rising desertions. In late August, he was greeted like a hero by many of Russia's upper-class elements at a Moscow State Conference called by Kerensky to rally support behind his policies. Although all shades of political opinion were supposed to be represented at the conference, the Bolsheviks boycotted it, and conservative and moderate elements supportive of "law and order" were most dominant. They included many Kadets who, during 1917, had moved from the left-center to the right-center of the political spectrum.

The conference, plus the fall of Riga to the Germans at the beginning of September, encouraged Kerensky and Kornilov to act. A confusing series of events followed, with the motivations of both men still not entirely clear. Kerensky asked Kornilov, who agreed, to send troops to Petrograd to help impose martial law and defend against a possible Bolshevik insurrection—unknown to Kerensky, Kornilov had already dispatched some troops closer to the capital. But less than a week later, largely as a result of the miscommunications of an intermediary and Kerensky's fears that Kornilov wished to unseat him and assume dictatorial powers, Kerensky dismissed Kornilov and, hours later, charged him with treason.

On September 9, Kornilov refused to resign and appealed to military commanders for their support, promising to lead the country to victory and the convening of a Constituent Assembly. Kerensky now veered to the Left and called upon supporters of democracy to save the revolution. He released many who had been jailed after the July demonstrations and armed the workers, including Bolshevik supporters. Fearful of a military coup and a counterrevolution, railway, telegraph, and other workers joined with many soldiers to protect Petrograd and dissuade and prevent Kornilov's troops from reaching the capital. The Kornilov rebellion was not cut down but melted away before ever reaching Petrograd. In mid-September, Kornilov was arrested.

The group helped most by Kornilov's failure was the Bolsheviks. In factory committees, unions, soviets, and local government organs, they now increased their numbers. Already by late September, they had obtained a majority in the Petrograd Soviet.

THE BOLSHEVIKS, CLASSES, AND NATIONALITIES

Crucial to the Bolsheviks' success was the support of workers. From mid-March until mid-May, workers won substantial gains from the Provisional Government and from commercial-industrial leaders. Worker and soviet pres-

FIGURE 8.2.
The Smolny Institute, earlier a school for noblewomen, became in 1917 the headquarters of the Petrograd Soviet and, for a few months after the November revolution, of Lenin's government. *(Sovfoto.)*

sure, plus the progressive views of industrialists such as Minister of Trade and Industry Alexander Konovalov, was especially influential in getting business leaders to agree to concessions. In Petrograd, factory and mill owners agreed to increase wages, approve an eight-hour day, and allow the establishment of factory committees. Other employers in Petrograd and elsewhere soon made similar concessions. In early May, the government recognized the right of factory committees to represent workers' interests in both private and state-owned industries. The conciliatory policy favored by Konovalov whetted the workers' appetite for more concessions, however, and by the end of May, when he resigned his cabinet position, strife between workers and employers was increasing.

As late spring turned into summer, Russia's economic problems grew worse: Coal, metals, and other resources became harder to obtain, and inflation spiraled upward. In such a climate, business leaders became increasingly resentful of growing wage and workplace demands and the power of factory committees. Moreover, the new coalition government of mid-May, with its six socialist ministers, increased the capitalists' sense of persecution. The government crackdown during the July days gave industrialists some hope, and some were encouraged by and supportive of Kornilov's desire to restore military discipline and curb the soviets. But the strengthening of the Left, following his failed attempt to take control of Petrograd, heightened owners' sense of alarm, and they attempted to roll back some of the growing powers assumed by factory committees.

The workers were also dissatisfied. Their wages were not keeping up with inflation; their jobs were often insecure; and their bosses frequently resisted implementing new workplace concessions.

The increasing polarization between employers and employees was evidenced not only in the factories, but also many lower-level white-collar workers organized, battled for gains, and sometimes struck. Postal and telegraph workers, office workers, sales clerks, cashiers, bookkeepers, and others demanded better treatment than they had received in tsarist Russia. Like factory workers, these employees often viewed their struggles in class terms: Some called themselves proletarians; a congress of postal and telegraph workers voted to abolish ranks, distinctions, and privileges among employees. Egalitarianism had a strong appeal in 1917, both in the cities and in the countryside. After relatively little strike activity in the spring, the number of strikes increased in the summer and even more so in the fall.

Although trade unions representing different crafts and occupations proliferated, factory and workplace committees, cutting across different trades, were most militant in 1917. Within them, the Bolsheviks were most successful. Already in June, the Bolsheviks dominated the First Conference of Petrograd Factory Committees, which called for workers' control over factory management. When an all-Russian conference of factory committees met about a week before the November revolution, 96 of 167 delegates were Bolsheviks.

Also vital to the Bolshevik success was the support of soldiers. Order Number One (March 14, 1917) led to the formation of soldiers' committees and more respectful treatment of enlisted men by their officers. Although the soldiers did not immediately desert the war effort, many backed the Soviet's call for a negotiated peace based on "no annexations and indemnities." As the year progressed, however, many soldiers abandoned this "defensist" position and became increasingly disillusioned with the Provisional Government and moderate socialists who supported war efforts. Miliukov's May note, Kerensky's July offensive, and Kornilov's attempts to restore military discipline and fight on to victory all helped the Bolsheviks win over growing numbers of soldiers to their call for an end to the "capitalist-imperialist war." In 1917, as Lenin later said, many soldiers voted for peace with their feet, as more than 1 million troops deserted the front.

Because most soldiers were peasants, many of them supported the Bolsheviks' call for peasant land seizures. Such seizures from state, noble, and even some independent peasant lands were often approved by village assemblies and committees operating under a variety of names, including "village soviet." As central government authority broke down in the countryside between March and November, the peasant commune and its members became the chief centers of local power. Although peasant disturbances slackened during periods of heavy agricultural labor, both disturbances and demands generally escalated from March to November.

Peasant turmoil was most prevalent in Russia's Central Black-Earth region and along the middle Volga. Although peasant actions varied from region to region, they included restricting landowners' access to hired (and prisoner-of-war) labor; reducing or ceasing payments for rented land; seizing equipment and crops; and asserting peasant rights to private or state-owned meadow, pasture, and timber lands. Although peasants engaged in some wanton violence and destruction and some who opposed peasant actions were killed, the peasants did not generally lust for blood.

In the countryside before 1917, the SRs were far more popular than the Bolsheviks and had been the first to advocate abolishing private landed property and turning it over to the peasants who worked it. Despite the participation of some SRs in a Provisional Government that insisted that any major land reform should await the convening of a Constituent Assembly, the SRs continued to have more support in the villages than did the Bolsheviks. Village peasants were slower to change and more distrustful of outsiders than were their fellow peasants in the army. Yet neither the SRs nor the Bolsheviks directed the peasants. Like many other social and national groups, the peasants acted mainly on their own. In dealing with the entire period 1917–1921, Christopher Read perhaps exaggerates when he states that "every social group, every nationality, every region, every town, every village, had its own revolution,"[2] but his statement contains much truth.

For their part, the Bolsheviks benefited from much of this turbulence. For example, village opposition to government policies and private landed interests helped reduce food and fuel supplies to the cities, thus further radicalizing urban opposition and undercutting the Provisional Government.

---

[2]*From Tsar to Soviets: The Russian People and Their Revolution, 1917–21* (New York, 1996), p. 1.

In Russian provincial capitals and in non-Russian areas of the empire, the Bolsheviks gained increasing support in the late summer and early fall of 1917. Liberal forces were generally weak, and moderate Menshevik and SR socialists (who had dominated most provincial soviets in the spring and early summer) lost ground. As class conflict sharpened, the Bolsheviks tarnished the other socialist parties by criticizing them for cooperating with the "capitalist" Provisional Government. Despite this general trend, there were regional variations, and moderate socialists continued dominant in some areas.

Among the other failings of the Provisional Government was its failure to spell out any appealing and coherent nationality policy. Such a policy was needed to satisfy a growing chorus of non-Russian appeals for autonomy or, less commonly, independence. From such areas as Poland, Ukraine, and Finland, such appeals rang out from national groups of varying size and importance. But the government's position was similar to its policy on land: The issue should await the convening of a Constituent Assembly. Although many non-Russian nationalist leaders distrusted the Bolsheviks, Lenin's nationality policy, which recognized the right to national self-determination, did gain the Bolsheviks some backing, or at least cooperation, from many non-Russians.

As Ronald Suny has pointed out, however, nationalist sentiments among the non-Russians were still weakly developed in 1917, frequently not extending much beyond a small number of urban intellectuals and students. More important to many non-Russians was the Bolsheviks' call for peace and its class-based policies dealing with economic, social, and political issues. These issues were especially crucial in the cities, where Russian and other nationalities together sometimes outnumbered the native nationality of a region. The Bolsheviks gained considerable backing from Russian and other ethnic workers and soldiers in multiethnic cities such as Baku. In some places—including Riga, where the dominant Baltic Germans were resented by Latvians—national and class hostilities combined to win converts to the Bolsheviks' promises.

Despite the Bolsheviks' growing popularity among the masses, most professional and upper-class elements continued to oppose Bolshevik ideas. Professors, for example, were almost unanimously antagonistic to the Bolsheviks. Although some writers and artists, such as the poet Maiakovsky, were sympathetic to the Bolsheviks' radical ideas, most intellectuals and the press were unsympathetic or downright hostile to the party of Lenin.

THE NOVEMBER REVOLUTION: THE BOLSHEVIKS COME TO POWER

By early October 1917, the Bolsheviks had gained a majority in both the Petrograd and the Moscow soviets. Leon Trotsky, who had returned to Russia in 1917 and decided to become a Bolshevik, now became the chairman of the Petrograd Soviet.

Late in October, Lenin returned to the capital after temporarily hiding in Finland and immediately called for a takeover of power. Despite the misgivings and hesitancy of some of Lenin's fellow Bolsheviks—especially Lev

Kamenev and Grigori Zinoviev—his urgings moved preparations forward. So too did Trotsky's persuasive and dynamic speeches to Soviet deputies, soldiers, and workers. He was, in Volkogonov's words, "the orator-in-chief of the revolution."

The Second All-Russian Congress of Soviets, which the Bolsheviks expected to control, was scheduled to meet in early November, and Trotsky suggested that it could legitimize a new Bolshevik-dominated government. On November 6, the day before it met, Kerensky inadvertently helped spark the Communist coup by ordering the closing of the Bolshevik press. Troops under the direction of Trotsky and the Petrograd Soviet's Military Revolutionary Committee took up positions to prevent any such "counterrevolutionary" moves and almost immediately assumed the offensive. On November 7, meeting little resistance, they took control of vital buildings in St. Petersburg.

While Kerensky escaped in an automobile and sought loyal troops outside the city, other members of his cabinet remained in the Winter Palace, weakly defended by cadets and a women's battalion. The palace takeover in the early morning hours of November 8, after surprisingly little bloodshed, completed the coup.

During the seizure of the Winter Palace, the Second All-Russian Congress of Soviets had begun its deliberations in the Smolny Institute. Deputies of the Mensheviks and many of the moderate SRs strongly objected to the coup, but

FIGURE 8.3.
The Cruiser Aurora. On the night of November 7, 1917, it fired on the Winter Palace as part of the Bolshevik takeover.

they were outnumbered by the Bolsheviks and their Left SR allies. Finally, in frustration, they stormed out in protest. Trotsky mocked those who left: "You are bankrupt. Your role is played out. Go where you belong: into the dustbin of history."

Shortly after this, in the early morning hours of November 8, A. Lunacharsky, soon to be named commissar of enlightenment, read to the remaining delegates a manifesto written by Lenin. It proclaimed that the Congress of Soviets would be assuming governmental powers from the deposed Provisional Government; that it would propose a democratic peace to all nations; oversee the transfer of landlord, imperial, and monastery land to peasant committees; establish workers' control over production; secure the right to self-determination to all nationalities of the country; and ensure the convocation of the Constituent Assembly. The reading was frequently interrupted by bursts of applause, before being finally approved overwhelmingly by the hundreds of remaining deputies.

Later that night, Lenin presented a Decree on Peace. In it he proclaimed "we have overthrown the government of the bankers," and he reiterated his call for an immediate armistice. Shortly thereafter, he introduced a Decree on Land, which mirrored an earlier SR position. The decree proposed abolishing all state and private land and making it available to those who worked it. The Congress delegates quickly endorsed both decrees. Then, before adjourning in the early hours of November 9, the Congress approved a new government—to last until the Constituent Assembly met. Lenin was made chairman of a Council of People's Commissars—"commissars" sounded more revolutionary and less bourgeois than "ministers." Among the most significant commissars were Trotsky, who was to oversee foreign affairs, and Stalin, who became commissar of nationalities.

These chief events of this all-night session of November 8–9 were interspersed with many others, and the Smolny scene was more cacophonous than the near unanimous agreement on the three main actions of the night suggests. Deputies and observers from among the leftist intelligentsia, soldiers, peasants, and workers intermingled amidst smoke and the smell of sweat. They argued, listened to speeches and telegrams of support from various regiments, and sang the Internationale as well as a funeral march for those who had died in the revolutionary struggle. They debated who should be arrested and who should be released. And they talked of the coming world revolution and a new age of brotherhood.

ANALYSIS OF THE NOVEMBER REVOLUTION

The Bolsheviks' success in coming to power was due to both their rivals' failures and their own abilities, plus a series of circumstances that favored the Bolsheviks. Chief among them were the unsuccessful war, the breakdown of government authority, class rivalries and suspicions, and peasant land hunger.

From the beginning, Provisional Government authority was checked by the Petrograd Soviet, and the new government was under considerable pressure from Russia's allies to continue its war effort. The Provisional Government, however, and the parties that participated in it—all the major parties except the Bolsheviks—compounded their difficulties by their political ineptness.

Although the government enacted progressive new laws and laid the groundwork for elections to a Constituent Assembly, it also continued an increasingly unpopular war and failed to appease the Russian peasants' demand for more land. On the land question and that of national minorities, the government generally took the position that those were issues to be dealt with in the future, following the convening of a Constituent Assembly. Although such a stand might be defended on democratic and liberal grounds, it satisfied few, distrustful as the masses were of the Provisional Government. This government, many believed, was too representative of upper-class society or the *burzhui*, a contemptuous popular term taken from the French *bourgeois*.

In contrast, the Bolsheviks obeyed a rule that many successful political parties have followed: Promise people what they want—regardless of whether all the promises can or will be fulfilled. The Bolshevik platform of peace, land, bread, and self-determination came closest to satisfying the desires of a majority of the empire's people. The Bolshevik slogan of "All Power to the Soviets" meant excluding the upper classes from sharing power—at least until a Constituent Assembly might decide differently—and this stand also proved popular with the masses. Finally, by working through the soviets and having the Second Congress of Soviets approve the new Bolshevik government, the Bolsheviks were able to cloak the coup in a certain degree of legitimacy.

Although the Bolshevik Party was neither as tightly disciplined nor controlled by Lenin as once thought, there is no denying that its success owed a good deal to his single-minded leadership. Trotsky's role in 1917 was also significant.

In recent years, some Russians have depicted the 1917 Communist revolution as an "anti-Russian" revolution. They point out that Marxism was a "Western" ideology, that many Bolshevik leaders were exiles who had lived in the West for years before 1917, and that many leading Bolsheviks were not ethnic Russians—Trotsky, Zinoviev, and Kamenev, for example, were Jewish; Stalin was Georgian; and Lenin was of mixed ancestry. Such an argument, however, tends to downplay the Bolsheviks' growing support in Russia during 1917 and ignores some of the indigenous reasons for that backing, even if it was based sometimes on falsely placed hopes. The Bolshevik victory in Petrograd and beyond in the years 1917–1921 was not some sort of "foreign" conquest. Although Marxism originated in the West, Lenin adapted it for Russian consumption, and Russian conditions proved favorable enough to enable Communist governments to remain in power for three quarters of a century.

SUGGESTED SOURCES

ABRAHAM, RICHARD. *Alexander Kerensky: The First Love of the Revolution*. New York, 1987.
ACTON, EDWARD. *Rethinking the Russian Revolution*. London, 1990.

ANWEILER, OSKAR. *The Soviets: The Russian Workers, Peasants, and Soldiers Councils, 1905–1921.* New York, 1974.

BASIL, JOHN D. *The Mensheviks in the Revolution of 1917.* Columbus, Ohio, 1984.

BROWDER, ROBERT P., and ALEXANDER F. KERENSKY, eds. *The Russian Provisional Government, 1917: Documents.* 3 vols. Stanford, 1961.

BURDZHALOV, E. N. *Russia's Second Revolution: The February 1917 Uprising in Petrograd.* Bloomington, 1987.

CARR, EDWARD H. *The Bolshevik Revolution, 1917–1923.* 3 vols. New York, 1951–1953.

CHAMBERLIN, WILLIAM H. *The Russian Revolution, 1917–1921.* Vol. 1. New York, 1935.

DANIELS, ROBERT. *Red October: The Bolshevik Revolution of 1917.* New York, 1967.

FERRO, MARC. *October 1917: A Social History of the Russian Revolution.* London, 1980.

———. *The Russian Revolution of February 1917.* Englewood Cliffs, N.J., 1972.

FRANKEL, EDITH ROGOVIN, JONATHAN FRANKEL, and BARUCH KNEI-PAZ, eds. *Revolution in Russia: Reassessments of 1917.* Cambridge, England, 1992.

GALILI, ZIVA. *The Menshevik Leaders in the Russian Revolution: Social Realities and Political Strategies.* Princeton, 1989.

GILL, GRAEME J. *Peasants and Government in the Russian Revolution.* London, 1979.

HARDING, NEIL. *Lenin's Political Thought.* 2 vols. New York, 1977–1981.

HASEGAWA, TSUYOSHI. *The February Revolution: Petrograd, 1917.* Seattle, 1981.

JACKSON, GEORGE D., and ROBERT J. DEVLIN, eds. *Dictionary of the Russian Revolution.* New York, 1989.

KAISER, DANIEL H., ed. *The Workers' Revolution in Russia, 1917: The View from Below.* Cambridge, England, 1987.

KATKOV, GEORGE. *Russia 1917.* 2 vols. London, 1967–1980.

KEEP, JOHN L. H. *The Russian Revolution: A Study in Mass Mobilization.* New York, 1976.

KERENSKY, ALEXANDER. *Russia and History's Turning Point.* New York, 1965.

KOENKER, DIANE. *Moscow Workers and the 1917 Revolution.* Princeton, 1981.

KOENKER, DIANE P., and WILLIAM G. ROSENBERG. *Strikes and Revolution in Russia, 1917.* Princeton, 1989.

MANDEL, DAVID. *The Petrograd Workers and the Fall of the Old Regime: From the February Revolution to the July Days, 1917.* London, 1983.

———. *The Petrograd Workers and the Soviet Seizure of Power: From the July Days, 1917 to July 1918.* London, 1984.

MCCAULEY, MARTIN, ed. *The Russian Revolution and the Soviet State, 1917–1921.* London, 1975.

MOYNAHAN, BRIAN. *Comrades: 1917—Russia in Revolution.* Boston, 1992.

October. A 1927 film of Sergei Eisenstein. Available on videocassette.

ORLOVSKY, DANIEL. "The Lower Middle Strata in Revolutionary Russia." In *Between Tsar and People: Educated Society and the Quest for Public Identity in Late Imperial Russia,* eds. Edith Clowes, Samuel Kassow, and James L. West. Princeton, 1991.

PIPES, RICHARD. *The Russian Revolution.* New York, 1990.

PITCHER, HARVEY. *Witnesses of the Russian Revolution.* London, 1994.

RABINOWITCH, ALEXANDER. *The Bolsheviks Come to Power: The Revolution of 1917 in Petrograd.* New York, 1976.

RALEIGH, DONALD J. *Revolution on the Volga: 1917 in Saratov.* Ithaca, N.Y., 1986.

READ, CHRISTOPHER. *From Tsar to Soviets: The Russian People and Their Revolution, 1917–1921.* New York, 1996.

REED, JOHN. *Ten Days That Shook the World.* New York, 1919.

ROSENBERG, WILLIAM G. *Liberals in the Russian Revolution; The Constitutional Democratic Party, 1917–1921.* Princeton, 1974.

SCHAPIRO, LEONARD. *The Russian Revolutions of 1917: The Origins of Modern Communism.* New York, 1984.

SERVICE, ROBERT. *Lenin: A Political Life.* Vol. 2, *Worlds in Collision.* Bloomington, 1991.

SMITH, S. A. *Red Petrograd: Revolution in the Factories, 1917–1918.* Cambridge, England, 1983.

SUKHANOV, N. N. *The Russian Revolution, 1917: A Personal Record.* New York, 1955.

SUNY, RONALD, and ARTHUR ADAMS, eds. *The Russian Revolution and Bolshevik Victory: Visions and Revisions.* 3d ed. Lexington, Mass., 1990.

THOMPSON, JOHN M. *Revolutionary Russia, 1917.* 2d ed. New York, 1989.

TROTSKY, LEON. *The History of the Russian Revolution.* 3 vols. New York, 1932.

VOLKOGONOV, DMITRI. *Trotsky: The Eternal Revolutionary.* New York, 1996. Ch. 2.

WADE, REX A. *Red Guards and Workers' Militias in the Russian Revolution.* Stanford, 1984.

———. *The Russian Search for Peace, February–October 1917.* Stanford, 1969.

WHITE, JAMES D. *The Russian Revolution, 1917–1921: A Short History.* London, 1994.

WILDMAN, ALLAN K. *The End of the Russian Imperial Army.* 2 vols. Princeton, 1980–1987.

CHAPTER 9

Anti-Bolshevism, Civil War, and Allied Intervention

Although the November revolution brought the Bolsheviks to power in Petrograd, maintaining it there and bringing other areas of the Russian Empire under Communist control was another task. The new government, motivated by both an ideology preaching class warfare and the conditions it found itself in, became increasingly undemocratic and authoritarian. This behavior provoked additional opposition to the Bolsheviks. Thus, from mid-1918 until 1921, civil war raged in Russia. Even before and after this period, however, armed opposition to the Bolsheviks existed, although insufficient in scale to be included in the Civil War parameters.

Many historians have defined the Civil War as a struggle between Bolshevik forces (the Reds) and their main domestic political and military opponents (the Whites). But extensive anti-Bolshevik as well as anti-White opposition also existed among peasants, workers, and non-Russian nationalities, and this too was part of the Civil War. Peasant, worker, and soldier/sailor resistance reached its height in early 1921, after the Whites had already been defeated. Only after the Communists overcame this final major challenge from below could the Civil War really be considered over.

To complicate the already chaotic Civil War further, the Reds also had to contend with the revolt of an anti-Bolshevik Czechoslovak Corps, the military intervention of Allied troops, and a war with Poland. Although the Communists overcame both domestic and outside opposition to win the Civil War, the human and economic costs of it were high, and it bequeathed to the future an authoritarian legacy.

EARLY OPPOSITION, NEW POLICIES, AND CLASS WARFARE

Although full-scale civil war did not break out until 1918, opposition to the Bolshevik government appeared already in the first week after the November revolution. Kerensky succeeded in mobilizing a small Cossack force that reached the outskirts of Petrograd. Within the capital, opposition socialists, Kadets, and other disgruntled elements formed an "All-Russian Committee for the Salvation of the Motherland and the Revolution." It called on the people to withhold support for the new government. Professionals and intellectuals were overwhelmingly against the Bolsheviks; and many white-collar workers, including government employees, refused to work. Military cadets seized some buildings in the capital. But all this opposition was poorly led, was divided, and underestimated the staying power of the Bolshevik government, which scattered, intimidated, or suppressed these original opponents.

Outside Petrograd, it was often more difficult to impose Bolshevik control, and political maneuvering and clashes occurred. In Moscow, opposition forces held off Bolshevik forces in bloody battles for about a week before finally succumbing in mid-November. In a majority of Great Russian cities, Bolshevik-dominated soviets soon ascended to power—in fact, in some urban areas, such as those of the Ivanovo-Kineshma region northeast of Moscow, such soviets had exercised the real power even before the November revolution. Bolshevik control over the countryside and non-Russian areas of the empire proved a more arduous task.

To assist it in its struggle to maintain power, Lenin's government curtailed civil liberties. During its first two months in power, it shut down opposition newspapers, replaced the old courts with revolutionary tribunals, and established the All-Russian Extraordinary Commission for Combating Counterrevolution and Sabotage (better known as the Cheka). Headed by Felix Dzerzhinsky, its job was to ferret out opponents to the new regime, who would then be tried in new revolutionary tribunals. But the Cheka almost immediately bypassed the tribunals and soon shot thousands of enemies without at trial. From the beginning of the Soviet state, Lenin insisted it had to use violence and was not squeamish if the violence sometimes seemed excessive.

Lenin's government also issued decrees designed to create a new order and abolish Russia's old patriarchal society. Its land decree of November 8, 1917 attacked noble land interests. Soon afterward, the state abolished all class distinctions, titles, and ranks, including military ranks—a new voluntary citizens' militia was to replace the old army. The government severed the age-old connection between the state and the Orthodox Church, confiscated church property, and prohibited religious instruction in the schools. By decreeing that only civil marriages were valid and that divorce could be easily obtained by mutual consent, Lenin's government also ended the church's dominant role over marriages.

The financial and economic policies of the new government aimed at creating a more egalitarian society but did not initially attempt to abolish private enterprise. Yet it still took over banks, insurance companies, and the means of communications and confiscated many assets of Russia's better-off citizens.

Such confiscations were part of the class warfare preached by the Bolsheviks. Shortly before the November revolution, Lenin had written that he was for strong state power when the state became "a machine for proletarian violence against the bourgeoisie."

In the winter of 1917–1918, the Petrograd Soviet ordered those it declared "rich" to donate blankets and clothing for soldiers. That same winter the government forced bourgeois "idlers"—a favorite term of abuse—to perform compulsory menial labor, including the digging of trenches. In the cities, soviets seized buildings and gave more living space to Soviet officials and workers. Former upper-class families who once occupied many rooms were fortunate if they were left with a few and not kicked out entirely. When Communist officials rationed foods and other goods during the Civil War, the former upper classes received little or none, unless they were "bourgeois" specialists who were willing to cooperate with the new regime and possessed talents needed by it. A new Soviet constitution, approved in July 1918, stated that one of its main aims was to suppress the bourgeoisie. It denied the vote to many upper-class people, specifically private traders, those who hired labor for profit, and those who lived on nonlabor income, such as interest or rents. (See Chapter 10 for more on this constitution.)

Just looking like a privileged person during this period could mean trouble. In early 1918, a Bolshevik was killed in Saratov because he was wearing a fashionable suit and mistaken for a *burzhui* (member of the upper class). Glasses also made a person suspect. Clean fingernails and uncalloused hands got some people shot by the Reds during the Civil War.

THE FATE OF THE CONSTITUENT ASSEMBLY AND GROWING SOVIET AUTHORITARIANISM

The Bolsheviks, like most other political parties, had agreed on the necessity of convening a Constituent Assembly to decide Russia's political fate. In the first few days of power, still on shaky ground, they reaffirmed this commitment and indicated their new government's provisional status, pending the assembly's convocation.

Despite some Bolshevik intimidation, the already scheduled and planned elections were allowed to proceed, beginning on November 25. Men and women turned out in large numbers to cast their votes in the freest, most democratic election Russia had ever witnessed. The result was a victory for the Socialist Revolutionaries (SRs). The SRs gained 370 delegates; the Bolsheviks, 175; and the Left SRs, 40 out of a total of 707. Various national groups obtained 86 delegates, and the Mensheviks and Kadets trailed far behind.

The results were not surprising. The vast peasant masses still in the countryside had been underrepresented in the soviets and the Second Congress of Soviets; among the peasants, despite some Bolshevik inroads, the SRs were still the most popular party. If the results gave some consolation to Bolshevik opponents, however, they also bore witness to how radical the Russian people had become by late 1917. For in many respects, the SRs economic and social policies were as far to the Left as those of the Bolsheviks. Lenin's November Land Decree, for example, reflected a position the SRs had adopted before Lenin had come around to it in the summer of 1917.

Between the election and the convening of the Constituent Assembly, friction among SR factions continued, and the Left SRs strengthened their position. For example, they dominated the Second Congress of Soviets of Peasants' Deputies, which met in December. That same month Lenin, under pressure from other Bolsheviks, brought some Left SRs into his government.

After considerable delay and the Soviet government's outlawing of the Kadet party, the Constituent Assembly was finally allowed to convene on January 18 at the Tauride Palace. After it became clear that the assembly would not follow Bolshevik guidance, Bolshevik delegates declared it a counterrevolutionary tool and departed. The assembly's one and only session continued until the early morning hours of January 19, when Red troops forced an end to it. Upon orders of the Soviet government, they also prevented any reconvening later that day.

This treatment of the democratically elected Constituent Assembly was in keeping with Lenin's Marxist views. He stressed class struggle, the proletariat, and the proletarian vanguard rather than democratic elections. Many other signs of growing Bolshevik authoritarianism in early 1918 further reflected Lenin's views, especially those regarding the leading role of the revolutionary intelligentsia. This growing authoritarianism was also a response to changing conditions: The Bolsheviks were now in power and no longer just a party attempting to broaden its support. And power brought difficult responsibilities: war with Germany, internal opposition, and a woeful economy.

Although early Soviet diplomacy is discussed in more detail in Chapter 12, some words concerning the new Soviet government's relations with Germany are necessary here. Although a Soviet-German armistice was signed and peace negotiations begun in December 1917, the Soviet government at first refused to accept Germany's harsh peace terms. Only after German troops marched toward Petrograd in February 1918 was Lenin able to convince a majority of other Bolshevik leaders to accept the distasteful Treaty of Brest-Litovsk (March 3, 1918).

The acceptance of the treaty, which deprived Russia of close to one-third of its empire's former cultivated lands and population, was bitterly opposed by other parties. The Left SRs now withdrew their officials from the Council of People's Commissars. In early July 1918, Left SRs assassinated the German ambassador in Moscow, where the capital had been moved because of the German threat to Petrograd. The plotters hoped the assassination would trigger renewed warfare with Germany.

Left SR opposition merged with that of other groups. In July, there were scattered uprisings in the provinces, and at the end of August, Lenin came close to losing his life when struck by two bullets. An SR terrorist, Fannie Kaplan, claimed responsibility for the crime. As a result of such opposition, the powers of the Cheka increased and Red terror against all enemies became more brutal.

By mid-1918, economic conditions were deteriorating. Chaotic developments in the countryside and little incentive to sell food to the cities decreased food deliveries to them. Government cutbacks on military contracts and the transition to worker-controlled factories contributed to a lessening of industrial productivity. In late spring, the government instituted policies designed to force peasants to give up "surplus" grain, and at the end of June it nationalized Russia's major industries (land had already been nationalized in February). With these steps, the state adopted an economic policy, later called War Communism, which strengthened state centralization and authoritarianism.

War Communism meant an increasing emphasis on industrial discipline and productivity and contributed to a further deterioration of worker autonomy in factory committees and trade unions. Concurrently the Bolsheviks and the Council of People's Commissars increased their control over other government organs, including local soviets.

Changes in the army paralleled those occurring in industry. Common soldiers, like common workers, became subject to more discipline and lost some of the rights gained in the early days of Soviet power. After Trotsky became head of the Red Army in March 1918, he ended the election of officers and won the right to recruit former tsarist officers. This last step was bitterly opposed by some Bolsheviks as well as by Mensheviks and Left SRs, but Trotsky argued that the expertise of these officers was needed. To insure their political reliability, the government instituted a policy of dual command, with political commissars acting as a check on military commanders from the company level to the highest command. During this same period, the government reinstituted the drafting of enlisted men.

REDS VERSUS WHITES AND ALLIED INTERVENTION

In the winter of 1917–1918, even before Trotsky had taken over command of the Red Army, the Soviet government had sent Red troops to peripheral regions of the empire to enforce Soviet rule. The two most significant areas were Ukraine and the lands of the Don Cossacks. By the end of February, Red troops had captured Kiev and Novocherkassk (the Don Cossack capital) and forced the retreat southward of a Volunteer Army formed by Generals Kornilov and Anton Denikin. Later German advances and the Treaty of Brest-Litovsk, however, soon nullified these Soviet gains (see Map 9.1).

The day after Brest-Litovsk, a small detachment of British marines landed in the northern port city of Murmansk. In the months that followed, more British troops, plus French, Japanese, U.S., and other Allied forces landed in such places as Murmansk, Archangel, and Vladivostok. At first, this "Allied intervention" was motivated primarily by concern with preventing Allied-sent equipment and Russian resources from falling into German hands as well as by the hope that anti-German opposition and a second front could be kept alive in Russia. But anti-Bolshevism also motivated the Allies, especially when Allied troops remained after World War I ended in November 1918. Geopolitical interests were another factor, especially in the case of Japan, which landed about 70,000 men in Vladivostok by the end of 1918. Some U.S. officials hoped that the much smaller U.S. force sent to Vladivostok, about 10,000 men, would help check any expanding Japanese influence in the Russian Far East.

The main stated reason for sending U.S. troops to Vladivostok, however, was to aid a Czechoslovak Corps that had gotten trapped in Siberia. Made up

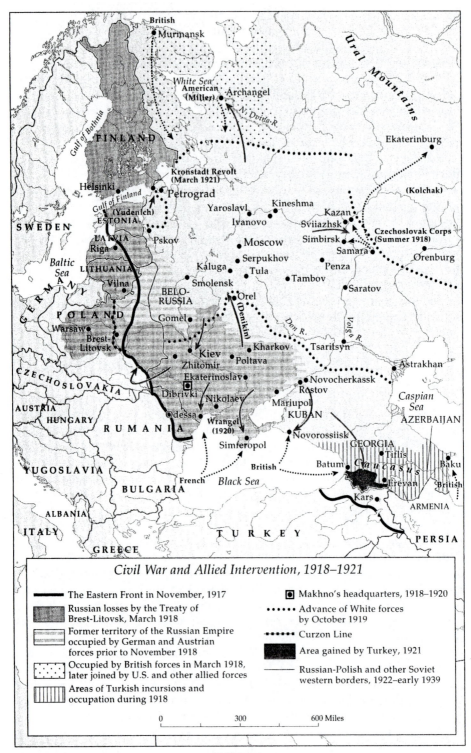

Civil War and Allied Intervention, 1918–1921

The Eastern Front in November, 1917

Russian losses by the Treaty of Brest-Litovsk, March 1918

Former territory of the Russian Empire occupied by German and Austrian forces prior to November 1918

Occupied by British forces in March 1918, later joined by U.S. and other allied forces

Areas of Turkish incursions and occupation during 1918

Makhno's headquarters, 1918–1920

Advance of White forces by October 1919

Curzon Line

Area gained by Turkey, 1921

Russian-Polish and other Soviet western borders, 1922–early 1939

0   300   600 Miles

MAP 9.1

chiefly of Russian-captured Czechoslovak prisoners-of-war and deserters, the Soviet government had promised to allow the approximately 40,000-man corps to leave Russia to fight on the Western front. They were to depart via the Trans-Siberian Railroad and Vladivostok. Because of changing circumstances, however, including the landing of Japanese and British troops in Vladivostok, the government changed its mind while the corps was en route. In May 1918, the corps resisted Soviet efforts to stop them and soon captured the main cities along the Trans-Siberian line.

Although the Soviet government had earlier brought these cities under its control, the Bolsheviks were relatively weak in Siberia—in the Constituent Assembly elections in Siberia, the SRs had gained more than seven times the votes received by the Bolsheviks. The corps' rebellion soon merged with local opposition and the Allied interventionists and marked the emergence of full-scale civil war in Russia.

During the next two years, the Bolsheviks faced opposition on four fronts. On their eastern front, numerous opposition governments formed. The most important initially were an SR-dominated Samara government and a more conservative government in Omsk, which contained some strong supporters of Siberian self-government. There was also a Transbaikal government, with its capital in Chita, under the Siberian Cossack Grigori Semenov. In September 1918, the Samara and Omsk governments, along with some smaller groups and authorities, agreed to form a Provisional All-Russian Government under a five-man Directory. In November, a rightist coup overthrew the Directory and named Admiral Alexander Kolchak the "Supreme Ruler and Commander-in-Chief of all Russia."

The second anti-Bolshevik front was the southern one, where for two years General Denikin headed the Volunteer Army, which was dominated numerically by Cossacks. The third front was in Estonia, where General Nikolai Yudenich commanded the Northwestern White Army. The final and least threatening front was in the north, where General Evgeni Miller was the chief commander of anti-Bolshevik forces.

All four White forces received varying help from the Allied interventionists. In the east, elements of the Czechoslovak Corps also offered considerable assistance in the anti-Red struggle. In the summer of 1918, they joined with troops formed by the Samara government to take the important Volga towns of Simbirsk (Lenin's birthplace) and Kazan. They also dominated the army that captured the Siberian Ural city of Ekaterinburg on July 25.

This threat to Ekaterinburg triggered the execution of former Tsar Nicholas II and his family, who were being held prisoners there. Fearful that the city would fall to the enemy, the Communist leadership in Moscow authorized the family's execution. It was carried out on July 17, 1918. Trotsky later claimed it was done to deprive the Whites of any banner to rally around, to dishearten them, and to show Bolshevik supporters "there was no turning back."

Despite capturing Ekaterinburg and some other territory in the summer of 1918, the Whites were unable to take the vital Volga town of Tsaritsyn (renamed Stalingrad in 1925 in honor of the role Stalin played in the city's defense). In August, Trotsky rushed in his specially equipped train to bolster Red

FIGURE 9.1.
Trotsky and an aide at a railway stop during the civil war.
(From Harrison Salisbury, Russia in Revolution, 1900–1930. *Holt, Rinehart and Winston, New York, 1978.)*

forces at Sviiazhsk, just across the Volga River from Kazan, from which Red forces had just retreated. Thanks largely to his efforts, his growing Red Army was able to retake Kazan and Simbirsk in September and Samara in October.

In November 1918, World War I ended, and a new phase in the Russian Civil War began. On Russia's western borders, Red troops began moving into the vacuum left by departing German forces, and for a brief period Soviet governments were established in Estonia, Latvia, and Lithuania. In early February 1919, the Red Army captured Kiev and soon followed it up with other Ukrainian conquests and the establishment of a Ukrainian Soviet Republic. The winter and early spring of 1918–1919 were a time of great hopes for the Soviet government in Moscow. The lands of the defeated World War I powers appeared ripe for revolution, and the establishment (in early spring of 1919) of soviet republics in Hungary and Bavaria seemed a sign of things to come.

Although the Allied victory over Germany and other Central Powers created new opportunities for Red advances, it also freed up the Allies to concentrate more on helping the Whites defeat the Reds. Lenin certainly feared such a turn of events. For a while, his fears seemed justified. In late 1918, British and French forces landed at Black Sea ports, now made more accessible by the Turks' recognition of defeat in World War I. Besides the port of Batum, the British also occupied other areas in Georgia and the important oil-producing city of Baku in Azerbaijan. But after some wavering and an unsuccessful attempt (in March–April 1919) by French troops to bolster the White cause on the Ukrainian Black Sea coast, the Western Allies began withdrawing their troops from Russia. Within a year, they were out, with only Japanese troops remaining in the Russian Far East. The decision to begin withdrawing Allied troops did not mean, however, that the Allies had given up offering other types of support to the Whites; they continued to provide supplies and weapons.

The Allies' main hope in the spring of 1919 was the White government and forces of Admiral Kolchak. By the end of April 1919, Kolchak's troops had advanced to within 75 miles of the Volga River. But there they were halted and subsequently pushed back. In the early summer, the Red Army drove them back beyond the Urals into Siberia, and in November it occupied Kolchak's capital, Omsk.

Meanwhile, in the summer and early fall of 1919, Denikin's forces in the south recorded one victory after another. They captured Kiev and other Ukrainian cities and reached and conquered Orel (October 14), just 100 miles from the weapons center of Tula and a little over 200 miles from Moscow. Less than a week after the fall of Orel, Petrograd itself was threatened by General Yudenich's army attacking from the west. Once again, however, Red counterattacks, in late October, reversed the momentum on both fronts. The Red Army survived its most crucial test.

By mid-November, Yudenich's army had retreated to Estonia and soon disbanded. In the south, Denikin's troops retreated toward the Black Sea, and by March 1920 were all but defeated. A month earlier, Red forces had executed Admiral Kolchak on the outskirts of the Siberian city of Irkutsk. (For Asian locations, see Map 4.1.) Only a brief Russo-Polish War (April–October 1920) prolonged the life of the White forces in the south. Under General Peter Wrangel, who replaced Denikin, they were able to regain some lost territory; once the war with Poland ended, however, Red troops pushed them back. In mid-November, Wrangel and his troops were forced to leave Russia by way of its Crimean ports.

In that same month, the Czechoslovak Corps completed its evacuation from the Russian Far East. By the end of 1920, the Communists had overcome the threat from White forces and Allied intervention. Nevertheless, it was not until late 1922 that the Japanese evacuated the Russian mainland—although remaining on Northern Sakhalin until 1925—and Russia absorbed the Far Eastern Republic. This buffer state, centered at Chita, had been created in 1920 and was recognized by Moscow until the Japanese departure made it no longer necessary.

NATIONALITIES AND THE RUSSO-POLISH WAR OF 1920

Although Allied intervention and the battle between the Reds and the Whites were the main occurrences of 1918–1920, other events were interwoven with them. On November 15, 1917, the new Soviet government issued the Declaration of the Rights of the Peoples of Russia. It espoused "the right of the peoples of Russia to free self-determination, even to the point of separation and the formation of an independent state." Yet, as seen previously, the espousal of the right of self-determination did not necessarily mean the Bolsheviks would actually let it occur among the nationalities of the former Russian Empire (see Chapter 8). Where the Soviet government was able to prevent secession, it generally did so.

Often, however, the chaotic conditions of 1917–1920 restricted Russia's options. It had little choice but to relinquish former Polish areas of the Russian Empire. After unsuccessful attempts to help install soviet Baltic governments, Lenin also finally had to recognize the establishment of non-Marxist independent governments in Finland, Estonia, Latvia, and Lithuania.

Ukraine, the Caucasus, and Central Asia, however, were a different matter. In Ukraine, a Central Rada (or council), made up primarily of representatives of Ukrainian nationalist and democratic parties and groups, came to power after the fall of the Russian Provisional Government in 1917. Although at first the Rada insisted only on Ukrainian autonomy and not complete independence, its actions soon awakened Bolshevik wrath. Attacks from local Bolsheviks and Red troops led to a Red takeover of Kiev in February 1918. But the Rada, already participating in the Brest-Litovsk peace talks, signed a separate peace treaty with Germany and, three weeks after being ousted, returned to Kiev with the help of German troops.

The Rada, however, remained in power less than two months. At the end of April, General P. Skoropadsky, with the complicity of German forces, overthrew it in a coup. The withdrawal of German troops at the end of World War I led to his own overthrow in December 1918. He was replaced by a Directory, which would duel with the Bolsheviks and others for control of Ukraine over the next two years.

During this period, Kiev and other parts of Ukraine changed hands frequently. Besides the Directory and the Bolsheviks, White, Green (peasant guerrilla forces), Allied (primarily French), and Polish troops became involved in the struggle. Green forces, fighting primarily for peasant interests, were led in Ukraine by the peasant anarchist Nestor Makhno. His army fought against the forces of Skoropadsky, the Directory, the Whites, and, finally, the Reds.

Both class differences and national or ethnic issues contributed to the

FIGURE 9.2.
Mariinskii Palace, built by Rastrelli in 1750–1755 (and restored in 1949). After the Bolsheviks temporarily took control of Kiev in 1919, the Ukrainian Council of People's Commissars established itself in this former tsarist palace.

Ukrainian conflict. Ethnic Ukrainians, Russians, Poles, and Jews all resided in Ukraine. In 1919–1920, tens of thousands of Jews lost their lives in pogroms, with White forces being the chief perpetrators.

In April 1920, Polish troops, along with others under Symon Petliura, head of the Ukrainian Directorate, launched an attack on Red forces once again in power in Ukraine. At stake were Ukrainian, Belorussian, and Lithuanian lands that both Poles and Russians had dominated at different times in the past. Petliura hoped to return to power in Kiev, and the Poles hoped he would create a friendly Ukrainian buffer state.

After a dramatic seesaw struggle, which in August 1920 brought the Red Army to the outskirts of Warsaw, both sides agreed to an armistice in October, followed by the Treaty of Riga in March 1921. By its terms, Russia and Poland divided Ukrainian and Belorussian lands between them, with the Russians receiving the largest share; an independent Lithuania was able to retain most of its territory. Nevertheless, Poland received more land than it would have if it had accepted the Curzon Line, earlier suggested by British Foreign Secretary Curzon as an appropriate Russo-Polish frontier.

Although Petliura was forced into exile in Poland, some of his forces and those of Makhno continued sporadic guerrilla operations against Bolshevik control in Ukraine. By the end of 1921, however, the Bolsheviks had crushed this dwindling opposition and were firmly in control.

In the Caucasus, firm Bolshevik control was also delayed for several years after the November 1917 revolution. In April 1918, Georgians, Armenians, and Azerbaijanis agreed to the formation of a Transcaucasian Federal Republic under a Georgian Menshevik president. It lasted only a month before rivalries split it apart, and three independent states were formed. The climate of the times, however, was not conducive to independence. First German and Turkish troops and then British military involvement in the region complicated an already complex situation in which national, ethnic, religious, and class differences made it difficult to establish or maintain peace and an independent existence. Armenia, for example, became entangled in territorial wars with Georgia, Azerbaijan, and Turkey and was finally forced at the end of 1920 to accept Soviet rule to prevent being crushed by Turkey.

Both the Whites and the Reds ultimately opposed the independent governments created in the region, and even before the sovietization of Armenia, the Bolsheviks had taken over Azerbaijan (April 1920). Georgia was the last to succumb; its capital, Tiflis (Tbilisi), fell to Red Army troops in February 1921.

In the overwhelmingly Moslem area of Central Asia, a Tashkent Soviet government, run by European Russian Bolsheviks and SRs, came to power in late 1917. In February 1918, its Red forces captured Kokand, slaughtered many of its Moslems, and crushed a rival Turkistan government dominated by Moslems. It was only after the defeat of Admiral Kolchak and the British withdrawal from the Caspian area in 1919, however, that the Red Army was able to insure Communist control over all of Central Asia. In 1920, the Red Army conquered the khanates of Khiva and Bukhara. This left the Basmachi guerrilla movement, with its slogan of "Turkistan for the Natives," as the only remaining significant anti-Red opposition. After 1922, however, it became gradually weaker and soon ceased to be an important concern.

OPPOSITION FROM THE MASSES

Although the White armies and main non-Russian nationality opposition were defeated by early 1921, the Communists now faced major upheavals from amidst the masses of peasants, workers, soldiers, and sailors. As Brovkin and others have convincingly demonstrated, strikes and rebellions had been building since 1918. They partly resulted from wartime conditions such as food and fuel shortages and wages that failed to keep up with inflation. Although some of this suffering was unavoidable during a civil war, Communist economic policies often made a bad situation worse. Despite the fact that government ministers such as Foreign Minister Chicherin might have had to suffer some deprivations, the masses perceived and often complained that the new Communist officials were receiving better food rations and more privileges than the common folk in whose behalf they claimed to fight. Workers and peasants also complained about being drafted into the Red Army and, when possible, many deserted.

Considerable resentment stemmed from the Communist government's increasing authoritarian ways. It limited the rights of workers and their organi-

Hunger, Cold, and Sickness: Winter 1919–1920

The following excerpt is taken from John Reed's "Soviet Russia Now—I," *Liberator* III (December 1920): 9–10. Reed was a radical U.S. journalist, sympathetic to the Communist revolution and author of *Ten Days That Shook the World* (1919), a first-hand account of the Bolshevik Revolution. Like some of those he described, he fell victim to typhus and died in Russia in 1920. He was buried near the Kremlin Wall in Moscow. I have changed a few spellings of names. Ellipses and bracketed material are mine.

The winter [1919–1920] was horrible beyond imagination. No one will ever know what Russia went through. Transport at times almost ceased, and the number of locomotives out of commission more and more exceeded those repaired. There was, and is, grain enough in the provincial storehouses to feed the whole country . . . but it cannot be transported. For weeks together Petrograd was without bread. So with fuel—so with raw materials. . . .

In the great cities like Moscow and Petrograd, the result was appalling. In some houses there was no heat at all the whole winter. People froze to death in their rooms. The electric light was intermittent—for several weeks in Moscow there were no street lights whatever—and the street cars crawled feebly along—in Moscow they stopped running altogether. Chicherin's hands were frost-bitten as he sat in the Commissariat of Foreign Affairs, and Krasin [commissar for transportation] worked in a room with a broken window, bundled up in a fur coat and hat and gloves. . . .

In January I went to Serpukov [Serpukhov], the center of a large textile industry—of which I shall speak again. Serpukov is a struggling country town, containing huge textile mills, and shading off into the country through a fringe of villages; all around it are other mills, to a distance of thirty versts.

The situation of the twenty-five or thirty thousand textile workers in and around Serpukov was unbelievable. Typhus was raging; in the Kontchin mill one worker a day was dying. In order to stop speculation by the peasants, and to centralize and equalize the distribution of food, a decree had been issued in the summer forbidding the people of the towns from making independent expeditions into the country after food; the government undertaking to supply a certain ration to the workers. But, except for the children, invalids and Soviet workers, the government had been unable to supply any bread in this region for six months. True, in the fall the local Soviet had authorized each factory to send a delegation to the villages to get food, but this had long been exhausted. Now the only way to get anything to eat was for the workers to go out to the villages by night, and take their chances of smuggling provisions past the soldiers on guard.

The workers would fall down from weakness as they stood at the machines. . . .

Typhus, intermittent fever, influenza raged among the workers; among the peasants, who could not get salt, pellagra ravaged whole villages.

zations (including other leftist political parties to which some workers belonged); forcefully requisitioned food, horses, and other items from the peasants; and unleashed the Cheka on all claimed enemies of the state.

The masses were just as hostile, if not more so, to White forces, which also acted in an authoritarian and often brutal fashion. Discontentment among the masses in White-occupied territories helped pave the way for Red advances in late 1919 and 1920, just as earlier hostility to Communist practices in Red-held territory had aided White advances. Once the White forces were defeated by the end of 1920, mass discontent was directed against the Communists, who attempted to tighten their hold and further Communist policies in all parts of the country.

The leading military opposition now came chiefly from the Green movement. It consisted mainly of numerous and scattered Red Army deserters and rebellious peasants—despite strenuous Communist efforts to recapture deserters, there were apparently at least 1 million of them who remained uncaptured in 1919. The Greens were generally based in forests and used hit-and-run guerrilla tactics.

In late 1920 and early 1921, Green resistance and spontaneous peasant rebellions increased in all directions: from the Kuban area to the Urals (especially in the Tambov Province and in the lower Volga), and from Ukraine to Siberia. In February and March 1921, workers in major industrial areas, sometimes supported by soldiers and sailors, engaged in a wave of strikes and issued demands. In late February, opposition even appeared among a group that Trotsky had once called "the pride and glory" of the revolution—the Kronstadt sailors.

They were located in the fortified town of Kronstadt (65,000 inhabitants before World War I) on the island of Kotlin in the Gulf of Finland and shared some of the hardships of nearby Petrograd. The Kronstadt sailors were upset with their conditions, including insufficient fuel and poor food and clothing,

FIGURE 9.3.
Kronstadt as viewed from the Gulf of Finland.

and were sympathetic to recent Petrograd strikers who had been harshly dealt with by the government. The sailors approved a rebellious resolution. It criticized the increasingly authoritarian and undemocratic policies of the government.

More specifically, the resolution stated that the existing soviets failed to represent the workers and peasants, and new soviets should therefore be elected by secret ballot. Furthermore, the peasants were to be free to use their land as they wished, provided that they did not employ hired labor. The rebels' listing of these and other demands (including freedom of speech, press, and assembly and the liberation of political prisoners) was primarily in behalf of peasants and workers as well as soldiers, sailors, and members of socialist and anarchist parties.

The government's answer to the rebels was to demand their unconditional surrender. When they refused, troops supervised by Trotsky and led by M. N. Tukhachevsky finally succeeded in crossing the ice on the Gulf of Finland and storming the Kronstadt fortress. Success, however, came at a high price. The campaign, waged from March 7 to March 18, cost the Red Army alone about 10,000 wounded, dead, or missing. Rebel losses were less, mainly because thousands of sailors fled across the ice to Finland before the fortress fell. Those who were unable to escape were either shot or sent to prison camps.

The Kronstadt rebellion, along with all the other signs of mass dissatisfaction, finally convinced the Communist leadership to back off from the forced requisitioning of crops and some of the other Communist economic policies. Soviet concessions, the first of which became operative in the spring of 1921, helped gradually end peasant and other resistance to the regime. So too did harsh repressions—full-scale military campaigns against the peasants were led by important commanders such as Tukhachevsky. Finally, a devastating famine, partially a result of the Civil War, struck Russia later in 1921, killing not only many peasants, but also lingering overt peasant opposition.

CONCLUSIONS, COSTS, AND LEGACY

Considering all the opposition the Bolsheviks faced from 1918 to 1921, their victory at first seems surprising. Upon closer examination, however, it is not. They were more unified, organized, and skillfully led than their enemies—even their application of repression and terroristic methods reflected this—and they controlled Russia's heartland, which contained most of its population.

Although it is possible to overestimate the Bolsheviks' efficiency, centralized control, and leadership qualities, there is no doubt of the disunity and generally poor leadership that characterized their enemies. On the ideological level, anti-Bolshevism was often the only common political sentiment they shared. Even White leaders such as Kolchak and Denikin were never able to control fully their own military forces, who often needlessly alienated the people over whom they temporarily ruled. The Allied interventionists, with their own sets of goals, probably hurt the White cause—partly by tainting it with "foreignness"—as much as they helped it. There was also little strategic or tactical coordination between the many different White fronts. Green opposition was even more localized and as hostile to Whites as to Reds.

The leadership of Lenin was an important reason for the greater unity of the Bolsheviks. Trotsky's skills in building up, administering, and, at times, rallying Red troops further contributed to the Red victory.

The Reds' control of the Russian heartland, including Petrograd and Moscow, gave them command over more people and industrial resources and provided a more homogeneous ethnic base than that enjoyed by the Whites, who were scattered around the periphery. The Reds' central position made it easier for them to move men and vital resources, including Trotsky's famed headquarters train, from one front to another. In contrast, the Whites were more dependent on the non-Russian areas of the former empire.

Although the Reds' policy toward the non-Russian nationalities promised much more than it delivered, the Whites steadfastly refused to pledge as much as the Bolsheviks. General Denikin's desire to maintain Russia as great and undivided was shared by most other White leaders and helped antagonize non-Russian nationalist feelings in such areas as Ukraine, the Caucasus, and Estonia.

This does not imply that nationalism was always strongly developed among the minority nationalities. It often went little beyond small groups of urban intellectuals and students; to many people, economic issues were more important than nationality. Furthermore, many non-Russian cities of the empire were heterogeneous, containing not only people from the dominant nationality of a region, but also significant numbers of Russians, Jews, and other nationalities. The support of at least some Russian workers in the cities of predominantly non-Russian regions often contributed to the Bolsheviks' success.

What worker and peasant support there was for the Communists—whether in Great Russian or non-Russian areas of the former empire—was partly motivated by the Bolshevik's class war against the landlords, bourgeoisie, and "rich peasants" (kulaks). Pitting poor peasants against more prosperous ones was one of the Bolshevik strategies in the countryside. Many workers and peasants feared the Whites would institute reactionary policies and disliked the generally superior attitude of White officers to the lower classes.

Yet any worker and peasant preference for the Reds versus the Whites should not be overemphasized, and there is little doubt that by the beginning of 1921, workers and peasants were far less enthusiastic about Communist policies than they had been at the end of 1917.

Although the Reds were victorious, victory came at a high price. Estimates vary widely as to the total Civil War deaths, but there were certainly more than a few million. Most of them were civilians, and most of the deaths, even in the armies, were not from being killed by the enemy. Because of Civil War conditions, diseases such as typhus and typhoid flourished. Hunger and malnourishment also contributed to many deaths.

Besides the deaths, Russia lost perhaps 2 million more people to emigration, a phenomenon especially noticeable among the educated elite. And the

Civil War contributed to multiplying the number of homeless children, which by 1921 reached into the millions.

Economic costs were also high, as various 1920 figures indicate. By then, inflation had made the ruble almost worthless; overall, industrial production was only one-fifth that of 1913 (large-scale industry had declined even more), and only about two-thirds as much grain was being produced as the average prewar (1909–1913) level. Both the country's industrial labor force and the combined populations of Petrograd and Moscow were now less than half of those of 1917. Finally, Russia's transport system, especially rail transport, was severely crippled.

The long-range legacy of the Civil War and Allied intervention is more difficult to pinpoint, but a few generalizations can be made. The warfare of 1918–1921 contributed to the increasing authoritarianism of the government and Communist party. Many non-Communist parties and autonomous social and political organizations that had been on the increase toward the end of the tsarist period were now disbanded. Moreover, even the soviets, trade unions, factory committees, and other more democratic aspects of Soviet political life were weakened. Allied intervention inadvertently strengthened this authoritarianism by giving the Soviet government a further excuse for it—to fight off foreign intervention effectively. In the future, the Communists often continued in a similar way to point to "capitalist encirclement" and hostility as a justification for authoritarian measures.

Thanks in part to Soviet propaganda, stories of Civil War heroism, both real and imagined, left their imprint on the mentality of the people. More significant, however, was the imprint the conflict left on the minds of the new Communist elite. The war, especially the campaigns directed against the Greens and peasants, increased their fear and suspicion of the peasants and their "backward" mentality. Furthermore, dealing with problems by military, command, and terroristic methods became a habit that was not easily forgotten. After being contained somewhat for seven or eight years, both that habit and the distrust of the peasants manifested themselves once again with a vengeance.

SUGGESTED SOURCES

ADAMS, ARTHUR E. *Bolsheviks in the Ukraine: The Second Campaign, 1918–1919.* New Haven, 1963.

AVRICH, PAUL. *Kronstadt, 1921.* Princeton, 1970.

BABINE, ALEXIS. *A Russian Civil War Diary: Alexis Babine in Saratov, 1917–1922.* Durham, 1988.

BENVENUTI, FRANCESCO. *The Bolsheviks and the Red Army, 1918–1922.* Cambridge, England, 1988.

BRINKLEY, GEORGE A. *The Volunteer Army and Allied Intervention in South Russia, 1917–1921: A Study in the Politics and Diplomacy of the Russian Civil War.* Notre Dame, Ind., 1966.

BROVKIN, VLADIMIR N. *Behind the Front Lines of the Civil War: Political Parties and Social Movements in Russia, 1918–1922.* Princeton, 1994.

BUNYAN, JAMES, ed. *Intervention, Civil War, and Communism in Russia, April–December 1918: Documents and Materials.* Baltimore, 1936.

BURBANK, JANE. *Intelligentsia and Revolution: Russian Views of Bolshevism, 1917–1922.* New York, 1986.

CONNAUGHTON, R. M. *The Republic of the Ushakovka: Admiral Kolchak and the Allied Intervention in Siberia, 1918–20.* London, 1990.

DAVIES, NORMAN. *White Eagle, Red Star—The Polish-Soviet War, 1919–1920.* London, 1972.

DENIKIN, ANTON. *The White Army.* London, 1930.

EMMONS, TERENCE, ed. *Time of Troubles, the Diary of Iurii Vladimirovich Got'e: Moscow, July 8, 1917 to July 23, 1922.* Princeton, 1988.

FIDDICK, THOMAS. *Russia's Retreat from Poland, 1920: From Permanent Revolution to Peaceful Coexistence.* New York, 1990.

FIGES, ORLANDO. *Peasant Russia, Civil War: The Volga Countryside in Revolution, 1917–1921.* Oxford, 1989.

FOGLESONG, DAVID S. *America's Secret War Against Bolshevism: U.S. Intervention in the Russian Civil War, 1917–1920.* Chapel Hill, 1995.

FOOTMAN, DAVID. *Civil War in Russia.* London, 1961.

GETZLER, ISRAEL. *Kronstadt 1917–1921: The Fate of a Soviet Democracy.* Cambridge, England, 1983.

HOVANNISIAN, RICHARD G. *The Republic of Armenia.* 4 vols. Berkeley, 1971–1996.

HUSBAND, WILLIAM B. *Revolution in the Factory: The Birth of the Soviet Textile Industry, 1917–1920.* New York, 1990.

KENEZ, PETER. *Civil War in South Russia, 1918: The First Year of the Volunteer Army.* Berkeley, 1971.

———. *Civil War in South Russia, 1919–1920: The Defeat of the Whites.* Berkeley, 1977.

KENNAN, GEORGE F. *Soviet-American Relations, 1917–1920.* 2 vols. Princeton, 1956, 1958.

KOENKER, DIANE, ed. *Party, State, and Society in the Russian Civil War: Explorations in Social History.* Bloomington, 1989.

KOTSONIS, YANNI. "Arkhangel'sk, 1918: Regionalism and Populism in the Russian Civil War," *RR* 51 (October 1992): 526–544.

KOWALSKI, RONALD. *The Bolshevik Party in Conflict: The Left Communist Opposition of 1918.* Pittsburgh, 1991.

LEGGETT, GEORGE. *The Cheka: Lenin's Political Police: The All-Russian Extraordinary Commission for Combating Counter-Revolution and Sabotage, December 1917 to February 1922.* Oxford, 1981.

LINCOLN, W. BRUCE. *Red Victory: A History of the Russian Civil War.* New York, 1989.

LUCKETT, RICHARD. *The White Generals: An Account of the White Movement and the Russian Civil War.* London, 1987.

MALET, MICHAEL. *Nestor Makhno in the Russian Civil War.* London, 1982.

MALLE, SILVANA. *The Economic Organization of War Communism, 1918–1921.* Cambridge, England, 1985.

MASSIE, ROBERT. *The Romanovs: The Final Chapter.* New York, 1995.

MAWDSLEY, EVAN. *The Russian Civil War.* Boston, 1987.

MCAULEY, MARY. *Bread and Justice: State and Society in Petrograd, 1917–1922.* Oxford, 1991.

MCFADDEN, DAVID W. *Alternative Paths: Soviets and Americans, 1917–1920.* New York, 1993.

PASTERNAK, BORIS. *Doctor Zhivago.* New York, 1958. A novel dealing mainly with the 1917 revolution and the subsequent civil war.

PIPES, RICHARD. *The Formation of the Soviet Union: Communism and Nationalism, 1917–1923.* Rev. ed. Cambridge, Mass., 1964.

———. *Russia under the Bolshevik Regime.* New York, 1994.

RADKEY, OLIVER H. *Russia Goes to the Polls: The Election to the All-Russian Constituent Assembly, 1917.* Ithaca, 1989.

———. *The Sickle Under the Hammer: The Russian Socialist Revolutionaries in the Early Months of Soviet Rule.* New York, 1963.

———. *The Unknown Civil War in Soviet Russia: A Study of the Green Movement in the Tambov Region, 1920–1921.* Stanford, 1976.

READ, CHRISTOPHER. *From Tsar to Soviets: The Russian People and Their Revolution, 1917–1921.* New York, 1996.

RESHETAR, JOHN S. JR. *The Ukrainian Revolution, 1917–1920: A Study in Nationalism.* Princeton, 1952.

RIGBY, T. H. *Lenin's Government: Sovnarkom 1917–1922.* Cambridge, England, 1979.

RSH 33 (Summer 1994). The entire issue is devoted to War Communism.

SAKWA, RICHARD. *Soviet Communists in Power: A Study of Moscow During the Civil War, 1918–21.* New York, 1988.

SCHAPIRO, LEONARD. *The Origin of the Communist Autocracy: Political Opposition in the Soviet State, First Phase, 1917–1922.* 2d ed. London, 1977.

SERVICE, ROBERT. *Lenin: A Political Life:* Vol 3, *The Iron Ring.* Bloomington, 1995.

STEINBERG, MARK D., and VLADIMIR M KHRUSTALËV. *The Fall of the Romanovs: Political Dreams and Personal Struggles in a Time of Revolution.* New Haven, 1995.

STITES, RICHARD. *Revolutionary Dreams: Utopian Vision and Experimental Life in the Russian Revolution.* New York, 1989.

TIRADO, ISABEL A. *Young Guard!: The Communist Youth League, Petrograd, 1917–1920.* New York, 1988.

WADE, REX A., ed. *Documents of Soviet History.* Vols. 1–3. Gulf Breeze, Fla., 1991–1995.

WHITE, JAMES D. *The Russian Revolution: 1917–1921: A Short History.* London, 1994.

CHAPTER 10

The Years of the New Economic Policy, 1921–1927

In early 1921, Lenin and the Communist party began a New Economic Policy (NEP). The earlier forced requisitioning of peasant crops, by both Reds and Whites, had created enormous peasant hostility. The Whites were now defeated, but numerous peasant uprisings continued, and the country was economically exhausted. The Kronstadt rebellion, partly fueled by dissatisfaction with shortages, helped Lenin convince Communist party delegates at the Tenth Party Congress (March 1921) that requisitioning should be replaced by an agricultural tax.

This new agricultural policy became the cornerstone of NEP, which restored some private trading and business enterprises and represented at least a temporary compromise with market principles. The government decided that more consumer goods were necessary to induce peasants to produce and sell enough crops to feed growing cities and provide surplus for foreign trade. After it soon became clear that the state alone could not produce and distribute enough such goods, the door was opened for private entrepreneurs and traders.

This limited toleration of bourgeois activities was distasteful to many Communists. Some stated that what NEP really stood for was "New Exploitation of the Proletariat." Lenin, however, who had earlier preached the necessity of class war, now believed that the path to communism ran through "state capitalism." While he worked hard to convince Communist doubters of the wisdom of NEP, he himself remained wary of Nepmen (private businessmen) and sometimes feared they were using the government more than the government was using them. The ambivalence of the party toward NEP and Nepmen was mirrored in Soviet laws and practices, and the Nepmen led a precarious, if occasionally prosperous, existence. Yet, however uncertain the political conditions were for Nepmen, by the end of 1927, NEP agricultural and industrial production had risen to roughly 1913 levels.

Meanwhile the Communist party strengthened its hold over the political process, and Stalin gradually succeeded Lenin as its most powerful figure. In the two years before his death in January 1924, Lenin was often ill and a succession struggle began during his illness. From 1923 until 1925, Stalin formed a triumvirate with Zinoviev and Kamenev to weaken Trotsky. After Trotsky was removed as war commissar in early 1925, the triumvirate split apart. Zinoviev and Kamenev now made common cause with Trotsky as part of a Left Opposition, while Stalin allied with a group on the Right led by Nikolai Bukharin (although the *Left* and *Right* labels used in the 1920s were at times misleading, they are maintained here for the sake of convenience). By his alliance with the leaders of the Right and by bringing in his own supporters to staff important positions, Stalin was able to expel Zinoviev, Kamenev, and Trotsky from the Communist party at the end of 1927.

NEW ECONOMIC POLICY AND THE FAMINE OF 1921–1922

Early in February 1921, before the Kronstadt revolt had broken out, leaders on the Communist party's Politburo agreed to put forward Lenin's proposal to end the forced requisitioning of peasant crops. By 1921, it had become clear that not only had such requisitioning awakened tremendous hostility among the peasants, but also it retarded agricultural production, thereby contributing to food shortages in cities including Moscow and Petrograd. Why should peasants produce as much as they could if the state was going to expropriate all but the barest minimum—and sometimes even that? To pacify peasant hostility and at the same time encourage more production, Lenin proposed that requisitioning be replaced by a tax in kind, which would allow peasants to sell any surplus at local markets.

While the Kronstadt campaign was being waged, the Tenth Communist Party Congress opened in Moscow; before it was over, hundreds of the almost 1,000 delegates left to assist in putting down the rebels. The rebellion helped overcome any lingering doubts about adopting Lenin's new peasant policy, and the congress approved it overwhelmingly.

Although this policy became the cornerstone of NEP, many other measures soon accompanied it. More often than not, they were dictated by subsequent developments rather than any ideological forethought. There was an overall purpose, however, which united most of the new steps: overcoming the economic misery and discontent of early 1921.

Most significant of the additional measures was the restoration of private trade and private small-scale industry, in part a response to increased peasant trading and purchasing. In addition, the in-kind tax paid by peasants was later replaced by a money tax, and foreign investment was encouraged and the currency stabilized.

Yet NEP was only a partial restoration of market or capitalistic forces. The state retained control over "the commanding heights" of the economy. Large-scale industry, most wholesale (and some retail) trade, banking, transportation, communications, and foreign trade remained in its hands. The government also attempted, although not always successfully, to regulate credit and many prices and wages, and to oversee general economic development.

FIGURE 10.1.
Famine victims in Samara, 1921.
(Radio Times Hulton Picture Library.)

NEP policies, however, did not come quickly enough to prevent a devastating famine from striking Russia in 1921 and 1922. Widespread drought in 1920 and 1921 was one cause of it; so too were the ravages of the Civil War, the forced requisitioning policies of both Reds and Whites, insufficient government surpluses, and an inadequate transportation system. Some 5 million people died, mostly in the Volga valley and southern Ukraine. There would have been many more deaths if outside assistance, primarily from the American Relief Administration, had not moved in to help. (See Chapter 15 for more on this and other famines in the early Soviet period.)

By late 1927, industrial and agricultural production returned to pre–World War I levels. Considering the problems and costs from 1914 to 1922—wars, Allied intervention, and famine—this was a notable achievement. Despite the economic growth, however, serious economic problems remained. One of the most troubling was increasing unemployment. By the beginning of 1927, well over 10 percent of the urban workforce was unemployed.

NEPMEN AND BOURGEOIS SPECIALISTS

Nepmen included a wide variety of manufacturers, financiers, speculators, merchants, artisans, and traders but not everyone engaged in selling; during NEP, many people on a part-time or occasional basis stood along market squares or streets selling personal or other items. Private manufacturers produced primarily food products (such as bread and other baked goods); clothing; and household goods, including furniture, tools, and utensils.

These products and others were bought and sold (or bartered) from permanent stores, shops, and kiosks; from temporary facilities at market squares, bazaars, and along streets; from the trays of peddlers; and from the bags and sacks of bagmen, who brought food and other village goods to the towns and city products to the countryside. The American anarchist Emma Goldman noted that NEP "turned Moscow into a vast market place. Trade became the new religion. Shops and stores sprang up overnight."

Besides the goods obtained from peasants, artisans, and private manufacturers, the private businesses and traders also purchased goods from state enterprises and from smugglers who brought goods in from abroad. As NEP progressed, so too did competition from state and cooperative stores. Yet, despite preferential government treatment and lower prices, these "socialist" stores were often considered inferior to private ones. The private stores generally offered speedier, more considerate service and a better quality and variety of goods.

The incomes earned by Nepmen varied considerably. Although a small percentage of them made large fortunes, few of these individuals were from the prewar business elite. Most Nepmen were small-scale traders who did not operate out of permanent facilities, and they were far from affluent. "Nepwomen" were overwhelmingly found in this category, but even here they were greatly outnumbered by men. The American writer Maurice Hindus noted that many Jews were prominent among the more successful Nepmen, and this was especially true in Ukraine.

During NEP "bourgeois" specialists as well as wealthy Nepmen temporarily joined party members in the upper ranks of the new Soviet society. Despite his hostility to the bourgeoisie as a class, Lenin had already become convinced that Russia could not be run without the knowledge and skills of specialists— whether they be the tsarist military officers recruited by Trotsky or civilian specialists, such as economists, agronomists, engineers, and professors. There were simply too few specialists among party members. Although "bourgeois" specialists and Nepmen might gain or regain economic and social status and often earn more than party officials, the party closely guarded its political prerogatives. Nepmen, for example, were not allowed to vote or arrange meetings, and they had to pay more for rent and public services than the working class.

These disadvantages did not keep Nepmen and specialists from being resented by many party and lower-class elements, who faulted or envied them for various combinations of attributes: their "bourgeois vices," high incomes, education and knowledge, good positions, and haughtiness. Because of the prominence of Jews among Nepmen, this resentment was often combined with antisemitism.

Among the bourgeois vices attributed to the Nepmen was the conspicuous consumption of those who could afford it. In Moscow, Petrograd (Leningrad), and some other cities expensive nightclubs and gambling houses operated, in some of which drugs and prostitutes were readily available. Like Berlin, Paris, and New York, the two major Soviet cities reflected some aspects of the Roaring Twenties.

The future dissident Lev Kopelev recalls in his memoirs that he "considered NEP the source of all our evils and misfortunes." Among these evils, he lists casinos, prostitution, grafters, bribe-takers, bickering among party leaders, and suicides, such as that of the poet Esenin.[1] The Comintern activist Victor Serge, returning from abroad to Leningrad in 1926, also reflects in his memoirs some of the anti-Nepmen hostility of the time. He criticized many of them as a "flock of vultures." He believed they had gained much of their money from "robbery," speculation, and racketeering and that money was corrupting everything, including Communist officials. Although it is not always clear who was corrupting whom, there were certainly numerous cases of bribery and other corrupt practices during the NEP years. Yet, if NEP produced its own brand of corruption, the practice of government officials taking money or other "favors" neither began nor ended with NEP.

CHANGES IN THE GOVERNMENT AND COMMUNIST PARTY

At the end of December 1922, the Union of Soviet Socialist Republics (USSR) came into being. Its member republics were Russia, Ukraine, Belorussia, and Transcaucasia. Russia was formally known as the Russian Soviet Federated Socialist Republic (RSFSR), which had been established by a 1918 constitution. Transcaucasia included Armenia, Azerbaijan, and Georgia, but it was replaced in 1936 by its three component parts, which were then recognized as separate union republics within the USSR. By the end of 1936, there were eleven union republics because by then five Central Asian Republics had been carved out of the RSFSR, some being upgraded from the lower status of "autonomous republics" (see Map 11.1).

A new constitution for the USSR was completed in 1924 and was basically modeled on the 1918 constitution for the RSFSR. Both constitutions, reflecting party distrust of the peasants, made each urban vote of the electorate worth five rural votes. According to the earlier constitution, supreme power in the RSFSR was vested in the All-Russian Congress of Soviets. Because the congress was not a permanent body, however, it elected an executive committee to act in its behalf between sessions, and the executive committee appointed the Council of People's Commissars. The 1924 constitution duplicated this basic structure on an "All-Union" basis but recognized some union republic rights, including the right to secede. It also established three types of commissariats: all-union, union-republic, and republic. The first type, such as the Commissariat for Foreign Affairs, existed just at the central level of government. The second, such as the Commissariat of Finance, existed at both the central and republican levels, with the latter responsible for carrying out the will of the cen-

---

[1]*The Education of a True Believer* (New York, 1980), pp. 166–167.

tral agency. The third type, such as the Commissariat of Internal Affairs, existed just at the republic level.

Yet both the 1918 and the 1924 constitutions were less important than the Communist party's monopoly on power, first in Russia and then in the other republics of the future USSR. Oskar Anweiler has noted that "the All-Russian Soviet Congress, as early as the Third Soviet Congress of January 1918 had played out its independent political role and increasingly turned into pure window dressing for Bolshevik rule."[2] Thus, even before the first constitution was promulgated in mid-1918, the Bolsheviks had created a reality that would vary considerably from that depicted in their constitution, in which the Communist party was not even mentioned. In the 1924 constitution, the promised right of secession was just as far from reality as the supposed power of the new All-Union Congress of Soviets. By the time the USSR was formed, the party was firmly in power in all of the republics, and it had no intention of allowing any secession.

In addition, the party did not wish to allow the growth of any conditions that might encourage pan-Turkic or pan-Islamic unity among the USSR's many Turkic and Moslem peoples. Throughout the 1920s and beyond, party policy divided Central Asia and other Moslem areas into territorial units designed to discourage any such development.

The party was willing, however, to allow the nonpolitical development of national cultures. Lenin advocated a policy of "national in form, socialist in content." He feared that attempts to prevent the evolution of national cultures by Russification would be counterproductive. In 1922, in the midst of a dispute about how best to facilitate Communist rule in Georgia, Lenin criticized Stalin and Grigori Ordzhonikidze (both Georgians) and Felix Dzerzhinsky (Polish and head of the Cheka and its successors, the GPU and OGPU) for their Russian chauvinism and lack of sensitivity to Georgian nationalist feelings. He also noted that assimilated non-Russians always overdid their pro-Russian attitudes. Before his death in January 1924, policies were introduced to help develop the use of national languages and cultures and to bring more non-Russians into the Communist party and government. In Ukraine, the amount of government business transacted in the Ukrainian language increased from 20 percent in 1922 to 70 percent by 1927.[3] During this same period, the non-Russian party membership in the country as a whole increased from 28 percent to 35 percent.

Although the soviets and congresses of soviets grew steadily weaker after 1917, the Council of People's Commissars (Sovnarkom) remained strong as long as Lenin remained healthy. As chairman of Sovnarkom, Lenin thought of himself as the head of the government and believed it should be responsible for the everyday running of the country.

Yet he recognized the authority of the Communist party to give overall di-

---

[2]*The Soviets: The Russian Workers, Peasants, and Soldiers Councils, 1905–1921* (New York, 1974), p. 226.

[3]Orest Subtelny, *Ukraine: A History*, 2d ed. (Toronto, 1994), p. 388.

rection to the government. Although he was clearly the leader of the party, his leadership resulted from the force of his personality, for he held no official party position designating him as "the leader." He could be, and occasionally was, outvoted on the chief party organs in which he participated.

After Lenin's health began to decline in late 1921—before his death in January 1924 he suffered several strokes—more government business passed into the hands of the party organs. In 1917, the chief Communist body had been the Central Committee of the party. By mid-1922, it had twenty-seven full members and nineteen alternates and had spawned three smaller bodies that became increasingly significant. The most important of them was the Politburo (Political Bureau). In 1922, its members were Lenin, Trotsky, Stalin, Kamenev, Zinoviev, A. Rykov, and M. Tomsky. There was also an Orgburo (Organizational Bureau) and a Secretariat. In April 1922, Stalin became the latter's first general secretary and slowly began fashioning that office into the key Communist post it would soon become. He was the only party member to sit on the Central Committee and all three of its offshoots.

Outside the hierarchy of the party, there were a little more than 730,000 full and candidate members in early 1921. By early 1924, however, several hundred thousand had been kicked out of the party—Lenin claimed many were "radish communists," red on the outside, white on the inside. Yet, by the beginning of 1927, a new recruiting drive had more than doubled the membership to more than 1 million full and candidate members—still less than 1 percent of the country's population.

On the local scene as well as in Moscow, the Communist party and not the soviet organizations exercised the real power, although following as always the general directions of the party leadership.

Decisions made by the Tenth Party Congress in March 1921 strengthened the role of that leadership by banning any factionalism in the party. Before the congress, several party factions had emerged criticizing the increasing authoritarianism, centralism, and bureaucraticism within the party. The most prominent of these groups was the Workers' Opposition (WO), led by Alexander Shliapnikov. He was rare among prominent Bolsheviks (commissar of labor in 1917–1918) in that he had actually been a factory worker, first in prewar Russia and then abroad. Another notable individual, Alexandra Kollontai (feminist and commissar of social welfare in 1917–1918), joined with him in opposition and wrote a pamphlet, *The Workers' Opposition*, to publicize better the faction's criticisms.

The WO's approach to achieving greater democracy and less authoritarianism within the party was to restore and expand the influence of workers and unions—the decline of industry and the deaths of many workers in the Civil War had contributed to the weakening of the proletarian element in the party. The WO wished to establish trade-union economic dominance and revive proletarian class consciousness among party members. It advocated that they engage in periodic manual labor and that nonproletarian elements be removed from the party.

In response to such criticism, Lenin acknowledged that the party had to become more vigilant in extending democracy and fighting bureaucraticism.

He also noted the need to expel unreliable elements that had "wormed their way" into the party. But he insisted that the forming of party factions to advocate such policies would only weaken party unity and play into the hands of counterrevolutionary enemies. He pointed to the Kronstadt rebellion to illustrate how dangerous factionalism could be and stated that the party was still surrounded "by a ring of enemies."

The Tenth Party Congress's decision to ban factionalism had important repercussions after Lenin's death and contributed to the rise of Stalinism.

At about the same time the party was cracking down on factionalism within its own ranks, it stepped up its curtailment of Menshevik and Socialist Revolutionary (SR) activity. Although the Mensheviks and right SRs had been banned in mid-1918, in less than a year they were again both permitted to operate. In 1921 and 1922, however, the Communists increasingly restricted their fellow leftists, culminating in arrests and a political trial of some leading SRs. Many other opposition socialist leaders emigrated.

During the Civil War, there had been complaints in the soviets about Cheka terroristic "excesses," and there were some fruitless attempts to see that it conformed to "revolutionary legality." In early 1922, with the Civil War now over, it was replaced by a new organization, the State Security Administration (GPU and later OGPU). Its head remained the same, Felix Dzerzhinsky, and the new organization was even given a right not enjoyed by the earlier Cheka—it could arrest party members.

Despite the Communists' increasing centralization of power and lack of tolerance of even leftist opposition, the NEP period was characterized by less ideological control and conformity than later existed under Stalin. This was especially evident in the cultural sphere (see Chapter 16).

STALIN'S RISE TO PROMINENCE

The decline of Lenin's health in the few years before his death in January 1924 provided an opportunity for Stalin to increase his powers. Born Joseph Djugashvilli in Gori, Georgia, in 1878 (not, according to newly discovered material, 1879, as previously thought), he was the son of a cobbler and the grandson of serfs. His mother wanted him to be a priest, and after graduating from a church school in Gori in 1894, he won a scholarship to the Orthodox theological seminary in Tiflis. There, however, he became more interested in revolutionary ideas than religion and left the seminary in 1899.

Not long afterward, he became a full-time Marxist agitator in Tiflis and other Caucasian cities. Beginning in 1902, he was often arrested, imprisoned, and exiled. Like many other political exiles, however, he often managed to flee exile before his term was completed.

According to police descriptions of the time, he was about 5 feet 4 inches tall and had a pockmarked face and an infirm left arm. Other evidence concerning his youth and early manhood indicate that he possessed a cold, coarse, ambitious, and authoritarian personality. He was not, however, immune to Georgian poetry and fiction, especially one tale that told of a Georgian avenger, Koba, who fought against Russian oppression. Later as a revolutionary, he adopted the name "Koba" as his own cover name, only later settling on "Stalin" (man of steel). His first wife, who died (in 1907?) a few years after their marriage, may have warmed his cold heart for a while. A friend of Stalin's later reported him saying: "This creature softened my heart of stone. She died and with her died my last warm feelings for people."[4]

Although later contrasts with the brilliant, cosmopolitan Trotsky sometimes made Stalin seem intellectually dull, he was more intelligent and well-read than often depicted. Writing of the mature Stalin, Robert Tucker has called him "a voracious reader," especially of historical and political works. Tucker also maintains that Stalin had his own political ideas and was not just an unprincipled opportunist taking up whatever ideas benefited him at the moment. Even after coming to power, he wrote many of his own articles and speeches.

Already a supporter of Lenin, Stalin first met him at a Bolshevik congress in Finland in 1905. During the next two years, Stalin attended congresses in Stockholm and London of the full Social Democratic Labor party—its Bolshevik and Menshevik factions not yet completely having severed ties. Back in the Caucasus, Stalin became involved in the planning of a rather unique method of Bolshevik fund raising—the robbing of banks. In 1912, Lenin brought Stalin onto the Bolshevik's Central Committee and also made him a member of a small Russian Bureau responsible for party activities inside the Russian Empire. That same year, Lenin asked him to write a work on Marxism and nationalism, which he completed to Lenin's satisfaction in 1913.

Like many other leading Bolsheviks who admired Lenin, Stalin occasionally differed with him, both before and after 1917. In that year, for example, Stalin returned to Petrograd about three weeks before Lenin, became an editor of the party's paper, *Pravda*, and approved its political stance, which was more moderate than Lenin's. Lenin communicated his views first from Switzerland and then in person, most notably in his "April Theses," but it took Stalin a little while before he was won over to Lenin's insistence on overthrowing the Provisional Government.

In spring 1917, Stalin was one of the most influential of the nine full members of the party's Central Committee, but he played a lesser role than either Lenin or Trotsky in the events surrounding the November revolution. During the Civil War, Stalin not only served as commissar of nationalities, but also on the Council of Workers' and Peasants' Defense and as a Red Army political commissar. The latter role brought him into sharp conflict with Trotsky because of Trotsky's use of former tsarist officers, a group greatly distrusted by Stalin. According to Khrushchev, Stalin's opposition to the use of such "bourgeois" specialists, military or civilian, earned him a reputation as a "specialist-eater." Stalin became a member of both the Politburo and an Orgburo in 1919, after the Eighth Party Congress approved their creation and the appointment

---

[4]Robert C. Tucker, *Stalin as Revolutionary, 1879–1929: A Study in History and Personality* (New York, 1973), p. 108.

of five Central Committee members to each. That same year, Stalin was named commissar of the Workers' and Peasants' Inspectorate, whose task was to ferret out and eliminate government incompetence and corruption and to help train Soviet civil servants. As Tucker summarizes the respective positions of Stalin and Trotsky at the end of the Civil War: "Whereas Trotsky emerged from the war with much glory and little power, Stalin emerged with little glory and much power."[5]

Stalin's work as a commissar in the Red Army, his reputation as a "specialist-eater," and his overseeing of the Workers' and Peasants' Inspectorate were in keeping with his distrust of "bourgeois" specialists and his views of government. To Stalin's mind, a main impediment in creating a new socialist order was bureaucratic resistance from specialists unsympathetic with communism as well as from party members corrupted by them. He believed that what Soviet Russia needed was a unified leadership capable of clearly spelling out a correct party line, selecting capable and loyal officials, and overseeing the fulfillment of leadership directives.[6]

The appointment of Stalin as general secretary of the party's Secretariat in April 1922 added to his powers. At first, however, few of his fellow Communists realized how significant this position would become. Although he lacked some of the qualities usually associated with being a good administrator, he was forceful and did not seem to mind dealing with the everyday party details that many other top leaders shunned. He was vitally interested in personal as well as party power and how it could be gained and used—he had read and been impressed by Machiavelli's *The Prince*. Now as the man most responsible for party personnel, he set out to find and promote those who would support him.

LENIN VERSUS STALIN

Although an ill Lenin supported Stalin's appointment as general secretary, he soon regretted it and suggested his removal. Lenin's doubts sprung, at least partly, from Stalin's dealings with Georgian leaders and his Russian chauvinistic position on the appropriate status of the non-Russian republics in the new Soviet Union. In a two-week span at the turn of 1922–1923, following strokes in May and December of 1922, Lenin dictated two criticisms of Stalin. By early March 1923, after discovering that Stalin had been rude to Krupskaia (Lenin's wife) back in December, Lenin wrote an angry letter to Stalin.

The rudeness occurred after Krupskaia had taken down a short letter to Trotsky dictated by the ailing Lenin. Even though his doctors had given him

[5]Ibid., p. 209.
[6]See Lars T. Lih's "Introduction" to *Stalin's Letters to Molotov, 1925–1936*, eds. Lars T. Lih, Oleg V. Naumov, and Oleg V. Khlevniuk (New Haven, 1995), pp. 10–11, especially for Stalin's frequent use of an "antibureaucratic scenario." Stalin later cited bureaucratism as a target of many of his purges of government and party officials.

FIGURE 10.2.
Lenin and Stalin, in early
1922.
(Tass/Sovfoto.)

permission to dictate it, Stalin called Krupskaia on the telephone and criticized her using crude and abusive language for allowing Lenin to exert himself. He also threatened to bring the matter before the party's Central Control Commission, which was responsible for monitoring the behavior of party members. Several days earlier, the Central Committee had authorized Stalin to oversee Lenin's treatment, a responsibility that Stalin attempted to use for his own benefit.

On the same day (March 5) that Lenin dictated his angry letter to Stalin, he dictated another to Trotsky asking for him to defend "the Georgian case" in the Central Committee, noting he could not trust Stalin's and Dzerzhinsky's handling of it. Several days later, Lenin suffered another stroke, depriving him of his speech. Although his condition improved somewhat in the summer and fall, he died on January 21, 1924, never having withdrawn his objections to Stalin.

Shortly before the Thirteenth Party Congress in May, 1924, Krupskaia passed on to the Central Committee Lenin's dictated notes of December 24–25 and the postscript to it of January 4, 1923. That the Central Committee refused to go along with Lenin's wishes and remove Stalin as general secretary reflects Stalin's astute political maneuvering among his fellow committee members.

Lenin's Growing Criticism of Stalin

The three criticisms of Stalin that follow reflect Lenin's growing wariness of him. The first and second criticisms are those just mentioned occurring at the turn of 1922–1923. The first is excerpted from notes Lenin dictated on December 24–25. These notes dealt with Lenin's concern about a possible future split in the party, and his criticism of Stalin is balanced somewhat by critical appraisals of the strengths and weakness of other party leaders (of which only those pertaining to Trotsky are here included). Lenin intended these observations for the Twelfth Party Congress, scheduled for the spring of 1923. The second criticism is a postscript of January 4, 1923 that Lenin added to his notes of December 24–25, and the third is his letter to Stalin of March 5, 1923. The first and second selections are found in V. I. Lenin, *Collected Works*, Vol. 36 (Moscow, 1966), pp. 594–596; the third selection is in Vol. 45 (Moscow, 1970), pp. 607–608.

Comrade Stalin, having become Secretary-General, has unlimited authority concentrated in his hands, and I am not sure whether he will always be capable of using that authority with sufficient caution. Comrade Trotsky, on the other hand, as his struggle against the C.C. [Central Committee] on the question of the People's Commissariat for Communications has already proved, is distinguished not only by outstanding ability. He is personally perhaps the most capable man in the preset C.C., but he has displayed excessive self-assurance and has shown excessive preoccupation with the purely administrative side of the work.

These two qualities of the two outstanding leaders of the present C.C. can inadvertently lead to a split, and if our Party does not take steps to avert this, the split may come unexpectedly.

Stalin is too rude and this defect, although quite tolerable in our midst and in dealings among us Communists, becomes intolerable in a Secretary-General. That is why I suggest that the comrades think about a way of removing Stalin from that post and appointing another man in his stead who in all other respects differs from Comrade Stalin in having only one advantage, namely, that of being more tolerant, more loyal, more polite and more considerate to the comrades, less capricious, etc. This circumstance may appear to be a negligible detail. But I think that from the standpoint of safeguards against a split and from the standpoint of what I wrote above about the relationship between Stalin and Trotsky it is not a detail, or it is a detail which can assume decisive importance.

Dear Comrade Stalin:

You have been so rude as to summon my wife to the telephone and use bad language. Although she had told you that she was prepared to forget this, the fact nevertheless become known through her to Zinoviev and Kamenev. I have no intention of forgetting so easily what has been done against me, and it goes without saying that what has been done against my wife I consider having been done against me as well. I ask you, therefore, to think over whether you are prepared to withdraw what you have said and to make your apologies, or whether you prefer that relations between us should be broken off.

Respectfully yours,
Lenin

STALIN AND HIS RIVALS, 1923–1927

Stalin was especially clever in playing upon the fears and ambitions of two Politburo colleagues, Grigori Zinoviev and Lev Kamenev. Zinoviev had spent a long time working with Lenin abroad before joining him for the return to Russia in April 1917. Although sometimes differing with Lenin, he generally came around to his viewpoint. In the early Soviet period, Zinoviev served as the party leader in Petrograd and also as the head of the Communist International (see Chapter 12). He was a vain and ambitious man.

Less ambitious, but more talented, was Kamenev. He had also worked closely with Lenin abroad but was later arrested in Russia and sent to Siberia in 1915. Along with Stalin he returned to Petrograd just weeks before Lenin, helped edit *Pravda*, and was criticized by the returning Lenin for his moderate policies. Along with Zinoviev, he had strongly resisted Lenin's call for an armed Bolshevik takeover in the fall of 1917. Despite these differences, Lenin relied heavily on Kamenev. He became head of the Moscow party organization and deputy chairman of the Council of People's Commissars. When Lenin became too ill to chair Politburo meetings, Kamenev usually took his place. When Stalin insulted Krupskaia, it was her friend Kamenev to whom she immediately turned for protection against Stalin's interference in her "personal life," noting that he (Kamenev) and Zinoviev were "closer comrades" to her husband than was Stalin.

As Lenin's health deteriorated, however, Zinoviev and Kamenev became more concerned with Trotsky than Stalin. They feared that the brilliant and talented head of the Red Army might succeed Lenin as the Soviet leader. Zinoviev, like Stalin, was especially hostile to Trotsky and apparently envisioned himself as the future leader. Stalin took advantage of their fixation on Trotsky to strengthen his own position cautiously without seeming too ambitious. Zinoviev and Kamenev relied on Stalin in their struggle against Trotsky; these two friends played the chief role within the Central Committee in preventing Lenin's wishes regarding Stalin from being realized.

The triumvirate of Zinoviev, Kamenev, and Stalin held together long enough to clip the wings of the man who had been referred to as the "young eagle." A great orator, brilliant writer, and a key figure in 1917 and the Civil War, Trotsky continued to head the Red Army and serve on the Politburo. But he was not a good politician. He was too proud to dirty his hands in the business of grubby political maneuvering, and he struck many other party leaders as aloof and arrogant.

Meanwhile, Stalin was using his skills, political allies, and position as general secretary to build up his following among the party. At the same time, he dispersed some of Trotsky's chief supporters to foreign posts. Stalin was on good terms with the OGPU head, Dzerzhinsky, and staffed the party's Central Control Commission with many of his own supporters, including its head, V. Kuibyshev. Both agencies became instrumental in helping Stalin weaken and eventually remove some of his rivals and their supporters from the party.

To lay claim to Lenin's unrivaled position as party leader, Stalin sought to establish himself as Lenin's most loyal follower and as the best interpreter of his ideas. At the time of Lenin's death, an ailing Trotsky was in the south of Russia, where he had gone for a "climatic cure." He did not return for Lenin's funeral, partly because Stalin misled him regarding its date. According to Volkogonov, his absence created a bad impression and was perhaps crucial in leading to his eventual downfall. Stalin himself played a prominent part in Lenin's Moscow funeral and in honoring the dead leader.

Several months later, in April and May 1924, Stalin's *The Foundations of Leninism* appeared in *Pravda*, and in late 1924 he began advocating his position of "socialism in one country." Russia, he said, could achieve socialism even without outside help from other countries. He contrasted this belief, which he claimed was also Lenin's, with Trotsky's idea of permanent revolution. Although Trotsky did maintain that achieving socialism required outside help (which proletarian revolutions in more advanced countries could help deliver), Stalin's polemics with his rival partially distorted both the ideas of Lenin and Trotsky. But Stalin's stance, along with his earlier *The Foundations of Leninism*, enhanced his reputation among party members. To many of them, he seemed a steady, reliable, optimistic leader, and his belief that Russia could achieve socialism on its own appealed to them.

Because he was somewhat of a loner and adept at concealing his real intentions, few party members knew the real Stalin. Although he apparently stated in a 1923 conversation that "the greatest delight is to mark one's enemy, prepare everything, avenge oneself thoroughly, and then go to sleep," he was generally much more cautious about revealing his ruthlessness.

By spring 1925, however, Kamenev and Zinoviev had seen enough of Stalin to realize that he was more of a threat to them than Trotsky. After helping to oust Trotsky as head of the Red Army in January, Zinoviev and Kamenev began attacking some of the policies espoused by Stalin. Meanwhile, Stalin had been strengthening his support from other Politburo members.

Three of them were Nikolai Bukharin, Alexei Rykov, and Mikhail Tomsky. Of the three Bukharin, editor of *Pravda*, was the most influential. In Lenin's comments on leading Communists in December 1922, he had said that the thirty-four-year-old "Bukharin is not only a most valuable and major theorist of the party; he is also considered the favorite of the whole party, but his theoretical views can be classified as fully Marxist only with great reserve." Rykov was an able and forthright administrator who had succeeded Lenin as chairman of the Council of People's Commissars, and Tomsky was the head of Russia's trade unions.

What united these three men of the "Right" was a common pro-NEP viewpoint best articulated by Bukharin. In the economic debates of the day, party leaders differed on how best to stimulate industrialization and peasant productivity. Trotsky and other "leftists," impatient with NEP, advocated more government planning, rapid industrialization (especially of heavy industry), and increased agricultural collectivization. They criticized NEP policies that enriched wealthy peasants (kulaks) and businessmen. In 1925, Zinoviev and Kamenev echoed some of the leftist criticisms, with Zinoviev charging that NEP was a retreat from Marxism-Leninism. In defense of their pro-NEP position, Bukharin's group cited Lenin's authority, especially as espoused in some of his final writings.

In these works, Lenin wrote of a long, slow process of enlightening the peasants and gradually winning them over to socialist methods. The Right, in turn, wanted to increase peasant productivity by incentives and use this increased productivity to help feed more industrial workers and fund increased industrialization. In 1925, the three leaders of the Right and Stalin approved a new policy that eased the tax burden on peasants and legitimized their right to lease land and hire labor.

The new policy did not reflect Stalin's own economic ideas, which were fully revealed only later. His alliance with the Right was a tactical maneuver, giving the temporary allies a majority on the seven-man Politburo, and strengthening Stalin's clout against Trotsky, Zinoviev, and Kamenev (the other three men on the Politburo). Meanwhile, Stalin continued placing loyal supporters in prominent positions. At the beginning of 1926, three Stalin supporters, Mikhail Kalinin, Viacheslav Molotov, and Kliment Voroshilov all became full members of the Politburo. The last two were especially close to the general secretary. Lenin had once called Molotov "the best file clerk in Russia." His dedication to working at his desk within the Secretariat earned him the unflattering nickname "Stony-Arse." Voroshilov served as a Civil War commander and in late 1925, after the death of Red Army head Mikhail Frunze (who had replaced Trotsky), Voroshilov took over his position.

As these supporters were being promoted to full Politburo status, Kamenev was being demoted to candidate membership. Although Zinoviev remained on the new nine-man Politburo, he soon lost his position as party chief in Leningrad. He and Kamenev had made the mistake of openly challenging Stalin at the Fourteenth Party Congress, held at the end of 1925.

In 1926, Zinoviev and Kamenev formed a Left-Opposition alliance with Trotsky, the man they had vilified not long before. The move reflected their desperation. By the end of 1926, charged with factionalism, all three men had been unseated from the Politburo and Zinoviev from heading the Comintern. In November and December 1927, after an intraparty struggle and heightened tensions, the three men were expelled from the party. Although Zinoviev and Kamenev were later readmitted in exchange for renouncing their views, Trotsky refused to do so and in January 1928 was exiled to Alma-Ata in Kazakhstan.

THE NEP PERIOD: SOME CONCLUDING REMARKS

Many past scholars viewed the NEP period as a purposeful interlude begun by Lenin, a temporary tactical retreat from his more hard-line Communist policies of the Civil War years. Stalin's subsequent ending of NEP was then perceived as a resumption of Lenin's earlier, more militant attempt to create a Communist society.

In recent years, however, historians have often criticized this approach as too simplistic. Indeed, this approach frequently paid insufficient attention to most causes of state policies aside from the decisions of the top political leaders. And it failed to capture the NEP period's complexity; its experimental, ad-hoc nature; and its open-ended possibilities. Although the decisions of Lenin and Stalin were certainly of utmost importance, both the policies of the NEP years and Stalin's ending of NEP also resulted from many other factors. Subsequent chapters dealing with economic, social, and cultural issues of the 1920s indicate some of these additional causes.

SUGGESTED SOURCES*

BALL, ALAN M. *Russia's Last Capitalists: The Nepmen, 1921–1929.* Berkeley, 1987.

BURANOV, YURI. *Lenin's Will: Falsified and Forbidden.* Amherst, N.Y., 1994.

CARR, E. H. *The Bolshevik Revolution: The Interregnum, 1924–1926.* New York, 1954.

———. *The Bolshevik Revolution: Socialism in One Country, 1924–1926.* Vols. 1 and 2. New York, 1958, 1959.

COHEN, STEPHEN. *Bukharin and the Bolshevik Revolution: A Political Biography, 1888–1938.* New York, 1973.

DANIELS, ROBERT V. *The Conscience of the Revolution: Communist Opposition in Soviet Russia.* Cambridge, Mass., 1960.

DAVIES, R. W., ed. *From Tsarism to the New Economic Policy: Continuity and Change in the Economy of the USSR.* Ithaca, N.Y., 1991.

DEUTSCHER, ISAAC. *The Prophet Unarmed: Trotsky, 1921–1929.* New York, 1959.

ERLICH, ALEXANDER. *The Soviet Industrialization Debate, 1924–1928.* Cambridge, Mass., 1960.

FITZPATRICK, SHEILA. *Cultural Revolution in Russia, 1928–1931.* Bloomington, 1978.

———. *The Russian Revolution.* 2d ed. Oxford, 1994.

———, Alexander Rabinowitch, and Richard Stites, eds. *Russia in the Era of NEP: Explorations in Soviet Society and Culture.* Bloomington, 1991.

GILL, GRAEME J. *The Origins of the Stalinist Political System.* Cambridge, England, 1990.

GLEASON, ABBOT, PETER KENEZ, and RICHARD STITES, eds. *Bolshevik Culture: Experiment and Order in the Russian Revolution.* Bloomington, 1985.

HINDUS, MAURICE. *Humanity Uprooted.* New York, 1929.

KENEZ, PETER. *The Birth of the Propaganda State: Soviet Methods of Mass Mobilization, 1917–1929.* Cambridge, England, 1985.

KOLLONTAI, A. *The Workers Opposition in Russia.* Chicago, 1921.

LEWIN, MOSHE. *Russian Peasants and Soviet Power: A Study of Collectivization.* London, 1968.

———. *Lenin's Last Struggle.* New York, 1968.

PETHYBRIDGE, ROGER. *One Step Backwards, Two Steps Forward: Soviet Society and Politics in the New Economic Policy.* Oxford, 1990.

PIPES, RICHARD. *Russia under the Bolshevik Regime.* New York, 1994. Chs. 8 & 9.

RADZINSKY, EDVARD. *Stalin.* New York, 1996. Chs. 1–11.

REIMAN, MICHAL. *The Birth of Stalinism: The USSR on the Eve of the "Second Revolution."* Bloomington, 1987.

SERVICE, ROBERT. *Lenin: A Political Life.* Vol. 3, *The Iron Ring.* Bloomington, 1995.

TUCKER, ROBERT C. *Political Culture and Leadership in Soviet Russia: From Lenin to Gorbachev.* New York, 1987.

TUMARKIN, NINA. *Lenin Lives!: The Lenin Cult in Soviet Russia.* Cambridge, Mass., 1983.

VOLKOGONOV, DMITRI. *Trotsky: The Eternal Revolutionary.* New York, 1996. Ch. 5.

VON HAGEN, MARK. *Soldiers in the Proletarian Dictatorship: The Red Army and the Soviet Socialist State, 1917–1930.* Ithaca, N.Y., 1990.

*See also books cited in footnotes.

CHAPTER 11

Stalin and Stalinism,
1928–1941

In 1928–1929, Stalin launched a "revolution from above" that compared in significance to the two revolutions of 1917. With help from many party members dissatisfied with NEP, he cast it overboard, attacked bureaucratism and "class enemies," and introduced the collectivization of agriculture and the USSR's first Five-Year Plan (FYP), with its emphasis on rapid industrialization. These changes, plus a "cultural revolution" that lasted from 1928 to 1931, were all part of Stalin's revolution.

Although it was a revolution from above, Stalin did not carefully plan all phases of it ahead of time. To some extent, he unleashed youthful and extremist energies on the country; allowed them to wreak their sometimes spontaneous havoc; and then, when his purposes had been served, once again restrained them.

Opposition to Stalin's revolution was great, especially among the peasantry, most of whom were forced onto collective farms. Millions of peasants left the countryside, some making their own way to the cities and others being exiled or sentenced to forced labor. Millions of others died in 1932–1933 in a "terror-famine" brought about by Stalin's policies.

Stalin's forced industrialization was successful in building up Soviet heavy industry and military preparedness but at the expense of other areas of Soviet life. Increasing government-party control over the economy was accompanied by the growth of the government and party and their increasing controls over people's everyday existence.

In contrast to Lenin, Stalin perpetrated a cult around himself, and it was difficult for most Soviet citizens to recognize his responsibility for many of the evils of his time. Although many of the seeds of Stalin's policies were sown during Lenin's years in power, Stalin placed his own unique stamp on the country. It began with his revolution from above and was also marked by a phenomenon of the mid 1930s that has been variously labeled "the revolution betrayed" (Trotsky), "the great retreat" (Timasheff), and "internal détente" (Tucker). Just as Lenin retreated from some Marxist revolutionary ideas during

NEP, so Stalin retreated from others during his "great retreat." As becomes clearer in later chapters devoted to social and cultural policies, Stalin's "retreat" diluted some strands of revolutionary Marxism-Leninism by placing more emphasis on stability, law and order, social hierarchy, Russian nationalism, and motherhood and family.

Stalin also left his mark by the Great Terror of 1936–1938. Its mass arrests and executions both disrupted and furthered some of the goals of his "retreat." As Volkogonov clearly indicates, the chief villain in Stalin's distorted mind was Trotsky, who was credited with masterminding many plots from abroad. Although Trotsky was most critical of Stalin for betraying the revolution, for retreating from Marxist-Leninist principles, his influence was nowhere near as great as Stalin feared.

WHY ANOTHER REVOLUTION?

After crushing the Left Opposition in late 1927, Stalin borrowed some of their economic ideas and began moving against the Right, led by Bukharin. In 1928–1929, while battling those he labeled the "Right danger," he began his new collectivization and industrialization policies.

At least six factors seem to have motivated his new policies: (1) a grain "crisis," accompanied by other economic problems; (2) military needs; (3) the legacy of the Civil War and War Communism (and to a lesser extent the legacies of Ivan the Terrible and Peter the Great); (4) the desire to increase party control over the economy and society; (5) Marxist ideological considerations and class resentments; and (6) Stalin's wish to weaken the Right, who were the most vocal advocates of maintaining NEP policies.

In late 1927, peasants sharply reduced the amount of grain they sold to the state, endangering urban food supplies and the growth of the cities. Decreasing state-set grain prices, a shortage of affordable manufactured goods, and war rumors (diplomatic relations had been broken with Great Britain) were among the causes for the peasants' behavior. This crisis came on the top of other economic difficulties, such as growing unemployment in the cities. Stalin could have increased state grain prices to end the food crisis but for a variety of reasons chose otherwise. Instead, he blamed kulaks ("rich" peasants) for trying to sabotage the government by withholding grain and threatening the cities with famine. In January 1928, he obtained unanimous Politburo agreement to extraordinary measures to deal with the shortages, primarily by confiscating grain from "kulak speculators."

Although the shortages provided Stalin the opportunity to begin his revolution from above, his hopes for the future of the USSR, emphasizing military-industrial strength, helped fuel it. Perhaps his most esteemed biographer, Robert Tucker, thinks that these aspirations were already present in the late 1920s and were clearly enunciated in a Stalin speech to industrial managers in February 1931.

It is Tucker's contention that Stalin believed that "capitalist encirclement"

Industrialize Rapidly or Be Crushed: Stalin's Speech to Industrial Managers

The following excerpt from a Stalin speech of February 4, 1931, is found in J. V. Stalin, *Works*, Vol. 13 (Moscow, 1955), pp. 40–41. Bracketed material is mine.

To slacken the tempo [of industrialization] would mean falling behind. And those who fall behind get beaten. But we do no want to be beaten. No, we refuse to be beaten! One feature of the history of old Russia was the continual beatings she suffered because of her backwardness. She was beaten by the Mongol khans. She was beaten by the Turkish beys. She was beaten by the Swedish feudal lords. She was beaten by the Polish and Lithuanian gentry. She was beaten by the British and French capitalists. She was beaten by the Japanese barons. All beat her—because of her backwardness, because of her military backwardness, cultural backwardness, political backwardness, industrial backwardness, agricultural backwardness. They beat her because to do so was profitable and could be done with impunity. You remember the words of the pre-revolutionary poet: "You are poor and abundant, mighty and impotent, Mother Russia." Those gentlemen were quite familiar with the verses of the old poet. They beat her, saying: "You are abundant," so one can enrich oneself at your expense. They beat her, saying "You are poor and impotent," so you can be beaten and plundered with impunity. Such is the law of the exploiters—to beat the backward and the weak. It is the jungle law of capitalism. You are backward, you are weak—therefore you are wrong; hence, you can be beaten and enslaved. You are mighty—therefore you are right; hence, we must be wary of you.

That is why we must no longer lag behind.

In the past we had no fatherland, nor could we have had one. But now that we have overthrown capitalism and power is in our hands, in the hands of the people, we have a fatherland, and we will uphold its independence. Do you want our socialist fatherland to be beaten and to lose its independence? If you do not want this, you must put an end to its backwardness in the shortest possible time and develop a genuine Bolshevik tempo in building up its socialist economy. There is no other way. That is why Lenin said on the eve of the October Revolution: "Either perish, or overtake and outstrip the advanced capitalist countries."

We are fifty or a hundred years behind the advanced countries. We must make good this distance in ten years. Either we do it, or we shall go under.

necessitated his revolution from above and the growth of state power to carry it out. (See Chapter 12 for the international situation in this period.) Stalin was familiar with the deeds of Ivan the Terrible and Peter the Great and with the justifications made for their policies in the name of strengthening the Russian state. He apparently saw himself following in their state-strengthening footsteps, especially Peter's, as well as in the Marxist revolutionary steps of Lenin.

The memory of the Civil War and War Communism sparked enthusiasm among many party members for a bold new drive toward the creation of a truly socialist order. Such a drive, led by them, promised new heroic opportunities. It also gave party members greater control over the economy and over the lives of Soviet citizens.

Still another factor contributing to Stalin's revolution was ideological and class dissatisfaction with NEP and the social groups thought to be benefiting from it. Marxian ideology stressed the proletariat and industrial development;

indeed, their advanced maturation was thought necessary before any final Communist order could be constructed. Many party members shared Marx's distrust of the peasantry and felt uncomfortable with the slow pace of NEP industrial development and social transformation. The NEP seemed too much of a compromise with capitalism. By 1928, the party and party-controlled press were increasingly playing upon lower-class resentments towards Nepmen, "bourgeois" specialists, and kulaks. When, at the end of the 1920s, Nepmen were kicked out of state housing, the great majority of other urban dwellers apparently welcomed the news that more housing space would now be available.

Finally, there was Stalin's political opportunism. By attacking NEP gradualism and launching his own "heroic" economic effort, Stalin could at the same time discredit the Right, which he charged with being corrupted by "bourgeois" specialists and views. It appears likely that in Stalin's mind strengthening his own powers and those of Soviet Russia, Marxism-Leninism, and the party were all interwoven. What must have made "revolution from above" so appealing to him is that he could work toward accomplishing all these goals at the same time.

STALIN, THE RIGHT OPPOSITION, THE FIRST FIVE-YEAR PLAN, AND COLLECTIVIZATION

Although Stalin had gotten Politburo members Bukharin, Rykov, and Tomsky to agree to grain confiscation from "kulak speculators," he soon went far beyond the measures these leaders of the Right had envisioned. Stalin himself later admitted that illegal searches and other methods were used and that peasants other than kulaks were affected. In Siberia, where he went in January 1928 to spur the collection of more grain, he urged a sharp increase in collective and state farms.

As 1928 progressed, so too did the split between Stalin and the Right Opposition. In August, Bukharin even turned to Kamenev, whom he had formerly attacked. According to Kamenev, Bukharin told him that Stalin was renewing War Communism and that his policies would provoke civil war. He referred to Stalin as "a Ghenghis Kahn" and as a man who was interested only in strengthening his own power.

Stalin became aware of this conversation and the following year used it against Bukharin. Meanwhile, he proceeded cautiously in his campaign to weaken the Right. In mid-1929, Tomsky was removed as the head of the trade unions, and Bukharin, who was attacked in the press, was unseated as chairman of the Comintern. In November, Bukharin was kicked off the Politburo. Later that month, Bukharin, Tomsky, and Rykov admitted the error of their ways and promised future unity with the party line, especially against any "right deviation."

Meanwhile, Russia began its first Five-Year Plan (FYP) in October 1928. A state planning agency, Gosplan, had been in existence since 1921, but its previous work was child's play compared to its preparation of the first FYP. In a book-length document, it set out growth targets for major categories such as industry, agriculture, national income, investment, and employment and provided detailed breakdowns for subcategories. In keeping with Stalin's military concerns, growth in heavy industry received top priority. In April 1929, Gosplan presented its final targets in two variants to the Sixteenth Party Congress, which approved the more optimistic of the two. Targets were later moved even higher. Stalin seemed bent on an unprecedented economic transformation of the country.

With the inauguration of the first FYP, the Soviet economy began assuming the characteristics that it would display for the next six decades. Although the new economic model was not fully settled upon immediately and a certain degree of groping in the dark occurred, nevertheless the model's main elements were constructed during the first FYP. Private enterprise became illegal. A "command economy" was introduced, and, with little concern for consumers' desires, government-party officials decided what should be produced throughout the country and in what quantity. One FYP would succeed another, all designed especially to increase heavy industrial output.

To pay for such rapid industrialization, Stalin believed it was necessary to squeeze more from the peasants. Until Bukharin was ousted from the Politburo in November 1929, this was done mainly by selective forced requisitioning and mandatory procurement quotas. After Bukharin's ousting, Stalin's drive to collectivize Russian agriculture proceeded rapidly. In December 1929, he insisted that the kulaks must be "liquidated as a class."

In 1928, less than 3 percent of Russia's farming was under the control of collective or state farms. The optimal FYP targets accepted by the Sixteenth Party Congress in 1928 called for these farms to produce only a little over 15 percent of agricultural production by the end of the first FYP. Yet by March 10, 1930, Stalin claimed that 58 percent of all peasant households had been collectivized.

Mistrusting the peasants and realizing that the number of party personnel in rural areas was insufficient to carry through collectivization, the party had sent some 25,000 urban workers and party activists ("the 25,000ers") into the countryside in January 1930. Their job was to lead the collectivization effort. Even earlier, state agents had begun expropriating peasant livestock as part of the forced-collectivization process. If the peasants opposed too strenuously, as many did, they were likely to be branded as kulaks or kulak sympathizers. OGPU (secret police) forces and party activists dealt severely with such opponents, often killing, deporting, or sentencing them to labor camps.

Apparently sensing the chaotic agricultural conditions such rapid collectivization was creating, Stalin, in a March 1930 article, blamed local officials for being "dizzy with success." He now emphasized a principle he had been most responsible for violating: Collectivization should be voluntary. And he conceded that peasant vegetable gardens and some domestic animals should not be collectivized. By June 1, 1930, government sources indicated that only 24 percent of all peasant households remained collectivized.

This, however, was only a temporary retreat. The government soon resumed its coercive collectivization drive. By July 1932, 62 percent of all peasant

FIGURE 11.1. Enemies of the 5-Year Plan. This Soviet poster depicts a landowner, kulak, corrupt journalist, capitalist (*top*) and a drunkard, priest, Menshevik, and White Army officer (*bottom*). The paper being read is the *Menshevik Herald*.
(*From J.P. Nettl,* The Soviet Achievement, *#65, p. 122, Harcourt, Brace & World, New York, 1967.*)

households were collectivized, and by July 1936, 90 percent. These figures included collective farms (kolkhozes) and state farms (sovhozes), both of which were tightly controlled by party-state functionaries. (For more on these farms and how they differed, see Chapter 15.)

In working out collectivization practices, the state in 1929 created Machine-Tractor Stations (MTS). The MTS were to possess and repair agricultural machinery such as tractors and combines and make them available, in exchange for payment in kind, to the kolkhozes. The MTS were indicative of the Soviet regime's great hopes for mechanizing agriculture—for example, tractor production jumped almost 100-fold from 1928 to 1936.

Besides their technical work, the MTS played an important political role. After the crusade of the 25,000ers was officially ended in December 1931, some of these outsiders remained in the countryside as MTS personnel or kolkhoz chairmen. The MTS became islands of party activism among a sea of peasants unsympathetic to the Communist regime.

Throughout the first FYP, peasants continued to resist collectivization, by such methods as killing and eating their animals so as not to hand them over to the collectives. By 1933, there were less than half the number of cattle, horses, hogs, goats, and sheep that had existed in 1929.

But such tactics could not deter Stalin. By the end of 1933, millions of peasant family members had been rounded up and deported to Siberia and other areas, many forced to work in dreadful labor camps. The Russian writer Alexander Solzhenitsyn, among others, has described in graphic detail the plight of many of these unfortunate people.

As a result of Stalin's policies in 1932 and 1933, millions of additional people starved to death. The government's exorbitant food procurements, often leaving peasants with nothing to eat, were the main cause, but collectivization, peasant hostility to it, and bad weather also helped bring the famine about. Although it struck the northern Caucasus, the lower and middle Volga, and some other areas, Ukrainian peasants were most decimated. Some historians, including Robert Conquest, have charged that Stalin's suspicion and hostility toward the Ukrainian nationality help account for why the Ukrainian losses were so great. To help pay for imported goods for industrialization, the government continued to export grain during the 1932–1933 famine, a famine it refused to acknowledge publicly or seek outside help to alleviate.

ACHIEVEMENTS AND FAILURES UNDER THE FIVE-YEAR PLANS, 1928–1941

At the end of 1932, nine months before a full five years had expired, Soviet officials announced that the exceedingly ambitious first FYP had been fulfilled. This was partly propaganda, and the statistics they released were far from reliable. With one plan now declared completed, Stalin launched another, the second FYP (1933–1937), and after that, a third FYP (1938–1942).

The second FYP projected less grandiose growth rates than the first FYP targets. Consolidation, efficiency, quality, and better living standards became the new watchwords. Yet, before the plan had been completed, Stalin's purges and his concerns with Nazi and Japanese aggression interfered with the fulfilling of these goals and also affected the third FYP, which was interrupted by Germany's attack on Russia in June 1941.

The net result of Russia's prewar industrialization drive was, however, impressive in many ways, especially in light of the worldwide depression of the 1930s. Many workers, especially young ones, accepted with enthusiasm the challenge of building a new socialist order. From 1928 to 1940, Russia's production of energy sources and ferrous metals, including iron and steel, more than quadrupled. Increases in machinery and chemical products were even greater. New and rudimentary industries developed rapidly, producing such goods as aircraft and agricultural machinery, tractors and tanks, and machine tools and munitions. During the 1930s, the production of most weapons increased tenfold or more. New industrial centers arose, such as Magnitogorsk in the Urals and Kuznetsk in southern Siberia. Although more than 1,200 miles apart, the two centers were linked together by rail to combine the ores of the former and the coal of the latter.

But this industrial growth came at a high price. While heavy industry benefited, other areas of the Soviet economy, such as agriculture, housing, and consumer goods, lagged far behind. The standard of living declined (see Chapter 15 for more on living conditions), and the situation of laborers worsened. New workers came to factories and mines not only of their own volition, sometimes in response to recruitment drives, but also as a result of government coercion. New measures tightened work discipline, especially after Stalin's purges of the late 1930s had disrupted it. In 1940, the increasing possibility of war furthered the tightening: New laws made absenteeism, lateness (by more than twenty minutes), or leaving one's job without permission criminal offenses.

The state also pressured workers in other ways. In 1935, a coal miner named Alexei Stakhanov became a "hero of socialist labor" by reportedly exceeding his work quota by fourteen times. Actually, his effort was stage-managed by the authorities, who soon afterward launched a "Stakhanovite movement" to hike up workers' norms. Another step that affected workers was the government's introduction in December 1932 of mandatory internal passports for urban dwellers. The passport was to list not only one's name, age, and nationality, but also one's place of employment and permanent residence. It was partly aimed at reducing the number of workers quitting their jobs to seek better ones in other towns.

A bigger target of the decree, however, was the peasants, who were denied these passports. Owing to collectivization, dekulakization, and famine—as well as industry's need for new workers—they had left the countryside in record numbers in the years 1930–1932. Millions of them moved into the cities, worsening urban housing and other conditions and hampering planning. The new law reduced the peasant influx, which thereafter became more moderate, industrial needs and peasant resourcefulness guaranteeing some continuation.

FORCED LABOR, SHOW TRIALS, PURGES, AND DEATHS

While the condition of "free" workers declined, an increasing number of forced laborers faced much harder conditions. Although labor camps and other forms of forced labor existed under Lenin and included political prisoners, under Stalin the system became a vast network. Estimates of the total forced-labor population by 1940 vary considerably, with figures both over and under 5 million often cited. Whatever the number, it became a major component of the Soviet labor force.

Many of these laborers were the so-called "kulaks," sent to labor camps and settlements in the early 1930s. They were soon joined by many others, including Ukrainians and members of other nationalities, religious believers of various types, soldiers, and intellectuals. Hardened criminals were often mixed in with the prisoners accused of political and economic crimes.

Forced laborers logged, mined, constructed, and performed other work under the NKVD, the successor of the OGPU. Conditions were often unbelievably harsh, and the death rate was high. Usually working in inhospitable environments, such as the Arctic region, prisoners typically labored 12 to 16 hours a day on insufficient rations and sleep and in inadequate clothing. Sometimes they were delivered to barren wastes and told to build their own camps, without the use of even the most basic tools. Barbed wire, vicious guard dogs, sadistic guards, and danger from fellow prisoners were also a part of camp life. In women's camps, prisoners were sometimes raped by other prisoners or by camp officials and guards.

Another aspect of Stalinist life was a series of public show trials beginning in 1928. The first few targeted primarily nonparty "bourgeois" specialists and reflected the renewed attack on class enemies (including kulaks and Nepmen) that was intertwined with the first FYP, collectivization, and the cultural revolution of 1928–1931. (See Chapter 16 for discussion of the cultural revolution.) These early show trials gave Stalin the opportunity to discredit the type of individuals Bukharin wished to use. They also offered up scapegoats, often labeled "wreckers," who were blamed for some of the economic failures of the period.

The first of the trials, in mid-1928, was aimed at a "wrecking organization" of engineers and technicians at the Shakhty coal mines. They supposedly had received aid from "counterrevolutionary capitalists in the West." In this and in subsequent show trials, it is difficult to know to what extent the highly suspicious Stalin really believed many of the accusations. In any case, enemies, whether real or imagined, internal or external, were necessary for Stalin's style of rule. After apparent OGPU "persuasion," some of the accused signed confessions—the only real "evidence"—and five of them were shot.

In 1930 and 1931, there were two more show trials, an Industrial party trial and a "Menshevik" trial. Both again involved technical specialists, so-called

FIGURE 11.2. So-called kulaks being deported during collectivization. (© *Illustrated London News.*)

economic sabotage, and alleged contacts with foreign elements, and both trials relied on coerced confessions as proof of guilt.[1]

In 1933, just a few months after the beginning of the second FYP, the Soviet government put on still another show trial of economic "saboteurs" in the Metro-Vikars trial. Among the accused were some British engineers who were found guilty but later released. (Foreign specialists had contributed to the first FYP; for example, the firm of the U.S. architect Albert Kahn oversaw the building of hundreds of factories in Russia and the training of more than 1,000 Soviet engineers and technicians.)

These early show trials foreshadowed the more dramatic ones that came later in the 1930s during Stalin's Great Terror. Still in the early 1930s, however, several other important events occurred that influenced the later trials.

First was the Riutin "plot," involving long-time party member Mikhail Riutin. In 1932, he and some others were arrested for issuing a lengthy "Appeal" to party members that criticized many of Stalin's past policies and called for removing him as head of the party. There are indications that Stalin desired Riutin's execution but that a Politburo majority would not agree. Riutin did, however, receive a ten-year sentence. In the show trials of the late 1930s, many of the accused confessed involvement in the "Riutin conspiracy," which was falsely portrayed as one of a series of plots masterminded by Trotsky.

According to some sources, a key figure in the Politburo decision not to execute Riutin was Sergei Kirov, the head of the Leningrad party. By late 1934, there is little doubt that Stalin saw Kirov as a possible rival, especially after the Seventeenth Party Congress in January and February of that year, in which some delegates suggested to Kirov that he replace Stalin as general secretary of the party. Another sign of displeasure with Stalin and of Kirov's popularity was the delegate vote for a new central committee. Many more delegates apparently crossed out Stalin's name than Kirov's.[2]

In December 1934, Kirov was assassinated in the Smolny building, where his office was located. It is likely that Stalin was implicated—by helping to arrange circumstances so that a disgruntled former party member named Leonid Nikolaev would be free to shoot Kirov.

Conquest has written that the Kirov murder was "the key moment in Stalin's road to absolute power and extreme terror."[3] While he was in Leningrad kissing the corpse of Kirov and acting as his chief pall-bearer, he ordered the issuing of new rules against terrorists such as Nikolaev. Henceforth,

---

[1] A Stalin letter quoted in *Stalin's Letters to Molotov, 1925–1936*, eds. Lars T. Lih, Oleg V. Naumov, and Oleg V. Khlevniuk (New Haven, 1995), pp. 195–196, strongly suggests that Stalin believed that the "conspirators" in the 1930 trial were working for foreign elements planning a new military intervention against the Soviet government.

[2] J. Arch Getty, however, in "The Politics of Repression Revisited," in *Stalinist Terror*, eds. J. Arch Getty and Roberta T. Manning (Cambridge, England, 1993), pp. 42–49, casts some doubt on the nature of this vote as well as on other Kirov material found in the books of Conquest, Tucker, and Medvedev.

[3] Robert Conquest, *The Great Terror: A Reassessment* (New York, 1990), p. 51.

they were to be allowed no defense lawyers or appeals, and.those receiving death sentences were to be immediately executed. Within the next several months, tens of thousands of people were arrested, including Zinoviev and Kamenev, and some, including relatives of Nikolaev, were shot—the arrest, and at times execution, of an accused's relatives was to become even more common between 1936 and 1938.

In 1935, hundreds of thousands of people suffered such fates as being kicked out of the party and sent to labor camps, and the Great Purge reached its most intense stage between late 1936 and the end of 1938.

These two years brought forth three big show trials, involving some of the party's most distinguished past members. Almost all of them confessed to crimes they never committed, including being involved in Trotskyite conspiracies. (On such confessions and the methods used to extract them, see Chapter 15.) In August 1936, Zinoviev, Kamenev, and fourteen other members of the former Left Opposition were tried, found guilty of being involved in the Kirov assassination, and shot. In early 1937, it was the turn of Karl Radek, Grigori Piatakov, and fifteen others who had once supported Trotsky. Besides being accused of being part of "an antiparty faction," they were also charged with having acted as a "fascist vanguard" in behalf of the German Gestapo and Japanese intelligence. Thirteen of the accused were shot; the other four were given sentences and died within several years. In March 1938 came the last of the big show trials, this time involving twenty-one notables. They included the Right Opposition leaders Bukharin and Rykov; former NKVD head, G. G. Yagoda, who had supervised the early stages of the purges, until purged himself in 1937; and a few union republic party leaders. Among other crimes, they were accused of attempting to dismember the Soviet Union. After being found guilty, Bukharin, Rykov, Yagoda, and most of the others were shot.

Being tried in these elaborately staged productions was reserved for only a small number of Stalin's most important victims. But many other leading members of the party were also purged. According to Khrushchev, of the almost 2,000 delegates at the Seventeenth Party Congress in 1934, more than half were subsequently shot, and of the 139 Central Committee members elected by the congress, 70 percent were executed.

Leading military officers, who were also party members, suffered a similar fate. In 1937, Marshal Tukhachevsky and some other top military leaders were accused of various crimes, including spying for Germany and Japan, and were shot. In 1937 and 1938, as Germany and Japan were becoming more dangerous potential enemies, Stalin all but decapitated his military leadership. The higher the rank, the more likely one was to be purged, including more than four-fifths of the marshals; admirals; and army, corps, and divisional commanders and commissars.

Although the terror lessened after 1938, it did not end. In early 1940, Nikolai Ezhov, who had taken over the NKVD after Yagoda, was himself shot. This "bloodthirsty dwarf," as he was labeled, had been replaced in December 1938 by Lavrenti Beria. According to Khrushchev, Beria liked to say about those he suspected: "Listen, let me have him for one night, and I'll have him confessing he's the king of England." In August 1940, Beria's men succeeded in organizing an assassination far from Soviet borders. In Mexico, from where Leon Trotsky continued criticizing Stalin, an assassin bashed Trotsky's head with an ice ax. Territorial acquisitions in 1939 and 1940 provided still more potential victims to keep the NKVD busy.

Although high-ranking party members and military officers suffered greater proportional losses than less significant people during the Great Purge, no one was immune from the terror of the late 1930s. The NKVD had arrest quotas to fulfill, and anyone might be awakened by an NKVD knock on the door in the middle of the night. Denunciations and informing assumed epidemic proportions. Some individuals engaged in such behavior to obtain an accused's job or apartment, to demonstrate party loyalty, or simply to settle old scores. Such acts as telling or laughing at a joke could get one arrested or having the wrong relative or friend. Solzhenitsyn tells the story of a woman who was jailed for coming to an NKVD office and inquiring what to do with the infant of an arrested neighbor—Solzhenitsyn's *The Gulag Archipelago*, which also mentions the dumping out of a child's body from his coffin in the midst of an NKVD search, is full of such individual sufferings.

Estimates of the number of arrested and executed in 1937–1938 vary considerably, as do those for the number of total deaths Stalin was responsible for throughout the whole period from 1928 until the German attack in 1941.[4] As more archival information is released, estimates will probably continue to change. (See also Chapter 15 for convictions from 1923–1953.) In the early 1990s, midrange "excess-death" estimates for the 1928–1941 period were about 10 to 12 million, with roughly half of that number resulting from the "terror famine" of 1932–1933. Besides dying of starvation, other chief causes of these excess deaths were inhumane camp conditions and being shot. Those shot were sometimes buried in mass graves, many of which have only been discovered in more recent times.

THE STALIN CULT: IMAGES AND REALITY

As the Great Terror of the late 1930s expanded to envelope more and more people in its webs, the Stalin cult continued to inflate. Even before 1936, it had reached large proportions. Numerous towns were named after him—for example, Stalingrad, Stalinbad, Stalino, Stalinogorsk. Writing of Stalin's image in 1935, Robert Tucker has noted that "photos of him appeared daily in the Soviet press, now in genial pipe-smoking profile . . . now hugging a returned airman-hero at the Moscow airport, now surrounded by young Pioneers [a Commu-

---

[4]One of these deaths was that of Stalin's second wife, Nadezhda. In 1932, dismayed by some of his policies and personal behavior, she apparently shot herself, although some rumors circulated that Stalin killed her. See Robert C. Tucker, *Stalin in Power: The Revolution from Above, 1928–1941* (New York, 1990), pp. 216–217.

FIGURE 11.3. The Stalin cult made it difficult to escape him, even at this beach resort. (*Sovfoto.*)

nist organization for young children], now in a country setting with an arm around his ten-year-old daughter Svetlana."[5]

Contributing to the Stalin cult were 300,000 copies of a Russian translation of a Stalin biography by the French Communist Henri Barbusse, published in 1936 at the affordable price of one ruble. In 1938, Stalin was more directly responsible for another flattering description. It appeared in *History of the All-Union Communist Party: Short Course*, a work that Stalin later claimed he wrote. It was the rewriting and falsifying of history to glorify himself. Before his death in 1953, almost 43 million copies had appeared in 67 languages.

The discrepancy between the real Stalin and the manufactured "heroic Stalin" leads to questions about Stalin's mentality and the attitude of the Soviet people toward him. Almost all reputable Stalin biographies agree that he was extremely suspicious and power-hungry and therefore intolerant of any opposition, however slight it might be. His remark to Khrushchev about certain de-

[5]Tucker, p. 330.

nunciations the latter thought unreliable are illustrative of Stalin's thinking: "Ten percent truth—that's already truth, and requires decisive measures on our part, and we will pay for it if we don't so act." His "ten percent truth" was often a mere suspicion, and his "decisive measures" included imprisonment and execution.

Stalin apparently thought of himself as a great leader, and he tended to purge those he suspected of thinking differently. Purging then created vacancies that could be filled with more trustworthy people, including new ones trained, with the help of works such as the *Short Course*, to see Stalin as he saw himself.

Without downplaying the influence of Lenin and Marxism on Stalin's thought, we should note (as Tucker has) that Stalin saw certain similarities between his actions and those of Peter the Great and Ivan the Terrible. Some of Peter's actions were comparable to Stalin's revolution from above and some of Ivan's to Stalin's Great Purge.

Stalin's view of Ivan was strongly influenced by that of R. Wipper's biography of the tsar (1922). Stalin was also probably aware of Gorky's view that folklore indicated that Ivan was popular with the common Russian people. By the late 1930s, Stalin saw numerous parallels between Ivan and himself: They were both strong, patriotic rulers, surrounded by foreign enemies and treasonable, unfaithful opponents at home. If Ivan had his boyars to contend with, Stalin had his "Old Bolshevik" opponents. But just as Ivan created an *oprichnina* of faithful followers and unleashed it on his opponents, so Stalin made use of the NKVD and promoted new men to take the place of the purged. If Stalin had any criticism of Ivan, it was that the tsar's religious scruples sometimes interfered with his being sufficiently thorough in his repressions.

Stalin was also familiar with Machiavelli's advice that if a ruler wished to avoid conspiracies against him, he should avoid unpopularity. Although it might seem that instituting mass purges was not the best way to gain popularity, there is ample evidence that in the mid and late 1930s Stalin took great pains to enhance his popular appeal. The Stalin cult he promoted was one means to this end. Encouraging a partial restoration of respect for Russian traditions was another.

During the mid and late 1930s the leader of a party that had prided itself on its internationalism and criticized "bourgeois nationalism" sanctioned the increasing use of terms like motherland (*rodina*). And he now approved of a new historical approach that glorified Russian heroes of the past, such as Ivan the Terrible, Peter the Great, and Generals Suvorov and Kutuzov. Eisenstein's film *Alexander Nevsky* (1938) was just one of numerous films, books, and plays that portrayed past Russian heroes in ways approved by Stalin, ways that often alluded to parallels between them and himself.

At the same time, Stalin's government allowed other aspects of Russia's past, like folk songs and dances, to become officially fashionable, and it permitted the recognition of the progressive role of Russian Orthodoxy in Russia's historical development.

This emphasis on Russian heroes and traditions was part of "the great retreat," a limited ideological retreat that served many purposes, including strengthening loyalty to the state and Stalin. Japan and Germany were becoming more threatening. If war came, Stalin wanted to insure the allegiance of the Russian people, who would be more likely to sacrifice their lives for their motherland than for communism. The film *Alexander Nevsky* ends with Nevsky's just uttered words being shown in big letters on the screen: "He who comes to us with a sword, by the sword shall perish. On that our Russian land takes and will forever take its stand." Although it is difficult to know exactly how much these and other stratagems helped to boost Stalin's popularity in the midst of the Great Terror, they undoubtedly helped.

Most people had no way of realizing to what extent Stalin orchestrated the Great Purge and that most of those purged were innocent victims. During the late 1930s, only the peasants, who never forgot Stalin's collectivization, were overwhelmingly hostile to him. Few city-dwellers had the insight of the poet Osip Mandelstam, who already by 1934 realized that killing was "a treat" for Stalin. Many intellectuals, even at the height of the Great Purge, refused to believe that Stalin was responsible for it. The writer Ilia Ehrenburg notes in his memoirs that the producer Meyerhold said, "They conceal it from Stalin," and that the poet Boris Pasternak exclaimed, "If only someone would tell Stalin about it." The historian Anton Antonov-Ovseenko noted many years later how he felt in 1939, not long after the execution of his father, the prominent old Bolshevik Vladimir Antonov-Ovseenko:

> A year has not passed since the death of [his father] and his son [Anton] was glorifying his murderer. For me, a youth of nineteen, Stalin's name was sacred. As for the executions of enemies of the people, what could you say? The state had the right to defend itself. Errors were possible in such matters, but Stalin had nothing to do with it.[6]

Although this son's naiveté might seem incredible, how could he or the average Soviet citizen realize what was really going on—for example, how could they know that the accused in the show trials were not really guilty as charged? Who could believe that the trials were concocted just for Stalin's benefit? Such a belief would fly in the face of all that people had been taught to believe about the "great leader." The trials even fooled some foreign diplomats, including U.S. ambassador Joseph Davies as well as the distinguished British historian of Russia, Sir Bernard Pares.

Ever-new accusations against traitors, saboteurs, and wreckers, including two former NKVD heads, reinforced the conviction that others were responsible for the terror of the times. Some citizens took comfort in such popular sayings as "when wood is cut, splinters fly" and rationalized that Stalin's "heroic" transformation of the country was bound to be accompanied by some suffering.

Many people believed in their country's mission and purpose and realized they were living in dangerous times. There were not only internal enemies, but also external ones. By 1937 or 1938, what other leader could citizens look to than Stalin? By late 1938, he had managed to destroy, as was his intention, any

---

[6]*The Time of Stalin: Portrait of a Tyranny* (New York, 1982), p. 231.

even semi-independent group that might serve as an anti-Stalinist rallying point.

Yet, it is true that some individuals, especially in the party leadership, knew or at least suspected much more than they later admitted. As in Hitler's Germany, guilt for atrocities cannot all be pinned on one man. Many cooperated with Stalin's policies because of fear or self-serving interests. Others, in many small ways, heroically resisted them. Still others attempted to stay as clear of politics as possible in such a society and kept any misgivings they had largely to themselves. The writer Isaac Babel said privately in the midst of the purges, "Today a man talks frankly only with his wife—at night, with the blanket pulled over his head." Although historians have debated how extreme, pervasive, and long-lasting were the fears and cautions of Soviet citizens in the late 1930s, there is little doubt that it was a perilous time for speaking out openly.

NATIONALITY AND CONSTITUTIONAL POLICIES

Soviet nationality policy of the 1920s had generally followed Lenin's dictum of "national in form and socialist in content." Form and content were not so easily divided, however. The promotion of non-Russian languages and cadres and the encouragement of national cultural manifestations inadvertently furthered the development of local nationalisms. During the 1930s, Stalin, always suspicious of non-Russian nationalisms, harshly attacked those non-Russians he labeled "bourgeois nationalists."

Stalin's policies of the 1930s were partly dictated by developments stemming from his economic initiatives of the late 1920s. The command economy that he introduced encouraged increased economic centralization and thus more Great Russian economic dominance. It also placed a premium on technical knowledge, and many Russian managers and skilled laborers moved to non-Russian areas, such as northern Kazakhstan, to help launch new industries. Opposition to collectivization was most intense in non-Russian areas such as Ukraine and Kazakhastan. In response, Stalin pursued policies that led to the execution, forced labor, and starvation of millions of Ukrainian, Kazakh, and other non-Russian peasants.

In addition, many other groups and individuals in the non-Russian regions were purged and arrested. In 1930, forty-five intellectuals were charged with belonging to a Union for the Liberation of Ukraine. During the next several years, more Ukrainian groups came under attack—for example, its Academy of Sciences, its Orthodox Church, and its Communist party. Stalin sent thousands of Russians to take over key Ukrainian positions. Large numbers of Ukrainian intellectuals were arrested, and from January 1933 to January 1934, about 100,000 members of the Ukrainian Communist party were purged. Most of these intellectuals and party personnel were charged with Ukrainian nationalist or counterrevolutionary activities and were shot, imprisoned, or exiled.

In August 1937, amidst the Great Purge, Stalin sent Molotov and Ezhov to Ukraine to wipe out what he considered the remnants of Ukrainian "bourgeois nationalism." By late January 1938, when Khrushchev, an ethnic Russian, arrived to take over as head of the Ukrainian party, almost all of the Ukrainian leadership had been purged. More than 150,000 Ukrainian party members had been arrested in 1937. As Conquest has summed up the situation in 1937–1938, "of the 102 members and candidate members of the Ukrainian Central Committee, 3 survived. All 17 members of the Ukrainian Government were arrested."[7] The NKVD charged many other leaders with Ukrainian nationalistic activities and purged them from fields such as education, the media, science, culture, industry, and local government.

Native elites in other non-Russian areas, including Belorussia, the Caucasus, and Central Asia, also suffered high losses during the Great Purge. In Uzbekistan, Tadzhikistan, and Kirgizia, the percentage of native people in the party declined noticeably by 1940.

Although it is difficult to be sure how many of the charges made against his enemies Stalin really believed, there are some indications that his suspicious mind feared attempts to dismantle the Soviet Union. In an impromptu speech of November 1937, which Tucker has cited as especially revealing of Stalin's thinking at the time, he spoke of how his major political enemies were planning to allow foreign powers to acquire many of the country's borderlands and even Leningrad.

Besides the purges, there were other indications of a changed nationality policy by the late 1930s. At first glance, a new constitution in 1936 seemed favorable to the non-Russian nationalities. As compared to the 1924 constitution, more of them were now recognized as legal units. The new constitution recognized eleven union republics, twenty-two autonomous republics, and nine each autonomous regions and national areas, and all units were given representation in a new Council of Nationalities (see Map. 11.1). Each union republic, including the large RSFSR—possessing about three-fourths of the Soviet Union's territory and well over half of its population—was allotted the same number of deputies. The Council of Nationalities was one body of a new bicameral Supreme Soviet that replaced the old Congress of Soviets. The other new house was a Council of Union, in which deputies were elected proportionate to population.

In other ways, however, the constitution weakened the powers of union republics. It took away, for example, some of their rights regarding legal codes and legislation. By establishing union-republic commissariats in the areas of agriculture, health, internal affairs, and justice, it subordinated the already existing union republics' commissariats in these areas to the new all-union ones.

All of the changes to the 1936 constitution, however, were not as significant as they might first appear; as noted previously, Soviet constitutions were misleading in regard to where the real power lay. It was not in the government, especially its legislative branch, but in the party. At the time of the purges, for example, Stalin held neither of the top two government positions, chairman of the Council of People's Commissars or chairman of the Supreme Soviet.

[7]Conquest, p. 232.

A more meaningful indicator of a changed nationality policy was the new party and government stance regarding Russian culture and history. In 1937, the party newspaper *Pravda* declared that Russian culture was the most advanced and humane in the world and that the RFSFR was "the first among equals" in the USSR. That same year, a new history text glorifying the Russian past appeared and was made mandatory in Soviet primary schools, Russian and non-Russian alike. The following year, *Against M. N. Pokrovsky's Conception of History* was published. Pokrovsky had been the dominant historian of the 1920s and had criticized much of the tsarist past, including its conquest and treatment of the non-Russian nationalities—"the prison of peoples," he had called the old Russian Empire. In contrast, the new historical approach saw the expansion of Muscovy and the Russian Empire as generally progressive and beneficial to the non-Russian nationalities.

By the late 1930s, the government was increasingly stressing the importance of the Russian language. After a rise in the proportion of non-Russian publications from 1921 to 1933, the tide turned in behalf of more Russian language publications. In 1938, a new law obligated non-Russian schools to institute Russian as a required subject.

Although the nationality policies of the late 1930s are often regarded as examples of Russification, Stalin preferred to regard them as steps in the making of a new Soviet nation and culture that would supersede old national loyalties and unite the "Soviet people." Furthermore, his policies not only harmed non-Russian cultures, but also Russian culture. Despite his approval of certain aspects of Russian folklore and his government's recognition that Russian Orthodoxy had once been a progressive force, his policies inflicted great harm on both traditional Russian peasant life and Russian Orthodoxy, two vital ingredients of Russia's past culture. Yet the use of Russian bricks, however selectively gathered from the past, to mix with the mortar of Marxism-Leninism certainly gave Stalin's new "Soviet nation" a neo-Russian look.

CHANGES IN THE GOVERNMENT AND PARTY

Under Stalin government and party functions and numbers both increased. The inauguration of five-year plans and collectivization, the expansion of defense industries and the military, and the growth of the government's repressive and penal operations all contributed significantly to this growth.

Although Marxist theory called for the gradual withering away of the state once a socialist order had been achieved (as Stalin said it had in 1936), Stalin proclaimed that this withering away during the transition to a full Communist society could not then occur. He blamed this primarily on the "capitalist encirclement" and dangerous situation that faced Russia in the late 1930s.

The 1936 constitution stipulated the revised government that subsequently came into being. The delegates to the new bicameral Supreme Soviet were to be elected by universal suffrage every four years. These "legislators," in turn, were to elect their own Presidium (at first consisting of 37 members), the

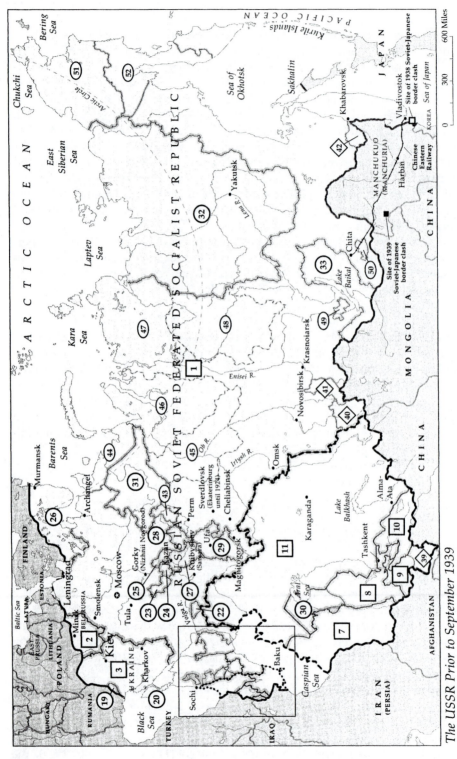

The USSR Prior to September 1939

MAP 11.1

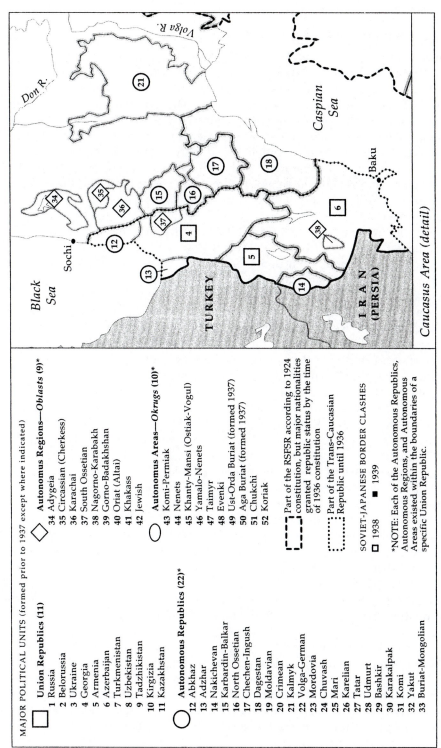

MAJOR POLITICAL UNITS (formed prior to 1937 except where indicated)

Union Republics (11)

1 Russia
2 Belorussia
3 Ukraine
4 Georgia
5 Armenia
6 Azerbaijan
7 Turkmenistan
8 Uzbekistan
9 Tadzhikistan
10 Kirgizia
11 Kazakhstan

Autonomous Republics (22)*

12 Abkhaz
13 Adzhar
14 Nakichevan
15 Karbardin-Balkar
16 North Ossetian
17 Chechen-Ingush
18 Dagestan
19 Moldavian
20 Crimean
21 Kalmyk
22 Volga-German
23 Mordovia
24 Chuvash
25 Mari
26 Karelian
27 Tatar
28 Udmurt
29 Bashkir
30 Karakalpak
31 Komi
32 Yakut
33 Buriat-Mongolian

Autonomus Regions—*Oblasts* (9)*

34 Adygeia
35 Circassian (Cherkess)
36 Karachai
37 South Ossetian
38 Nagorno-Karabakh
39 Gorno-Badakhshan
40 Oriat (Altai)
41 Khakass
42 Jewish

Autonomus Areas—*Okrugs* (10)*

43 Komi-Permiak
44 Nenets
45 Khanty-Mansi (Ostiak-Vogul)
46 Yamalo-Nenets
47 Taimyr
48 Evenki
49 Ust-Orda Buriat (formed 1937)
50 Aga Buriat (formed 1937)
51 Chukchi
52 Koriak

Part of the RSFSR according to 1924 constitution, but major nationalities granted republic status by the time of 1936 constitution

Part of the Trans-Caucasian Republic until 1936

SOVIET-JAPANESE BORDER CLASHES

☐ 1938   ■ 1939

*NOTE: Each of the Autonomous Republics, Autonomous Regions, and Autonomous Areas existed within the boundaries of a specific Union Republic.

Caucasus Area (detail)

MAP 11.1

Council of People's Commissars (the chief executive organ), and the Supreme Court and procurator general (the chief judicial organs).

Because the Supreme Soviet was normally to meet only twice a year, and then for only several days on each occasion, the Presidium was given wide powers to act in its name between sessions. The chairman of the Presidium was considered the president of the country, whereas the chairman of the Council of People's Commissars was considered its premier.

The governments at the republican and more local levels mirrored the governmental structure at the federal level, with their soviets theoretically holding the supreme power. Of course, now more than ever, real power at every level continued to reside in the party and increasingly in the hands of its general secretary, Stalin.

For the first time, a Soviet constitution emphasized the leading role of the Communist party. According to it, the party was "the core of all organizations of the working people, both public and state." This was certainly the case— from party cells in villages and factories to the upper reaches of the government and military, it was party bodies that made the most crucial decisions.

Party membership grew rapidly from 1928 to 1933, but purges from 1934 through 1939 reduced party numbers. Not until 1941 did party membership surpass the total in 1933. Taking the 1928–1941 period as a whole, however, the number of full and candidate party members almost tripled, reaching almost 4 million, or roughly 2 percent of the overall population.

Stalin's purges created opportunities for rapid advancement. About half the party members at the party congress in 1939 were under thirty-five. The early career of Alexei Kosygin (1904–1980), later premier of the USSR, illustrates how fast individuals could rise. Son of a worker, he joined the party in 1927, graduated from a textile institute in 1935, became head of the textile industry commissariat in 1939, and deputy premier of the USSR in 1940. Kosygin's lower-class and technical background were increasingly typical of the rapid advancers in the government and party structures.

Advancements were normally decided upon based on the nomenklatura system, which matched suitable candidates with available positions and the benefits that accompanied them, from housing and health care to special stores and subsidized vacations. Cadre departments at various party levels, along with the NKVD, kept these lists current. At the highest level, the nomenklatura system was directed by a Secret Department-Special Sector office of the Central Committee, headed by one of Stalin's closest followers, Alexander Poskrebyshev.

To be admitted into the party, one had to be recommended by other party members and serve a trial period, pay dues, and play an active role in furthering party goals. By the late 1930s, party members increasingly entered the party after having served in Communist youth organizations.

For the young children there was first the Little Octobrists and then, upon reaching age ten, the Pioneers. At age fourteen, a smaller proportion of youths joined the Komsomol (or Young Communist League), where they could remain from ages fourteen through twenty-eight. During the late 1920s and early 1930s, Komsomol members furnished much of the energy, idealism, and intolerance that accompanied Stalin's industrialization and collectivization drive. At that time, Komsomol membership, although larger than that of the party, was still relatively small. In the mid-1930s, the organization became less elitist, and it possessed 9 million members in 1939, as compared to 2.3 million full and candidate party members.

By the beginning of 1928, Stalin had already brought many of his own followers into key party positions. The Right Opposition also had a substantial following, but by the end of that year Stalin had purged many of them. Even after this, he continued to face some opposition within the party, and the party's Politburo apparently maintained some restraints upon him. The assassination of Kirov in December 1934 enabled him to remove these remaining constraints gradually and become more of a dictator. Dmitri Volkogonov has noted, "Gradually Stalin's decisions were accepted by everyone as those of the party. From the mid-1930s his directives were being registered as orders from the Central Committee or as general instructions. His power became virtually unbounded."[8]

A quick look at some chief party institutions underlines Volkogonov's point. Although eleven party congresses had met between 1918 and early 1934, not one was held again until 1939. Stalin's purge of 70 percent of the Central Committee elected in 1934 is ample evidence of the decline of that body's power. In 1934, Stalin had the Central Control Commission of the party abolished. Even the Politburo (with ten full members throughout most of the 1930s) became little more than a sounding board for Stalin's ideas. Politburo "meetings" often took the form of dinners at Stalin's Kuntsevo home in the countryside, to which frequently only some Politburo members were invited. Molotov (who had replaced Rykov as premier in 1930), Voroshilov, and Kaganovich seemed to be the three Politburo members closest to Stalin during this period.

Not all historians, however, agree that Stalin's powers had become "virtually unbounded" by 1939. Just as some historians have argued that no tsarist autocrat ever really exercised full autocratic powers, so some historians have made similar arguments regarding Stalin.

J. Arch Getty, for example, has emphasized that the inefficient and sometimes chaotic condition of the party in the late 1930s hampered any efficient centralized control and enabled local leaders to protect and sometimes even increase their powers. He has also downplayed Stalin's involvement in the daily running of the country and called attention to rivalries and differences between Stalin's key followers. Getty's points provide a needed reminder of the practical difficulties of running a huge country such as the Soviet Union; there were practical limitations on how much power Stalin could effectively exercise. Other party people did implement and sometimes interpret how Stalin's policies would be carried out. Moreover, at times such as 1928–1931 and 1937–1938, Stalin unleashed violent forces including collectivization, cultural revolution, and terror and denunciations that worked to his benefit, but that he

[8]Dmitri Volkogonov, *Stalin: Triumph and Tragedy* (Rocklin, Calif.), p. 219.

could not completely preprogram. Yet, in the final analysis, what strikes the Western observer of the powers of Stalin, like those of Ivan the Terrible, is not the limitation that reality placed upon them; rather it's their magnitude, which left almost everyone else in the country at Stalin's mercy.

STALINISM AND THE LENINIST LEGACY

After years of generally presenting Lenin and Stalin in a similar way, scholars in recent decades began debating whether or not there were any essential differences between the policies of Lenin and Stalin.

The case for essential differences (as made by Tucker, Cohen, Medvedev, and others) can be summarized briefly. Whereas Lenin was the chief oligarch in a government run by a small elite, Stalin was more autocratic or dictatorial. Whereas Lenin advised evolving out of the NEP gradually and by persuasion, not revolutionary force, Stalin rejected this advice and instead launched his revolution from above. Whereas Lenin was opposed to building a cult around any individual leader, including himself, Stalin not only helped construct a Lenin cult, but even more, one revolving around himself.

Among others, Tucker has not denied that the Lenin of 1917–1920, as opposed to the more moderate Lenin of 1921–1923, had a significant impact on the launching of Stalinism. Yet Tucker has also cited other important factors influencing Stalinism, including Stalin's own mind and personality and the heritage of tsarist Russia. Opposing this "revisionist" view, the Russian writer Alexander Solzhenitsyn has criticized it for mitigating Lenin's responsibility for Stalin's crimes and suggesting a strong link between Stalinism and the tsarist heritage.

A more unique position has been that of the Russian biographer of both Stalin and Lenin, Dmitri Volkogonov. In his Stalin biography of the late 1980s, he perceived an essential difference between the two men, but in his more recent Lenin work, he has written: "Everything done in Soviet Russia after Lenin's death was done according to his blueprint, his precepts and his principles."[9] Among the evils he lists flowing from Lenin are totalitarianism, bureaucratism, atheism, the planned economy, exploitation of labor, militarization of the country, and a constant search for new enemies. Yet even Volkogonov admits that Lenin probably would not have acted like Stalin by killing his Politburo comrades or millions of peasants. Although Volkogonov's Lenin biography reflects the passion of one who has become enlightened after decades of believing falsehoods, his new view carries substantial weight because of his use of many previously unused archival materials.

Another related debate has been over totalitarianism and how well that term describes the Stalinism of the 1930s. Once thought to be a good word for describing the similarities of Nazi Germany and Stalinist Russia, it has been criticized in more recent times. Getty, for example, has argued that the Soviet

---

[9]Dmitri Volkogonov, *Lenin: A New Biography* (New York, 1994), p. 450.

administration of the 1930s was too chaotic and technologically unsophisticated to merit the term. And he and other scholars have noted that it offers an inadequate explanation for local political leaders and others who pursued goals of their own within the larger Stalinist system. As so often has been the case in recent scholarship related to Russian/Soviet history, more empirical social studies have discovered that peasants, industrial workers and managers, and others were not just passive tools of the ruling elite. Rather they often violated or bent laws to serve their own purposes, even in such an oppressive atmosphere as the 1930s.

Yet, despite these criticisms of the term, many scholars (including Volkogonov) continued to find it helpful. They used it to describe single-party governments such as Stalin's that relied on terror and propaganda to help them exercise controls over various phases of public life, including ideology, the judiciary, the military, police forces, the economy, education, the media, and cultural institutions.

In the final analysis, the debate over similarities and differences between Leninism and Stalinism and that on totalitarianism have intersected. Despite the many similarities of Lenin's rule and Stalin's, state-party control and oppression were greater, more "totalitarian," under Stalin than under Lenin.

SUGGESTED SOURCES*

CONQUEST, ROBERT. *The Harvest of Sorrow: Soviet Collectivization and the Terror-Famine.* New York, 1986.

———. *Stalin and the Kirov Murder.* New York, 1989.

DALLIN, ALEXANDER, and BERTRAND M. PATENAUDE, eds. *Stalin and Stalinism.* New York, 1992.

DANIELS, ROBERT V., ed. *The Stalin Revolution: Foundations of the Totalitarian Era.* 3d ed. Lexington, Mass., 1990.

DAVIES R. W. *The Socialist Offensive: The Collectivization of Soviet Agriculture, 1929–1930.* Cambridge, Mass., 1980.

GETTY, J. ARCH. *Origins of the Great Purges: The Soviet Communist Party Reconsidered, 1933–1938.* Cambridge, England, 1985.

GETTY, J. ARCH, GÁBOR T. RITTERSPORN, and VIKTOR N. ZEMSKOV. "Victims of the Soviet Penal System in the Pre-war Years: A First Approach on the Basis of Archival Evidence," *AHR* 98 (October 1993): 1017–1044.

GINZBURG, EVGENIIA. *Journey Into the Whirlwind.* New York, 1975.

GROSSMAN, VASILY. *Forever Flowing.* New York, 1972. A novel.

HINDUS, MAURICE. *Red Bread: Collectivization in a Russian Village.* New York, 1931; Reprint, Bloomington, 1988.

HUGHES, JAMES. *Stalin, Siberia, and the Crisis of the New Economic Policy.* Cambridge, England, 1991.

KHELVNIUK, OLEG V. *In Stalin's Shadow: The Career of "Sergo" Ordzhonikiaze,* ed. Donald J. Raleigh. Armonk, N.Y., 1995.

KOESTLER, ARTHUR. *Darkness at Noon.* London, 1973. A novel.

*See also books cited in footnotes.

LAQUEUR, WALTER. *Stalin: The Glasnost Revelations*. New York, 1990.

LEWIN, MOSHE. *Russian Peasants and Soviet Power: A Study of Collectivization*. London, 1968.

MEDVEDEV, ROY A. *Let History Judge: The Origins and Consequences of Stalinism*. Rev. ed. New York, 1989.

NOVE, ALEC, ed. *The Stalin Phenomenon*. New York, 1992.

RADZINSKY, EDVARD. *Stalin*. New York, 1996. Chs. 12–21.

REIMAN, MICHAL. *The Birth of Stalinism: The USSR on the Eve of the "Second Revolution."* Bloomington, 1987.

RYBAKOV, ANATOLI. *Children of the Arbat*. Boston, 1988. A novel.

SCOTT, JOHN. *Behind the Urals, an American Worker in Russia's City of Steel*. Boston, 1942.

SIEGELBAUM, LEWIS H. *Stakhanovism and the Politics of Productivity in the USSR, 1935–1941*. Cambridge, England, 1988.

SOLZHENITSYN, ALEKSANDR I. *The Gulag Archipelago, 1918–1956: An Experiment in Literary Investigation*. 3 vols. New York, 1974–78.

TIMASHEFF, NICHOLAS. *The Great Retreat*. New York, 1946.

TROTSKY, LEON. *Stalin, an Appraisal of the Man and His Influence*. New York, 1941.

———. *The Revolution Betrayed: What is the Soviet Union and Where is It Going?* Garden City, N.Y., 1937.

TUCKER, ROBERT C., ed. *Stalinism: Essays in Historical Interpretation*. New York, 1977.

TUCKER, ROBERT C., and STEPHEN F. COHEN, eds. *The Great Purge Trial*. New York, 1965.

VAKSBERG, ARKADY. *Stalin's Prosecutor: The Life of Andrei Vyshinsky*. New York, 1991.

VIOLA, LYNNE. *The Best Sons of the Fatherland: Workers in the Vanguard of Soviet Collectivization*. New York, 1987.

———. *Peasant Rebels under Stalin: Collectivization and the Culture of Peasant Resistance*. New York, 1996.

VOLKOGONOV, DMITRI. *Trotsky: The Eternal Revolutionary*. New York, 1996. Chs. 6–7.

WARD, CHRIS. *Stalin's Russia*. London, 1993.

WEISSBERG, ALEXANDER. *The Accused*. New York, 1951.

CHAPTER 12

Soviet Foreign Policy, 1917–1941

During Russia's interwar years, primarily two institutions implemented Soviet foreign policy—the Commissariat for Foreign Affairs and the Comintern (Communist or Third International). The first generally pursued conventional foreign policy goals, such as obtaining trade, diplomatic recognition, and credits. The second concentrated more on encouraging revolutionary and anticolonial activity abroad. Although the two organizations sometimes seemed to be working at cross purposes, they were really two sides of the same foreign-policy coin, minted primarily by Lenin and later Stalin.

By the mid-1920s, Soviet hopes for any immediate Communist revolutions in the West had receded, and foreign policy became entangled in the power struggle to succeed Lenin. Once Stalin emerged as the clear successor, his foreign policy was primarily concerned with strengthening the Soviet Union and guarding against foreign dangers—by 1933, both Nazi Germany and an increasingly aggressive Japan were major sources of Soviet concern. At the same time, however, Stalin was vigilant for an opportunity to expand Soviet borders. In late August 1939, the USSR gained such an opening by signing a Nazi-Soviet nonaggression pact along with a secret protocol indicating German and Soviet spheres of influence.

Although the treaty and protocol freed Germany to invade western Poland without fear of Soviet reprisals, the invasion of September 1, 1939, led Britain and France to declare war on Germany. During the year after the invasion, with these three major European powers at war, the Soviet government incorporated eastern Poland, Latvia, Estonia, Bessarabia, Bukovina, almost all of Lithuania, and some Finnish border areas into the USSR. Only the addition of Finnish territory required a war—the 1939–1940 "Winter War" with Finland.

Although at first Stalin thought of the Nazi-Soviet Pact as a great triumph, Germany's rapid 1940 advances in Western Europe made it seem less so. In late 1940, Nazi-Soviet relations worsened, and before the year ended Hitler ordered preparations for a spring 1941 attack on the USSR.

OVERVIEW AND THE BEGINNINGS OF SOVIET DIPLOMACY

In October 1939, Winston Churchill, soon to become British prime minister, declared that he could not predict future Soviet behavior because it was "a riddle wrapped in a mystery inside an enigma." But he thought that perhaps there was a key to the locked door of Soviet foreign policy, and that was "national interest."

Both before and after this time, Soviet foreign policy was a riddle to many Western observers. They debated, for example, whether national interest or Communist ideology was more important in determining it. Those who emphasized national concerns tended to see more continuity between tsarist and Soviet foreign policy, and they placed more emphasis on traditional factors such as geopolitical considerations. The riddle continued for so long partly because the Soviet system was a closed one, and the thinking that influenced particular diplomatic decisions was seldom aired openly, even decades afterward.

It now seems fairly clear that Communist leaders generally interpreted their Marxian ideology in such a way as to serve what they considered "Soviet national interest," which often coincided with their own personal political interests. This does not mean that Communist ideology played an insignificant role in shaping foreign policy; it did, for example, strongly influence Soviet leaders' perceptions of the world. Stalin's foreign policy, for example, reflected a Marxian perspective combined with his effort to defend and expand Soviet borders and to further his own personal power.

Although under Lenin, key foreign policy decisions were made in the party's Central Committee, and by the beginning of 1920s in the smaller Politburo, Lenin was clearly the dominant shaper of them. After his death, the Politburo continued to make important foreign as well as domestic policies. As Stalin consolidated his power, however, he increasingly dictated his own foreign policies. Letters recently published from Stalin to Molotov indicate that even in the mid and late 1920s Stalin was more concerned with foreign affairs than many scholars previously thought. The main task of the two chief commissars of foreign affairs, Georgi Chicherin in the 1920s and Maxim Litvinov in the 1930s, was to implement policy, not make it.

Because the first few years of Soviet foreign policy have already been touched upon, they can be summarized briefly here. Lenin's early thinking was strongly affected by two convictions: (1) that World War I was an imperialist war and (2) that a socialist revolution in one or more advanced industrialized countries was necessary for the survival of the Bolshevik government. The first belief influenced the new Soviet government's decision to withdraw from the war and renounce traditional diplomacy as well as tsarist debts, obligations, and commitments. The second belief linked Soviet "national interest" with fomenting revolutionary activity abroad.

Initial Soviet diplomacy was especially unconventional, as most colorfully demonstrated at the Brest-Litovsk negotiations with the Germans, begun in December 1917. There at the bargaining table were the military and frock-coated diplomatic elite of Germany and its allies; across from them sat a Soviet delegation that included, among others, a woman who had once assassinated a Russian general, a worker, soldier, sailor, and peasant. The peasant had been walking along a street when Kamenev and Adolf Ioffe—the capable head of the Russian delegation—realized they had no representative of Russia's most numerous class. So they talked him into accompanying them to the train station and then on to Brest-Litovsk.

According to German General Max von Hoffmann, at the first diplomatic dinner together, the worker used his fork only to clean his teeth; and the long-bearded peasant, when asked his choice of two wines, replied whichever was stronger.

Not only was the appearance of the Soviet delegation unconventional, but also its approach. Weeks after the opening of negotiations, Trotsky arrived on the scene to take charge of the Russian negotiating. With him on a train was the fiery revolutionary activist and political writer Karl Radek. Radek's first action upon arriving was to distribute revolutionary pamphlets among the German soldiers at the train station; this appeal over the heads of government, directly to their people, would become a characteristic trait of Soviet foreign policy. After the Germans eventually presented their harsh terms to Trotsky, he replied with a "no war–no peace" response, which meant that the new Soviet government would neither renew war with Germany nor agree to its draconian peace terms. As Trotsky later explained in a speech to the Petrograd Soviet, he believed that a renewed German attack on Russia was unlikely because it would provoke a "mighty revolutionary protest by the German workers."[1]

Before Trotsky's compromise position was authorized by the party Central Committee, a stormy debate among its members occurred. Bukharin, for example, argued for waging a revolutionary war against Germany and Austria. He thought that making peace would be a betrayal of international revolutionary goals. Foreshadowing a policy line that would become increasingly common in the years ahead, Lenin argued that saving the new Soviet government must come first. Even Trotsky, while admitting that the West might be pregnant with revolution, noted that Russia had already given birth to a healthy revolutionary infant who must be protected.

After his "no war–no peace" formula failed to prevent German troops from marching toward Petrograd, Trotsky and a majority of the Central Committee agreed with Lenin that the German terms had to be accepted. One-third of the old Russian Empire's cultivated lands and population was lost (see Map 9.1) by the Treaty of Brest-Litovsk (March 3, 1918), including its Polish and Ukrainian territories, Finland, Estonia, Latvia, Lithuania, and some small concessions to Turkey in the Caucasus. The treaty was annulled, however, in November 1918 by the German acceptance of the Allied armistice terms for ending World War I. The question of how much of the lost territory would be regained then became intermingled with the Russian Civil War, Allied intervention, and the Russo-Polish War of 1920.

The Soviet government's early relations with the Allies were hardly better

---

[1]Quoted in Dmitri Volkogonov, *Trotsky: The Eternal Revolutionary* (New York, 1996), p. 112.

FIGURE 12.1. Lenin and Trotsky plotting world revolution, from a White Army poster. *(From J.P. Nettl,* The Soviet Achievement, *#31, p. 58, Harcourt, Brace & World, New York, 1967, British Museum photo, Freeman.)*

than those with Germany. Its refusal to abide by previous Russian obligations, including Russia's huge foreign debts; its proclaimed hostility to Western "bourgeois governments"; and its call for international revolution alarmed the Allies. Partly for these reasons, and because Soviet authority was being contested in the Civil War, the Allies did not invite Lenin's government to participate in the Paris Peace Conference of 1919. The Bolshevik side also had its grievances, primarily the Allied intervention that coincided with the Russian Civil War.

In these early years, the Soviet government pursued some traditional diplomatic measures. It signed, for example, peace treaties in 1920 recognizing the independence of the Baltic states. For some time, however, it also continued to count on revolutions in the West, especially in Germany.

In spring 1919, Communist governments were briefly in power in Hungary and German Bavaria, and the U.S. diplomat Colonel House thought that "Bolshevism was gaining ground everywhere." In such a climate, Soviet leaders were especially hopeful. Zinoviev wrote: "Civil War has flared up throughout Europe. The victory of communism in Germany is absolutely inevitable. In a year Europe will have forgotten about the fight for communism, because all of Europe will be Communist."[2]

This bold prediction appeared in the first issue of the journal of the Comintern, the body having come into being in early March 1919 with Zinoviev as its chairman and Radek its secretary. Theoretically, it was an "International Workingmen's Association" devoted to the overthrow of capitalism and the establishment of Communist governments around the world. Its founding congress had few genuine foreign representatives, however, and the Comintern was clearly established to serve Soviet government interests, including the ending of Allied intervention. Of course, Soviet leaders believed that fomenting world revolutionary activity would serve the workers of the world as well as the security of the new Soviet state.

The second congress of the Comintern, with Communist representatives from roughly forty countries meeting in 1920, was more truly international. But its twenty-one conditions for national Communist parties to join the organization included the necessity of modeling themselves on the Russian Communist party and on their willingness to give "unconditional support to any Soviet republic."

At the congress, Lenin stressed the necessity of Communist parties working with colonial liberation movements against Western colonialism—he especially wished to weaken British colonialism, thereby weakening Russia's greatest global rival. Shortly thereafter, in September 1920, the Comintern organized a Congress of Peoples of the East, which was held in Baku. With many Moslems in attendance, from both inside and outside Soviet borders, Zinoviev summoned the delegates to a "holy war" against "British imperialism." The foreign Asian delegates were also reminded of the Soviet government's "enlightened" nationality policy toward its own Asian peoples.

In early 1921, in an effort to lessen British influence in Afghanistan, Persia, and Turkey, the Soviet government signed treaties with these neighbors, even relinquishing some earlier tsarist diplomatic gains. Criticism of Western imperialism and the courting of its colonial subjects remained important characteristics of Soviet foreign policy for many decades. If imperialism was the last stage of capitalism, as Lenin believed, encouraging anti-imperialist movements in the capitalists' colonies was an important step to bringing about the collapse of capitalism and capitalist governments.

NEP YEARS

During the New Economic Policy (NEP) years, 1921–1927, the balance between fomenting revolutionary activity abroad and pursuing more traditional diplomatic goals increasingly tipped toward the latter. The government now

---

[2]Cited in Mikhail Heller and Aleksandr M. Nekrich, *Utopia in Power: The History of the Soviet Union from 1917 to the Present* (New York, 1986), p. 123.

stressed furthering trade and obtaining diplomatic recognition and economic credits. Of the three goals, obtaining credits was the hardest to achieve, especially because the Soviet government had renounced the repayment of tsarist debts.

As traditional diplomacy became more important, so too did the role of Georgi Chicherin. He was from a noble family; his father had been in diplomatic service, and his uncle was the well-known liberal Boris Chicherin. Before leaving Russia in 1904, Georgi himself had worked as a diplomatic historian in the archives of the tsarist Ministry of Foreign Affairs. Abroad, he became involved in Marxist émigré politics, first siding with the Bolsheviks and later the Mensheviks. By the time he returned to Russia in January 1918, he was once again ready to join with the Bolsheviks, who were happy to make use of his knowledge, skills, and revolutionary sympathies. He became Trotsky's deputy at the Commissariat for Foreign Affairs and replaced him as commissar in mid-1918, after Trotsky had resigned to take up his post as commissar of war.

During the years 1918–1920, the Allies had supported the birth and rebirth of buffer states along Russia's western borders, hoping they would act as a *cordon sanitaire* to keep communism contained within the new Soviet state. By the beginning of 1921, the new Soviet state was not only exhausted by years of war and intervention, but also was more geographically separated from the major powers than when tsarist Russia had shared borders with both Germany and Austria-Hungary. The political scene in Western Europe was also a little more stable. The times seemed to dictate more moderate policies abroad as well as at home.

An important early breakthrough came in March 1921, with the signing of the Anglo-Soviet Trade Agreement. With it, the Soviet government achieved tacit (de facto), although not official (de jure), diplomatic recognition and from a country Lenin thought of as its chief capitalist-imperialist enemy. Lenin believed that Russia needed to buy Western machinery to rebuild its economy, the sooner the better, for he was convinced it had to become economically independent before the capitalist nations resumed their war against it. (For more on Soviet foreign trade in this period, see Chapter 15.)

For such nations to help the Soviet state strengthen its economy might seem like they would be "digging their own grave." In a speech just a few days after the signing of the agreement, that is exactly what Kamenev, citing Marx, said they would do. Marxism-Leninism led the Soviet leadership to believe that the capitalists' competition for profits would not only lead them to strengthen their Communist rival inadvertently, but also could be used to fan economic rivalry between the capitalist nations. Such rivalry, Lenin hoped, would keep these nations, at least temporarily, from launching any united military effort against the Soviet state.

As part of the Anglo-Soviet agreement, the British insisted that the Soviet government refrain from propagandizing abroad against British interests or the British Empire, especially in Asia. In exchange, the British agreed to forgo foreign propaganda against the new Soviet state. Both in this agreement and in future ones, extracting such general promises from Soviet leaders seldom changed Soviet behavior.

While Britain, despite the new agreement, remained the chief capitalist enemy, Germany held out the best hope for friendlier relations with a major European country. Weakened and resentful because of World War I and the Allied-imposed Treaty of Versailles, Germany joined Soviet Russia as the chief European outcasts. Between 1920 and early 1922, Soviet-German talks led to agreements on trade, the repatriation of war prisoners, and the beginnings of secret military cooperation. Then, amidst a Genoa Conference of European powers, dealing with economic problems, Chicherin and German Foreign Minister Walter Rathenau agreed to a treaty of their own. It was called the Treaty of Rapallo, after the nearby Italian resort area where it was signed on Easter Sunday in April 1922.

By the treaty, the Soviet government established for the first time official diplomatic relations with a major Western power. The pact also renounced past debts and war claims from either side and pledged favorable trade relations and cooperation. With the signing of the treaty, the Soviet government had one less cause to worry about any unified capitalist anti-Soviet coalition. Following the treaty, German-Soviet economic as well as military cooperation increased.

The secret military collaboration was to continue for more than a decade. It enabled Germany to avoid some of the prohibitions of the Treaty of Versailles. It also provided Russia with German assistance in rebuilding its armament industry and in training its military, especially its officers.

In 1924, fearful that Germany would dominate trade with the USSR, other leading European powers, plus some smaller ones, followed Germany's lead and extended official diplomatic recognition to the Soviet Union. Of the major Western governments, only that of the United States now refused to exchange ambassadors with the Soviet state. It did, however, play a major role in helping to alleviate the Russian famine of 1921–1922, and it was favorable enough toward U.S.-Soviet trade for the United States to become by 1930 the leading exporter of goods to the Soviet Union.

Yet, despite all these steps in the normalization of relations, the Soviet government of the NEP period did not completely abandon its earlier hopes for Western revolutions. This was best illustrated by Comintern efforts encouraging German Communists to seize power in late 1923, a year marked by both the French occupation of Germany's Ruhr Valley and record-breaking German inflation. Although the German government had little trouble suppressing the German Communists' rebellious efforts, Soviet interference in German affairs harmed the more positive atmosphere created at Rapallo. It also helped stimulate Germany's subsequent efforts to improve relations with France and England. Despite the success of the German efforts, culminating in the Locarno treaties of 1925 and its admission into the League of Nations in 1926, Chicherin succeeded in limiting the damage to Soviet-German relations. In 1926, Germany and the Soviet Union signed the Treaty of Berlin, which pledged both powers to neutrality if either were attacked by a third country.

Real and suspected hostile Soviet activities also hampered more normal re-

Europe, 1924–Early 1941

■ Soviet territorial gains, 1939–1940

Changes in Czechoslovakia, 1938–1939
1 Sudetenland, annexed by Germany 1938
2 Protectorate of Bohemia-Moravia, created by Germany 1939
3 Slovakia, independent, then German protectorate 1939
4 To Hungary 1938, 1939
5 To Poland 1938

▨ Germany after Anschluss, 1938

▧ Western areas overrun by Germany, spring of 1940

▨ Areas in Central and Eastern Europe annexed by Germany, under German occupation, or a German protectorate by May 1941

▥ Countries allied with or friendly to Germany by May 1941

0   200   400 Miles

MAP 12.1

lations with Britain. In October 1924, an apparent letter from Zinoviev, the head of the Comintern, caused a furor in the midst of a British election campaign. The letter, later determined a forgery, called on British Communists to increase their subversive activities. The turmoil caused by the letter helped defeat the Labour party, whose government earlier in the year had officially recognized the Soviet government. Anglo-Soviet relations, however, were not broken off.

Three years later, in mid-1927, Britain's Conservative government authorized a London raid on a Soviet trade delegation and a British-Soviet trading company. Already angered by the Soviet encouragement of strikers in the British general strike of 1926, the British government undertook the raid hoping to find incriminating subversive material. Although some debate exists as to how damaging the seized materials were, the Conservative government broke off diplomatic relations a week after the raid.

Stalin now used this break and several other foreign developments of 1927 to exaggerate the danger of Western aggression against the USSR. The primary reason for this exaggeration was to aid him in his own political struggle against Trotsky, Zinoviev, and Kamenev. He claimed, for example, that by threatening to split the Communist party in such perilous times, Trotsky was forming "something like a united front" with British Foreign Minister Austen Chamberlin.

The 1927 war scare was not the first foreign policy development to strengthen Stalin's hand. The Comintern failure in Germany in 1923 helped to weaken Trotsky's case for emphasizing international revolution and, conversely, aided Stalin's subsequent stress on "socialism in one country" (see Chapter 10). The failure in Germany also dimmed the luster of Zinoviev, Comintern head and later rival of Stalin, who lost his Comintern post in late 1926.

In 1927, Stalin had his own foreign policy failure. Even before Lenin's death, the Comintern had begun to support China's nationalist and anti-imperialist Kuomintang (KMT) party and urged the infant Chinese Communist party (CCP) to become part of the Kuomintang without losing its own identity. After the death of Kuomintang founder Sun-Yat-sen in 1925, his successor Chiang Kai-shek successfully began to unite China by defeating many of its provincial warlords. Believing that Chiang offered the best hope of minimizing British, Japanese, and other imperialistic activity in China, Stalin supported him and the continuing CCP participation within the Kuomintang. But Chiang, growing increasingly suspicious of the Comintern and the CCP, began to turn on them, culminating in a massacre of Communists and their supporters in Shanghai in April 1927.

Trotsky was especially critical of Stalin's misguided China policy but mainly after its disastrous consequences became clear. Just a week before the massacre, Stalin had assured Moscow party workers that Chiang was reliable and would be "squeezed out like a lemon" until he had fulfilled his purpose, after which he could be flung into the garbage can of history. Instead of Chiang, however, it was the CCP that was squeezed, although not of all its vital juices. After additional KMT anti-Communist actions, the Soviet government broke off diplomatic relations with China in December 1927.

FOREIGN POLICY DURING THE FIRST
FIVE-YEAR PLAN, 1928-1932

By the end of the 1920s, several important developments occurred that affected Soviet foreign policy. Stalin had launched his "revolution from above" and consolidated his own power; the Great Depression, which would soon become a global one, had just begun in the United States (October 1929); and Maxim Litvinov had taken over increasing foreign-affairs responsibilities from an ailing Chicherin.

In the period of upheaval that accompanied collectivization and the first Five Year Plan (FYP), the USSR was in a poor position to defend itself from any outside enemies and had to pursue a cautious foreign policy. Although Stalin exaggerated the danger of war in 1927 for his own political benefit, his public and private statements taken together suggest that he was generally inclined to perceive greater foreign threats than actually existed. At the end of 1927, shortly before beginning his revolution from above, he told the Fifteenth Party Congress that "the threat of war remains in force. . . . Hence the task is to take into account the contradictions in the camp of the imperialists, to postpone war by 'buying off' the capitalists and to take all measures to maintain peaceful relations." On September 1, 1930, he wrote privately to Molotov: "The Poles are certain to be putting together (if they have not already done so) a bloc of Baltic states (Estonia, Latvia, Finland) in anticipation of a war against the USSR. . . . This means that they will go to war *as soon as they have secured the bloc* (they'll find an excuse)."[3]

From the Soviet perspective, the Great Depression further complicated foreign policy. On the one hand, it held out hopes for the collapse of capitalist governments; on the other hand, it threatened to increase international tensions, which might then adversely affect the Soviet Union. Moreover, the decline of world commodity prices (such as on grain) and the wave of economic protectionism that swept the world threatened Soviet export profits. In this period, they were more needed than ever to balance the cost of imports required for the first FYP.

In such a climate, Chicherin's assistant, Maxim Litvinov, proved a good choice to replace him, as he officially did in mid-1930. The son of a Jewish bank clerk, Litvinov was intelligent, outgoing, and familiar with the West. Before 1917, he spent considerable time in Western Europe and in 1917 had married an Englishwoman, Ivy Low. Although the USSR did not join the League of Nations until 1934, Litvinov was well known in Geneva, where, beginning in late 1927, he advocated sweeping Soviet disarmament proposals. (Although made partly for propagandistic purposes, they would have served, if accepted, Soviet interests at a time when the USSR was especially vulnerable militarily.)

Among the highlights of Soviet foreign policy in this period were the restoration of diplomatic relations with Great Britain (1929) and China (1932), increasing fears of Japan, a series of nonaggression pacts in 1932, and certain

[3]*Stalin's Letters to Molotov, 1925–1936*, eds. Lars T. Lih, Oleg V. Naumov, and Oleg Khlevniuk (New Haven, 1995), p. 208.

miscalculated steps that helped smooth Hitler's rise to power in Germany. The restoration of full ties with Britain at the end of October 1929 was largely due to a new British Labour government, but British manufacturers eager for Soviet trade also helped. Full relations with China were resumed because of a more dramatic occurrence—Japanese aggression in Manchuria in 1931–1932. Harmed by the global depression and hungry for Manchurian resources, Japan established there the puppet state of Manchukuo. With Japanese troops now just across the Soviet border, the Soviet government patched over differences with Chiang Kai-shek and signed a Soviet-Chinese nonaggression treaty in June 1932.

Alarmed by Japanese developments in the East and always fearful that western border states might act in collusion with one or more of the major European powers, the Soviet government pressed for nonaggression pacts with its western neighbors. In the course of 1932, Litvinov oversaw the signing of treaties with Finland, Latvia, Estonia, and Poland. Because Poland was an ally of France, the Polish treaty, plus France's growing apprehensions regarding Germany, helped propel France into signing its own non aggression treaty with the Soviet Union, which it did in November 1932. In addition, a Soviet-Lithuanian treaty of friendship and neutrality already existed (first signed in 1926 and then renewed in 1931). In contrast, negotiations with Rumania were not able to overcome differences regarding Bessarabia, which Rumania had kept following World War I.

Of all the Soviet diplomatic developments of this time, however, none was more ultimately significant than the Soviet policy toward Hitler and his Nazi party. This policy was influenced by the Stalinist position enunciated at the Sixth Comintern Congress in 1928, which was hostile to any cooperation between communist and socialist parties. Cooperation between the German Communist party (KPD) and the German Social Democratic party (SDP) might have prevented Hitler from coming to power, as he did in January 1933.

Some historians have attributed Stalin's noncooperation policy in Germany to the belief that a Nazi government would represent just a brief dying gasp of the old German capitalist order. But Robert Tucker has argued that Stalin realized that Hitler's reign might last some time but hoped it would increase tensions between Germany and the former Western allies. That would then reduce the chances of any combined great-power, anti-Soviet coalition. It might even eventually lead to a war between the "European imperialists," a war from which the Soviet Union could benefit.

SEARCH FOR SECURITY, 1933–1939

After Hitler became chancellor of Germany in January 1933, Stalin initially hoped that the Soviet-German cooperation that had existed since Rapallo could continue. At first, Hitler also seemed willing. Although Hitler persecuted German Communists, and both leaders were aware of the deep ideological differences between their beliefs, it did not prevent them from extending the Treaty of Berlin in mid-1933.

At the same time, however, the Soviet Union was keeping other options open. It was not only concerned about Germany's future intentions, but also about those of Japan. Dominant in Manchuria, it posed a threat to Soviet control of that region's Chinese Eastern Railway, to the neighboring Soviet satellite of Mongolia, and perhaps to Soviet territory itself. Because the United States was also concerned about Japanese imperialism, this mutual concern helped overcome remaining hurdles to the establishment of full U.S.-Soviet diplomatic relations. This occurred in November 1933, after Litvinov came to Washington and he and the new U.S. president, Franklin D. Roosevelt, agreed to the final details.

By the end of that year, Hitler's behavior was causing heightened anxiety in the Kremlin. Friendly German words about "good will toward France" and the appearance of a new edition of Hitler's *Mein Kampf*, complete with its call for conquering *lebensraum* (living space) within the Soviet Union, were a few of the causes of alarm. In the late fall of 1933, Soviet authorities began ending more than a decade of German-Soviet military collaboration on Soviet soil.

Shortly afterward, in late December 1933, Litvinov gave an important speech to Soviet government officials in which he identified Germany and Japan as the greatest threats to peace and to the Soviet Union. While expressing a desire to live in peace with both countries, he made it clear that the Soviet Union would cooperate with other countries prepared "to oppose any violators of peace."

In January 1934, the signing of a German-Polish ten-year nonaggression pact furthered Soviet suspicions of Germany. The following month, the French Communists signaled a change in Moscow's Comintern policy when they formed a "popular front" with French Socialists against extreme right-wing French forces.

While keeping the door open to better relations with Germany, Stalin allowed Litvinov to build whatever "collective-security" coalitions he could against potential Nazi aggression aimed at the USSR. In May 1934, the Soviet Union extended the Polish and Baltic nonaggression treaties signed in 1932 into ten-year pacts. The following month, it established diplomatic relations with Czechoslovakia and Rumania—despite its unhappiness with the loss of Bessarabia to Rumania. In September 1934, by which time both Japan and Germany had already dropped out of the League of Nations, the Soviet Union joined this organization it had once referred to as a "League of Imperialist Robbers."

The new momentum continued into 1935. In May, the Soviet government signed two mutual defense treaties, first with France and then with Czechoslovakia. In the first treaty, both sides pledged assistance "in case of an unprovoked attack on the part of a European state." The second pact was similar except that the Soviet Union was obligated to assist Czechoslovakia only if France did so first. The fact that Germany and the USSR did not share a border was relevant to both treaties. So was the position of Poland and Rumania between the Soviet Union and Czechoslovakia. To attack Germany (in aid of France) or to reach Czechoslovakia would first require Soviet troops to cross through at least one neighboring country.

As Litvinov continued pursuing his policy of collective security, Stalin continued to hope that Soviet-German relations could be improved. In April 1935, a German-Soviet trade agreement was concluded. After Hitler sent German troops to remilitarize the Rhineland in March 1936, thereby weakening French security, Premier Molotov stated that the Soviet government continued to believe in the possibility of improved Soviet-German relations.

But a variety of complications prevented any warming of the icy relations that were developing. Playing upon Western anticommunist sentiments, which competed with antifascist feelings in both France and Britain, Hitler encouraged the belief that he was more benign toward the two Western powers than to the Soviet Union. In the first half of 1936, popular-front, antifascist governments were elected in both France and Spain. In France, the Soviet Union supported the socialist-led government and instructed French Communists, who supported but did not join in the new government, not to let strikes jeopardize the strengthening of the French military.

In Spain, matters were more complicated. In July 1936, General Francisco Franco began a rebellion against the government. It soon turned into a civil war, complicated by outside intervention. Although France and Great Britain decried such interference, Germany and Italy intervened on the side of Franco and, more cautiously and belatedly, the Soviet Union on the side of government forces.

Spain created a dilemma for Stalin. On the one hand, failure to intervene might have handed a quick victory to Franco's forces, strengthened Western fascism, and disillusioned leftist antifascists throughout the world. And Stalin was then courting leftist opinion by such means as his 1936 constitution, which he declared was "the most democratic . . . in the world." On the other hand, involvement might mean further alienating Hitler. Too great a Soviet involvement, especially if followed by a victory for government forces, might also inadvertently help fan the flames of anticommunism in France and Great Britain and strengthen anti-Soviet forces in both countries. Moreover, Stalin distrusted any leftist forces not completely loyal to Soviet interests. This suspect category included most of the Spanish and foreign leftists, especially Trotskyites and anarchists, who participated in the Spanish conflict.

Thus, Stalin's response was to (1) furnish limited Soviet aid (including a few thousand military, technical, NKVD, and other personnel), (2) support the creation of antifascist "International Brigades," (3) weaken the influence—sometimes by murder—of any leftists not loyal to him, and (4) encourage government social and economic policies moderate enough not to alarm the Western bourgeoisie. Rather than any quick radical leftist victory over Franco, a continuing war that helped keep Hitler and the nonintervening Western democracies focused on Spain was probably more to Stalin's liking. The conflict in Spain, however, helped exacerbate international ideological conflict, and from late 1936 to late 1937, Germany, Italy, and Japan joined together in an "Anti-Comintern" coalition pledged to resist communism.

Japan's involvement in this expression of hostility to communism was a reminder of the continuing eastern danger faced by the Soviet Union. Although in 1935 the Soviet government had bowed to Japanese pressure and sold to

Manchukuo the Soviet share of the Chinese Eastern Railway, Japan continued its aggressive policies. In mid-1938, a year after launching its eight-year war with China, Japanese forces clashed in a bloody battle with Soviet troops over disputed territory along the Soviet border with Manchukuo and Korea. A year after that, in July–August 1939, another Soviet-Japanese battle occurred along the Mongolian frontier. In both these battles, Soviet forces were able to hold onto the territory the Japanese had hoped to gain.

Meanwhile, Hitler's successes in central-eastern Europe were increasing the Nazi threat to the USSR. In March 1938, Hitler succeeded in uniting Austria with Germany. Although unification with Austria was a violation of post–World War I treaties, Great Britain and France did nothing more than protest. Hitler then began pressuring Czechoslovakia, which included a German populated area (the so-called Sudetenland).

Although France and the USSR had signed a mutual defense pact in May 1935, relations between the two powers (and Anglo-Soviet relations) were hardly warm. Because of French conservative opposition, the Franco-Soviet Pact was not ratified until late February 1936. The two signatories had not drawn up any concrete military convention between them. Anticommunist sentiments in France and Britain were one hindrance. The Soviet purges of 1937 and 1938, which weakened the military, also undercut any Western confidence in the USSR.

Stalin more than reciprocated this distrust. In a conversation with the U.S. ambassador, Joseph Davies, in June 1938, Stalin told him that British Prime Minister Neville Chamberlain was trying to strengthen Germany against the Soviet Union. Besides such suspected malevolence, there was the question of will: whether France and Britain had the backbone to stand up to Hitler.

This mutual distrust continued up to and beyond the Munich Conference of September 29, 1938. While Britain and France were there and approved the Munich Agreement that paved the way for Germany's gaining of Czechoslovakia's Sudeten borderlands, neither the Soviet Union nor Czechoslovakia were invited to the conference. Doubts about whether the Soviet military could or would come to Czechoslovakia's aid in case of a German attack did, however, contribute to the concessions made to Hitler.

With the Japanese danger still looming in the east and Great Britain and France willing to appease at least some of Hitler's eastward desires, Stalin stepped up efforts to come to terms with Hitler. Toward the end of 1938, Soviet and German diplomats agreed to reduce media attacks against each other and to renew a trade agreement. The Soviet Union also cut back its involvement in Spain, perhaps intending to send another positive signal to Hitler.

But the Soviet Union's position remained precarious: Unless a deal was struck with Hitler, there seemed little on the horizon to prevent additional eastward moves on his part; Soviet distrust of France and Great Britain continued to mount; and the danger from Japan, possibly allied with Germany, seemed a real threat to Soviet leaders. On March 10, 1939, before delegates of the Eighteenth Party Congress, Stalin gave his analysis of major developments, foreign and domestic, since the last party congress in 1934. He said that a new imperialist war had begun, with Germany, Japan, and Italy being the aggressors. He reviewed Soviet attempts to foster collective security. At a time when most countries were still suffering from the effects of the Great Depression, he emphasized the growing economic strength of the Soviet Union and called it "the only country in the world where crises are unknown and where industry is continuously on the upgrade." Most notable were his words explaining the appeasing policies of the major Western democracies and the chief aims of Soviet foreign policy.

Stalin's speech has often been interpreted as a signal to Hitler that the So-

---

Stalin on Appeasement and Soviet Foreign Policy, March 1939

The following excerpt is taken from Stalin's Report to the Eighteenth Party Congress. The source is *Leninism, Selected Writings by Joseph Stalin* (New York, 1942), pp. 439–440, 444. Ellipses are mine.

It is a distinguishing feature of the new imperialist war that it has not yet become universal, a world war. The war is being waged by aggressor states, which in every way infringe upon the interests of the non-aggressive states, primarily England, France and the USA, while the latter draw back and retreat, making concession after concession to the aggressors. . . .

To what are we to attribute this one-sided and strange character of the new imperialist war? . . .

. . . The chief reason is that the majority of the non-aggressive countries, particularly England and France, have rejected the policy of collective security, the policy of collective resistance to the aggressors, and have taken up a position of non-intervention. . . .

The policy of non-intervention means conniving at aggression, giving free rein to war, and, consequently, transforming the war into a world war. The policy of non-intervention reveals an eagerness, a desire, not to hinder the aggressors in their nefari-

ous work: not to hinder Japan, say, from embroiling herself in a war with China, or, better still, with the Soviet Union; not to hinder Germany, say, from enmeshing herself in European affairs, from embroiling herself in a war with the Soviet Union, to allow all the belligerents to sink deeply into the mire of war, to encourage them surreptitiously in this; to allow them to weaken and exhaust one another; and then, when they have become weak enough, to appear on the scene with fresh strength, to appear, of course, "in the interests of peace," and to dictate conditions to the enfeebled belligerents.

Cheap and easy! . . .

The tasks of the party in the sphere of foreign policy are:

1. To continue the policy of peace and of strengthening business relations with all countries.

2. To be cautious and not allow our country to be drawn into conflicts by warmongers who are accustomed to have others pull the chestnuts out of the fire for them.

3. To strengthen the might of our Red Army and Red Navy to the utmost.

4. To strengthen the international bonds of friendship with the working people of all countries, who are interested in peace and friendship among nations.

viet Union would not be drawn into anti-Nazi war unless Soviet interests were violated—in other words, that a Nazi-Soviet understanding was possible. Adam Ulam, however, has deciphered it primarily as a message to the Western powers: "We don't need you, but you may need us; if so, better hurry up."[4] It seems likely that the speech was intended to keep both options open. From Stalin's viewpoint, it was probably still too early to tell whether Hitler would desire a *rapprochement* with the Soviet Union or whether France and Great Britain would realize the folly of their ways and come humbly forth seeking closer antifascist ties with the Soviet Union. If he were lucky, perhaps both would occur, and then he could take his choice from the highest bidder.

Just days after his March 10 speech, Germany took over control of most of the rest of Czechoslovakia and later that month forced Lithuania to allow German annexation of the port city of Memel. After Hitler increased the pressure on Poland to make concessions regarding Danzig and the Polish Corridor, the British and French pledged support to Poland if threatened by Germany. Two weeks later, in mid-April, they made a similar pledge to Rumania.

These pledges did not put to rest Soviet fears of British and French intentions; mutual distrust, along with negotiations, continued during the spring and early summer. Although Stalin and some of the other Soviet leaders were often overly suspicious of Britain and France and sometimes mistaken because of ideological blind spots or faulty intelligence information, there is also no doubt that British and French diplomacy was at times inept and faulty in allaying Soviet suspicions.

Meanwhile, Stalin continued to encourage better Soviet-German relations. In May, he sent a strong new signal to Hitler by appointing Molotov as foreign minister in place of Litvinov, who was Jewish and had been the major Soviet proponent of antifascist collective security. Stalin also told Molotov to purge his new ministry of Jews. In mid-June, a Soviet diplomat in Berlin apparently let it be known that although the Soviet Union was keeping its options open, it preferred a nonaggression treaty with Germany to a pact with Great Britain and France.[5]

After further maneuvering and bargaining, Hitler struck a bargain with Stalin. Hitler was ready to start a war with Poland and hoped to prevent British and French intervention by depriving them of any Soviet assistance. In a public Nazi-Soviet nonaggression pact, dated August 23, 1939, both sides pledged neutrality if either country was "the object of belligerent action by a third Power."

At the same time, Molotov and German Foreign Minister von Ribbentrop

---

[4]*Expansion and Coexistence.* 2d ed. (New York, 1974), pp. 263–264.

[5]For a different interpretation of Stalin's policy in early 1939, see Geoffrey Roberts, *The Soviet Union and the Origins of the Second World War: Russo-German Relations and the Road to War, 1933–1941* (New York, 1995), pp. 62–86. In general, Roberts downplays Soviet initiatives toward Germany and insists that a treaty with France and Great Britain remained Stalin's main objective until at least the end of July 1939. Although Roberts claims that his position is supported by primary materials first made available in the late 1980s and early 1990s, these materials continue to allow for different interpretations of Stalin's policies.

FIGURE 12.2. Molotov signs 1939 Nazi-Soviet Pact as Stalin looks on.
(*UPI/Bettmann.*)

signed a secret protocol. It marked out Lithuania and western Poland as a German sphere of interest, and eastern Poland, Latvia, Estonia, Finland, and Bessarabia—still part of Rumania—fell into the Soviet sphere. (A month later, the two powers agreed that almost all of Lithuania could become part of the Soviet sphere in exchange for allowing Germany a slightly larger share of Poland.)

At first glance, before subsequent events provided greater perspective, the Nazi-Soviet Pact seemed a major triumph for Stalin. In contrast to Britain and France, Germany was willing to grant him a free hand in a broad belt of territory from the Baltic to the Black seas. Moreover, at a time that border conflict with Japanese troops was occurring, the pact freed him from any immediate concern about having to wage a two-front war. According to Nikita Khrushchev's later testimony, Stalin was most pleased with the treaty, thought he had outsmarted Hitler, and was confident the treaty would enable the Soviet Union to save its strength. Khrushchev surmised that Stalin hoped the British and French would exhaust Germany, thereby thwarting Hitler's plan later to turn eastward.

Reaction to the nonaggression pact was less jubilant, sometimes hostile, in many areas outside the Kremlin, even among many Soviet citizens and foreign Communists. Many were puzzled and dismayed. In a speech to the Supreme Soviet on August 31, 1939, Molotov referred to "voices" asking "how the Soviet Union could consent to improve political relations with a state of the fascist type." His explanation was that the Western democracies had not negotiated with the Soviet Union in good faith and that it was the duty of Soviet leaders to prevent a Soviet-German war. For the next half-century, Soviet writings, including the memoirs of Khrushchev and long-time foreign minister Andrei Gromyko, arrived at the similar misleading conclusion that Great Britain and France left Stalin little real choice.

SOVIET "NEUTRALITY," SEPTEMBER 1939–JUNE 1941

On September 17, 1939, two weeks after France and Great Britain had declared war on Hitler for his September 1 invasion of western Poland, Stalin sent Soviet troops into eastern Poland. Molotov falsely declared it was to protect Ukrainians and Belorussians. Besides these two peoples, the area was also populated with Poles, Jews, and other ethnic groups.

Despite his treaty with Hitler, Stalin remained wary of Germany. For this and other reasons, in late September–early October, Molotov pressured the Estonians, Latvians, and Lithuanians into accepting treaties permitting Soviet troops and bases on their soil. Soviet demands on Finland were even greater, including insistence on territorial adjustments to make strategic areas such as Leningrad more secure.

At the end of November, after Finland had refused to acquiesce fully, Soviet troops began invading that small country of 4 million people. Although the outnumbered Finns put up surprising resistance in the ensuing "Winter War," they were finally forced, in March 1940, to agree to a treaty relinquishing certain border areas to the Soviet Union. The poor performance of the Soviet military, so recently decimated by his purges, angered Stalin, but, typically, he blamed it on others. Although Molotov proclaimed that the war had resulted in 48,745 Soviet deaths, the real number was many times that figure.

In the summer of 1940, on a variety of pretexts and without having to wage war, the Soviet Union claimed its final Nazi-Soviet pact gains. It forced Estonia, Latvia, and Lithuania into the USSR. From Rumania, it took not only Bessarabia, but also northern Bukovina, which had not been mentioned in the Nazi-Soviet pact.

Moscow incorporated the new areas into the union republic structure of the Soviet Union and imposed Communist political and socioeconomic structures. Somewhat like Ivan the Terrible centuries before, after acquiring new territories Stalin and his authorities ordered the arrest, killing, internment, or deportation of many inhabitants. Roughly 2 million people, or close to ten percent of the areas' population, were so victimized before Hitler's troops arrived on the scene in the summer of 1941. Among those deported were many women, children, and old people, whereas some of the more feared opponents, or potential opponents, of the new Communist order were shot. Most of the deportees were loaded upon freight trains and shipped to Siberia or other remote destinations, some dumped in settlements and others into forced-labor camps. Among those executed, the most notable were the almost 5,000 Polish officers whose remains were discovered by the Germans during World War II in Katyn forest near the city of Smolensk. Another 10,000 Polish officers seized by Soviet authorities also "disappeared."

While these new areas were receiving their welcome into Stalin's world, Hitler was achieving great successes in the West. In spring 1940, German armies defeated and occupied Denmark, Norway, the Netherlands, Belgium, Luxembourg, and France. Khrushchev noted that after hearing of the rapid fall of France, Stalin cursed the British and French governments for not putting up more resistance and stated that Hitler would now surely "beat our brains in."

Yet the fall of France, a fatal blow to Stalin's hopes for a protracted war in the west, was partly his own doing. His pact with Hitler had allowed the German dictator the luxury of concentrating almost all of his troops in the west. Furthermore, both before and after France's collapse, the Soviet Union was a major supplier of vital materials to Germany. Petroleum, manganese, copper, nickel, chrome, platinum, phosphates, lumber, and grain were among the important supplies Germany was able to import from the USSR. The Soviet government also bought and shipped other materials, such as rubber, to Germany and aided it in other ways.

Although Stalin wanted to give Hitler no excuse for turning eastward and attacking the Soviet Union, the personalities and territorial appetites of the two dictators offered little hope for any prolonged peace. A variety of tensions sprang up. Among their causes were the Soviet seizure of Bukovina, Balkan differences, and the sending of German troops to Finland in September 1940. That same month, Germany, Italy, and Japan signed a Tripartite Pact, promising each other assistance if one were attacked by a country not already involved in the European or Sino-Japanese wars.

Meanwhile, Britain's stiff air resistance against the German Luftwaffe led Hitler to postpone plans to invade Britain, and he secretly ordered his generals to plan an invasion of the Soviet Union.

Concealing his intentions and appearing conciliatory, Hitler invited Molotov to Berlin in November 1940. Ribbentrop and Hitler encouraged the USSR to join with Germany, Italy, and Japan in world dominance and attempted to focus Soviet territorial appetites southward "in the direction of the Indian Ocean." They also promised German help in improving Russia's position regarding the Black Sea Straits. In the talks and in a follow-up note, the Soviet government pressed the Germans for greater concessions, including the removal of German troops from Finland.

Molotov's hard bargaining confirmed Hitler's belief that the Soviet Union had to be smashed, the sooner the better. In December, he approved Operation Barbarossa, by which the German military was to be prepared to attack the Soviet Union by May 15, 1941.

SUGGESTED SOURCES*

BELOFF, MAX. *The Foreign Policy of Soviet Russia, 1929–1941.* 2 vols. London, 1947–1949.
BORKENAU, FRANZ. *World Communism: A History of the Communist International.* Ann Arbor, 1962.

* See also books mentioned in footnotes.

BRANDT, CONRAD. *Stalin's Failure in China, 1924–1927*. Cambridge, Mass., 1958.

CARR, E. H. *Twilight of the Comintern, 1930–1935*. New York, 1982.

CLARKE, J. CALVITT. *Russia and Italy Against Hitler: The Bolshevik-Fascist Rapprochement of the 1930s*. Westport, Conn., 1991.

COOX, ALVIN. *Nomonhan: Japan Against Russia, 1939*. Stanford, 1985.

———. *The Anatomy of a Small War: The Soviet-Japanese Struggle for Changkufeng-Khasan, 1938*. Westport, Conn., 1977.

CRAIG, GORDON, and FELIX GILBERT, eds. *The Diplomats: 1919–1939*. Princeton, 1953.

CROWE, DAVID M. *The Baltic States and the Great Powers: Foreign Relations, 1938–1940*. Boulder, 1993.

DEBO, RICHARD K. *Revolution and Survival: The Foreign Policy of Soviet Russia, 1917–1918*. Toronto, 1979.

———. *Survival and Consolidation: The Foreign Policy of Soviet Russia, 1918–1921*. Montreal, 1992.

DEGRAS, JANE, ed. *The Communist International, 1919–1943: Documents*. 3 vols. London, 1956–1965.

———, ed. *Soviet Documents on Foreign Policy, 1917–1941*. 3 vols. London, 1951–1953.

DYAKOV, YURI, and TATYANA BUSHUYEVA. *The Red Army and the Wehrmacht: How the Soviets Militarized Germany, 1922–1933, and Paved the Way for Fascism*. Amherst, N.Y., 1995.

EUDIN, XENIA J., and H. H. FISHER, eds. *Soviet Russia and the West, 1920–1927: A Documentary Survey*. Stanford, 1957.

———, and ROBERT C. NORTH. *Soviet Russia and the East, 1920–1927: A Documentary Survey*. Stanford, 1957.

———, and ROBERT M. SLUSSER, eds. *Soviet Foreign Policy, 1928–1934: Documents and Materials*. University Park, Penn., 1966.

FISCHER, LOUIS. *Russia's Road from Peace to War: Soviet Foreign Relations, 1917–1941*. New York, 1969.

———. *The Soviets in World Affairs: A History of the Relations Between the Soviet Union and the Rest of the World, 1917–1929*. 2d ed. 2 vols. Princeton, 1951.

FREUND, GERALD. *Unholy Alliance: Russian-German Relations from the Treaty of Brest-Litovsk to the Treaty of Berlin*. New York, 1957.

GOLDBERG, HAROLD J., ed. *Documents of Soviet-American Relations*. 2 vols. Gulf Breeze, Fla., 1993–1995. Both volumes deal with the 1917–1933 period.

GROSS, JAN T. *Revolution from Abroad: The Soviet Conquest of Poland's Western Ukraine and Western Belorussia*. Princeton, 1988.

HASLAM, JONATHAN. *Soviet Foreign Policy, 1930–33: The Impact of the Depression*. New York, 1983.

———. *The Soviet Union and the Struggle for Collective Security in Europe, 1933–39*. New York, 1984.

———. *The Soviet Union and the Threat from the East, 1933–41: Moscow, Tokyo, and the Prelude to the Pacific War*. Pittsburgh, 1992.

HILGER, GUSTAV, and ALFRED G. MEYER. *The Incompatible Allies: A Memoir-History of German-Soviet Relations, 1918–1941*. New York, 1953.

HOCHMAN, JIRI. *The Soviet Union and the Failure of Collective Security, 1934–1938*. Ithaca, N.Y., 1984.

KENNAN, GEORGE F. *Russia and the West under Lenin and Stalin*. Boston, 1961.

KOCHAN, LIONEL. *Russia and the Weimar Republic*. Cambridge, England, 1954.

MAISKY, IVAN. *Memoirs of a Soviet Ambassador*. New York, 1968.

O'CONNOR, TIMOTHY. *Diplomacy and Revolution: G. V. Chicherin and Soviet Foreign Affairs, 1918–1930*. Ames, Iowa, 1988.

PAUL, ALLEN. *Katyn: The Untold Story of Stalin's Polish Massacre*. New York, 1991.

PHILLIPS, HUGH D. *Between the Revolution and the West: A Political Biography of Maxim M. Litvinov.* Boulder, 1992.

READ, ANTHONY, and DAVID FISHER. *The Deadly Embrace: Hitler, Stalin, and the Nazi-Soviet Pact, 1939–1941.* New York, 1988.

ROBERTS, GEOFFREY K. *The Unholy Alliance: Stalin's Pact with Hitler.* Bloomington, 1989.

SABALIUNAS, LEONAS. *Lithuania in Crisis: Nationalism to Communism, 1939–1940.* Bloomington, 1972.

SONTAG, RAYMOND J., and JAMES S. BEDDIE, eds. *Nazi-Soviet Relations, 1939–1941: Documents from the Archives of the German Foreign Office.* Washington, D.C., 1948.

SUVOROV, VIKTOR. *Icebreaker: Who Started the Second World War?* London, 1990.

TROTTER, WILLIAM R. *A Frozen Hell: The Russo-Finnish Winter War of 1939–1940.* Chapel Hill, 1991.

TUCKER, ROBERT C. *Stalin in Power: The Revolution from Above, 1928–1941.* New York, 1990.

ULDRICKS, TEDDY, J. *Diplomacy and Ideology: The Origins of Soviet Foreign Relations, 1917–1930.* London, 1979.

VOLODARSKY, M. I. *The Soviet Union and Its Southern Neighbours: Iran and Afghanistan, 1917–1933.* Portland, Or., 1994.

WATT, DONALD CAMERON. *How War Came: The Immediate Origins of the Second World War, 1938–1939.* New York, 1989.

———, and KENNETH BOURNE, eds. *British Documents on Foreign Affairs—Reports and Papers from the Foreign Office Confidential Print.* Part II, *From the First to the Second World War.* Series A, *The Soviet Union, 1917–1939.* 17 vols. Frederick, Md., 1984–1986.

WEINBERG, GERHARD L. *Germany and the Soviet Union 1939–1941.* Leiden, 1972.

WHEELER-BENNETT, JOHN WHEELER. *Brest-Litovsk: The Forgotten Peace, March, 1918.* London, 1938.

WHITE, STEPHEN. *The Origins of Detente: The Genoa Conference and Soviet-Western Relations, 1921–1922.* Cambridge, England, 1985.

WILBUR, C. MARTIN. *Missionaries of Revolution: Soviet Advisers and Nationalist China, 1920–1927.* Cambridge, Mass., 1989.

CHAPTER 13

The Great Patriotic War, 1941–1945

For the Soviet government and citizens, World War II was primarily their "Great Patriotic War" against Germany and its allies. It was a horrendous yet heroic experience. Estimates of the mid-1990s suggest that at least 27 million Soviet people lost their lives (some estimates are much higher); yet the Soviet military turned back Hitler's forces and in 1945 pursued them all the way to Berlin. Tens of thousands of Soviet towns, villages, plants, and schools were destroyed; yet the Soviet Union gained new territories and established the basis for an Eastern European empire.

ON THE EVE OF BATTLE

Although Hitler had hoped to attack the Soviet Union in May 1941, late flooding in Eastern Europe (more so than a Balkan campaign in Yugoslavia and Greece) delayed his plans. Meanwhile in April, Soviet diplomacy accomplished a major goal by signing a Soviet-Japanese pact that promised neutrality if either country were attacked by a third power. The strong Soviet military performance in border clashes in 1939 had influenced Japan to direct its aggression elsewhere. Now, if war came with Germany, at least the Soviet Union would not have to fight a two-front war.

But Stalin still hoped a war with Germany could be avoided or at least postponed. This hope was one of the reasons he ignored intelligence information and other warnings that a German attack was imminent in mid-1941. As late as a week before the German attack on June 22, Stalin indicated that he thought such an attack was unlikely during that year. He convinced himself that Western warnings were a trick designed to instigate a Soviet conflict with Germany and that it was necessary not to provoke Hitler.

This mentality contributed to the Soviet Union's lack of preparedness for Germany's massive surprise attack. Even if Stalin had taken the warnings more seriously, the situation would have remained precarious. Despite a significant Soviet increase in combat readiness since 1939, the military still had not recovered from the Great Terror; new defense fortifications in the territories acquired in 1939–1940 were woefully inadequate; and the Soviet defense plan was poorly thought out.

Khrushchev's Secret Speech of 1956 and the memoirs of Marshal Zhukov reveal several examples of Stalin's mentality on the eve of the German attack. Khrushchev stated that the head of the Kiev Military District warned of an imminent German attack and suggested that 300,000 people be evacuated and that trenches and antitank ditches be dug. But Moscow replied that such actions would be a provocation, and Hitler should be given no pretext for an invasion. Zhukov noted that on the evening of June 21, after being told that several German deserters had revealed plans for a German attack later that night, Stalin stated that it might still be possible to deal with the situation by "peaceful means." Stalin then said, "I think Hitler is trying to provoke us. He surely hasn't decided to make war?"

WARFARE AND MAJOR BATTLES, JUNE 1941–MAY 1945

On June 22, 1941, at 4:00 A.M. Moscow time, Germany and its allies launched their attack on the Soviet Union. On a broad front from the Baltic to the Black seas, they advanced rapidly. By the beginning of September, they had begun the siege of Leningrad; later that month, they captured Kiev; and in October they were approaching Moscow from three sides and were close to its outskirts. As November gave way to December, they briefly were within 15 to 20 miles of the Kremlin.

Immediately following the initial German invasion, Stalin had been in a state of near shock. Although he tried to rally the Soviet people when he finally made his first wartime radio speech on July 3, his words had little immediate effect on the German advance. In the middle of October, he had ordered government ministries evacuated to Kuibyshev and planned to go there himself. At the last minute, however, he decided he could not leave the capital and that it would be defended "to the last drop of blood." Several weeks later, at anniversary celebrations of the Communist revolution, he appealed to Russian patriotism by calling to mind numerous national heroes from Alexander Nevsky to Leo Tolstoy. He was finally beginning to display the leadership needed if Soviet forces were to reverse the German onslaught. From this point on, Soviet troops went into battle shouting "For the motherland and Stalin!"

Just as significant as Stalin's leadership were the other obstacles now faced by the Germans. Their forces had advanced so far and so rapidly that it became increasingly difficult to provide front-line troops with adequate fuel, food, munitions, and other equipment. A Soviet scorched-earth retreat contributed to their shortages. As early as November, their lack of warm clothing caused numerous cases of frostbite. The December cold was even worse, reaching lows in the Moscow area of about −30°C (−22°F). The freezing temperatures wrecked havoc on German troops, vehicles, and weapons.

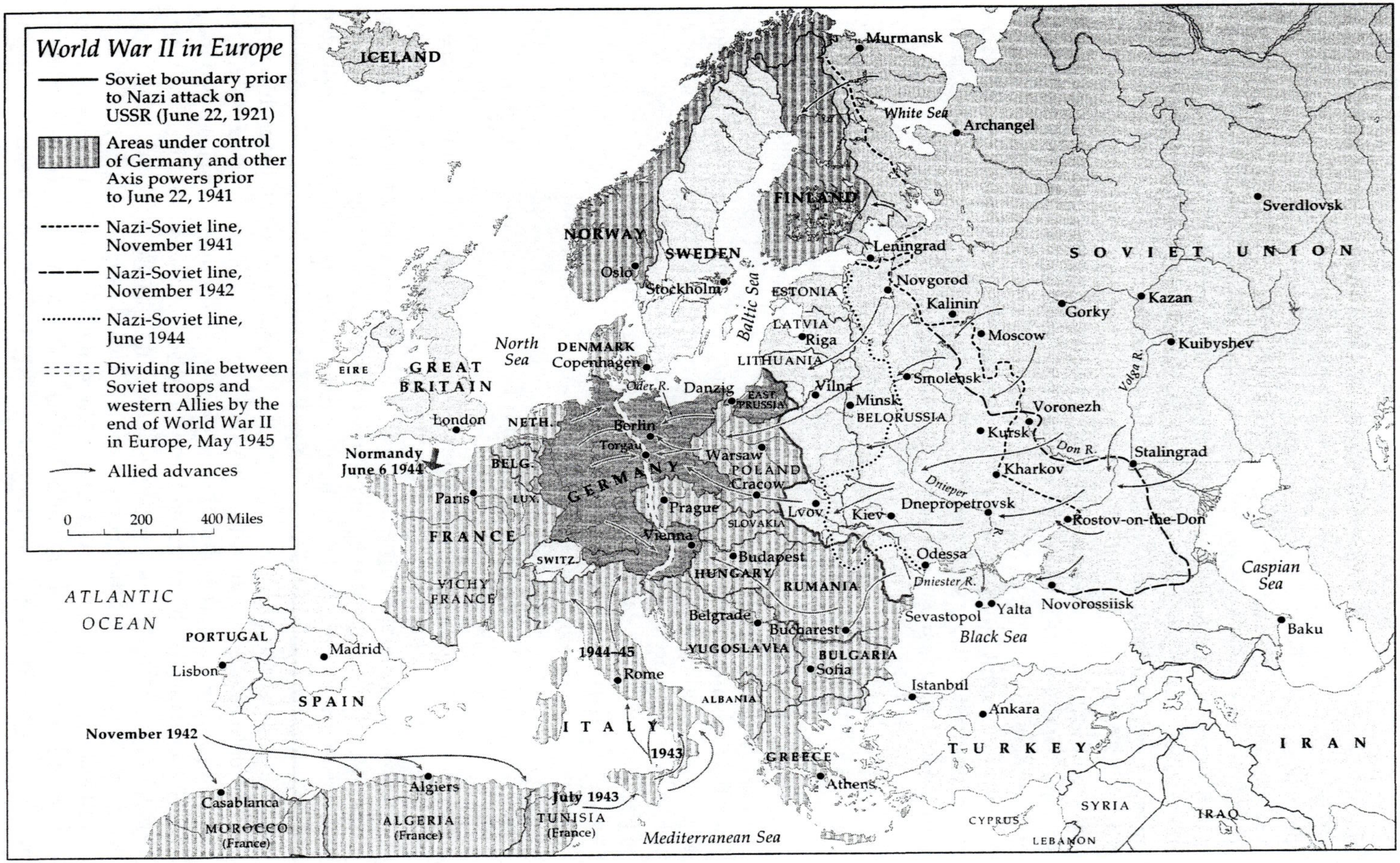
World War II in Europe
Soviet boundary prior to Nazi attack on USSR (June 22, 1921)
Areas under control of Germany and other Axis powers prior to June 22, 1941
Nazi-Soviet line, November 1941
Nazi-Soviet line, November 1942
Nazi-Soviet line, June 1944
Dividing line between Soviet troops and western Allies by the end of World War II in Europe, May 1945
Allied advances
0
200
400 Miles
ICELAND
Murmansk
White Sea
Archangel
Sverdlovsk
FINLAND
NORWAY
SWEDEN
Oslo
Stockholm
Baltic Sea
Leningrad
Novgorod
SOVIET UNION
ESTONIA
Kalinin
Moscow
Gorky
Kazan
Kuibyshev
Volga R.
LATVIA
Riga
LITHUANIA
Vilna
Minsk
BELORUSSIA
Smolensk
Voronezh
Kursk
Don R.
Stalingrad
Kharkov
Dnieper
Dnepropetrovsk
Rostov-on-the-Don
Kiev
Lvov
Odessa
Dniester R.
Caspian Sea
Novorossiisk
Yalta
Sevastopol
Black Sea
Baku
North Sea
DENMARK
Copenhagen
EIRE
GREAT BRITAIN
London
NETH.
BELG.
LUX.
Oder R.
Danzig
EAST PRUSSIA
Berlin
Torgau
Warsaw
POLAND
Cracow
GERMANY
Prague
SLOVAKIA
Vienna
Budapest
HUNGARY
RUMANIA
Normandy June 6 1944
Paris
FRANCE
SWITZ.
VICHY FRANCE
ATLANTIC OCEAN
PORTUGAL
Madrid
Lisbon
SPAIN
1944–45
Rome
Belgrade
Bucharest
YUGOSLAVIA
BULGARIA
Sofia
Istanbul
Ankara
ALBANIA
ITALY
1943
GREECE
Athens
TURKEY
IRAN
November 1942
Casablanca
MOROCCO (France)
Algiers
ALGERIA (France)
July 1943
TUNISIA (France)
Mediterranean Sea
CYPRUS
SYRIA
LEBANON
IRAQ

MAP 13.1

The Soviet forces of General Zhukov were better prepared; halted the German advance; and, in December, began slowly pushing it back, giving Moscow some breathing room. The nonaggression pact with Japan and intelligence information indicating that Siberia would not be a Japanese target had helped Zhukov. He was able to reinforce his troops with soldiers, horses, and equipment brought from Siberia and suitable for harsh-weather combat. Aided by the forests around Moscow, Soviet partisans disrupted German operations, and effective weapons such as the T-34 tank and the Katiusha rocket launcher also helped stop the German forces. For the first time, Nazi troops were halted and pushed back, suffering heavy casualties. The Battle of Moscow was an important victory and morale boost for the Soviet Union. Combined with the U.S. entry into World War II at about the same time, it gave new hope to all who had been battered by the Germans during the past two years.

In other Soviet areas, the news was not so encouraging, especially in Leningrad. Despite the evacuation of many people, including most of the city's children, about 2 million inhabitants remained in the besieged city, and there was not enough food. Inadequate planning and German air attacks had deprived the city of any emergency supplies. And the amount of food that could be brought in by the only supply route open—over Lake Ladoga, frozen by the end of November—was insufficient. People ate whatever they could to stay alive, including their pets, birds, rats, carpenter's glue, and hair oil. Yet it was not enough. In December 1941, more than 50,000 Leningraders perished, mainly from hunger.

What the courageous Leningraders endured in the winter of 1941–1942—and altogether for about 900 days—is almost unimaginable. Hunger; German shelling and bombing; and severe cold, both inside and outside of dwellings, took their toll. Although matters improved somewhat after the first winter, the siege was not lifted until late January 1944. Altogether about 1 million Leningraders lost their lives during the siege, most of them from hunger and cold.

Although unsuccessful in capturing Moscow or Leningrad, German troops continued their advance in southern areas during the spring and summer of 1942. Sevastopol and Rostov-on-the-Don fell in July (Germany had already held the latter for ten days the previous November). German troops now headed toward the rich Caucasian oilfields and the city of Stalingrad, which sat on the west bank of the Volga River. Hitler planned to capture it and sever the Volga supply line. He then hoped to send his troops north along the river line, cutting off Moscow's links with the rest of the country. Although German forces reached the north Caucasus and the suburbs of Stalingrad by late August, they could not capture the main oil fields or Stalingrad itself.

The Battle of Stalingrad was a turning point in the war. During the battle's first few months, Soviet forces were on the defensive, with German bombing and shelling destroying much of the city. Amidst charred and smoking ruins, Soviet troops defended the city, building by building, in bitter hand-to-hand combat. In late November, however, they went on the offensive. By then, the Soviets finally had more armaments than the Germans.

In early February 1943, German Field Marshal von Paulus surrendered,

FIGURE 13.1. Statue representing the Motherland at Piskarevskoe Cemetery, St. Petersburg. About a half-million Leningraders were buried here in mass graves during 1941–1943.

and more than 90,000 German soldiers, including two dozen German generals, became Soviet prisoners. Overall, the aggressors lost about 800,000 troops in the Stalingrad campaign. According to statistics uncovered in military and KGB archives in the early 1990s, Soviet losses in the Battle of Stalingrad numbered 1.1 million people. Fifty years after the battle, countless human bones still lie scattered over steppes near the city. Although some important battles remained ahead—especially "the greatest tank battle in history" at Kursk in July 1943—after Stalingrad, the Germans were in retreat.

By D-Day, June 6, 1944 (the day the Western allies landed on Normandy Beach in France), Soviet forces had almost completed recapturing Soviet territory, and in some areas (such as Rumania) they had gone beyond their pre-1939 borders. Thus, in the months that followed, Soviet troops could now move westward into east-central Europe while Western Allied forces were moving eastward toward Germany. This military-geopolitical reality would have important consequences for east-central European countries and for Allied diplomacy.

The Battle of Stalingrad
as Seen by Vasili Grossman

Vasili Grossman (1905–1964) was a Soviet writer born into a Ukrainian Jewish family. A war correspondent for *Krasnaia Zvezda* (*Red Star*), his pieces were widely read. After the war, he wrote several controversial novels dealing with Stalingrad. The last and most famous, *Life and Fate*, was seized in manuscript form by Soviet authorities in 1961. Although it paid tribute to the heroism and goodness of ordinary people, the many parallels it indicated between Nazism and communism prevented its publication until it first appeared in the West in 1980. The following two excerpts are taken from his wartime sketches as found in his *The Years of War* (1941–1945) (Moscow, 1946), pp. 216, 224–225. Ellipses are mine.

Here was a tremendous elemental clash of two states, of two worlds battling in a life and death struggle, combined with a mathematically and pedantically precise battle for a single storey of a house, or for a street crossing. . . .

The Volga was seething. The blue flame of exploding German mortar shells hissed on the waters. Death-bearing splinters were whining. Our heavy bombers droned angrily in the dark skies. Hundreds of screaming blue, red and white tracer bullets sent by the German AA batteries sped after them. The bombers spewed forth the white trajectories of machine-gun bursts on the German searchlights. On the other side of the Volga it seemed as if the whole universe shook with the mighty roar of the heavy guns and the deafening blast of our powerful artillery. On the right bank the ground trembled with the explosions. Vast conflagrations caused by bombs flared up over the factories, and the

earth, the sky, the Volga—everything was enveloped in flames. And one felt that the fate of the world was being decided here in the titanic struggle in which calmly, solemnly, amidst the smoke and the flame, our people were battling.

October 20, 1942
Stalingrad

Fighting has been raging in Stalingrad itself for seventy days—one hundred days if one includes the battles at the distant approaches to the city. . . .

And now this city lies before us in ruins, some of which are still smoking and warm, like corpses not yet grown cold; others are frigid and gruesome. At night the moon lights up the gutted buildings and the stumps of trees mown down by shells. In the cold greenish moonlight the desolate asphalted squares glisten like ice-bound lakes, and the huge dark patches of the craters made by high-explosive bombs look like holes in the ice. The shell-battered factories stand silent; no smoke curls from the chimney-stacks, and the flower beds which once ornamented the factory grounds look like burial mounds.

A dead city? No, Stalingrad lives! Even during the short lulls in the fighting, life is astir in every wrecked house, in every factory. Keen-eyed snipers are ever on the lookout for the enemy; shells, bombs and cases of cartridges travel along the communication trenches in the ruins. . . .

But most often the houses, the squares and the factories are an inferno of roaring guns and bursting shells and bombs. Life is not easy in Stalingrad just now.

November 5, 1942
Stalingrad Front

In the late summer of 1944, the Red Army entered Bucharest and Sofia, the capitals of Rumania and Bulgaria. In the fall, it occupied Belgrade, Yugoslavia. In January 1945, after earlier stalling while Germany destroyed most of Warsaw and its staunch resistance fighters, the Red Army finally captured the Polish capital. The following month, it occupied Budapest. On May 2, a few days after Hitler had committed suicide, it took Berlin. The war in Europe officially ended on May 8, 1945.

GOVERNMENT AND PEOPLES; PARTISANS AND PRODUCTION

By November 1942, the government for many former Soviet citizens was that of the German occupying forces—the territory gained by them had contained about 45 percent of the Soviet prewar population. Although millions of people fled eastward, the great majority remained.

At first, many non-Russians, such as the Ukrainian grandfather depicted in the novel *Babi Yar*, welcomed the Germans as liberators from Stalin's yoke. Some former Soviet citizens served in Axis armies or in local administrative posts. Many peasants were happy for an opportunity to pull out of Soviet collective farms. In 1941–1942, many Muslims among the Crimean and Northern Caucasian peoples welcomed the opportunities offered them by the occupying forces to expand their religious freedoms and reopen some closed mosques. In these same years, the Germans captured 5 million Soviet prisoners of war, partly because not all of them were ready to die for a Stalinist Soviet Union. Even some who had been willing to die were convinced after capture to come out against Stalin's government.

One such person was General Andrei Vlasov, a man of peasant background who considered himself a patriotic Russian. Captured by the Germans in 1942, they recruited him to sign anti-Soviet leaflets critical of Stalin and to form a liberation army, made up primarily of his fellow prisoners-of-war and other former Soviet citizens. It saw no action until 1945, however, and then on only a limited and insignificant scale.

The underutilization of Vlasov's army was symptomatic of Hitler's overall failure to make sufficient use of anti-Stalinist sentiments. Considering Nazi racial policies and ideology, this is hardly surprising. Although Hitler's greatest hostility was directed at Jews, who were numerous in the Soviet western borderlands seized in 1941, he also regarded all Slavs as subhuman. His plan was to enslave the Slavic peoples and use them for German purposes. The Nazi long-range plan was to send tens of millions of those who survived the Nazi onslaught and exterminations to Siberia. With the *lebensraum* (living space) thus gained, Hitler planned to repopulate it with Germans and other "superior" peoples.

With few exceptions, the Soviet peoples under German occupation were soon disillusioned from any hopes of better treatment. More than 4 million Soviet citizens were rounded up and sent to Germany, where they performed industrial and agricultural work in segregated and often humiliating conditions.

Although many peasants rejoiced over the German abolition of Soviet kolkhozes, they quickly discovered that the working conditions and quotas imposed by their new German masters were no improvement. The Soviet prisoners-of-war captured by the Germans were treated much worse, and most of them did not survive the war. Worst of all was the fate of Soviet Jews and others who were exterminated at sites such as Babi Yar (see Chapter 21) or at death camps such as Treblinka (near Warsaw) and Auschwitz (near Cracow).

As a result of German occupation policies, the number of Soviet partisans springing up behind German lines steadily increased. At first, it was primarily a spontaneous movement combining soldiers separated from their units with local inhabitants, including some party and government officials. The partisans were especially active in forest and wooded areas in Belorussia, Ukraine, and Great Russia, including the Novgorod and Leningrad regions. Their activities included blowing up railway tracks, trains, and bridges; killing German occupation officials and soldiers; and punishing collaborators.

The Soviet government urged the partisans on, sometimes directed their activities, and glorified the movement's heroes. One such individual was the eighteen-year-old Moscow schoolgirl Zoia Kosmodemianskaia, who was hanged by the Germans in December 1941 for attempting to blow up an ammunition dump. By 1942, the government had prepared a thick *Partisan's Guide*. It included instructions for wrecking havoc on the Germans and surviving under terrible conditions. Only after the Battle of Stalingrad, however, was the government able to provide considerable material assistance, including guns, food, and medicine, to the partisans. Because of this increased aid and because a Soviet victory now seemed more likely, partisan numbers grew rapidly in 1943 and 1944.

The German reaction to partisan warfare was ruthless. Already by late 1941, German generals were ordering the taking of hostages related to partisans or suspected of being in contact with them. The German XXX Army Corps ordered the killing of ten of these hostages for every German soldier killed by partisans. The fate of the 151 people of the village of Khatyn, about 30 miles from the Belorussian capital of Minsk, illustrated the German policy. In March 1943, the German SS accused them of aiding partisans, forced them into a barn, and torched it. All but one of the villagers, half of them children and the other half mainly women and old men, were killed, either in the barn or trying to escape from it.

Although partisans operated behind German lines, volunteer People's Militia units arose in Soviet-controlled cities. Overall, millions of men and women volunteered. With little training and inferior weapons, militia units were sometimes thrown into battle to defend cities such as Moscow and Leningrad. In such cases, their losses were often heavy, especially in 1941.

These militia units were indicative of the wartime relationship between the Soviet people and their government. The people performed heroic acts of self-sacrifice to defeat the enemy; the government encouraged and made use of such acts, although often inefficiently, causing more Soviet deaths than necessary.

Of course, Stalin had never been finicky about individual lives, and he retained great authority during the war. About six weeks before the German invasion, he had taken over the premiership from Molotov. About a week after the attack, a small State Defense Committee was established and given absolute power over all aspects of Soviet life. Of course, Stalin was its chairman. He also assumed the position of Supreme Commander of the military. Although he made many mistakes early in the war, he became more effective as the conflict continued. Although he was vested with supreme powers, he relied heavily on others, including Molotov, Malenkov, Beria, Voroshilov, Kaganovich, Nikolai Voznesensky, Anastas Mikoian, and Marshal Zhukov. He sometimes accepted their advice and recommendations, and he delegated considerable authority to them.

Although the central leadership attempted to exercise maximum power, the chaos of wartime conditions sometimes prevented this. As Moskoff and Barber and Harrison have indicated, local initiative, adaptability, and flexibility played a greater role in the eventual Soviet victory than is often recognized.

Despite wartime losses, the size of the Communist party increased after the early stages of the war. By January 1943, the number of full and candidate members was about what it had been in 1941. By January 1945, the total number reached about 5.76 million members, a gain of almost 2 million as compared with 1941. Especially noticeable was the increase in military members, who composed about half the party's total by war's end. Party leaders expanded military membership to encourage and reward military loyalty and to stress nationalism and patriotism. In keeping with these tendencies, and with less emphasis on revolutionary Marxism, the role of political commissars in military units was reduced in late 1942: They were no longer to interfere in military combat operations.

Although many Soviet citizens welcomed the new spirit and hoped for freer days after the war, the government's distrust of its citizens continued to manifest itself. Throughout the war, the NKVD kept a close watch on soldiers' behavior as well as their mail (see Chapter 21 for Alexander Solzhenitsyn's letter that cost him a decade of imprisonment and exile). Deserters and suspected traitors, including those who allowed themselves to be captured by the enemy, were dealt with ruthlessly if later apprehended by the NKVD.

The NKVD was also active overseeing the deportation of several million people who were members of nationalities suspected of German sympathies or collaboration. The first group to suffer during the war was the Volga and other ethnic Germans of the USSR. By the end of 1941, many of them had been deported to Central Asia and Siberia, where they often ended up in NKVD camps. After Soviet forces recaptured earlier German-held Soviet territory in 1943 and 1944, NKVD and army forces arrested and deported not only individuals accused of collaborating with the enemy, but also entire nationalities. Moslem and Turkish peoples of the Caucasus and Black Sea areas, such as the Balkars, Chechens, Crimean Tatars, Ingushi, Karachai, Kalmyks, and Meskhetians, all suffered such a fate.

Besides the millions of deportees sent eastward, millions of other people moved more willingly in the same direction, many of them accompanying relocated industrial enterprises. By the end of 1941, more than 1500 enterprises had been moved, primarily to the Urals, the Volga Basin, Central Asia, and western Siberia. Although this massive relocation of people and industry was accompanied with its share of problems and inefficiencies, it nevertheless was vital to a war industry threatened by the rapid German advance of 1941. Marshal Zhukov later wrote that it helped determine his country's fate as much as did the great battles of the war.

Along with relocation, the reconversion of factories was essential for the war effort. All sorts of changeovers occurred. In Leningrad, a toy factory began producing grenades; some musical-instrument shops turned out antitank mines; and distilleries, appropriately enough, made explosive Molotov cocktails—bottles filled with gasoline or alcohol. In Moscow, a bicycle factory began producing flame-throwers, and a typewriter enterprise turned to making rifles and ammunition. In various locations, tractor factories converted to producing tanks.

Factory hours were extended. In his memoirs, Andrei Sakharov wrote of his munitions plant in Ulianovsk following the national schedule of two eleven-hour shifts per day, seven days a week. Other figures indicate that in 1942 the average work week for all industrial workers, many of them now women and youths, was around 55 hours.

Despite the loss of the country's most industrialized prewar territory to German occupation, and despite food shortages and other harsh conditions, Soviet military production steadily increased. By 1944, it was roughly four times as large as in 1940 and had become greater than that of German war industries. By this time, Soviet factories were producing (per month) thousands of planes, tanks, guns, and mortars; about 200,000 rifles; and millions of bombs, shells, and mines. This advantage over the Germans was crucial to the Soviet victory.

LEND LEASE AND ALLIED DIPLOMACY

Besides its own production, the Soviet military effort was greatly assisted by Allied aid. Especially helpful was the U.S. Lend-Lease program, which furnished almost 11 billion dollars worth of assistance. Although thousands of Allied planes, tanks, and guns reached the Soviet Union, goods such as trucks, food, and boots arrived in greater quantities and proved more vital. Other supplies delivered included steel and nonferrous metals, chemicals and petroleum products, machine tools and jeeps, wire and cable, and locomotives and flat cars. These goods arrived in ports such as Murmansk or by way of Iran. Although some British and U.S aid arrived in late 1941 and 1942, most of it came after the Battle of Stalingrad and was instrumental in aiding Soviet forces to mount the successful offensive that took them all the way to Berlin.

Allied diplomacy during the war revolved around Stalin, U.S. President Franklin Roosevelt, and British Prime Minister Winston Churchill ("the Big Three"). The British leader had been an early and harsh critic of Soviet communism. Despite Roosevelt's establishment of diplomatic relations with the Soviet Union in 1933, U.S.-Soviet relations had never been warm, and the Soviet war on Finland in 1939–1940 further chilled U.S.-Soviet relations. Yet, following the German invasion—and months before the U.S. entry into the war in December 1941—both Churchill and Roosevelt declared their willingness to aid the Soviet Union. For not the first time in history, a greater enemy propelled countries toward an alliance, a "Grand Alliance" as Churchill liked to say.

Stalin's chief war aim was to defeat Germany and expel its troops from Soviet territory. To accomplish this task, he desired much more from Churchill and Roosevelt than mere material assistance. On September 3, 1941, he wrote to Churchill about the "mortal danger" of the German advance and then stated that the only way out was "to open a second front this year . . . that would divert 30–40 German divisions from the Eastern Front." Stalin, however, did not get his second front in 1941, or in 1942, or in 1943.

Instead, for three years, Soviet troops faced at least nine-tenths of Germany's front-line forces, even after Western Allied campaigns in North Africa and Italy diverted some German troops. Only in June 1944, with the Allied D-day invasion of France, did the major second front Stalin desired finally arrive.

Despite complex military reasons for this delay, not the least of which was the U.S. war against Japan, it fed the suspicions of Stalin and other Soviet leaders about their capitalist allies. More than two decades after the war's end, a retired Nikita Khrushchev still harbored these suspicions. In his memoirs, he stated that the delay's main cause was probably the Western allies desire to bleed the USSR dry so they could then come in and determine the world's fate.

Despite Stalin's overwhelming concern with stopping the German advance and eventually defeating Germany, he never forgot other priorities. Chief among them was maintaining the Soviet frontiers gained in the period of the Nazi-Soviet Pact. When British Foreign Secretary Anthony Eden came to Moscow in mid-December 1941, Stalin pressed him on this issue and continued pressing both Britain and the United States thereafter.

The Western allies were reluctant to acquiesce in frontiers that meant Poland's loss of territory and the Baltic republics' loss of independence. Thus, they suggested postponing any decisions on the matter. Despite the rhetoric of the Atlantic Charter of 1941—in which Roosevelt and Churchill had recognized "the right of all peoples to choose the form of government under which they will live"—both Western leaders were willing to make exceptions to the principle. (Churchill, in fact, insisted that it did not apply to the British colonial subjects.) Rather, it was more practical considerations that delayed Western acceptance of Stalin's proposed frontiers. For example, Churchill had to deal with the Polish government in exile ("the London Poles"), with whom Stalin broke relations in 1943 after denying Soviet responsibility for the 1940 Katyn massacre of Polish officers. Roosevelt, as he privately told Stalin at the first summit of the Big Three at Tehran (November–December, 1943), could not ignore Polish-American sentiments with a presidential election approaching in 1944.

Yet, reluctant or not, the two Western leaders finally agreed to Stalin's western border demands. Much has been made of the appeasement of Roo-

FIGURE 13.2. Churchill, Roosevelt, and Stalin at the Yalta Conference, 1945. *(AP/Wide World.)*

sevelt and Churchill to Stalin at Tehran and especially at a second summit at Yalta (February 1945), and not just on the question of borders. Although the diplomacy of the two Western leaders was certainly flawed, some of the constraints placed upon them must also be acknowledged. First, they feared alienating Stalin and, on occasion, the possibility of a separate Soviet-German peace. Second, by the time D-Day was launched in June 1944, Soviet troops had already begun penetrating beyond their pre-1939 borders; given the lateness of D-Day and its Normandy-coast location, there was little the Western allies could do to prevent Soviet troops from occupying much of east-central Europe. Third, Roosevelt and Churchill desired Soviet cooperation in the postwar period.

For his part, Stalin exploited U.S.-British differences. By such means as abolishing the Comintern in 1943, he also encouraged the belief that the Soviet Union had become less concerned with overthrowing or weakening capitalist governments abroad.

Because of these factors and others, including Western illusions about Stalin and the Soviet Union, Stalin gained acceptance of much of what he wanted at Tehran and Yalta. At the Potsdam Conference of July–August 1945, Churchill was replaced after a week by a new British prime minister, Clement Attlee, and President Harry Truman took the place of Roosevelt, who had died in April. Despite Truman's more hard-line approach,[1] the new U.S. president was unable to prevent Stalin from consolidating his gains.

At Tehran, Yalta, and Potsdam, four major topics received most attention: Poland, Germany, Japan, and the United Nations. In compensation for allowing the USSR to keep interwar Polish territory seized in 1939 (actually these were overwhelmingly Ukrainian, Belorussian, and Lithuanian lands), Poland received a lesser amount of German territory. The new government of Poland was to be Communist dominated, although Stalin agreed to allow the London Poles some representation and to permit future free Polish elections. Regarding Germany, the Soviet right to the Königsberg (later Kaliningrad) region of East Prussia was recognized, and the rest of Germany was divided into Soviet, U.S., British, and French occupation zones. All four powers were to receive reparations and jointly administer Berlin.

At Yalta, Stalin agreed to enter the war against Japan within three months of Germany's surrender. In exchange, the USSR was to gain the Kurile Islands, Southern Sakhalin, and additional Asiatic concessions, but Truman later insisted that Russia was to play no part in the postwar occupation of Japan. Stalin also acceded to most of Roosevelt's desires regarding the formation of a United Nations (UN), and the Soviet leader scaled down his original demand for sixteen UN seats. He had originally insisted on one seat for each of the Soviet republics, whose number had increased in 1940 when republic status had been conferred upon Estonia, Latvia, Lithuania, Moldavia, and the Karelo-Finnish lands. The USSR still obtained three seats, the extra two being for Belorussia and Ukraine.

Besides Poland, the fate of other Eastern European peoples was determined more by the presence of the Red Army than by diplomacy. But at a conference with Stalin in Moscow in October 1944, Churchill proposed spheres of influence in Eastern Europe that recognized Soviet predominance in Rumania and Bulgaria. At Yalta, U.S. officials pressed for and obtained agreement on a Declaration on Liberated Europe. It espoused democratic principles in keeping with the Atlantic Charter. It had little practical effect, however, except to provide later ammunition for Western charges that Stalin failed to live up to it.

Although Allied diplomacy maintained enough unity to win a difficult war and to establish the United Nations, it failed not only to deal adequately with east-central Europe, but also with the nuclear weapons' question. At Potsdam, Truman merely mentioned to Stalin that the U.S. possessed a new weapon of great destructive power.

Part of the reason for the first failure was the belief that some questions, especially regarding Germany, could be dealt with in the future, for example, at a peace conference. Once the wartime enemies were defeated, however, there was little glue left to hold the Allies together. The ideological and geopolitical differences that had been toned down during the war once again resounded.

---

[1] On June 24, 1941, Truman (then a senator) had been quoted in the *New York Times*, p. 7, as saying: "If we see that Germany is winning we ought to help Russia and if Russia is winning we ought to help Germany and that way let them [each] kill as many as possible."

THE END OF WORLD WAR II AND
SOVIET GAINS AND LOSSES

On August 8, 1945, the USSR declared war on Japan and attacked Japanese troops in Manchuria soon after midnight, August 9, local time. It thus fulfilled its commitment to combat Japan within three months of the war's end in Europe. Stalin was anxious to keep his word so as to give his allies no excuse to deny Russia all of its promised postwar gains. Earlier the U.S. government had thought that Soviet participation against Japan would save numerous U.S. lives. But the dropping of atomic bombs on Hiroshima (August 6) and Nagasaki (August 9) convinced the Japanese to accept Allied surrender terms, which they did on August 14. On September 2, 1945, World War II ended with the signing of peace terms aboard the *U.S.S. Missouri*.

For its brief Asiatic effort, the Soviet Union was rewarded, as promised, with Southern Sakhalin, the Kurile Islands, and other concessions. Altogether, Soviet territorial gains, east and west, between 1939 and 1945 amounted to lands larger than France and containing (in 1945) about 24 million people. Besides part of East Prussia and gains made during the 1939–1941 period, another annexed western land was the Carpatho-Ukrainian territory, which had been part of Czechoslovakia before the war. In addition, with its army occupying most of east-central Europe, the Soviet Union was now in a solid position to dominate the region.

For Stalin and the political and military elite, the successful conclusion of the war meant increased prestige at home and abroad. For decades afterward, the Communist party and Soviet government repeatedly emphasized the Soviet leadership's vital role in overcoming the Nazis.

The costs of Soviet victory had been mind-boggling—at least 27 million Soviet war dead and almost as many left homeless. In the city of Leningrad alone, war deaths were more than twice the entire U.S. wartime losses. Thousands of bridges, boats, and locomotives; tens of thousands of towns, villages, plants, schools, libraries, and railway tracks; and millions of livestock were destroyed. It is little wonder that the war left an indelible mark on the Soviet citizens who survived this monstrous conflict.

SUGGESTED SOURCES

ANDREYEV, CATHERINE. *Vlasov and the Russian Liberation Movement: Soviet Reality and Émigré Theories.* Cambridge, England, 1987.

BARBER, JOHN, and MARK HARRISON. *The Soviet Home Front, 1941–1945: A Social and Economic History of the USSR in World War II.* London, 1991.

BARROS, JAMES, and RICHARD GREGOR. *Double Deception: Stalin, Hitler, and the Invasion of Russia.* DeKalb, Ill, 1995.

BIALER, SEWERYN. *Stalin and His Generals: Soviet Military Memoirs of World War II.* Boulder, 1984.

CLARK, ALAN. *Barbarossa: The Russian-German Conflict, 1941–1945.* New York, 1965.

CLEMENS, DIANE SHAVER. *Yalta.* New York, 1970.

CONQUEST, ROBERT. *The Nation Killers: The Soviet Deportation of Nationalities.* New York, 1970.

COOPER, MATTHEW. *The Nazi War against Soviet Partisans, 1941–1944.* New York, 1979.

CRAIG, WILLIAM. *Enemy at the Gates: The Battle for Stalingrad.* New York, 1973.

DALLIN, ALEXANDER. *German Rule in Russia, 1941–1945: A Study of Occupation Policies.* London, 1981.

DOUGLAS, ROY. *From War to Cold War, 1942–1948.* London, 1981.

EDMONDS, ROBIN. *The Big Three: Churchill, Roosevelt, and Stalin in Peace and War.* New York, 1991.

ERICKSON, JOHN. *The Road to Stalingrad: Stalin's War with Germany.* London, 1975.

————. *The Road to Berlin: Continuing the History of Stalin's War with Germany.* Boulder, 1983.

————, and DAVID DILKS, eds. *Barbarossa: The Axis and the Allies.* Edinburgh, 1994.

FEIS, HERBERT. *Churchill, Roosevelt, Stalin: The War They Waged and the Peace They Sought.* Princeton, 1967.

FUGATE, BRYAN I. *Operation Barbarossa: Strategy and Tactics on the Eastern Front, 1941.* Novato, Calif., 1984.

GLANTZ, DAVID M., and JONATHAN M. HOUSE. *When Titans Clashed: How the Red Army Stopped Hitler.* Lawrence, Kan., 1995.

GROSSMAN, VASILY. *Life and Fate: A Novel.* New York, 1986.

KOCHINA, ELENA. *Blockade Diary.* Ann Arbor, 1990.

KUZNETSOV, ANATOLI. *Babi Yar.* New York, 1970. A novel.

LANE, ANNE, and HOWARD TEMPERLEY, eds. *The Rise and Fall of the Grand Alliance, 1941–1945.* New York, 1995.

LINZ, SUSAN J., ed. *The Impact of World War II on the Soviet Union.* Totowa, N.J., 1985.

LYONS, GRAHAM. *The Russian Version of the Second World War: The History of the War as Taught to Soviet Schoolchildren.* Hamden, Conn., 1976.

MASTNY, VOJTECH. *Russia's Road to the Cold War: Diplomacy, Warfare, and the Politics of Communism, 1941–1945.* New York, 1979.

MINER, STEVEN MERRITT. *Between Churchill and Stalin: The Soviet Union, Great Britain, and the Origins of the Grand Alliance.* Chapel Hill, 1988.

MOSKOFF, WILLIAM. *The Bread of Affliction: The Food Supply in the USSR during World War II.* Cambridge, England, 1990.

MULLIGAN, TIMOTHY PATRICK. *The Politics of Illusion and Empire: German Occupation Policy in the Soviet Union, 1942–1943.* New York, 1988.

NEKRICH, A. M. *"June 22, 1941": Soviet Historians and the German Invasion.* Columbia, S. C. 1968.

PAUL, ALLEN. *Katyn: The Untold Story of Stalin's Polish Massacre.* New York, 1991.

PAVLOV, D. V. *Leningrad 1941: The Blockade.* Chicago, 1965.

PERLMUTTER, AMOS. *FDR and Stalin: A Not So Grand Alliance.* Columbia, Mo., 1993.

PLIVIER, THEODOR. *Moscow.* Garden City, N.Y., 1954. A novel.

PORTER, CATHY, and MARK JONES. *Moscow in World War II.* London, 1987.

RAACK, R. C. *Stalin's Drive to the West, 1938–1945: The Origins of the Cold War.* Stanford, 1995.

RADZINSKY, EDVARD. *Stalin.* New York, 1996. Chs. 22–24.

REYNOLDS, DAVID, WARREN F. KIMBALL, and A. O. CHUBARIAN, eds. *Allies at War: The Soviet, American, and British Experience, 1939–1945.* New York, 1994.

SAKHAROV, ANDREI. *Memoirs.* N.Y., 1990.

SALISBURY, HARRISON E. *The 900 Days: the Siege of Leningrad.* New York, 1969.

SCHMIDT, PAUL K. *Hitler Moves East, 1941–1943.* Boston, 1965.

————. *Scorched Earth: The Russian-German War, 1943–1944.* Boston, 1970.

SEATON, ALBERT. *Stalin as Warlord.* London, 1976.

————. *The Russo-German War, 1941–45.* London, 1971.

SIMONOV, KONSTANTIN. *Days and Nights.* New York, 1945. A novel dealing with the Battle of Stalingrad.

SNELL, JOHN L. *Illusion and Necessity: the Diplomacy of Global War, 1939–1945.* Boston, 1963.

Stalin's Correspondence with Churchill, Attlee, Roosevelt, and Truman: 1941–45. 2 vols. in 1. New York, 1958.

TUMARKIN, NINA. *The Living and the Dead: The Rise and Fall of the Cult of World War II in Russia.* New York, 1994.

VAN TUYLL, HUBERT P. *Feeding the Bear: American Aid to the Soviet Union, 1941–1945.* New York, 1989.

VITUKHIN, IGOR, ed. *Soviet Generals Recall World War II.* New York, 1981.

WERTH, ALEXANDER. *Russia at War, 1941–1945.* New York, 1984.

ZHUKHOV, GEORGII. *The Memoirs of Marshal Zhukov.* New York, 1971.

CHAPTER 14

Postwar and Cold War, 1945–1953

Both inside and outside the Soviet Union, many people believed that postwar life under Stalin would be freer and better than in the purge-filled 1930s. The Soviet wartime alliance with Great Britain and the United States, accompanied with a deemphasis on Communist ideology, contributed to such a belief.

The postwar Soviet reality turned out more bleak than most people had foreseen. The cost of restoring the war-ravaged country was immense. Just as importantly, the victory over Germany strengthened the already strong cult of Stalin, and he soon returned to many of his practices of the 1930s: purges, massive deportations to forced-labor camps, and new five-year plans emphasizing heavy industry and defense rather than consumer goods. He justified his economic priorities partly by pointing to the dangers threatening the Soviet Union from its former wartime allies, the United States and Great Britain.

Even before World War II had ended, tensions between the USSR and its Western allies were increasing. Differing ideologies, geopolitical interests, and mutual suspicions now helped generate a Cold War that continued long after Stalin's death in 1953.

The attitude of the Soviet peoples to postwar developments varied considerably. Among newly annexed Western Ukrainians, Estonians, Latvians, and Lithuanians, guerrilla movements battled against Soviet control. But a Harvard research project based mainly on interviews in the early 1950s of Soviet refugees revealed more positive attitudes as well, especially toward the Soviet socialist economic system. The Soviet interviewees also generally took great pride in the Soviet war effort, its postwar reconstruction, and its achievement of status as a world power. Although often critical of Soviet "police terror," the refugees displayed little appreciation or interest in constitutional guarantees and were unable to envision a meaningful alternate system of rule for their former country. They simply believed that what the Soviet Union required was "good rulers," who cared about the people and their economic well-being—an attitude similar to the earlier belief that all Russia needed was a good tsar.

The Harvard project also found that "most Soviet citizens seem to have accepted the main outlines of the official image of foreign affairs disseminated by the official media." They saw the U.S. government dominated by powerful groups apparently "committed to waging a war of destruction against the Soviet Union." In such an atmosphere, most Soviet citizens seemed inclined to leave world politics in the hands of Soviet leaders, "who understand these things, and know best."[1]

Such views about domestic and foreign affairs, which are generally corroborated by other evidence, offer a partial explanation for the staying power of Soviet rule. So too does the material Vera Dunham presented in her book *In Stalin's Time*, in which she analyzed postwar popular fiction and indicated how it reflected what she called "the Big Deal." This "deal," never made explicit, was between the regime and what Dunham called the Soviet "middle class," which included, among others, administrators, engineers, and professionals. The "deal" recognized as legitimate the middle class's desires for career advancement, better consumer goods and housing, and more leisure. These were not Marxist revolutionary values, and this Stalinist concession could be seen as an extension of the "great retreat" of the 1930s (see Chapter 11) and as a means to solidify middle-class backing for the regime.

STALIN'S POSTWAR DOMESTIC POLICIES

During Stalin's final years of rule (1945–1953), he concentrated on primarily three challenges: economic reconstruction, political loyalty to the Soviet government, and strengthening his own power.

The daunting task of economic reconstruction was approached in a manner similar to the command-economy methods of previous five-year plans. This meant a continuing stress on heavy industry and a relative neglect of light industry and agriculture. And once again, economic results mirrored the priorities.

By the end of the Fourth Five-Year Plan—begun in 1946 and declared overfulfilled months ahead of time in 1950—Soviet figures indicated that the annual production of cement, coal, electricity, oil, pig iron, steel, and tractors had all surpassed the prewar figures of 1940. The chemical and machine tool industries also displayed impressive growth, and overall industrial production was considerably greater than prewar levels.

Once again, this growth came because of the exhausting work of Soviet laborers, who continued to work longer hours than they had in the immediate prewar period. Additionally, in December 1947, Soviet citizens were forced to turn in their old rubles for new ones, but received only one for every ten exchanged. Unlike most peasants, those fortunate enough to have small deposits in bank savings accounts did receive a one-to-one exchange on deposits of less than 3,000 rubles.

[1]Alex Inkeles and Raymond A. Bauer, *The Soviet Citizen: Daily Life in a Totalitarian Society* (New York, 1968), pp. 381–382.

Although workers' living standards gradually improved after 1947, they still had not surpassed 1928 levels by the time of Stalin's death in 1953. Despite the massive rebuilding and construction of housing, living space remained crowded, and many new buildings were poorly constructed. Consumer goods remained scarce and of poor quality—in 1949, however, Stalin did enhance his popularity by reducing the prices of some basic commodities such as bread, meat, and vodka.

Agriculture and peasants suffered more than industry and urban workers. Largely because of government policies, per capita agricultural production by 1953 was no better than in 1940. Although during the war peasants had managed to treat some kolkhoz land as their own, the government now ended that practice. It also consolidated the kolkhozes, reducing their number and forcing peasants into larger units.

Besides hurting many peasants by the forced exchange of currency, government policies insured low peasant incomes. Nove has estimated that in 1948–1950 it would have required more than a year's pay for the average kolkhoz peasant to buy a suit and—more significant to many peasants—about twenty days to buy a bottle of vodka. Only additional income earned from their private plots kept matters from being worse. Although these plots constituted less than 2 percent of the land, they accounted for well over two-thirds of the country's meat, potatoes, and dairy products and almost half its vegetables.

Soviet postwar economic growth was aided by Axis reparations worth billions of dollars. During and after the war, plants and equipment were seized from such areas as eastern Germany, Rumania, and Manchuria and brought back to the USSR. New satellite states in east-central Europe that had not been on the Axis side were also forced to contribute to Soviet economic recovery by a variety of means, including one-sided trade agreements. UN, British, and Swedish aid were less significant but still helpful, as was the forced labor of foreign prisoners-of-war, some of whom were not released until after Stalin's death. Finally, Soviet convict and conscript laborers contributed to the country's economic reconstruction.

The prison camp population expanded after the war, mainly owing to Stalin's desire to insure loyalty to his regime. He was aware of the Decembrists and their revolt of 1825. Many of them had been officers exposed to foreign influences after crossing Russian borders to pursue Napoleon's forces. During World War II, Soviet soldiers and others had likewise been exposed to many foreign influences—by German occupation forces, as occupiers or prisoners abroad, and by contacts with Western allies. (In Alexander Solzhenitsyn's realistic novel *One Day in the Life of Ivan Denisovich*, naval Captain Buinovsky receives a 25-year sentence merely because a British admiral he had served with sends him a gift as a token of gratitude.)

Millions of prisoners-of-war, civilians sent to Germany to work, and refugees from Soviet lands were liberated by Western forces, and many of them did not wish to return to the Soviet Union. Most of them were forced to, however, because Western leaders desired cooperative relations with Stalin and the return of Western prisoners-of-war liberated by Soviet troops.

There were also peoples whose loyalty was suspect because they had not been part of the Soviet Union before 1939. Because of this and because of postwar guerrilla resistance among these peoples, lasting into the early 1950s, many West Ukrainians, Estonians, Latvians, Lithuanians, and others were deported, the men usually ending up in forced-labor camps.

Those not deported faced a new campaign emphasizing the superiority of the Russian people. In May 1945, Stalin toasted the Russian people as "the most outstanding of all the nations that constitute the Soviet Union" and stated that they had earned this recognition because of their wartime efforts. Russians were sent to reside and assume important positions in the new western borderlands, and "bourgeois nationalist" tendencies among the non-Russian nationalities were squelched.

In the postwar years, Stalin displayed an increasing hostility and suspiciousness toward Soviet Jews, especially after the establishment of Israel in 1948. The warm welcome that some Soviet Jews gave to the new Israeli ambassador to the USSR, Golda Meir, contributed to a stepped-up antisemitic campaign. Jewish schools were closed, and many leading Jews were purged and some executed. Among those arrested was Polina Molotov, wife of one of Stalin's most faithful and long-time political associates. In 1952, some two dozen Jewish writers were tried and shot; in 1953, a majority of the nine doctors accused of a Doctors' Plot against the Soviet leadership were Jewish. It is likely that if Stalin had not died soon thereafter many Jews would have been deported to remote Soviet areas.

The purging of Jews went along with a campaign against "rootless cosmopolitanism" and was in keeping with a major ideological offensive started earlier against foreign influences. Begun in August 1946 and spearheaded by former Leningrad party boss Andrei Zhdanov, this attack berated writers, artists, composers, and others for kowtowing to Western ideas and culture (see Chapter 16 for some specific examples). Such behavior, claimed Zhdanov, was not "becoming" to those who were part of a Soviet culture vastly superior to the emaciated and depraved Western "bourgeois culture." The Zhdanov attack was also marked by an emphasis on Soviet superiority in other realms and extravagant claims for Soviet "firsts" in all sorts of past inventions and discoveries. Although Zhdanov died in August 1948, the cultural narrowness he displayed during the *Zhdanovshchina* (the time of Zhdanov) continued after him.

In his final years, Stalin took various steps to weaken anyone who might conceivably threaten his powers. Top military leaders were an early target, including Marshal Zhukov, who was relegated to a minor command post, and some leading admirals, who were imprisoned.

Even more severe was the fate of some prominent Leningrad officials and others who had been close to Zhdanov. In 1949, these men, including Politburo member N. A. Voznesensky, were arrested and shot the following year. One factor in their fall was that Zhdanov and his followers were considered too friendly toward Yugoslavia's Communist party, which split with Moscow shortly before Zhdanov's death in 1948.

Two Politburo members who had been eclipsed by Zhdanov after the war benefited from this "Leningrad Case," as Georgi Malenkov and former NKVD

FIGURE 14.1. Soviet leaders at the 1946 funeral of M. Kalinin. From left to right in the front are Malenkov, Beria, Molotov, and Stalin.
(*Sovfoto.*)

head Beria once again became more prominent. But Stalin was careful not to allow any subordinate too much power and deliberately played one off against another. In his memoirs, Khrushchev left behind a vivid picture of the suspicious, coarse Stalin of these final years and the indignities he inflicted upon his circle of political subordinates. He forced them, for example, to get drunk and dance, made them the butt of practical jokes, and arrested some of their relatives (such as Molotov's wife).

At the Nineteenth Party Congress (October 1952), the first such congress since 1939, Stalin introduced a number of changes that boded ill for some old party leaders. The Orgburo was ended, and, more ominously, the eleven-member Politburo was abolished, both being replaced by a larger Presidium with a smaller, informal Bureau within it. Molotov and Mikoian were left off the Bureau and seemed destined for a worsening fate.

Malenkov, Beria, and Khrushchev seemed more secure and remained in Stalin's inner circle, but under Stalin there was no real security, and there were signs that Beria might be the next to lose favor. On the night of February 28–March 1, 1953, these three subordinates plus Nikolai Bulganin, a more recent addition to the inner circle, dined and drank with Stalin at his Kuntsevo dacha, about five miles from the Kremlin. After heavy and late drinking, Stalin retired to his quarters.

The next day, March 1, his body was discovered on the floor. A stroke apparently had felled him, but he was still alive. (Radzinsky thinks it more likely Stalin fell victim to some sort of a conspiracy masterminded by Beria). Beria and Malenkov were eventually reached, but they seemed in no hurry to summon doctors, who did not arrive until the morning of March 2, about six hours after Beria and Malenkov had arrived on the scene. For three more days, Stalin lingered on and finally died an agonizing death on March 5, 1953.

THE EARLY COLD WAR

In 1947, the term *Cold War* became popular to describe the international tensions between the Soviet Union and the major Western nations, tensions that continued for another four decades.

During these decades, political scientists and historians wrote many thousands of pages about the early Cold War—the years of Stalin's postwar rule and Harry Truman's postwar U.S. presidency. At first, most Western scholars blamed Stalin and "Soviet expansionism" for the conflict. During the 1960s, an increasing number of revisionist scholars insisted that the United States deserved much of the blame for the start of the Cold War. Still later, during Mikhail Gorbachev's years in power, new materials about Stalin began emerging, the Cold War ended, and the Soviet Union disintegrated, all of which stimulated further rethinking about early Cold War tensions.

What is most important, however, is to understand that the Cold War emerged from the different ideologies and geopolitical concerns of the Soviet and Western leaders—and their different experiences in World War II. Once the war ended, which had temporarily made allies of these otherwise incompatible leaders, there was little to hold the wartime alliance together.

In his retirement years Molotov noted that "my task as minister of foreign affairs was to expand the borders of our Fatherland. And it seems that Stalin and I coped with this task quite well."[2] At a minimum, Stalin desired to make the best of Soviet World War II gains to enhance Soviet security and help rebuild the Soviet economy. The presence of Soviet troops in east-central European countries and northern Iran gave the USSR considerable leverage. Yet Stalin had to be cautious about how he used his advantages because it made little sense to alienate the Western powers needlessly. Their good will might enable the Soviet Union to settle favorably still unresolved diplomatic issues such as the final fate of Germany.

But Stalin's view of the West and his postwar domestic policies hindered chances for continuing cooperation with his former allies. His extremely suspicious nature as well as his Marxist ideology affected his perception of Western policies. Although historians dealing with Stalin's many purges have generally recognized his "persecution mania" (even the faithful Molotov mentioned it in

---

[2]*Molotov Remembers: Inside Kremlin Politics: Conversations with Felix Chuev*, ed. Albert Resis (Chicago, 1993), p. 8.

his memoirs), scholars have placed relatively little emphasis on how this "mania" and extreme mistrust affected his postwar foreign policy.

In February 1946, in a speech to the Supreme Soviet, Stalin attributed World War II to developments growing out of "monopoly capitalism." He declared that Soviet victory in the war had been due to the correctness of the party's earlier policies—for example, rapid industrialization, collectivization, and the successful campaign against internal enemies (e.g., Rightists) who tried to divert the Soviet economy to the "capitalist path of development." The war, he stated, had proven the superiority of the Soviet system over "any non-Soviet social order." To prepare for any future military threats, he called for sharp increases in the production of such vital materials as pig iron, steel, coal, and oil. He suggested that the Soviet Union would soon make up for its lack of atomic weapons by overtaking and surpassing other countries in scientific achievements.

This speech, accompanied later that year by Zhdanov's attacks on Western influences, made it clear that Stalin intended to proceed as he had in the prewar years. Stalin's view of the West not only helped to determine his foreign policy, but also served his domestic purposes. To spur the Soviet people to herculean industrial efforts and new sacrifices, while increasing government controls over them, a crisis atmosphere was needed. Stalin and the party claimed credit for their role in saving the country from Nazism; the Cold War now provided a justification for the people's continuing subordination to a government that would protect them from the new international dangers of an atomic age.

The United States was at this point the only country possessing the atomic bomb and was uncontested in terms of economic strength. What it desired was a peaceful postwar world dominated by market economies open to U.S. trade and capital. Stalin realized that the Soviet economy was in no position to compete with the U.S. economy and that he could not open up the Soviet Union to Western capital and economic influence without threatening his own grip on power. What his government needed was an economic sphere of its own.

Despite differences and difficulties at the Potsdam Conference in July and August 1945, many U.S. government officials and citizens were still hopeful about Soviet postwar intentions before Stalin's speech of February 1946. That speech and several other events in February and March 1946 led to a marked reevaluation of the Soviet Union. The other events included the announcement of a new Communist government in North Korea, news of the uncovering of a Communist spy network in Canada, George Kennan's "Long Telegram" (which the Soviet expert and junior diplomat sent from the U.S. Embassy in Moscow), and Winston Churchill's famous "Iron Curtain" speech in Fulton, Missouri.

In Kennan's telegram to the U.S. State Department, he indicated that the Soviet government looked upon the capitalist powers as foes and would try to weaken them but without taking "unnecessary risks." He believed that aggressive Soviet policies should be met with strong diplomatic resistance—indicating a willingness to use force if necessary—and that such a firm stand would usually lead to a Soviet diplomatic retreat. A year later in his famous article signed "X" (*Foreign Affairs*, July 1947), he wrote of the necessity of "a long-term, patient but firm and vigilant containment of Russian expansive tendencies." Despite certain ambiguous phrases in both of these pieces, Kennan's "containment" ideas had considerable influence on U.S. foreign policy for decades to come.

Although Kennan's telegram had an immediate impact on U.S. policymakers, it was Churchill's "Iron Curtain" speech that alarmed Kremlin leaders. Although Churchill was no longer British prime minister, Truman's attendance at his speech suggested the president's endorsement of its main ideas. Churchill spoke of the iron curtain that now separated eastern from western Europe. He spoke of Soviet expansionism and, like Kennan, indicated that the Soviet government respected force. He called upon the English-speaking peoples to unite against the Soviet danger in an effort to remove "every temptation to ambition and adventure."

According to Khrushchev, Churchill's speech ruined Soviet relations with its former Western allies and marked the start of the Cold War. Khrushchev also stated that it was mainly this speech that led Stalin to exaggerate the Western powers' strength and their intention to "unleash war" on the Soviet Union. A week after Churchill's speech, Stalin stated that Churchill was calling for war against the Soviet Union and that any Western armed intervention in Eastern Europe would be "thrashed," as was the Allied intervention of 1918–1919.

Although Churchill's speech was no doubt important, Khrushchev and other Soviet commentators on it tended to overestimate its significance. The basic tensions, growing out of different views of the world, were already there and the Cold War was already emerging, with or without Churchill's speech.

A major source of tensions was Germany and Eastern Europe—as the Cold War developed, "Eastern Europe" became the common term for referring to the area west of the Soviet Union and east of the Western German zones, an area that for four decades would be dominated by Communist parties.

The main differences over Germany revolved around its future status (unified or divided, socialist or capitalist) and Soviet efforts to extract maximum reparations from it—the Soviet government also obtained significant reparations from Hungary and Rumania. In Poland, Czechoslovakia, Hungary, Rumania, Bulgaria, Yugoslavia, and Albania, Communist parties (with varying names), usually with the backing of Soviet occupation forces, gradually took over government controls. At the time of Churchill's speech, this process had not been completed, but the Western powers feared it soon would be. A Czech Communist takeover in February 1948 finalized the process.

Another source of tension was the U.S. intention to make use of its possession of the atomic bomb to strengthen its negotiating pressure on the USSR and, conversely, Stalin's determination to resist such an effort.

Although there is little doubt that some Soviet actions abroad from 1946 to 1953 were a reaction to earlier Western initiatives, Western revisionist historians often have gone too far in pointing to such initiatives as causes for Soviet policies. The Marshall Plan, for example, in which Czechoslovakia expressed an interest, might have influenced the timing of the Communist takeover in Czechoslovakia, but it is unlikely that Stalin would have long tolerated anything less in such a vital area. It bordered on the Soviet Union (specifically its rebellious Western Ukrainian region) as well as the eastern and western zones of Germany, Poland, Hungary, and Austria (which, like Germany, was under four-power occupation) (see Map 14.1).

Diplomatic differences also arose in 1945–1946 over Iran and Turkey. Soviet wartime forces were slow to withdraw from northern Iran and did so (in the spring of 1946) only after Western protests over their continued presence. Even then, the withdrawal might not have occurred if Iranian negotiators had not signed an agreement favorable to Soviet interests in northern Iran—after the withdrawal, however, the Iranian parliament rejected the agreement.

From Turkey, the Soviet government attempted to gain a few areas lost in previous wars as well as bases in the Black Sea Straits. In August 1946, tensions escalated after the Kremlin sent a note to Turkey demanding that the Soviet Union, along with Turkey, be jointly responsible for defending the Turkish Straits. Viewing the proposal as a sign of Soviet determination to dominate Turkey, the United States rejected such a Soviet role and dispatched part of the U.S. fleet to the eastern Mediterranean.

Truman Doctrine, Marshall Plan, and the Berlin Blockade

In February 1947, the British informed Washington that it could no longer afford military and economic aid to Turkey and Greece. The latter was then in the midst of a civil war, with an authoritarian Greek government struggling against Communist-dominated guerrillas. Contrary to Washington beliefs, however, the chief outside support of these guerrillas originated in Yugoslavia, not the USSR.

In March 1947, President Truman asked the U.S. Congress for economic aid and authorization to send civilian and military personnel to Greece and Turkey. He indicated that this was to be part of an overall policy (soon dubbed the Truman Doctrine) based upon the premise that "it must be the policy of the United States to support free peoples who are resisting attempted subjugation by armed minorities or by outside pressures."

In mid-1947, U.S. Secretary of State George Marshall proposed another idea, the European Recovery Plan (or Marshall Plan) for blunting the perceived threat of expanding communism. Observing the poor economic conditions of Europe and believing that communism might grow stronger in such an environment (Communist parties were already strong in France and Italy), Marshall recommended U.S. aid to help fund European financial reconstruction. He also believed that the plan would eventually expand U.S. market opportunities abroad.

Although all European countries were invited to participate, the Soviet Union, after some apparent indecision, declined involvement. It also pressured Czechoslovakia and other Eastern European countries to decline participation. Why Stalin took this stance was indicated in September 1947 by Andrei Zhdanov at the founding congress of a new Communist organization, the Cominform (Communist Information Bureau). The gathering occurred in Poland, and

MAP 14.1

The Russian Response
to the Marshall Plan

In his speech to Cominform delegates, Zhdanov spoke of the postwar emergence of two camps: the "imperialist and antidemocratic camp" (composed of the former Western allies) and the "anti-imperialist and democratic camp" (led by the Soviet Union). He also spoke more specifically about U.S. intentions and its motivations for the Truman Doctrine and Marshall Plan. Although the speech was partly propaganda, it also apparently reflected the thinking of Stalin and Zhdanov at the time. The source for the following excerpt is A. Zhdanov, *The International Situation* (Moscow, 1947), pp. 13, 32, 35–36. Ellipses are mine.

In the new post-war conditions the Wall Street bosses adopted a new policy. . . . to establish the world supremacy of American imperialism. . . .

At this present juncture the expansionist ambitions of the United States find concrete expression in the "Truman doctrine" and "Marshall plan." Although they differ in form of presentation, both are an expression of a single policy, they are both an embodiment of the American design to enslave Europe. . . .

Acting on instructions from Washington, the British and French governments invited the Soviet Union to take part in a discussion of the Marshall proposals. This step was taken in order to mask the hostile nature of the proposals with respect to the U.S.S.R. The calculation was that, since it was well known beforehand that the U.S.S.R. would refuse American assistance on the terms proposed by Marshall, it might be possible to shift the responsibility on it for "declining to assist the economic restoration of Europe," and thus incite against the U.S.S.R. the European countries that are in need of real assistance. If, on the other hand, the Soviet Union should consent to take part in the talks, it would be easier to lure the countries of East and Southeast Europe into the trap of the "economic restoration of Europe with American assistance." Whereas the Truman plan was designed to terrorize and intimidate these countries, the "Marshall plan" was designed to test their economic staunchness, to lure them into a trap and then shackle them in the fetters of dollar "assistance."

In that case the "Marshall plan" would facilitate one of the most important objectives of the general American program, namely, to restore the power of imperialism in the new democracies and to compel them to renounce close economic and political cooperation with the Soviet Union.

Cominform members included the Communist parties of the USSR, the Eastern European nations (excluding Albania), France, and Italy.

The Cominform itself accomplished little except expelling from its ranks (in June 1948) the Communist party of Yugoslavia, led by Joseph Tito. He had come to power on his own, had his own ideas of how to construct a Yugoslavian Communist state, and refused to be Stalin's puppet. Among other Tito actions angering Stalin was his continuing support of Communist guerrillas in Greece. For his own reasons, Stalin wanted an end to the civil war there. Angered with Tito and his "nationalist" tendencies, Stalin attempted to prevent

"Titoism" in other countries more firmly under Soviet control: In the next several years, many Eastern European Communists suspected of "Titoism" were purged. Furthermore, the satellite states were ordered to bring their political, economic, and social institutions more in line with the Soviet model.

Although trade terms with its European satellites were already determined by the Soviet Union, it announced in January 1949 that it and five other Soviet bloc states were forming a Council for Mutual Economic Assistance (CMEA or COMECON). Albania joined the following month and East Germany in 1950. Under Stalin, however, COMECON's role was not significant. It seems to have been mainly a belated propaganda response to the Marshall Plan, which by then was already operating.

Meanwhile, the Soviet government had become alarmed at increasing steps taken by its former Western allies to reunite Germany and build up its economy. Unable to arrive at a four-power agreement, the United States and Britain had agreed in late 1946 to create a "bizone" out of their separate zones. In the spring of 1948, the two Western powers, along with France, announced their intention of creating a united West German government out of the western occupation zones, and in mid-June they announced a currency reform in the western zones.

Stalin's response was the Berlin blockade, which prevented the Western powers from using rail and road links from their zones across the Soviet zone to Berlin. Only a massive and continuous Western airlift (some 275,000 flights) was able to provide West Berliners with sufficient supplies. After almost a year (June 1948–May 1949), Stalin realized the Western powers could not be forced out of their Berlin zones and ended the blockade. Soon afterwards, still in 1949, separate West and East German governments came into existence, the former called the German Federal Republic and the latter the German Democratic Republic.

Stalin feared that West Germany would be remilitarized and become another antagonistic Western power. In 1952, he proposed the existence of a united but neutral Germany, even allowing that it could possess enough military to defend itself. How serious the offer was is debatable. The former Western allies countered with the suggestion that free elections first be held in both Germanys. Nothing came of the two proposals.

NATO, China, and the Korean War, 1949–1953

Besides the end of the Berlin blockade, the year 1949 witnessed three other important Cold War developments: the formation of the North Atlantic Treaty Organization (NATO), the first testing of a Soviet atomic bomb, and the establishment by the Chinese Communists of the People's Republic of China. The NATO countries, initially consisting of the United States and eleven other Western nations, pledged themselves to military cooperation and mutual assistance against aggression. The significance of the Soviet A-bomb test was that it broke the U.S. nuclear monopoly, although not yet its nuclear superiority. The victory of the Chinese Communists in their civil war against Kuomintang

FIGURE 14.2. The rebirth of German militarism, aided by the United States, Great Britain, and France, a 1951 cartoon from the Soviet magazine *Krokodil*.
(From J.P. Nettl, The Soviet Achievement, *#111, p. 187, Harcourt, Brace & World, New York, 1967, British Museum photo, Freeman.)*

forces meant that the most populous country of the world (China) now joined the biggest country in the world (USSR) in being under Communist governments. The new Chinese leader, Mao Zedong, who had received some Soviet support (although not as much as wished), came to Moscow and negotiated with Stalin. The outcome, in February 1950, was a Sino-Soviet mutual assistance treaty.

Several months later, in late June, North Korean troops attacked South Korea. Stalin had been consulted ahead of time and before and during the ensuing war furnished support to North Korea, including Soviet planes and pilots. Among other motivations, Stalin was influenced by a desire to weaken U.S. and Japanese influence in the Far East—he apparently feared that the United States might allow a Japanese military resurgence and that South Korea might then become a staging area for Japanese anti-Soviet operations.

The United States used the opportunity of a temporary Soviet absence from the United Nations (UN) to get UN backing for military support for South Korea. After initial UN troop advances under U.S. General Douglas MacArthur, China followed Soviet advice and sent troops to aid North Korea and drive UN forces back. By mid-1951, the front had stabilized near the original boundary between the two Korean states, and both sides agreed to armistice talks. They began in July 1951 but were then frequently interrupted, and the war did not finally end until several months after Stalin's death in early 1953.

That an armistice was not signed earlier was due primarily to Stalin. Although he did not want any direct Soviet-American confrontation and feared any sharp escalation of the war, he also did not want the United States to extricate itself from the Korean quagmire. The large loss of lives on the part of his Communist allies apparently did not bother him, and the war had the added benefit of reminding Communist China how dependent it was on the Soviet Union for various types of assistance. The wrath Stalin displayed against Tito was an indication of Stalin's belief that Moscow alone should formulate and direct Communist policy, and Communist China was potentially a much more serious challenger to Stalin's desire for supreme and unquestioning Communist leadership.

STALIN'S POSTWAR FOREIGN POLICY: AN ASSESSMENT

By the early 1950s, Soviet postwar foreign policy seemed amazingly successful to many in the Western world. Whereas before World War II there had been one Communist country, by 1950 there were numerous others from Albania on the Adriatic Sea to China on the Pacific Ocean. With the exception of Yugoslavia, Eastern Europe was firmly under Soviet control. Moreover, the Soviet Union had joined the United States as the only other nuclear power.

On more careful examination, however, the Soviet postwar policy was not as successful as it appeared—and it was not as premeditated or well thought out as many in the West believed. The creation of a Soviet bloc in east-central Europe had been primarily because of Soviet wartime successes. Soviet-Yugoslavian relations had deteriorated and been terminated. Soviet policies had helped create just what Soviet leaders did not desire: a stronger, unified, hostile Western coalition symbolized by NATO. The Chinese Communist victory over Kuomintang forces owed little to Soviet help and was not necessarily better for Soviet interests than a weak, divided China. Finally, the Soviet Union became involved in an arms race with the wealthiest country in the world. Only decades later did it become clear how high a price that race imposed on the Soviet economy.

Most of that cost, however, was paid not by members of the Soviet elite but by common Soviet citizens, many of whom were convinced that both massive Soviet defense spending and the Communist government that preached its necessity were essential for their protection. For more than three decades after Stalin's death, party leaders continued to reinforce this conviction.

The arms race, of course, involved two sides, and the United States and its allies also bore some responsibility for it. U.S. policy makers sometimes failed to appreciate the intensity of USSR security concerns after its horrendous suffering in World War II and the U.S. development of the A-bomb. Nevertheless, as long as Stalin was alive, it is difficult to perceive how U.S. policies could have greatly improved U.S.-Soviet relations—without harming U.S. interests or those of other peoples (such as the Iranians or the Turks).[3]

In autumn 1945, the U.S. ambassador in Moscow, Averell Harriman, ran into former Soviet foreign commissar Maxim Litvinov at a theater. They spoke briefly and Harriman asked Litvinov what the United States could do to improve their countries' relations. Litvinov replied, "Nothing." Other evidence, including a "bugged" Litvinov conversation with a U.S. correspondent, confirms that in the mid-1940s Litvinov believed U.S. concessions to Stalin would accomplish nothing except the demand for more concessions. (In his memoirs, Molotov, who had succeeded Litvinov in 1939, declared that the treasonous Litvinov deserved the highest punishment, and he apparently would have received it, although somewhat belatedly, if he had not died a natural death in 1951.) Although Litvinov hated Molotov and had been unhappy since being recalled as U.S. ambassador in 1943, even Molotov later admitted that he was intelligent and knowledgeable about international affairs.

While recognizing Litvinov's possible bias against Molotov and the foreign policy he implemented, Harriman thought Litvinov's assessment in late 1945 was important. More than a half-century later, it still seems so.

SUGGESTED SOURCES*

AKSYONOV, VASILLY. *The Winter's Hero*. New York, 1996. A novel.

BANAC, IVO. *With Stalin against Tito*. Ithaca, N.Y., 1988.

Bulletin of the Cold War International History Project. A good source for keeping up with latest archival revelations, published by the Wilson International Center for Scholars, 1992– . Volume 6–7 (Winter 1995/1996), for example, includes many new materials and analysis (by Kathryn Weathersby and others) on the Korean War, Sino-Soviet relations, and other aspects of the Cold War in Asia.

DUNHAM, VERA S. *In Stalin's Time: Middleclass Values in Soviet Fiction*. Rev. ed. Durham, 1990.

DUNMORE, TIMOTHY. *Soviet Politics, 1945-1953*. New York, 1984.

———. *The Stalinist Command Economy: The Soviet State Apparatus and Economic Policy, 1945–1953*. New York, 1980.

ELLIOT, MARK R. *Pawns of Yalta: Soviet Refugees and America's Role in Their Repatriation*. Urbana, Ill., 1982.

GADDIS, JOHN LEWIS. *The United States and the Origins of the Cold War, 1941–1947*. New York, 1972.

GONCHAROV, SERGEI N., JOHN W. LEWIS, and XUE LITAI. *Uncertain Partners: Stalin, Mao and the Korean War*. Stanford, 1993.

HAHN, WERNER G. *Postwar Soviet Politics: The Fall of Zhdanov and the Defeat of Moderation, 1946–1953*. Ithaca, N.Y., 1982.

HAMMOND, THOMAS T., ed. *The Anatomy of Communist Takeovers*. New Haven, 1975.

HARRIMAN, W. AVERELL. *Special Envoy to Churchill and Stalin, 1941–1946*. New York, 1975.

---

[3]For a similar conclusion, see David Holloway, *Stalin and the Bomb: The Soviet Union and Atomic Energy, 1939–56* (New Haven, 1994), pp. 369–371.

* See also books cited in footnotes.

KENNAN, GEORGE F. *Memoirs, 1925–1950*. Boston, 1957.

KENNEDY-PIPE, CAROLINE. *Stalin's Cold War: Soviet Strategies in Europe, 1943 to 1956*. Manchester, England, 1995.

KHRUSHCHEV, NIKITA. *Khrushchev Remembers*. Boston, 1970.

KOSTYRCHENKO, GENNADI V. *Out of The Red Shadows: Anti-semitism in Stalin's Russia: From the Secret Archives of the Soviet Union*. Amherst, N.Y., 1995.

LaFEBER, WALTER. *America, Russia, and the Cold War, 1945–1990*. 6th ed. New York, 1991. Chs. 1–6.

MASTNY, VOJITECH. *The Cold War and Soviet Insecurity*. New York, 1996.

NEKRICH, A. M. *The Punished Peoples: The Deportation and Fate of Soviet Minorities at the End of the Second World War*. New York, 1978.

NETTL, J. P. *The Eastern Zone and Soviet Policy in Germany, 1945–1950*. New York, 1951.

NOVE, ALEC. *An Economic History of the U.S.S.R., 1917–1991*. London, 1993.

RADZINSKY, EDVARD. *Stalin*. New York, 1996. Chs. 25–28.

RAPOPORT, LOUIS. *Stalin's War Against the Jews: The Doctors' Plot and the Soviet Solution*. New York, 1990.

RAPPORT, YAKOV. *The Doctors' Plot of 1953*. Cambridge, Mass., 1991.

SOLZHENITSYN, ALEXANDER. *One Day in the Life of Ivan Denisovich*, trans. Max Hayward and Ronald Hingley. New York, 1963. A novel.

TAUBMAN, WILLIAM. *Stalin's American Policy: From Entente to Detente to Cold War*. New York, 1982.

THOMAS, HUGH. *Armed Truce: The Beginnings of the Cold War, 1945–46*. New York, 1987.

ULAM, ADAM B. *Expansion and Coexistence: Soviet Foreign Policy, 1917–73*. New York, 1974. Chs. VIII–X.

CHAPTER 15

An Economic and Social Transformation, 1917–1953

Marxist ideology, the modernizing and military needs of the Soviet state, and the personalities of Lenin and Stalin helped determine Soviet economic and social life. So too did the USSR's peoples and the nature of pre-Soviet Russia. In many social spheres, such as family life, the new Soviet government began with utopian hopes; by the late 1930s, however, socioeconomic traditions and realities, plus Stalin's political desires, had ended most revolutionary utopianism. This transition was marked by Stalin's "great retreat" of the mid 1930s, or "the revolution betrayed," as Trotsky called it (see Chapter 11). One aspect of this betrayal was increased social stratification and heightened privileges for party members.

Yet while Stalin retreated from revolutionary utopianism, he increased state terrorism. From 1935 through 1938, record numbers of Soviet citizens were prosecuted for "crimes against the state." Although the terror subsequently lessened, it remained at higher levels throughout Stalin's rule than during the NEP years.

ECONOMIC OVERVIEW AND ANALYSIS

Despite the ideological compromises of the NEP, the first decade of Soviet power produced notable long-range economic changes. The government expropriated imperial, upper-class, and church lands and took over and maintained control over "the commanding heights" of the Soviet economy. It also enacted social welfare measures, such as sick, unemployment, and medical benefits for workers.

By 1928, the country's economy was at about the level it had been before the wreckages of 1914–1921. During the next twenty-five years, it underwent a huge transformation. By 1940, the USSR's industrial output was second only to that of the United States—a position it still held in 1953 despite its horrendous losses in World War II. In 1913, it had been fifth in the world. At that time, four-fifths of its people were peasants; by 1953, less than half were. The qualifications of the Soviet industrial workforce improved significantly; in the years 1928–1941 alone, the number of Soviet graduate engineers increased more than sixfold.

Another Soviet achievement was reducing its dependence on foreign imports. Soviet foreign trade was generally lower in the interwar period than in 1913, partly because of interwar global conditions, including the Great Depression. The decrease in valuable strategic imports, such as machine tools, also reflected the Soviet desire to become more self-reliant. After World War II, in Stalin's final years, Soviet foreign trade expanded from the levels of the late 1930s, but the trade was overwhelmingly with other Communist countries and on terms favorable to the USSR.

By the time of Stalin's death in 1953, the Soviet Union's economy was admired by many people in less developed regions of the world. The USSR had become one of the world's two superpowers, and its "command" economy offered a model for rapid transformation from backwardness to modernity.

The command economy, which developed under Stalin, was characterized by state determination of the types, amounts, and prices of goods produced. Of course, it was up to the Soviet people to fulfill government plans, and this was not always done. Moreover, there was always an unknown amount of illegal black market buying and selling. In addition, the government allowed some produce, such as most of that from a peasant's personal plot, to be sold on the market for whatever price its seller could obtain.

The institution of a command economy enabled economic growth to move more rapidly in the direction desired by the state. By such means as determining salaries, taxes, and prices (including those paid to collective farmers for mandatory deliveries to the government), the state was able to increase revenues by keeping most of the population at little more than a subsistence level. It could then invest in whichever sectors it wished, such as heavy industry and defense, largely ignoring the type of consumer demand that exists in market economies.

Beneath the surface of the economic gains trumpeted by Soviet leaders and media, serious structural problems existed. Collective and state farms were inefficient, and the command economy depended upon a large bureaucracy to manage it. The first priority of party personnel and industrial enterprises was "meeting the plan," fulfilling the production quotas handed down from above. This obsession, in turn, contributed to an emphasis on quantity not quality and to the shrinkage of individual economic and entrepreneurial initiative. Moreover, the economic gains came not only on the backs of "free" workers and consumers, but also on those of millions of forced laborers.

Although few paid much attention to it at the time, the environmental cost of Stalin's "planned economy" was also high. As two modern scholars put it: "For the environment, the central planning system became Frankenstein's monster. . . . The plan and its fulfillment became engines of destruction geared

"How is the cattle population?"
"On the increase!"

FIGURE 15.1. When "meeting the plan" could not be accomplished, those responsible often attempted to fool their superiors into believing otherwise, as this *Krokodil* cartoon from the Khrushchev era illustrates.
(Courtesy of Roger Swearingen.)

to consume, not to conserve, the natural wealth and human strength of the Soviet Union."[1]

For decades after Stalin's death, many scholars maintained that Stalin's forced industrialization was necessary for Soviet survival and that it helped prevent a Hitler triumph. Some still hold this position. It is by no means proven, however, that Stalin's economic approach was the best or only way to fulfill that task. In considering Stalin's economic methods, it is difficult to separate them from his politics. If the immense taking of civilian and military lives during his purges are considered, it is even more difficult to maintain that Stalin's policies were the best way of preparing for Hitler's eventual onslaught.

[1] Murray Feshbach and Alfred Friendly, *Ecocide in the USSR: Health and Nature Under Siege* (New York, 1992), p. 40.

POPULATION, TOWNS, AND URBAN LIFE

As a result of the loss of territory and lives in the 1914–1922 period, the population of the Soviet Union was only about 134 million in 1923, as compared to about 168 million in the Russian Empire at the beginning of 1914. During the 1930s and 1940s, famine deaths, Stalin's purges, and World War II killed off many more millions. By 1953, even though the Soviet Union had gained new territory in World War II and was now about the same size as the Russian Empire in 1914, it contained only about 188 million people. Thus, four decades brought about a growth of only about 20 million people, whereas normal birth and death rates for these years would have increased the population many times that.

Despite all the demographic catastrophes, the population was able to grow to the extent it did because in "normal years" many more people were born than died. Both birth and death rates dropped noticeably in this period but especially the latter: In 1953, there were only about three-fifths the births and about one-third the deaths per 1,000 people that there had been four decades earlier.

During the Lenin and Stalin years, there were numerous population shifts. Civil War conditions led many people to leave the cities for rural areas, but by 1926 the percentage of urban dwellers was back around where it had been in 1913, at about 18 percent of the total population. Then, during the 1930s, urban growth increased in unprecedented proportions, largely because of Stalin's industrialization, collectivization, and purges—inmates of forced-labor camps of more than 5,000 people were counted as part of the urban population. The 1939 census listed 33 percent of the people living in urban areas. By 1953, the urban population was about 43 percent. Although still less urban than Western industrialized countries and Japan, the Soviet Union was by Stalin's death much more urbanized than most parts of the world.

Rural-urban movements overlapped those from one region of the USSR to another. Stalin's purges and deportations, the building of new factories and towns in the Urals and further east, and the German occupation during World War II all led to regional population shifts. Under Stalin, for example, millions of people settled, willingly and unwillingly, in Siberia. By 1939, the "urban" population of eastern Siberia had more than tripled from 891,000 in 1926.

Some of the fastest-growing cities were east of the Volga, including Novosibirsk, Cheliabinsk, Perm, Omsk, Ufa, Krasnoiarsk, Karaganda, and Magnitogorsk. By 1953, Moscow and Leningrad were still the two largest cities in the Soviet Union, although Leningrad had not yet completely recovered from World War II—the 1959 census (the first since 1939) indicated that Leningrad's population was about 3.3 million, which was about what it had been in the 1939 census. Moscow was the largest city in the USSR in both 1939 and 1959, with 4.6 million in 1939 and 6.1 million people in 1959.

Other large cities in both censuses included Kiev, Baku, Kharkov (Kharkiv), Gorky (Nizhnii Novgorod), and Tashkent. By 1959, Novosibirsk,

Kuibyshev (Samara), and Sverdlovsk (Ekaterinburg) were also among the ten largest cities.

Moscow and Magnitogorsk

Among the many differences in urban life during this period were those between Moscow and provincial cities. One young Communist of the early 1930s later wrote of his impressions after coming to the capital from the provinces. He noted that compared to Dnepropetrovsk or Kharkov, Moscow "seemed a haven of plenty. The lines outside shops were not so long, the shelves inside not so bare." He observed newly asphalted streets, new modernistic buildings, and people better dressed than in the provinces. He impressed one of Stalin's chief officials and was afterward driven to one of the city's best hotels, the Metropole, in a Lincoln. In the Metropole's restaurant, a jazz band played amidst tropical plants and well-dressed patrons, foreign and Soviet.[2]

During these years, the planning and initial construction of the Moscow metro was underway, and the first line opened up in 1935. With its escalators and gilded and marble stations, the Moscow subway system soon became the showpiece of the city. The subway was just one of the government's plans for transforming the capital. Some streets were widened or newly constructed, new buildings sprung up, and Stalin hatched even more grandiose plans. (See Chapter 16 for plans for a gigantic Palace of Soviets.)

One of the individuals most responsible for overseeing Moscow's new construction, especially the metro, was the future Soviet leader Nikita Khrushchev. Although proud of his efforts, he also recognized that the capital's sewage and water drainage systems were outdated, most streets were either cobblestone or unpaved, and horsedrawn transport was still much in use. In his memoirs, he refers to the housing situation as a "nightmare."

With about 2 million peasants coming to the capital to work between 1929 and 1939, many had to live in factory dormitories. There some rotated the use of a bed with someone working on another shift. Such beds were often lined up one against another and without pillows or blankets. Even then, however, there sometimes were not enough beds, and some workers slept on the floor. Many newcomers could find housing only on the capital's outskirts, where some of them constructed mud huts, underground dugouts, or makeshift shanties. The majority of newcomers lacked running water in their dwellings; in fact, in 1931, only about two-fifths of all Moscow housing possessed such a convenience.

Most apartment-dwellers lived in communal apartments, where families had to share kitchens, bath and toilet facilities, and sometimes even a single living and sleeping room with other families. (See Boym's book listed at the

[2] Victor Kravchenko, *I Chose Freedom: The Personal and Political Life of a Soviet Official* (New York, 1946), pp. 82–83. Anatoli Rybakov's novel *Children of the Arbat* (New York, 1988) offers a good depiction of Moscow life in 1934, especially as seen through the eyes of young people.

end of this chapter for an insightful treatment of communal apartments.) Although most families had a room to themselves, in 1935, there were about four times more Moscow renters (usually families) that occupied only *part* of a room than there were renters residing in more than one room.

Although Moscow had its hardships, they palled in comparison to Magnitogorsk, which in the course of five years (1929–1934) went from a village to a town of about 200,000. Located on the Ural River in former Bashkir territory, it became one of the great hopes of Stalin's industrialization drive. A Soviet booklet of 1932 indicated that it was to contain the world's largest, most modern iron-and-steel plant and be a model of city planning, with ample greenery, no pollution problems, and attractive worker housing.

It was true that by the end of the 1930s the plant had become a great steel producer, and the city boasted of numerous schools, cultural-recreational facilities, and clinics, although no churches. But most of its inhabitants still lived in miserable dwellings without running water and sewerage. The American John Scott, who was one of hundreds of foreigners who worked there in the 1930s, estimated that in 1938, three-fourths of the population lived in mud huts, underground dugouts, barracks, or temporary wooden structures. If families in huts were fortunate enough to own a cow, pigs, or chickens, these animals also usually shared the family hut.

Yet living accommodations had improved considerably as compared to the early 1930s. Besides enthusiasts who had willingly come to Magnitogorsk to help build this Communist "dream," tens of thousands of others were sent there. The largest group of involuntary laborers were peasant kulaks shipped there in 1931 and 1932 in closed railway boxcars. After arriving, the kulaks spent their first winter in tents, and most children and many adults died within months from cold and hunger.

In the decades to come, Magnitogorsk continued to be a great steel-producing center—it produced steel for half of the Soviet tanks of World War II—but it never became a model city. By the beginning of the 1990s, pollution-related sicknesses were widespread in the city.

Trends in Urban Housing and Living

Not only in Moscow and Magnitogorsk, but also throughout the Soviet Union, housing remained a major problem. About the only positive aspect was that rents were cheap, absorbing a much smaller percentage of the average worker's income than in the pre–World War I period.

During the revolution and Civil War, hundreds of thousands of urban buildings were wrecked, and urban living space decreased, although the departure of many town-dwellers for the countryside temporarily lessened urban housing needs. Shortages of brick and cement made it difficult to repair or replace anything but wooden structures. During the NEP, little money was invested in urban housing, and what was built was often of poor quality. As more people migrated to cities in the 1920s, urban living space became more scarce, and the number of homeless sleeping outdoors or in such places as train stations increased.

Then, as peasants flooded into the cities in the 1930s, matters got worse. One example was the life of Boris Yeltsin's family. His father gave up farming to work as a construction worker in Berezniki, a city in the Perm Region, near the Ural Mountains. Yeltsin's autobiography depicted the family (including a goat) living there for a decade, crowded into one drafty room in a communal barracks of twenty small rooms. The barracks had no "modern conveniences," such as indoor toilets or running water.

At least the Yeltsins were fortunate enough to be far enough east to escape German occupation during World War II. During the war years, so many buildings were destroyed in the occupied-and-then-recaptured area that almost half of its urban living space was wiped out. Millions were forced to live in earth dugouts.

After the war, new construction gradually housed more and more people, but the government's first priority was on factories, not housing. Major cities were rebuilt first, and a decade after the war some smaller cities were still mostly in ruins. In Belorussia in 1947, 34,000 families were still living in earth dugouts. In Moscow, which had suffered relatively little war damage, most residents during Stalin's final years still lived in overcrowded communal apartments.

Like housing, other urban living conditions left much to be desired but varied over time. The years of the Civil War and World War II were difficult. Although most Soviet urban inhabitants did not suffer the way the people of Leningrad did during the 900-day German siege, overall living standards dropped sharply during World War II.

Peacetime conditions varied but were generally better. More food and other goods were available under NEP than during the subsequent first Five-Year Plan (FYP). Then, in the mid-1930s, during the "great retreat," the government slightly improved the lot of wage earners and consumers, and some people talked about the coming of a "little NEP." In 1935, most rationing ended, which had been in effect in the cities since late 1928–early 1929, and more consumer goods appeared on shop shelves.

By 1937, most townspeople were better off financially—although in the midst of the purges probably not psychologically—than five years earlier. The average worker's standard of living, however, still lagged behind that at the end of the NEP (or the eve of World War I), and prices remained high. In late 1936, a pair of shoes cost a typical worker more than a month's wages; sewing machines, radios, gramophones, cameras, and bicycles remained luxury items. Throughout the Stalin years, automobiles remained far beyond the reach of almost all workers, and crowded trams and trolley-buses were the most common means of urban transport.

Although individual wage earners saw sharp declines in their purchasing power in the decade from 1928 to 1937, household purchasing power declined less because more family members found jobs. Moreover, overall unemployment was sharply reduced, and more people received free state services such as health care and education.

From 1938 until mid-1941, as more revenue was diverted to military preparation, the production of many consumer items declined. After World War II, urban conditions gradually improved. By 1952, however, average real wages (which factor in inflation) were still below those of 1928, and the currency "reform" of 1947 had wiped out most savings of any substance.

SOCIAL STRUCTURE AND THE NEW ELITE

Although urban conditions changed from city to city and from time to time, they also varied from one group to another. Within a few years of coming to power, the Communists had largely destroyed the old upper classes, while favoring the workers (for example, with better rations and social welfare benefits). The leading members of the Communist party, however, many of whom were not of working-class background, became the new elite.

Party of Privilege

Lenin was aware of lower-class hostility—indeed had encouraged it—toward the privileges of the old elite; he attempted to keep Communists from engendering a similar animosity. He insisted, for example, that party officials' salaries be kept close to those of skilled workers. But there was more to elite status than money. Party membership was the key to the levers of power, and with power came privileges that could not be measured in money alone.

During the NEP, wealthy Nepmen and educated "bourgeois" specialists temporarily joined party members in the upper ranks of Soviet society. Some Communist purists, such as Victor Serge, believed that the Nepmen corrupted party officials. He wrote of party men who took bribes and who lived in fine flats with antique furniture they had expropriated. But as long as the Nepmen and "bourgeois" specialists remained prominent, popular resentment, at least in the cities, was more directed at them than at party members.

During the first FYP, Stalin lifted the former lid on party salaries, and during the 1930s the lifestyle of leading party members grew more lavish, although the party took pains to conceal the heightened privileges.

Top party people enjoyed a world of special shops, dining facilities, dachas (summer homes), special resorts, and chauffeur-driven limousines. The American John Scott described the house of the director of the Magnitogorsk plant, a high-ranking party member. In 1938, it was a new structure containing fourteen rooms, including a billiard room, a music room, and a playroom, and the house's furnishings were valued at more than twice the cost of the house. Another eleven large houses were constructed for the director's leading assistants.

In Moscow by the mid-1930s, many important party people and their families lived in the so-called Government House. This was a huge complex of several large buildings completed in 1931 and located across the Moscow River from the Kremlin. The ensemble contained some 500 large, furnished apartments, a library, theater, cinema, gymnasium, clinic, restaurant, and special shops. The apartments were supplied with central heating, gas, always-available hot water, and a telephone (which remained a luxury for decades). Numerous "service personnel" (the preferred term because servants sounded too bourgeois) also served the apartment-dwellers. Although the size of the apartments varied, the former Soviet officer and diplomat Alexander Barmine recalled a family he knew who lived there and had eight "luxuriously furnished" rooms "and two servants."

Besides these new constructions, the party elite took over for their collective use old royal and upper-class estates. Some of these, for example in the Black Sea region, were turned into vacation retreats. On other estates, palatial homes became the dachas of party leaders. One such dacha, near Moscow, was that of the Armenian Anastas Mikoian, who oversaw Soviet trade and became a full member of the Politburo in 1935. Stalin's daughter, Svetlana, later described it: "Inside are marble statues imported from Italy. . . . downstairs the windows are of stained glass. The garden, the park, the tennis court, the orangery, stables and greenhouses are all exactly as they have always been."[3]

The party elite also included high-ranking military officers—military personnel in general more than doubled from 1927 to 1937. One senior officer, Alexander Barmine, later described a recently constructed officers' rest house where he vacationed in 1935. It was in Sochi, on a high rock overlooking the Black Sea. It contained eight five-storied buildings, each with a plate-glass view of the sea. Although all the buildings were luxurious, some were more so than others. The higher the rank, the more opulent the building and furnishings, with the top generals having a building to themselves. Funicular cable cars transported the officers back and forth to their private beach.

Yet Barmine's additional comment is worth noting: "Readers who are made envious by my account . . . may comfort themselves with the knowledge that fully 90 percent of those who stayed there in the next three years were either shot or disappeared in the purge."[4]

Despite the leadership's attempts to conceal many of its privileges from public knowledge, chauffeured limousines, expensive clothes, and other signs of privileged status were not difficult to detect, and memoirs and documents of the period indicate some grumbling about elite Communist party lifestyles.

Even some party members were unhappy with the "corrupting action of privilege, place, and patronage on the part of those in power." These words were written in 1928 by an exiled Christian Rakovsky, a friend of Trotsky and a former Soviet ambassador to France. A year earlier the Left Opposition, to which Trotsky and Rakovsky belonged, had criticized the "swollen and privileged administrative apparatus." In *The Revolution Betrayed* (1937), Trotsky, by

[3]Svetlana Aliluyeva, *Twenty Letters to a Friend* (New York, 1968), p. 39.
[4]Alexandre Barmine, *One Who Survived: The Life Story of a Russian Under the Soviets* (New York, 1945), p. 274.

FIGURE 15.2. Black Sea resort areas such as Sochi and Yalta (pictured above) were popular vacation spots for top leaders.

then in Mexico, quoted these words and Rakovsky's and extensively criticized increasing elite privileges, inequalities, and bureaucracy.

Workers and the Intelligentsia

Among the inequalities Trotsky criticized in 1937 were those among workers, especially those resulting from Stalin's Stakhanovite movement to increase worker productivity. As early as mid-1931, Stalin had defended wage differentials, and they had subsequently increased. Including the favors dispensed on the elite Stakhanovite workers as part of their real income, Trotsky calculated it to be twenty to thirty times that of poorer workers.

The number of workers as a whole increased rapidly after 1928, as did white-collar employees. According to Soviet figures, which include dependents, in 1928 the workers made up 12.4 percent of the population; in 1939, 33.7 percent; and in 1959, 50.2 percent.[5] White-collar employees increased from 5.2 percent in 1928 to 16.5 percent in 1939 and to 18.1 percent in 1959.

---

[5]Soviet statistics classified peasants on state farms as "workers," but they were only a small percentage of the farming population until the 1950s. The realities of work life were always more varied and complex than Soviet categories and statistics suggested. See, for example, David L. Hoffmann, *Peasant Metropolis: Social Identities in Moscow, 1929–1941* (Ithaca, N.Y., 1994), and Lewis H. Siegelbaum and Ronald Grigor Suny, eds., *Making Workers Soviet: Power, Class, and Identity* (Ithaca, N.Y., 1994).

Soviet sources tended to consider most of these white-collar employees as mental-workers (or "intelligentsia"). Western sources have generally defined the Soviet "intelligentsia" more narrowly, often limiting it to people in administrative, scientific-technical, cultural, and professional positions or to the well educated.

Whereas the bourgeoisie and landowner category (including kulaks) was listed at about 5 percent in 1928, this category ceased to exist in later census figures. The "bourgeois" specialists, however, disappeared more in name than in fact, as many of them now became reclassified as part of the "nonparty intelligentsia." After the cultural revolution of 1928–1931 had removed some of them from their positions, Stalin signaled that the process had gone far enough, sometimes too far. Although he insisted that the *"working class must create its own industrial and technical intelligentsia"* (Stalin's emphasis), he also concluded that the Soviet Union could not yet dispense with the services of co-operative nonparty intelligentsia.

Stalin made this point already in mid-1931, in the same speech in which he defended salary differentials. Although some members of the nonparty technical and cultural intelligentsia later became victims of the Great Terror, others prospered. The Soviet government rewarded the adaptable Alexei Tolstoi (1883–1945), former nobleman and author of the novel *Peter I*, with sumptuous rewards, allowing him to live in a style that surpassed that of many of his illustrious ancestors.

In a speech about the Draft Constitution of 1936, Stalin stated that the Soviet transitional phase from capitalism to socialism had been completed and that the "exploiting classes" had been liquidated. He claimed that only three classes remained: the workers, the peasants, and the intelligentsia (of which, according to Stalin, 80 to 90 percent had come from among Soviet working people, including peasants).

Peasants

While the percentage of manual and white-collar workers increased, the percentage of peasants decreased. Excluding those categorized as kulaks, official figures listed the collective and individual peasants (plus a small percentage of handicraftsmen) as 77.8 percent of the population in 1928, 49.8 percent in 1939, and 31.7 percent in 1959.

The most momentous events in the lives of the peasants during this era were the Bolshevik Land Decree (November 1917), the Civil War, the institution of NEP (1921), the famine of 1921–1922, the collectivization of agriculture (late 1929–early 1930s), the famine of 1932–1933, and World War II.

The nationalization of crown, noble, and church lands in 1917 resulted in some arable-land gains for most peasants but not much. In European Russia, peasants apparently added an average of several acres per household to their holdings, plus obtaining access to nationalized forests and meadows.

By the end of the NEP, Russian peasants were still living in ways similar to that of their predecessors. They overwhelmingly belonged to a peasant commune (*mir*), and most of them continued plowing their own scattered strips with horse-drawn plows, although now generally metal rather than wooden. Three-fourths of the land devoted to grains was still sown by hand, and more than two-fifths of it was harvested with scythes and sickles, as opposed to horse-drawn mechanical implements.

The big change in the peasants' way of life came with Stalin's forced collectivization. In the years 1928–1932, about 12 million people left the countryside, willingly or unwillingly.[6] Most peasants who remained became members of collective farms (kolkhozes) or state farms (sovkhozes).

Although at first the government failed to specify what type of collective farm the peasants were to be herded into, by the mid-1930s, trial and error had delivered the answer. Although supposedly a cooperative venture of its peasant members, the kolkhoz was controlled by state regulations, a rural soviet, and, above it, district officials. Although the kolkhoz chairman (only occasionally a woman) was supposedly elected by the kolkhoz members, he was usually imposed upon them.

Life in the kolkhoz was different than life in the *mir*. The peasants no longer farmed their own strips but now worked collectively, earning labordays. These were based on a combination of hours worked and the type of job performed. The number earned determined a peasant's pay, which was primarily paid in grain. Before the peasants received any payment, however, various obligations had to be met. The kolkhoz as a whole as well as individual kolkhoz members (kolkhozniks) had to pay high taxes (both in money and in crops) to the state. Most, if not all, of the remaining kolkhoz grain and other crops had to be sold to the state at extremely low state-set prices. Obviously the state's main concern was to squeeze as much as possible from the kolkhozniks. Not surprisingly, many peasants viewed collectivization as a new form of serfdom.

Before collectivization, the peasants farmed not only their own holdings (generally in strips), but also small garden plots around their huts. In 1930, Stalin conceded that these plots could remain separate from the collectivized peasant holdings, along with a small number of farm animals. In 1935, the government specified that the plot of a kolkhoznik household generally should be between one-fourth to one-half a hectare (or 0.6–1.2 acres), but 1938 statistics indicated that the average kolkhoznik plot was nearer the minimum.

Stalin was not being generous in this concession; from the private plots and retained animals, the peasants had to sell produce, meat, and milk to the state, again at state-determined prices. Only afterward could they sell (as of 1932) at the kolkhoz market what the state had not procured or they had not eaten or stored away for themselves. Even on this income, the peasants paid taxes over and above other taxes owed by both their kolkhoz and individual households.

Although the peasant owned his hut sitting amidst his private plot, he did not own the plot itself. If he were kicked out of the kolkhoz, the kolkhoz could

---

[6] For this figure and much of the material for this section, I am indebted to Sheila Fitzpatrick, *Stalin's Peasants: Resistance and Survival in the Russian Village after Collectivization* (New York, 1994).

reassign it. Yet the fact that his household could keep or sell (at free prices) some of what it produced was incentive enough for the household to devote its greatest care to its plot. An official estimate of 1937 indicated that although the private plots made up only about one-twentieth of the total sown area of the kolkhozes, they produced about one-fourth of total kolkhoz production (the true figure might even have been higher). This private productivity remained a Communist embarrassment throughout the remainder of the Soviet period. And whenever state pressure eased and the kolkhoznik gained the opportunity to expand his private plot at kolkhoz expense, he did so—as was evidenced during World War II.

Despite its Marxian ideological appeal, the state farm (sovkhoz) did not play as important a role as the kolkhoz. Because workers on the sovkhozes received regular wages, the sovkhozes proved less economically efficient for the government than the kolkhozes. Although the average sovkhoz was larger than the average kolkhoz, there were far fewer of them, and they collectively farmed much less land than all the kolkhozes combined.

From the perspective of most peasants, collectivization brought with it numerous unwelcome changes in their personal lives. One was the decline of peasant crafts and the income that went with them. This occurred for various reasons, one being that many craftsmen were declared kulaks and persecuted accordingly. The decline of bootmaking, shoemaking, tailoring, and weaving made peasants more dependent on store-bought goods, which were often of poor quality and too expensive for peasant incomes.

Peasants generally believed—and correctly so—that they were treated less favorably than urban workers and consumers. They certainly had fewer goods available to them in rural stores. Periodic shortages of kerosene meant that many peasants could not use their lamps but had to use candles or the centuries-old lighting splinters (*luchiny*). As late as 1950, only about one-sixth of the country's kolkhozes possessed electricity—certainly a smaller percentage than envisioned by Lenin, who had said that "Communism is Soviet Power plus the electrification of the whole country" and that for the peasants electricity would replace God.

Except for increased educational opportunities, the Soviet government furnished little to make up for what the peasants lost during collectivization. Accompanying collectivization was the closing of many rural churches and taverns, two different sources of traditional solace for the peasants. Instead, peasants were coerced into going to more meetings or lectures run by local authorities. By the late 1930s, a growing minority of peasants were able to purchase radios, and peasants increasingly viewed films, although they often had to go to district towns to do so. By the end of Stalin's rule, however, few peasants' huts or housing yet possessed indoor plumbing or telephones, and rural roads were almost exclusively unpaved.

Yet in the countryside, as in the cities, some people were better off than others. Government and party officials, kolkhoz administrators, and MTS (Machine-Tractor-Station) workers earned more money and had greater privileges than almost all full-time kolkhoz peasants. So too did Stakhanovite peasants, who received awards (including consumer goods such as gramophones) and publicity for setting agricultural production records. Sovkhoz workers and peasants who were not immediately collectivized also earned more than the average kolkhoznik. (By 1940, however, only about 3 percent of peasant households were still outside the kolkhozes and sovkhozes, down from 38 percent in mid-1932.) Another group of peasants better off than the average kolkhoznik were those who spent part or all of their time working in a factory or at another location outside the kolkhoz. Often a husband, while retaining kolkhoz membership, worked in town while his wife worked on the kolkhoz.

Thus, although collectivization got rid of most kulaks and supposed kulaks, or at least took their "wealth" from them, it did not end economic differences among the peasantry. Along with lingering resentments from past battles in the countryside, these differences helped sow hostility and conflicts among the peasants themselves.

Despite all its efforts, the party was often frustrated in its attempts to mold the peasants into ideal kolkhoz workers. Communist personnel in the countryside were not plentiful, especially after purges in the mid and late 1930s. By 1938, for example, only one-fifth of the kolkhoz chairmen were party members. The peasants often found ways, ranging from slack work performance to stealing, to ease or evade burdens that the shorthanded party tried to impose upon them. During the purges of the 1930s, peasants were sometimes able to get even with unpopular kolkhoz chairmen or other bosses or officials by denouncing them (on real or invented grounds) to higher authorities.

A minority of peasants took advantage of limited opportunities offered for upward mobility. Becoming a kolkhoz administrator (like future Soviet leader Mikhail Gorbachev's grandfather) or an MTS driver (like Gorbachev's father) were two such paths. Although many rural youngsters left the kolkhoz and never returned after military service or after completing secondary or higher education, few rural students ever got the opportunity Mikhail Gorbachev did—the chance to study at such a prestigious institution as Moscow State University.

FOOD AND FAMINE; DRINKING AND HEALTH

When the Bolsheviks came to power, food was scarce in the cities and rationing was already in existence, a practice that they continued throughout the Civil War. With the institution of NEP, the government ended food rationing but reintroduced it from 1929 to 1935. During late 1941, the government once again imposed it in the cities, and the policy continued after the war, until ended in late 1947.

At first, rationing discriminated primarily according to class. During World War II, when rationing applied to most citizens except kolkhoz workers and the unemployed, the government distributed rations primarily based on one's occupation and importance for the war effort. Soldiers and coal-miners, for example, received much higher rations than most white-collar workers.

Most fortunate of all were important party members. In 1942, Victor Kravchenko was given an important State Defense position in Moscow and along with it the right to elite monthly rations at a special location. Besides Soviet fish, fowl, vegetables, vodka, wine, and cigarettes, he also received from U.S.-furnished supplies bacon, butter, canned goods, flour, salt pork, and sugar. Even during the siege of Leningrad, such privileged individuals received special food supplies, such as fresh fruit.

Most of the urban population, however, was kept alive by bread; in 1944, it provided 85 to 90 percent of the proteins and calories almost all civilian groups received from rationed food. Many people did not receive enough food, however, either from rations or from other sources. Although Leningraders suffered the most severely during World War II—most of the city's 1 million deaths resulted from hunger—they were not alone. Hunger afflicted most townspeople, and death caused or exacerbated by malnutrition was common. In the countryside during the war, most peasants survived primarily by relying on potatoes from their private plots. Extreme hunger in Leningrad and other places led people to eat all sorts of things not normally consumed, including acorns, tree bark, grass, wallpaper paste, dogs, cats, and mice. Even isolated cases of cannibalism occurred.

Besides World War II, the two great famines of 1921–1922 and 1932–1933 killed off 10 million or more additional people. A less severe famine in 1947 took lives not in the thousands (as historians once thought) but in the hundreds of thousands. Although drought played a role in all three famines, many more deaths resulted from the government's excessive demands on peasant crops than from bad weather.

When war or famine was not contributing to hunger, most peoples' staples were bread and other grain-based foods, potatoes, and a few vegetables, especially cabbage. The average person ate best during the NEP, a time when more meat and dairy products were available. During the first FYP, both rural and urban food consumption declined, before improving somewhat in the mid and late 1930s.

After World War II, the food situation improved more for city-dwellers than for collective farm workers, especially after price cuts beginning in 1949. At the time of Stalin's death in early 1953, the average peasant's diet was still inferior to what it had been in 1926–1927.

Not only did the peasants have more to eat during the late NEP period, they also had more to drink. Privately owned village taverns existed, and by 1928, about two-fifths of the Russian peasant households made their own home-brewed vodka (*samogon*).

The Soviet government's alcohol policy was in some ways similar to that of the tsarist government: Both governments recognized the social evils flowing from alcoholism, but both governments were even more strongly influenced by the desire for alcohol revenues. In September 1930, for example, Stalin wrote to Molotov about the necessity of increasing Soviet military forces but noted that it would require more money. He then added: "Where can we find the money? I think vodka production should be expanded (to the extent possible). We need to get rid of a false sense of shame and directly and openly promote the greatest expansion of vodka production possible for the sake of a real and serious defense of our country."[7]

At first the Soviet government continued the World War I prohibition policies of its predecessors. During the Civil War, it forbade the distilling of *samogon*, although many peasants continued to turn their grain into the more easily concealed *samogon* rather than handing it over to either Reds or Whites. Later, during the NEP, government militia detachments raided stills and fined or arrested those caught violating the continued ban on *samogon*. The lower government grain prices fell, as they did toward the end of NEP, the stronger the inducement to produce *samogon* and the greater the state's effort to repress it. Thus, the peasant's production of *samogon* became part of the continuing peasant-state battle over trade terms and prices, a battle Stalin hoped to put an end to by collectivization.

In late 1921, the government once again permitted the sale of beer and wine, which it taxed, and in the mid-1920s renewed selling government-produced vodka. The state declared that such vodka would be both less dangerous and less wasteful of grain than *samogon*. The state's vodka monopoly did not, however, reduce *samogon* production. In the late NEP period, both legal vodka and *samogon*, as Lewin states, "flowed like water in the countryside." Although there was less *samogon* in the cities, drinking and drunkenness also increased there during the late NEP years, as numerous observers and government statistics indicated.

The growth of *samogon* production was finally stopped by collectivization. With most grain now ending up in state hands, much less of it was available for illegal distilling. Furthermore, as most people's real incomes declined sharply during the early 1930s, both in the villages and towns, legal drinking became harder to afford. Thus, from 1932–1935, per capita alcoholic consumption dropped below that of the late 1920s.

As real wages began improving in the late 1930s, alcohol sales spurted upward from 1937–1939. The best grain harvest of the decade in 1937 also made more grain available for government vodka production.

Although the Soviet government did not institute prohibition after being attacked by Germany in World War II, the state did raise, by about sixfold, prices on vodka, wine, and beer. Although this increase slowed down consumption, soldiers were given a vodka ration, and partisans often found ways to obtain *samogon* from sympathetic villagers.

For Stalin, obtaining alcohol was no problem. Once after visiting him toward the end of World War II, Yugoslavia's Marshal Tito declared: "I don't know what the devil is wrong with these Russians that they drink so much."[8] In his memoirs, Khrushchev noted the heavy postwar drinking of Soviet leaders. Like Peter the Great, Stalin sometimes forced those around him to get drunk.

---

[7] *Stalin's Letters to Molotov, 1925–1936*, eds. Lars T. Lih, Oleg V. Naumov, and Oleg V. Khlevniuk (New Haven, 1995), p. 209. In contrast to Stalin, Trotsky (in 1923) had objected strongly to any increased reliance on alcohol revenues.

[8] Milovan Djilas, *Conversations with Stalin* (New York, 1962), p. 115.

Heavy drinking in the postwar years was also evident among workers and others. Michel Gordey, a capable French correspondent born of Russian parents, spent two months in the Soviet Union in 1950 and was amazed at the amount of drinking he observed. He recalled, for example, standing at a Moscow kiosk one morning when a truck driver pulled up, jumped down, and ordered seven ounces of vodka. After finishing it off in one gulp, he drank another three and a half ounces and drove off.

Despite such cases of indulgence, most Soviet citizens were living much longer by the 1950s than their predecessors had at the end of the nineteenth century. Official statistics give at least an approximate indication of the country's health improvements. They indicate that by 1955–1956, average life expectancy at birth was sixty-seven years, slightly more than double what it had been in the fifty provinces of European Russia in 1896–1897. One reason for the increase was the sharp decline in infant mortality, another was the dramatic increase in doctors, most of them women.

But the Soviet health care system also had its shortcomings. As in many aspects of the command economy, the emphasis was often on the quantity (number of doctors), not the quality of what was produced (health care). Rural medical facilities lagged noticeably behind urban ones, and shortages of needed medicines often occurred. From the doctors' perspective, there were additional defects. Although private medical practice (for example, in one's home) was never completely outlawed, it was strongly discouraged, and the state controlled the health profession. Partly because the party originally perceived most doctors as "class enemies" and because most Soviet medical care was free and the state was always short of money, doctors' salaries were usually inferior to those of highly paid workers.

Finally, any summation of Soviet health should note the physical and psychological effects of collectivization, purges, forced-labor camps, executions, and famine-producing state policies. If terrible plagues such as the Black Death were a thing of the past, Solzhenitsyn's reference to dekulakization and collectivization as "the Peasant Plague" is a fitting analogy.

WOMEN AND FAMILY LIFE

Like Soviet health policy, the Soviet position on women and family life was strongly affected by Marxist ideas. Marx and Engels believed that the capitalist family exploited women, while providing a means for passing on accumulated capital from one male generation to another.

Before 1917, the Bolsheviks insisted on equal rights for women, including the right to vote. They also advocated maternity benefits and the lessening of household chores, which were to be increasingly handled by public institutions such as day care centers, laundries, and communal dining rooms. (On women and housework, Lenin noted in 1919: "Woman continues to be a *domestic* slave, because *petty housework* crushes, strangles, stultifies and degrades her, chains her to the kitchen and nursery.") Some Bolsheviks even predicted the eventual withering away of the family.

Between 1917 and 1920, the Soviet government legislated the political and legal equality of women, removed marriage from church control and made it a civil matter, allowed divorce at the request of either spouse, legalized abortion, and mandated maternity leaves. By these means and by its abolition of property inheritance and the legal distinctions between legitimate and illegitimate children, the government intended to extinguish capitalist family practices, while laying the groundwork for socialist ones.

Lenin and other Bolsheviks also hoped that their backing of women's rights would win them more female support. But in the face of traditional patriarchal ideas, especially in the countryside, this was no easy task.

There were, however, several energetic women, including Alexandra Kollontai and Inessa Armand, who worked hard to improve women's lives and gain their support. In late 1917–early 1918, Kollontai served briefly as the commissar of social welfare. In late 1918, both women were leaders in convening a large Congress of Women Workers and Peasants. In late 1919, Armand became head of *Zhenotdel*, a new Woman's Department of the Communist party's Central Committee. A year later, after her death because of cholera, Armand was succeeded by Kollontai, until she was replaced in 1922, largely because of her key role in the Workers' Opposition Movement (see Chapter 10).

Although the successors of Armand and Kollontai were less prominent, *Zhenotdel* continued to exist until January 1930, when the Politburo abolished it and subordinated women's issues to Stalin's new priorities.

During its decade of existence, *Zhenotdel* published millions of copies of magazines, books, and pamphlets; organized workshops, classes, readings, speeches, and conferences attended by millions of women throughout the Soviet Union; and promoted and encouraged the establishment of female internships, day care centers, cafeterias, and laundries. It also encouraged Central Asian women to resist Moslem female exclusion by such means as publicly burning their veils. Such actions, however, led to violent retaliations by many Moslem men, which caused the deaths of hundreds of Moslem women and *Zhenotdel* workers in the late 1920s.

One of the first realities forced upon the Soviet government after it won the Civil War was its limited financial resources. In the early 1920s, it reduced spending for child care and some other social service programs. One of its hopes had been to create sufficient state institutions to care for homeless children; not only could they be cared for there, but also they could be brought up with solid socialist values. Partly for this reason, in 1918, the state forbade private adoptions.

By 1922, however, years of war and famine had produced about 7 million homeless children, and the government was unable to fund sufficient orphanages. Although the problem of homeless children gradually declined, partly because the state changed its opposition to adoption, it did not disappear.

One reason the problem lingered on was the increasing breakup of families, mainly in the big cities; in Moscow in 1926, there were almost half the number of divorces as there were marriages. A new Russian (RSFSR) Family Code of 1926, besides giving some protection to wives of unregistered, common-law marriages, made divorce easier. One of the spouses could now dissolve a marriage at the registry office, which would then relate the news to the other spouse via a postcard. Not surprisingly, divorce rates spurted higher the following year. The divorces left many women without adequate financial support to care for their children, and some of these children ended up alone on the streets. Thus, the homeless problem continued into the late 1920s; and during future major disruptions, including collectivization, the 1932–1933 famine, and World War II, the number of homeless children once again rose.

By 1930, the party had recruited many new members, but women made up only 13 percent of the total party membership. Furthermore, many new male party members were less cosmopolitan, less utopian, and less committed to female equality than most old Bolsheviks had been. In the 1930s, they followed Stalin's lead in deemphasizing women's issues. Gail Lapidus has noted that an index of party resolutions and decrees for the years 1917 to 1930 listed 301 entries on women, whereas for the following three decades there were only 3 entries.

What was important to Stalin was creating a more educated, technically advanced workforce, and this did open up opportunities for women. Whereas in 1926 only about two-fifths of females aged 9 to 49 could read, by 1939 about four-fifths of them were literate. The number of women completing secondary and higher education also rose sharply.

Although female unemployment and prostitution increased during the NEP, both rates plunged during the 1930s. From 1928 to 1940, women went from about 28 percent of the nonagricultural workforce to about 40 percent of it. In 1940, about three-fifths of the doctors and teachers were women. By then a majority of workers on the kolkhozes and in the cotton, clothing, and printing industries were women. Even in the metal industries, traditionally dominated by men, the number of female workers increased noticeably.

The percentage of women in important government and party positions, however, remained low. After Kollontai was replaced as commissar of social welfare in 1918, there would not be another female commissar/minister until the mid-1950s. During this same period, there were also no female members on the party's Politburo or Orgburo. Also low, especially before World War II, was the number of women in important positions in the countryside, where conservative gender attitudes were strong. In 1936, less than 3 percent of the kolkhoz heads were women. Partly because women held less important offices than men, however, fewer of them were shot or sent to labor camps during the purges.

Although Stalin's rapid industrialization opened up new career opportunities for women, it also reduced some of the their job protections. During the late 1930s, for example, pregnancy leaves were shortened. Women also suffered disproportionally from the government's budget priorities. With most state financing going to heavy industry and defense, little was left for social services and consumer items that might have made women's household chores easier. They did most of the housework, including standing in line for scarce goods.

In 1920, Lenin noted that "few men . . . realize how much effort and trouble they could save women, even quite do away with, if they were to lend a hand in 'woman's work.' But no, that is contrary to the 'right and dignity of a man.' "[9] Lenin's words, however, had little effect on changing male attitudes.

What did change, however, was Soviet family policy. As part of the "great retreat" of the mid-1930s, divorce became harder to obtain. In 1936, the government banned all abortions except when the mother's health was endangered. Two years earlier, there had been 2 to 3 abortions for every birth in Moscow's hospitals and clinics, and birth rates were declining. As a government official told a U.S. journalist, "The Boss says we must have more children."[10] Before the banning, the government permitted a limited public discussion of the issue. Most letters (although not most *printed* letters) to leading Moscow newspapers were opposed to stricter limits on abortions, citing such factors as unavailable contraceptives and crowded living quarters.

Although the new party line stressed family life, large families, and the importance of correctly raising children, the Great Terror disrupted family life by its arrests and by encouraging children to reject any "counterrevolutionary" values held by their parents. During the purge years, a young boy named Pavlik Morozov was glorified for having testified against his father. Because the boy was subsequently killed, supposedly by kulaks but actually by his grandfather and cousin, Soviet media treated him like a Communist martyr.

World War II produced further disruptions in traditional family life. Men (and some women) left home to fight, and women and children took over many of their civilian jobs. By 1943, women made up 53 percent of industrial workers, compared to 41 percent in 1940. By 1942, youth under eighteen years of age composed 15 percent of industrial employees, compared to 6 percent in 1940.

Besides those working as civilians, more than 1 million women served in the armed forces. Except for partisans and thousands of women who received combat assignments (in such positions as tank drivers, pilots, snipers, and machine gunners), the women served in theoretically noncombative capacities (such as doctors, nurses, telephone operators, and truck drivers).

The chaos of the war and great Soviet loss of life in its early years stimulated additional steps to promote the formation of families, keep them together, and encourage childbirth. In 1944, the government decreed the recognition of only registered marriages and made divorces more expensive and difficult to obtain. It also denied certain rights to illegitimate children and condemned sexual libertarianism, which had been encouraged by some early Bolsheviks, although not Lenin. Finally, it encouraged women to have many children by paying bonuses to mothers for each child after the second and awarding medals and making "mother-heroines" of those who had more than six children.

The war also turned millions of children into orphans and left many women widowed or with reduced chances of marrying. In 1950, there were about 100 Soviet women for every 78 men. Among those in the age groups that did most of the fighting in the war, the gap was much larger—census data in-

---

[9] Clara Zetkin, *Reminiscences of Lenin* (New York, 1934), p. 57.
[10] Louis Fischer, *Men and Politics: Europe between Two World Wars* (New York, 1966), p. 347.

Women in War

The following excerpts are taken from Vasili Grossman's wartime sketches as found in his *The Years of War: 1941–1945* (Moscow, 1946) pp. 183–184. They are based on his observations as he traveled on roads from Moscow to Stalingrad in the late summer of 1942. Ellipsis marks are mine.

We travel on through the lovely countryside that is in the grip of war. Women are working everywhere, reaping, threshing, guiding their horse-drawn ploughs, driving tractors and harvesters, sitting behind the wheels of trucks and tackling their dangerous and difficult jobs at advanced railroad sidings. They were the first to fight the fire started by the Germans at Yasnaya Polyana manor [the former estate of Leo Tolstoy near Tula]; it was they who levelled the endless road over which pass tanks, ammunition, and supply trucks. Russian women shouldered the burden of the tremendous harvest—cutting the ears, binding the sheaves, threshing the grain and delivering it to the granaries. Their sunburned hands know no rest from sunrise to sunset. It is they who rule the land just behind the frontline with the help of the youngsters and the old people. The work is not easy for the women.

Wiping the sweat from their brows, they help the horses pull heavily-loaded carts out of the sand in which they are stuck fast. They swing axes in the woods, felling great pine trunks; they drive locomotives; man the ferries at river crossings; carry mail; and work all night long in collective farm, state farm and machine-and-tractor station offices. They spend nights making the rounds of the granaries, guarding the grain. They do not shrink from hard work, and the ominous nights just behind the frontline hold no terrors for them; they gaze calmly at the distant lights of flares as they patrol the village streets. . . .

The Russian woman has assumed the tremendous burden of work in field and factory. But the weight she carries in her heart is heavier than the burden of labour. She does not sleep nights, mourning the loss of her dead husband, son, brother. She waits patiently for a letter from her dear ones who have been reported missing. Her warm, generous heart and unclouded mind help her to live through all the painful setbacks of war. How much grief is there in her words, how keenly she understands the danger that threatens our country; how kind, humane and patient she is!

---

dicate, for example, that among those 40 to 49 years of age in 1959, there were 62 men for every 100 women.

LAW AND LAWLESSNESS

After Stalin's death, the writer Ilia Ehrenburg revealed that his daughter once had a poodle trained to close the dining-room door anytime visitors began speaking in a secretive way. This is just one example of the many effects Stalinist terror had on everyday life. According to one estimate (that of V. P. Popov) based on archival information, more than 40 million people were convicted of crimes in the RSFSR alone between 1923 and 1953.

FIGURE 15.3. As this Khrushchev-era *Krokodil* cartoon suggests, the large loss of men in World War II prevented women hoping to marry from being too choosy.
(Courtesy of Roger Swearingen.)

"I am willing to be your wife, professor."
"I am so happy, Natasha; just help me up!"

The coin of terror sprung from two sides: government laws and government lawlessness. The poet Osip Mandelstam captured the spirit of the first when he referred to Stalin's laws as being "flung like horseshoes at the head, eye or groin."[11] After Stalin's death, Khrushchev referred to the other side of the coin when he spoke of Stalin's "brutal acts of violation of socialist legality." This dual source of terror, although on a smaller scale, began already in Lenin's day and emanated partly from the Marxist-Leninist view of law.

A lawyer by training, Lenin followed Marx in considering all law as having a class character. In the new Soviet state, it was to be used as a state instrument to deal with "enemies of the people" and to help construct socialist society. When the state finally withered away with the establishment of full communism, laws, crimes, courts, and punishments would also disappear.

In the meantime, one way of dealing with counterrevolutionaries was through new revolutionary tribunals (revtribunals) that sprung up toward the end of 1917. A December decree of the Council of People's Commissars stipulated that the personnel for these tribunals should be selected by local soviets. The same decree abolished older existing judicial institutions and replaced justice of the peace courts with local courts (later people's courts), which were to deal with minor civil and criminal cases.

[11] Cited in Nadezhda Mandelstam, *Hope Against Hope: A Memoir* (New York, 1983), p. 13.

The judges in all these courts seldom had any legal training and often no higher education. Their main qualification was their sympathy with the revolution, and their main criterion for dispensing justice was to be their "revolutionary conscience." In these early Soviet days, no body of Soviet laws yet existed to guide the judges, even had they possessed the training to interpret their application. These factors helped give birth to the principle of analogy, later written into Soviet criminal codes. By this principle, a court could find someone guilty of a "socially dangerous act" if it was analogous to any specific code-stipulated crime. During 1918, revtribunals were given the right to sentence individuals to capital punishment and, in 1920, the ability to deny a defendant the right to appear before the court.

Meanwhile, the Cheka was less concerned with legal restrictions of any sort. (See Chapter 9 for the Cheka's early years and the Glossary for it and other Soviet secret-police acronyms.) Although not given any judicial powers when instituted in December 1917, it soon began sentencing people. Thus, it often arrested, investigated, sentenced, and executed "enemies of the people." In 1918 and the first half of 1919, according to one Cheka official, it alone sentenced and carried out more than 8,000 executions in just twenty Russian provinces.

In early 1922, with the Civil War now over, the Cheka was replaced by the GPU (OGPU after the formation of the USSR). It was to operate under the authority of the Commissariat of the Interior and no longer hand down its own sentences. But secret police personnel remained the same and soon regained sentencing powers.

During NEP, Lenin realized that changed economic and political circumstances necessitated new laws and a revised court system. Although revtribunals now disappeared, Lenin continued to use terror as a political weapon to intimidate political enemies. After receiving a new criminal-code outline in 1922, he informed his commissar of justice that a "formula" should be found to connect Socialist Revolutionary (SR) and Menshevik activities "with the international bourgeoisie," and that the death penalty should be handed out for actions that assisted them. He also informed his justice commissar: "The courts must not ban terror . . . but must formulate the motives underlying it, legalize it as a principle, without any make-believe or embellishment. It must be formulated in the broadest possible manner, for only revolutionary law and revolutionary conscience can more or less widely determine the limits within which it should be applied."

Lenin's thoughts were incorporated into the Criminal Code of 1922 and further expanded in the infamous Article 58 of the Criminal Code of 1926. As Alexander Solzhenitsyn, who was sentenced under it in 1945, later noted: "There is no step, thought, action, or lack of action under the heavens which could not be punished by the heavy hand of Article 58. The article itself could not be worded in such broad terms, but it proved possible to interpret it this broadly."[12]

---

[12] *The Gulag Archipelago: 1918–1956*, Vol. I (New York, 1974), p. 60.

Almost immediately after its completion, the 1922 code was used to prosecute a large group of SRs. They were found guilty of many crimes, including working with foreign enemies against the Soviet state. Many later courts also followed up on Lenin's suggestion of linking domestic political opponents with the foreign bourgeoisie. As in many later trials, the guilt of the defendants was decided before they ever stepped into the courtroom.

To be the judge in the Shakty trial of 1928, the government appointed the long-time Marxist Andrei Vyshinsky, rector of Moscow University and professor of criminal law. His main concern was getting the accused to confess their guilt, which some did after being coerced by OGPU interrogators. (The main headquarters of the OGPU was Moscow's infamous Lubianka. About it, Ehrenburg had written in 1923, "Shake someone awake at night and say the word 'Lubianka' and he will stare at his bare feet, say goodbye to everybody, and even if he's young, and healthy as an ox, he'll break down and cry like a baby."[13])

In the late 1930s, by which time Vyshinsky was procurator-general of the USSR, he prosecuted the defendants at the major show trials of the Great Terror. At this time, Vyshinsky shared the sixteenth-century conviction that "confession is the queen of evidence." As in that earlier time, authorities often used torture to obtain confessions. In a telegram of 1939, Stalin himself defended the "application of methods of physical pressure in NKVD practice." Because the defendants in the show trials had to look presentable in court, however, NKVD methods that left no visible traces were preferable. In *The Gulag Archipelago*, Solzhenitsyn lists thirty-one different psychological and physical methods used to obtain confessions. The methods ranged from threats to harm a prisoner's loved ones to a variety of gruesome physical tortures.

Although much of the Soviet state's concern was with political "criminals," there were also more ordinary criminals to be dealt with, although the line between the two categories became increasingly blurred. Under pressure from higher government and party officials, judges in the 1930s often found minor ordinary crimes and behavior such as telling a political joke to be "crimes against the state."

During the NEP, ordinary crime increased, an increase some criminologists blamed on capitalist influences. The true causes were more complex and included poor urban housing conditions, high unemployment, and the numerous homeless youths who had become thieves or worse.

From 1928 to 1933, crime rates continued rising, partly because an ever-widening list of job-related failings now became crimes. The unstable environment created by collectivization, rapid industrialization, and cultural revolution was also responsible for the rising rates. In the countryside, where no regular police forces existed beneath the district (*volost*) level, unhappy peasants increasingly resorted to arson, banditry, hooliganism, and murder against

---

[13] Cited in Mikhail Heller and Aleksandr M. Nekrich. *Utopia in Power: The History of The Soviet Union from 1917 to the Present* (New York, 1986), p. 220.

kolkhozes and their personnel. In the cities, declining living standards and overcrowding helped increase crimes such as theft and hooliganism.

Although the tendency during NEP had been toward more lenient sentences, this trend was reversed during Stalin's revolution from above. In 1932, for example, the government decreed the death penalty for any theft of public property, unless mitigating circumstances were present, in which case the sentence was to be ten years.

The new trend produced so many arrests that by 1933 they were overburdening the courts and prison system. Stalin and Molotov (chairman of the Council of People's Commissars since late 1930) now ordered a more restrained arrest policy. The new Stalin-Molotov position can be seen as part of Stalin's "great retreat," or "internal détente" of the mid-1930s. Just as utopian talk about the family withering away now disappeared, so too did similar comments about law. Vyshinsky began advocating more emphasis on legality, legal training, and professionalism; in 1936, Stalin said the USSR required "stability of laws now more than ever."

But Lenin's advice about legalizing state terror was not forgotten. The decree issued right after Kirov's murder on December 1, 1934, took several new steps in this direction by allowing state terror more scope against terrorists plotting or acting against "functionaries of Soviet power." The new decree stipulated that terrorists were to be tried without being present and that they were to be executed immediately after being found guilty. In the months that followed, the always adaptable Vyshinsky helped provide the appearance of legality to what Tucker has called terror-law.

Despite the law's assistance to the Great Terror, the latter destabilized legal procedures and institutions and purged almost half the legal officials of the time. On the eve of the German invasion of 1941, a majority of judges, procurators, and criminal investigators still possessed little or no legal or higher education.

During Stalin's postwar rule, lawlessness continued to plague the country. As one scholar has stated: "Conditions for law and order could hardly be worse after World War II. . . . Stalin's one-sided preoccupation with crimes against the state and crimes against socialist property and his neglect of preventive measures left society open to disorder and delinquency from below alongside lawlessness from above. . . . his social controls against ordinary crimes of everyday life turned out flaccid, spiritless, and bumbling."[14]

Although the government encouraged more legal training and professionalization, few party leaders had any legal background, and a law career remained an unpopular choice among Soviet youth. In 1950, when Mikhail Gorbachev began studying law (a five-year undergraduate program) at Moscow State University, only a small percentage of higher-education students chose it.

---

[14] Peter H. Juviler, *Revolutionary Law and Order: Political and Social Change in the USSR* (New York, 1976), p. 67.

And when he graduated, Gorbachev, like many other law graduates, did not pursue a law career. When, in 1980, he became a full member of the Politburo, he also became its only member trained in law.

*SUGGESTED SOURCES**

AKSYONOV, VASSILY. *Generations of Winter.* New York, 1994. A historical novel.

ALLILUEVA, SVETLANA. *Only One Year.* New York, 1969.

ANDREEV-KHOMIAKOV, GENNADY. *Naturally Resourceful: Enterprise in the Russian Provinces, 1935–1941.* Boulder, 1995.

BAILES, KENDALL E. *Technology and Society under Lenin and Stalin: Origins of the Soviet Technical Intelligentsia.* Princeton, 1978.

BALL, ALAN M. *Russia's Last Capitalists: The Nepmen, 1921–1929.* Berkeley, 1987.

BARBER, JOHN, and MARK HARRISON. *The Soviet Home Front, 1941–1945: A Social and Economic History of the USSR in World War II.* London, 1991.

BOYM, SVETLANA. *Common Places: Mythologies of Everyday Life in Russia.* Cambridge, Mass., 1994.

BURBANK, JANE. "Lenin and the Law," *SR* 54 (Spring 1995): 23–44.

Burnt by the Sun. A 1994 film set in 1936, directed by Nikita Mikhailov. Available on videocassette.

CHASE, WILLIAM J. *Workers, Society, and the Soviet State: Labor and Life in Moscow, 1918–1929.* Urbana, Ill., 1987.

CLEMENTS, BARBARA EVANS. *Daughters of Revolution: A History of Women in the U.S.S.R.* Arlington Heights, Ill., 1994. Chs. 1–4.

COLTON, TIMOTHY J. *Moscow: Governing the Socialist Metropolis.* Cambridge, Mass., 1995. Chs. 2–4.

CONQUEST, ROBERT. *The Harvest of Sorrow: Soviet Collectivization and the Terror-Famine.* New York, 1986.

COOPERSMITH, JONATHAN. *The Electrification of Russia, 1880–1926.* Ithaca, N.Y., 1992.

DAVIES, R. W. *The Soviet Collective Farm, 1929–1930.* Cambridge, Mass., 1980.

DAVIES, R. W., MARK HARRISON, and S. G. WHEATCROFT, eds. *The Economic Transformation of the Soviet Union, 1913–1945.* Cambridge, England, 1994.

ELWOOD, R. C. *Inessa Armand, Revolutionary and Feminist.* Cambridge, England, 1992.

FARNSWORTH, BEATRICE. *Aleksandra Kollontai: Socialism, Feminism, and the Bolshevik Revolution.* Stanford, Calif., 1980.

FILTZER, DONALD. *Soviet Workers and Stalinist Industrialization: The Formation of Modern Soviet Production Relations, 1928–1941.* Armonk, N.Y., 1986.

FITZPATRICK, SHEILA. *The Cultural Front: Power and Culture in Revolutionary Russia.* Ithaca, N.Y., 1992.

FITZPATRICK, SHEILA, ALEXANDER RABINOWITCH, and RICHARD STITES, eds. *Russia in the Era of NEP: Explorations in Soviet Society and Culture.* Bloomington, 1991.

GARROS, VERONIQUE, NATASHA KORENEVSSKAYA, and THOMAS LAHUSEN, eds. *Intimacy and Terror: Soviet Diaries of the 1930s.* New York, 1995.

* See also books cited in footnotes.

GELB, MICHAEL, ed. *An American Engineer in Stalin's Russia: The Memoirs of Zara Witkin, 1932–1934.* Berkeley, 1991.

GOLDMAN, WENDY Z. "Industrial Politics, Peasant Rebellion, and the Death of the Women's Proletarian Movement in the USSR," *SR* 55 (Spring 1996): 46–77.

———. *Women, the State and Revolution: Soviet Family Policy and Social Life, 1917–1936.* Cambridge, England, 1993.

GORDEY, MICHEL. *Visa to Moscow.* New York, 1952.

GORSUCH, ANNE E. *Flappers and Foxtrotters: Soviet Youth in the "Roaring Twenties."* The Carl Beck papers . . . , no. 1102. Pittsburgh, 1994.

HUSKEY, EUGENE. "A Framework for the Analysis of Soviet Law," *RR* 50 (January 1991): 53–70.

INKELES, ALEX, and RAYMOND A. BAUER. *The Soviet Citizen: Daily Life in a Totalitarian Society.* Cambridge, Mass., 1961.

JAKOBSON, MICHAEL. *Origins of the GULAG: The Soviet Prison Camp System 1917–1934.* Lexington, Ky., 1993.

KHRUSHCHEV, NIKITA. *Khrushchev Remembers.* Boston, 1970.

KNIGHT, AMY W. *Beria: Stalin's First Lieutenant.* Princeton, 1993.

KOTKIN, STEPHEN. *Magnetic Mountain: Stalinism as a Civilization.* Berkeley, 1995.

KUROMIYA, HIROAKI. *Stalin's Industrial Revolution: Politics and Workers, 1928–1932.* Cambridge, England, 1988.

LAPIDUS, GAIL WARSHOFSKY. *Women in Soviet Society: Equality, Development, and Social Change.* Berkeley, 1978.

LENIN, V. I. *On the Emancipation of Women.* Moscow, 1974.

LEWIN, MOSHE. *Russian Peasants and Soviet Power: A Study of Collectivization.* New York, 1975.

LINZ, SUSAN J., ed. *The Impact of World War II on the Soviet Union.* Totowa, N.J., 1985.

MAGGS, PETER B. *The Mandelstam and "Der Nister" Files: An Introduction to Stalin-era Prison and Labor Camp Records.* Armonk, N.Y., 1995.

MCNEAL, ROBERT H. *Bride of the Revolution: Krupskaya and Lenin.* Ann Arbor, 1972.

NOVE, ALEC, ed. *The Stalin Phenomenon.* New York, 1993.

POPOV, V. P. "State Terror in Soviet Russia, 1923–1953 (Sources and Their Interpretation)," *RSSR* 35 (September–October 1994): 48–70.

ROSENBERG, WILLIAM G., ed. *Social and Cultural History of the Soviet Union: The Lenin and Stalin Years.* New York, 1992.

ROSENBERG, WILLIAM G., and LEWIS SIEGELBAUM, eds. *Social Dimensions of Soviet Industrialization.* Bloomington, 1993.

SCOTT, JOHN. *Behind the Urals: An American Worker in Russia's City of Steel.* Bloomington, 1989.

SEGAL, B. M. *The Drunken Society: Alcohol Abuse and Alcoholism in the Soviet Union: A Comparative Study.* New York, 1990.

SERGE, VICTOR. *Memoirs of a Revolutionary, 1901–1941.* London, 1967.

SIEGELBAUM, LEWIS H. *Soviet State and Society Between Revolutions, 1918–1929.* Cambridge, England, 1992.

SOLOMON, PETER H., JR. *Soviet Criminal Justice under Stalin.* Cambridge, England, 1996.

SOLZHENITSYN, ALEKSANDR I. *The Gulag Archipelago: 1918–1956.* 3 vols. New York, 1974–1978.

THURSTON, ROBERT W. *Life and Terror in Stalin's Russia, 1934–1941.* New Haven, 1996.

TROTSKY, LEON. *Problems of Everyday Life, and Other Writings on Culture and Science.* New York, 1973.

————. *The Revolution Betrayed: What Is the Soviet Union and Where Is It Going?* New York, 1957.

TUCKER, ROBERT C. *Stalin in Power: The Revolution from Above, 1928–1941.* New York, 1990.

VIOLA, LYNN. *Peasant Rebels under Stalin: Collectivization and the Culture of Peasant Resistance.* New York, 1996.

VOSLENSKY, M. S. *Nomenklatura: Anatomy of the Soviet Ruling Class.* London, 1984.

YELTSIN, BORIS. *Against the Grain: An Autobiography.* New York, 1990.

CHAPTER 16

Religion and Culture, 1917–1953

Even more so than its tsarist predecessor, the Soviet government attempted to shape the fundamental beliefs of its subjects. Thus, it increasingly strengthened its controls over religion, education, and culture. As in other areas of Soviet life, however, government controls were never as absolute as party leaders desired: Religious and cultural life was more an amalgamation reflecting both official desires (not always uniform) and those of the people.

From 1917 to 1929, the Marxist intellectual Anatoli Lunacharsky served as Russia's commissar of enlightenment, with jurisdiction over education, theaters, libraries, museums, publishing, and films. Lunacharsky tolerated most non-Marxist artists and intellectuals not openly opposing the government and attempted to maintain many of Russia's earlier cultural monuments and artifacts.

Few priests or professors welcomed the new government. Feelings among artists were more varied; for example, the writers Ivan Bunin and Marina Tsvetaeva were hostile to it and emigrated when circumstances permitted, but the futurist poet Vladimir Maiakovsky and the painter/sculptor Vladimir Tatlin supported it.

Before World War I, artists such as Maiakovsky and Tatlin had been involved in modernist movements advocating experimentation and criticizing traditional artistic practices. World War I heightened the alienation of such artists from the old European order and made them more receptive to a new, nonbourgeois, sociopolitical order.

For their part, the Bolsheviks believed they could create a new culture, one that integrated artistic works more into the everyday life of the masses. ("Art belongs to the people," said Lenin.) To help them create such a culture, the Bolsheviks at first employed many of the prerevolutionary avant-garde artists.

For some artists, the chance to use their creative talents in such a way, free from the shackles of the past, seemed like a golden opportunity. In his poem "Order No. 2 to the Army of the Arts" (1921), Maiakovsky wrote: "Comrades, give us a new art—one that will pull the republic out of the mud." Earlier, in

1918, he had declared: "We do not need a dead mausoleum of art where dead works are worshipped, but a living factory of the human spirit—in the streets, in the tramways, in the factories, workshops and workers' home."[1]

During the Civil War years, some artists shared the utopian revolutionary hopes of the new regime. Together with it, they helped narrow the gap between high and popular culture in such spheres as literature, music, and art. They created artistic works and sets for Bolshevik holidays, street pageants, and revolutionary plays. They helped produce political posters and cartoons. They put on factory concerts and poetry readings for the workers. They created works for "agitational" trains and ships that traveled around the country bringing art and Bolshevik propaganda to the masses. They helped establish new museums and free art schools. And they created statues of revolutionary heroes, monuments to the revolution, and designs for new structures such as government buildings and workers' clubs and housing.

Some of the planned creations were gigantic in scope. "The Storming of the Winter Palace" was a massive spectacle appearing on Petrograd's Palace Square during the third anniversary of the Bolshevik takeover. Some 6,000 performers appeared in the production. In 1919, Vladimir Tatlin was commissioned to construct a *Monument to the 3rd International*. It was to be taller than the Empire State Building and made up of a spiral steel framework containing rotating geometric shapes. Like many other plans of these early years, it was too utopian ever to be realized.

During the early and mid 1920s, many artists became disillusioned, and some emigrated abroad. Causes of the disillusionment included in-fighting among rival artistic groups, government policies, unappreciative masses, and the philistinism of Nepmen.

In 1928, Stalin supported extremist groups such as the Russian Association of Proletarian Writers (RAPP), which desired to wage a "cultural revolution" against bourgeois influences, cultural bureaucraticism, and NEP's relative cultural tolerance. This revolution lasted into 1931 and weakened former cultural authorities and tendencies. The Commissariat of Enlightenment was purged of "rightists," accused of following Bukharin and his colleagues; and in 1929, Lunacharsky was replaced as its head. The commissariat also lost control over some aspects of the educational system.

After the cultural revolution had served Stalin's purposes, he brought it to an end in 1931. He now imposed further state controls, which made those of the NEP period look mild in comparison. Stalin's new policies ended most revolutionary and cultural utopianism, some aspects of which had been reinvigorated by the cultural revolution.

During the mid-1930s, as part of what Timasheff has called "the great retreat" (see Chapter 11), a new Stalinist culture emerged. The party operated through a single union for each profession (for example, writers or composers) to oversee culture in an authoritarian manner. The new cultural style was to be comprehensible to the masses, antiexperimental, conformist, optimistic, and

---

[1] Cited in Camilla Gray, *The Russian Experiment in Art, 1863–1922* (New York, 1962), p. 219.

puritanical—the pre-Soviet cultural fascination with sexuality was declared decadent. Culture was to glorify Stalinist socialism and its construction and development; to depict socialist heroes (especially Stalin) winning out over antisocialist villains, both domestic and foreign; and to foster Soviet patriotism.

One means to achieve the last goal (at least among Great Russians) was through a selective glorification of Russia's past, pre-Soviet as well as Soviet. "Russia is a great nation because she gave Pushkin and Lenin to the world" is the way one slogan put it on the centennial of Pushkin's death in 1937. Wherever possible, artists were to draw appropriate analogies between the Russian past and Soviet present, especially between the heroes of yesterday and Stalin. In this respect and in some others, Eisenstein's film *Alexander Nevsky* (1938) was indicative of the times, although its high quality was much less typical.

Although often didactic and controlled from above, Stalinist culture had considerable popular appeal. Its accessibility and optimism, simplistic depiction of good versus evil, and selective glorification of Russia's past struck responsive chords in the hearts of many. So too did the culture's romanticized presentations of the folklife, songs, and dances of the Russians and other Soviet nationalities. These peoples' happy, harmonious relations were part of the fantasy world of Stalinist culture.

Some artists resisted this culture or refused to participate in its construction. Many such individuals were arrested; for example, from 1934 to 1940, more than 1,000 writers suffered such a fate, with some of the greatest, such as the poet Osip Mandelstam, soon perishing. Many of their works never reached the public during Stalin's lifetime. Other works, however, such as some of those of the composer Dmitri Shostakovich, slipped past Soviet censorship even though they contained elements contrary to official Stalinist culture. As in tsarist times, authorities were not always able to decipher the hidden meanings that a piece of literature, music, or art communicated to those skilled in interpreting them.

The perilous Nazi threat during World War II helped produce, as one of the characters in Boris Pasternak's *Doctor Zhivago* later stated, "a breath of fresh air." It brought the Soviet state and many of its citizens closer together. With both religious leaders and ordinary citizens focused on the titanic struggle with Hitler's forces, the government allowed more cultural expression of genuine emotions, especially of patriotic sentiments.

The USSR's World War II alliance with the democratic United States and Great Britain contributed to a less repressive religious-cultural policy. Conversely, however, the end of World War II and the rise of Cold War were accompanied by new Soviet cultural repressions, especially those associated with party spokesman Andrei Zhdanov.

When the Frenchman Michel Gordey visited the Soviet Union in 1950, he noticed that the word *kultura* (culture) appeared everywhere and was used in the broadest sense. Soviet culture was proclaimed the most progressive and advanced in the world. Economic gains; educational, scientific, and technological advances; artistic productions, and victories in international sports competition were heralded as proof of this superiority. The regime contrasted its accomplishments to those of tsarist Russia in such areas as literacy, enlightenment, and death rates and promised an even brighter future.

The official media informed postwar Soviet citizens that good manners and politeness were also signs of being cultured. As Vera Dunham noted: "The regime, especially after the chaos of war, cared a lot about the manageable, predictable, and 'proper' manners of its citizens."[2] It equated good manners with officially accepted behavior.

CHURCH AND STATE

Conflict between the new Communist state and Russian Orthodoxy manifested itself almost immediately. Lenin and the Communists, following Marx, believed that religion was the *"opium* of the people" and that the ruling classes fostered it to keep the masses diverted from their earthly oppression. Lenin's hostility to the Orthodox Church was heightened by its past cooperation with the tsarist government and his fear that it would oppose his new regime.

In the first two months of its existence, the Soviet government issued numerous decrees affecting the Orthodox Church. By these laws, Orthodox landed property and educational institutions were nationalized, and marriage and divorce jurisdiction was handed over to civil authorities.

Meanwhile, in November 1917, the Orthodox Church had taken advantage of the collapse of tsarism and reestablished (after two centuries) the patriarchy. Patriarch Tikhon lost little time in condemning the new Soviet measures. On February 1, 1918, he called upon the Orthodox faithful to rise up in spiritual defense against such acts as the seizure of church lands by the "atheistic masters of the darkness of this world."

Several days later, the government issued the "Decree on Separation of Church from State and School from Church." It ended all state religious subsidies and prohibited religious instruction in any schools "where general educational subjects" were taught. Further, it forbade religious groups from owning any property, including religious buildings and sacred items (such as icons). Instead, such property could be leased, without charge, from the state. The state was also free to use church buildings for other purposes, such as holding political meetings.

Because the February decree ended the former privileged position of the Orthodox Church and promised that "every citizen may profess any religion or none," non-Orthodox religions, with the notable exception of the Catholic Church, generally supported the new law. For a while, some religious groups, including Moslems, Baptists, and sectarians, were treated better than the Orthodox. By the end of the 1920s, however, they too suffered increasing discrimination.

During the Civil War and famine of 1921–1922, the Soviet government

---

[2] *In Stalin's Time: Middleclass Values in Soviet Fiction.* rev. ed. (Durham, N.C., 1990), p. 22.

closed many churches and monasteries and arrested many Orthodox clergy, executing some of them for pro-White and anti-Soviet activities. The Communists used the famine as an opportunity to demand that the Orthodox Church contribute valuables, including consecrated objects, for famine relief.

Soviet policy in these early years and throughout the NEP aimed at countering Orthodoxy by encouraging factional and atheistic competition to the formerly established church. Examples of such were the "progressive" Orthodox splinter group the *Living Church*, formed in 1922, and the League of the Militant Godless, founded in 1925. The latter carried out extensive antireligious propaganda.

Meanwhile, before his death in 1925, Patriarch Tikhon had declared that the Orthodox Church was "nonpolitical," neither Red nor White. Following his death, the government allowed no new patriarchal election, but it did permit Metropolitan Sergei, after several months' imprisonment in late 1926–early 1927, to act as an Orthodox spokesman. In July 1927, he issued a statement of reconciliation that went far beyond Tikhon's more modest final pronouncements. Sergei called on Orthodox believers to display loyalty to the Soviet government and stated that "every blow directed against the [Soviet] Union . . . we regard as a blow directed against us."

Sergei's statement was rejected by many Orthodox believers, including some of the country's leading metropolitans and bishops. Schisms threatened to tear apart the Russian Orthodox Church. Various factions, however, were allowed little time to debate religious differences: During the cultural revolution and first FYP, the government and atheistic enthusiasts (especially Komsomol youth) accelerated their oppression of religion. The government was especially harsh with factions that refused to accept Sergei's reconciliation policy; Komsomolists closed down many rural churches, often burning icons and engaging in other blasphemous activities.

Before Stalin's revolution from above, the Soviet government had experienced some success in weakening religious convictions, especially among younger people. But the forced closing of many rural churches alienated most peasants and helped revive religious passions in the countryside. As Hoffmann has noted, many of the peasants who migrated to Moscow after 1928 also held onto their religious beliefs.

Although persecution of the Orthodox Church lessened slightly during the mid-1930s' "great retreat," it increased again during the Great Terror of the late 1930s, when many Orthodox clergy were arrested. By 1937, with many arrests still to occur, there were only two-fifths as many priests and other religious ministers in the country as there had been in 1926. According to the long-suppressed 1937 census, however, almost three-fifths of the adult population claimed to be religious believers. If believers wished to go to church, many fewer were open than at the end of the 1920s. In Moscow, for example, Colton estimates that in 1930 there were still 224 functioning Orthodox churches, but by 1938 the number had been reduced to 16.

Stalin's policies of the late 1920s and 1930s drove many Orthodox and other believers into underground religious activities. Often acting without the participation of priests or other clergy, underground groups continued to function up to, and beyond, Stalin's death. During and after World War II, they were especially strong in areas that had fallen under German occupation, and they often sided with opposition to the reinstitution of Soviet controls. In the absence of hierarchical religious supervision over them, their religious practices and beliefs grew more varied, sometimes crossing the line separating Orthodoxy from sectarian and other beliefs.

Although hostile to Orthodoxy, Stalin realized that the help of Metropolitan Sergei and other Orthodox believers was vital to defeat Germany in World War II. After Sergei offered to raise money for tank production in 1942, Stalin accepted his help and in 1943 allowed him to be elected patriarch and increase the number of clergy and functioning churches. Stalin also disbanded the League of the Militant Godless. For the next fifteen years, an uneasy compromise characterized Orthodoxy's relations with the state: In exchange for some support, the state allowed it officially to exist and provide liturgical services, but little else, to Orthodox believers.

The fate of other believers during and after the war varied considerably. The state treated some (such as the Baptists) better than others (such as Ukraine's Catholic Uniates). The latter were forced to unite with Orthodoxy, although many continued to practice their religion illegally.

EDUCATION, SCIENCE, AND SCHOLARSHIP

After coming to power, the Bolsheviks hoped to transform schools "from a weapon of bourgeois class rule . . . into a weapon of the Communist rebirth of society." A decree of September 1918 declared that tsarist primary and secondary schools were to be replaced by free, coeducational, nine-year Unified Labor Schools that would be mandatory for those aged eight to seventeen.

These new schools were to be polytechnical. In theory, this meant that students would combine work experiences with learning and be active learners, not passive recipients, and that much of their learning would relate to economic and labor conditions. Champions of this type of education, however, distinguished it from mere vocational education, which they charged was too narrow.

The Bolsheviks made special efforts to overcome illiteracy and to educate further workers and future Communist leaders. Literacy rates rose from less than half to three-fourths of the population aged 9 to 49 in the first two decades (1917–1937) of Soviet rule. New workers' schools in factories attempted to make up for previous educational deficiencies and to prepare at least some individuals (including future party leader Nikita Khrushchev) for additional higher schooling. Although older universities continued to exist, new institutions such as the Sverdlov Communist University in Moscow and the Institute of Red Professors taught primarily Marxist social science to future leaders.

Early Soviet educational theorizing was influenced not only by Marxist ideas, but also by those of Western educators such as John Dewey. As a result, Soviet theorists discouraged many traditional approaches, such as relying on textbooks, homework, examinations, grades, and authoritarian classroom practices.

Yet despite all these revolutionary efforts and utopian hopes, stubborn realities and ideological disagreements often blocked aspirations from being realized. In the schools, new ideas warred against older traditions, sometimes winning out and sometimes not.

During the Civil War, chaotic conditions lessened the availability of teachers and school buildings. Throughout the first decade of Soviet rule, financial shortages and a lack of sufficient trained personnel hampered faster educational advances. By 1925, many children were still not in schools; of those who attended, less than half of them completed three years of schooling. The compulsory nine-year Unified Labor Schools that Lenin had decreed in 1918 were still mainly a dream, with only a small percentage of schools even offering the first five primary years of education. To the dismay of Lenin's widow, Krupskaia, who worked in the Commissariat of Enlightenment, the polytechnical idea was gradually losing out to more specialized vocational training.

In the universities, most professors had been opposed to the Bolsheviks coming to power, and some emigrated or were imprisoned or deported. Those that remained failed to gain the autonomy they desired. According to a 1921 university constitution, the chief university official (the rector) was appointed by the Commissariat of Enlightenment. Moreover, Communist students received preferential admissions treatment and often exercised considerable powers.

Yet, because of a shortage of their own professors, the Communists during the NEP years continued to rely on nonparty professors, thus limiting party control over university education. By 1927, most professors were living fairly well and still exercising some freedoms in regard to their teaching and research, especially outside the ideologically charged social sciences. Professors' demands in 1927 (at a Congress of Scientific Workers) indicate that they overestimated the strength of their position. Unfortunately for them, its precariousness soon became evident.

During the cultural revolution of 1928-1931, attacks on leading "bourgeois" professors and scholars intimidated others into becoming more accommodating to party wishes. Two important scholars who suffered arrest and imprisonment or exile were the historians S. F. Platonov and E. V. Tarle. Many of the most important scholars in the country, such as Platonov, were members of the Academy of Sciences, and the Academy leadership had been in the forefront of defending the interests of the scholarly community. From 1929 to 1933, the Academy was transformed as many Academy staff were arrested or dismissed and hundreds of Communists became Academy members.

This attack on the old specialists and transformation of the Academy was part of the cultural revolution's aim of producing a new cultural elite more representative of the masses. As Stalin declared in February 1931, "Bolsheviks must master technique. It is time that Bolsheviks themselves became experts." From 1927-1928 until 1932-1933, higher-education enrollment (often in technical institutes) tripled, with students of working-class origin increasing from one-fourth to one-half the total. Among future Soviet leaders, Khrushchev,

Brezhnev, and Kosygin all received varying amounts of higher technical training in this period.

Another aspect of the cultural revolution in education was a renewed attack on traditional educational methods that had failed to disappear during NEP. Some critics even talked of the eventual withering away of classroom learning. From 1928 to 1931, schools were placed under increasing factory sponsorship and emphasized more vocational education and political indoctrination.

The cultural revolution in education produced considerable chaos. In 1930, universities outside Moscow and Leningrad were shut down. Some industrial enterprises exploited the labor of schoolchildren, and teachers and professors became more intimidated by politically conscious adult students—by 1931, two-thirds of the higher-education students were 23 years old or older. One army veteran, for example, placed his loaded pistol in front of his professor before submitting to his oral examination. Eventually, educators, parents, and government officials responsible for industry helped bring an end to the educational turmoil.

In June 1931, Stalin called for a cessation of excessive specialist harassment, and in August the party Central Committee criticized schools on several counts. They were accused of failing to provide sufficient general knowledge and higher educational preparation in such basic fields as the natural sciences, mathematics, "native language," and geography. At about the same time, closed universities were reopened but concentrated almost exclusively on the teaching of science.

After the ending of education's cultural revolution in mid-1931, the state increasingly imposed traditional educational practices: standardized textbooks and curriculum, teacher discipline, examinations, and homework. In 1934, the party's Central Committee and the government called upon teachers to teach history by aiding students to remember chronological sequence and important facts and persons and not by spewing out "abstract sociological schemes." That same year, the government reorganized the school system into four-, seven-, and ten-year schools.

Although seven years of schooling was supposed to become mandatory for all children by the end of the decade (up from the four years decreed in 1930–31), this was not fully accomplished, especially in the countryside. Yet from 1932–1933 to 1940–1941, the number of rural pupils in grades five to seven did increase more than threefold.

Grades eight to ten were necessary for higher schooling, which continued to expand, although not as quickly as it had from 1927 to 1933. During the mid and late 1930s, higher institutions selected their applicants primarily based on educational qualifications and not their class origins. The percentage of working-class students declined, and their opportunities were further reduced in 1940, when the government imposed fees for grades eight through ten and for higher education. World War II necessitated educational adjustments and brought with it the destruction of more than 80,000 schools, but in Stalin's postwar years the general trends of the mid and late 1930s continued.

Closely connected to education was the fate of science and scholarship.

Some of the most important scientific achievements in the Stalin years were made in physics. The geneticist and later dissident Zhores Medvedev has attributed this not only to the government's strong support for physics (especially during and after World War II), but also because Stalin granted physicists considerable scientific leeway. Medvedev quotes Stalin as supposedly saying: "Do not bother our physicists with political seminars. Let them use all their time for their professional work."[3] One of the physicists who benefited from this leeway was future dissident Andrei Sakharov, whose work helped the USSR explode its first H-bomb in 1953.

Most scientists and scholars were less fortunate. The most notable case of Stalin's interference in science was connected with the theories of T. D. Lysenko (1898–1976). An agronomist and biologist, Lysenko achieved prominence in the 1930s. He challenged traditional teachings about genetics and heredity. He claimed that environmentally changed plants could pass on their acquired characteristics and that his research could greatly boost crop yields. For ideological and other reasons, Lysenko's view appealed to Stalin, and by 1938 he was president of the Academy of Agricultural Scientists. He helped purge some of the more reputable geneticists, and his destructive influence continued for several decades.

In history, the pivotal figure was the militant M. N. Pokrovsky (1868–1932). This Marxist historian served as a deputy commissar under Lunacharsky and also as the head of the Institute of Red Professors. He was extremely critical of Russian tsars and the former upper classes and believed that the attainment of wealth and capital was their main concern. He also criticized tsarist imperialism and its nationality policy.

In the mid-1930s, his ideas and followers were attacked, as Stalin oversaw the revision of historical writing and teaching. For Stalin, who now selectively glorified Russia's past, Pokrovsky had been too negative toward many aspects of pre-Soviet history, including the reigns of rulers such as Ivan the Terrible and Peter the Great.

Among the many other scholars who suffered under Stalin was the literary theorist Mikhail Bakhtin (1895–1975), who was arrested and exiled in 1929. His many original ideas subsequently exercised a notable influence on literary criticism, linguistics, and cultural studies, both in the USSR and abroad.

LITERATURE

As in the final tsarist decades, so in the early years of the new Soviet state, some of Russia's best literature was its poetry. This was largely because of the continuing presence of many of Russia's finest prewar poets. In 1918, Alexander Blok completed two of his most famous poems, the epic poem *The Twelve* and "The

---

[3] *Soviet Science* (New York, 1978), p. 46. For more on Stalin and Soviet physicists, see David Holloway, *Stalin and the Bomb: The Soviet Union and Atomic Energy, 1939–56* (New Haven, 1994), pp. 200–213.

Scythians." Andrei Bely's poem "Christ Has Risen" appeared that same year. At first, both Blok and Bely appeared to welcome the Bolshevik revolution for their own unique mystical-religious reasons. But Blok's *The Twelve*, which compares twelve Red soldiers with Jesus Christ's twelve apostles, remains open to many interpretations. And two of Blok's final poems, "To Pushkin House" and "On the Poet's Calling" (both 1921), suggest that his love of freedom would have led to increasing disillusionment with the Soviet regime had he not died that same year. By 1921, Bely's enthusiasm for the new order had also cooled, and he left the Soviet Union for a few years, before returning to spend his final decade writing largely apolitical poetry, novels, and memoirs.

Vladimir Maiakovsky (1893-1930) offered more ardent and sustained support to the revolutionary cause. A rebellious, iconoclastic personality who detested the bourgeoisie, Maiakovsky was both a Marxist and a Futurist poet before World War I. He signed the famous Futurist manifesto of 1912—entitled "A Slap in the Face of Public Taste." It called for throwing overboard, from the "steamship of contemporary life," most of the art of the past, including the works of Pushkin, Dostoevsky, and Tolstoy.

After the 1917 revolutions, Maiakovsky preached the necessity of bringing art to the people. Not only did he recite his poems to worker audiences, but also as a gifted graphic artist, he worked for the Russian Telegraph Agency

FIGURE 16.1. The poet (and graphic artist) Vladimir Maiakovsky. (*Sovfoto*.)

turning out propagandistic cartoonlike window posters, accompanied with verse captions. The multitalented Maiakovsky also wrote film scenarios and plays, including two satires, *The Bedbug* (1928) and *The Bathhouse* (1930).

In contrast to most propagandists of the new order, Maiakovsky was a man of great talent. His poetry, both lyrical and political, reflects skilled craftsmanship, imagination, and emotional intensity. Always a moody, stormy personality, Maiakovsky grew increasingly disenchanted with Soviet bureaucraticism. In his two satirical plays, he poked fun at it as well as at the NEP bourgeoisie. Political and personal unhappiness led him to commit suicide in 1930.

Five years earlier, another prominent poet, Sergei Esenin (1895–1925), had also committed suicide. Although Maiakovsky was primarily a poet of the city and new technology, Esenin described himself as "the last village poet." His best poems were marked by simplicity and melodiousness and either celebrated nature and the joys of village life or nostalgically bemoaned their passing or that of his own happier days. Although an early supporter of the revolution, he became disillusioned more quickly than Maiakovsky, and the early 1920s was a period of rocky instability for him. These years were marked by a failed marriage to the American dancer Isadora Duncan, travel abroad, and increasing alcoholism. Many of his late poems reflect his instability and bohemian tavern life. His final poem was written in his own blood. Although officially out of favor for some time, Esenin's melodiousness and simplicity, his nostalgia and sentimentality for the countryside, and his tragic life endeared him to generations of Russian readers, many of whom had also been brought up in the countryside.

Although Maiakovsky and Esenin were the most visible poets of the early 1920s, Pasternak, Akhmatova, Mandelstam (who some regard as the best twentieth-century Russian poet) continued writing and sometimes publishing their poetry. So too did many other poets who had begun writing during Nicholas II's era.

The regime's attitude during the NEP was generally to allow a variety of literary expressions, provided that they were not anticommunist. Lenin, Trotsky, Bukharin, and Lunacharsky all favored such a policy and were more tolerant of past creative works and noncommunist writers than were many of the writers associated with new cultural groups that sprang up during and after 1917.

One of these groups was LEF (Left Front of Art), under Maiakovsky's leadership, and another was the less avant-garde, more plebeian, Proletcult (the Association of Proletarian Cultural and Educational Organizations). Formed in 1917, Proletcult's literary goals were to train and encourage proletarian writers and to create a proletarian literature. Although it declined in significance by the mid-1920s, it produced several offshoots.

But most of the best NEP writers were less political and belonged to neither the Communist party nor the proletarian class. They included such prose writers as Isaac Babel, Mikhail Bulgakov, Leonid Leonov, Yuri Olesha, Boris Pilniak, Alexei Tolstoi, Evgeni Zamiatin, and Mikhail Zoshchenko.

Among the topics dealt with by these and other writers were (1) the revolutionary and Civil War struggles and (2) the role of the individual, imagination, and spontaneity in the new collectivist state that emphasized technology, order, and its own brand of rationalism.

An example of the first concern was Babel's collection of Civil War stories, *Red Cavalry.* Another was Bulgakov's *The White Guard,* a novel that became a popular play under the title *The Day of the Turbines* (1926). Despite some radical writers' criticism of the play (for being too sympathetic to White officers), Stalin liked it and saw it many times. He thought it reflected the ultimate persuasiveness of Bolshevism. The play was revived in the 1930s and again proved popular—the future dissident Raisa Orlova later wrote that she saw it about fifteen times.

Examples of the second topic mentioned were Olesha's *Envy* and Zamiatin's *We* (first published abroad in 1924). The latter is an antiutopian novel that later influenced George Orwell's classic *1984.* The main character of the novel, D-503, is forced at the end of the novel to undergo an operation to eliminate his imagination. In such works as *The Naked Year* and *Machines and Wolves,* Boris Pilniak dealt, in his own complex manner, with spontaneous (and primitive) ways versus the rationalistic-technological approach of the new Communist elite.

At first, the new Soviet state was hostile to most of the tsarist popular "boulevard fiction," believing it a reflection of earlier degenerate values. With the revival of private printing during the NEP, however, some of this earlier popular fiction was permitted to reappear. Foreign works such as the Tarzan stories and novels of Jack London and Upton Sinclair were also popular. So too was science fiction, which included foreign translations and works by some talented Russian writers, including Alexei Tolstoi, Ilia Ehrenburg, and Andrei Platonov. Science fiction lent itself well to the utopianism of the era and to the glorification of technology.

Although it permitted nonideological fiction, the state preferred that which reinforced Communist ideas. Although readers often turned away from propagandistic literature lacking readability, works occasionally appeared containing Communist heroes that endeared themselves to popular tastes. One such hero was the Red Civil War guerrilla leader Chapaev, immortalized in Dmitri Furmanov's *Chapaev* (1923). This novel was subsequently reprinted over and over again and in 1934 became the basis of the immensely popular film of the same name.

Also popular with the public were older works by writers such as Pushkin, Leo Tolstoy, Chekhov, and Gorky. Despite spending most of the 1920s abroad, Gorky remained especially popular during the 1920s and 1930s, partly because his views generally coincided with those of the regime. Russian readers greatly enjoyed the comic satire contained in the stories of the talented Mikhail Zoshchenko and, in the late 1920s and 1930s, in the novels of the satirists Ilf and Petrov, who combined to write *The Twelve Chairs* and *The Golden Calf.*

During the first FYP, the Russian Association of Proletarian Writers (RAPP) gained considerable control over literature and encouraged works praising industrialization and collectivization. Fedor Gladkov's *Cement,* which had appeared in 1925, now became a model for novels dealing with the heroic buildup of Russian industry. In 1932, one of the better examples of these new "production novels" appeared, Valentin Kataev's *Time Forward*, which dealt with the construction of a factory in Magnitogorsk. That same year, the Soviet leadership eliminated previously legitimate literary groups (including RAPP) and established a Union of Soviet Writers to dictate party demands.

The style writers were to follow—and this remained true for the next half-century—was "socialist realism." By its dictates, writers were to portray life in such a way as to help foster the creation of the socialist order and were to do so in a "realistic" manner that could be understood by the people. The new doctrine had no place for "bourgeois formalism, experimentalism, and aestheticism." Gorky's works, along with novels such as *Chapaev*, *Cement*, and *Time Forward*, were held up as positive examples of socialist realism. Although the state had previously restricted writers, by the mid-1930s it was forcing them to write about certain topics and in a certain style. If they did not, their works remained unpublished, and they risked the wrath of the state.

Considering the state's literary demands, it is surprising that any worthwhile works appeared. Mikhail Sholokhov's four-volume *The Quiet Don* (1928–1940), which dealt with Don Cossack life from 1912 to 1922, was one of the best. Alexei Tolstoi's historical novel *Peter the First* (1929–1945) was another quality work.

Two of the best prewar works were not published until decades later. Anna Akhmatova's *Requiem* is a series of poems dealing with the sufferings of those who saw their loved ones victimized by the Stalinist terror—the author's own son fell into NKVD hands beginning in 1935. Bulgakov's *The Master and Margarita* depicts a novelist (the "master") who is writing a book about Jesus and Pontius Pilate and lives in Moscow, where the devil pays a visit. Although the novel's bizarre events violate the tenants of socialist realism, they capture the grotesque spirit of Stalin's rule better than any work following that cultural doctrine.

The relatively freer atmosphere of World War II allowed several works of genuine merit to be published. One was Alexander Tvardovsky's epic poem *Vasili Terkin*, a long work that appeared in serial form from 1942 to 1945 and was aired over the radio. This tale of a common, colorful soldier with folk hero–like qualities was very popular. Two other poets, Vera Ibner and Olga Berggolts, wrote moving poems emanating from their experiences in besieged Leningrad. And first-rate poets such as Akhmatova and Pasternak benefited from the relative ideological relaxation of the war to publish new poems. Konstantin Simonov's *Days and Nights* (1944), dealing with Stalingrad, and some of his war poems won him wide acclaim and popularity.

In August 1946, a party resolution criticized two literary journals, *Star* and *Leningrad*, for publishing the "shallow and insipid" works of Mikhail Zoshchenko and the "decadent" poetry of Akhmatova. Party cultural spokesman Andrei Zhdanov signaled out Zoshchenko's story "Adventures of a Monkey" for special criticism because he thought this story about a monkey who got free from his zoo cage and roamed a town suggested that life was better in a zoo cage than in Soviet society. Citing one of Akhmatova's love poems,

---

Cement: *An Early Socialist Novel*

Cement appeared in millions of copies in the decades after its appearance in 1925. In the novel, Gleb Chumalov returns from the Civil War to find his factory and his wife Dasha greatly changed. The factory no longer operates, and Dasha (liberated by new Soviet ideas and experiences) is no longer a submissive wife. Despite the difficulties that Gleb has adjusting to Dasha's transformed personality and the death of their daughter Nurka, he valiantly gets the factory running again. The excerpts below are taken from F. V. Gladkov, *Cement*, trans. A. S. Arthur and G. Ashleigh (New York, [1929?]), pp. 309–311. Ellipses and bracketed material are mine.

Badin [Chairman of the local District Economic Council] was speaking [to the factory workers and staff]. . . .

"And here is one of our victories on the economic front: a great superhuman victory. The re-starting of our factory. . . . On this day, the fourth anniversary of the October Revolution, we celebrate a new victory on the proletarian revolutionary front. In the course of the struggle the proletariat produces its organisers and heroes. Can our working masses ever forget the name of that fighter, the Red soldier, who gave his life willingly to the great cause of the revolution, can they ever forget the name of Comrade Chumalov? And here we see him, on the labour front, the same self-denying hero as he was on the field of battle. . . .

[Gleb then addresses the group.]

". . . Keep your heads firm on your shoulders and get the work well in hand. That's how you have to look at it! It's no merit when we struggle consciously at the construction of our proletarian economy—! All of us—! United and of one mind. If I am a hero, then you are all heroes, and if we don't work with all our guts towards that kind of heroism, then to hell with us all! But there's one thing I want to say, Comrades: we'll do everything, build up everything, and give points to everyone, and be damned to them! If we only had more technologists like our Engineer Kleist and a bit more of some other things—we'd put it all over Europe in no time. And we'll do it, Comrades! It must be! We've staked our blood on it, and with our blood we'll set fire to the whole world. And now, tempered in fire, we're staking everything on our labour. Our brains and our hands tremble—not from strain but from the desire for new labours. We are building up socialism, Comrades, and our proletarian culture. On to victory, Comrades!"

Zhdanov referred to her as "half-nun and half-whore." Both writers were kicked out of the Writer's Union, and Akhmatova had to scrub floors to make a living.

The actions against the two authors became part of the new party assault against foreign influences and deviations from socialist realism, an assault that continued throughout the rest of Stalin's reign.

ART AND ARCHITECTURE

Early Soviet art, like early Soviet literature, benefited from the continuing presence of many gifted artists whose careers had begun before 1917. Lunacharsky's Commissariat of Enlightenment established a Department of Fine Arts (IZO) in 1918 and artists such as Vladimir Tatlin, Mark Chagall, Vasili Kandinsky, and Alexander Rodchenko worked under its jurisdiction to bridge the gap between art and the people. In 1922–1923, however, several of the more notable artists emigrated.

Among them was Marc Chagall. In 1918–1919, he had served as art commissar in his native region of Vitebsk and as head of the Vitebsk School of Art. On the first anniversary of the Bolshevik revolution, his multicolored animal creations decorated Vitebsk's streets for the celebration, but some Communists wanted to know what a flying horse or green cow had to do with Marx and Lenin. Kasimir Malevich, the founder of Suprematism, who championed geometrical, abstract, nonrepresentational art, criticized Chagall's art from a different perspective. Malevich declared it insufficiently abstract. In 1919, Malevich led an artistic revolt against Chagall at the Vitebsk art school and soon replaced him as its head. Chagall then moved to Moscow, where he became art director of the Moscow State Jewish Theater (1919–1922). He painted murals in the theater and worked on production sets. Again, however, his work was insufficiently appreciated, and a government arts' committee decided that he deserved only a meager state stipend. In 1922, he settled abroad.

That same year Kandinsky also emigrated. Like many other leading artists, he had become active in the Institute of Artistic Culture, established under IZO in 1920. But in 1920 and 1921, a majority of the institute's members rejected Kandinsky's belief that art was primarily an expression of the "inner spirit"; with artists such as Tatlin and Rodchenko in the forefront, they believed that the artist must become more like an engineer, using his tools and materials for the good of society. Instead of remaining in Russia, Kandinsky accepted a position at the Bauhaus school in Germany, where he helped make it one of the most important modernistic artistic influences of the twentieth century.

Two other artists who found themselves swimming against the tide of the new artistic utilitarianism were Anton Pevsner and his younger brother Naum Gabo, and they also emigrated. Both had spent time in Western Europe before 1917, where they familiarized themselves with Cubism and other new artistic techniques. In 1920, they wrote a manifesto declaring that art had an absolute and independent value, regardless of what role it played.

For their part, Tatlin and his supporters attempted to be useful to the masses. Besides his design for a *Monument to the 3rd International* (mentioned earlier), Tatlin designed such products as an energy-efficient stove and workers' clothes—other artists such as Malevich, Rodchenko, and Natalia Popova also worked to design clothes for the new Soviet man and woman.

In the early 1920s, several proletarian artists founded the Association of Artists of Revolutionary Russia, proclaiming that their group would reflect the daily life of the masses. This organization became stronger as the decade proceeded; their type of "heroic realism" increasingly became the type of art favored by party leaders. A 1975 Soviet reference book lists what it considered to be some of the notable paintings and sculptures of the 1923–1932 period: various statues and portraits of Lenin; *The Cobblestone Is a Weapon of the Proletariat;*

Worker, Sower; A Woman Deputy and the Chairwoman; and *Meeting of a Village Party Cell.*

The avant-garde painters who did remain in Russia increasingly turned away from painted canvases and sculpture. They followed Tatlin's example of branching into other areas. Besides designing clothing, furniture, and buildings, they created stage and film sets (most notably for the great theater director Vsevolod Meyerhold) and poster and typographical designs.

An early breeding ground for new architectural ideas was the Higher Artistic and Technical Workshops in Moscow (VKhUTEMAS), which originated as a result of the merger of two pre-Soviet art schools. VKhUTEMAS had various departments, including separate ones for painting, sculpture, and architecture, and there was considerable cross-fertilization between the different departments.

In 1923 and 1925, two competing architectural groups emerged from the VKhUTEMAS faculty. The first was the Association of New Architects, which was influenced by the modernist ideas and art of such individuals as Malevich. The second was the Association of Contemporary Architects, which became the bastion of Constructivist (or Functionalist) architects, who believed that modern technology and materials and the utilitarian purpose of a building should determine its form.

Of the two groups, the Constructivists built the most buildings. One example is the *Izvestiia* newspaper building (1925–1927). Its stress on pure geometrical shapes, devoid of aesthetic compromises, is typically Constructivist. Horizontal and vertical lines, squares and circles, asymmetrical balconies, and the newspaper's masthead at the top of the facade are among its most notable features (see Figure 16.2).

The buildings of the Constructivists bore some similarities to the Functional architecture of Western architects such as Le Corbusier (who visited the Soviet Union on several occasions) and Walter Gropius. Throughout the 1920s, Soviet architects continued to have contacts with Western counterparts.

Meanwhile, however, competition and name-calling between the two main architectural associations weakened both groups, and party controls over architecture tightened. An important step in the process occurred in 1932, when all independent architectural groups were abolished and a single Union of Soviet Architects was formed. Constructivism was increasingly criticized, and a new Stalinist monumental architecture, characterized by eclectic borrowings, came to the forefront.

An early indication of it can be seen in the plans for a new Palace of Soviets. To make way for it, Stalin approved the destruction of the massive Cathedral of Christ the Savior (see Figure 7.1). After it was blown up in 1931, proposals for the new building were submitted. By 1937, after considerable preparation, work was begun digging out the foundation pit. The plans called for a building with a main hall that would seat 21,000 people. Although Lenin was already being honored in countless ways, including the display of his body in a new Red Square mausoleum completed in 1930, the new Palace of Soviets was to honor him further (as well as Stalin). It was to be topped by an

FIGURE 16.2. Izvestiia
Building, Moscow, 1927,
architect G. Barkhin.
(From A History of Russian
Architecture *by William
Craft Brumfield, Cambridge
University Press 1993,
p. 471.)*

aluminum Lenin statue, more than twice as tall as the Statue of Liberty—
Lenin's index finger alone was to be over 19 feet long. The whole structure was
to be higher than the Empire State Building, then the tallest building in the
world. But like many of Stalin's grandiose plans, this project was never completed—the foundation pit was, however, put to good use: Two decades after it
was dug out, a vast outdoor swimming pool was constructed there. (See Chapter 22 for the rebuilding of the Cathedral of Christ the Savior during the 1990s.)

Other monumental buildings were built, however, such as the Leningrad
House of Soviets (1936–1941), which was 220 meters (about 240 yards) long.
After World War II, seven tall similar buildings arose to dominate the Moscow
skyline. They were in the monumental Soviet mold, but reflected various other
domestic and foreign historical influences. According to Khrushchev, Stalin
wanted them built to impress foreigners.

The most dominant of the seven new buildings was the main structure
of Moscow State University, constructed (partly by prison laborers) from
1949–1953. With its elaborate decorations and its wasted spaces, it was contrary to Constructivist functionalism. To Stalin, however, space was just as dis-
pensable as were humans; what mattered was the building's symbolism. Indeed, it symbolized the Stalin era well. Although Stalin undoubtedly thought

FIGURE 16.3. Moscow State University, 1949–1953, architects L. Rudnev, P. Abrosimov and A. Khriakov.

that it would reflect the power of the Soviet state, its cultural achievements, and his own heroic transformation of the country, others have thought it more symbolic of other aspects of Stalinism. The Yugoslavian Mihajlo Mihajlov found that its ominous mass made one feel helpless and insignificant. Khrushchev, although no great art critic, saw in it "an ugly, formless mass," as well as a great "waste of money."[4]

MUSIC

Although the nature of music made it less susceptible to government dictates than literature and art, the party still interfered in the musical world, especially under Stalin. During this era, the NEP period experienced the greatest musical diversity. Russian and Western classical music could be heard along with revolutionary songs and marches. Bands played jazz and Western and domestic

[4] In a stimulating reappraisal of "The Stalinist Skyscraper" at the 1994 National Convention of the American Association for the Advancement of Slavic Studies, Anatole Senkevitch, Jr., indicated, however, that there was much more to the seven tower buildings than first meets the eye. He stated that they were a significant departure from the socialist realism that ruled in most other artistic cultural spheres. Paradoxically, they were more in keeping both with Moscow's architectural tradition (especially its medieval architecture) and with U.S. utopian architectural thinking than most critics of the buildings have realized.

popular music for dances such as the foxtrot, waltz, and tango. Although Igor Stravinsky had settled in Western Europe before the 1917 revolutions and the young Sergei Prokofiev (1891–1953) began a fifteen-year stay there in 1918, their music was performed in their native land. Other composers sympathetic to modernist music remained in Russia, where during the NEP years they could still hear the music of modern Western composers such as Arnold Schoenberg. The Association for Contemporary Music (ASM) was affiliated with the International Society for Contemporary Music and prided itself on keeping up-to-date with the latest musical developments. Finally, in the spirit of the revolution, Russian musicians experimented with revolutionary musical initiatives, such as establishing a conductorless orchestra. "The First Symphonic Orchestra without a Conductor," which continued in existence for a decade after its founding in 1922, attempted to put collectivist principles in practice by doing away with the autocratic position of conductor.

During the cultural revolution of 1928–1931, the Russian Association of Proletarian Musicians (RAPM), with party approval, dominated music. It prevented the playing and publishing of a wide range of music, such as the modernist music championed by ASM, much of the older classical repertoire, jazz, and most lighter music.

After Stalin ended the cultural revolution in 1931 and RAPM in 1932, some of the purged music, including jazz, made a strong comeback. But as with writers and other cultural figures, composers in 1933 were brought under tighter control with the establishment of a single party-dominated union, the Union of Soviet Composers.

The next major development began in 1936 when Stalin and his followers unleashed an attack on cultural formalism (modernism). After Stalin and Molotov attended a performance of Shostakovich's opera *Lady Macbeth of the Mtsensk District*, the party newspaper *Pravda* attacked it in an editorial entitled "A Muddle Instead of Music." Up until this point, the opera had been performed on an average of once a week in both Moscow and Leningrad since first appearing in early 1934. But the editorial now suddenly discovered it to be too avant-garde, dissonant, jazz-influenced, vulgar, pornographic, and decadent. It stopped being performed, and the attack on it marked the beginning of other assaults on similar "formalist" works in other artistic spheres, including the theatrical productions of Meyerhold, Constructivist architecture, and the poems of Pasternak.

After some confusion, the new musical parameters became clear. Outside them were musical dissonance, avant-garde experimentation, and Western jazz; inside were melody, folk influences, classical music, sterilized Soviet jazz, and optimistic popular tunes.

During World War II, music reflected not only the heartfelt patriotism of many Soviet citizens, but also the influence of new allies. Jazz, for example, threw off some of its prewar restraints and became more like U.S. jazz—wartime enthusiasm for jazz was so great that pilots, cooks, and even the NKVD formed jazz groups of their own.

In 1948, Shostakovich again found himself under attack, along with several other prominent composers including Sergei Prokofiev and Aram Khachaturian. Shostakovich had earlier managed to restore his Soviet reputation by such works as his Seventh Symphony, which was awarded a Stalin prize in 1942. Prokofiev, after his return to Russia in 1934, had composed symphonic, ballet, opera, and other music, including the score for Eisenstein's film *Alexander Nevsky*. In 1948, however, Zhdanov and others attacked him as well as Shostakovich and Khachaturian for their modernistic music, which Zhdanov thought reflected too much Western influence and too little harmony. (As with Shostakovich earlier, Prokofiev later regained official favor, being awarded a Stalin prize in 1952 for his Seventh Symphony.)

As part of the *Zhdanovshchina* of the late 1940s, the government also turned against jazz and Western-influenced popular music. In 1949, declaring that jazz was a means of spreading U.S. imperialism, it banned the saxophone.

The treatment of two corpses in March 1953 serves as a final commentary on Stalin and Soviet music. One corpse was Stalin's, the other was Prokofiev's. They both died on the same day, March 5th. Because all the available flowers in the city went for Stalin's funeral, there were none left for Prokofiev's. Because of the vast crowds trying to make their way to obtain one last glimpse of the body of the "Leader and Teacher of All Times and All Peoples," few people could get through police barriers to attend Prokofiev's funeral. Finally, because the name Stalin dominated the newspapers, there was no room for a Prokofiev obituary.

POPULAR CULTURE AND THE STATE

As in other cultural areas, the party attempted to mold popular culture to serve its own purposes. Yet despite its control over the powerful twentieth-century mediums of film and radio, it was only partly successful. During the 1920s, party and Komsomol leaders often criticized frivolous bourgeois activities such as dancing the foxtrot or other Western dances; but Komsomol clubs eventually recognized that to attract Soviet youth they had to permit such dancing. Government propaganda presented John Ford's 1940 classic *Stagecoach* (renamed *The Journey Will Be Dangerous*) as a frontier battle of native Indians resisting white imperialists, but such propaganda could not prevent Soviet viewers from appreciating the U.S. film for their own reasons. After Mikhail Gorbachev, then a young Moscow State University student, viewed the musical film *Kuban Cossacks* (1949), he told a Czech friend that it painted a false picture of collective-farm life.

Some elements of popular culture were carryovers from more traditional pastimes. Throughout this period, in both urban and rural areas, most leisure time was spent talking and interacting with friends. Such interaction included drinking, singing, dancing, and playing games such as cards, and it occurred primarily in each other's homes and apartments or outside in streets, yards, courtyards, and parks. Many of the peasants who became urban workers continued associating with other former peasants and engaged in entertainment they had enjoyed in their villages, such as folk dancing or singing to the accompaniment of an accordion. People also still went ice skating, sledding, swimming, and mushroom-gathering and, where possible, attended circuses and puppet shows.

Traditional activities lasted longest in the countryside, and modern innovations such as films and radios penetrated the countryside more slowly than in urban areas. Yet by the late NEP period, older peasant parents grew increasingly alarmed to see rural youth dancing the foxtrot or tango rather than more traditional folk dances.

Of the new museums, libraries, and parks, some, such as Moscow's Lenin Museum, served mainly a political purpose. Parks such as Moscow's large Park of Culture and Rest (Gorky Park), despite propaganda on posters and loudspeakers carrying Radio Moscow, also offered genuine relaxation— swimming, rowing, walking, dancing, chess, and rides including a ferris wheel.

Some of the most popular Soviet productions, such as the novel and film *Chapaev*, managed to propagandize Soviet values by building upon traditional Russian ones—the Civil War hero Chapaev possessed qualities that would have endeared him to Russian audiences of earlier times. Other productions became popular because they appealed to people's desires. Vera Dunham has indicated how, after World War II, the Stalinist regime encouraged the creation of fictional heroes and writings that appealed to the aspirations of the Soviet "middle class" (see Chapter 14).

Despite some on-again-off-again restrictions, foreign imports such as jazz, Western dances, and selected Western films and literature became a permanent part of Soviet popular culture. The most popular films shown at Moscow University during Gorbachev's years there were the Tarzan films. After their showings, students displayed their enthusiasm by crying out Tarzan-like howls.

Although the Tarzan movies were primarily escapist, rather than ideological, Soviet leaders preferred propagandistic films. Lenin declared in 1922 that "the cinema is the most important of all the arts." According to Robert Tucker, Stalin personally approved new films before they were shown to the public. He also frequently gave personal directions to directors like Eisenstein. No doubt, films such as Eisenstein's *Battleship Potemkin* (1926), *October* (1927), *Alexander Nevsky* (1938), and *Ivan the Terrible* (Part I, 1945) served to reinforce Soviet ideology.

The more Stalin interfered, the more directors and films suffered. Peter Kenez has referred to the 1925–1929 period as the Golden Age of Soviet cinema. It was followed, however, by a cultural revolution in which the works of great silent film directors and theorists such as Eisenstein, A. Dovzhenko, L. Kuleshov, V. Pudovkin, and D. Vertov came under increasing attacks, partly for being too "formalist" and experimental. Their films were criticized for not being more accessible to the tastes of peasants and workers—it was true that most viewers of the 1920s preferred simpler films of adventure, comedy, or romance, such as foreign films starring Douglas Fairbanks, Charlie Chaplin, and Mary Pickford.

Although Soviet movie attendance increased in the 1930s, as it did worldwide, fewer Soviet films were produced per year than in 1928. Few foreign films were imported. Soviet scripts were closely scrutinized, and "movies for the millions" were turned out, including adventure stories, comedies, and musicals. Stalin especially liked films depicting himself acting in a heroic manner, but he also enjoyed some of the musicals of the decade.

As in literature, so in films, the works of World War II were more full of genuine emotion than earlier or later Stalinist productions. Three of the best war films, *The Rainbow, Zoia* (about Zoia Kosmodemianskaia), and *She Defends the Motherland* revolved around heroic female partisans. *Once There Lived a Little Girl* was a simple but powerful film about a little girl during the siege of Leningrad.

Stalin's final years were dismal ones for the Soviet film industry. Relatively few films were produced, and a higher proportion were heavily propagandistic, often depicting Stalin as a heroic war leader. Films about Russian heroes of the past, especially scientists, composers, writers, and admirals, also characterized these final Stalinist years.

Along with films, sporting events, especially soccer, attracted many spectators. During the early NEP years, various groups put forth competing positions regarding sports. A group of exercise advocates called the "Hygienists" opposed spectator sports and wanted to eliminate grandstands. By the late 1920s, however, the party had given its blessing to spectator sports, and in 1928 the Dynamo Stadium was erected in Moscow with 35,000 seats. Other large stadiums were soon constructed in other cities. By 1939, 10 million spectators viewed soccer games throughout the country.

Before World War II, no indoor arena could seat more than 2,000 people, thus limiting the popularity of indoor contests. In the winter, hockey teams played outdoors, and track and field competitions were held in milder weather, but neither type of competition attracted large crowds.

During Stalin's final years, the popularity of soccer continued to grow. The same was true for hockey, even though indoor ice arenas remained nonexistent. Two reasons for the growth of interest in hockey were the adoption in 1946 of Canadian hockey (different than the earlier Russian hockey) and the participation of Soviet teams against those of foreign countries.

After a lull at the end of the 1940s, Soviet participation in international competitions picked up in the early 1950s. This was best evidenced by the USSR's first Olympic participation, in the 1952 summer Olympic games at Helsinki. Soviet athletes, male and female, performed well there, especially in gymnastics, weightlifting, and wrestling, and the men's basketball team made it to the finals before losing to the U.S. team. Although Soviet sources contended that overall the Soviet athletes had tied U.S. athletes for dominance at the games, Western sources gave a small edge in the total unofficial count to the U.S. team.

From almost its beginning, the Soviet state emphasized the importance of good physical health and training. It maintained that healthy bodies increased the country's military preparedness and the productivity of workers. In 1931, the Komsomol put forward the "Ready-for-Labor-and-Defense" series of fitness tests, which helped to popularize physical fitness. In 1935, the head of Komsomol urged Soviet athletes to surpass world records. In 1948, the Communist party called for Soviet dominance in international sports competition as proof of socialism's superiority, and the good Soviet showing at the 1952 Olympics was cited as proof of the advanced development of Soviet culture.

Yet, despite its best efforts, the state could not completely control and manipulate the world of sports for its own purposes. Soccer players and fans alike, for example, often manifested behavior that Soviet officials considered uncultured. In the late 1940s, the Soviet press criticized the frequent "hooliganism" of soccer players, and a campaign was begun to encourage more gentlemanly behavior. Soon the press was reporting that some soccer players were avidly studying Marxism-Leninism, going to museums, and attending poetry readings and lectures on classical opera. Ultimately, however, this campaign to make Soviet athletes more "cultured" did little good. The state had its sports priorities, and athletes and fans had theirs. As in other areas of popular culture, these priorities did not always coincide.

SUGGESTED SOURCES*

BAILES, KENDALL. *Science and Russian Culture in an Age of Revolutions: V. I. Vernadsky and His Scientific School, 1863–1945*. Bloomington, 1990.

BOWLT, JOHN E. *Russian Art of the Avant-Garde: Theory and Criticism, 1902–1934*. New York, 1976.

BROOKS, JEFFREY, "Socialist Realism in *Pravda*: Read All about It!" *SR* 53 (Winter 1994): 973–991.

BROWN, EDWARD J. *Russian Literature since the Revolution*. Cambridge, Mass., 1982.

BROWN, MATTHEW. *Art Under Stalin*. Oxford, 1991.

CHAGALL, MARC. *My Life*. London, 1965.

CLARK, KATERINA. *Petersburg: Crucible of Cultural Revolution*. Cambridge, Mass., 1995.

COLTON, TIMOTHY J. *Moscow: Governing the Socialist Metropolis*. Cambridge, Mass., 1995. Chs. 2–4.

CURTISS, JOHN SHELTON. *The Russian Church and the Soviet State, 1917–1950*. Boston, 1953.

EDELMAN, ROBERT. *Serious Fun: A History of Spectator Sports in the USSR*. New York, 1993.

ENTEEN, GEORGE M. *The Soviet Scholar-Bureaucrat: M. N. Pokrovskii and the Society of Marxist Historians*. University Park, Penn. 1978.

FITZPATRICK, SHEILA. *The Commissariat of Enlightenment: Soviet Organization of Education and the Arts under Lunacharsky, October 1917–1921*. Cambridge, England, 1970.

———. *The Cultural Front: Power and Culture in Revolutionary Russia*. Ithaca, N.Y., 1992.

———. *Education and Social Mobility in the Soviet Union, 1921–1934*. Cambridge, England, 1979.

———, ed. *Cultural Revolution in Russia, 1928–1931*. Bloomington, 1978.

Freeze, Gregory L. "Counter-reformation in Russian Orthodoxy: Popular Response to Religious Innovation, 1922–1925," *SR* 54 (Summer 1995): 305–339.

Fulop-Miller, René. *The Mind and Face of Bolshevism: An Examination of Cultural Life in Soviet Russia*. New York, 1965.

GLEASON, ABBOTT, PETER KENEZ, and RICHARD STITES, eds. *Bolshevik Culture: Experiment and Order in the Russian Revolution*. Bloomington, 1985.

GRAHAM, LOREN R. *Science and Philosophy in the Soviet Union*. New York, 1972.

* See also books cited in footnotes, and note that many of the literary works mentioned in the text are available in English translations and some of the films are available on video.

GÜNTHER, HANS, ed. *The Culture of the Stalin Period*. New York, 1990.

HOFFMANN, DAVID L. *Peasant Metropolis: Social Identities in Moscow, 1929–1941*. Ithaca, N.Y., 1994.

HOLMES, LARRY E. *The Kremlin and the Schoolhouse: Reforming Education in Soviet Russia, 1917–1931*. Bloomington, 1991.

HUDSON, HUGH D., JR. *Blueprints and Blood: The Stalinization of Soviet Architecture, 1917–1937*. Princeton, 1994.

JORAVSKY, DAVID. *The Lysenko Affair*. Cambridge, Mass., 1970.

———. *Soviet Marxism and Natural Science, 1917–1932*. New York, 1961.

JOSEPHSON, PAUL R. *Physics and Politics in Revolutionary Russia*. Berkeley, 1991.

KENEZ, PETER. *Cinema and Soviet Society, 1917–1953*. Cambridge, England, 1992.

KOPELEV, LEV. *The Education of a True Believer*. New York, 1980.

LINZ, SUSAN J, ed. *The Impact of World War II on the Soviet Union*. Totowa, N.J., 1985.

MACDONALD, IAN. *The New Shostakovich*. Boston, 1990.

MAGUIRE, ROBERT A. *Red Virgin Soil: Soviet Literature in the 1920's*. Princeton, 1968.

MALLY, LYNN. *Culture of the Future: The Proletcult Movement in Revolutionary Russia*. Berkley, 1990.

MANDELSTAM, NADEZHDA. *Hope Against Hope: A Memoir*. New York, 1970.

MAYAKOVSKY, VLADIMIR. *The Bedbug and Selected Poetry*. New York, 1970.

MEDVEDEV, ZHORES A. *The Rise and Fall of T. D. Lysenko*. New York, 1969.

MIHAJLOV, MIHAJLO. *Moscow Summer*. New York, 1965.

O'CONNOR, TIMOTHY E. *The Politics of Soviet Culture: Anatolii Lunacharsky*. Ann Arbor, 1983.

ORLOVA, RAISA. *Memoirs*. New York, 1983.

PERIS, DANIEL. "Commissars in Red Cassocks: Former Priests in the League of the Militant Godless," *SR* 54 (Summer 1995): 340–364.

POSPIELOVSKY, DIMITRY. *A History of Soviet Atheism in Theory and Practice, and the Believer*. 3 vols. New York, 1987–1988.

———. *The Russian Church under the Soviet Regime, 1917–1982*. 2 vols. Crestwood, N.Y., 1984.

PROFFER, CARL R., et al., eds. *Russian Literature of the 1920s: An Anthology*. Ann Arbor, 1987.

RAEFF, MARC. *Russia Abroad: A Cultural History of the Russian Emigration, 1919–1939*. New York, 1990.

READ, CHRISTOPHER. *Culture and Power in Revolutionary Russia: The Intelligentsia and the Transition from Tsarism to Communism*. New York, 1990.

ROBIN, REGINE. *Socialist Realism: An Impossible Aesthetic*. Stanford, 1992.

ROSENBERG, WILLIAM G., ed. *Bolshevik Visions: First Phase of the Cultural Revolution in Soviet Russia*. Ann Arbor, 1984.

SCHWARZ, BORIS. *Music and Musical Life in Soviet Russia, 1917–1981*. Rev. ed. Bloomington, 1983.

SHENTALINSKY, VITALY. *Arrested Voices: Resurrecting the Disappeared Writers of the Soviet Regime*. New York, 1996.

SINYAVSKY, ANDREI. *Soviet Civilization: A Cultural History*. New York, 1990.

SOIFER, VALERII. *Lysenko and the Tragedy of Soviet Science*. New Brunswick, N.J., 1994.

STARR, S. FREDERICK. *Red and Hot: The Fate of Jazz in the Soviet Union, 1917–1980*. New York, 1983.

STITES, RICHARD. *Revolutionary Dreams: Utopian Vision and Experimental Life in the Russian Revolution*. New York, 1989.

———. *Russian Popular Culture: Entertainment and Society Since 1900*. Cambridge, England, 1992. Chs. 2–4.

———, ed. *Culture and Entertainment in Wartime Russia*. Bloomington, 1995.

STRUVE, GLEB. *Russian Literature under Lenin and Stalin, 1917–1953*. Norman, Okla., 1971.

TAYLOR, RICHARD, and DEREK SPRING, eds. *Stalinism and Soviet Cinema*. London, 1993.

TROTSKY, LEON. *Literature and Revolution*. Ann Arbor, 1960.

VISHNEVSKAYA, GALINA. *Galina: A Russian Story*. San Diego, 1984.

VON GELDERN, JAMES. *Bolshevik Festivals, 1917–1920*. Berkeley, 1993.

———, and RICHARD STITES, eds. *Mass Culture in Soviet Russia: Tales, Poems, Songs, Movies, Plays, and Folklore, 1917–1953*. Bloomington, 1995.

YOUNGBLOOD, DENISE J. *Movies for the Masses: Popular Cinema and Soviet Society in the 1920s*. New York, 1992.

ZHDANOV, ANDREI A. *Essays on Literature, Philosophy, and Music*. New York, 1950.

CHAPTER 17

The Khrushchev Era: Destalinization, Coexistence, and Confrontation

From 1953 to 1964, the colorful and energetic Nikita Khrushchev served as first secretary of the Communist party. He was never as powerful as Stalin had been, however, and in 1964 he was overthrown.

Those who removed him criticized him for his erratic ways and abuse of power, and Richard Nixon, who was U.S. vice-president when Khrushchev came to power, later wrote of his "brutal will to power." In the United States, Khrushchev was perceived as the "Butcher of Budapest" (for putting down the Hungarian Revolt of 1956) and as a warmonger. Although Khrushchev later insisted that his words had been twisted, U.S. citizens believed he had threatened them in 1956 with the phrase "We will bury you!" His role in the construction of the Berlin Wall in 1961 and the Cuban Missile Crisis of 1962 further strengthened his warmongering reputation.

Yet Khrushchev was more complex than these perceptions suggest. Despite his often erratic ways, his policies were shaped not only by his own "will to power," but also by several consistent ideas. He thought that Stalin had deviated from Leninism, that a main purpose of the party's activity was to raise Soviet living standards, and that in a nuclear age peaceful coexistence was necessary.

In 1956, in a "secret speech" to the Twentieth Party Congress, Khrushchev disclosed some of Stalin's crimes and harshly criticized him. For decades afterwards, the Stalin issue would remain central to Soviet political life. How much of the Stalinist past should be revealed? Which Stalinist practices should be maintained and which rejected? Khrushchev's main political accomplishment was in raising these questions and in taking steps to free the USSR from part, although not all, of the Stalinist legacy.

KHRUSHCHEV'S BACKGROUND, CHARACTER, AND BELIEFS

At the time of Stalin's death, Khrushchev was fifty-eight years old. He had begun life in a peasant hut in Kalinovka, a village in the Kursk Province. As a young teenager, however, he moved with his family to the outskirts of Yu-zovka (later called Stalino and then Donetsk). In Yuzovka, he learned the metal-fitting trade and became a skilled worker in foreign-owned factories and plants connected with the local mining industry. In his memoirs, Khrushchev stated that in Yuzovka he observed firsthand the capitalist ex-ploitation of workers that he later learned more about from the teachings of Marx.

During World War I, Khrushchev's work in Yuzovka gained him a military exemption. In 1918, he became a Bolshevik, and during the Civil War he served as a junior commissar in the Red Army. During or just after that internal strug-gle, his first wife died of typhus, leaving him a widower with two young chil-dren; in 1924, he married his second wife Nina. Between the end of the Civil War and the German attack on the USSR in 1941, Khrushchev served mainly in party positions, first in and around Yuzovka, then in Ukraine, Moscow, and again back in Ukraine. Along the way, he upgraded his limited formal school-ing by furthering his education at the Yuzovka Workers' Faculty and the Moscow Industrial Academy. His rise in party ranks was rapid—in 1934 he be-came a member of the Central Committee and in 1939 a full member of the Politburo.

During World War II, Khrushchev served as a leading political commissar with the rank of major general. Among the war's millions of deaths was Khrushchev's son Leonid, a pilot, who died in mysterious circumstances. After Ukraine was liberated, Khrushchev resumed his position as first secretary of the Ukrainian party and became chairman of the Ukrainian Council of Minis-ters. Although temporarily replaced as Ukrainian party head in early 1947, he regained this post by year's end, relinquishing his less important government position. From late 1949 until Stalin's death, he was back in Moscow heading the Moscow party, serving in the party Secretariat, and acting as one of Stalin's top subordinates, especially for agricultural matters.

Khrushchev was earthy and energetic and enjoyed mixing with people—as the Soviet leader, he was critical of bureaucrats reluctant to interact with the common people. Despite his limited education, he possessed a sharp mind and learned more from conversations and observations than from reading. He be-lieved ardently in communism's superiority but was also a flexible politician. Not as innocent as his memoirs suggest, he could never have arisen to the po-sitions he had if he had not supported Stalin's policies. But exactly how much he knew during Stalin's lifetime of all the dictator's crimes is uncertain. Like many other "true believers," Khrushchev was willing to make sacrifices—and see others sacrificed—to advance toward the inauguration of his dream, communism.

Although extremely cautious, as one had to be to survive under Stalin, Khrushchev later demonstrated that he was also willing to take high risks, as he did in moving against the dangerous Beria or later when he placed missiles in Cuba. During his final years in power, his impulsiveness, impatience, and paternalistic authoritarianism became more evident.

Khrushchev on the Superiority of Communism Over Capitalism

Khrushchev often stated his belief that communism was superior to capitalism, and this ardent belief influenced many of his policies, both domestic and foreign. The following excerpt from his report to the Twenty-First Party Congress in 1959 is taken from his *Socialism and Communism: Selected Passages, 1956–1963* (Moscow, 1963), pp. 118–120. Ellipses are mine.

To achieve communism, the most just and perfect human society, in which all the finest moral traits of the free man will unfold to the full, we must bring up the man of the future today. Communist ethics should be developed among Soviet people, ethics founded on devotion to communism and intolerance of its enemies, on a sense of social duty, active participation in work for the good of society. . . .

It is well known that in the capitalist *system man withdraws into his shell and depends only on his own strength, because he has no one else to rely on. He knows that if he should be out of work, he would be deprived of the means of livelihood, would be doomed to poverty and starvation.*

The situation is different under socialism. Here each man feels the solicitude of society, of the state. That is why the urge of aggrandizement, of private property, is disappearing from the mind of the Soviet citizen, whereas the spirit of collectivism and concern for public welfare is gaining in him. . . .

. . . Foremost Soviet men and women do not go to distant parts because they are lured by the "golden calf," not for the sake of personal enrichment, but to build new factories and plants, plough up virgin soil, erect new towns for all society, for our children, for our future, in the name of the triumph of communism.

STALIN'S SUCCESSORS AND THE EXECUTION OF BERIA

Stalin's death on March 5, 1953, shocked the Soviet people. Many wept, both for the loss of a man who had dominated their lives for a quarter of a century and because they feared an uncertain future.

By mid-March, with Stalin's body now sharing the heretofore "Lenin Mausoleum" with Lenin's corpse, Stalin's successors had parceled out his powers among themselves. Malenkov became premier (chairman of the Council of Ministers), and Beria, Molotov, Bulganin, and Kaganovich became first deputy ministers. All five of these leaders also remained members of the party Presidium (the old Politburo). So too did Khrushchev, Voroshilov (who also served as titular president of the USSR), Mikoian, M. Saburov, and M. Pervukhin. Molotov once again became foreign minister. On March 14, Malenkov resigned from the party Secretariat, leaving Khrushchev as the senior secretary in the Secretariat—only in September did Khrushchev become the official first secretary of the party.

Besides his other powers, Beria became head of a more powerful Ministry of Internal Affairs (MVD), which oversaw both state security and traditional internal affairs. Beria not only had the secret police and its military force under his control, but also exercised considerable influence over the less willful Malenkov.

Within the USSR, Beria attempted to strengthen his popularity by advocating several reforms, and he went further regarding East Germany, where he suggested abandoning the forceful construction of socialism. The suggestion confused East German leaders, and in the uncertain days of June 1953, demonstrations broke out throughout East Germany until Soviet tanks helped restore order.

The East German crisis provided Khrushchev with the final ammunition he needed to destroy his most feared political rival. At the end of June, with the consent of Malenkov and some of the other leaders, he masterminded Beria's arrest by trustworthy military officers. In late December 1953, Soviet newspapers announced that Beria and six followers were found guilty (under the infamous Article 58) of conspiracy and other crimes and were to be shot. Although it is possible that Beria was executed even before the announcement, he was certainly dead by the end of 1953.

DOMESTIC POLITICS AND KHRUSHCHEV'S POLICIES

After Beria's death, Khrushchev gradually strengthened his powers. Although in many ways he eventually proved to be a reformer, he also accepted the basic economic structure he had inherited from Stalin and attempted to remain true to Lenin's legacy. As the Soviet people became less terrorized, they became bolder and more willing to voice their grievances. If individuals or groups became too bold and critical of government actions or inactions, however, they were often arrested or punished.

Khrushchev Versus Malenkov

Once Beria was removed, the main political struggle was between Malenkov and Khrushchev. The chief area of contention was the economy. Malenkov wished to increase agricultural production primarily through incentives for peasants and more mechanization and fertilization. And he proposed increasing consumer goods by converting some heavy industrial enterprises to light industry. In contrast, Khrushchev emphasized his virgin-lands policy. It was designed to open up to agricultural production millions of new acres in areas such as northern Kazakhstan and southwestern Siberia. The new lands would produce not only more food, but also help to increase cattle, hides, and cotton, therefore giving a boost to consumer products using leather and cotton.

In the political struggle, Khrushchev had several advantages. First, he was more decisive and had more experience heading party organizations than did Malenkov, whose strength lay in his bureaucratic abilities—Molotov called him a good "manager by telephone." Second, as first secretary of the party, Khrushchev was able to increase his supporters within it, and party and Komsomol activists soon played an important part in implementing his virgin-lands program. Third, the weather and grain harvest were not especially good in 1953, spurring serious consideration of the virgin-lands plan. Conversely, the weather and harvest were good on the small number of virgin lands opened up in 1954, further boosting the plan's popularity and expansion. Finally, Khrushchev was able to play upon the anxieties of top party and military leaders who feared that Malenkov would divert too much state investment from heavy industry.

By February 1955, Khrushchev had won the struggle: Malenkov resigned as premier, although he remained on the party Presidium, and Defense Minister Nikolai Bulganin succeeded him. In contrast to Malenkov, the agreeable and unremarkable Bulganin never contended with Khrushchev for the political spotlight.

Khrushchev's Secret Speech and Destalinization

In February 1956, the Twentieth Party Congress convened in Moscow—the first party congress since 1952. According to Khrushchev's later recollections, he convinced the party Presidium that newly discovered abuses of power by Stalin (which "came as a complete surprise to some of us") should be reported to the congress's delegates. The Presidium selected him, as first secretary, to perform the task. He had argued that Stalin's abuses and the innocence of many of his victims could not much longer be suppressed and that it was better for the party leadership to speak out immediately than later be accused of concealing such information.

Regardless of how accurate or self-serving Khrushchev's recollections are, there were additional reasons to go ahead with the disclosure of selected Stalinist crimes. Only a break from Stalinist oppression could free the party and country from past fears and allow groups and individuals to operate more creatively in solving the country's problems. Khrushchev, especially, had too many ideas of his own and too much energy to remain long content with Stalinism's constraints. Besides, he believed that turning the term Stalinist into one of abuse would harm mostly Molotov, Malenkov, Voroshilov, and Kaganovich, all of whom had been closer to Stalin. Thus, destalinization became a tool he could use in his power struggle against these men. Finally, it is possible that a genuine, although somewhat overdue, revulsion against Stalin's crimes motivated Khrushchev's desire to unmask them.

In his four-hour secret speech, delivered to the congress's delegates in a closed session, Khrushchev implicated Stalin in the 1934 assassination of Kirov and criticized him for overseeing subsequent campaigns of mass repression, tortures, and other violations of "socialist legality." He contrasted Stalin's methods with "Lenin's wisdom in dealing with people" and read aloud some of Lenin's final criticisms of Stalin. Further, Khrushchev blamed Stalin for the USSR's inadequate defenses in June 1941 and for other wartime failings that caused the deaths of countless Soviet troops. Among Stalin's postwar failures, Khrushchev mentioned Stalin's break with Yugoslavia and his new repressions, including those against the so-called doctor-plotters and his likely plans "for the annihilation of the old Political Bureau [Politburo] members." If Stalin had not died, Khrushchev informed the delegates, "Comrades Molotov and Mikoian would probably have not delivered any speeches at this congress." Khrushchev attributed most of Stalin's errors to the cult he constructed around himself—"the cult which became at a certain specific stage the source of a whole series of exceedingly serious and grave perversions of party principles, of party democracy, of revolutionary legality."

Despite this harsh criticism, Khrushchev acknowledged Stalin's role in the "preparation and execution of the Socialist revolution, in the Civil War, and in the fight for the construction of socialism in one country." Furthermore, Khrushchev stated that Stalin was correct in resisting the ideas of some of his political opponents "because the political line of both the Trotskyite-Zinovievite bloc and of the Bukharinites led actually toward the restoration of capitalism and capitulation to the world bourgeoisie." Finally, although critical of Stalin for creating a cult of personality, Khrushchev still spoke of the sincerity of Stalin's concern for the masses, for communism, and for the party.

Thus, Khrushchev's speech only went partway in condemning Stalin—for example, it left unmentioned the horrors that Stalin inflicted on the country from 1928 through 1933. As often, Khrushchev's words reflected some combination of what he himself believed and what political circumstances seemed to dictate.

The secret speech left many delegates in a state of shock. Although not printed or reported on in the USSR, it did not long remain secret, either in the Soviet Union or abroad. At home, rumors about it spread quickly, and it was read aloud and discussed at closed party meetings; an editor at the party's theoretical journal, *Kommunist*, privately referred to the speech as a time bomb, whose impact on Communist ideology was incalculable. In the West, the speech soon appeared in print, and in Poland and Hungary it helped ignite demonstrations in the summer and fall of 1956. In Hungary, demonstrations turned into a full-scale rebellion in October 1956, a rebellion that the Red Army soon crushed.

The Hungarian rebellion forced Khrushchev to proceed more cautiously in his destalinization campaign. At the Twenty-Second Party Congress in 1961, however, he and his supporters launched another major attack on Stalin; only this time, the criticism received Soviet media coverage. Shortly thereafter, Stalin's body was removed from the Lenin Mausoleum and his name from cities, streets, and other places; Stalingrad, for example, became Volgograd.

Antiparty Group and Khrushchev's Victory

Along with the Hungarian revolt, other developments of 1956 and early 1957 increased Presidium dissatisfaction with Khrushchev. First, there were the growing demands for punishing those guilty of Stalinist crimes, demands that became more frequent as millions returned from forced-labor camps and exile. Then there was Khrushchev's early 1957 plan to create more than 100 *sovnarkhozy* (regional economic councils) and abolish most central industrial ministries. The plan had the backing of the Central Committee (CC), more than half of which consisted of party secretaries of republics, provinces, and territories. Khrushchev had appointed many of them, and they viewed the plan as an opportunity to decentralize some of Moscow's powers into their own hands.

In June 1957, a majority of Khrushchev's Presidium colleagues attempted to remove him as party first secretary, accusing him of various failings including sowing disunity in the party and overstepping his powers. But Khrushchev rejected their decision, maintaining that he could be removed only by a vote of the CC. He then moved quickly and decisively; with help from leading military men such as Marshall Zhukhov, he convened a special session of the CC and won its support.

Khrushchev's victory spelled the end of the political influence of those who had tried to unseat him—"the antiparty group," as they were subsequently called. Molotov, Malenkov, Kaganovich, and Saburov were kicked off the party Presidium and the CC. At least they suffered lesser fates than they would have for opposing Stalin: Molotov was made ambassador to Mongolia and Malenkov became head of a hydroelectric plant in Kazakhstan. Three other Presidium members who had initially opposed Khrushchev, including Bulganin, were treated less harshly.

To replace the ousted Presidium members and to stack it with more of his own followers, Khrushchev enlarged the Presidium to 15 full members. Among the newcomers were Marshall Zhukhov, Leonid Brezhnev, and the first woman ever to obtain full status on the Politburo-Presidium, E. A Furtseva.

Zhukhov's tenure on the Presidium was brief. Apparently fearful that Zhukhov, who was also defense minister, might pose a future threat, Khrushchev removed him from both of his important positions in October 1957. The following year it was Bulganin's turn; in March, Khrushchev succeeded him as premier, and in September Bulganin lost his Presidium seat.

Khrushchev's Economic, Social, and Cultural Policies: Successes and Reforms

In his early years as first secretary, Khrushchev was aided by his economic, social, and cultural policies, which suggested he was a leader with enough energy and ideas to lead the country. The challenge for any post-Stalinist leader was to deal effectively with the numerous problems facing the USSR, while maintaining the support of powerful forces such as the party and military elite.

Agriculture had been a perennial problem, but by 1958 Khrushchev's policies, especially his virgin-lands policy, seemed to be working. Soviet statistics indicated that the average yearly grain harvest for the years 1955–1958 was about two-fifths greater than for the years 1950–1953. The 1958 grain harvest was especially good, reported to be about three-fifths higher than the 1950–1953 average.

In scientific-technological spheres with important military implications, Khrushchev's early policies also seemed successful. In 1957, there was the test of an intercontinental ballistic missile and the launching of Sputnik I, the first artificial earth satellite. Such triumphs continued into the early 1960s; especially notable was Yuri Gagarin's 1961 achievement, the first manned space flight around the earth (only in the 1990s were serious problems with that flight revealed). In perhaps the most highly valued field of twentieth-century activity (science and technology), Khrushchev and the USSR had displayed that communism could not only compete with capitalism, but also sometimes prove victorious.

By 1957, Khrushchev was confident enough about the Soviet economy to predict that within several years Soviet meat and dairy production would surpass that of the United States. In 1961, he told the Twenty-Second Party Con-

FIGURE 17.1. A rocket similar to the one that put Yuri Gagarin into orbit around the earth in 1961. USSR Economic Achievements Exhibition, Moscow, 1990.

gress that by 1980 the USSR "will leave the United States far behind in industrial and agricultural output per head of the population."

By the early 1960s, more housing and consumer goods were becoming available and so too were opportunities for intellectual and cultural development. One reason that Khrushchev allowed publication of works such as Alexander Solzhenitsyn's novel *One Day in the Life of Ivan Denisovich* (1962) was that he perceived them as aiding him in his destalinization campaign.

Along with most other people, writers and artists were now freer to express themselves than they had been under Stalin. New criminal codes based on legislation of 1958 attempted to establish the principle that individuals should be free from arrest and punishments unless they violated a specific law.

Khrushchev's Economic, Social, and Cultural Policies: Failures and Repressions

The party's control over the media and Khrushchev's increasing dominance of the party meant that his policies received favorable domestic coverage. Positive accomplishments received much more attention than failures, which often went unreported.

Although the launching of Sputnik I in late 1957 received enormous publicity, an important technological failure of the same year received none. An explosion at a Urals nuclear site at Kyshtym, near Cheliabinsk, blasted tons of radioactive material skyward. It contaminated a large area, killed an unknown number of people, and led to the evacuation of thousands of peoples from their homes. Like a great deal more environmental damage in the USSR, this event went unreported in the Soviet media until the Gorbachev era.

The slowdown in economic growth that characterized Khrushchev's final years in power was harder to conceal. After the leader's original successes with his virgin-lands campaign and the record-breaking harvest of 1958, the agricultural record was especially disappointing.

The virgin lands were risky in terms of climate, with drought occurring more frequently than in older farming areas. By the time of Khrushchev's fall in 1964, wind storms and ecologically unsound soil practices had damaged millions of acres of these new farm lands. Meanwhile, in his desire to overtake the United States in meat and dairy production, Khrushchev insisted that some older agricultural areas like Ukraine devote more of their lands to the production of corn (maize). It was good cattle fodder, and with the virgin lands adding to wheat supplies, Khrushchev thought some older farming areas could afford to switch to corn. These developments, plus others such as the abolition of Machine-Tractor Stations in 1958, led to some confusion, mistakes, and new inefficiencies. On top of these problems, the year 1963 brought little rainfall, and the combined effect was the lowest grain harvest since 1957.

In his effort to improve the economy and people's lives, Khrushchev was constantly tampering and reorganizing Soviet economic administration. After establishing regional economic councils in 1957, he gradually undermined many of their powers and recentralized economic administration, culminating in the creation of the USSR Supreme Economic Council in 1963.

He left unchanged, however, the basic command economy instituted by Stalin. In the course of his political battles, Khrushchev often criticized bureaucratic practices and advocated more trust of the masses. Yet, the command economy was a living reflection of the party's distrust of the masses—distrust of their tendency to care more for their own economic welfare than for any collective beyond the family, including the state.

Thus, despite Khrushchev's tinkering, the party-government structure alone remained legally empowered to decide what and how many products to produce and how much to charge for them. The only exception was on the small private plots, which the collective and state farmers were allowed to own. As long as the party-government retained such power, major problems and inefficiencies were bound to continue. This fact, plus heavy defense spending (despite Khrushchev's attempts to restrain it), the failure to meet consumer demands adequately, and the overriding concern with fulfilling economic plans imposed from above, continued to foster all sorts of abuses. Among them were poor quality consumer products, attempts to fool superiors, theft from state enterprises, blackmarketeering, and corruption.

Even if Khrushchev had taken a more realistic view of the economic nature of human beings and realized some of the fundamental flaws of the command economy, he would have found it difficult to do much to improve matters. The party's political power was intricately connected with its economic controls. As Mikhail Gorbachev later discovered, any tampering with the basic economic structure was fraught with dangers, both for the leader and for the party.

In other spheres of Soviet life, Khrushchev's rejection of Stalinist terrorism and advocacy of socialist legality went hand-in-hand with continuing restraints on freedom and punishments for those who overstepped permissible boundaries. In 1956, one individual who wrote to the Central Committee demanding that it fully investigate Stalin's crimes soon found himself being forcefully institutionalized in a psychiatric hospital. The following year, a Moscow historian and others were arrested and convicted after distributing leaflets calling for strikes and reforms and criticizing Khrushchev. In 1958, Khrushchev launched a new antireligious campaign and closed many places of worship. (See Chapter 21 for more on state-church relations.)

From 1958 until 1960, the writer Boris Pasternak was severely criticized in the media and by officials for allowing his novel *Doctor Zhivago* to be published abroad in 1957. After it was announced that he had won the Nobel Prize for literature in 1958, Soviet authorities successfully pressured him into renouncing it. Following his death in 1960, the love of his late years, Olga Ivinskaia, was arrested, tried, and sent to a Siberian prison camp for her alleged dealings with the Western publisher of *Doctor Zhivago*.

Working-class dissent was also treated harshly. In 1962, after the government increased meat, dairy, and vodka prices, strikes and demonstrations broke out in about a dozen cities. To restore order in the Don Region's city of Novocherkassk, KGB troops ended up firing upon rioters, killing two dozen of them and wounding even more.

Nationalities: Reform and Repression

Like his cultural policies, Khrushchev's nationality policies reflected both reform and repression. His criticism of Stalin at the Twentieth Party Congress included reference to Stalin's violations of Lenin's nationality policy and "monstrous" deportations of entire peoples during World War II. "The Ukrainians," Khrushchev told the delegates, "avoided meeting this fate only because there were too many of them and there was no place to which to deport them."

Two years earlier (in 1954), Khrushchev had attempted to gain Ukrainian support by placing the Crimea under the Ukrainian SSR. Because all of the USSR was then under firm party control, this transfer from RSFSR jurisdiction did not then seem significant. Later, however, following the 1991 breakup of the USSR, it became a point of contention between Russia and Ukraine.

During the mid-1950s, deported peoples were freed from forced labor camps and exile. Most of the nationalities, including the Chechens, Ingushi, and Kalmyks, had their rights restored and were allowed to return to their homelands. Their return created some friction with those who had moved onto their former lands; for example, after the restoration of the Chechen-Ingush Autonomous Republic in 1957, tensions during the next few years led to bloodshed and the exodus of some of the ethnic Russians and others who had settled in the area after the deportations.

Although released from camps and settlements, the Volga Germans and Crimean Tatars (the two largest deported nationalities) were prevented from returning to their homelands. Many of them now made new homes in Kazakhstan and Uzbekistan. Not until 1964 and 1967 did the government officially declare the USSR's Germans and Tatars free of any collective guilt for wartime collaboration with the enemy.

Other Khrushchev policies that affected the nationalities were those connected with his weakening of centralized industrial ministries and creation (in 1957) of regional economic councils. The furthering of local economic responsibilities strengthened the powers of the union republics and other national units. Some non-Russian elites, especially in the Caucasus and Central Asia, assumed not only more economic duties, but also more control of local political patronage.

Predictably, however, non-Russian aspirations soon went beyond what Khrushchev considered acceptable, and he lashed back against "national narrow-mindedness." After he initiated an educational reform in 1958, conflict emerged over the language of instruction to be used in the republics' schools. Non-Russians feared the reform would encourage the use of Russian while discouraging the use of the native language. Differences between Khrushchev and local leaders led to some of them being replaced: From 1959 through 1961,

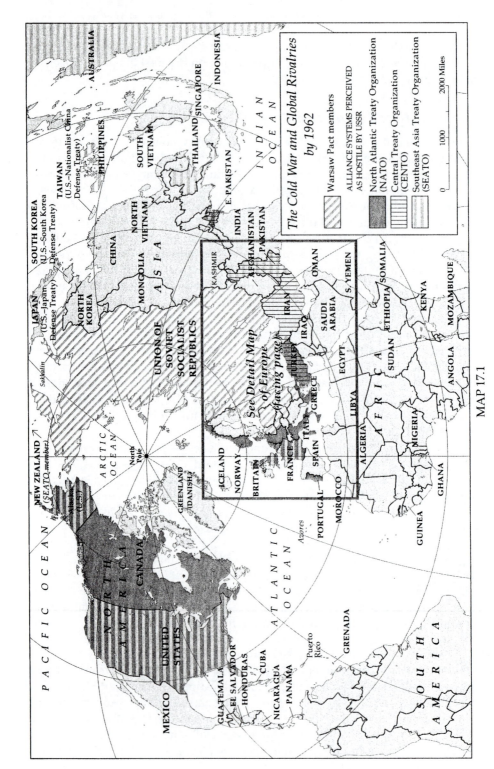

The Cold War and Global Rivalries by 1962

	Warsaw Pact members
	ALLIANCE SYSTEMS PERCEIVED AS HOSTILE BY USSR
	North Atlantic Treaty Organization (NATO)
	Central Treaty Organization (CENTO)
	Southeast Asia Treaty Organization (SEATO)

0   1000   2000 Miles

MAP 17.1

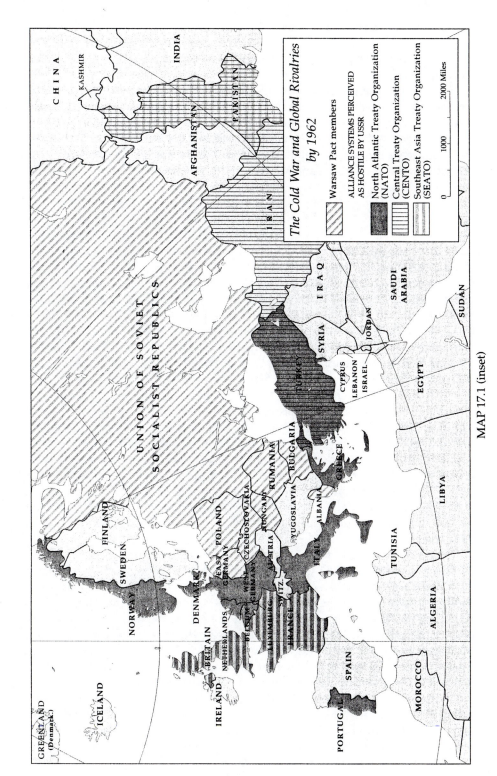

The Cold War and Global Rivalries
by 1962

Warsaw Pact members

ALLIANCE SYSTEMS PERCEIVED
AS HOSTILE BY USSR

North Atlantic Treaty Organization
(NATO)

Central Treaty Organization
(CENTO)

Southeast Asia Treaty Organization
(SEATO)

0   100   2000 Miles

MAP 17.1 (inset)

365

the number of native party first secretaries at the republican level decreased by more than half.

Other steps the government took against "national narrow-mindedness" included repressing newly formed nationalist groups and reducing the expanded economic powers recently bestowed upon the republics. Although economic recentralization, which culminated in 1963 with the creation of the USSR Supreme Economic Council, was motivated primarily by economic considerations, it was also a means of overcoming "localism."

FOREIGN POLICY

As in domestic policy, so in foreign policy, Khrushchev gradually became the chief decision maker. Malenkov had talked of ending the Cold War, and Molotov continued to advance a more Stalinist hard-line approach; but as their political powers waned, they exercised less influence on foreign affairs. Although Molotov remained foreign minister until mid-1956, Khrushchev's foreign policy strategy had clearly become dominant a year earlier. In 1957, Andrei Gromyko, whom Khrushchev privately referred to as "a dry old stick," began his long tenure as foreign minister. During the Khrushchev era, however, he was not part of the policy-making party Presidium.

Although Khrushchev's impetuousness harmed his foreign policy and sometimes made it seem inconsistent, his goals remained the same throughout his years in power. His primary concern was Soviet security interests. Surrounded by U.S. bases and missile sites from Western Europe to Japan and from Alaska to Turkey, he attempted to lessen the imbalance he perceived in the global balance of forces (see Map 17.1). This attempt sometimes led to dangerous actions, especially his placing of missiles in Cuba in 1962. Yet Khrushchev was also aware of the dangers of a nuclear holocaust and wished to minimize the chances of war by pursuing what he called "peaceful coexistence."

Although willing to take some steps to reduce the threat of nuclear war, Khrushchev was unwilling to reduce tensions by withdrawing Soviet support for Third World anti-Western movements. Marxism-Leninism taught that history was on the side of the "oppressed masses" and that Western imperialism was a backward-looking force attempting to prevent the national liberation of colonial peoples. (During the Khrushchev years, there were many anticolonial movements around the world, and in the early 1960s alone, more than two dozen countries ceased being colonies and became independent nations.) From Khrushchev's Marxian perspective, the USSR had more of a right to support anticolonial and anticapitalist forces than the West did in trying to suppress them. Thus, both for ideological reasons and because the weakening of the West's colonialism and Third World influence would serve Soviet security interests, he supported anti-Western "liberation movements." He saw their success as a symbol of socialism's coming global victory over capitalism.

FIGURE 17.2. Khrushchev and U.S. Vice-President Nixon debate capitalism versus socialism at a U.S. exhibition in Moscow, 1959. Brezhnev stands to the right of Nixon. *(UPI/Bettmann.)*

Meanwhile, however, Khrushchev faced his own challenges within the Communist world—an area where "oppressed masses" and imperialism also existed, although unacknowledged by Soviet authorities. He improved relations with Yugoslavia's Tito, but in 1956 Hungary revolted and threatened to pull out of the Soviet bloc. During the early 1960s, after years of simmering, Sino-Soviet differences boiled over into open ideological conflict, threatening Communist unity and Soviet leadership of the Communist movement.

First Steps, 1953–1956

Soviet actions abroad during the first two post-Stalin years reflected the insecurities, uncertainties, and lack of unanimity among the new collective leadership. As Khrushchev later noted, Stalin had not contributed to his successors' confidence by telling them "when I'm gone the imperialistic powers will wring your necks like chickens." The Soviet ambivalence in East Germany (encouraging liberalization and then sending in tanks to put down demonstrators), concessions to Communist China, and conciliatory steps toward the West and Yugoslavia characterized this early diplomacy.

In July 1953, partly because of increased Soviet flexibility, an armistice was finally signed ending the conflict in Korea. Later that year, Moscow agreed to provide financial backing, technicians, and technology for more than 100 construction projects in Communist China. In a display of increased respect for the Chinese leadership, Khrushchev and Bulganin journeyed to Beijing in 1954, the first of many foreign trips Khrushchev made as party leader. There he and Bulganin agreed to remove Soviet forces from Port Arthur, occupied since 1945, and provide increased economic assistance to China.

In May 1955, the Soviet Union signed a treaty to end the four-power occupation of Austria, and Austria pledged itself to neutralism. In July, building upon this peace momentum, heads of the four powers (Britain, France, the United States, and the USSR) gathered in Geneva for a summit. For the first time as leaders of their country, Khrushchev and Bulganin met with U.S. President Eisenhower, supported by his hard-line secretary of state, John Foster Dulles. The future of Germany was a major topic of discussion. (See Map 14.1 for postwar Europe.) The absence of any official postwar settlement had left it divided into West Germany, which in May had joined NATO, and East Germany which was a Soviet satellite. The Soviet leaders attempted to stop the ongoing remilitarization of West Germany and to obtain Western recognition of East Germany but were unsuccessful. Nor was any progress made toward eventual German reunification—in his memoirs, former Soviet ambassador to the United States Anatoly Dobrynin maintains that Khrushchev "opposed the reunification of Germany on any terms."[1]

Yet the involved leaders considered the Geneva talks a limited success, and "the spirit of Geneva" came to mean a willingness to talk and negotiate, not just threaten. Khrushchev later expressed satisfaction that the Soviet leaders had held their own—they could, after all, deal with the "imperialistic powers" without getting their necks wrung.

In September, the "spirit of Geneva" continued. During a Moscow visit by West German Chancellor Konrad Adenauer, the USSR and West Germany agreed to establish regular diplomatic relations. That same month, the USSR signed a treaty with Finland that stipulated the Soviet withdrawal from a naval base near Helsinki.

The most significant turnabout in Soviet foreign policy, however, was regarding Yugoslavia and its leader Tito, upon whom Stalin had heaped so much abuse and who increasingly pursued his own brand of socialism. In May 1955, Khrushchev led a delegation to Belgrade. Less than two weeks earlier, partly to counter West Germany's admission into NATO, the USSR and its Eastern European satellites had signed the Warsaw Pact, legitimizing the Soviet military

---

[1] *In Confidence: Moscow's Ambassador to America's Six Cold War Presidents (1962–1986)* (New York, 1995), p. 121.

presence in Eastern Europe and officially providing for a unified military command. Khrushchev now hoped to entice Yugoslavia back into the Soviet bloc.

During and after his visit, Khrushchev made concessions. A joint communiqué released at the end of the visit recognized what Stalin had been unwilling to allow—that each socialist country had the right to determine its own concrete form of socialism. In his secret speech in February 1956, Khrushchev conceded that the break with Yugoslavia in 1948 was overwhelmingly Stalin's fault. In April, Cominform was abolished; it had accomplished little since its founding in 1947 except expelling the Yugoslavian Communist party from its ranks. Yet, despite a gradual warming of Soviet-Yugoslavian relations, Tito remained committed to his own socialist path, having no desire to become just another junior member of the Soviet bloc.

Poland and Hungary in 1956

In Poland and Hungary, the USSR's apologetic behavior to Tito, along with Khrushchev's secret speech, produced unintended consequences. Khrushchev desired to establish a less oppressive relationship with the Eastern European satellite countries and to encourage limited destalinization there—a process already begun before 1956. He failed to appreciate, however, that such policies might inadvertently encourage more radical anti-Soviet feelings. That is exactly what happened in Poland and Hungary.

At the end of June 1956, riots broke out in Poznan, Poland, and their repression caused hundreds of casualties. Polish Communist leaders then attempted to increase their party's popularity with the Polish people by returning former party leader Wladislaw Gomulka, earlier purged and imprisoned as a "Titoist," to his old position as party first secretary.

Khrushchev and his colleagues feared that Gomulka might be too independent-minded. On October 19, soon after learning that Gomulka was about to resume his old position, Khrushchev, Molotov (recently replaced as foreign minister), Kaganovich, and Mikoian rushed to Warsaw, and Soviet troops in Poland prepared for action. After a stormy session with the Polish leadership and assurances that Poland would remain loyal to the USSR, the Soviet leaders acquiesced in Gomulka's appointment.

Although Gomulka soon brought meaningful reforms to Poland, these were changes that the Soviet leaders could grudgingly accept. In Hungary, however, in late October, matters escalated beyond such a point.

Sparked by Polish developments, Hungarian demonstrators demanded the withdrawal of Soviet troops stationed in Hungary and the reinstatement of Imre Nagy as premier. This moderate reformer had held that position from mid-1953 to early 1955, before being ousted by Hungarian leaders less sympathetic to reforms. With pressures increasing from below, Hungarian party leaders agreed to Nagy's appointment. The same day Nagy assumed office (October 24), Soviet tanks appeared on the streets of Budapest to put down anti-Soviet demonstrators.

This show of force inflamed the situation, and the rebellion spread. Rebels hurled Molotov cocktails at Soviet tanks, and many Hungarian soldiers joined the rebellion. By the end of October, it seemed like the continuing Hungarian resistance had won the rebels important gains. A cease fire was proclaimed, and Soviet troops pulled out of Budapest. Then, from October 30 to November 1, Nagy announced that Hungary would restore multiparty democracy, withdraw from the Warsaw Pact, and become a neutral country. All three steps went beyond what Soviet leaders thought permissible. On November 4, Soviet troops poured back into Budapest and other cities and installed a new government under János Kádár, who had become party first secretary on October 25. Although labeled a Titoist during Stalin's final years and imprisoned, he was now willing to cooperate with Soviet forces. Within ten days, Soviet troops crushed all significant armed resistance. Thousands of rebels were killed, and about 200,000 Hungarians fled their country. After leaving the Yugoslavian embassy, where he had sought refuge until promised safe conduct, Nagy was kidnapped by Soviet forces and eventually tried and executed in 1958.

The suppression of the Hungarian rebellion created new Soviet-Western tensions. Through such media instruments as the Voice of America and Radio Free Europe, the Eisenhower administration had for some time encouraged Hungarian resistance to Soviet control. This urging was part of Dulles's "roll-back-the-iron-curtain" policy. Soviet statements about the rebellion criticized the West for encouraging and supporting the "Nagy counterrevolution." Yet, much to the dismay of Hungarian rebels, the Western powers did nothing substantial to help them.

Soviet leaders were fortunate that in the midst of the crisis, France, Great Britain, and Israel attacked Egypt after it nationalized the Suez Canal. Soviet criticisms of this attack against Egypt now countered Western criticisms of the Soviet repression of Hungarian rebels.

Khrushchev's memoirs suggest he never abandoned his belief that the crushing of the "Nagy counterrevolution" served the interests of most Hungarians, for it threatened to overthrow Hungarian socialism. Yet the use of force in Hungary must have shaken Khrushchev's hopes that a common belief in Marxism-Leninism, rather than Stalinist exploitation, could hold the Soviet bloc together. Ultimately, only force, or at least its threat, could maintain the Soviet empire. Not surprisingly, Soviet relations with Tito, despite his support for the suppression in Hungary, grew cooler. After the Hungarian rebellion, the Soviet leadership saw more clearly that it was dangerous to boost the popularity of the independent-minded Tito. Yugoslavia was not part of the Warsaw Pact, and emulation of its independent ways could only threaten the unity of the Soviet bloc.

From Sputnik to the U-2 Incident, 1957–1960

The successful Soviet testing of an intercontinental ballistic missile (ICBM) and the launching of Sputnik I, both in 1957, inaugurated the space and missile age. Khrushchev boasted about Soviet missile superiority and attempted to take diplomatic advantage of it.

In the West, Khrushchev's most immediate concern was the German question. His main goals regarding the two German states remained what they had been earlier, to obtain Western treaty recognition of East Germany and to reduce the West German military threat. U.S.-led NATO forces in West Germany possessed nuclear weapons, and in NATO circles there was talk of allowing West Germany to have its own such weapons. In late 1957–early 1958, Polish Foreign Minister Adam Rapacki put forward a Soviet-backed proposal to create a nuclear-free zone, which would include both Germanys, Poland, and Czechoslovakia.

After the Western powers rejected the plan, Khrushchev attempted a new approach. In November 1958, he hinted at another Berlin blockade if the four-power occupation of Berlin did not end within six months. Khrushchev stated that instead of an occupied Berlin, a free and demilitarized Berlin could be created. He added that the best way to insure the city's future would be for both East and West Germany to withdraw from their respective military alliances and retain only minimal self-defense forces.

Within a few months, Khrushchev began backing away from his six-month time limit but kept pressuring the Western powers regarding Berlin. In mid-1959, shortly after the death of Secretary of State Dulles, the Eisenhower administration invited Khrushchev to visit the United States, in exchange for a later Eisenhower trip to the USSR. This proposal delighted Khrushchev and further postponed any decisive Soviet steps regarding Berlin.

In September 1959, Khrushchev and his wife Nina came to Washington to begin a colorful twelve-day U.S. visit. After additional stops in New York, California, Iowa, and Pennsylvania, the trip ended with two days at the presidential retreat at Camp David. Little of substance was achieved. Eisenhower agreed, however, to begin arranging a summit of the four Berlin occupying powers and to expand U.S.-Soviet cultural and other exchanges. The U.S. media played up the positive "spirit of Camp David," and Khrushchev spoke of Eisenhower as a man who sincerely wished to end the Cold War.

On May 1, 1960, however, before the proposed summit could occur, a U.S. spy plane was shot down in the middle of the USSR and along with it the "spirit of Camp David." Since 1956, the CIA-piloted U-2 planes had been flying high over Soviet airspace, taking pictures with high-powered cameras that could decipher a license plate from twelve miles above. The Kremlin had objected but previously had been unable to shoot one down. Because the flights provided valuable intelligence information—such as the fact that the USSR had not raced ahead of the United States in constructing missile sites—Eisenhower continued them.

The clumsy U.S. handling of the incident and the Soviet revelation that the shot-down pilot, Gary Powers, had been captured alive produced a propaganda coup for the USSR. But the incident also embarrassed Khrushchev, who had praised Eisenhower as a peace-loving man.

Several weeks later, on May 16, the four-power summit opened in Paris. Khrushchev demanded that Eisenhower denounce the U-2 flight before the summit continued. Eisenhower refused. Consequently, Khrushchev ended the summit and announced that Eisenhower's earlier planned visit to the USSR was now indefinitely postponed.

Berlin, Cuba, and the Test Ban Treaty, 1961–1963

In a press conference before leaving Paris, Khrushchev stated that he hoped that in six to eight months he could again meet with Western leaders in more favorable circumstances. He knew that by early 1961 the United States would have a new president, and he was pleased when it turned out to be John Kennedy and not the man he called in his memoirs "that son-of-a-bitch Richard Nixon."

Soon after Kennedy took office, negotiations began for a meeting between the two leaders. But before such a summit could occur, another incident, the Bay of Pigs invasion of Cuba, threatened to derail summit preparations.

Following Fidel Castro's 1959 assumption of power in Cuba, the U.S. government became increasingly upset with Castro's growing closeness to the Soviet Union. Eisenhower authorized the CIA to recruit and prepare anti-Castro Cuban émigrés to invade Cuba; after succeeding Eisenhower, Kennedy approved of the invasion. It took place in April 1961, but Castro's forces defeated the anti-Castro émigrés in a few days. Although Khrushchev harshly criticized the United States for its support of the émigrés, he and Kennedy soon agreed to hold their summit in Vienna in early June.

At the two-day summit, a confident and bullying Khrushchev tried to intimidate the young and inexperienced U.S. president, especially regarding Berlin. The Soviet leader informed Kennedy that the stalemate in Berlin had to end. If the Western powers would not cooperate, the USSR would sign a treaty with East Germany before the end of 1961, turning over to it control of Berlin access rights. If the West then interfered with East German controls, Khrushchev threatened war. Kennedy left Vienna visibly shaken.

In the months that followed, Kennedy attempted to convince Khrushchev of U.S. resolve by such means as activating army reservists. But Khrushchev remained confident, and in August he took a step that created another crisis. On August 13, the East German government announced that a Berlin Wall would be constructed. The main purpose of the wall and other new barriers was to prevent the continuing large exodus of East Berliners and other East Germans into West Berlin. During early August alone, more than 20,000 refugees, many of them professional and skilled people, had poured into West Berlin.

In the weeks and months that followed, tensions remained high. The USSR announced its resumption of atmospheric nuclear testing, which had been suspended in 1958, and the United States sent additional U.S. troops and equipment to Europe. Once again, Khrushchev gradually backed off his timetable for turning over control of Berlin access routes to East Germany.

The year 1962, however, produced an even greater Cold War scare—the Cuban Missile Crisis. President Kennedy later estimated that the chances of a Soviet-U.S. war resulting from this October crisis were between "one out of three and even." And it probably would have been a nuclear war.

The crisis grew out of Khrushchev's decision to place medium-range and intermediate-range nuclear missiles in Cuba that were to be targeted on the United States. Castro accepted the idea partly because he was aware of U.S. actions (Operation Mongoose) supporting sabotage in Cuba. In his memoirs, Khrushchev stated that he took the step to safeguard Cuba against the United States and to equalize the "balance of power."

To Khrushchev, the latter reason was the more important of the two, especially if "balance of power" is seen in its broadest possible context. Despite Sputnik, the USSR was far behind the United States in terms of nuclear strength, and U.S. missile sites and bomber bases surrounded the USSR. When vacationing along the Black Sea, Khrushchev sometimes pointed out to his guests that U.S. missiles aimed at the USSR were just across the sea in Turkey. (Actually, by late 1962 these missiles in Turkey were out of date and not significant to overall U.S. nuclear strategy.) Before Castro came to power, the Soviet Union was not able to place Soviet land-based missiles as close to the United States. Another Soviet option, the production and deployment of significantly more ICBMs, which could reach the United States from the USSR, would be costly at a time Khrushchev was attempting to invest more in civilian sectors. Thus, placing less costly missiles in Cuba was more affordable and, as Khrushchev saw it, would give Americans "a little of their own medicine."

Some analysts of the crisis have suggested that by placing the missiles in Cuba, Khrushchev later hoped to strike a bargain with the United States. For example, the missiles could be withdrawn in exchange for a U.S. withdrawal of its missiles in Turkey or for Western recognition of East Germany and a pledge not to allow West Germany to possess nuclear weapons.

On October 16, the CIA displayed to Kennedy detailed U-2 photographs of Soviet missile installations being constructed in Cuba. In the days that followed, U.S. officials and military leaders engaged in intense debate on how to deal with this information. Some advocated a military attack; others, a blockade—decades later, Soviet sources revealed that the Soviet military in Cuba possessed tactical nuclear weapons and would have used them against U.S. forces attacking Cuba.

On October 22, in a nationwide television address, Kennedy revealed the discovery of the missile installations and announced a naval blockade of Cuba. He also stated that any missile launched from Cuba would be considered an attack by the Soviet Union, and in words revealing his concern about a possible Cuban-Berlin linkage, he proclaimed that an attack "on Berlin would be an attack on the United States."

For almost a week after Kennedy's address, as the crisis ebbed and flowed, nuclear war was a real possibility. October 24 and 27 were especially tense days. On the 24th, the world waited to see if Soviet ships would attempt to run the blockade—they did not. On the 27th, a U-2 pilot was shot down and killed flying over Cuba. Kennedy and Khrushchev exchanged many communications, and Robert Kennedy and Soviet Ambassador Dobrynin often met together late at night trying to resolve the crisis. Finally, Khrushchev backed down. In exchange for a U.S. promise not to attack Cuba, and an unofficial (and nonpublicized) assurance that the United States would remove its missiles from Turkey in four or five months, Khrushchev announced on October 28 that the USSR would dismantle its missile sites and return its missiles to the USSR. Castro was bitterly disappointed that Khrushchev had not gained greater concessions for Cuba, such as the removal of U.S. forces from their long-standing base at Cuba's Guantanamo Bay.

The crisis made both Khrushchev and Kennedy aware of the necessity of avoiding or minimizing such crises in the future. In his memoirs, Ambassador Dobrynin related that during the tense days of October, with the avoidance of nuclear war seeming to hinge on successful negotiations, he had used Western Union to send coded cables to Moscow. He could only hope that the bicycle messenger delivering his cables would take them directly to the Western Union office "and not stop to chat on the way with some girl!"[2] In June 1963, Kennedy and Khrushchev agreed to establish a Moscow-Washington "hot line" to facilitate mutual emergency communication. In August 1963, the USSR, the United States, and Great Britain signed a nuclear test ban treaty banning all but underground nuclear testing.

Sino-Soviet Split and Soviet Third World Policy

After Communist China heard of the 1963 test-ban treaty, it accused the USSR of "allying with the United States to oppose China." This charge was just one of many coming from Beijing in the early 1960s, and by 1963, Sino-Soviet relations were more antagonistic than U.S.-Soviet relations.

The roots of the Sino-Soviet conflict were deep. By 1963, for example, China was criticizing tsarist Russian policies that had imposed unequal treaties on China and enabled Russia to gain vast border territories. These treaties, the Chinese insisted, should now be renegotiated. The Chinese also remembered and resented some of Stalin's policies toward them.

The immediate causes of the Sino-Soviet split, which erupted openly in 1960, stemmed from differing national priorities and Communist visions. China was unsympathetic with Khrushchev's continuing criticism of Stalinism and his desire for peaceful coexistence with the West. Mao Zedong wanted Soviet help in modernizing China, developing a nuclear force, and supporting Communist China's desire to annex Taiwan. Khrushchev was critical of Mao's grandiose plan ("the Great Leap Forward") to achieve full communism, wanted to prevent China from obtaining nuclear weapons, and was unwilling to risk war with the United States over Taiwan.

In the summer of 1960, Khrushchev ended Soviet economic and technolog-

---

[2] Dobrynin, p. 96.

ical aid to China and recalled Soviet experts. The following spring, he took similar actions against Albania, which had sided with China in the dispute.

An additional aspect of the Sino-Soviet antagonism was the two countries' difference regarding Third World nations. Mao called for bold revolutionary action to help bring Communists to power in such countries and was less concerned than Khrushchev with any response of the "paper tiger," as he labeled the United States.

Although also desiring communism to advance around the globe, Khrushchev's Third World priorities reflected more traditional Soviet foreign-policy goals. While avoiding war with the West, he sought to weaken Western colonialism and imperialism, even if it meant supporting nationalist non-Communist movements and leaders. Khrushchev also wished to weaken Western-initiated alliances, such as the Baghdad Pact (later CENTO) and the Southeast Asia Treaty Organization (SEATO), which he believed were directed against the USSR. In keeping with these goals, the Soviet Union greatly expanded its Third World aid to countries such as Egypt, Indonesia, and India.

From 1960 to 1964, Sino-Soviet name-calling escalated. Khrushchev called Mao "un-Leninist," an "adventurist," and a "racist." The Chinese referred to Khrushchev as a "buffoon," and accused Soviet leaders of the unpardonable Marxist sin of "revisionism."

At first, few in the West realized the significance of the Sino-Soviet split and how it might be affecting Soviet policies—the belief in a monolithic communism directed from Moscow was not easily forsaken. But for decades to come, the split reverberated throughout the Communist world, weakening Communist unity and ideology.

KHRUSHCHEV'S DECLINE AND FALL

By 1964, dissatisfaction with Khrushchev was increasing among important and frequently overlapping Soviet groups. His growing authoritarian, erratic, and intemperate ways were partly responsible, but so too were his economic and international failures and his actions that threatened those fearful of further destalinization, defense reductions, and party reforms.

When his opponents had tried to remove him from power in 1957, Marshal Zhukov had supported him. By 1964, however, he had alienated many military leaders. In an effort to divert more government spending to the civilian sector, Khrushchev made sharp cuts in military personnel, reducing their number by a few million from 1955 to 1961. (According to Soviet figures, the armed forces in 1955 stood at a little less than 6 million troops.) In exchange for these cuts, Khrushchev promised new investments in missiles and other military technology. Yet, as the Cuban Missile crisis made clear, in the five years following the Sputnik launch in 1957, Soviet nuclear weapons' development lagged behind that of the United States.

In 1957, Khrushchev had stayed in power not only because of military backing, but also because of party support in the Central Committee (CC) and among local party leaders. In his effort to improve economic performance, Khrushchev increasingly became more populist, antibureaucratic, and critical of party members more concerned with their privileges and prerogatives than the welfare of the country. In 1961–1962, he alienated many by initiating party changes. First, new party rules stated that at least one-quarter of the CC membership were to be replaced at each "election," with even higher replacement ratios at lower party levels. Second, in November 1962, Khrushchev decreed that local party organizations were to be split in two: One part would be responsible for overseeing agriculture and the other for overseeing industry and construction. Like most bureaucrats, party members deeply resented and resisted changes that threatened to disrupt their everyday existence.

In October 1964, other members of the party Presidium moved to oust Khrushchev from power. The plot was backed by Soviet security forces, now referred to as the KGB, under V. E. Semichastny. On October 12, a vacationing Khrushchev was summoned back to Moscow by other Presidium members. After he returned the next day, they criticized him for his errors and failings.

FIGURE 17.3. Visitors to Khrushchev's Memorial in Novodevichii Cemetery, Moscow, discuss its meaning, 1987.

On October 14, party ideologist M. Suslov read a list of Presidium charges to a meeting of the Central Committee. That same day, Leonid Brezhnev, one of the chief conspirators, replaced Khrushchev as first secretary, and the following day Alexei Kosygin assumed Khrushchev's position as premier. Khrushchev was, however, allowed a comfortable retirement. During the years remaining before his death in 1971, his most notable achievement was tape-recording his memoirs. After authorities told him to hand over his tapes, he and his son Sergei conspired to smuggle them out of the USSR. In 1970, the first of several volumes was published in the United States.

Of course, those who removed Khrushchev exaggerated some of his failings and attempted to conceal or downplay their own political ambitions and responsibilities. As Presidium members, they had joined with Khrushchev in making most of the important decisions. Nevertheless, as party leader, the major blame for such failures as the poor harvest of 1963, declining economic growth, and the missile retreat from Cuba quite naturally fell on Khrushchev.

Not only his policies alienated many, but also his style. Many party people were tired of his erratic ways and constant tinkering and changes. Despite his genuine desire for reforms, he was by nature authoritarian, and the longer he was in power, the more he displayed this trait. Critics, both inside and outside the party, thought of him as somewhat of a buffoon. At a United Nations' appearance in 1960, he had pounded a desk with a shoe for emphasis. One party member and later dissident recalled that during his reign, she and her friends were indignant about his shoe pounding and other "idiotic" antics. Only later did she come to the conclusion that "in his uneven and boorish way, Khrushchev was one of the greatest leaders Russia ever had."[3]

In fact, Khrushchev was neither a buffoon nor a great leader, but he was a reformer, and Soviet life did improve under him. After his removal, his reputation within the Soviet Union fluctuated. It remained low during the Brezhnev years, but after Mikhail Gorbachev came to power, it shot up during the late 1980s, when Khrushchev was perceived as a Gorbachev precursor. The fall of Gorbachev and the collapse of the Soviet Union (both in 1991), along with subsequent developments, have led to still further reappraisals of Khrushchev. In the final analysis, the white and black memorial at Khrushchev's grave, symbolizing good and evil, captures well his mixed record. (See Chapter 21 for more on this memorial.)

*SUGGESTED SOURCES**

AUSLAND, JOHN C. *Kennedy, Khrushchev, and the Berlin-Cuba Crisis, 1961–1964.* Oslo, 1996.
BESCHLOSS, MICHAEL R. *The Crisis Years: Kennedy and Khrushchev, 1960–1963.* New York, 1991.

[3] Ludmilla Alexeyeva and Paul Goldberg, *The Thaw Generation: Coming of Age in the Post-Stalin Era* (Boston, 1990), p. 105.
* See also sources cited in footnotes.

————. *Mayday: Eisenhower, Khrushchev, and the U-2 Affair*. New York, 1986.

BIALER, SEWERYN. *Stalin's Successors: Leadership, Stability, and Change in the Soviet Union.* Cambridge, England, 1980.

BLIGHT, JAMES G. *Cuba on the Brink: Castro, the Missile Crisis, and the Soviet Collapse.* 2d ed. New York, 1993.

BRENNER, PHILIP, and JAMES G. BLIGHT, "Cuba 1962: The Crisis and Cuba—Soviet Relations: Fidel Castro's Secret 1968 Speech." In *BCWIHP* 5 (Spring 1995): 1, 81–85.

BRESLAUER, GEORGE W. *Khrushchev and Brezhnev as Leaders: Building Authority in Soviet Politics.* London, 1982.

BURLATSKY, FEDOR. *Khrushchev and the First Russian Spring: The Era of Khrushchev Through the Eyes of His Advisor.* New York, 1991.

CHOTINER, BARBARA ANN. *Khrushchev's Party Reform: Coalition Building and Institutional Innovation.* Westport, Conn., 1984.

COHEN, STEPHEN F., ALEXANDER RABINOWITCH, and ROBERT SHARLET, eds. *The Soviet Union since Stalin.* Bloomington, 1980.

CRANKSHAW, EDWARD. *Khrushchev: A Career.* New York, 1966.

ELLISON, HERBERT J., ed. *The Sino-Soviet Conflict.* Seattle, 1982.

FRANKLAND, MARK. *Khrushchev.* New York, 1967.

GARTHOFF, RAYMOND L. *Reflections on the Cuban Missile Crisis.* 2d ed. Washington, D.C., 1989.

GRIFFITH, WILLIAM E. *The Sino-Soviet Rift.* Cambridge, Mass., 1964.

KELLEY, DONALD R. *The Sons of Sergei: Khrushchev and Gorbachev as Reformers.* New York, 1992.

KHRUSHCHEV, NIKITA. *Khrushchev Remembers.* Boston, 1970.

————. *Khrushchev Remembers: The Glasnost Tapes.* Boston, 1990.

————. *Khrushchev Remembers: The Last Testament.* Boston, 1974.

KHRUSHCHEV, SERGEI. *Khrushchev on Khrushchev: An Inside Account of the Man and His Era.* Boston, 1990.

KIRALY, BELA K., and PAUL JONAS, eds. *The Hungarian Revolution of 1956 in Retrospect.* New York, 1978.

LEONHARD, WOLFGANG. *The Kremlin since Stalin.* New York, 1962.

LINDEN, CARL A. *Khrushchev and the Soviet Leadership: With an Epilogue on Gorbachev.* Baltimore, 1990.

McCAULEY, MARTIN. *The Khrushchev Era: 1953–1964.* London, 1995.

————, ed. *Khrushchev and Khrushchevism.* London, 1987.

MEDVEDEV, ROY A. *Khrushchev.* Garden City, N.Y., 1983.

————, and ZHORES A. MEDVEDEV. *Khrushchev: The Years in Power.* New York, 1976.

MEDVEDEV, ZHORES A. *Nuclear Disaster in the Urals.* New York, 1979.

MICUNOVIC, VELJKO. *Moscow Diary.* Garden City, N.Y., 1980.

NATHAN, JAMES A. *The Cuban Missile Crisis Revisited.* New York, 1992.

PC 41 (Spring 1992). Special Issue.

RICHTER, JAMES G. *Khrushchev's Double Bind: International Pressures and Domestic Coalition Politics.* Baltimore, 1994.

ROTHBERG, ABRAHAM. *The Heirs of Stalin: Dissidence and the Soviet Regime, 1953–1970.* Ithaca, N.Y., 1972.

TATU, MICHEL, *Power in the Kremlin: From Khrushchev to Kosygin.* New York, 1969.

TOMPSON, WILLIAM J. *Khrushchev: A Political Life.* New York, 1995.

ULAM, ADAM B. *The Communists: The Story of Power and Lost Illusions, 1948–1991.* New York, 1992. Chs. 4–7.

WERTH, ALEXANDER, *Russia under Khrushchev*. New York, 1962.

WHITE, MARK J. *The Cuban Missile Crisis*. Basingstoke, England, 1996.

WOLFE, BERTRAM. *Khrushchev and Stalin's Ghost: Text, Background, and Meaning of Khrushchev's Secret Report to the Twentieth Congress on the Night of February 24–25, 1956*. New York, 1957.

ZAGORIA, DONALD S. *The Sino-Soviet Conflict, 1956–1961*. New York, 1964.

CHAPTER 18

From Stability to Stagnation, 1964–1985

From late 1964 until his death in November 1982, Leonid Brezhnev was party first secretary, retitled general secretary in 1966. Up into the early 1970s, collective leadership was emphasized. Others, notably Premier Alexei Kosygin, shared power with Brezhnev. But like Khrushchev, Brezhnev gradually strengthened his powers over both domestic and foreign policies, achieving more successes in the early and middle years of his rule than toward the end. Also like Khrushchev, Brezhnev presided over alternating periods of Cold War tensions and relaxations, the use of armed force against an Eastern European reform movement (Czechoslovakia in 1968), continued ideological clashes with China, and Soviet support for "national liberation movements" in the Third World.

Yet for all these similarities, the public differences between the two party leaders were the most striking. Whereas Khrushchev was colorful, erratic, down-to-earth, and risk-taking, Brezhnev was less colorful, steady, fond of luxuries and presents, and politically cautious—it is fitting that the Russian word for cautious or careful is *berezhnyi*. (Outside the public eye and political arena, Brezhnev was less cautious, as U.S. President Nixon discovered to his alarm when he accompanied Brezhnev as he speedily drove a new car presented to him around the curves of the U.S. presidential retreat at Camp David.)

In their policies, Khrushchev was a reformer who pushed destalinization; Brezhnev was a conservative who eased back on it. Khrushchev angered the military by cutbacks and threatened party-government personnel with constant changes; Brezhnev appeased the military with increases and emphasized the "stability of [party-government] cadres." Khrushchev spoke of completing "the foundations of communism" by 1980, Brezhnev was more cautious, claiming only that the USSR was the first country to achieve "developed socialism"—a stage still far removed from the final goal of communism. Finally, Khrushchev constantly spoke of the future and what Soviet communism would achieve, whereas Brezhnev was inclined to sentimentalize about the past.

After achieving many apparent successes under Brezhnev's leadership, Soviet domestic and foreign policies were less successful during the last half-decade of his life. The USSR seemed to mirror his own declining health. Its political leadership, economy, and quality of life reflected stagnation. Following Brezhnev's death in 1982, the stagnation continued under his next two successors. Neither 68-year-old Yuri Andropov, who ruled fifteen months before dying, nor 72-year-old Constantine Chernenko, who lasted only thirteen months, was physically up to the job of providing vigorous leadership.

LEADERS AND LEADERSHIP

During the late 1960s, the four most important leaders were Brezhnev, Kosygin, Nikolai Podgorny, and Mikhail Suslov. They were all born between 1902 and 1906 and came from similar backgrounds. For a while, Alexander Shelepin, a younger member of the party Presidium, also competed to become a major influence, but his political fortunes soon waned. Although the other four men agreed on pursuing collective leadership and preventing any new cult of personality, they each possessed distinctive positions on domestic and foreign policies.

Of the four leaders, Brezhnev and Kosygin were the most important, although the ideological specialist Suslov always lurked in the background. Although an ethnic Russian, Brezhnev grew up in Ukraine, the son of a metalworker. After receiving a technical education, he served as an agricultural administrator in the Ural Mountain region. By 1931 (the year he joined the party), he had returned to his hometown to renew his education, graduating as an engineer in 1935 from the Dneprodzerzhinsk Metallurgical Institute.

During the next three decades, Brezhnev rose steadily within the party hierarchy, first in Ukraine and then in other areas. During World War II, he was a political officer in the army, ending the war with the rank of major general. During the 1950s, he first was party leader in the Moldavian republic and later held a similar position in Kazakhstan, where he oversaw Khrushchev's virgin-lands program. He also served in the party Secretariat in Moscow and, in the early 1960s, as chairman of the Presidium of the Supreme Soviet (government president). At the time of Khrushchev's fall, Brezhnev was once again back in the party Secretariat, where he was outranked only by Khrushchev, his patron for some years. His full membership on the party Presidium dated from 1957.

Like Stalin and Khrushchev before him, Brezhnev was underestimated at the time he became chief party secretary. But this was generally a plus, for individuals who stood out, such as Trotsky and Beria, aroused too much opposition from jealous rivals. Brezhnev's mind, tastes, and cultural level, though not his political skills, were undistinguished. The Soviet adviser Georgi Arbatov later wrote that "when he did read something for his own pleasure, it was usually a magazine like *Circus*."[1] Besides his appreciation for the circus, he liked to hunt, go boating, and follow such sports as hockey and soccer.

Although not a charismatic leader, Premier Alexei Kosygin was more intellectually impressive. The future premier was born into a St. Petersburg working-class family. He served in the Civil War, joined the party in 1927, and in 1935 graduated as an engineer from the Leningrad Kirov Textile Institute. Benefiting from the many vacancies created by Stalin's purges, in 1938 he became party chief in Leningrad; the following year, still in his mid-thirties, he became head of the Commissariat for Light Industry. In 1940, he was promoted to deputy chairman of the Council of People's Commissars and retained that position throughout Stalin's remaining years. In 1948, he also became a full member of the Politburo, only to lose this position in 1952 during Stalin's final Politburo-Presidium shakeup.

After Stalin's death, Kosygin's career only slowly regained its momentum. Although Kosygin was never one of Khrushchev's protégés, the new leader recognized his talents, especially his knowledge of the economy. In 1960, he became Khrushchev's deputy premier and once again a full member of the party Presidium (Politburo after 1966).

Partly because of his economic knowledge and background, Kosygin was more sympathetic than Brezhnev with economic reforms and more government investment in the civilian sector. In foreign policy, he was more open to improving U.S.-Soviet relations, especially before Brezhnev moved in his direction and began advocating détente at the beginning of the 1970s. As had often occurred before in Kremlin politics, Brezhnev's reorientation was intertwined with political maneuvering. His new stance favoring détente positioned him between Kosygin and the more hard-line Podgorny and Suslov.

Although collective leadership continued to be official policy, Brezhnev's preeminence increased during the early 1970s. He moved more of his protégés, friends, and supporters into important positions. But he also proved effective in overseeing a consensus politics, which took into consideration the desires of all major elite groups. In 1973, for example, the heads of the KGB, foreign affairs, and defense became full members of the Politburo. That body continued to oversee all major initiatives—A. Dobrynin (former Soviet ambassador to the United States) writes that Brezhnev had to follow Politburo-approved guidelines when negotiating with foreign leaders, even though most Politburo members knew little about foreign affairs.

During the years 1976–1978, Brezhnev acquired more titles and honors. In 1977, he assumed one of the top two government positions when he replaced Podgorny as president. His ghostwritten memoirs were published and awarded the country's highest literary prize, an award reflecting more the subservience of the Writers' Union than any literary quality of the memoirs. By early 1980, a Soviet article mentioned that more than 17 million copies of "the

---

[1] Georgi Arbatov, *The System: An Insider's Life in Soviet Politics* (New York, 1992), p. 246. Another side of Brezhnev, however, is depicted by his niece in a work that is fairly objective. Luba Brezhneva, *The World I Left Behind: Pieces of a Past* (New York, 1995), p. 315, writes that her uncle "loved Yesenin and Pushkin and knew most of their verses by heart."

remarkable works" of Brezhnev were in print. A growing Brezhnev cult was clearly evident.

POLITICAL DECLINE, CORRUPTION, AND THE PARTY

Unfortunately for Brezhnev, however, the cult rose just as his health seriously declined. His slowed movements, slurred speech, and faltering memory became increasingly evident. An unconventional healer whom he increasingly relied upon did more harm than good, and in his final years he often seemed disoriented in his public appearances.

The health of other leaders was also deteriorating, and Kosygin died in 1980 and Suslov in early 1982. With Podgorny already having been removed from his leadership positions in 1977 and serious problems accumulating in the country, the times seemed to call for new and vigorous leadership.

Yet in the higher reaches of the party, there was little to be found. The average age of the fourteen full members of the Politburo was sixty-eight in mid-1978, and, as a group, they were anything but vigorous. Inertia and drift, along with increasing corruption and nepotism, marked Brezhnev's final years. Brezhnev's fondness for expensive presents and luxuries was shared by some of his family members, relatives, and other party leaders who resorted to a variety of methods to obtain them.

One member of the party elite who was less acquisitive was KGB chief Andropov. After the death of the ailing Suslov in January 1982, Andropov attempted to deal with the mounting corruption. Those soon arrested, in this case for illegal trade and smuggling, included the director of the national circus, his wife, and a minor entertainer, Boris the Gypsy. All were close friends of Brezhnev's daughter Galina, whose third husband was deputy minister of internal affairs. Growing corruption among the Soviet elite flowed partly from their heightened security and privileges. As fear of reprisals for shady dealings faded under Brezhnev, so too did the elite's inhibitions about engaging in them.

One of the first steps of the new leaders in 1964 was to end Khrushchev's unpopular division of the party into agricultural and industrial sections. They also ended Khrushchev's policy which insisted that a significant ratio of new members be elected whenever "elections" were held to party bodies. Partly because of increased job security and other benefits, party membership increased by a greater percentage than overall population growth, going from about 10 million full members in 1964 to about 17 million (or almost 10 percent of the adult population) in 1982. Just as significantly, the turnover on key bodies and in key positions declined significantly, and the average age of holders of important positions increased. "Stability of cadres" and "trust in cadres" were not just idle words to Brezhnev.

One of the most trusted and valued leaders on the republican level was the party boss in Azerbaijan since 1969, Geidar Aliev. This republic was an extreme example of the corruption that was increasingly engulfing the country. Formally the republic's KGB head, Aliev made a reputation for himself as an anticorruption fighter, earning the nickname "hammer of the mafia."

Yet as a party boss, this "hammer" was selective in his "mafia" targets, striking at those who refused to cooperate with his government and officials but rewarding those who did. Corruption, bribes, and nepotism continued to flourish under Aliev, as he relied on a strong patronage system to keep various "mafias" in line. They dealt in black-market petroleum, caviar, and a whole host of other products and even controlled their own airplanes and railway cars.

Aliev kept Moscow happy by producing what it wanted (especially cotton), by his personal connections, and by generous gift-giving. In 1978, when Brezhnev visited Baku, Aliev presented him with an expensive gold and diamond ring, an enormous hand-woven carpet, and a Brezhnev portrait decorated with rare gems. (The gems had originally been used to decorate a Khrushchev portrait, but the less acquisitive Khrushchev had rejected such an ostentatious present.) Four years later, in preparation for another visit, Aliev ordered a palace built for Brezhnev and presented him with another sixteen-jeweled ring, the jewel in the center representing Brezhnev and the fifteen more modest ones encircling it, the fifteen Soviet republics. The ring was named "The Unbreakable Union of Republics of the Free," and before millions of Soviet television viewers, a deeply touched Brezhnev accepted this gift.

Aliev was not alone in running his republic like a mafia "godfather." Later, under Gorbachev, decades of political corruption in the Caucasus and Central Asia would be exposed, nepotism being especially prevalent in these areas because of traditionally strong kinship ties. Political corruption, however, went

FIGURE 18.1. Baku, where Brezhnev visited in 1978.

far beyond these regions and permeated the entire country. Already in 1982, a Soviet émigré with a great deal of legal experience wrote: "Massive and ubiquitous corruption at the district level of the party-state apparat has forged such close ties between it and the criminal world that there is every justification for saying that a system of organized crime has come into existence in the Soviet Union."[2]

Before Aliev's ardent courting of Brezhnev, Aliev was already a protégé of Andropov, who stepped up his anticorruption efforts after replacing Brezhnev as general secretary in November 1982. Andropov even brought Aliev to Moscow and made him deputy premier and a full Politburo member. How much Andropov knew of or was willing to overlook Aliev's own corrupt ways in Azerbaijan is not clear, for Andropov's anticorruption policy was partially based on political expediency.

Andropov himself remains somewhat of a mystery. A worker's son, he was born in 1914 in the Stavropol Province. He received a technical education, became a Komsomol official, and later held important party posts in what was briefly the Karelo-Finnish SSR. At the time of the Hungarian revolt in 1956, he had already been Soviet ambassador to Hungary for two years. The year after the revolt, he returned to Moscow and became head of the Central Committee's department dealing with other Communist countries. From 1967 to early 1982, he served as KGB chief, vacating the post only months before Brezhnev's death to become the number-two man in the party Secretariat.

Despite his role in putting down the Hungarian rebels and his long tenure as KGB head, Andropov was sometimes depicted during the early 1980s as a "liberal." This was hardly an accurate portrayal. He was, however, more intelligent and more knowledgeable about life inside and outside the USSR than most other Soviet leaders.

After becoming party chief, he attempted to reenergize the country, both by attacking corruption (though selectively) and by bringing some new blood into party posts. He also attacked poor workplace discipline and indifference. Police raided public baths, movie houses, restaurants, stores, and other places to catch bosses and workers who had absented themselves from work to pursue other interests. Unfortunately for Andropov, however, his own energy did not last long. After seriously ailing for months, he died of kidney failure in February 1984.

One of the newer breed of party leaders given more responsibilities by Andropov was Mikhail Gorbachev, the Politburo's youngest member. He often acted in Andropov's name during the ailing leader's final months and was apparently the leader's choice as his successor. Yet the older Politburo members were still unready to confer the leadership upon such a "young" (almost fifty-three years old) man. Instead, they turned to a man two decades older, Constantine Chernenko.

Born a Siberian peasant's son, he worked in the early 1950s in Moldavia

---

[2] Konstantin M. Simis, *USSR—the Corrupt Society: The Secret World of Soviet Capitalism* (New York, 1982), p. 94.

under Brezhnev, who became his political patron and advanced his career. In 1956, he came to Moscow and began working in the Central Committee, overseeing propaganda. A decade later, under Brezhnev, he began supervising daily party matters; in 1977, he became a full member of the Politburo. Lacking good health, energy, vision, and leadership qualities, Chernenko was hardly the man to deal with the country's growing problems. He died on March 10, 1985, after a lackluster thirteen-month rule.

THE ECONOMY: FROM THE COMMAND SYSTEM TO BLACK MARKETEERING

A frank assessment of the overall Soviet economy in 1965 came from an unpublicized speech by the Novosibirsk economist Abel Aganbegyan. He noted that Soviet economic growth had slowed during the previous six years and that the Soviet industrial structure was the most backward of the major industrial nations. He spoke of economic inefficiencies, waste, poor-quality products, lack of economic incentives, poor farming conditions, unrealistic pricing policies, the low pay of kolkhoz peasants, and rising unemployment. Despite Khrushchev's efforts to cut military spending, Aganbegyan estimated that the defense industry engaged 30 to 40 percent of the Soviet workforce. The main causes of such trends and poor performance he attributed to Soviet efforts to match U.S. defense spending, overemphasis on heavy industry, overly centralized planning, and insufficient economic information. He claimed that the Soviet Statistical Administration's statistics were misleading and often wrong and that the agency could not do its job, partly because it possessed no computers.

Like Khrushchev, the new leaders made some attempts to reform the economy while retaining its basic command structure. In 1965, for example, Kosygin presented a plan to make industry more efficient. He proposed stressing profits—not just the quantity of production—increasing incentives for managers and workers, and freeing managers from some centralized bureaucratic controls.

The plan was implemented piecemeal, but from the beginning it contained inconsistencies and encountered difficulties. Bureaucrats resented any loss of their powers, there was little ideological support for economic innovations, and the overall economy was not yet bad enough to risk major changes. After the overthrow of the Czechoslovakian reform movement in 1968, opposition to any reforms, economic or otherwise, hardened within the USSR.

Yet until the late 1970s, when the economic picture became increasingly dark, the Soviet economy supported a military buildup that brought the USSR up to nuclear parity with the United States. At the same time, it improved living standards, partly by sharply increasing agricultural investment. It spent more on rural wages and benefits, farm equipment, fertilizers, irrigation, rural electrification, and procurement payments for agricultural goods.

Considering the level of increased investment, however, farm outputs were disappointing, especially after 1978. Although weather conditions produced sharp disparities from year to year and meat and dairy production increased, the grain crop from 1979 through 1985 never came close to reaching the levels of 1973, 1976, or 1978. To maintain improved Soviet diets, the state increasingly depended on grain imports to make up for bad harvests.

Fortunately for the Soviet Union, the years 1973–1981 were ones of escalating world energy prices. Expanding petroleum production, especially in Siberia, made the USSR (beginning in 1974) the world's largest oil producer. The export of oil and other energy sources was primarily responsible for enabling the country to retain a favorable trade balance even though it imported rising amounts of grain, other foodstuffs, and Western and Japanese advanced technology.

Like agriculture, overall economic growth slowed noticeably after 1978. Although Soviet economic statistics are notoriously unreliable, there is general agreement that in each of the three succeeding five-year-plan (FYP) periods after 1966–1970, the growth of both the economy and per capita consumption was smaller than in the preceding FYP period. Some economists have argued that during Brezhnev's final years there was no overall economic growth.

Yet both before and after the late 1970s, one economic sphere did grow—private (including black-market) economic activities. The Brezhnev regime tolerated such activities as a way of maintaining the command economy while compensating for its failure to provide adequate consumer goods and services. The range of private economic activities became wider, with many shadings between legal and illegal dealings.

The growth of the private, or "second," economy can also be seen in a wider context. Writing in the late 1980s, Vladimir Shlapentokh viewed it as part of a larger process by which Soviet citizens from the late 1950s on began channeling more of their time, energy, and enthusiasm away from public and state sectors into their own private spheres. Economic activities such as the illegal channeling of state goods into private hands were just one part of this larger process, as was bribe-taking, nepotism, and other forms of political corruption.

During the Brezhnev years, the state adopted a more favorable attitude toward the previously tolerated peasant private plots. (Khrushchev had attempted to prevent peasants from diverting too much attention to them as opposed to their kolkhoz or sovkhoz duties.) Furthermore, the government encouraged city-dwellers to farm garden plots in the nearby countryside, especially if they owned dachas (country huts or houses). By the mid-1980s, many urban families possessed such garden plots. Despite the fact that all the private plots together made up only about 3 percent of the country's arable land, they produced about one-fourth of the country's total crop, including about three-fifths of its combined vegetable and potato yield and more than one-fourth its meat and dairy products.

Besides earning income by selling their produce in markets, there were numerous other private ways people made money: They tutored, repaired vehicles and appliances, produced and sold illegal goods, traded in foreign goods and currencies, gave people rides in their cars or in the state cars they drove, sold off state goods (including gasoline from state vehicles and goods from the factories and stores they worked in), stood in lines for people, and took bribes in exchange for better service.

Sometimes no money exchanged hands, only goods or favors. A foreign-made VCR given as a "gift" to a college official might gain a desired admission, or a few tickets to a sold-out concert might insure a prompt and thorough medical examination at a "free" state health clinic. Almost all Soviet citizens, including party-government officials and police, participated in some form of illegal or quasilegal economic activity.

PUBLIC OPINION, NATIONALITIES, AND DISSENT

As economic growth declined and corruption increased, the mood of the Soviet public turned increasingly negative. Among the most dissatisfied were the young and the best educated. The young had not lived long enough to experience the marked long-term improvement in living standards, and, along with the highly educated, they were more likely to be affected by, or knowledgeable about, foreign ways. Many young men served in the military in Eastern Europe, and the number of Soviet tourists there increased more than tenfold between 1960 and 1976. In cities such as Budapest, East Berlin, Prague, and Warsaw, Soviet tourists had the opportunity to observe more plentiful and higher-quality consumer goods.

Although sons and daughters of the top Soviet political elite were a notable exception, few Soviet citizens were able to travel to the West. The détente of the 1970s, however, did increase cultural exchanges and Western tourists to the USSR. Through such contacts (including Western films), Soviet citizens, especially the young and educated, became more familiar with Western ways and consumer styles. Even before détente, Finnish tourists and television had begun having an increasing influence on Estonians, whose language was linguistically related to Finnish. By the late 1970s, the growing economic dissatisfaction of Soviet citizens was probably due as much to increased opportunities for foreign comparisons as it was to the decreasing growth in their own living standards.

The attitude of Soviet citizens toward their government was also affected by their nationality. In the two decades following Khrushchev's removal, ethnic relations worsened, and local nationalisms increased, both fueling discontent with the Kremlin.

Census figures from 1959 and 1979 indicate that during these years the Great Russians declined as a percentage of the USSR population from 54.6 to 52.4, but the percentage of people of Moslem background increased rapidly. For example, the Uzbeks, Kazakhs, Tatars, Tadjiks, Turkmens, Kirgiz, and Azerbaijanis collectively went from about 10 percent to a little over 14 percent. These demographic developments concerned the top Kremlin leadership, which was dominated by Great Russians.

The Brezhnev regime continued Kremlin efforts to contain any non-Russian nationalism. In 1972, for example, the head of the Ukrainian Communist

FIGURE 18.2. Two U.S. male students receive bread and salt (a traditional welcoming gift) and flowers from youth in Kishinev including the two women to their left, mid-1980s.

party, P. Shelest, was replaced after being accused of encouraging Ukrainian nationalism and "localism." During 1972–1973, thousands of other Ukrainian party officials and cultural leaders also lost their positions. The new party leader, V. Shcherbitsky, though like Shelest a Ukrainian, was much more willing to appease Kremlin fears regarding any "localism."

The continuing movement of ethnic Russians into some areas such as Estonia and Latvia increased ethnic resentments. The most contentious issue between Moscow and the union republics, however, was that of language. The central government continued pushing the learning and use of Russian throughout the USSR, especially during Brezhnev's final years in power. The increasing use of Russian was to be one of several tools that would eventually create a supranational "Soviet people," who would share a single ideology and multiethnic culture. After the USSR adopted a new constitution in late 1977, new union-republic constitutions were prepared. In that process during 1978, Moscow attempted to end the right of the dominant native language in Armenia, Georgia, and Azerbaijan to be the only official one in each republic. The Kremlin backed away from this step only in the face of Caucasian demonstrations.

Despite such Kremlin efforts, native leaders and cadres were allowed to become more prominent in the union republics, provided that they conformed to the party's nationality policy. Although some Soviet citizens thought that

Russians in the non-Russian republics obtained the best housing and jobs, other citizens believed that the dominant nationality in each republic gained the most opportunities. Certainly, there were educational, occupational, and political openings for non-Russians, especially for individuals adept at conforming, or seeming to conform, to central party policies. At the same time, they could take advantage of local patronage and clan networks, such as those in Central Asia and Transcaucasia.

Yet, despite some maladroit Kremlin actions and its habit of favoring things Russian (provided that they were compatible with what Siniavsky has called "Soviet civilization"), the nationality policy of Brezhnev and his two brief successors was generally cautious. It reflected the realization that nationality was a touchy area and that it would be dangerous to try to move too rapidly down the road of overcoming national differences and creating one "Soviet people."

This caution, however, did not prevent a sharp increase in dissident activity among non-Russians. It was especially notable in the Ukrainian SSR, the Baltic republics, the Georgian SSR, and among Jews and Crimean Tatars.

In late 1965, about two dozen Ukrainian intellectuals were arrested and accused of "defamation of the Soviet system." Their true crime was calling for more destalinization and less Russification. Their trials aroused protests, with one of those protesting being the young journalist Viacheslav Chornovil. In 1967, his efforts led to his arrest, trial, and sentencing to a prison camp.

Other signs of Ukrainian dissent were the underground journal *Ukrainian Herald*, which began appearing in 1970, and the Ukrainian Helsinki Watch Group, which first appeared in 1976 to monitor Ukrainian compliance with the 1975 Helsinki Accords regarding civil rights.

In Lithuania, the Catholicism of many of its citizens provided a focus for national feelings. In 1972, Catholic activists began publishing the underground *Chronicle of the Catholic Church of Lithuania*. For more than fifteen years, this journal, devoted to religious and other human rights, continued intermittently to appear. In 1972, another noteworthy occurrence was the tragic death of the student Romas Kalanta, who burned himself to death protesting a lack of Lithuanian freedom. Many other signs of anti-Soviet resentments in Lithuania and in the other two Baltic republics also appeared during the 1970s and early 1980s.

In Georgia, the writer Zviad Gamsakhurdia was a leading spokesman for the Georgian language and culture and a critic of human rights violations. In 1978, a year of pro-Georgian language demonstrations in the streets of Tbilisi, he was tried and convicted of spreading anti-Soviet propaganda.

Although Jewish culture and religion (Judaism) had long suffered from Soviet discrimination, the Arab-Israeli war of 1967 awakened increased anti-semitism. Partly in reaction, Jews became more outspoken in their criticism of the government's Jewish policies and more inclined to attempt emigration. During the 1970s, partly as a result of U.S. pressures during the détente era, more than 200,000 Jews, or about one-tenth of the Jewish population, emigrated. Permission was not easily obtained, however, and applicants for emigration usually suffered further discrimination and harassment before some of them were allowed to leave.

After many years of submitting petitions for permission to return to their Crimean homeland, the Crimean Tatars (most of whom were in Uzbekistan) also became more outspoken in the late 1960s. Thanks in part to the efforts of a former Ukrainian general, P. Grigorenko, their cause became part of a broader human rights movement that flourished in the late 1960s and early 1970s. Yet, despite all their efforts, only a small percentage of Crimea Tatars were allowed to return to the Crimea.

Among the causes of the broader human rights movement was the stifling of the destalinization momentum begun under Khrushchev. In the Russian heartland, this stifling was indicated in 1966 with the trial of Andrei Siniavsky and Yuli Daniel. The critical and satirical works of these two writers had been appearing abroad for years under the respective pseudonyms of Abram Tertz and Nikolai Arzhak. In a bizarre trial, the two men were accused of anti-Soviet propaganda and sentenced to Soviet labor camps. Siniavsky received seven years and Daniel five.

Their trial and sentences, plus additional trials and violations of human rights, sparked only greater opposition (including petitions) from Soviet intellectuals. The Soviet invasion of Czechoslovakia in 1968 aroused still more dissent. Underground self-published literature (*samizdat*), usually circulating in typed or mimeographed copies, and foreign-published forbidden works of Soviet authors (*tamizdat*) proliferated. Often *samizdat* works soon became *tamizdat* ones, such as *A Chronicle of Current Events*, which appeared regularly from 1968 to 1972 and intermittently thereafter. Portions of this and other works were also read over Western radio stations that beamed broadcasts to the USSR. This chronicle was a Moscow-based underground journal that recorded opposition and human rights violations, including those against individual dissenters (often writers or scientists), ethnic minorities, and religious groups.

During the 1970s, the dissident movement reflected many different approaches. Three of them, sometimes labeled neo-Slavophile, liberal, and Marxist reformist, were respectively represented by three of the most important dissidents: the writer Alexander Solzhenitsyn, the nuclear physicist Andrei Sakharov, and the historian Roy Medvedev.

Author of *One Day in the Life of Ivan Denisovich* (1962) and other works (see Chapter 21), Solzhenitsyn was called a "neo-Slavophile" because he eventually came to represent a position grounded in respect for the pre-Soviet Russian cultural and religious traditions.

One of the fathers of the Soviet hydrogen bomb, Andrei Sakharov became increasingly concerned during the 1960s about domestic and international political issues, including human rights and nuclear weapons control. During the late 1960s and the 1970s, many of his works were circulated in *samizdat* and published abroad. His approach was most admired in the West because his thinking was closest to Western liberalism with its emphasis on human rights, legality, and due process of law. For his activities, he was awarded the Nobel Peace Prize in 1975, although the Soviet government would not grant him a

Dissident Voices Protest the Czechoslovakian Invasion

The following selection is an excerpt from *A Chronicle of Current Events*, No. 3 (August 30, 1968), as edited and translated by Peter Reddaway, *Uncensored Russia: Protest and Dissent in the Soviet Union: the Unofficial Moscow Journal, A Chronicle of Current Events* (New York: American Heritage Press, 1972), pp. 99–100. Bracketed material and ellipses are mine. The selection was written by the poet Natalia Gorbanevskaia, one of the chronicle's founders and editors. On August 25, she wheeled her baby in its carriage, along with protest banners and a Czechoslovakian flag, to Red Square to join six other protesters.

At midday we ... unrolled banners with the slogans LONG LIVE FREE AND INDE-PENDENT CZECHOSLOVAKIA (written in Czech), SHAME ON THE OCCU-PIERS, HANDS OFF CZECHOSLOVA-

KIA, FOR YOUR FREEDOM AND OURS.[3] Almost immediately a whistle blew and plainclothes K.G.B. men rushed at us from all corners of the square. They were on duty in Red Square, waiting for the Czechoslovak delegation's departure from the Kremlin. They ran up shouting "They're all Jews!" "Beat the anti-Soviet-ists!" We sat quietly and did not resist. They tore the banners from our hands. They beat Victor Fainberg in the face until he bled, and knocked his teeth out. They hit Pavel Litvinov [grandson of the former Soviet foreign minister] about the face with a heavy bag. ... They shouted at us, "Disperse, you scum!" But we remained sitting. After a few minutes cars arrived. ... In the car they beat me. ... After the search I was released, probably because I had two children to look after [on the fate of the protesters, see below].

[3] In a later work, *Red Square at Noon* (New York, 1972), Gorbanevskaia slightly modified her account of the banners. The slogan "FOR YOUR FREEDOM AND OURS" was borrowed from Alexander Herzen, who used it a century earlier to indicate his sympathy with Polish rebels.

visa to leave the USSR to receive it personally. Instead his wife, Elena Bonner, went for him. She herself was an important dissident, a charter member of Moscow's Helsinki Watch Group, which was established in 1976 and helped launch other branches later that year in Ukraine and Lithuania.

A member of the Academy of Pedagogical Sciences, the historian Roy Medvedev served as the chief editor of still another *samizdat* publication called *Political Diary*, which appeared from 1964 to 1971. Medvedev's approach was that of a reforming Communist, who blamed most of the USSR's problems on Stalin and his legacy. Medvedev's *Let History Judge: The Origins and Consequences of Stalinism* was first published in the West in 1971 and became one of the most valuable sources of information on the Stalin years.

Determined to squash the growing dissident movement, the government increased its repression. Under Andropov, the KGB grew stronger and more sophisticated. In dealing with hard-core dissidents, the state relied primarily upon three methods: (1) sentencing them to forced labor camps, prison, or exile; (2) allowing or forcing them to emigrate; and (3) incarcerating them in psychiatric facilities. Among Gorbanevskaia's fellow protesters against the invasion of Czechoslovakia, five of them were dealt with by the first method, and another received the third treatment, as eventually did Gorbanevskaia, before she finally emigrated in 1975.

By 1980, most of the earlier active dissidents had been dealt with by these methods. Solzhenitsyn, for example, was forcibly expelled in 1974, and Roy Medvedev's twin brother, Zhores, a prominent geneticist, was one of a distinguished group who involuntarily spent some time in a mental institution. He later became an émigré after his citizenship was stripped from him while abroad in 1973.

Primarily because of Sakharov's international prominence, he was not imprisoned or made to perform forced labor. Following an Andropov suggestion, the Politburo exiled him in January 1980 to the Volga city of Gorky (Nizhnii Novgorod), a city off limits to foreigners. This action followed his denunciation of the Soviet intervention in Afghanistan the previous month. For the next seven years, he remained in Gorky, forcefully isolated from many of his former contacts.

In 1980, an authoritative account of the dissident movement stated: "At least for the moment, dissent is less visible and less vocal than it has been at any time since the Khrushchev years."[4] This account and others attributed this weakness primarily to repressive government measures, divisions among the dissidents, and the gap between dissidents and the average Soviet citizen, who often thought of them as unpatriotic. The average citizen was more concerned with bread-and-butter issues. Moreover, the state-controlled media often deliberately misinformed the public about prominent dissidents such as Sakharov.

Compared to the intelligentsia's dissident activity, there was relatively little active political protest by workers and peasants. Although industrial strikes, demonstrations, and disturbances did occasionally occur, they were scattered, spontaneous, and never threatened to snowball into a significant political movement.

FOREIGN POLICY: CONFRONTATIONS AND DÉTENTE

After Khrushchev's fall, his successors pursued a less erratic foreign policy. They remained, however, committed to his major goal of enhancing Soviet security and avoiding nuclear war. As before, peaceful coexistence, including the détente of the 1970s, did not rule out Soviet support for "liberation struggles" in Third World countries. Indeed, in his first major speech after overthrowing Khrushchev, Brezhnev maintained that peaceful coexistence would contribute to the success of such struggles.

During the late 1960s, the most significant Soviet foreign policy develop-

---

[4] Marshall S. Shatz, *Soviet Dissent in Historical Perspective* (Cambridge, England, 1980), p. 180.

ments centered around other Communist countries (especially Czechoslovakia and China), Western Europe, and the Third World. During the 1970s and early 1980s, U.S.-Soviet relations moved to the forefront.

Czechoslovakia and the "Brezhnev Doctrine"

Following the Sino-Soviet split of the early 1960s, Rumanian Communist dictator Nicolae Ceausescu carved out a more independent Rumanian role. Although not happy about Ceausescu's drive for more economic and foreign-policy autonomy, Moscow tolerated it, as it did other variations from Soviet-style communism among other bloc countries. In Hungary under the Kádár regime, there was less reliance on centralized economic planning; in Poland under Gomulka, there was more private farming; and in both countries, there was greater personal and religious freedom.

Definite limits remained in place, however, as Czechoslovakia tragically discovered in 1968. Up until then, it was ruled by Antonín Novotny. But Czechoslovakian discontent with his Stalinist ways, plus Soviet acquiescence in his ousting, led to his fall. In January, he was replaced as party head by the Slovakian Alexander Dubcek and in March as president by Ludvík Svoboda. Driven by public opinion, the new leadership set out to create "socialism with a human face." What came to be called "the Prague Spring" was characterized by an expansion of freedom of expression and other civil liberties.

By the summer of 1968, Soviet leaders were becoming increasingly alarmed about these developments and talk of closer Czechoslovakian-Western economic relations. Most importantly, they feared that the Czechoslovakian leadership could not keep reform within acceptable bounds or boundaries and that the Czechoslovakian Communist party might itself lose political control. Czechoslovakia's crucial strategic position, forming a corridor between the USSR's Ukrainian republic and West Germany as well as bordering on East Germany, Poland, Hungary, and Austria heightened Soviet fears (see Map 14.1). Dissidents and reformers in Ukraine and other Soviet areas might become bolder if the Czechoslovakian reform movement continued to develop. Other Communist leaders, especially Gomulka of Poland and Ulbricht of East Germany, feared that winds from Prague might carry the Prague-Spring "virus" to their own countries.

In mid-July, leaders of the USSR, Bulgaria, East Germany, Hungary, and Poland met in Warsaw and drafted a letter to the Central Committee of the Czechoslovakian Communist party. The letter stated that "it is our deep conviction that the offensive of the reactionary forces, backed by imperialism . . . threatens to push your country off the road of socialism and thus jeopardizes the interests of the entire socialist system. . . . We cannot agree to have hostile forces push your country from the road of socialism." In the weeks that followed, Soviet leaders twice met with those of Czechoslovakia and became convinced that persuasion would not roll back reform.

Thus, on the night of August 20–21, greater than a half-million Soviet and other Warsaw Pact troops from Bulgaria, East Germany, Hungary, and Poland launched a surprise attack on Czechoslovakia. It was met by passive resis-

FIGURE 18.3. Soviet invasion of Prague, 1968.
(Keystone Press Agency)

tance, but the occupying forces soon controlled the country with little loss of blood. Meanwhile, Czechoslovakian leaders were brought to Moscow. From August 23 to 26, they were subjected to intense Kremlin pressures and reluctantly agreed to take a harder line against "antisocialist" elements. In exchange, most of them were allowed to continue in their positions—at least temporarily.

About a month after their return to Prague, the Soviet newspaper *Pravda* provided a justification for the August invasion. In the West, this justification was labeled the "Brezhnev Doctrine." It stated that "every Communist party is responsible not only to its own people but also to all the socialist countries" and that "the sovereignty of each socialist country cannot be set up in opposition to the interests of the socialist world."

In the months that followed, Soviet troops remained in Czechoslovakia, and Kremlin pressures were exerted on Dubcek. Finally, in April 1969, he was forced to resign and was succeeded by Gustav Husák, who had supported the "Prague Spring" but after the invasion cooperated with Moscow. Not long after coming to power, he began forcing many unrepentant Dubcek supporters from their party and government positions.

Among other Communist parties, the reaction to the Soviet invasion of 1968 was mixed. Both the Italian and the Chinese parties, though far apart ideologically, were critical. In general, the invasion further divided and weakened international communism.

China, Non-European Marxists, and the Third World

After the fall of Khrushchev, the new Soviet leadership made modest attempts to improve Sino-Soviet relations but to little avail. The Chinese complained of

"Khrushchevism without Khrushchev." In late 1966, after China sent Soviet students back to the USSR, the Soviet government reciprocated by expelling Chinese students.

In 1968, the Soviet invasion of Czechoslovakia and its "Brezhnev-doctrine" justification stimulated new fears and actions from the Chinese. If the doctrine could be applied to Czechoslovakia, could it not also be applied to China or Eastern European countries friendly to China? Although Albania was most supportive of China in its dispute with the USSR, Rumanian-Chinese relations were also good and grew closer following the invasion, in which Rumania had refused to participate. Just a few days after the Soviet attack, China's Zhou Enlai, while lashing out against the invasion, assured Rumania of future Chinese support. China also improved relations with Yugoslavia, a step that was facilitated by China's new line of verbal attack on the Soviet Union. Although formerly China had criticized both Yugoslavia and the USSR for Marxist revisionism, the new line criticized only the USSR and not for revisionism but for "social [Soviet] imperialism."

In 1969, polemics escalated into serious border clashes and Soviet hints of possible strikes against China's nuclear installations, then still in their early stages. From March to September, skirmishes occurred at various points along the more than 4,500-mile-long border that the USSR and its satellite Mongolia shared with China. By late summer, the Soviet Union was sending out signals through newspapers, secret correspondence, and diplomats that escalating Sino-Soviet tensions could lead to war, possibly involving the Soviet use of nuclear weapons. By this time, Soviet bombers newly moved to Siberia and Mongolia were practicing for possible attacks against Chinese nuclear facilities. The exact mixture of Soviet bluff and genuine preparations remains unclear.

Also unclear is to what extent the Soviet threats and actions influenced the Chinese leaders. Whatever the case, in September 1969, Kosygin and China's Zhou Enlai met briefly in Beijing and agreed to upgrade their strained diplomatic relations by once again exchanging ambassadors rather than just lesser diplomatic officials.

Although Sino-Soviet relations improved slightly and border clashes diminished, the Soviet government continued its Asian military buildup, increasing and upgrading its military divisions, missiles, and planes. During the late 1970s, it greatly strengthened the Soviet Far Eastern navy. For its part, China in the 1970s developed delivery systems capable of launching nuclear missiles thousands of miles into the Asiatic portion of the USSR and, in the early 1980s, into the European portion as well. Continuing tensions between the two Communist giants were also affected by their relations with other Communist and Third World countries and with the United States.

Partly to counter China, the Soviet Union continued to support India, whereas China backed India's rival Pakistan. In 1966, Premier Kosygin mediated an end to the latest Indo-Pakistani conflict over Kashmir. In 1971, the USSR increased its weapons deliveries to India; in December, India militarily intervened in the Pakistani civil war, assisting East Pakistan to defeat West Pakistan and establish its own independent state, Bangladesh.

Indochina was another area where the USSR and China supported rival powers, only this time rival Communists. After furnishing North Vietnam with billions of dollars worth of weapons during the Vietnam War, the Soviet Union continued thereafter to support a united Vietnam. Although China had also aided North Vietnam during the war, its postwar relations with Vietnam were more antagonistic. In 1978–1979, Vietnam defeated the Chinese-backed Pol Pot regime in Cambodia (Kampuchea) and established a puppet government there. In response, in early 1979, Chinese troops crossed over into Vietnam, beginning two weeks of combat before returning to China.

For years afterward, China cited Vietnamese control over Cambodia as one of three major obstacles to improved Sino-Soviet relations. The other two were the continuing presence of powerful Soviet military forces along the Sino-Soviet border and the presence of Soviet troops in Afghanistan, troops that were first sent in December 1979.

Key Politburo members—primarily Andropov, Defense Minister D. Ustinov, and, less enthusiastically, Gromyko—convinced the ailing Brezhnev that troops had to be sent to protect Soviet security interests. Afghanistan shared a 2,500-kilometer border with portions of Soviet Central Asia, and the peoples on both sides of the border were ethnically related.

For a year and a half before the invasion, a Marxist government had ruled in Afghanistan. Having come to power primarily by its own efforts, it soon received Moscow's backing. Soviet leaders, however, increasingly viewed it as inefficient and suspect. Moslem rebellions against it increased, as did outside aid for the rebels. Moslem countries such as Iran (where a new Moslem fundamentalist government was now in power), Libya, Saudi Arabia, and Pakistan supported the rebels, and Moscow feared that the United States and China were encouraging such support. Furthermore, Afghanistan's Marxist ruler, Hafizullah Amin, displayed growing signs of turning away from the USSR and finding support elsewhere. Soviet leaders feared an increasing U.S. role.

With the loss of less than 100 Soviet lives, the Soviet military occupied Kabul, toppled Amin (who died in the takeover), and replaced him with the more accommodating Afghan Marxist, Babrak Karmal. In mid-January 1980, Brezhnev declared that the intervention had been essential to prevent an "imperialist military bridgehead" from being established in Afghanistan. Although Soviet leaders overestimated the "imperialist" danger, they underestimated the difficulties and complications a Soviet invasion might produce, both inside Afghanistan and with other countries.

In other Third World areas, Soviet diplomacy had earlier suffered both setbacks and gains. In Indonesia in the mid-1960s, the military slaughtered hundreds of thousands of Communists and other leftists, weakened and eventually (1967) deposed President Sukarno, and inherited large amounts of Soviet military equipment that had been sent to him. In 1966, the government of N. Nkrumah was overthrown in Ghana and Soviet technicians sent home. The following year, Arab forces, armed with many Soviet weapons, were crushed by Israel in the Six-Day War. In 1972, despite Soviet assistance in rebuilding and strengthening its military, Egypt expelled most Soviet advisers. During the late 1970s, Egypt's President Anwar Sadat moved closer to the United States, recognized Israel, and further cooled Soviet-Egyptian relations.

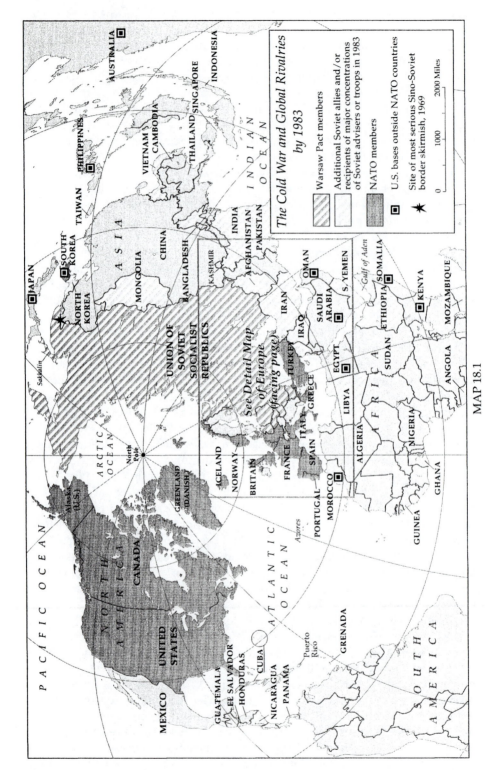

The Cold War and Global Rivalries by 1983

Warsaw Pact members

Additional Soviet allies and/or recipients of major concentrations of Soviet advisers or troops in 1983

NATO members

▣ U.S. bases outside NATO countries

✴ Site of most serious Sino-Soviet border skirmish, 1969

0   1000   2000 Miles

MAP 18.1

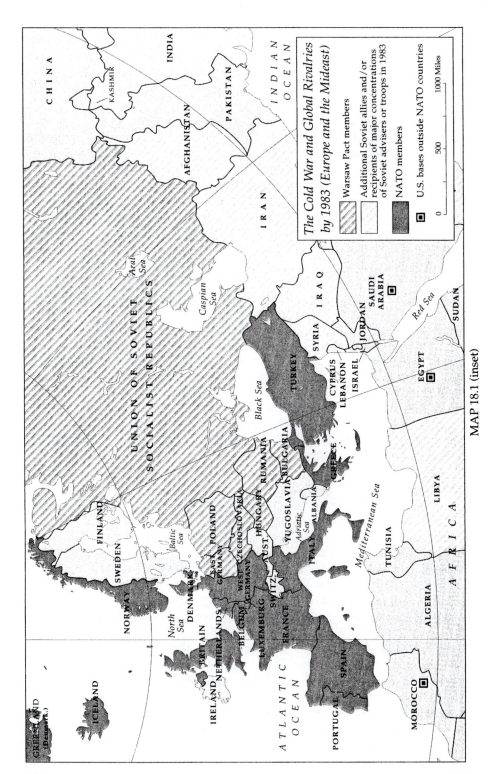

The Cold War and Global Rivalries by 1983 (Europe and the Mideast)

▨ Warsaw Pact members

☐ Additional Soviet allies and/or
recipients of major concentrations
of Soviet advisers or troops in 1983

▰ NATO members

◩ U.S. bases outside NATO countries

0   500   1000 Miles

MAP 18.1 (inset)

On a more successful note, in 1975–1976, the faction that Soviet aid and Cuban troops supported in the Angolan civil war won out over U.S.-backed and Chinese-backed groups and South African military forces. In 1977–1978, Soviet support and Cuban troops also aided an Ethiopian Marxist government in its struggle against secessionists and neighboring Somalia (formerly supported by the USSR). Across the Gulf of Aden from Somalia, the self-proclaimed Marxist republic of South Yemen granted port and air facilities to the USSR and supported the Soviet-Cuban assistance of Ethiopia. These facilities gave the USSR supply stations on the strategically important Arabian Peninsula.

The gains in South Yemen reflected an expansion of Soviet global strategic power and influence during the late 1960s and 1970s. This heightened outreach, however, was becoming increasingly costly. By the early 1980s, Cuban aid alone was costing the USSR several billion dollars per year. Moreover, the expansion alarmed the United States and contributed to an escalation of an arms race the Soviet Union could ill afford.

Soviet-Western Relations: The Rise and Fall of Détente

Before the expansion of Soviet power helped cool Soviet-U.S. relations at the end of the 1970s, they had earlier improved during the heyday of détente (or the relaxation of tensions) in the early 1970s. From the Soviet viewpoint, détente came about primarily because the Soviet military buildup of the late 1960s had overcome Soviet nuclear inferiority and brought about a rough nuclear parity: The United States now realized that it had to deal with the USSR on more equal terms. Although this was one factor, there were others, including the costs of the escalating arms race, European and Asian developments, and mutual desires for greater trade.

Before the U.S. movement toward détente, Western Europe had begun to move in that direction on its own. Later U.S. efforts were partly an attempt to regain leadership on the issue.

Before his resignation in 1969, French President Charles de Gaulle had encouraged détente as part of his effort to lessen Western European dependence on the United States. After becoming West German chancellor in October 1969, Willy Brandt began implementing his *Ostpolitik* (Eastern Policy). It aimed at improving East-West relations as a first step toward eventual German reunification. In November, West Germany signed the Nuclear Nonproliferation Treaty, which the U.S. and USSR had signed in 1968 to prevent the transference of nuclear weapons or their components to nonnuclear states. In August 1970, Brandt and Kosygin signed a nonaggression treaty, which implicitly accepted the Oder-Neisse boundary separating East Germany and Poland. The following year, in a new agreement with the three other Berlin-occupying powers, the USSR gave new assurances regarding access to West Berlin. In December 1972, the two Germanys signed a treaty extending diplomatic recognition to each other.

While the U.S. Nixon administration had some reservations about Brandt's

Ostpolitik, the Soviet Union had a serious concern of its own—the warming of U.S. relations with Communist China. Not only was 1969 a year of acute Sino-Soviet tensions, but also it marked the beginning of a decade-long process of establishing full U.S.-Chinese diplomatic relations. By February 1972, when Nixon spent a week in China, Soviet leaders already had good reason to fear that if they did not improve Soviet-American relations, the USSR might become increasingly isolated as the United States moved closer to China.

In June 1967, Premier Kosygin had met with U.S. President Lyndon Johnson in Glassboro, New Jersey, and the two powers signed the Nuclear Nonproliferation Treaty a year later. But the Vietnam War and the Soviet invasion of Czechoslovakia in 1968 hampered further U.S.-Soviet efforts to improve relations.

By the early 1970s, however, President Nixon was trying to end the Vietnam War and needed both the USSR and China to help him persuade North Vietnam to reach a compromise settlement. Furthermore, he and his chief foreign policy adviser, Henry Kissinger, had developed a diplomatic strategy of simultaneously improving U.S.-Chinese and U.S.-Soviet relations. In May 1972, Nixon came to Moscow, where he signed ten agreements. Two of them had developed from Strategic Arms Limitation Talks (SALT), which had been underway for several years. The first SALT treaty limited each side to two antiballistic missile (ABM) sites. (ABMs were defensive missiles that could shoot down incoming missiles.) The fear of both superpowers was that massive deployment of ABMs would encourage more spending on offensive missiles to overcome the ABMs. The second SALT treaty was an Interim Agreement good for five years that capped the number of intercontinental ballistic missiles (ICBMs), missile-launching submarines, and submarine-launched ballistic missiles (SLBMs) that either side could deploy.

Another agreement that received great attention in the USSR was that on the Basic Principles of Mutual Relations between the United States and USSR. By it, both sides agreed to conduct "their mutual relations on the basis of peaceful coexistence" and "equality." Other agreements provided for cooperation on health research, science and technology, space exploration, and the prevention of incidents at sea. Although increased trade was important to Brezhnev, the only significant summit trade agreement was to establish a joint trade commission. But the summit set the stage for other trade agreements later that year, and by year's end the Soviet Union had bought (partly on credit) more than $1 billion worth of U.S. grain and other agricultural products.

From 1973 to 1975, the two superpowers signed additional economic, cultural, and arms agreements and held new summits. In 1973, Brezhnev visited the United States, and in 1974, Nixon returned to the USSR. In November 1974, following Nixon's Watergate resignation, President Gerald Ford met with Brezhnev at Vladivostok in the Soviet Far East, where the two leaders agreed to new limitations on the total number of strategic arms carriers, including bombers. A Vietnam cease-fire and the removal of U.S. troops in 1973 was another step furthering détente. In July 1975, there was a joint U.S.-Soviet space rendezvous and docking, symbolizing the new spirit of cooperation. Later that same month, the USSR, thirty-two other European countries, and the United States and Canada convened in Helsinki to approve the Final Act of the Conference on Security and Cooperation in Europe (CSCE).

The Final Act contained three accords or "baskets." The Soviet Union pushed hardest for most aspects of the first and second baskets, which in effect finally sanctioned (after thirty years) postwar European boundaries and provided for increased scientific, economic, and other cooperation. Western nations successfully bargained to include most provisions of the third basket, which pledged the participating countries to recognize various human rights, including those of their own subjects. It was the honoring of these provisions that concerned the Helsinki Watch groups established in the USSR and other countries.

Despite the apparent successes of détente by mid-1975, the bargaining over the third Helsinki basket indicated the strains threatening to derail the détente process. U.S.-Soviet trade had not developed to the extent hoped for by Moscow because it had become linked with U.S. congressional pressures regarding the civil rights of Soviet citizens, particularly the rights of Jews to emigrate.

Other pressures were also building. Continuing arms talks aimed at more drastic measures than the 1972 Interim Agreement aroused fears among military-industrial forces in both countries. And both powers continued developing new weapons and feared the other side might spurt ahead. Although the number of ICBM and SLBM missiles had been capped in 1972, there had been no agreement then as to how many warheads each missile could have. Before 1972, the United States had already tested a multiple independently targeted reentry vehicle (MIRV) system, by which one missile could be launched containing several warheads, each directed at a different target. At Vladivostok in 1974, the two superpowers agreed to limit the number of MIRVed missiles to 1,320, but this still allowed for ample escalation—the first Soviet ICBM MIRV deployment did not come until 1975.

Finally, the two superpowers had never clarified their differences regarding Third World involvement and what actions were and were not in keeping with détente. During the Arab-Israeli War of 1973, there had been some tense moments between the two superpowers because of their support of different sides, but the better relations created by détente helped them to overcome the crisis.

By late 1975–early 1976, however, cooperation was becoming increasingly difficult, and support of different factions in Angola contributed to eroding détente. In the months surrounding Angola's gaining of independence (from Portugal) in November 1975, Soviet-Cuban aid competed with U.S., Chinese, and South African assistance to different Angolan factions—although the U.S. Congress cut off U.S. covert aid in December 1975. By March 1976, when the civil war ended, there were about 17,000 Cuban troops in Angola. The U.S. government regarded Soviet-Cuban actions in Angola as incompatible with détente; Soviet decision makers, however, saw no contradiction and maintained that Soviet aid was in keeping with its long-standing commitment to national-liberation movements.

Despite continuing arms talks and a new summit in 1979, highlighted by the signing of a SALT II arms agreement, détente eroded further in the late 1970s. The new U.S. president, Jimmy Carter, strongly emphasized human rights, once calling it "the soul of our foreign policy." But Soviet leaders thought that his strong expressions of support for Soviet dissidents violated the spirit of détente. Despite SALT I and the signing (though not ratifying) of SALT II, the arms race and mutual suspicions continued escalating because of more MIRVed missiles and other new military technology and movements. Soviet Third World activities continued to alarm many U.S. officials and politicians. Finally in 1979–1980, the Soviet invasion of Afghanistan and the U.S. response to it dealt a death blow to détente and insured that SALT II would not be ratified.

Although the Soviet government saw its action in Afghanistan as comparable to U.S. intervention in places such as the Dominican Republic (1965), U.S. President Carter called the Soviet invasion "the greatest threat to peace since the Second World War." A whole series of U.S. retaliatory measures followed from embargoing U.S. grain sales to the USSR to boycotting the 1980 summer Olympic Games in Moscow. Shortly before leaving office in January 1981, Carter sought to increase the previous year's U.S. defense budget by 15 percent.

Soviet Foreign Policy on the Defensive, 1981–1984

U.S. President Ronald Reagan believed that détente had been a mistake and that the Soviet Union had obtained much more from it than had the United States. Although he did not use the words until 1983, he had long thought that the Soviet Union was an "evil empire" and the "focus of evil in the modern world." He believed in "peace through strength," and along with the U.S. Congress, he now increased U.S. military spending well beyond the 15 percent increase requested by Carter. He also desired not only to contain communism, but to overthrow Marxist governments in such places as Afghanistan, Angola, Nicaragua, and Grenada, where U.S. troops were sent in 1983.

Meanwhile the Soviet Union faced a major crisis in a country of vital interest to it—Poland. In 1980, after the Polish government attempted to increase meat prices, protests erupted. They were more widespread and coordinated than similar disturbances over price increases in 1970 and 1976, although the 1970 crisis had been enough to force Gomulka from power. In 1980, a powerful and genuinely independent labor union called Solidarity emerged to lead the opposition. The government bargained with it and made major concessions. The Catholic Church, whose head was the Polish pope John Paul II, worked along with Solidarity and its leader Lech Walesa to increase freedoms in Poland.

With the Polish Communist party growing steadily weaker, the amount of freedom gained in Poland during 1980–1981 soon went beyond what Czechoslovakians had obtained in the spring of 1968. Moscow again made threatening noises. In December 1981, recently appointed party leader General Wojciech Jaruzelski, fearful of Soviet troop intervention, established martial law and outlawed Solidarity.

Correctly believing that the USSR bore a "heavy and direct responsibility for the repression in Poland," the U.S. government responded with sanctions against both Poland and the USSR. In the summer of 1982, the U.S. government began a covert support program to aid the outlawed Solidarity.

Faced with the Polish crisis and the hostility of the new Reagan administration, plus continuing Chinese animosity and growing economic problems at home, the aging Soviet leadership kept hoping that détente was still salvageable. They simply had no new overall strategy to replace it. Yet, despite renewed arms talks that showed little sign of progress, there was almost no indication of any chance for improved relations.

On the contrary, in 1983 relations worsened. Early that year, President Reagan not only publicly referred to the Soviet Union as the "evil empire" and "focus of evil," but also called for a new weapons system, the Strategic Defense Initiative (SDI), often called "Star Wars." By it, U.S. missiles in space would be able to destroy Soviet missiles launched toward the United States. Andropov and other Soviet leaders believed such a plan could be used to prevent the Soviets from launching a retaliatory attack in response to a U.S. nuclear "first strike."

In the late summer of 1983, a Soviet plane shot down a Korean civilian jetliner (KAL 007) that had overflown Soviet airspace along its Far Eastern border. The Soviet military had mistaken the jetliner carrying 269 passengers for a spy plane, and the Soviet government covered up details regarding the incident. President Reagan erroneously declared that "there is no way a pilot could mistake this for anything other than a civilian airliner." He called the shooting "an act of barbarism," and he lashed out at the Soviet system and its deceitfulness, calling into question its reliability in any negotiations.

Toward the end of 1983, the United States deployed Pershing II and cruise missiles in Western Europe. Although the deployments had been planned under President Carter in response to new Soviet SS-20s missiles targeted on Western Europe, Soviet officials had hoped to prevent the deployment of these feared U.S. missiles. But negotiations in ongoing arms talks in Geneva and pressure on West Germany and other countries not to allow them on their soil proved fruitless. When the United States went ahead with the decision, Soviet negotiators ended arms talks in Geneva.

The following year was a presidential election year in the United States, and President Reagan spoke a little more about peace and improving U.S.-Soviet relations. Yet there were still numerous causes for tension. In August 1984, Reagan tested a radio microphone by joking: "I have signed legislation to outlaw Russia forever. We begin bombing in five minutes." The "joke" was reported in the press and was not thought humorous in the Soviet Union.

The Soviet leadership, now under Chernenko, was convinced that the Reagan administration sought nuclear superiority and was attempting to ruin the Soviet economy. Being much poorer, the USSR could not match the heightened U.S. defense spending without severely harming its economy. Nevertheless, in

November 1984, the Soviet government announced a major increase in its defense budget.

Yet in keeping with the slight signs that relations might arise from the depths of 1983, the superpowers agreed in January 1985 to resume Geneva arms negotiations on March 12. By that date, however, Chernenko was dead, and Mikhail Gorbachev had just become his successor.

*SUGGESTED SOURCES**

ANDERSON, RICHARD D., JR. *Public Politics in an Authoritarian State: Making Foreign Policy during the Brezhnev Years*. Ithaca, N.Y., 1993.

BIALER, SEWERYN. *The Soviet Paradox: External Expansion, Internal Decline*. New York, 1986.

BONNER, ELENA. *Alone Together*. New York, 1986.

BRESLAUER, GEORGE W. *Khrushchev and Brezhnev as Leaders: Building Authority in Soviet Politics*. London, 1982.

BROWN, ARCHIE, and MICHAEL KASER, eds. *Soviet Policy for the 1980's*. Bloomington, 1982.

BRUCAN, SILVIU. *The Post-Brezhnev Era: An Insider's View*. New York, 1983.

BYRNES, ROBERT F., ed. *After Brezhnev: Sources of Soviet Conduct in the 1980s*. Bloomington, 1983.

CHORNOVIL, VIACHESLAV. *The Chornovil Papers*. New York, 1968.

COCKBURN, ANDREW. *The Threat: Inside the Soviet Military Machine*. New York, 1984.

COHEN, STEPHEN F., ed. *An End to Silence: Uncensored Opinion in the Soviet Union*. New York, 1982.

COHEN, STEPHEN F., ALEXANDER RABINOWITCH, and ROBERT SHARLET, eds. *The Soviet Union since Stalin*. Bloomington, 1980.

COLTON, TIMOTHY J. *The Dilemma of Reform in the Soviet Union*. Rev. ed. New York, 1986.

DAWISHA, KAREN. *The Kremlin and the Prague Spring*. Berkeley, 1984.

DOBRYNIN, ANATOLY. *In Confidence: Moscow's Ambassador to America's Six Cold War Presidents (1962–1986)*. New York, 1995.

DODER, DUSKO. *Shadows and Whispers: Power Politics Inside the Kremlin from Brezhnev to Gorbachev*. New York, 1986.

DORNBERG, JOHN. *Brezhnev: The Masks of Power*. New York, 1974.

DUNLOP, JOHN B. *The Faces of Contemporary Russian Nationalism*. Princeton, 1983.

EDMONDS, ROBIN. *Soviet Foreign Policy: The Brezhnev Years*. Oxford, 1983.

FREEDMAN, ROBERT O., ed. *Soviet Jewry in the Decisive Decade, 1971–80*. Durham, 1984.

GARTHOFF, RAYMOND L. *Détente and Confrontation: American-Soviet Relations from Nixon to Reagan*. Rev. ed. Washington, D.C., 1994.

———. *The Great Transition: American-Soviet Relations and the End of the Cold War*. Washington, D.C., 1994.

GELMAN, HARRY. *The Brezhnev Politburo and the Decline of Detente*. Ithaca, N.Y., 1984.

GOLDMAN, MARSHALL I. *U.S.S.R. in Crisis: The Failure of an Economic System*. New York, 1983.

GRIGORENKO, PETRO G. *Memoirs*. New York, 1982.

GROMYKO, ANDREI. *Memoirs*. New York, 1989.

* See also books cited in footnotes; many works by individual dissidents are also available.

HAYWARD, MAX, ed. *On Trial: The Soviet State Versus "Abram Tertz" and "Nikolai Arzhak."* New York, 1967.

HOLLOWAY, DAVID. *The Soviet Union and the Arms Race.* New Haven, 1984.

HOUGH, JERRY F., and MERLE FAINSOD. *How the Soviet Union is Governed.* Cambridge, Mass., 1979.

KRAMER, MARK. "Poland, 1980-81: Soviet Policy during the Polish Crisis," *BCWIHP* 5 (Spring 1995) 1, 116–26.

MEDVEDEV, ZHORES A. *Andropov.* New York, 1983.

———. *A Question of Madness.* New York, 1971.

MILLAR, JAMES R., ed. *Cracks in the Monolith: Party Power in the Brezhnev Era.* Armonk, N.Y., 1992.

NIXON, RICHARD. *Leaders.* New York, 1982.

SAKHAROV, ANDREI. *Memoirs.* New York, 1990.

SCAMMELL, MICHAEL. *Solzhenitsyn: A Biography.* New York, 1984.

———, ed. *The Solzhenitsyn Files: Secret Soviet Documents Reveal One Man's Fight against the Monolith.* Chicago, 1995.

SHLAPENTOKH, VLADIMIR. *Public and Private Life of the Soviet People: Changing Values in Post-Stalin Russia.* New York, 1989.

STEELE, JONATHAN. *World Power: Soviet Foreign Policy under Brezhnev and Andropov.* London, 1983.

TÖKÉS, RUDOLF L., ed. *Dissent in the USSR: Politics, Ideology, and People.* Baltimore, 1975.

VALENTA, JIRI. *Soviet Intervention in Czechoslovakia, 1968: Anatomy of a Decision.* Baltimore, 1991.

VAKSBERG, ARKADY. *The Soviet Mafia.* London, 1991.

ZEMTSOV, ILYA. *Chernenko: The Last Bolshevik: The Soviet Union on the Eve of Perestroika.* New Brunswick, N.J., 1989.

CHAPTER 19

Gorbachev and the End of the USSR, 1985–1991

From March 1985 until December 1991, Mikhail Gorbachev was the key actor in one of the most compelling dramas of the twentieth century. During the first act, he presided over sweeping reforms in the Soviet Union. During the second, he struggled with mounting crises at home while helping end the Cold War and accepting the collapse of Soviet hegemony over Eastern Europe. And during the third act, he saw the USSR disintegrate into fifteen countries and along with it his own political powers. On Christmas day 1991, with no country to rule, he resigned as president of the USSR. Although his own mistakes contributed to his downfall, the task he set for himself—transforming the USSR into an efficient and humane socialist society—was almost impossible from the start.

GORBACHEV: THE MAKING OF A REFORMER

Gorbachev was born in 1931 in the village of Privolnoe, a steppe area in the North Caucasus Foreland region of Stavropol. Although his ancestors were mainly Russian, his mother was also partly Ukrainian. Both his grandfathers were peasants, one becoming a kolkhoz administrator; both had been victimized in the 1930s, one being sent to Siberia, the other imprisoned for more than a year. Gorbachev's father, an MTS (Machine-Tractor Station) driver, remained loyal to the party and during World War II was away at the front.

An only child, Gorbachev grew up in a two-room peasant hut and went to the village school. He later attended secondary school in a nearby town, where he received almost perfect marks, joined the Komsomol, and acted in school plays. In the summers, the young Gorbachev worked on the collective farm and won an award for his harvesting efforts working on a combine. From 1950 to 1955, he was a student at Moscow State University and became a Komsomol leader in the Law Faculty, in which he was enrolled. In 1952, he joined the Communist party. The following year, he married Raisa Titorenko, a philosophy student, who had finished first in her secondary school class.

After graduating in 1955, he returned to the Stavropol region and worked in the Komsomol and party, while completing correspondence studies at the Stavropol Agricultural Institute. In 1970, he became party boss for the Stavropol province, an area rich not only in good farm land, but also in famous North Caucasian mineral-health resorts visited by top Soviet leaders. Welcoming them to the province gave Gorbachev an opportunity to impress them. In 1971, he became a member of the Central Committee and in 1978 went to Moscow, where he worked in the party Secretariat overseeing Soviet agriculture. Two years later, he became a full member of the Politburo. In late 1983–early 1984, he became the ailing Andropov's right-hand man.

In many ways, Gorbachev reflected the attitudes of a newer generation of leaders. His relationship with his wife was one indication. After Krupskaia (Lenin's wife), the wives of Soviet leaders seldom played a prominent public role. By the early 1980s, the Gorbachevs' only child, Irina, was an adult, and Raisa Gorbachev, who meanwhile had obtained the equivalent of a Ph.D., lectured on Marxism-Leninism at her alma mater, Moscow State University. Throughout her husband's years in power, she was much in the news, and he told an interviewer in 1987 that he discussed "everything" with her.

Gorbachev was intelligent, self-confident, and well mannered and knew how to please superiors without seeming obsequious, but he had few close friends. He was open to new ideas and approaches, although after coming to power he sometimes seemed a know-it-all and displayed irritation when crossed. In general, however, until his political problems began to mount in the late 1980s, he impressed most people he met, whether older Communists such as Andropov, Kosygin, and Suslov; dissidents such as Sakharov; or foreign leaders such as British Prime Minister Margaret Thatcher. After meeting with Gorbachev in London in late 1984, Thatcher announced: "I like Mr. Gorbachev. We can do business together."

This final important foreign trip before assuming the Soviet leadership several months later helped broaden Gorbachev's international awareness. By early 1985, he had visited more Western countries, including Canada (1983), than had any other post-Lenin party chief before coming to office.

DOMESTIC REFORMS: THE FIRST STAGE

By March 11, 1985, just a day after Chernenko's death, the Politburo (minus a few of its full ten members), followed by the Central Committee, agreed that Gorbachev should be the new general secretary. Some Central Committee members thought that an energetic, dynamic leader was needed to address the country's mounting problems: economic stagnation, political corruption, poor working habits, mass cynicism, declining birth and rising death rates, major environmental problems, growing ethnic tensions, and antagonistic foreign relations with both China and the West. But the majority of leaders, especially on the Politburo, had no intention of elevating a man who would pursue radical reform. Had they realized what a radical reformer he would become, they would never have selected Gorbachev.

One of Gorbachev's first priorities was to solidify his position. Within about a year, he had managed to rid the Politburo of several old members and to promote individuals more supportive of reform. By the spring of 1986, about half the members of the Politburo, Secretariat, and Central Committee were new, although not all were hand-picked by Gorbachev, especially on the several-hundred-member Central Committee. In the tradition of new party bosses, still hemmed in by "collective leadership," Gorbachev's powers to remove and appoint the party elite were still restricted. Among the most important new full Politburo members and Gorbachev supporters in 1985 was former Georgian party boss Eduard Shevardnadze, who also replaced Gromyko as foreign minister.

In December 1984, several months before coming to power, Gorbachev foreshadowed his later reforms in a speech in which he used words that would soon capture world attention—*glasnost* (openness), *perestroika* (restructuring), and *demokratizatsiia* (democratization). Yet at this time, they did not necessarily imply all they would later. Like Peter the Great before him, Gorbachev wanted to refashion the structure he had inherited, not destroy it, but he possessed no specific blueprint indicating exactly how to go about his task. From the beginning he intended to be more radical than he revealed to other party leaders. Realizing that his ideas were more radical than those of other Soviet leaders, he knew that he had to proceed cautiously or risk being replaced as head of the party. But Gorbachev also became a more radical reformer as his horizons expanded and other reformers from below pressured him to go further.

During Gorbachev's early months in power, it was still possible to see him as a younger, more vigorous version of Andropov. Like his former supporter, Gorbachev attacked poor worker discipline and talked of accelerating economic growth. The most notable reform of 1985 was an attempt to improve the performance of both the workers and the economy via a "vodka reform" that increased alcohol prices and made it more difficult to obtain.

From the beginning, Gorbachev benefited from the support of reform-minded individuals within the party. Some of them had once been Andropov advisers or had at least been given some encouragement under him. Among the latter were two academics based at Akademgorodok, a relatively free enclave near the Siberian city of Novosibirsk. One was the economist Abel Aganbegyan, and the other was the economist and sociologist Tatiana Zaslavskaia. In 1983, Andropov had authorized her and some of her colleagues to present him with a frank analysis of Soviet socioeconomic problems, and her *Novosibirsk Report* did just that. Before and after assuming power, Gorbachev met with some of these Akademgorodok experts, seeking their advice and being influenced by it.

By 1986, Gorbachev and his supporters were trumpeting the need for *glasnost* and *perestroika* and continued to do so thereafter. One stimulant to both policies as well as to a growing environmental movement was a terrible nuclear accident in April 1986 at Chernobyl, north of Kiev. A nuclear reactor exploded, spewing tons of radioactive particles into the atmosphere. Winds then carried contamination into other nations. Although the number of immediate Soviet deaths was officially stated to be only thirty-one, it was widely suspected that there were more, and there was little doubt that the eventual death toll resulting from radiation damage would be much higher. (A decade later, estimates of combined deaths that had already occurred and future deaths from Chernobyl aftereffects varied from thousands to hundreds of thousands.) Subsequent costs for clean-up and the eventual resettlement of at least 200,000 people were also high.

At first, the government only reluctantly released information about the accident. Gorbachev soon realized, however, that an accident of this magnitude, affecting both Soviet and foreign peoples, demanded more *glasnost*.

GLASNOST, PERESTROIKA, AND DEMOCRATIZATION

Glasnost meant more freedom of expression and less censorship and government secrecy. A main reason for government support of it was to stimulate creative economic developments, while exposing corruption and other economic problems. In short, Gorbachev viewed it primarily as an instrument to promote *perestroika*, specifically economic "restructuring."

Although Gorbachev encouraged *glasnost*, it also took on a life of its own. In the years following Chernobyl, writers became increasingly free to criticize without fearing punishment, and many dissidents were released from detention—one of the most famous, Andrei Sakharov, was freed from his Gorky exile in December 1986. Critics of Soviet life and other Soviet citizens also became freer to emigrate and travel abroad (Jewish emigration in 1990 was about 200 times the level of 1986). Most Soviet intellectuals supported Gorbachev's policies, and films, plays, and books that had long been forbidden suddenly appeared, including Boris Pasternak's *Doctor Zhivago*.

The government tolerated some demonstrations, strikes, and the formation of independent political associations. It took a more liberal attitude toward religious believers and broadened the legal rights of Soviet citizens. In December 1988, it suspended the jamming of foreign radio broadcasts, including the Russian-language programs of U.S.-financed Radio Liberty.

One of the most essential aspects of *glasnost* was what the journalist David Remnick has called "the return of history." So crucial was this return that he believed "once the regime eased up enough to permit a full-scale examination of the Soviet past, radical change was inevitable. Once the System showed itself for what it was and had been, it was doomed."[1]

In mid-1986, Gorbachev was still reluctant to encourage too much looking backward, fearing it would divert energies needed for the present and future. *Glasnost*, however, unleashed a thirst for historical facts that became greater with every gulp, and he himself gradually became more critical of the party's past. At first, the media concentrated primarily on the errors and crimes of the Brezhnev and Stalin years. The NEP and Khrushchev years were regarded more favorably, both seeming to offer positive lessons for the late 1980s. Grad-

---

[1] *Lenin's Tomb: The Last Days of the Soviet Empire* (New York, 1993), p. xi; see also his chapter, "The Return of History."

ually, however, the criticism broadened—by the end of the decade, even Lenin was starting to be tainted by it. (See Chapter 21 for more on *glasnost* and cultural, educational, and religious developments under Gorbachev.)

Although a term eventually applied to *restructuring* in various spheres, *perestroika* originally referred chiefly to economic restructuring. Chapter 18 discussed some of the major economic problems of the previous two decades. From the beginning, improving the economy was Gorbachev's major challenge. At first, the dilemma he faced was how to do so without abandoning the state socialism in which he believed. This is why for some time reformist Communist economic systems such as Hungary's, China's, or the USSR's own past NEP seemed more relevant than Western-style market economies. Yet for many reasons, the Hungarian and Chinese situations were different than the USSR's, and the world had changed much since NEP days.

By the mid-1980s, the world had entered the Information Age. At a time when computers and telecommunications were becoming increasingly important in business and economic affairs, the Soviet Union was falling further behind the United States and many other nations in Europe and Asia. As late as 1988, personal computers in the Soviet Union numbered in the tens of thousands, while there were about 20 million in the United States. The director of Moscow's Institute for Space Research admitted that to find adequate computers for his institute he had to buy U.S.-made ones on Moscow's black market.

After about two years of trying to renovate the old command economy, Gorbachev realized that more radical measures were needed. In 1987–1988, four such measures appeared. First, the government legalized private cooperative or collective business activity in certain spheres, especially in the long-neglected area of services, such as restaurants and repairs. Second, the government encouraged peasants to lease state lands and establish their own family and cooperative agricultural arrangements on them, selling their surplus product on the open market. Third, the state permitted joint Soviet-foreign business ventures, which slowly sprang up, providing goods and services from dental fillings and hotel construction to fast foods such as McDonald's. Finally, primarily because of a 1987 Enterprise Law that became effective in January 1988, state enterprises were encouraged to begin switching to a system of "self-management," "self-financing," and "self-accounting."

The ultimate goal of the Enterprise Law was to transform more economic decisions from centralized ministries to individual enterprises. The latter were to sign contracts with the government and other enterprises and be primarily responsible for planning their own production, wage rates, and other expenditures and for selling their products. Not only were factory directors to be given more powers, but so too were workers within a factory. The Enterprise Law, for example, called for the election of factory directors and other supervisory personnel.

Such elections were an example of Gorbachev's third watchword, *demokratizatsiia* (democratization). More generally, the principle aimed at increasing Soviet citizens' participation in the political process. Gorbachev had finally come to realize that along with *glasnost*, democratization was necessary for any thorough *perestroika*. Otherwise, entrenched interests could never be overcome.

FIGURE 19.1. The first McDonald's in Moscow. Even though this was the largest Mc-Donald's in the world, lines to get in were often several blocks long in the summer of 1990. (From Goff, Richard, et al. *The Twentieth Century: A Brief Global History.* 4th ed. New York, McGraw-Hill, 1994, p. 291.)

In mid–1988, at the Nineteenth Communist Party Conference, Gorbachev told delegates that the party's history of monopolizing power and exercising centralized control had "straight-jacketed society." He therefore proposed changes designed to reduce the role of the Communist party in the everyday political and economic life of the nation and called for the creation of more democratic governmental bodies. The delegates then approved measures calling for secret-ballot, multiple-candidate (although not multiparty) elections to soviet bodies at all levels, and they suggested limiting the term of elected government officials to a maximum of ten years in any position. The party also agreed to similar changes for its own structure.

A new Soviet Congress of 2,250 deputies, which met in the spring of 1989, reflected some of the proposed changes. Although many of the 750 deputies selected by "social organizations" faced little or no competition to obtain their seats, three-fourths of the other 1500 deputies gained their places by winning *contested* elections. Moreover, some prominent local party leaders who ran for the Congress were defeated. The Congress's spirited two-week televised session presented to Soviet citizens the most open political debates they had witnessed in seven decades of Soviet rule. Before adjourning, the Congress elected by secret ballot a new, more powerful 542-member Supreme Soviet, with Gorbachev as its president (he also had served as head of the earlier Supreme Soviet).

By 1989, it was clear that Gorbachev wished to create a far more humane system than any of his Soviet predecessors had done and one that was neither totalitarian nor terroristic. He continued to insist that he was following in the footsteps of Lenin (the Lenin of the NEP), but he was deluding himself. Although, as of yet, he displayed no intention of working for a Western-style multiparty system with a capitalist economy, his concept of a desirable Soviet socialism was slowly evolving closer to that of Western democratic socialism.

GORBACHEV'S THREE CRISES, 1988–1991

In his last years in power, Gorbachev faced three intertwined crises: growing nationality tensions, diminished political authority, and serious economic decline. They resulted from the clash of long-standing Soviet patterns with all the hopes, fears, and confusion unleashed by *glasnost*, *perestroika*, and democratization. Alexis de Tocqueville's famous words of the previous century, "The most dangerous time for a bad government is when it starts to reform itself," now once again seemed relevant; so too did the reforming experiences of Tsar Alexander II. Allowing pent-up dissatisfactions a public voice proved much easier than solving the country's problems.

The Nationalities Crisis

Despite increasing nationality tensions before the mid-1980s, order had been maintained by a combination of repressing non-Russian nationalisms and granting local Communist leaders and non-Russian elites some leeway. As we have seen with party boss G. Aliev in Azerbaijan, he could get away with nepotism, favoritism, and corruption as long as he made Brezhnev and the Kremlin happy by gifts, flattery, and his republic's economic performance.

In his quest for reform, Gorbachev attacked the old corrupt ways, many of which were exposed for the first time as a result of *glasnost*. The first major ethnic outbreak of his regime occurred in December 1986 after he replaced the corrupt party chief of Kazakhstan, D. Kunaev, with the Russian G. Kolbin. Students and others took to the streets of the republic's capital shouting "Kazakhstan for the Kazakhs and only the Kazakhs!" A show of force (tanks and other weapons) finally ended the outbreak after two days, and Gorbachev attempted to appease local feelings by replacing a Russian with a Kazakh as the number-two party man in the republic.

Yet the crisis revealed a fact that would become increasingly apparent in the next five years—Gorbachev's lack of sensitivity to nationality issues. What he saw as a struggle to "clean up" Kazakhstan's government and make it more efficient was not seen in such simple terms by the Kazakhs. Complex ethnic rivalries existed in this and other republics and, as Gorbachev admitted in 1990, he underestimated "the forces of nationalism and separatism."

Some conflicts were between non-Russian nationalities themselves, the most significant case being that of Armenians and Azerbaijanis over Nagorno-Karabakh (see Map 19.1). It was located in the Azerbaijan republic but peopled

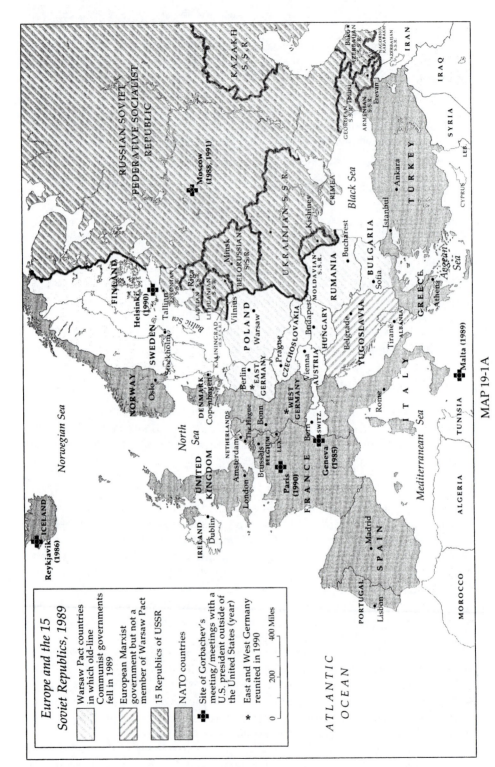

Europe and the 15 Soviet Republics, 1989

Warsaw Pact countries in which old-line Communist governments fell in 1989

European Marxist government but not a member of Warsaw Pact

15 Republics of USSR

NATO countries

Site of Gorbachev's meeting/meetings with a U.S. president outside of the United States (year)

* East and West Germany reunited in 1990

0   200   400 Miles

MAP 19-1A

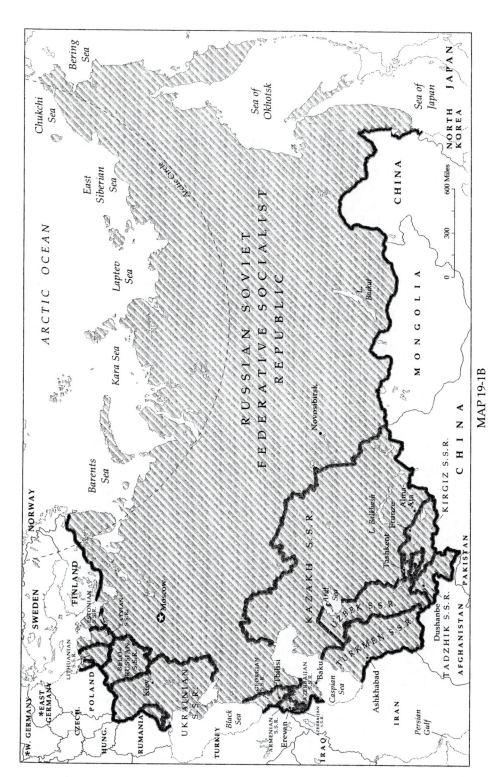

MAP 19-1B

415

primarily by Armenians, who wanted it unified with Armenia. In February 1988, Armenian demonstrations in favor of the idea were countered by Azerbaijani demonstrations opposing it. At the end of the month in Sumgait, near Baku, Azerbaijani youth initiated an especially bloody pogrom against Armenians, who were the second largest nationality in Azerbaijan. The months that followed produced massive demonstrations, strikes, and additional casualties in the two Caucasian republics as well as the flight of hundreds of thousands Armenians and Azerbaijanis who had been living in the republic dominated by the other. Only a devastating earthquake that struck Armenia in December temporarily diverted attention from this ethnic rivalry.

Both before and after the Sumgait pogrom, local hostility to Moscow also existed. In the aftermath of Chernobyl, environmental issues became more important to Armenians (as well as to other nationalities), and some of them protested Moscow's apparent indifference to spreading industrial pollution in their region. In Azerbaijan, there was dissatisfaction when Aliev was removed from the Politburo in late 1987. Yet at the beginning of 1988, many proponents of change in the Caucasus, especially in Armenia, still thought of themselves as backers of Gorbachev's reforms. After the Sumgait pogrom, Gorbachev attempted to reduce conflict through political compromise, culminating in the placing of Nagorno-Karabakh under Moscow's direct rule (January 1989). But the compromise pleased neither side.

Meanwhile, in the three Soviet Baltic republics of Estonia, Latvia, and Lithuania, nationalism took another form. In these republics, where the history of the 1939 Nazi-Soviet Pact and subsequent Soviet deportations remained vivid, national or popular front organizations came into being in 1988.

Participants in these organizations initially supported some of Gorbachev's reforms and worked in behalf of them and other issues, such as environmental ones. Obtaining more national autonomy naturally emerged as their most important goal. Thanks in part to Gorbachev's democratization policies, the fronts were able to display their popularity in local elections. The republics' Communist parties had little choice but to go along with the rising national tides. At the end of 1989, a large majority of the Lithuanian Communist party declared its independence from the all-union party; a minority opposed them, causing a split into two Lithuanian Communist parties. A similar development then occurred in the other two Baltic republics.

During early 1990, the governments of all three republics declared their independence, although none was yet able to make it a reality. In January 1991, amidst other signs that Moscow was unwilling to allow complete Baltic independence, Soviet troops stormed a government press building in Vilnius, Lithuania, killing fourteen people. According to Archie Brown and other sources, Gorbachev did not order the attack. Rather, it seems to have been part of a larger effort on the part of conservative forces, including some generals, to sow seeds of discord between Gorbachev and his reform supporters.

Other republics soon followed the Baltic example of proclaiming their sovereignty, especially after the huge Russian republic (RSFSR) declared its sovereignty from the federal government in June 1990. Partly in reaction to anti-Russian sentiments among non-Russian nationalities, Russian nationalism

FIGURE 19.2. Estonian demonstrators in Tallinn demanding independence, summer 1990. (From Goff, Richard, et al. *The Twentieth Century: A Brief Global History*. 4th ed. New York, McGraw-Hill, 1994, p. 512.)

intensified. Right-wing nationalist organizations such as *Pamiat* became stronger, and its antisemitism stimulated the desire of many Soviet Jews to emigrate. In Ukraine, a leader of its popular front (called *Rukh*) was the long-time dissident Viacheslav Chornovil, who became mayor of Lvov (Lviv) in the spring of 1990.

Gorbachev's Declining Political Authority

While the federal or nationalities crisis threatened the USSR with disintegration, other forces more specifically challenged Gorbachev's own political authority. From 1985 to early 1990, he battled mainly against conservative Communist party members who feared change and often stalled, delayed, and weakened reforms.

Yet by the end of the 1980s, Gorbachev also clashed with those who thought him too moderate. Although most deputies to the new Supreme Soviet that met in mid-1989 were opposed to sweeping reforms, a more liberal minority of deputies formed the "Inter-Regional Group." For a while, its chief spokesman was the former dissident Andrei Sakharov, but ill health led to his death at the end of 1989. Boris Yeltsin then emerged as the group's leading voice. For the next two years, the political and personal struggles between Gorbachev and Yeltsin proved crucial.

Although the two men were the same age, were equally ambitious, and had both risen through party ranks, they differed greatly in style and temperament. From December 1985 to November 1987, Gorbachev had attempted to make use of Yeltsin's talents by having him act as Moscow's party boss. By the latter date, however, the burly former head of the Sverdlovsk party must have seemed to Gorbachev like the proverbial bull in a china shop. Yeltsin's outspokenness and populist enthusiasm threatened to disrupt the precarious consensus for managed change that Gorbachev was attempting to orchestrate among party leaders. Yeltsin's critical remarks and disagreements with other leaders, including Gorbachev, at an October 1987 Central Committee meeting led to Yeltsin being removed as Moscow party chief in November. In February 1988, he also lost his position as a candidate member of the Politburo.

His treatment by Gorbachev and other party leaders, however, just endeared him more to Muscovites. So too did his criticism in mid-1988, at the widely covered Nineteenth Party Conference, of corruption and party privileges. Running for Moscow's at-large seat in the March 1989 elections to the new Soviet Congress of People's Deputies, Yeltsin captured 89.4 percent of the vote. In his *Against the Grain*, published in 1990, he presented a detailed list and scathing indictment of elite privileges. The book was widely read, further enhancing his popularity.

In it Yeltsin rejected the charge that he was pandering to those desiring "equal misery for all." Many observers, Soviet and foreign, believed such a desire characteristic of Soviet life. A "culture of envy" some called it. The dissident historian Andrei Amalrik believed that the desire that "nobody should live better than I do" was the "most destructive aspect of Russian psychology."[2] Soviet authorities had encouraged this psychology, especially in the early Soviet years, by their attacks on bourgeois greed, private property, Nepmen, and kulaks. It now came back to haunt them as Yeltsin's popularity increased, and that of the party, perceived as a privileged class, declined.

By 1990, other voices were also speaking out for an acceleration of reform. Gorbachev's democratization policies had made possible the emergence of many thousands of informal, voluntary groups on all levels from city to all-union. Some of them, such as the popular fronts in the Baltic republics, were large, primarily political, and pro-reform.

In early February 1990, on the eve of an important meeting of the party's Central Committee (CC), the voices of the people were heard in a massive pro-democracy demonstration in Moscow. The next day Gorbachev proposed to his fellow Communists that they agree to allow a multiparty system, and a few days later, following a bitter debate, the CC voted to accept his proposal. Later in the year, a new Law on Public Associations legalized the proposal.

Gorbachev himself, however, was unwilling to submit to the democratic

---

[2] Andrei Amalrik, *Will the Soviet Union Survive until 1984?* (New York, 1970), p. 35.

Yeltsin Attacks Party Privileges

In his autobiography, after several pages of detailing elite perks and sumptuous privileges, Yeltsin contrasts his own position (in 1989) with that of Gorbachev. The excerpt is from Boris Yeltsin, *Against the Grain: An Autobiography* (New York, 1990), pp. 164–167. Ellipses and bracketed material are mine.

It may be a somewhat controversial opinion of mine, but I do believe that perestroika would not have ground to a halt, despite the tactical mistakes that have been made, if only Gorbachev had been able to get rid of his reluctance to deal with the question of the leadership's privileges—if he himself had renounced all those completely useless, though pleasant, customary perquisites; if he had not built a new house for himself on the Lenin Hills and a new dacha outside Moscow; if he had not had his dacha at Pitsunda rebuilt and then an ultramodern one put up at Thorosin in the Crimea. . . .

. . . He likes to live well, in comfort and luxury. In this he is helped by his wife. She, unfortunately, is unaware of how keenly and jealously millions of Soviet people follow her appearance in the media. . . .

And what about his wife's ZIL [a Soviet automobile]? What about Gorbachev's proposal to raise the salary of Politburo members? Such things cannot be kept secret; people will always find out somehow. My daughter, at her place of work, is given one small cake of soap per month, which is barely enough for her. When my wife has to spend two or three hours a day in shopping lines and still cannot buy the most elementary products to feed her family, even she, a calm, balanced woman, becomes irritated, nervous, and distressed. . . .

When people say behind my back that I refused all such privileges—dachas, special rations, special hospitals, etc.—for the sake of cheap popularity, to play up the feelings of the mob, which wants everything to be leveled and demands equal misery for all, I pay no attention and am not offended.

test of a general popular election. Realizing that party powers were diminishing, in March 1990 he succeeded in having the Soviet Congress of People's Deputies elect him to a new strengthened presidency. Only subsequent presidents would have to be elected in popular elections.

Meanwhile, elections to local and republican parliaments further strengthened the hand of those desiring faster reforms. In May 1990, despite Gorbachev's opposition, the Russian Republic's Congress of People's Deputies elected Yeltsin chairman of its Supreme Soviet (president of the republic). From this platform, he trumpeted not only the Russian Republic's sovereignty, but also he continued to criticize Gorbachev for being too timid in pushing reforms.

By the fall of 1990, the rivalry between the two men helped push Gorbachev temporarily closer to conservatives. The military-industrial complex, the KGB, managers of state enterprises, and many party members were becoming increasingly alarmed at the pace of reform, and Gorbachev may have feared a military takeover if he did not slow it down. In December 1990, reform-minded Foreign Minister Shevardnadze warned that reactionary forces were on the rise and "a dictatorship was approaching." What type of dictator

FIGURE 19.3. By the summer of 1990, Moscow entrepreneurs were offering a new service: You could have your picture taken next to a mock-up of Gorbachev or his rival
Yeltsin.

would come to power, he could not be sure, but in protest to the oncoming developments, he resigned as foreign minister.

By the beginning of 1991, Gorbachev was increasingly perceived as someone who was out of tune with democratic elements. In a national poll in January, people favored Yeltsin's views to Gorbachev's by a two-to-one margin.
With Yeltsin and reformist mayors in cities such as Moscow and Leningrad
often challenging Gorbachev within the Russian Republic itself, his authority
was eroding there just as it was in the non-Russian republics.

The Economic Crisis

Gorbachev's third crisis, the economic one, also grew more acute from 1988
to 1991. Even before this, Gorbachev had been hampered by bad luck. Poor
farming weather in 1985–1987, the Chernobyl disaster of 1986, and the Armenian earthquake of 1988 all hurt the economy. Because the USSR was the
world's largest oil producer, declining world petroleum prices worsened the
problem, helping produce large budget deficits. Yet the worst was yet to come.

Although some scholars maintain that Gorbachev's inconsistent economic
ideas and lack of any long-range economic blueprint worsened economic conditions in Russia, Brown discounts this view. He admits that Gorbachev's economic ideas changed—slowly evolving from maintaining much of the command economy to finally accepting the necessity of market principles—but
believes the major cause of economic deterioration by 1991 was widespread

entrenched and powerful resistance to Gorbachev's economic plans. This resistance greatly increased the difficulties and complexities of evolving from a command to a market economy, and the economic policies that were enacted under Gorbachev represented political compromises and realities as well as Gorbachev's ideas. Even if Brown is correct, however, Gorbachev failed to communicate any clear economic vision to the Soviet peoples, any vision that might have inspired more individuals to back him and accept the necessity of a rocky transition to a better economic future.

During Gorbachev's first two years in power, he emphasized investing in high technology, producing better quality products, and improving worker discipline. But the vodka reform, partly aimed at improving worker performance, greatly reduced state vodka revenues. Moonshine production increased and along with it demand for sugar, contributing to a sugar shortage and sugar rationing. Other shortages also increased.

The economic polices of 1987–1988 produced their own set of problems, some related to the suspicion of "bourgeois greed" already discussed. There was increased grumbling about the high prices that cooperatives and private entrepreneurs charged for goods and services. The embryonic state of commercial laws, the confusion of the times, and the well-developed interlocking system of black marketeering and political graft contributed to shady dealings on the part of some new enterprises, further tarnishing their image. Peasants brave enough to risk leasing state land to establish family or cooperative farming arrangements were often called "kulaks" and faced bureaucratic obstacles. By the spring of 1990, there were only about 20,000 private farms in the USSR, with only a few hundred of them in the Russian republic.

The 1987 Enterprise Law helped weaken the old command planning system before workable market mechanisms were in place. And factory directors, now elected by their workers, increased workers' wages to an inflationary extent.

By 1990, the nationalities crisis and increasing political discord were playing their part in worsening the economy. Among other effects, they disrupted trade patterns between areas, making it harder for both consumers and manufacturers to obtain needed products. As a CIA report stated it: "The nationwide breakdown of distribution has been aggravated by the efforts of republics and local authorities to insulate their own territories from the effects of ubiquitous shortages." Ukrainians sent out less grain, Georgians less fruit, and so forth; industrial cities found it harder to obtain food. The economy was now characterized by the growth of all of the following: inflation, budget deficits, unemployment, shortages, bartering, and rationing.

Faced with the growing economic crisis, Gorbachev finally seemed ready to switch to a market economy. For a while, he hovered between two plans, both designed to privatize the economy and most property. The more drastic of the two, the 500-Day Plan, would relegate many economic powers (such as taxation) to the USSR's fifteen republics; the other plan would take longer, about five years to implement fully, and would dispense less economic authority to the republics. Yeltsin supported the first plan, and for a while in the late summer of 1990, it seemed that he and Gorbachev were in accord.

Gorbachev soon backed away, however, and asked the economist Aganbegyan to synthesize the two plans, which Yeltsin compared to trying to mate a snake with a hedgehog. But Gorbachev did not accept the subsequent plan either. Instead, in October, about the time he began his political retreat to appease conservative forces, Gorbachev and the USSR's Supreme Soviet approved a plan that reflected more a political compromise than sound economic thinking.

The October plan did, however, still call for a gradual transition to a market economy. Among other steps in that transition, the plan necessitated reducing budget deficits, controlling inflation, and decontrolling state-subsidized prices. The last step would allow prices to reflect more the true cost of producing them as well as market supply and demand. Thus, in January 1991, the government ordered a partial currency changeover, directed at confiscating illegal income, thereby reducing money supply and inflation. In April, it raised many prices in state stores, a move intended to increase state revenues and bring prices more in line with market supply and demand. But the immediate impact of these measures was to erode people's purchasing power without making more goods available. One estimate for 1991 stated that less than one-tenth of the food and consumer products thought essential for everyday life were regularly available in the state stores.

GORBACHEV'S "NEW-THINKING" FOREIGN POLICY AND THE END OF THE COLD WAR

While Gorbachev used the term *perestroika* to refer to his domestic reforms, he chose the phrase "new thinking" to characterize his foreign policy. It was indeed new in many ways and, with the help of his hand-picked foreign minister (July 1985–December 1990), Eduard Shevardnadze, he soon exercised more direct control over foreign policy than Brezhnev had ever done. Soviet détente policies of the 1970s had aimed at decreasing superpower tensions but without abandoning ideological struggle, especially in the Third World. Gorbachev was now willing to jettison such "struggle" and proclaimed that the backbone of his new thinking was that universal human values were more important than class struggle.

Although there were numerous reasons for his new-thinking foreign policy, Soviet economic difficulties were at the top of the list. The Cold War and the arms race were becoming too expensive. Gorbachev and his arms negotiators at Geneva displayed a new willingness to make arms concessions, and he changed Soviet strategic doctrine to emphasize "reasonable sufficiency." In November 1985, he stated that such sufficiency was "far lower" than what the two superpowers then possessed. He admitted that the Soviet Union bore some responsibility for the past arms race and got the Nineteenth Party Conference in 1988 to declare that "foreign policy activity should contribute ever more to releasing the nation's resources for peaceful construction, for *perestroika*."

At about the same time, the Soviet government admitted it had been wrong not to give its full support to the United Nations because the world needed a stable structure for international affairs. In the sphere of regional conflicts, the government renounced exporting revolution or counterrevolution and expressed its desire to help find solutions to conflicts in such places as Angola, Cambodia, the Middle East, and Latin America.

Of course, Gorbachev's new policies did not evolve in diplomatic isolation. The memoirs of A. Dobrynin, the former Soviet ambassador to the United States, make clear that U.S. President Ronald Reagan as well as Gorbachev displayed some initiative in improving Soviet-Western relations. The beginning of Reagan's second term in office coincided with Gorbachev's assumption of power; and for reasons of his own, Reagan was by then more interested in improving relations with the country he had labeled the "evil empire."

From 1985 to 1988, Gorbachev and Reagan met on five occasions: in Geneva (November 1985), Reykjavik (October 1986), Washington (December 1987), Moscow (May–June 1988), and New York (December 1988). Preparing for these summits and meeting each other turned out to be positive experiences for both leaders, helping them overcome some prejudices and put to the side remaining differences (such as Reagan's continuing commitment to his Strategic Defense Initiative or "Star Wars"). Out of these summits came agreements that helped reverse the deteriorating relations of the early 1980s.

Although these agreements covered a wide variety of areas from fishing rights to increased student, cultural, and scientific exchanges, the most important of them was the Intermediate Nuclear Forces (INF) Treaty. It was signed at the 1987 summit and ratified in 1988. An unprecedented achievement, it mandated the destruction of a whole class of weapons—all Soviet and U.S. land-based nuclear missiles in the 300- to 3400-mile range. The treaty contained strict verification procedures. Because the USSR possessed more such missiles, it had to destroy more.

After George Bush became the U.S. president, disarmament talks and summit diplomacy continued. In November 1989, Gorbachev and Bush met in Malta, where Bush promised economic assistance to the USSR. In late May 1990, Gorbachev arrived in Washington, where he and Bush approved a treaty reducing stockpiles of chemical weapons and ending their production. In September, the two leaders met briefly in Helsinki, where they supported UN resolutions condemning Iraq for invading Kuwait. In November 1990, Gorbachev, Bush, and twenty other NATO and Warsaw Pact leaders met in Paris, where they signed the most sweeping arms control treaty in history. This Conventional Forces in Europe (CFE) Treaty committed the signatories to destroy tens of thousands of howitzers, tanks, and other conventional weapons.

In July 1991, Bush came to Moscow, where the two leaders signed the Strategic Arms Reduction Talks (START) treaty. It promised approximately a 30 percent cut in long-range nuclear weapons over the next seven years. In late September, Bush announced several additional unilateral disarmament steps, and a week later Gorbachev went even further, promising among other steps to observe a one-year moratorium on nuclear testing.

Meanwhile, other foreign and domestic events were occurring that affected and would continue to affect arms treaties signed in this period. One of

FIGURE 19.4. Gorbachev and Reagan at their Geneva summit, November 1985. *(Reuters/Bettmann)*

these developments was the collapse of Communist governments in Eastern Europe.

Although the Eastern European peoples' hostility to Soviet hegemony was central to ending it in 1989–1990, such hostility was nothing new. What was new was Gorbachev's decision not to send in Soviet troops to maintain Communist governments.

Just as he failed to realize that *glasnost, perestroika,* and democratization in the USSR would spin out of his control, so too he failed to foresee the consequences of unleashing such forces in Eastern Europe. Once again, as with the Soviet nationalities, he underestimated the strength of nationalism. It is difficult to understand how he could believe, for example, that Poland would remain loyal to the USSR if given a choice.

Yet in fairness to Gorbachev, he had few other options in Soviet bloc countries besides continuing the Brezhnev doctrine, which he had no desire to do. Like the USSR, bloc governments were facing economic hard times and a lack of popular support. If the USSR needed reform, so too he thought did the satellite nations. Furthermore, like British and French leaders in the decades following World War II, he faced the question of whether it any longer made economic sense to attempt maintaining an empire by force. The cost of the Afghanistan occupation, which continued until 1989, certainly suggested such a policy could grow more costly wherever resistance to Soviet hegemony increased.

Once the breakup of the Soviet bloc began in 1989–1990, the political cost of trying to prevent it escalated. Gorbachev's entire policy was built upon domestic and foreign-policy reform. To resort now to military force would have been contrary to his earlier efforts and met with much more opposition at home and abroad than faced by either Khrushchev's action in Hungary in 1956 or Brezhnev's in Czechoslovakia in 1968. It would have imperiled East-West relations, endangering all the fruits of Gorbachev's summit diplomacy. Thus, as one East European nation after another renounced communism and, eventually, the Warsaw Pact, Gorbachev attempted only to gain what concessions he could from grateful Western leaders such as West Germany's Helmut Kohl.

The first bloc nation to renounce communism was Poland. In early 1989, its Communist government agreed once again to legalize Solidarity, to revamp Poland's parliament, and to allow Solidarity to participate in elections. In June 1989, Solidarity candidates won greater than 99 percent of the seats they were allowed to contest. A few months later, for the first time in a Soviet bloc nation, a coalition government was formed with a non-Communist prime minister.

After it became clear that the Soviet Union had no intention of intervening to maintain Communist dominance in Poland, other bloc governments, lacking popular support, began collapsing like dominos. By the end of 1989, old-line Communist leaders had been replaced throughout the bloc nations.

In some countries, reformist Communists or coalition governments took over, as in Rumania and Bulgaria, but in others, such as Czechoslovakia, power fell to people the Communists had once persecuted. In December 1989, playwright and often imprisoned human rights advocate Vaclav Havel became president of Czechoslovakia. As was generally the case in the region, the changeover in Czechoslovakia (the "Velvet Revolution") was surprisingly non-bloody. In 1990 and 1991, democratic forces continued to develop in east-central Europe—as we shall hereafter refer to the region because *Eastern Europe* was more a political concept encompassing Communist countries west of the USSR and east of West Germany.

The internal political changes in the region affected foreign policy developments. Its nations improved Western ties, and in 1991 the Warsaw Pact military alliance came to an end and Soviet troops began leaving the area's nations.

One result of the collapsing communism in east-central Europe was the reunification of Germany. After elections in March 1990 brought a non-Communist coalition to power in East Germany, it agreed to reunification with West Germany, which came about in October under the West German leadership of Helmut Kohl. A divided Germany had symbolized the Cold War. The Cold War was now over.

Kohl was just one of Western Europe's leaders with whom Gorbachev established good relations. Others included Thatcher of Great Britain, F. Mitterand of France, and F. González of Spain, a socialist who influenced Gorbachev's own evolving concept of socialism. Gorbachev stressed Soviet links with Western Europe, advocating "the end of the schism of Europe" and referring to it as our "common home." Like the United States, Western European nations granted economic assistance to the USSR or, toward the end of its existence, directly to the increasingly independent republics.

In other parts of the world, ending the Afghanistan occupation was the number one priority, although Gorbachev also cut back on expensive support for other Marxist regimes, such as that of Castro in Cuba. The conflict in Afghanistan, where the U.S. government increased covert aid to the rebels, was one of several regional disputes involving the two superpowers. Although settling such conflicts was important to improving superpower relations, Gorbachev had other reasons to end what he came to call a "bleeding wound," or what others called the "Soviet Vietnam." Before Soviet troops finally completed their decade-long occupation in early 1989, more than 14,000 Soviet troops had died, more than 50,000 had been wounded, and even more had become sick from infectious diseases.

At a Politburo meeting of November 1986, Gorbachev stressed the need to remove Soviet troops in a year or two and to make sure that the United States did not move into the vacuum. Diplomatic consultations led to UN-sponsored accords on Afghanistan, signed in April 1988. These agreements stipulated that the USSR would withdraw all of its troops by February 1989, and the two superpowers agreed on Afghanistan's future "nonalignment" and that they would "refrain from any form of interference and intervention in the internal affairs of the Republic of Afghanistan."

As indicated in Chapter 18, the Soviet occupation of Afghanistan had been one of three major impediments to improving Sino-Soviet relations. The withdrawal helped improve matters, as did Gorbachev's reduction of Soviet forces along the Chinese border and encouraging Vietnam to withdraw its troops from Cambodia. In May 1989, Gorbachev visited China, and relations between the two Communist giants were normalized after almost thirty years of strain. Yet massive pro-democracy rallies that embarrassed the Chinese government during his visit, and were crushed two weeks after he left, highlighted the fact that different approaches to communism still existed between the two powers.

Gorbachev's moves to improve Soviet-Chinese relations were symptomatic of his efforts to better Soviet relations in Asia as well as in Europe. He sought increased trade on both continents and help from Asian capitalist nations for Siberian development. In April 1991, Gorbachev visited Tokyo, but Japan's unhappiness over Soviet unwillingness to return the Kurile Islands taken after World War II kept the summit from being more successful.

THE COUP THAT FAILED AND ITS AFTERMATH

By 1991, Gorbachev was admired far more abroad than at home. His role in ending the Cold War and Soviet control over east-central Europe earned him the gratitude of people in numerous countries. In the Western democracies, he was perceived as a westernizer, attempting to make the USSR more like the West. Although many Soviet citizens also appreciated these accomplishments and efforts, others were embittered by the collapse of the Soviet empire and too much westernization. Although Soviet society generally welcomed Gorbachev's policies of *glasnost* and democratization, it was less enthusiastic about government economic policies, which only worsened conditions. Finally, his conservative retreat in late 1990 alienated many of the democratic elements he had earlier encouraged.

After months of political retreat, Gorbachev moved back toward the reformers in the spring of 1991. In doing so, he was partly motivated by huge reform demonstrations and strikes, especially a widespread miners' strike in March. In late July, he spoke in behalf of a free-market economy and called for the Communist party to abandon many of its Marxist-Leninist ideas.

Meanwhile, however, his own powers were declining as each of his three intertwined crises (economic, political, and federal) continued to worsen. In June, his chief political opponent, Boris Yeltsin, further strengthened his position by trouncing his rivals in a popular election for the office of president of the Russian Republic—Gorbachev, by contrast, had never participated in a direct democratic election. Yeltsin now became even more insistent on diverting powers from the federal government to the national republics, a process already proceeding at breakneck speed.

With his own powers diminishing, Gorbachev gave ground and agreed to a new compromise union treaty, officially transferring many powers to the republics. It was to be signed on August 20th with Yeltsin and four of the five Central Asian leaders. By then, Gorbachev was willing to concede that the three Baltic and three Caucasian republics would not sign the treaty, but follow their own independent paths, but he hoped that Ukraine and the remaining republics would sign later in the year.

Two days before the August 20 signing could occur, however, conservative leaders, including the head of the KGB and the defense minister, attempted a coup. By weakening federal powers, the new union treaty threatened to erode further the personal powers of such leaders, and information gained from an illegal wiretap gave them cause to fear that Gorbachev would soon replace several of them. Yet they were not just driven by personal concerns. From their viewpoint, the USSR was disintegrating into chaos, and Gorbachev's newthinking foreign policy had been a great failure. They believed he had made too many unreciprocated concessions to the West, lost the Soviet empire, and squandered away the country's superpower status. They viewed themselves not as restorers of totalitarianism, as Gorbachev later characterized them, but as national saviors.

On August 18, they put Gorbachev under house arrest while he was vacationing in the Crimea. The next morning, the plotters announced that Gorbachev was sick and that an eight-member Emergency Committee had assumed power. But bad luck, poor planning, their own irresolute behavior, the defection of some military units, and the resistance of Boris Yeltsin and other supporters of democracy prevented them from solidifying their control. Yeltsin and a growing number of resisters to the coup stood their ground, facing tanks, at the Russian parliament building (the "White House"), and by August 21 the coup leaders recognized defeat. The feared attack on the White House never occurred. On the morning of August 22, Gorbachev returned to Moscow. Coup leaders except one who committed suicide were arrested, and Yeltsin became the hero of the day.

Gorbachev quickly wrote his own account of the August coup, severely criticizing the plotters. But many Soviet citizens thought that he deserved part of the blame, that perhaps in some convoluted way he was even in on it, allowing the plotters to do the dirty work before he came back to some sort of power. Such an extreme suspicion, however, was unfounded.

The events that followed the failed coup were almost as dramatic as the coup itself. It created an immediate backlash against the Communist party. After first defending his party, Gorbachev backtracked. A few days after his return, he resigned as its general secretary. He also followed Yeltsin's example as president of the Russian republic and suspended the party's political activities throughout the Soviet Union.

But if the Communist or Soviet aspect of the Soviet Union was rapidly disintegrating, so too was the union itself. Within a few weeks, the Soviet government officially recognized the independence of the three Baltic republics. Other republics also rushed to declare their independence. On December 8, the presidents of the three founding members of the USSR in 1922—Russia, Ukraine, and Belorussia (now Belarus)—agreed to disband the union and instead to form a Commonwealth of Independent States (CIS). On December 21, eight other former Soviet republics joined them in the CIS. Besides the three Baltic republics, Georgia also remained outside the new commonwealth. Gorbachev, now a president without a country, resigned his office on December 25, 1991.

THE COLLAPSE OF THE SOVIET UNION: A SUMMARY AND ANALYSIS

The disintegration of the Soviet Union was a complex phenomenon lending itself to many interpretations. It consisted of two intertwined collapses, first that of more than seven decades of Communist power and second that of a union of nationalities, most of which had been unified for a much longer period. Risking oversimplification, here the two collapses are treated as one, and the main reasons for it are summarized.

Among the reasons for the fall are seven overlapping background causes—which for decades had been weakening the Soviet system—and one immediate cause.[3] The first list consists of the following (in no particular order of importance): (1) economic and social decline, including rising alcoholism, death

---

[3] This list is indebted to that found in Alexander Dallin, "Causes of the Collapse of the USSR," in *The Soviet System: From Crisis to Collapse*, rev. ed., eds. Alexander Dallin and Gail W. Lapidus (Boulder, 1995), pp. 673–695. Dallin's article also briefly summarizes some other different approaches to the subject, such as that of Martin Malia, which is also found in this collection. Malia has updated his views in his *The Soviet Tragedy: A History of Socialism in Russia, 1917–1991* (New York, 1994), especially Chapter 13.

rates, and corruption; (2) growing disillusionment and anger with the Soviet system and its privileged elite; (3) the ideological erosion of Marxism-Leninism-Stalinism; (4) the weakening of party controls over Soviet citizens; (5) social developments such as the growth of a more urbanized and better educated population; (6) nationality differences; and (7) foreign influences. All seven of these background causes were already at work when the immediate cause of the USSR's collapse—Gorbachev—took center stage and inadvertently accelerated the process.

Of the background causes, the first, second, and sixth have already been treated in this and the preceding chapter, and more light is shed upon them in succeeding chapters. Regarding these three causes, we need here only note that decades of heroic efforts by dissidents such as Sakharov helped pave the way for increasing disillusionment with the Soviet system. By the time of his death in December 1989, Sakharov exercised great moral influence on his fellow citizens. More than 100,000 of them, including Gorbachev, paid homage at his open coffin.

The third and fourth causes—ideological erosion and the weakening of party controls—were both primarily post-Stalin phenomena. Ideological erosion can be viewed from many different angles. To begin with, Marxism-Leninism-Stalinism contained significant inherent flaws. Simply put, its view of reality was skewed, poorly equipping the USSR to deal with late-twentieth-century technological, economic, and other global developments. As time passed, the gap between ideological promises and Soviet performance seemed less and less likely to be bridged. Because of the ideology's undemocratic nature, reforming it was difficult: Any loosening up of repression and the command economy threatened to erode party control.

Before Gorbachev, Khrushchev's destalinization policies and challenges from outside Communists (especially in China and Eastern Europe) helped split the Communist world into different factions, further undermining communism's credibility. By the mid-1980s, Soviet party members seemed more interested in their own careers and material comforts than in their professed ideology.

For decades, some individuals such as Roy Medvedev had believed that the problem was not Marxism-Leninism, only Stalinism. Glasnost and "the return of history," however, helped reveal Lenin in a harsher light, and his once-mighty image began to crumble just as Stalin's had earlier. As for Marx, he was a foreigner, "a German Jew," as some right-wing, antisemitic nationalists now emphasized.

As Communist ideology eroded after Stalin, so too did party control over Soviet life. Khrushchev deliberately cut back on terroristic and other controls. People began to feel freer to talk among their friends and in their kitchens—a development assisted by more people gaining housing with private kitchens. Under Brezhnev, despite the crackdown on dissidents, Soviet citizens channeled increasing amounts of time, energy, and money away from state sectors into private areas.

The fifth and seventh background causes—social changes and foreign influences—are closely related. As indicated in succeeding chapters, Soviet society was much different in 1985 than it had been in 1953. Especially important was the fact that it was more urbanized and professionalized, better educated, and less provincial. By the early 1980s, many Soviet citizens believed too few career opportunities existed for them. Times were far different than in the 1930s, when purges, economic needs, and a shortage of trusted experts made rapid career advances possible—provided that one was not among the purged.

The better-educated Soviet population of the 1970s and early 1980s traveled abroad more, even if only to other Communist countries, and came into contact more with foreigners and foreign ways and ideas. In an Information Age of increasing global interdependence, professionals desired more access to foreign materials. Inevitably, comparisons with countries better able to provide for their people increased discontent with the Soviet government and system.

It is more difficult to be precise about the effect of any specific Western policies on the USSR's collapse. Yet from the early days of containment, through détente and the West's emphasis on human rights, up to the Western diplomatic policies of 1985–1991, Western actions had a cumulative effect on Soviet life and played at least a small part in bringing about the fall of the USSR.

Political developments in other Communist-governed countries combined to make up still another foreign influence. From Eastern Europe to China, from Afghanistan to Cuba, political and economic developments had a cumulative effect and not just an ideological one. After Gorbachev came to power, the subsequent collapse of Communist governments in the Eastern European satellite states certainly encouraged the breakup of the USSR itself.

Yet, in the final analysis, the main reason that both the breakup of the Soviet bloc and the USSR itself occurred when and how they did was Gorbachev and his policies, although Boris Yeltsin was also an important catalyst for the collapse of the USSR. In contrast to Khrushchev or Brezhnev, Gorbachev was unwilling to hold the Soviet empire together by force, and within the USSR he presided over a transformation that by 1991 had eliminated many characteristics of the earlier Soviet system.

By means of his *perestroika* policies, assisted by *glasnost* and democratization, Gorbachev attempted to transform the USSR into an efficient and humane socialist society. But despite his intelligence and many political talents, he was unable to hold his country together. This was partly because of his own failings. After a year or two in power, he became increasingly impatient to institute changes in both domestic and foreign policy, and he sometimes failed to think through the consequences of policies before he enacted them.

Compared to someone like Yeltsin, Gorbachev was never as comfortable among the common people, and he failed to realize how deeply feelings such as nationalism and resentment toward Communist privileges ran among Soviet citizens. Despite his charismatic appeal in the West, he increasingly was unable to inspire the Soviet peoples with his vision of the future, partly because it was somewhat murky, always changing and evolving. Although Brown has argued convincingly that Gorbachev's political values by 1991 had evolved far from Leninism, Gorbachev remained reluctant to renounce Lenin and communism openly—he did not resign as Communist party head until

August 24, 1991. This reluctance helped Yeltsin and others to depict Gorbachev as someone not sufficiently converted to new democratic principles.

Yet, given the difficulties he faced (including reactionary resistance and ambitious politicians such as Yeltsin), decades of Communist rule and misrule, and the natural aspirations of many non-Russians for national independence, it is hardly surprising that he failed to hold the Soviet Union together. In many other ways, however, he did not fail. In addition to being mainly responsible for ending the Cold War, he set in motion changes that helped bring much greater freedom to many peoples in the world, including those in east-central Europe as well as in most of the former USSR.

*SUGGESTED SOURCES**

ARBATOV, GEORGI. *The System: An Insider's Life in Soviet Politics.* New York, 1992.

ASLUND, ANDERS. *Gorbachev's Struggle for Economic Reform.* Rev. ed. Ithaca, N.Y., 1991.

BILLINGTON, JAMES H. *Russia Transformed: Breakthrough to Hope: Moscow, August 1991.* New York, 1992.

BOETTKE, PETER J. *Why Perestroika Failed: The Politics and Economics of Socialist Transformation.* London, 1993.

BOLDIN, V. I. *Ten Years That Shook the World: The Gorbachev Era as Witnessed by His Chief of Staff.* New York, 1994.

BROWN, ARCHIE. *The Gorbachev Factor.* New York, 1995.

CARRÈRE D'ENCAUSSE, HÉLÈNE. *The End of the Soviet Empire: The Triumph of the Nations.* New York, 1993.

COHEN, STEPHEN F., and KATRINA VANDEN HEUVEL, eds. *Voices of Glasnost: Interviews with Gorbachev's Reformers.* New York, 1989.

DALLIN, ALEXANDER, ed. *The Gorbachev Era.* New York, 1992.

DANIELS, ROBERT V. *The End of the Communist Revolution.* London, 1993.

———, ed. *Soviet Communism from Reform to Collapse.* Lexington, Mass., 1995.

DAVIES, R. W. *Soviet History in the Gorbachev Revolution.* Bloomington, 1989.

DAWISHA, KAREN. *Eastern Europe, Gorbachev, and Reform: The Great Challenge.* 2d ed. Cambridge, England, 1990.

DOBRYNIN, ANATOLY. *In Confidence: Moscow's Ambassador to America's Six Cold War Presidents (1962–1986).* New York, 1995.

DODER, DUSKO, and LOUISE BRANSON. *Gorbachev: Heretic in the Kremlin.* New York, 1990.

DUNLOP, JOHN B. *The Rise of Russia and the Fall of the Soviet Empire.* Princeton, 1993.

GARTHOFF, RAYMOND L. *The Great Transition: American-Soviet Relations and the End of the Cold War.* Washington, D.C., 1994.

GOLDMAN, MARSHALL I. *What Went Wrong with Perestroika.* New York, 1992.

GORBACHEV, MIKHAIL. *The August Coup: The Truth and the Lessons.* New York, 1991.

———. *Memoirs.* New York, 1996.

———. *Perestroika: New Thinking for Our Country and the World.* Rev. ed. New York, 1988.

GRACHEV, ANDREI S. *Final Days: The Inside Story of the Collapse of the Soviet Union.* Boulder, 1995.

HOGAN, MICHAEL J., ed. *The End of the Cold War: Its Meaning and Implications.* Cambridge, England, 1992.

* See also books cited in footnotes.

HOSKING, GEOFFREY A. *The Awakening of the Soviet Union.* Cambridge, Mass., 1990.

HOSKING, GEOFFREY A., JONATHAN AVES, and PETER J. S. DUNCAN. *The Road to Post-Communism: Independent Political Movements in the Former Soviet Union, 1985–1991.* London, 1992.

KAGARLITSKY, BORIS. *The Disintegration of the Monolith.* London, 1992.

KAISER, ROBERT G. *Why Gorbachev Happened: His Triumphs and His Failure.* New York, 1991.

KIERNAN, BRENDAN. *The End of Soviet Politics: Elections, Legislatures, and the Demise of the Communist Party.* Boulder, 1993.

LAPIDUS, GAIL, and VICTOR ZASLAVSKY, eds. *From Union to Commonwealth: Nationalism and Separatism in the Soviet Republics.* Cambridge, England, 1992.

LAQUEUR, WALTER. *Black Hundred: The Rise of the Extreme Right in Russia.* New York, 1993.

———. *The Dream that Failed: Reflections on the Soviet Union.* New York, 1994.

LEWIN, MOSHE. *The Gorbachev Phenomenon: A Historical Interpretation.* Berkeley, 1988.

LIEVEN, ANATOL. *The Baltic Revolution: Estonia, Latvia, Lithuania and the Path to Independence.* New Haven, 1993.

LIGACHEV, YEGOR. *Inside Gorbachev's Kremlin.* New York, 1993.

LIKHACHEV, DMITRII S. *Reflections on Russia.* Boulder, 1991.

MATLOCK, JACK F., JR. *Autopsy of an Empire: The American Ambassador's Account of the Collapse of the Soviet Union.* New York, 1995.

MILLER, JOHN. *Mikhail Gorbachev and the End of Soviet Power.* New York, 1993.

MOTYL, ALEXANDER J., ed. *The Post Soviet Nations: Perspectives on the Demise of the USSR.* New York, 1992.

NOVE, ALEC. *Glasnost' in Action: Cultural Renaissance in Russia.* Boston, 1989.

ORTTUNG, ROBERT. *From Leningrad to St. Petersburg: Democratization in a Russian City.* New York, 1995.

POPOV, NIKOLAI. *The Russian People Speak: Democracy at the Crossroads.* Syracuse, 1995.

PRYCE-JONES, DAVID. *The Strange Death of the Soviet Empire.* New York, 1995.

RALEIGH, DONALD J. *Soviet Historians and Perestroika: The First Phase.* Armonk, N.Y., 1989.

SAKHAROV, ANDREI. *Moscow and Beyond, 1986–1989.* New York, 1991.

SATTER, DAVID. *The Age of Delirium: The Decline and Fall of the Soviet Union.* New York, 1996.

SENN, ALFRED ERICH. *Gorbachev's Failure in Lithuania.* New York, 1995.

SHEVARDNADZE, EDUARD. *The Future Belongs to Freedom.* New York, 1991.

SHLAPENTOKH, VLADIMIR. *Public and Private Life of the Soviet People: Changing Values in Post-Stalin Russia.* New York, 1989.

SMITH, HEDRICK. *The New Russians.* New York, 1991.

SPRING, D. W., ed. *The Impact of Gorbachev: The First Phase, 1985–90.* London, 1991.

SUNY, RONALD GRIGOR. *The Revenge of the Past: Nationalism, Revolution, and the Collapse of the Soviet Union.* Stanford, 1993.

TIMOFEYEV, LEV. *Russia's Secret Rulers.* New York, 1992.

VAKSBERG, ARKADY. *The Soviet Mafia.* New York, 1991.

VOGT-DOWNEY, MARILYN. *The USSR 1987–1991: Marxist Perspectives.* Atlantic Highlands, N.J., 1993.

WALKER, RACHEL. *Six Years That Shook the World.* New York, 1993.

WHITE, STEPHEN. *After Gorbachev.* Cambridge, England, 1993.

ZASLAVSKAIA, T. I. *The Second Socialist Revolution: An Alternative Soviet Strategy.* London, 1990.

CHAPTER 20

Economic and Social Life, 1953–1991

By the mid-1980s, Soviet citizens had higher incomes, better housing, more social services, and more leisure than at the time of Stalin's death. More of them were better educated and resided in cities. Yet economic progress had slowed and then stagnated in the 1970s and early 1980s, and the standard of living in the USSR remained far behind that of other major industrialized powers. Environmental devastation grew worse, as did alcoholism. Life expectancy, after at first increasing, was lower in 1980–1981 or 1990–1991 than it had been in the mid-1960s.

The party elite remained the Soviet ruling class and reached the height of their privileges under Brezhnev. At the same time, however, professional expertise became more important. Conditions for workers and collective farmers improved; but within the family, women continued to bear the heaviest burden, combining full-time jobs with most of the housework. Soviet law continued to serve as an instrument of party rule until almost the end of the USSR's existence.

Gorbachev's policies from 1985 to 1991 not only were influenced by economic and social developments, but also, in turn, helped transform the economic-social sphere. These years were transitional ones from the old command economy and Communist dominance to a new post-Soviet Russia that was still crystallizing in the mid-1990s.

ECONOMIC AND ENVIRONMENTAL OVERVIEW

Despite the economic problems of the last decade and a half of Soviet rule, the overall economic picture from 1953 to 1991 had its positive aspects. Before 1990–1991, there were few years when the Soviet economy actually declined. Blessed with many natural resources, including the greatest land mass in the world, the USSR steadily increased its industrial production. It was during this period, for example, that it became the world's largest petroleum producer. By the end of the 1980s, it was also the world's largest producer of numerous other products, including cadmium, iron and steel, mercury, mineral fertilizers, nickel, natural gas, railway tracks, tractors, and most textiles; and it was second in producing wood and in its fish catch. It was also a major producer of aluminum, asbestos, coal, cement, copper, diamonds, gold, lead, manganese, potash, silver, zinc, leather goods, and, despite many of its farming woes, agricultural products.

Most importantly, by the late 1980s, most Soviet citizens were better housed, clothed, and fed and possessed more consumer goods than in 1953. From 1955 to 1964, official statistics indicated that the production of refrigerators, washing machines, vacuum cleaners, and televisions all increased fivefold or more, much more in the case of washing machines. Yet in 1965, only about one-fourth of all families possessed a television, one-fifth a washing machine, and one-tenth a refrigerator. By 1989, according to a Soviet survey of more than 300,000 urban and rural families, there was an average of one television set per family; about three-fourths of the families possessed washing machines, and nine-tenths possessed refrigerators or freezers. Additionally by then, of all families surveyed except those of collective farmers, three-fifths owned vacuum cleaners and sewing machines, one-half tape recorders, and one-fifth automobiles.

State welfare provisions increased sharply, beyond free health care, primary education, and only small fees or payments for more advanced educa-

FIGURE 20.1. Cutting and raking grass outside a hotel in Kishinev, 1986. Many consumer products (such as lawnmowers) taken for granted in the West were seldom available in the USSR.

tion and rental housing. Under Khrushchev, the educational fees were eliminated. Legislation, especially in 1956 and 1964, raised pensions and extended them to more people, with the general age for availability being age 60 for men and 55 for women. By 1986, there were about seven and a half times as many old-age pensioners as in 1960, making up about 15 percent of the population. Under Khrushchev and Brezhnev, the state increased expenditures for housing, children of poor families, preschool child care, public health, paid maternity leaves, and student stipends. As might be expected, free or low-cost state-provided services were one of the most popular aspects of Soviet rule.

Under Gorbachev, the government legislated (in 1990) new family-allowance benefits and a new state pension law. In January 1991, it set up the USSR's first unemployment-compensation system. (After the 1920s and before Gorbachev's rule, unemployment was officially nonexistent and had actually been quite low compared to unemployment in capitalist countries.) Although designed to aid the unemployed, the new legislation also reflected the government's desire to move away from the old command economy toward a more market-driven system. In the transition, some new safety-nets were to compensate for phenomena such as inflation and unemployment, but overall the government intended the population to become less dependent on the government, not more.

Yet, despite its resources, increases in production, and expanded social services, the Soviet economy remained the most backward of the major industrial nations. The quality of Soviet telecommunications, roads, and consumer goods and services was especially poor. Someone once referred to the USSR as "Upper Volta with rockets." Although an exaggerated and unfair comparison with a poor African country (Burkina Faso since 1984), the comparison contained a grain of truth.

After the 1960s, Soviet economic growth slowed decade after decade. According to U.S. CIA estimates (1990), which at a minimum accurately reflect the overall trend, the growth of the gross national product (GNP) in the 1950s and 1960s averaged about 5 percent per year, only about half that for the 1970s, and only about half the 1970s average during the 1980s. In the late 1980s, the USSR's per capita GNP was well under half that of the United States, Japan, West Germany, and many other Western European countries. In the midst of the Information Age, the gap was widening, not narrowing.

The reason for this relatively poor economic performance was primarily the command economy already examined in previous chapters. This economy produced not only slowing growth, but also poor-quality consumer goods. Although defense-related and space-related products were better made, even vital constructions such as nuclear reactors were not up to the standards of other major powers. A secret 1979 KGB report, for example, found numerous "deviations and violations" in the construction of the Chernobyl Nuclear Power Plant.

Mention of Chernobyl, the site of the terrible nuclear disaster of 1986, brings us to the most damaging long-range consequence of the Soviet economy—environmental damage. The combination of state secrecy, control, and obsession with increasing production at almost any cost proved deadly for the environment. One Russian minister in the early 1990s summed up the problem this way: "The situation is not bad, but desperate. Sixteen percent of the territory of the former USSR, where something on the order of 45 million to 50 million people . . . live, lies within ecological hazard or disaster zones." After citing this quote, a leading Western expert indicated that his own earlier estimate that it would cost six to seven times the USSR's yearly GNP to clean up the problem was much too low.[1]

Although Gorbachev's *glasnost* helped spur the Soviet environmental movement, his administration took few concrete steps to halt the continuing devastation. In some respects, the problem grew worse. During the late 1980s, a much publicized environmental cause was that of Lake Baikal, the deepest lake in the world. Yet, despite some government attention to the problem of dumping wastes from processing plants into its once pristine waters, plant wastes continued to pour into this "pearl of Siberia."

The environment and economy under Gorbachev, however, must be viewed in a larger context. Although the economy declined more in 1991 than in any previous post-Stalin year and the government found it increasingly difficult to provide all the promised social services, the Gorbachev years were transitional ones. In such a period of turmoil, it is hardly surprising that little immediate economic or environmental progress was made or that there was even some regression. At least, however, some of the major problems were publicly recognized, a necessary first step for any subsequent improvements. And beginning in the late 1980s, politicians and citizens in the USSR began the difficult trial-and-error process of addressing the economic and environmental legacy of the previous seven decades of Soviet rule.

FOREIGN TRADE AND INVESTMENT

As the Soviet production of fuels and energy increased, so too did their export. According to Soviet statistics, in 1960 they comprised about one-sixth the total value of exports, but in the early 1980s, they made up more than half of the total before decreasing below that percentage beginning in 1986. Other significant exports in this era were ores and metals; machinery; and, to a lesser extent, chemical and timber products.

The chief imports throughout the last four decades of Soviet rule were machinery and transport equipment, which generally hovered between about one-third to two-fifths the total value of imports. Other significant imports were foodstuffs, consumer goods, and various raw materials needed for industry.

As was true during Stalin's final years, other Communist countries, especially in Eastern Europe, were the USSR's chief trading partners. Although the Soviet Union purchased such items as advanced technology from Western

[1] Murray Feshbach, "Environmental Calamities: Widespread and Costly," in *The Former Soviet Union in Transition*, ed. Richard F. Kaufman and John P. Hardt for the U.S. Congress, Joint Economic Committee (Armonk, N.Y., 1993), pp. 579, 589.

countries and Japan, its trade with any of these countries never came close to matching that with East Germany, its principle Soviet bloc trading partner.

In most years, the value of Soviet exports exceeded that of imports, and trade volume grew until the Gorbachev years. Yet compared to major trading countries such as the United States, West Germany, and Japan, the USSR's total foreign trade remained small. Under Gorbachev, decreasing world energy prices and then increasing Soviet political and economic instability led to falling export earnings, which forced a cutback in imports. After decreasing in 1990, foreign trade plunged in 1991. By 1990, declining export earnings and the general economic decline also made it increasingly difficult for the government to pay off foreign companies and investors.

As the Soviet Union moved away from its command economy, so too it ended its practice of channeling almost all foreign trade through its Ministry of Foreign Trade. The government began permitting some businesses to trade with foreign companies on their own. The Gorbachev transition years also witnessed Soviet attempts to become more integrated into the world trading community by joining international economic organizations like GATT (General Agreement on Tariffs and Trade), in which it was granted observer status. One major drawback to expanding foreign trade and doing business in the USSR was the inconvertibility of the Soviet ruble.

Despite this continuing inconvertibility, the Gorbachev government for the first time since the 1920s encouraged foreign investment, mainly through joint (Soviet-foreign) ventures. Despite complex economic, political, and cultural obstacles for foreign companies and entrepreneurs, the foreign presence steadily increased. According to one account, in 1991 the number of joint ventures almost doubled, reaching about 1200 by the end of the year.

POPULATION, TOWNS, AND URBAN CONDITIONS

In the absence of major wars, famines, or murderous Stalinist actions, the USSR's population increased from about 188 million in 1953 to about 287 million in 1989. Compared to the rest of the world, Soviet population growth was more rapid than that of Western Europe, but less than that of Third World countries.

Within the USSR, the fastest growth was in Central Asia, primarily because of its higher birth rates. This region also had a higher percentage of younger people than in the Russian republic (RSFSR) or the European USSR; and by the 1989 census, the RSFSR contained only about 51 percent of the country's population, down from about 56 percent in the 1959 census.

By 1989, the population density of the USSR was still much lower than that of most Western European countries—for example, only one-eighth that of France. Except for its far northern portion, however, European Russia was more densely populated than the USSR as a whole, whereas Siberia and Central Asia were less so. Partly because of the need to develop valuable resources, the government encouraged migration to certain regions such as Siberia, but Siberia's generally harsh conditions inhibited any great exodus to it.

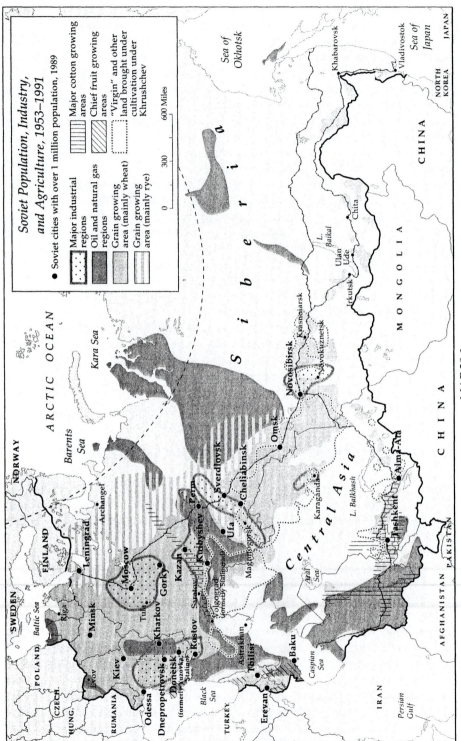

Soviet Population, Industry, and Agriculture, 1953–1991

● Soviet cities with over 1 million population, 1989

Major industrial regions

Oil and natural gas regions

Grain growing area (mainly wheat)

Grain growing area (mainly rye)

Major cotton growing areas

Chief fruit growing areas

"Virgin" and other land brought under cultivation under Khrushchev

MAP 20-1

More significant than any migration from one region to another was that from the countryside to the city. In 1959, three Soviet cities had more than 1 million people; in 1989, twenty-three such cities existed (see Map 20.1). During those same three decades, the urban population increased from 48 percent to 66 percent. The 1989 figure, however, masked significant regional disparities, for in the RSFSR about three-fourths of the population lived in cities, whereas in Central Asia and Moldavia less than half did. Of the twenty-three largest cities, none were further east than Novosibirsk, which is closer to Leningrad (renamed St. Petersburg again in 1991) than to Vladivostok.

Among these large cities in 1989, Moscow towered over the others with 8.8 million people. Leningrad was only about half as big with about 4.5 million. The next eight largest cities in order of size were Kiev, Tashkent, Kharkov, Minsk, Gorky (Nizhnii Novgorod), Novosibirsk, Sverdlovsk (Ekaterinburg), and Tbilisi.[2]

Increasing post-Stalin urbanization placed great pressure on urban housing, already scarce because of World War II's destructive effects. In response, the state oversaw the construction of block after block of new prefabricated apartment buildings—from 1955 to 1988, an average of more than 10 million people a year (counting all family members) obtained new apartments or other housing, mostly in the cities. State-owned apartment buildings constituted most of the new urban housing, although private and cooperative structures as well as dormitories were also constructed. Because of this building boom, most urban families were able to move out of communal apartments and obtain less crowded ones with their own kitchen and bathroom. (In smaller towns and rural areas, conditions were not quite so crowded, and there were more private houses.)

Because space was scarce in large cities, the state kept building taller and taller apartment buildings. Before 1960, it was unusual for them to have more than five stories; by the mid-1980s, three or four times that height and more was common for the high-rise apartments of major cities like Moscow and Leningrad.

By Western standards, Soviet apartments continued to be overcrowded and inferior. Buildings were usually poorly constructed and drab. Plumbing and maintenance were also poor. As late as 1989, almost a quarter of state-owned, public, and cooperative urban housing still possessed no hot water.

Yet the perspective of Soviet citizens was different than that of outsiders. Before Brezhnev's death in 1982, most adults, especially older people, compared their situation more with that of their past than with Western housing conditions. A Soviet Interview Project, conducted by James Millar and others, found that only one-third of recent émigrés had been dissatisfied with their housing conditions during Brezhnev's final years in power.

Those most dissatisfied were those who had been unable to obtain separate quarters. As late as 1989, about one-fifth of urban households still lived in

---

[2] City rankings do not factor in the inhabitants of outlying areas. Toward the end of Gorbachev's rule, many cities reverted to their former names, preferring no longer to be named after Communist-era heroes like Lenin, Gorky, and Sverdlov.

FIGURE 20.2. Typical Soviet apartments, Kiev, 1985.

communal apartments or dormitories or shared a private house. If all the households containing young couples still living with parents or in-laws but desiring a place of their own were counted in, the figure would have been still higher. Obtaining a separate apartment was often an arduous chore, taking many years.

Under Gorbachev, citizens' dissatisfaction with their living conditions rose or at least became more vocal. As magazines received more letters from their readers and as investigative journalism became more common, public complaints about Soviet housing or the lack thereof increased. The Chernobyl contamination of large areas, the Armenian earthquake of December 1988 (where destruction was great partly because of poor construction), the increasing number of refugees fleeing ethnic unrest, and the soldiers returning from east-central Europe all placed new burdens on housing. So too did the increasing decay of many of the earlier poorly built apartments.

Before *glasnost*, Soviet propaganda painted Western housing worse than it was by overemphasizing the problems of slums and homelessness, problems that supposedly did not exist in the USSR. By the late Gorbachev years, the Soviet media often reversed this picture. It viewed housing in the West through rose-colored glasses, exposed Soviet homelessness and shantytowns, and found poor and overcrowed housing conditions a major cause of everything from alcoholism and crime to family strife and pilot errors.

Furthering this dissatisfaction were all the letters and stories that now appeared exposing the favoritism and privileges operating throughout Soviet housing as well as all other aspects of Soviet life. The old saying *"blat* [pull or influence] is higher than Stalin" indicates that Soviet citizens had long been aware of the prevalence of favoritism throughout their system. Yet it still irritated many of them to read about someone who obtained a new apartment through *blat* while others remained for years, sometimes for more than a decade, on a waiting list.

During Gorbachev's final years, private construction cooperatives came into being, more private housing was built, and laws were passed to facilitate transferring state-owned housing to its tenants. This latter step, however, did not get far before the collapse of the USSR.

Besides housing, other sources of urban frustration were goods shortages and waiting in lines. These conditions varied from time to time and place to place. Moscow, for example, was better supplied than outlying areas, so much so that in the early 1980s about a million "outsiders" a day invaded the capital to shop. Despite variations, however, the total time expended on purchasing life's necessities was incredible. Living in Moscow as a *New York Times* correspondent in the 1970s, Hedrick Smith estimated that the average woman spent about two hours a day, seven days a week, making such purchases. The Soviet Interview Project found the greatest standard-of-living dissatisfaction related to shortages, poor quality, and waiting in lines. Public opinion polls of the late 1980s indicated continuing, massive dissatisfaction with growing shortages and lines.

Until the Gorbachev years, most Soviet cities had few of the amenities except parks that make city life more pleasant. Except in some of the non-Russian republics, outdoor cafes were almost nonexistent, and public toilets throughout the USSR were scarce, poorly maintained, and unsanitary. In contrast, Soviet subways in the country's largest cities were among the best in the world and were continually being extended. Although the changes of the Gorbachev years brought some improvements in urban life, they also brought new fears and dissatisfactions, concern with increasing crime being one of the most significant.

RULING CLASS, SOCIAL STRUCTURE, AND CIVIL SOCIETY

In the quarter-century after the 1959 census, the number of party members more than doubled to over 18 million. Only a small percentage of them, however, constituted the party elite, the ruling class, the *nomenklatura*. As already mentioned, their privileges and perks aroused much resentment, and Yeltsin later used this hostility to help end Communist rule.

Beneath this ruling class, Soviet society changed considerably by 1984, the last year before Gorbachev's coming to power. Using the Soviet categories we have already looked at (see Chapter 15), which include dependents, official figures indicate the following: Workers went from 50.2 percent of the population in 1959 to 61.5 percent in 1984; white-collar employees from 18.1 percent to 26 percent; and collective farmers from 31.4 percent down to 12.5 percent (in 1959, statistics still included 0.3 percent individual farmers and handicraftsmen, but this category disappeared in later census figures).

Without further explanation, however, these categories, are misleading. Among other drawbacks, they fail to identify certain groups, such as millions of military personnel (about 4 million in 1980), and they include state-farm (sovkhoz) workers in the "worker" category. The number of sovkhoz workers more than doubled from 1959 to 1984, becoming almost as large a group as collective-farm (kolkhoz) workers—thus, about one-fourth of the workforce still worked for collective and state farms, as compared to about two-fifths in 1959. Sovkhoz and white-collar workers increased their percentage of the workforce at a much faster rate than blue-collar workers, whereas the percentage of kolkhoz workers dropped sharply.

The increase in white-collar employees was especially significant, particularly the jump in professionals and other well-educated individuals. From 1959 to 1984, the percentage of people of working age who had received some higher education went from 3.3 percent to 11.6 percent. When Gorbachev came to power in 1985, he was well aware of the increasing significance of better-educated citizens, and his reforms appealed more to them than to those less educated.

Ironically, however, it was becoming more difficult by the mid-1980s for high school graduates to get into universities, and opportunities for upward social mobility were less than they had been under Khrushchev. During this same period, salary differentials among employees and occupations decreased, and attitudes toward work and occupations also changed.

In the 1960s and early 1970s Soviet industrial workers had more prestige and farmers less than their U.S. counterparts, but professional and other occupations requiring higher education had the highest prestige in both countries. By the mid-1980s, however, good pay and an opportunity to obtain goods were becoming more important than ever to Soviet citizens. The job of a bus or truck driver, whose pay often exceeded that of doctors or professors, was becoming more valued. So too were jobs in commerce and services, which usually provided opportunities for obtaining scare consumer goods or services before the general public had its chance.

The developments of the Gorbachev years began a process of even more significant changes, from top to bottom of the social hierarchy. The prestige of the military declined rapidly as Gorbachev reduced military spending, returned troops from Afghanistan and east-central Europe, and decreased military personnel. Private enterprise increased the purchasing power of some, whereas inflation decreased that of many. To maintain a decent standard of living, some academics and other professionals became full-time or part-time entrepreneurs. In a climate in which laws for new commercial practices were either nonexistent or poorly defined and understood, new fortunes were often made using methods that were legally questionable.

Despite such changes, many among the old ruling class, including Yeltsin, became part of the new ruling class; and many privileged individuals managed to use their positions to enrich themselves as the Communist order was collapsing around them.

If in some ways the last years of the USSR recalled the era of the entrepreneurial Nepmen, in other ways, it was reminiscent of the last decades of the tsarist empire. In both earlier periods, there had been autonomous organizations not dictated to by the state. The proliferation of such organizations in the final tsarist decades signaled the ongoing development of a civil society—an independent social sphere standing between the government and individuals or families. But this evolution was dealt a mortal blow by the Bolshevik revolution of 1917. Although a much smaller number of autonomous organizations were still permitted under NEP, Stalin's "revolution from above" quickly ended even that concession. Although political repression declined after Stalin's death, his successors, until Gorbachev, still hampered any development of civil society. Unions, for example, remained under party control. Most of the small number of independent organizations that did manage to emerge before 1985 were either repressed or at least harassed.

All this changed during the Gorbachev years. By 1990, there were at a minimum 11,000 independent organizations in the USSR—many times that according to other estimates—and scholars talked about the emergence of a civil society. Organizations came in all shapes, sizes, and forms: political and nonpolitical, countrywide and local, left-wing and right-wing, religious and secular, devoted to preserving the past and safeguarding the future (especially its environment), devoted to animals and children, devoted to leisure activities and workers' rights, and devoted to business and charity. Not only industrial workers, but also professionals, peasants, veterans, peace advocates, women, the disabled, and others banded together to further their causes through such methods as meetings and publications.

One such organization was Memorial, which dedicated itself to collecting testimony and other information about Stalin's millions of victims. By early 1989, it had branches in almost 200 Soviet cities. Another organization, founded in 1988, was the Democratic Union. Although smaller than Memorial, it placed the creation of a civil society at the top of its agenda. It perceived Gorbachev as a defender of party interests and favored overthrowing the old system by starting from the beginning with a new constituent assembly. It led the charge for political pluralism, a multiparty system, and respect for minority rights. In its own organization, including its regional branches, it practiced what it preached, for it contained liberal democrats, social democrats, democratic communists, Christian democrats, anarchists, socialist revolutionaries, and constitutional monarchists.

Thanks in part to the Democratic Union's efforts, the USSR did become more pluralistic: In late 1991, one publication identified more than 300 political parties. And there were at least 2,000 others, if one counts all the local parties spread out among the union republics.

BLUE-COLLAR WORKERS: GAINS AND LOSSES

Besides sharing in the general economic and social-service gains made by Soviet citizens under Khrushchev and Brezhnev, Soviet blue-collar workers made specific gains of their own. Scattered labor disturbances such as that in Novocherkassk in 1962, triggered by price increases, served as a reminder to the ruling elite of the importance of avoiding worker alienation. Some scholars have written of a tacit "social contract" that post-Stalin authorities concluded with the workers: In exchange for political compliance, the workers received not only guaranteed jobs, increased purchasing power, and state services, but also reduced labor discipline. In 1956, for example, the government canceled the harsh 1940 laws that had made absenteeism, tardiness, and changing jobs without permission criminal offenses.

With labor more scarce because of World War II deaths, declining birth rates, and a shrinking pool of rural recruits, many workers took advantage of their freedom to change jobs. Although labor turnover was highest in the period immediately after the 1956 changes, it still remained high during subsequent years, with about one-fifth of the workforce changing jobs per year during the quarter century before Gorbachev's rule. Not only were workers free to work somewhere else, but also they were permitted to work less, both officially and unofficially. For most of them, the work week went from six days a week to five and from 48 hours a week in 1955 to 40 by the end of the 1960s.

The amount of effort put into each work week also declined. During the late 1950s, the future dissident Vladimir Bukovsky worked briefly in a Moscow bus factory, where he recalled only one man working conscientiously, and his co-workers hated him for it. Many of them were often drunk or hungover. Although perhaps an extreme example of workers' indifference to work, it was by no means an isolated exception. If anything, the problem of worker indifference seemed to grow in subsequent decades, as did the repetition of the joke about the worker who stated: "I'll pretend to work as long as they pretend to pay me."

As indicated in Chapter 18, Andropov's efforts to deal with poor workplace discipline included police raids to round up absentee workers. The 1985 vodka reform was also intended to improve labor discipline. Many of Gorbachev's later policies undermined both sides of the "social-contract" bargain, as both government paternalism and workers' political subservience were reduced. The Enterprise Law of 1987, for example, threatened job security, making layoffs more probable, but also it called for workers to elect their own factory managers.

From the beginning, workers had been less enthusiastic about Gorbachev's reforms than were most professionals. By 1990–1991, the workers' standard of living had clearly eroded along with their job security. To many of them, their legal right to strike, granted in late 1989, and to form truly independent trade unions was little recompense for their new insecurities and hardships.

Even before they were legally permitted to strike, a half-million miners had done so in the summer of 1989. Largely ignoring their own union officials, miners organized their own strikes. Sobered by the experience, the All-Union Central Council of Trade Unions, supposedly representing 140 million members, proclaimed a new policy: It would no longer carry out the wishes of the Communist party but instead would focus more on the welfare of its members. In 1990, it reorganized and renamed itself the General Confederation of Trade

Unions (GCTU). Although it was able to gain government recognition as the voice of Soviet workers and play some role in labor negotiations, it was not destined to live long.

As the USSR disintegrated, so too did this all-union worker confederation. In the RSFSR and then in the new independent Russia, one of the GCTU branches, the Federation of Independent Trade Unions of Russia, emerged as the strongest labor organization, but there were also other smaller union organizations, including the Independent Miners' Union, founded in 1990.

As labor unrest increased during Gorbachev's final years in power, he was forced to make concessions to workers, concessions that slowed down the transition to a less paternalistic system. Yet labor was far from forming a united front. Rather, it reflected the chaotic and transitional nature of the times.

LIFE IN THE COUNTRYSIDE

From 1959 to 1979, the Soviet rural population declined by 10 million people. From 1979 to 1989, the decline was much smaller, a little less than 1 million. Most rural workers performed agricultural work, but by the late 1980s, only a little over one-fifth of all Soviet laborers were engaged in such work.

As compared to the urban population, those who lived in the countryside were more likely to be children under age 15 or older people over age 60. Like the young Gorbachev, many teenagers left their villages, often permanently, to seek better schooling or a better life in the city. For those who remained, there were real improvements under Khrushchev and Brezhnev, especially for collective-farm workers (kolkhozniks), whom Stalin had treated shabbily. Khrushchev increased the prices the state paid kolkhozes for their crops; from 1964 to 1970, new decrees extended pensions, a guaranteed minimum wage, and government-backed health insurance to kolkhozniks. Although the incomes of kolkhozniks and other rural workers still lagged behind those of urban workers, by the mid-1980s, the gap had noticeably narrowed as compared to three decades earlier.

A similar picture existed regarding many other urban-rural comparisons, from obtaining education to material comforts: Rural conditions improved but still lagged behind those in urban areas. In 1953, almost nine-tenths of the country's sovkhozes were electrified but only a little over two-tenths of its kolkhozes. By 1965, almost all of both types of farms had electricity. By 1980, seven-tenths of rural households possessed televisions and six-tenths washing machines and refrigerators. By this time, however, most rural households still had no indoor toilets, running water, central heating, or telephones, and few rural settlements possessed paved roads.

Changes in the size and number of sovkhozes and kolkhozes produced significant changes in Soviet village life. From 1953 to 1988, the number of sovkhozes increased almost fivefold, whereas the number of kolkhozes decreased by more than two-thirds. The average size of the latter, however, grew much larger, though still smaller than the average sovkhoz. The decrease in the number of kolkhozes and their increasing size broke the earlier connection between kolkhozes and villages and led to the abandonment of many of the latter.

This development did not trouble the government, which had always intended eventually to eliminate the "socio-economic and cultural distinctions between town and country." In the party Program adopted at the Twenty-Second Party Congress in 1961, this goal was once again stated, and the Program proclaimed that kolkhoz villages would be amalgamated into modern urban communities.

In keeping with this concept, many agro-towns or central villages of perhaps 1,500 to 2,000 people were established and resettlement encouraged. Houses in them were usually wooden and placed close to each other, but public buildings for administrative or communal purposes (for example, a school, post office, medical center, or library) were often brick or concrete. As so often happened, reality usually fell short of rhetoric, with the services available being less than promised.

Spurred on by government policy, the number of villages kept declining. By 1975, there were less than one-third the number of settlements in the Siberian Buriat ASSR as there had been in 1959. In the Perm province of Central Russia, the government planned by the year 2000 to eliminate more than nine-tenths of the more than 5,000 rural communities still in existence in 1980; in Belorussia, almost as large a percentage of villages were scheduled to disappear.

Not all villagers were happy about these resettlement plans. Such dissatisfaction was echoed by a group of Russian "village-prose" writers who lamented the increasing standardization of the larger central villages, the decline of more traditional villages and Russian village customs, and the erosion of good peasant work habits and respect for the land (see Chapter 21, for more on these writers).

Despite government-encouraged standardization, many rural and agricultural differences remained between the various Soviet republics. Estonian farmers, for example, were much more prosperous than their Russian counterparts and less demoralized.

Although Gorbachev came from a farming background, his agricultural policies accomplished little. Neither agricultural administrators nor farmers were enthusiastic about his 1988 plan encouraging the leasing of state land to establish family or cooperative farming arrangements.

The leasing option threatened to lessen the powers of the administrators and was too full of uncertainties for most farmers. For centuries, Russian peasants had farmed primarily in one type or another of collective arrangement and had been distrustful of innovations from above. Soviet rule, collectivized agriculture, and, more recently, expanded welfare policies further discouraged private entrepreneurial activity and risk-taking. Uncertainties about obtaining sufficient capital, equipment, selling markets, and cooperation from government officials all helped undercut Gorbachev's plan. So too did justifiable fears that some future political authority might reverse Gorbachev's policy and leasers' private gains would be seized from them just as they had from the kulaks under Stalin. It is little wonder that at the time of the USSR's breakup in 1991, state and collective farms continued to dominate Soviet agriculture.

FOOD AND DRINK; SICKNESS AND HEALTH

Despite agricultural shortcomings, the post-Stalinist USSR was no longer plagued by sporadic famine, and the diet of its people gradually improved. By the late 1980s, Soviet citizens' caloric intake was comparable to that of Western citizens. Although the former still relied more heavily on bread, potatoes, and other foods high in starch and fats, their diet had become more varied. Even with all the food problems in 1990, Soviet statistics indicated that the caloric intake was greater and the reliance on grains and potatoes less than in 1980. Only in 1991, amidst the disintegration of the USSR, did per-capita food consumption for foods except grains and potatoes decline.

Beneath these generalizations, however, there was a wide variety of differences, especially between regions of the USSR and between the fortunate and unfortunate of Soviet society. During the 1980s, for example, diets in the Baltic republics were the most varied and least starchy, whereas those in the Central Asian republics were at the other end of the scale. The unfortunate in the USSR had insufficient income to purchase higher-priced but more varied foodstuffs available in farmers' markets. They had to rely on state stores, where prices were subsidized, but meat, vegetables, fruit, and dairy products were more scarce. The most fortunate were the party elite with access to special stores and foods.

Throughout this period, Soviet eating habits remained more traditional than in Western industrialized nations. With a scarcity of good restaurants and almost no fast foods available (only under Gorbachev did a few franchises such as McDonald's and Pizza Hut begin to appear), most Soviet citizens ate their breakfast and evening meal at home.

Foreign visitors to the USSR were often amazed at the amount of food (and drink) Soviet citizens consumed on special occasions, which they loved to celebrate with a first-class feast. It generally included *zakuski* (appetizers), soups such as borscht or *shchi* (cabbage soup), followed by another course, and then the main meal and dessert. Alcohol, often including vodka, wine, and champagne, also tended to be plentiful at such feasts. The amount of time and income spent to gather all the ingredients for such a feast was usually great.

Although diets improved in the post-Stalin years, alcohol abuse worsened, at least up until the mid-1980s. Although statistical comparisons can be misleading, they give a general idea of the problem. One expert (Segal) has estimated that in 1984–1985, Soviet per capita alcohol consumption for those over age 15 was about two and a half times as high as in the United States. During the 1980s, he estimated that about one-sixth of the Soviet adults over age 21 were alcoholics, with men being much worse abusers than women.

The causes of such heavy drinking were many. Among them were cultural habits that had long encouraged excessive alcohol consumption, the need for

FIGURE 20.3. The author and his wife (third from left) with gracious Russian hosts and friends after a sumptuous meal, Akademgorodok, Siberia, 1993.

state revenues (about 13 percent of the government budget in the early 1980s), more purchasing power and leisure time, inadequate leisure alternatives, and increasing frustration and disenchantment with Soviet life. Some older people blamed the increasing alcoholism of younger generations on their moral emptiness, sometimes adding that Western influences contributed to the decay of Soviet morals. But such charges at best contained only half-truths.

The effects of alcoholism were pervasive throughout Soviet society. It raised rates of all of the following: worker absenteeism, crimes, industrial accidents, sickness and death, and family strife and abuse.[3] As a result of the vodka reform of 1985, vodka consumption temporarily declined (despite greater moonshine production), but bounced back to 1984 levels during the early 1990s.

Overall, life expectancy at birth increased until the mid-1960s, when it reached a reported high of about 70 years, with women projected to live to age 74 and men to age 66. In contrast to the general pattern in other industrialized countries, by 1980–1981, life expectancy had gradually decreased by a few years, before slowly rising again almost to reach the mid-1960s figure in 1987. By 1990–1991, however, amidst the chaos of a disintegrating country, death rates increased and life expectancy again declined. Regardless of the difficul-

---

[3] For an excellent treatment of drinking's social effects in the USSR during this period, see Stephen White, *Russia Goes Dry: Alcohol, State and Society* (Cambridge, England, 1996), pp. 41–55.

ties of comparing Soviet and Western statistics, there is little doubt of the over-all patterns and that USSR death rates during its final two decades of existence were higher than those in other major industrialized countries.

During the 1960s, vaccines, antibiotics, and other public health measures brought sharp decreases in diseases such as polio, diphtheria, measles, whooping cough, scarlet fever, tetanus, and typhoid. A Soviet reference book of the mid-1970s claimed that the USSR had "almost one-third of the world's doctors" and noted long-term and recent advances in the number of hospital beds and hospitals. Some Soviet specialists, for example, eye surgeons, made important contributions to world medicine.

Meanwhile, however, alcohol and environmentally related diseases were killing off growing numbers; heavy smoking also was a health problem. In their book *Ecocide*, Feshbach and Friendly cite ample evidence to document the health consequences of increasing levels of radioactivity and other types of air and water pollution. To cite just a few of their statistics, they point out that between 1949 and 1981, bronchial asthma rose sevenfold among Moscow's children, and by 1990, one-sixth of the children, and one-fourth of the country's adults were chronically ill.

The *glasnost* era made clear many of the enormous healthcare problems facing the USSR in the late 1980s. Most of them could be summed up in two words—sanitation and shortages. Public toilets were a sanitary scandal, and conditions in crowded apartments, at factories, restaurants, and other places were below Western hygienic standards. Close to half the rural hospitals and polyclinics were without sewer connections, and four-fifths of them were without hot water. Such sanitation problems were worsened by shortages, such as a lack of disposable syringes.

Other medical equipment was also in short supply; for example, only half of the country's hospitals and polyclinics possessed x-ray machines. Well-trained doctors were another shortage. Although possessing more physicians than any country in the world, their training often left much to be desired. According to the Russian Academy of Sciences, almost half of the 1990 medical school graduates could not read an electrocardiogram.

During the USSR's final few years, medical and food shortages increased, and the growing number of ethnic conflicts and refugees worsened Soviet health conditions. Further worsening the situation, the percentage of children receiving vaccinations for such diseases as diphtheria, tetanus, whooping cough, polio, measles, and mumps decreased. In Moscow in 1991, there were 1,100 cases of diphtheria, twenty-four times the 1988 number. Although acquired immunodeficiency syndrome (AIDS) cases remained well below U.S. figures, rising Soviet drug abuse, along with a shortage of disposable syringes, gave cause for future AIDS concerns.

WOMEN, FAMILY, AND GENDER ISSUES

For decades after World War II, the war continued to affect male to female ratios. The gap between the number of men and women gradually receded as the effects of the war grew more distant: women made up 55 percent of the population in 1959 and 53 percent in 1989, and part of the gap was because of women's greater longevity.

Increases in the percentage of women in higher education, the workforce, and the Communist party from the early 1960s until the late 1980s, however, were more a continuation of their upward prewar trends than an aftereffect of the war. Although in 1960, women composed 43 percent of higher education students (as they had in 1937) and made up 47 percent of the workforce, by 1970 their percentages were 49 percent and 51 percent. Continuing to hover around half of the workforce in the next few decades, by 1988 women had risen to 54 percent of the students in higher institutions. Within the Communist party, their percentage increased from 20 to 29 percent between 1961 and 1989.

Yet, as before World War II, women tended to be more prominent in lower-paid jobs and fields, for example, health, education, trade, banking, and insurance. Throughout the post-Stalin Soviet period, they provided more than two-thirds the combined number of teachers, doctors, and dentists, but these were not high-paying Soviet professions. Soviet women performed more than nine-tenths of the secretarial work, but they also worked at more heavy, unskilled labor than did Western women.

Soviet women made little progress in rising to the country's top economic and political posts. In a 1989 survey of the percentage of women in the top managerial positions of various enterprises and organizations, they held less than 1 percent of such positions in transport and construction and between 6 and 10 percent of those in agriculture, communications, and industry. During the 1980s, the percentage of women on the party's Central Committee never climbed over 5 percent. In 1957, E. A. Furtseva was the first woman ever to be appointed a Politburo member, but she was demoted several years later. In 1988, the Politburo obtained its second female appointment (this time a candidate member) in seven decades, but by then the body was beginning to lose its former significance. In the new Congress of People's Deputies elected in 1989, women gained 16 percent of the seats, but prejudice against women holding high political offices remained strong.

There was also continuity with the Stalinist years in the continuing double burden that almost all women faced: They held full-time jobs like their husbands, while also performing most household duties. More so than men, women cleaned, cooked, watched over the children, and—often most taxing of all—waited in lines. The cumbersome Soviet retail system, necessitating food purchases at different stores and markets and often waiting in three different lines in any one store, meant long and tiresome hours spent shopping each week. Because most women (and men) did not possess an automobile, they could buy no more at one time than they could carry home on public transportation.

Although women continued to be overburdened and have less leisure than men, they did benefit from the overall improvement in Soviet living standards and social services that marked the Khrushchev and Brezhnev years. The expansion of maternity benefits and day care facilities was especially important to women.

As in the earlier Soviet decades, government policies regarding abortion and divorce wavered between Marxist-Leninist principles and Soviet desires to increase the population, especially among Russians and other Slavs. In 1955, the government reversed Stalin's earlier policy and once again legalized abortion. Partly because of its desire to increase family size, however, the government's policy toward providing sufficient contraceptives remained negative.

Inadequate urban housing space and women's "double burden," however, prevented couples from sharing the government's enthusiasm for larger families. In the cities, one-child families became the most common. To prevent more children, Soviet women had numerous abortions. By the late 1970s, their number greatly outnumbered those of live births, and most Soviet urban women in the European part of the country had six or more (sometimes many more) abortions during their lifetime. Although legal, the conditions under which most of them were performed were generally crude by Western standards.

New regulations and reduced fees under both Khrushchev and Brezhnev made divorces easier to obtain, and they steadily increased, ending nearly half of all marriages by the mid-1970s. Like abortion rates, divorce rates varied considerably among regions and nationalities. In the 1980s, they were highest in the Estonian, Latvian, and Russian republics and lowest in Moslem areas and among Armenians and Georgians.

Feminist institutions and attitudes were barely visible under Khrushchev and Brezhnev. Khrushchev did establish "women's soviets" (*zhensovety*) to help remedy women's problems, especially at the workplace. But these local bodies generally exercised little influence; not until Gorbachev's rule, when a Soviet Women's Committee was established, were women allowed any national representation.

Female dissenters, like the women radicals of the late tsarist period, were more concerned with battling against government oppression in general than with any feminist agenda. Although a feminist underground journal, *Almanac: Woman and Russia*, appeared at the end of 1979, it was soon suppressed, and only under Gorbachev did Soviet feminist writings and independent associations legally begin appearing in the USSR.

Although influenced and encouraged by Western feminists, Soviet feminists of the late 1980s found it difficult to make much headway. They had to overcome long-dominant institutional and attitudinal obstacles to improving women's lives, and their collective voice had to compete with numerous others under increasingly chaotic conditions. Although the Gorbachev years brought some improvements for women, they also brought new problems, including more prostitution and layoffs (higher among women than men).

Among young men, a major concern was the military draft. According to the 1967 conscription law, eighteen-year-olds were liable to be drafted for a minimum of two years unless they received an exemption for educational or other purposes. During the 1980s, concern with being sent to Afghanistan led

FIGURE 20.4 Although divorce rates were lower among Armenians, Georgians, and Moslem peoples, birth rates were higher and children more plentiful. Erevan, 1985.

to rising youth opposition to Soviet military service. So too did increasing anti-Soviet sentiments in the republics and *glasnost* media revelations about the brutalities of military life. In the fall 1990 draft in Georgia, less than one-tenth of those called up reported for Soviet service. Such opposition, plus the poor health of potential draftees, became major headaches for military authorities in the final Soviet years.

Among other phenomena that received media attention and some sympathy for the first time under Gorbachev was Soviet homosexuality. In the 1950s, *The Great Soviet Encyclopedia* had defined it as "an expression of moral decadence by the ruling classes" in capitalist countries and suggested it was rare in the USSR. Soviet criminal codes made homosexual relations between men a criminal offense (those among women, perhaps considered more unthinkable, were not even mentioned). A new criminal code still being worked on in 1991 was supposed to decriminalize homosexual relations, but this did not come about in Russia until after the breakup of the USSR.

LAW AND LAWLESSNESS

Khrushchev's criticism of Stalin's violations of "revolutionary socialist legality" did not change the fact that the law and Soviet courts remained tools of the party almost until the end of the Soviet regime. The term *telephone justice* described the phenomenon of a party official dictating by phone a verdict to a judge or procurator. Although Khrushchev oversaw the enactment of important legal reforms—including ending the courtroom use of "analogy" and insisting that confessions were not alone enough for convictions—he remained faithful to Lenin's view of the role of law in Soviet society (see Chapter 15 for "analogy," confessions, and Lenin's legal views).

Although Khrushchev truly wanted to rule more by law and less by coercion and terror, the socialist cause he believed in always came first. After first approving of a reduction in the application of the death penalty, in 1961 he extended the penalty to more crimes, including major economic offenses. He especially wanted it applied to two big-time currency dealers who had already been tried and sentenced. The story was later told that when his procurator-general told him that such a retroactive action would be a violation of socialist legality, Khrushchev replied: "Which is more important to you: your legality or your socialism."[4] Whether these were Khrushchev's exact words or not, they capture perfectly the attitude of the party elite toward any "rule of law." The two dealers were subsequently shot, the standard method of execution.

Khrushchev, Brezhnev, and their colleagues attempted to rule less arbitrarily than Stalin by improving the criminal codes to make it easier to prosecute criminals according to the law. Typical was the treatment of dissidents such as Siniavsky and Daniel. Like them, many others were charged with violating Article 70 of the 1960 RSFSR Criminal Code or comparable articles in other republics' codes. Violating this article could result in as much as seven years "deprivation of freedom" as well as additional exile for up to five years. The article's prohibition of agitation or propaganda carried on to subvert or weaken the Soviet regime left Soviet judges plenty of room for interpretation and arriving at a guilty verdict.

In the absence of a jury system, all criminal and civil cases except in higher courts of appeal were decided theoretically by a judge and two "people's assessors." In reality, the judge's influence almost always predominated over the lay assessors, who possessed no legal training.

In early 1964, the unconventional poet Joseph Brodsky was arrested and sentenced to five years of administrative exile for being a "parasite," who avoided socially useful work. The parasite law was another Khrushchev-era innovation. Because Brodsky was not an officially recognized poet, his defense that he worked writing poetry got him nowhere—or rather only to the Arctic region of Archangel.

Although Soviet constitutions, such as the 1977 all-union constitution and the 1978 RSFSR constitution, were party instruments, they also served a propagandistic function. If dissidents took certain articles too literally, for example, regarding freedom of speech, courts ruled against them anyway. Higher courts of appeal existed, including a USSR Supreme Court, but they too were under party control, and no court could rule that any law was unconstitutional. Only

---

[4] Cited in Geoffrey Hosking, *The First Socialist Society: A History of the Soviet Union from Within*. 2d ed. (Cambridge, Mass., 1993), p. 353.

an occasional defense attorney, such as those of some of the dissidents, dared to act against party wishes, although that did not save their clients from convictions. One Soviet dissident noted that among 424 known political trials in the decade following 1968, there were no acquittals in any of them.

In other types of criminal and civil cases—the latter dealing with such matters as inheritance, libel, alimony, apartment evictions, and employment terminations—justice was not so infrequent. But even where the party's vital interests were not at stake, there were still impediments to a fair trial, the main one being judicial bribe-taking. Dina Kaminskaya, a leading Soviet defense attorney for many years, later wrote that during the early post-Stalin years "judges who did not take bribes were a phenomenon so unusual as to be incredible." She believed there was a strong link between judges' subservience to the party and their corruption. Because justice did not come before political directives, why should it come before judges' enriching themselves? Although Khrushchev attempted to curtail bribe-taking, he enjoyed only mixed success. Decades later, the problem still existed.

If the party elite and judges placed other considerations above the law, it is hardly surprising that those with less power did likewise—for example, in regard to buying or selling on the black market or stealing from their places of employment.

By the time Gorbachev came to power in 1985, there were indications of even less respect for law. In his book *Perestroika*, first published in late 1987, the

---

Widespread Theft

The following excerpt is taken from *A Chronicle of Current Events*, reporting on a 1970 *samizdat* (underground) pamphlet. The excerpt is a condensed version of that edited and translated by Peter Reddaway in *Uncensored Russia: Protest and Dissent in the Soviet Union; the Unofficial Moscow Journal, A Chronicle of Current Events* (New York, 1972), pp. 360–361. Ellipses are mine.

"Simplicity is worse than theft" is a pamphlet about how in our country *"an enormous number of conscientious citizens steal things in one way or another, some a little at a time, others by the wagon-load; they steal primitively or with miraculous ingenuity, for friends or for themselves, to get rich or to get drunk. They steal meat and* butter, instruments and medicines, planks, semi-conductors, engines, paper, young currant-bushes and cement, bricks and slate and anything under the sun. . . . People steal because it is much simpler, more convenient and more profitable to do so than to go mad trying to push one's way through crowds of fellow shoppers, all driven frantic by the constant shortage of one commodity or another. People steal because while it is still considered shameful to steal private property, it is an amusing game to take what belongs to the State." This is the way the lower strata of society think. And what example of moral behaviour is offered from above? The second part of the pamphlet deals with this. "The ruling élite insatiably gobbles up all the tastiest morsels of the common cake."*

law-trained Gorbachev wrote that "democracy cannot exist and develop without the rule of law, because law is designed to protect society from abuses of power and guarantee citizens . . . rights and freedoms."

In 1988, he began speaking of the necessity of creating a "law-based state." Moreover, he obtained the Central Committee's agreement to various legal measures including an extensive review of law codes. That same year, almost one-third of the 1977 constitution was amended. In 1989, the new Congress of People's Deputies agreed to Gorbachev's suggestion that a commission be established to draft an entirely new constitution for the USSR.

By this time, enthusiasm for a "law-based state" was growing, especially among liberal deputies to the new Congress and the smaller Supreme Soviet, which it elected from its midst. One of the most enthusiastic for the idea was Anatoli Sobchak, who for years had been a professor of law in Leningrad and in 1990 became mayor of that city. In his recollections of the stormy parliamentary sessions of 1989–1990, he states that the idea of the party leadership learning to stay within the law became his "mantra," which he often repeated to his fellow deputies and others. In one of his preelection speeches, he borrowed the cadence of Martin Luther King's famous "I Have A Dream" speech and listed a law-governed state as one of his dreams.

Sobchak credited Gorbachev for advancing the concept, an idea the Leningrad mayor came to believe "represented a knife in the very heart of the [old Communist] system." Sobchak also recognized the importance of the work of Andrei Sakharov for advancing the cause of a law-based society. The earlier efforts of dissidents such as Valeri Chalidze were also important. He pursued a legal approach to human rights and persuaded Sakharov to join with him and fellow physicist Andrei Tverdokhlebov in founding the Human Rights Committee in 1970.

Yet creating a "law-based state" was easier said than done, especially in a society that had never displayed much respect and appreciation of the law. Furthermore, users of the new term did not necessarily mean the same thing by it. In his *Perestroika*, Gorbachev not only called for the rule of law, but also inaccurately pictured Lenin as one who cherished it, strictly remaining within its bounds. Moreover, Gorbachev himself, after all his fine speeches, continued to make use of illegally obtained KGB wiretaps on politicians distrusted by the KGB. Adding to the difficulty was the need for many new commercial, criminal, and civil laws and the fragmentation of political power. Although all sorts of new laws were passed on various governmental levels, they often contradicted each other. This further confused the legal situation and led to talk of a "war of laws."

Meanwhile, as the command economy and centralized power were collapsing, random and organized crimes were increasing, along with people's fears. Official estimates placed the number of organized crime groups in 1991 at slightly over 5,000. The reported number of mercenary crimes such as robbery and aggravated assault especially increased, both of them more than tripling in the Russian republic between 1987 and 1991.

Although Soviet "mafias" cooperating with politicians such as Aliev in

Azerbaijan were already powerful under Brezhnev, they now got stronger. They took advantage of economic and political weaknesses and gained new opportunities. They benefited from the 1985 vodka reform by organizing the illegal vodka trade and the sugar needed for moonshine. In the last two Soviet years, they made the equivalent of billions of additional dollars. They controlled the drug trade, obtaining drugs such as opium from such sources as North Korea and Afghanistan and then selling them in the rising USSR market or abroad. They also engaged in vast illegal foreign currency exchanges; sold stolen art, antiques, and weapons abroad; controlled many prostitutes and businesses; and demanded "protection" payments from still others. The mafias committed murders and bought the cooperation of numerous people necessary for their operations. Among them were government, police, military, border, and customs personnel, including high officials and KGB officers. Becoming stronger than ever at the time of the USSR's collapse, organized crime was just one more troubling legacy for the USSR's successor states.

SUGGESTED SOURCES*

ADELMAN, DEBORAH. *The "Children of Perestroika": Moscow Teenagers Talk about Their Lives and the Future.* Armonk, N.Y., 1991.

ALEKSEYEVA, LIUDMILA, and PAUL GOLDBERG. *The Thaw Generation: Coming of Age in the Post-Stalin Era.* Boston, 1990.

BARRY, DONALD D. *Toward the "Rule of Law" in Russia?: Political and Legal Reform in the Transition Period.* Armonk, N.Y., 1992.

BINYON, MICHAEL. *Life in Russia.* New York, 1983.

BIRMAN, IGOR. *Personal Consumption in the USSR and the USA.* New York, 1989.

BUCKLEY, MARY, ed. *Redefining Russian Society and Polity.* Boulder, 1993.

———. *Perestroika and Soviet Women.* Cambridge, England, 1992.

BUKOVSKY, VLADIMIR. *To Build a Castle: My Life as a Dissenter.* New York, 1979.

CHALIDZE, VALERY. *Criminal Russia: Essays on Crime in the Soviet Union.* New York, 1977.

CLARK, WILLIAM A. *Crime and Punishment in Soviet Officialdom: Combating Corruption in the Political Elite, 1965–1990.* Armonk, N.Y., 1993.

CLEMENTS, BARBARA EVANS. *Daughters of Revolution: A History of Women in the U.S.S.R.* Arlington Heights, Ill., 1994. Chs. 5–6.

COLTON, TIMOTHY J. *Moscow: Governing the Socialist Metropolis.* Cambridge, Mass., 1995. Chs. 5–7.

CONNOR, WALTER D. *The Accidental Proletariat: Workers, Politics, and Crisis in Gorbachev's Russia.* Princeton, 1991.

COOK, LINDA J. *The Soviet Social Contract and Why It Failed: Welfare Policy and Workers' Politics from Brezhnev to Yeltsin.* Cambridge, Mass., 1993.

DALLIN, ALEXANDER, and GAIL W. LAPIDUS, eds. *The Soviet System: From Crisis to Collapse.* Rev. ed. Boulder, 1995.

DANIELS, ROBERT V., ed. *Soviet Communism from Reform to Collapse.* Lexington, Mass., 1995.

* See also books cited in footnotes. Soviet life is also revealed in many literary works and films that are available in English translations. See Chapter 21 for a discussion of some of them.

FEOFANOV, YURI, and DONALD D. BARRY. *Politics and Justice in Russia: Major Trials of the Post-Stalin Era.* Armonk, N.Y., 1996.

FESHBACH, MURRAY, and ALFRED FRIENDLY, JR. *Ecocide in the USSR: Health and Human Nature Under Siege.* New York, 1992.

FILTZER, DONALD. *Soviet Workers and the Collapse of Perestroika: The Soviet Labour Process and Gorbachev's Reforms, 1985–1991.* Cambridge, England, 1994.

GILINSKII, YAKOV L. "Crime in Russia: The Past, Present, and Future," *CPER* 3, no. 4 (1994): 215–231.

GOLDMAN, MARSHALL I. *What Went Wrong with Perestroika.* New York, 1992.

HANSSON, CAROLA, and KARIN LIDEN. *Moscow Women: Thirteen Interviews.* New York, 1983.

HINDUS, MAURICE. *House without a Roof: Russia after Forty-three Years of Revolution.* Garden City, N.Y., 1961.

———. *The Kremlin's Human Dilemma: Russia after Half a Century of Revolution.* Garden City, N.Y., 1967.

HOFFMANN, ERIK P., and ROBIN F. LAIRD, eds. *The Soviet Polity in the Modern Era.* New York, 1984.

HOLLAND, BARBARA, ed. *Soviet Sisterhood.* Bloomington, 1985.

JONES, ANTHONY, and WILLIAM MOSKOFF. *Ko-Ops: The Rebirth of Entrepreneurship in the Soviet Union.* Bloomington, 1991.

JONES, ANTHONY, WALTER CONNOR, and DAVID E. POWELL, eds. *Soviet Social Problems.* Boulder, 1991.

KAMINSKAYA, DINA. *Final Judgment: My Life as a Soviet Defense Attorney.* New York, 1982.

KERBLAY, BASILE. *Modern Soviet Society.* New York, 1983.

KNIGHT, AMY W. *The KGB: Police and Politics in the Soviet Union.* Boston, 1988.

KON, IGOR, and JAMES RIORDAN, eds. *Sex and Russian Society.* Bloomington, 1993.

KOTKIN, STEPHEN. *Steeltown, USSR: Soviet Society in the Gorbachev Era.* Berkeley, 1991.

LANE, DAVID. *Soviet Economy and Society.* New York, 1985.

———. *Soviet Society under Perestroika.* Rev. ed. London, 1992.

———, ed. *Russia in Flux: The Political and Social Consequences of Reform.* Brookfield, Vt., 1992.

LAPIDUS, GAIL WARSHOFSKY. *Women in Soviet Society: Equality, Development, and Social Change.* Berkeley, 1978.

LEVINE, IRVING R. *Main Street, U.S.S.R.* Garden City, N.Y., 1959.

MAMONOVA, TATYANA, ed. *Women and Russia: Feminist Writings from the Soviet Union.* Boston, 1984.

MANDEL, DAVID. *Rabotyagi: Perestroika and After Viewed from Below: Interviews with Workers in the Former Soviet Union.* New York, 1994.

MILLAR, JAMES R., ed. *Politics, Work, and Daily Life in the USSR: A Survey of Former Soviet Citizens.* Cambridge, England, 1987.

MILLER, WRIGHT. *Russians as People.* New York, 1961.

MOSKOFF, WILLIAM. *Hard Times: Impoverishment and Protest in the Perestroika Years: The Soviet Union 1985–1991.* Armonk, N.Y., 1993.

ORLOV, YURI. *Dangerous Thoughts: Memoirs of a Russian Life.* New York, 1991.

ORLOVA, RAISA. *Memoirs.* New York, 1983.

POCKNEY, B. P. *Soviet Statistics since 1950.* New York, 1991.

POSADSKAYA, ANASTASIA, ed. *Women in Russia: A New Era in Russian Feminism.* London, 1994.

RICHARDS, SUSAN. *Epics of Everyday Life: Encounters in a Changing Russia.* New York, 1991.

RIORDAN, JAMES. *Soviet Youth Culture.* Bloomington, 1989.

RIORDAN, JAMES, and SUE BRIDGER, eds. *Dear Comrade Editor: Readers' Letters to the Soviet Press under Perestroika.* Bloomington, 1992.

RYAN, MICHAEL. *Contemporary Soviet Society: A Statistical Handbook.* Brookfield, Vt., 1990.

RYWKIN, MICHAEL. *Soviet Society Today.* Armonk, N.Y., 1989.

SEGAL, B. M. *The Drunken Society: Alcohol Abuse and Alcoholism in the Soviet Union: A Comparative Study.* New York, 1990.

SHLAPENTOKH, VLADIMIR. *Public and Private Life of the Soviet People: Changing Values in Post-Stalin Russia.* New York, 1989.

SIMIS, KONSTANTIN M. *USSR—the Corrupt Society: The Secret World of Soviet Capitalism.* New York, 1982.

SOBCHAK, ANATOLY. *For a New Russia: The Mayor of St. Petersburg's Own Story of the Struggle for Justice and Democracy.* New York, 1992.

SMITH, HEDRICK. *The New Russians.* New York, 1991.

———. *The Russians.* New York, 1976.

VLADIMIROV, LEONID. *The Russians.* New York, 1968.

VOZLENSKY, MICHAEL. *Nomenklatura: The Soviet Ruling Class.* New York, 1984.

YAKOVLEV, ALEXANDER M. *Striving for Law in a Lawless Land: Memoirs of a Russian Reformer.* Armonk, N.Y., 1996.

CHAPTER 21

Religion and Culture, 1953–1991

In the post-Stalinist era, religion and culture continued to reflect both official policies and the spiritual and creative activities of the peoples of the USSR. Up until the Gorbachev years, socialist realism (with its emphasis on portraying Soviet life in a positive and easily comprehensible manner) remained the ruling doctrine for the arts. And the party insisted that religious policy, the arts, and education serve the interests of the country, as determined by the party. One such vital interest was improving the Soviet economy and Soviet socialism, as the country attempted to complete the groundwork for the transition from socialism to communism.

In delivering the Central Committee report to the Twenty-Second Party Congress in 1961, Khrushchev stated: "The party maintains that the purpose of art is to educate people above all by depicting positive examples from life, to educate them in the spirit of communism. . . . We must give Soviet people interesting works which reveal the romance of Communist labor, which spur their initiative and perseverance in achieving their aims."

The Brezhnev regime took a similar approach. A late 1970s Soviet reference book noted that "the supreme goal of Soviet socialist culture is the moulding of the new man, an active builder of communism, a collectivist, an internationalist, a fighter for communist ideals."

Even Gorbachev thought that Soviet culture's main task was to help create a better socialist order. He just defined such an order differently, and it required greater religious and artistic freedom. Just as Khrushchev allowed publication of works such as Solzhenitsyn's *One Day in the Life of Ivan Denisovich* to battle against Stalinism, so Gorbachev hoped that allowing *glasnost* would build religious and artistic support for his *perestroika* policies.

Another continuity was the official insistence that Soviet culture incorporated the best traditions of each of the national cultures of the USSR. Yet, in fact, the Soviet culture recognized by the state overwhelmingly emphasized the Russian as well as Marxist basis of that culture.

Still another continuity was the pride the party-state took in spreading and extending education and "culture" to a growing number of people within the country. Numerous Soviet publications cited ever-escalating statistics regarding levels of education and the number of libraries, museums, theaters, cinemas, and books published. The international renown of such companies as the Bolshoi Ballet was also a source of great pride.

Before the late 1980s, official publications often linked Soviet cultural achievements with "overcoming the considerable backwardness inherited from the old [tsarist] regime." During Gorbachev's final years, however, a growing number of Soviet citizens expressed doubts about the superiority of Soviet culture over pre-1917 culture.

Despite the general continuities under Khrushchev and Brezhnev, there were important variations regarding the government's religious and cultural controls. In 1958, Khrushchev launched a new and vigorous antireligious campaign, which ended up closing almost two-fifths of the country's places of worship within six years. Under Brezhnev, there were no new antireligious crusades, although there was continuing discrimination against believers and the oppression of religious dissidents. The government's arts policy displayed a different pattern: First, it eased cultural controls under Khrushchev, then tightened them again under Brezhnev, though not as tightly as under Stalin. There were also variations within the reigns of each of the post-Stalinist rulers; under Khrushchev, for example, after considerable cultural liberalization, the party in late 1962–early 1963 mounted a major campaign criticizing writers and artists for taking too many artistic liberties.

Under Gorbachev, both religious and cultural freedoms bloomed, at first slowly and then with increasingly rapid speed. By 1991, hundreds of different beliefs, viewpoints, and artistic approaches competed openly with each other.

RELIGIOUS LIFE: FROM REPRESSION TO RESURGENCE

It did not take long for the post-Stalinist leadership to indicate its displeasure with postwar religious developments. In 1954, the party insisted that more ideological struggle was needed against religion, which party leaders feared had become stronger since World War II.

Yet only in 1958 did the party begin a new full-scale antireligious campaign. The Central Committee called for increasing atheistic propaganda and decreasing religious pilgrimages to places still revered by believers. In 1959, the first issue of a new atheist magazine, *Science and Religion*, appeared. It was published by the Znanie (Knowledge) Society, founded twelve years earlier, mainly to replace the defunct League of the Militant Godless. The newer society sponsored an increasing number of atheist lectures. Finally, from 1958 to 1962, new laws appeared making it easier to prosecute almost any religious activity except services in an official place of worship.

Unfortunately for believers, the number of such places decreased sharply under Khrushchev. According to Anderson's figures, from January 1958 to January 1964, almost 7,000 out of a little over 18,500 places of worship were closed. Although almost all denominations suffered such closings, the Orthodox Church lost the largest percentage. It also witnessed the elimination of half of its ten teaching establishments and three-quarters of its sixty-nine convents and monasteries.

The new party-state attacks stemmed primarily from Khrushchev's impatience to hasten the onset of full communism. The draft Party Program he presented to the Twenty-Second Party Congress in 1961 promised that the "material and technical basis for communism" would be built by 1980 and stressed that "the shaping of a scientific world outlook" was of "prime importance" for the transition to communism. To help shape this outlook, the program emphasized overcoming "religious prejudices" by educating people to realize that science left "no room for religious inventions about supernatural forces."

In religious policy, as in other areas, Khrushchev's successors proceeded more cautiously than the man they accused of "harebrained schemes" and excesses. Although some religious denominations, including the Orthodox Church, suffered additional "closings" during the next two decades, by 1986 the overall number of registered places of worship was slightly higher than it had been in 1964. Among those benefiting from this rise were Roman Catholics, Baptists, Lutherans, Mennonites, and Seventh-Day Adventists.

Yet the party-state continued its strict control over religious organizations and punished believers who refused to comply with imposed limitations. Within the party, the Central Committee's Ideological Commission and Ideology Department were heavily involved in antireligious efforts. After Khrushchev's fall, two state agencies were merged to form a Council for Religious Affairs (CRA), whose duties included exercising control over the Russian Orthodox Church's Holy Synod and patriarch and approving hierarchical appointments. Patriarch Pimen, selected in 1971 to succeed Alexei I, proved especially cooperative. For example, following the Afghanistan invasion, he praised "Brezhnev, the beloved peacemaker." The KGB also helped control religion by recruiting agents and collaborators among religious groups.

Although Orthodox religious leaders cooperated with the state, not all of them did so with equal enthusiasm, and some bishops made great efforts to strengthen the Orthodox faith through all legal means available to them. Lower on the ecclesiastical ladder, some priests and believers were critical of the hierarchy for being too subservient. One of the most outspoken was Father Gleb Yakunin, who openly criticized the Orthodox leadership in 1965 and a decade later formed the Christian Committee for the Defense of Believers' Rights. Yakunin was finally arrested in 1979 and spent most of the 1980s in prison camps and Soviet exile.

Like Yakunin, many Baptists proved willing to risk state displeasure and were the chief victims of repressive campaigns such as that of 1966, when close to 200 of them were arrested. The state treated such individuals similarly to Yakunin and other types of dissidents. It also sometimes took children away from fervent religious parents, claiming that the parents were harming the children by infecting them with their religious teachings. Even believers who stayed within the limits of the law suffered various discriminations, for example, in regard to educational or job opportunities.

Yet, despite repression and Khrushchev's earlier hopes of rapidly overcoming "religious prejudices," religious belief, activities, and sympathies appeared stronger by 1980 than they had been two decades earlier. Some observers even spoke of a religious renaissance or revival. Although earlier those who had partaken in Orthodox services had been overwhelmingly old women, now more younger and better-educated people, male and female, were participating.

The disappointments and discontent of the 1970s left many people looking for deeper meaning than that provided by Soviet atheism, science, and secular rituals. Some émigré writers, especially Alexander Solzhenitsyn, called for a return to Russia's Orthodox roots. Within the USSR, interest in the past increased under Brezhnev, and this helped stimulate interest in Orthodoxy, with which Russian history had been so closely intertwined. Concern also rose with preserving parts of the pre-Soviet heritage and the Russian land from further destruction. In the 1970s, more than 10 million people belonged to the All-Russian Society for the Preservation of Historical and Cultural Landmarks. Russian writers of "village prose" contributed their part to greater appreciation of older traditions, and some members of the party elite encouraged fondness for the Russian past, partly to strengthen Russian nationalism. Although many involved in these movements were indifferent or even hostile to Orthodox doctrine, the overall effect of the movements was to create a more positive attitude toward Orthodoxy's historical and cultural contributions.

Among other nationalities, growing nationalist feelings also often had a religious dimension. Lithuanian Catholics received a major injection of hope with the election of the Polish Pope John Paul II in 1978 and the growth of the Catholic-influenced Solidarity movement in Poland. By 1980, an Islamic resurgence, apparent in places such as Iran and Afghanistan, affected Soviet Moslems.

During the Brezhnev years, foreign relations with Middle Eastern and other countries—for example, the United States during the détente years—became more interconnected with domestic religious policies. The desire to create a better impression abroad sometimes led to an easing of Soviet religious repressions. Meanwhile, Pope John Paul II and Protestant and Jewish leaders more actively pursued religious rights for their co-religionists in the USSR.

As in other spheres, the Gorbachev years brought momentous changes to religious life. By 1987–1988, some of them were already on the horizon. Initial steps included the drafting of a new law on freedom of conscience, the release of some religious prisoners, the official recognition of more religious communities, the opening of new places of worship, and Gorbachev's meeting with Orthodox hierarchs (April 1988). At the meeting, he pledged to work cooperatively with church leaders to improve Soviet life.

Gorbachev's desire for *perestroika* was a prime motivation for his more favorable religious policies. He wished to make positive use of the energies, values (such as sobriety), and charitable inclinations of believers to help solve some of the country's economic and social problems. More Soviet religious tolerance also would be a plus in helping improve relations abroad, for example, with Western and Islamic countries.

The fact that 1988 marked the 1,000-year anniversary of the Rus adoption of Christianity was of great significance. This millennium occurred just when many Soviet citizens were beginning to look for values and a sense of national identity to replace those offered by the increasingly discredited Communist party. The anniversary stimulated a rising tide of debates concerning church-state relations and the role of Christianity and the Orthodox Church in Russian history. In June, a week was devoted to celebrating the millennium. As part of the celebrations, an unprecedented event in Soviet history occurred: A church service was held inside the Kremlin. Another ceremony celebrating the millennium took place in Moscow's Bolshoi Theater and was attended by Raisa Gorbachev.

Although the path forward was far from smooth, in October 1990, after extensive public debate, the Supreme Soviet finally passed a new law "On Freedom of Conscience and Religious Organizations." In general, it granted to citizens and religious organizations the same types of rights and status enjoyed in most Western democracies. Among other rights, such organizations could lease or own buildings and other property and start their own schools. The new law generally adhered to the principal of separation of church and state, enunciating it specifically in regard to education and in the prohibition of any state financing of "religious organizations or atheistic propaganda."

By this time, religion was much more popular than communism, but religious conditions themselves were becoming extremely complex. The Soviet republics were passing their own laws, and differences among believers were coming to the surface. In Ukraine, for example, the Greek Catholic Church (whose adherents were also known as Uniates) contested with the Orthodox Church for restoration of properties it had lost when Stalin brought its existence to an end in 1946.

Within the Orthodox Church itself, splits were occurring, primarily because of a challenge from the long-standing Russian Orthodox Church in Exile. It criticized the Moscow Patriarchate for its collaboration with the Soviet government; for its ecumenical sympathies; and because it refused to recognize the last tsar, Nicholas II, as a saint and Christian martyr. By the end of 1991, the Church in Exile had gained the adherence of a small percentage of Orthodox communities and priests, who called themselves the Free Russian Orthodox Church.

Another issue on which many Orthodox differed was church-state relations and politics in general. Some priests, including Yakunin, became members of the Supreme Soviet. And priests and other Orthodox believers were active in a wide range of political parties, including those adhering to Christian Democratic and monarchist programs. Although some Orthodox believers supported extreme right-wing organizations such as *Pamiat*, whose slogan included a call "For Faith, Tsar, and Fatherland," other Orthodox Christians found its extreme views and frequent antisemitism repugnant.

EDUCATION, SCIENCE, AND SCHOLARSHIP

As with religious suppression, so too with education, Khrushchev attempted bolder policies than Brezhnev. From lower-class origins himself and with little formal education, he tried to increase educational opportunities for children of workers and peasants. At the same time, he attempted to make it more difficult for the new Soviet elite to pass on elite status to their children through educational favoritism. Such thinking influenced his policy of ending fees for more advanced secondary schooling and higher education.

But this was only a first step. More radically, he wished students, after eight years of school (one more than had heretofore been compulsory), to end or suspend their full-time schooling and work for a few years. After such work experience, those who qualified could go on to higher education. He coupled this idea with more emphasis on vocational training and his larger scheme of narrowing the gap between school and work. He thought that such a narrowing would produce more skilled workers and boost the economy.

Most ruling-class parents, however, resisted the idea of their youngsters performing factory or farm work. Partly because of such resistance, neither the educational reform of 1958 nor subsequent educational developments went as far as Khrushchev desired. And some of the changes that were put into effect— such as adding an extra secondary school year to fit in sufficient trade training—were later rescinded.

Although the Brezhnev regime took a more cautious and piecemeal approach, it continued Khrushchev's general line: It attempted to strengthen vocational, technical, and specialized education and tailor learning more to the needs of the Soviet workplace and economy. By 1980–1981, for example, close to half of the students completing their secondary schooling (ten years were by then mandatory) were in technical or specialized schools. At the same time, institutes with a similar narrow focus outnumbered universities by more than ten to one among the approximate 800 higher educational establishments. Overall, higher education produced many more engineers than students majoring in the arts or humanities.

Besides stressing state economic needs, Soviet education emphasized Soviet ideals and conformity. In the USSR, a much higher percentage of children ages one to six received preschooling than in the United States. From these early years, Marxist-Leninist and other Soviet values, including collectivism as opposed to individualism, shaped the school day. These values were reinforced by successive youth organizations (Young Octobrists, Young Pioneers, and the Komsomol) that were closely linked to the party and the schools. Most youngsters belonged to them, though less to the Komsomol, usually entered at ages fourteen or fifteen, than in the two groups for younger children.

Because all schooling was under state control and molded to fit state, not individual, preferences, education placed a heavy emphasis on subjects the government thought most important. As compared to U.S. students, Soviet students had to take much more science, mathematics, and foreign languages. They also put in more class and homework time, going to school six days a week.

FIGURE 21.1. As children prepare to return to school after summer vacation in 1978, this Moscow banner tells them: "Pioneers and schoolchildren, get ready to become active fighters for the cause of Lenin and for communism."

Still another difference from U.S. schooling was the extreme Soviet educational uniformity, with similar lessons and texts being used from Leningrad to Vladivostok. Schools, institutes, and universities offered few electives and little opportunity for discussion, instead heavily emphasizing the memorization and comprehension of fundamental materials, taught in uniform curricula. Only the existence of different types of schools and institutes and those offering instruction in different languages of the Soviet Union (with Russian being a required second language) offered much educational variety.

There were also other differences that U.S. university students might note in Soviet higher educational institutions. Class attendance was required, and Soviet institutions offered much less in the way of organized social activities, especially of a nonideological type. Another difference was that Soviet students received free tuition, and most of them attending full-time also received stipends. Graduates, however, had to accept jobs wherever their institutions sent them for their first two years after graduation.

In the early 1980s, the percentage of Soviet people receiving higher education was still smaller than in the United States but had surpassed the British or Canadian percentages. Within the Soviet Union, the Russian republic's percentage was the highest. In the country as a whole, two-fifths of all higher education students in 1980 were pursuing their studies in the evening or by correspondence.

The reforms and developments of the Gorbachev years changed many earlier educational practices, though not the concern with better preparing students for the workplace. (Some of the changes were already called for in 1984 but not implemented until after Gorbachev came to power.) The year of beginning compulsory education was dropped from age seven to six, thus extending it to eleven years instead of the earlier ten. Some new subjects, such as information science and computer technology, were introduced into the secondary schools; the content of other subjects, such as history, changed radically. Teaching and learning methods also were affected: Teachers were encouraged to be less authoritarian and students more inquisitive and creative. Although some teachers and professors resisted the new tendencies, they were fighting a losing battle.

Another notable change was that education became less centralized and more diverse, a process furthered in 1990–1991 by Soviet republics seizing many powers once centered in Moscow. The Russian republic, for example, developed its own program for educational reform. As compared to earlier Soviet programs, it was based more on humanistic principles and student needs and designed to prepare students better for life in a democratic society with a market economy.

Unfortunately for education, however, the governmental and individual economic hardships of 1990–1991, accompanied by other disruptions, severely hurt the educational process. Adequate physical facilities, supplies, and equipment, never abundant, now became even more scarce. The salaries of teachers, professors, and researchers could not keep up with inflation, and some of them left their positions to pursue more lucrative ventures.

These developments also harmed the scientific community not engaged in teaching. In the USSR, much scientific research was done in thousands of research institutes and laboratories. Overall, by the 1970s the USSR possessed the world's largest scientific community, with the Academy of Sciences (including its many branches) being especially significant. Soviet scientists made valuable contributions, primarily in areas emphasized by national security policies such as physics, mathematics, and space sciences.

Under Khrushchev, Soviet genetics continued to suffer the destructive effects of Lysenko's theories (see Chapter 16). Although he temporarily lost influence under Khrushchev, he regained it by siding with him in disputes with more reputable scientists and agricultural experts. Only after Khrushchev's fall was Lysenko discredited.

Under Khrushchev and Brezhnev, scientists such as the geneticist Zhores Medvedev and physicist Andrei Sakharov became more outspoken, criticizing Lysenko, extensive nuclear testing, and other dangerous environmental practices. Such scientists eventually made up a significant proportion of Soviet dissidents.

As compared to Western scientists, Soviet scientists had to deal with more government bureaucracy, less opportunities to exchange information with foreign scientists, and a woeful lack of computers. Although the Gorbachev administration attempted to correct these deficiencies, the crises of 1990–1991 bequeathed numerous economic and other problems to the scientists of Russia and the other successor states.

The situation of post-Stalin social scientists resembled that of other educators and scientific researchers. Yet, more so than most natural sciences, the social sciences remained dominated by Marxist-Leninist thinking. Gradually, however, the Khrushchev and Brezhnev governments allowed some leeway to social scientists. The state increasingly relied on them more for more accurate information, obtained by such means as public opinion polls and research done in places such as the Institute of World Economics and International Relations and the Institute for Study of the USA and Canada.

Until Gorbachev's rule, however, the Marxist-Leninist overview continued to reign supreme. In history, for example, some excellent works dealing with the pre-Soviet past appeared, but their main contribution was in the empirical material they provided. The only overall viewpoint or interpretive framework allowed by the party-state was the Marxist-Leninist one.

Soviet historians were especially hampered from making any objective study of the Soviet period. As late as 1988, Yuri Afanasiev (a leading historian, rector of the Moscow State Historical Archive Institute, and political activist) charged that history textbooks dealing with the Soviet period were still full of lies. Mainly because of such falsifications, the government canceled all final history examinations for primary and secondary school students at the end of the 1987–1988 school year.

By 1988, however, there were numerous signs of positive changes. Two leading historical journals were taken over by reform-minded editors, and the Institute of the History of the USSR elected a similar-type director. In the final three Soviet years, many historians, along with the public in general, became increasingly critical first of Lenin and then of the whole Soviet experience. Soviet archival information became more available, further fueling anti-Soviet sentiments. Although these new developments did not guarantee historical objectivity—some historians went too far in praising the old tsarist order—they were favorable to freeing historians from party dominance and promoting the competition of opposing historical viewpoints.

LITERATURE: FROM THE THAW TO GLASNOST

In December 1953, an article entitled "On Sincerity in Literature" appeared in the Soviet journal *Novy Mir*. It criticized the falsity of postwar literature—a literature dominated by a socialist realism that was anything but realistic. In 1954, the first part of Ilia Ehrenburg's novel *The Thaw* appeared. Although lacking great literary merit, its depiction of characters struggling to free themselves from the frozen rigidities of Stalin's times had a strong public impact. The term "The Thaw" was soon applied to the whole cultural unfreezing that followed Stalin's death. Another influential work of this early post-Stalinist period was Vladimir Dudintsev's *Not by Bread Alone*. Serialized in *Novy Mir* in 1956, it was unconventional in its sympathy for a lonely inventor struggling against Soviet bureaucracy.

Frightened by the Hungarian revolt of late 1956, the government retightened cultural controls before loosening them again later in the decade. Such fluctuations were especially common under Khrushchev and reflected both internal party struggles over cultural policy and Khrushchev's own uncertainties regarding it—in his memoirs, published after his removal from power, he regretted not allowing more artistic freedom.

Pasternak and Solzhenitsyn

The period from 1958 to 1964 witnessed not only the persecution of Boris Pasternak for allowing *Doctor Zhivago* to be published abroad (1957), but also the later publication of such unconventional works as Solzhenitsyn's *One Day in the Life of Ivan Denisovich*. *Doctor Zhivago* was a worthy successor to the great nineteenth-century novels of Tolstoy and Dostoevsky. Dealing mainly with the revolutionary and Civil War years, it not only captured some of the era's complexities, but also dealt with artistic and philosophic-religious questions. As we have earlier seen, Pasternak was primarily a poet, and he included two dozen poems at the end of his novel, which add to its beauty and symbolism. For almost three decades after Pasternak's death in 1960, the novel remained unpublished in the USSR.

Solzhenitsyn's *One Day in the Life of Ivan Denisovich* was a much shorter novel, but also one of the best of the Soviet period. It depicted a day in the life of a labor-camp prisoner under Stalin. It first appeared in 1962 in *Novy Mir*, whose editor, the poet Alexander Tvardovsky, published some of the best literature of the period. The novel marked Solzhenitsyn's literary debut.

Born in 1918, Solzhenitsyn served as an officer in World War II, before being arrested in 1945 for an unflattering reference to Stalin in a letter. He then spent the next decade in prison, camps, and exile before being rehabilitated and settling down to teach mathematics in a Riazan secondary school. In 1963, *Novy Mir* printed three of his short stories and in 1966 a fourth. But the latter date was the year of the Siniavsky-Daniel trial, and by then Solzhenitsyn was having increasing difficulties with the authorities, who would not allow his new novel, *The First Circle*, to appear. During the late 1960s, he was also frustrated in his attempt to have still another novel, *Cancer Ward*, published in the USSR. Unauthorized by him, however, the two novels were soon printed abroad. After Solzhenitsyn battled with the Union of Soviet Writers for several years, accusing it of serving the government more than the writers it supposedly represented, the union expelled him in 1969.

The following year, the Swedish Royal Academy honored him (as it had Pasternak earlier) with the Nobel Prize for literature, noting his "ethical force." In 1971, he allowed his new novel, *August 1914*, to be published in Paris, and two years later he permitted the publication there of the first volume of his *The Gulag Archipelago*. In 1973, he also sent a *Letter to the Soviet Leaders* (eighty-one pages long in its English-language edition). It clearly indicated that Solzhenitsyn was willing to speak out on a whole range of issues from Sino-Soviet relations to Soviet family life.

Accused of treason and deported from the USSR in 1974, Solzhenitsyn remained abroad, primarily in the United States, until returning to Russia in 1994. During his years abroad, he published two more volumes of *The Gulag*

Archipelago. He thereby completed his massive and detailed account of the Soviet punishment system from 1918 to 1956, much of it based on what he and other *Gulag* sufferers had experienced and heard during their years in the prisons, camps, and exile. He also occasionally commented on current conditions in the USSR as well as in the West. In 1990, by which time his forbidden works had begun to be published in the USSR, a new essay of his was printed in the Soviet press, entitled "How Shall We Organize Russia."

The major project of his two decades of exile was an enormous multivolume work of fiction called *The Red Wheel*, dealing with the years 1914–1917. Its first volume (of over 800 pages) was a reworked and expanded *August 1914*, and it also included a revised portion of *Lenin in Zurich* (1975).

In a 1989 interview, Solzhenitsyn was asked about frequent comparisons between him and Tolstoy and Dostoevsky. He responded that he resembled Tolstoy more in his narrative technique and in his variety of characters and situations but Dostoevsky more in his spiritual interpretation of history. Solzhenitsyn's life and experiences, marked by imprisonment, spiritual rebirth, and the adoption of a Russian Orthodox neo-Slavophile outlook, were also more similar to those of Dostoevsky. But Solzhenitsyn resembled Tolstoy more, especially the Tolstoy of *War and Peace*, in his contempt for many historians and his attempt to capture history better than they (especially in *The Red Wheel* and in the nonfictional *The Gulag Archipelago*). Like both of his illustrious predecessors, Solzhenitsyn combined the roles of writer and moral prophet, thought the West was morally declining, and wanted Russia to mold a non-Western type of future based on spiritual values.

Poets and Satirists

Before Solzhenitsyn's literary debut in 1962, a number of younger writers had come to the forefront of Soviet literary life. Several of them were poets, including Evgeni Evtushenko and Andrei Voznesensky, both born in 1933. Both men gave poetry readings in the USSR attended by large audiences (over 10,000 people on some occasions), and both of them became well-known abroad—they both visited the United States for the first time in 1961. That same year, Evtushenko's poem "Babi Yar" appeared, criticizing Soviet antisemitism and noting that no monuments appeared at Babi Yar, a ravine on the outskirts of Kiev, where Nazi forces killed perhaps 100,000 Soviet citizens in 1941, about nine-tenths of them Jewish. In 1962, Evtushenko's "Stalin's Heirs" warned against any resurgence of Stalinism.

The content of Voznesensky's poetry tended to be less controversial and contentious than Evtushenko's, often dealing with personal or broad issues such as the role of the artist or science and technology in the modern world. It was more his concern with poetic style and his stylistic experimentation that led to sporadic criticism of him for being a "bourgeois formalist," a criticism applied to writers the authorities thought were more concerned with form than socialist content.

Less well-known abroad but a celebrity in the USSR was Bella Akhmadulina (born in 1937), whose first volume of poetry appeared in 1962. Already famous because she had been the subject of love poems written by Evtushenko (her first husband), her poetry was marked by its strong lyric quality.

A more influential young prose writer was Vassily Aksyonov (born in 1932). During most of his childhood and youth, he had been separated from his parents, who fell victims to Stalin—his mother, Evgeniia Ginzburg, later related her *Gulag* experiences in two moving volumes published abroad (*Journey into the Whirlwind* and *Within the Whirlwind*). Aksyonov's short novel *Ticket to the Stars* was published in the journal *Yunost* (Youth) in 1961 and became perhaps the best-known example of "youth prose." The novel dealt with a group of teenagers more interested in sports, jazz, and the opposite sex than lofty party goals and slogans. Their language was full of slang and Western borrowings. Like Evtushenko and Voznesensky, Aksyonov and his iconoclastic characters and style were often criticized by more conservative writers and authorities.

The same age as Aksyonov, Vladimir Voinovich was another writer of a 1961 story, "We Live Here," which fit in the "youth-prose" category but with a collective-farm setting. Like much of Aksyonov's prose, it was marked by its inventiveness, irony, and satire.

After their independent ways led to sporadic problems with Soviet authorities—for example, in 1979, Aksyonov had been one of the editors of an uncensored literary collection (*Metropol*) that was denied Soviet publication—both Aksyonov and Voinovich were forced to emigrate in 1980. Their prose, written both before and after their forced emigration, has heightened their reputations as two of Russian literature's most gifted satirists. Aksyonov's novels published abroad in the 1980s and dealing with Soviet life include *The Burn*, *The Island of Crimea*, and *Say Cheese!*; among Voinovich's works are *The Life and Extraordinary Adventures of Private Ivan Chonkin*, *The Ivankiad*, *Pretender to the Throne: The Further Adventures of Private Ivan Chonkin*, *The Anti-Soviet Soviet Union*, and *Moscow 2024*.

By 1980, many of Russia's finest writers had been forced out of the country. In 1987, the poet Joseph Brodsky (1940–1996), by then an émigré for a decade and a half, followed in the footsteps of Pasternak and Solzhenitsyn by being awarded a Nobel Prize for literature. Ironically, in 1991, while many critics considered him the best poet writing in Russian and Russian audiences were becoming more familiar with his poetry (often of a complex, philosophic nature), he was named U.S. poet laureate.

Writers of Village Prose

Within the USSR, the most notable and long-lasting movement was that of "village prose," which flourished in the 1960s and 1970s. Writers who produced such works included Fedor Abramov, Viktor Astafiev, Vasili Belov, Valentin Rasputin, Vasili Shukshin, Vladimir Soloukhin, and Sergei Zalygin. Solzhenitsyn's 1963 story "Matryona's Home" was also an important village-prose piece, although Solzhenitsyn is not generally listed as a "village writer."

Village prose was characterized by its sympathy with village life and people. The village writers tended to be suspicious of modern "progress" and

FIGURE 21.2. Tourists and cows in the Lake Baikal fishing village of Listvianka, 1993. A long-term concern of the writer V. Rasputin has been preserving Siberia's Lake Baikal region.

technology and concerned with the preservation of village values, nature, and Russian tradition. One of the best of such works was the Siberian Rasputin's *Farewell to Matyora* (1976), which dealt with the government-mandated destruction of an island village in the Angara River (for reasons of "progress").

Village writers considered themselves Russian patriots and were not dissidents, but their rural sympathies were hardly in the spirit of Marx, who had criticized the "idiocy of rural life." Furthermore, their emphasis on the Russian (not Soviet) people troubled some critics and authorities who stressed the USSR's mutinational makeup. Yet, despite these concerns, the village writers continued to be published.

Although village writers were unhappy with the destruction of village life and their prose was often filled with nostalgia, it was generally subdued, more suggestive than didactic. It called to mind more the bleak realism of the late Chekhov than the socialist and future-oriented optimism of novels such as *Cement* and Kataev's 1932 novel, *Time Forward*. Village writers concerned themselves with human bonds and roots and with the rhythms and cycles of nature, and they attempted to capture the language of the village people they described.

During the Gorbachev years, the village writers became more politically active and village prose fragmented. In 1989, Belov, Rasputin, and Zalygin be-

Village Prose: An Excerpt from Vasili Belov's That's How It Is

The following selection comes at the end of Belov's 1966 novella *That's How It Is*, as translated by Eve Manning in *Soviet Literature* no. 1 (1969): 131. The novel begins with a drunken Ivan Afrikanovich talking to his horse and ends with this same poor peasant trying to reconcile himself to the death of his wife, who had died six weeks earlier. After a lakeside reflection on nature's cycles finally brings him some peace of mind, he goes to visit his wife's grave. Ellipses are in the original translation.

Ivan Afrikanovich sat on his wife's grave and looked at the river and the clearly-etched golden birches beyond. He mused and smoked.

Rubbish, not cigarettes. Smoke more matches. One pull and it's out again. Well, Katya, don't hold it against me. I've not been before, not visited ye, first one thing, then another. But I've brought ye some rowan berries. Ye used to like plucking them, autumn. And how am I going on without you? Well, just going on, looks like I'm beginning to get used to it. I don't drink now, Katerina, getting old maybe, and sort of lost the wish. You used to scold me. . . . The children are all well. We've sent Katyushka to Tanya and Mitka, and Anatoshka's at the building trade school, he'll soon be on his feet. And Mishka and Vaska—well, I took them to a children's home, now don't be angry wi' me. It was more than your mother could manage, with

them all. She got right thin and kept saying her arms hurt her, and you know yourself, Katya, she's getting along in years. And they're rascals, anyway, those twins of ours. They stopped there as if they'd been there all their lives. Never a tear. I've dug the potatoes. And we'll get a new cow, Mishka Petrov's got a calf, I'll buy it of him. Aye. Well, wife, so you can see how it's all turned out. I was a fool, I took bad care of you, you know yourself. And now I'm alone. It's like treading on fire when I tread the earth over you, forgive me. It's bad without you, Katya. So bad I thought to follow you. But then I came to myself. I mind your voice, Katya. And all of you, I mind you so clear that. . . . Aye. So don't ye worry about the children. They'll get on their feet. And the youngest, Vanyushka, he can say a word or two already. He's a real clever boy and eyes like yours. I've already—aye. Well, so I'll come and visit you here, and you wait for me sometimes. Katya. . . . Katya, where are you? My own, my darling, I'm—I'm—well, what's to be done . . . here, I've brought you some rowan berries . . . Katya, my darling. . . .*

Ivan Afrikanovich shook from head to foot. But nobody saw how grief stretched him out on the bare, cold earth, nobody saw.

A noisy flock of starlings flew over the church. There was the acrid, ancient scent of fires. The sky was blue. And somewhere beyond the brightly coloured forest the first breath of winter stole towards the village.

came delegates to the Congress of People's Deputies; whereas the first two spoke from a conservative nationalist viewpoint, Zalygin (who had become editor of *Novy Mir*) adopted a more liberal stance.

In 1985–1986, Belov, Rasputin, and Viktor Astafiev each published a work depicting moral decay in an urban environment (Belov's *Everything Lies Ahead* and Astafiev's *A Sad Detective*) or new settlement (Rasputin's "The Fire"). Belov's novel was the most scathing, having as its chief villain a Jew. It was a bitter attack on Western influences; Moscow intellectuals; and an urban existence full of crime, decadent sex, rock music, alcoholism, and drugs.

Rasputin and Astafiev shared Belov's fears for what lay ahead for Russia. Like Solzhenitsyn and the nineteenth-century Slavophiles and conservative nationalists, all three men wanted Russia to get back to its roots and avoid too much Western influence. Their fears and passions led them, especially Belov and Rasputin, to sometimes side with extreme right-wing elements such as *Pamiat*, although they did not support all of that organization's positions.

Aitmatov, Iskander, Trifonov, and Tendriakov

The writer Chingiz Aitmatov shared some of the concerns of the village writers except that the objects of his sympathies were the native people and traditions of Central Asia. Although a Kirgiz who set most of his works in Central Asia, he wrote primarily in Russian. His novel *The Day Lasts More than A Hundred Years* (1980) was immensely popular—among Aitmatov's many admirers was Gorbachev, who listed him as his favorite writer. Aitmatov's 1986 novel *The Execution Block* (translated into English as *The Place of the Skull*) reflected some of the same moral concerns regarding drugs, the environment, and other issues as expressed by writers such as Belov and Rasputin in the mid and late 1980s. Like them, Aitmatov also became more active politically, though generally supporting the Gorbachev government, which appointed him ambassador to Luxembourg in late 1990.

Like Aitmatov, Fazil Iskander was a non-Russian who wrote in Russian and contributed significantly to late Soviet literature. His works were generally set in his native Abkhazia, located in the northwestern part of the Georgian republic. Primarily a prose writer, his *Sandro of Chegem* (containing a series of interrelated stories with frequent new additions) best displays his wide-ranging gift of humor. His comic touch was humane but biting enough to upset Soviet censors, who until the late 1980s allowed only portions of *Sandro* to be published within the USSR.

The urban Russian settings of the works of Yuri Trifonov (1925–1981) set him apart from the village writers, Aitmatov, or Iskander. His moral earnestness and honesty in portraying his characters (many of them officials or professionals) won him a large following. He shared the late Soviet interest in history, and in such works as *The House on the Embankment* (1976), he dealt with earlier Soviet times. His novel *Impatience* (1973) went further back, dealing with the revolutionary People's Will of the nineteenth century.

Vladimir Tendriakov (1923–1984) was another major Russian writer interested in both moral questions and history. Some of his prose fit into the village-prose category, but other novels and stories had urban settings. Although a prolific writer for decades, several of his works were published only after his death. His novel *Attack on Mirages*, published in 1987, dealt extensively with historical causation.

Popular Fiction, Guitar Poetry, and the Glasnost Era

Historical fiction was popular during the 1970s and 1980s, especially that of Valentin Pikul, who specialized in this genre and appealed to Russian nationalist sentiments. The village-prose writer Zalygin also wrote novels dealing with the early Soviet period, and the poet\singer Bulat Okudzhava wrote four novels set in the nineteenth century.

Okudzhava (of Georgian\Armenian background) was one of the originators of guitar poetry, singing his own lyrics, beginning in the mid to late 1950s. Although collections of some of his poems and songs were published—for example, in *Arbat, My Arbat* (1976)—many of his songs circulated on *magnitizdat* (underground tape recordings).

As popular as Okudzhava was, his popularity was overshadowed in the 1970s by that of another guitar poet, Vladimir Vysotsky (1938–1980), whose poem-songs circulated in *magnitizdat*. He also acted in films and on the stage of the best Soviet theater of his time, the Taganka. In a 1970 questionnaire, Vysotsky listed Marlon Brando as his ideal man. Although he played Hamlet on stage, in his movies he often portrayed "tough guys"; in one of his poems, he wrote that he feared neither words nor bullets.

Many people loved Vysotsky's harsh-voiced songs. They thought of him as a hard-drinking, hard-living man, who experienced many of the same joys and sorrows as they did. Yuri Trifonov wrote of his "daredevil spirit" and of his "quintessential Russian mentality." The writer Tatiana Tolstaia in a 1994 interview explained Boris Yeltsin's initial appeal to the Russian people by saying that Russians love those who have been victims. Such sympathy for the victimized helps account for Vysotsky's appeal, for he sympathized with them while satirizing the complacent and privileged. Although his poetry and songs were primarily an underground phenomenon before his death, in 1988 (on the occasion of the fiftieth anniversary of his birth) there was a tremendous media outpouring devoted to Vysotsky.

By this time, the media was paying more attention to people's desires. Although historical fiction, science fiction, and detective and spy fiction had long been popular and available, censorship had still prevented publication of many works. What characterized the *glasnost* era was the availability of so many previously forbidden books—fiction and nonfiction, religious and pornographic, by Soviet authors and those living abroad, whether émigré or foreign. Controversial plays, such as those of Mikhail Shatrov criticizing Stalin but favorable to Lenin, were also produced and published. Despite all these works, there was some lamentation in the press that the Soviet people (known for their fondness for reading) were now reading less. Others complained that people were reading more "junk."

In the late 1980s, while many writers were becoming more didactic in their writings, others rejected such a function for literature. They placed aesthetic considerations ahead of ideological or educative ones. One critic labeled their writing "alternative prose." The stories of Tatiana Tolstaia (born 1951), which began appearing in 1983, are one example of such literature. She stated that "real writers transcend politics," and her short stories have a poetic quality and deal with a wide range of ordinary people.

Liudmila Petrushevskaia (born 1939) also wrote "alternative prose," usually dealing with ordinary people, especially women. Like Tolstaia's style, hers was more complex and less straightforward than that dictated by socialist realism. More than Tolstaia, however, she concentrated on the dark side of life, its brutality and suffering; her stories are full of catastrophic occurrences, including murder. This type of concentration delayed the publication of many of her stories as well as some of the "tough" and "cruel" fiction of other writers until the Gorbachev years. Before then, she was known more for her plays and screenwriting—her scenario for *Fairy Tale of Fairy Tales* (1979) won her several international awards.

During Gorbachev's final years in power, Petrushevskaia wrote several fantasy stories, including "A Modern Family Robinson" and "A New Gulliver." The first was subtitled "An End-of-the-Twentieth-Century Chronicle," and the second featured a sick man fantasizing about miniature people constructing a civilization. They somehow seemed appropriate for this transitional period of Russian history.

ART AND ARCHITECTURE

In art, as in literature, a "thaw" occurred under Khrushchev, allowing more exposure to both modern Western art and that of the earlier Soviet avant-garde. Although socialist realism continued dominant in state-approved art, artists were able to broaden the parameters of what the doctrine allowed. Some artists rejected it altogether and went their own way.

In December 1962, Khrushchev let such independent artists know what he thought of their work. This occurred at an exhibition of "Thirty Years of Moscow Art" at the Manezh gallery near the Kremlin. In addition to the dominant officially approved art, there was another small collection suddenly put on display in a separate area just before Khrushchev's visit. It contained nonrepresentational painting and sculpture. Officials (including some from the Artists' Union) opposed to such art arranged for Khrushchev to see it, hoping he would condemn it. They were not disappointed.

The earthy Khrushchev compared one painting to "dog shit." He asked if the artists painting such pictures were pederasts or normal people. And he insisted that such art was incomprehensible (he admitted he did not understand Picasso either), anti-Soviet, and amoral and that it failed to arouse people to "great deeds," as he believed art should.

One of the artists present to hear Khrushchev's words of abuse was the sculptor Ernst Neizvestny. Ironically, it was the talented Neizvestny whom Khrushchev's son, Sergei, sought out, after his father's death in 1971, to create a memorial to his father. In a long chapter in his book on his father, Sergei recounts the whole lengthy process Neizvestny and himself had to go through before Neizvestny's memorial finally appeared in 1975 at Khrushchev's grave in the Novodevichii Cemetery (see Figure 17.3). The white and black of the tombstone, which Neizvestny intended to symbolize the conflict between good versus evil, the progressive versus the reactionary, aroused the most opposition. Bureaucrats were not sure what to make of the contrast, and Sergei had to assure one of them that the black did not represent Brezhnev.

After it appeared, the memorial continued to arouse controversy. Why did the bronze head appear cut off? What did the white and black symbolize? Why did the sculptor keep his name secret? (He did not, but his name, meaning "unknown" in Russian, confused some who had not heard of him.) To the authorities, who wanted Khrushchev's spirit as well as his body permanently buried, the memorial opened up unwanted controversies. Before long, Neizvestny was forced to emigrate, and most of the cemetery, including the Khrushchev site, was closed to the public. Only a decade later, under Gorbachev, was it reopened.

In 1974, police forces bulldozed, burned, and firehosed an open-air exhibit by Moscow artists who dared to exhibit their works without permission. This was just another indication of the fate of artists attempting to work outside the confines dictated by the Brezhnev regime and the Artists' Union.

The government allowed some latitude, however, to representational art appealing to Russian nationalist sentiments, even though it fell outside the boundaries of socialist realism. The best example was that of Ilia Glazunov, whose 1978 exhibition in Moscow displayed Russian historical figures and old churches and villages, although one of his paintings that included Tsar Nicholas II was not displayed. Glazunov's pictures appealed to the same thirst for pre-Soviet history and depictions of traditional Russia that attracted readers to village prose and Pikul's historical fiction.

Under Gorbachev, a joint party-government resolution of 1986 attempted to fortify the cause of socialist realism and called for the visual arts to help advance the "Communist education of the workers." By then, however, socialist realism was already fighting a losing battle. That same year, Glazunov was able to display more fully his nationalist and pre-Soviet sentiments in an exhibit that attracted millions of viewers in Moscow and Leningrad. By 1991, the Soviet art scene was characterized by artistic pluralism, with hundreds of different tendencies, representational and nonrepresentational, competing with each other.

In architecture, Khrushchev's approach was less traditionalist than in painting and sculpture. Like many Western architectural modernists, he advocated functionalism—a building's function should determine its form. It was primarily because he believed it was not "functional" that Khrushchev in his memoirs criticized the new main building of Moscow State University, which was constructed under Stalin (see Chapter 16). Khrushchev thought that from a distance it looked more like a church and that for the same amount of money three times as many students could have been accommodated in a more functional building.

Khrushchev's successors continued to emphasize the functionalist approach, and because the party-state dominated architecture even more than other arts (there being little private building), functionalism continued to reign supreme. A good example were the nine tall buildings constructed from 1964 to 1969 on the new Kalinin Prospect. Five of them were apartment buildings with shops on the bottom floors, and across the street were four commercial buildings of about the same height. Under the direction of the dominant Moscow architect, Mikhail Posokhin, they reflected a Soviet adaptation of the International Style.

Kalinin Prospect and its modernist buildings contrasted sharply with nearby older buildings. The road was carved out of the Arbat district, one of Moscow's most picturesque historic districts. The Palace of Congresses (1959–1961), which was built inside the Kremlin walls, and the Hotel Rossiia (1964–1969), constructed in an old district near the Kremlin, were two further examples of such contrasts. Fears of further "violations" of Moscow's historical character helped energize Moscow's historic preservation movement.

Besides reflecting the functionalist approach, the Hotel Rossiia (with 3,200

FIGURE 21.3. The first of five apartment buildings on Kalinin Prospect rises up next to the seventeenth-century Church of Simon Stylites.

rooms) and the Palace of Congresses (with 800 rooms and halls and an auditorium seating 6,000 people) testified to a continuing party-state fondness for large structures. Under Gorbachev, however, the collapse first of the command economy and then of the Soviet party-state structure began a transition toward more privately commissioned and smaller-scaled architecture.

MUSIC: FROM CLASSICAL TO ROCK

In music, Aram Khachaturian and Dmitri Shostakovich once again became prominent composers and remained so until their respective deaths in 1978 and 1975. An Armenian born in Georgia, Khachaturian's music was lively and often reflected Armenian and Georgian folk influences. His "Saber Dance," from an otherwise forgettable 1942 ballet about a collective-farm heroine, was internationally popular. In 1953, he wrote an article calling for an end to bureaucratic interference in musical composition. His own works during the next quarter-century included his much-performed ballet *Spartacus*, choreographed in several different versions after its first appearance in 1956.

Shostakovich, however, was the more significant of the two composers. As earlier, his compositions and actions sometimes pleased authorities and sometimes not. His Eleventh Symphony (1957), subtitled *The Year 1905*, and his Twelfth Symphony (1961), subtitled *The Year 1917*, were in the first category, but his Thirteenth Symphony (1962), coming shortly after Khrushchev's criticism of modern art at the Manezh gallery, was banned after two performances.

What occasioned the ban was Shostakovich's collaboration with the poet Evtushenko and the use of "Babi Yar" and several other Evtushenko poems in the symphony. In the reactionary phase following the gallery incident, Soviet authorities were in no mood to allow public performances and publicity to a symphony featuring "Babi Yar." Khrushchev publicly denied that antisemitism still existed in the USSR.

When Soviet authorities could not rely on a composition's words to determine its appropriateness, they found it more difficult to decide what was appropriate. At times, composers such as Shostakovich were able to disguise their intentions.

The musical taste of Khrushchev and most other Soviet leaders was similar to their taste in art. Khrushchev liked revolutionary, patriotic, and classical music as well as traditional folk songs, and he disliked any modern music that he considered discordant. Nevertheless, in the 1960s and 1970s, Soviet music gradually began reflecting more modern influences. A visit by the native-born Stravinsky to the USSR in 1962 furthered this process, as did increased Western cultural contacts.

The music of younger composers such as S. Slonimsky, R. Shchedrin, and A. Shnitke, all born in the early 1930s, indicated a wide familiarity with both modern and traditional Western compositions as well as with their own native musical heritage. Although Khrushchev had earlier criticized most jazz—he compared it to radio static and "gas on the stomach"—in the 1970s some of Slonimsky's compositions incorporated jazz elements.

By the 1970s, however, Soviet authorities were much more frightened of rock music than of jazz, which was now permitted wide latitude. Among youth, rock had steadily grown in popularity. Beginning in the mid-1950s, this growth was aided by the Voice of America, which beamed rock as well as jazz and other music into the USSR. The music of Bill Haley, the Beatles, Chubby Checker, and the Rolling Stones became known to Soviet youth. As rock's popularity grew and illegal rock tapes circulated, officials responded in various ways: criticism; promoting new Soviet dances; and finally allowing a mild, censored form of rock to appear.

During the early 1980s, the number of rock groups, official and unofficial, numbered in the hundreds of thousands, but in that period the state record company, Melodiia, released fewer than a dozen rock albums. Most rock performers, such as Boris Grebenshchikov of Aquarium, were known by their live performances and, more so, by the vast numbers of underground tapes in circulation. After a performance at the Tbilisi Music Festival in 1980, where he lay down to play his guitar, Grebenshchikov was kicked out of the Komsomol. Finally, in 1987, Melodiia released an album by him.

A rock star who received better treatment under Brezhnev was Stas Namin, who was allowed to record and become a member of the Union of Composers. The fact that he was the grandson of former Politburo member Anastas Mikoian undoubtedly helped. Some groups such as the popular Time Machine went from underground status to being officially recognized and allowed media appearances and the opportunity to perform abroad.

Although rock (both Soviet and foreign) became the most popular music among youth by the time of Brezhnev's death in 1982, other types of music continued to appeal to a Soviet public long appreciative of music. Classical and folk music, songs by guitar poets, jazz, blues, and popular music by such singers as Alla Pugacheva all had their fans. Nostalgic and sentimental songs and those about World War II continued to appeal to many older people.

Following the decline of détente and Brezhnev's death in 1982, there was a brief crackdown on rock. Later in the decade, however, the Gorbachev government removed most restraints on it. Soviet rock fans, especially in Moscow and Leningrad, were now able to view Western groups, such as Britain's UB-40, which came to the USSR in 1986. By the end of the 1980s, the party youth newspaper, *Komsomolskaia Pravda*, was reporting on Pink Floyd and the Talking Heads, and Soviet youth could legally buy records of such groups as Led Zeppelin. Although this accessibility pleased many youth, the right-wing *Pamiat* denounced rock groups as satanistic, and some of the conservative writers were also upset at rock's growing visibility.

ADDITIONAL ASPECTS OF POPULAR CULTURE

During the post-Stalinist era, most people's free time increased. As before, however, most of it was spent inside apartments or houses or outside walking, talking, or playing games with friends. Going out for entertainment such as films or participating in organized leisure activities took up much less time.

Men had more leisure than women, especially married women, who generally did much more of the housework and tedious shopping.

Under Khrushchev and Brezhnev, more films appeared, and their range broadened considerably. Up until the 1960s, some of the best films still dealt with World War II. But such movies as *The Cranes Are Flying* (1957) and *Ballad of A Soldier* (1959) also concerned themselves with the war's homefront and personal concerns such as love and adultery.

In the quarter-century from 1960 to 1985, the most popular films were Soviet and foreign melodramas, but comedies, science fiction, romances, musicals, and other types of films also attracted viewers. Although the state continued to control film production tightly and it was not difficult to tell the "good guys" from the "bad guys" in KGB versus CIA melodramas, films were less propagandistic than under Stalin. More foreign films were also shown, though not sexually explicit ones, which were often thought to reflect Western "decadence."

The Soviet Union's most internationally acclaimed director in this era was Andrei Tarkovsky (1932–1986), who directed the compelling *Andrei Rublev* (1965) and the science-fiction film *Solaris* (1973). But he had trouble with Soviet authorities, and none of his films were as popular in the USSR as some of the era's more commercial, less artistic, films. In the 1980s, he permanently left the USSR and made his final film, *The Sacrifice* (1986), abroad.

The most popular film of the Brezhnev era was *Moscow Does Not Believe in Tears* (1980), which received a U.S. Academy Award as best foreign film in 1981. It depicts a woman who, after overcoming many hardships, becomes a factory director, obtains a nice apartment and automobile, and finally finds a good man. On his first visit to her apartment, he tells her to rest while he puts on an apron and prepares the evening meal—hardly a realistic Soviet occurrence. Lest Soviet men think he is not man enough, he and a friend successfully defend her daughter's boyfriend against five young toughs.

During the Gorbachev years, numerous films that had earlier been banned were released; and in 1986, reform-minded filmmakers took over the Union of Cinematographers. Among the earlier-made films that appeared in 1985–1986 was *Agony* (available abroad under the title *Rasputin*), which had been considered too sympathetic to Tsar Nicholas II. Two others were *My Friend Ivan Lapshin* and the Georgian film *Repentance*, both of which were stylistically innovative and dealt with Stalinism in their own unique and critical ways.

New films that appeared included *Little Vera* (1988), an unflattering depiction of Soviet alienated and sexually active youth, urban ugliness, crowded housing, alcoholism, and stressful family relations. Other films, including documentaries, dealt realistically with aspects of Soviet life that had earlier been ignored or downplayed, such as Soviet prostitution, homosexuality, and organized crime and corruption. The war in Afghanistan was now also depicted honestly for the first time.

Developments in television were interconnected and parallel to those in literature, art, music, and film. Some works of popular fiction later found their way to the television screen. A good example in 1984 was the novel *Tass Is Au-*

thorized to Announce (1979) by Julian Semenov, one of the USSR's most popular writers of crime and spy thrillers. Musical groups and stars, such as Alla Pugacheva, appeared frequently on TV, and the film *My Friend Ivan Lapshin* first appeared on national television.

During the 1970s, TV sets made their way into the overwhelming majority of Soviet homes. Attendance at movie houses and sporting events declined; leisure became more privatized, and an increasing amount of indoor free time was devoted to TV watching. (One of the characters in *Moscow Does Not Believe in Tears* complains that "people have forgotten how to communicate; they sit in their apartments watching television and don't even know their neighbors.")

As compared to U.S. television, there were no commercials or sitcoms, and production techniques were less developed. Before the Gorbachev years, besides musical programs, Soviet TV (all state-owned) consisted of news, sports, films, documentaries, and a variety of other entertainment from circuses and puppet shows to the comic routines of the USSR's most popular comedian Arkadi Raikin.

Raikin and other comedians, whether appearing on stage or on television, were allowed to satirize a limited range of subjects, as was the humor magazine *Krokodil*. Poor-quality consumer goods, crowded apartments, bureaucracy, and drunkenness were among their targets. Under Gorbachev, the permissible range of satire expanded much further, both in live performances in new clubs and theaters and on TV.

During the same final Soviet years, hard-hitting investigative television journalism became popular with such programs as Leningrad's nightly *600 Seconds*. Another investigative program was Leningrad's *Fifth Wheel*, which also featured new historical information. Call-in shows, such as the three-hour *Public Opinion*, began appearing, as did commercials for products like Pepsi-Cola.

Although sports were among the most popular television programs, especially among men, such programs were not as readily available as in Western Europe or the United States. An exception was made for the Olympics, which received extensive coverage.

Emphasizing Olympic success to demonstrate Soviet superiority remained a chief characteristic of Soviet sports. Although the Soviet athletes were the world's most successful in Olympic competition, this one-sided emphasis led to many abuses. Among them were the use of steroids and payments to athletes—until the last few years of the USSR, all its athletes were supposedly amateurs.

Soccer continued to be the most popular spectator sport, with hockey being in second place and men's basketball a distant third. Sports teams were officially the product of sports societies, generally sponsored by trade unions, although the two most successful groups of teams were those supported by the military and the security forces in various cities.

In 1956, the Luzhniki Sports Complex, including Lenin Stadium, with its seating capacity of 103,000 people, opened in Moscow. The nearby Palace of

Sport, opening the same year, gave Moscow an indoor facility for hockey and basketball that could seat 14,000. Later constructions, including those for the 1980 Olympics in Moscow, expanded sports facilities. Yet by 1989, there were still more large stadiums (seating over 50,000) and twice the number of large indoor arenas (seating over 10,000) in the United States state of California than in the entire USSR. In short, domestic sports competition in the Soviet Union did not play as important a role in society as it did in the United States or Western Europe.

Although the Soviet regime continued to emphasize national fitness, especially in the schools, by the beginning of the 1980s many more adults were watching sports on television than participating in them. One of the problems was the shortage of adequate sports facilities for individual or small, unofficial group use.

In 1981, alarmed by growing signs of poor physical fitness and its implications for the economy and military readiness, the state attempted to reorient its sports priorities. It tacitly recognized that it had overemphasized producing top athletes at the expense of the sports needs of the masses. Under Gorbachev, these needs were given even more attention. Yet despite an improvement in television exercise programs and an increased interest in physical fitness and weight control, especially among young adults, not much headway was made. Increasing economic problems hampered the state from doing more and chipped away at people's leisure time, as they spent more time trying to provide for themselves and their families.

In the USSR's final years, the disintegration of the old command economy and the Soviet Union itself affected both participatory and spectator sports. As with most other aspects of Soviet culture and entertainment, sports were supposed to become more self-supporting and less reliant on state funding. This new approach led to more emphasis on commercialization and the open recognition of the professional nature of many athletes. One means of making money was for the sports societies to sell Soviet athletes to foreign teams. As this was done and as some athletes began negotiating contracts abroad, more Soviet soccer, hockey, and basketball players took up residence in Western countries.

An increased emphasis on profits and private business activity also led to the growth of cooperative health and sports clubs as well as the promotion of spectator sports that promoters hoped would make them money. Professional boxing and wrestling matches (including women's boxing and wrestling), U.S.-style football, and erotic ice shows were among the new phenomena appearing in the final Soviet years.

The increasing ethnic nationalism that marked these years stimulated some fan violence at sporting events when teams from different national regions played each other. The disintegration of the USSR itself, partly stemming from this same ethnic nationalism, meant that by the end of 1991 Soviet sports ceased to exist. This was symbolized by the end of Soviet Olympic participation, though not of Russia and other newly independent states of the former USSR. The 1988 Olympic games were the last ones to display the "CCCP" (USSR) logo.

SUGGESTED SOURCES*

AKSYONOV, VASILY, et al. *Metropol: Literary Almanac.* New York, 1983.

ANDERSON, JOHN. *Religion, State, and Politics in the Soviet Union and Successor States.* Cambridge, England, 1994.

BAIGELL, RENEE, and MATTHEW BAIGELL, eds. *Soviet Dissident Artists: Interviews after Perestroika.* New Brunswick, N.J., 1995.

BALZER, HARLEY. "Science, Technology, and Education in the Former U.S.S.R." In *The Former Soviet Union in Transition,* eds. Richard F. Kaufman and John P. Hardt for the U.S. Congress, Joint Economic Committee. Armonk, N.Y., 1993.

BROWN, DEMING. *The Last Years of Soviet Russian Literature: Prose Fiction, 1975–1991.* Cambridge, England, 1993.

———. *Soviet Russian Literature since Stalin.* Cambridge, England, 1978.

BURBANK, JANE, and WILLIAM G. ROSENBERG, eds. *Perestroika and Soviet Culture.* A special issue of *Michigan Quarterly Review* 28 (Fall 1989).

DAVIES, R. W. *Soviet History in the Gorbachev Revolution.* Bloomington, 1989.

DAVIS, NATHANIEL. *A Long Walk to Church: A Contemporary History of Russian Orthodoxy.* Boulder, 1995.

DUNSTAN, JOHN, ed. *Soviet Education under Perestroika.* London, 1992.

EDELMAN, ROBERT. *Serious Fun: A History of Spectator Sports in the USSR.* New York, 1993.

ELLIS, JANE. *The Russian Orthodox Church: A Contemporary History.* Bloomington, 1986.

GLAD, JOHN, ed. *Conversations in Exile: Russian Writers Abroad.* Durham, 1993.

GOSCILO, HELENA, ed. *Lives in Transit: A Collection of Recent Russian Women's Writing.* Ann Arbor, 1995.

HORTON, ANDREW, and MICHAEL BRASHINSKY. *The Zero Hour: Glasnost and Soviet Cinema in Transition.* Princeton, 1992.

JOHNSON, PRISCILLA. *Khrushchev and the Arts: The Politics of Soviet Culture, 1962–1964.* Cambridge, Mass., 1965.

IVINSKAYA, OLGA. *A Captive of Time: My Years with Pasternak.* Garden City, N.Y., 1978.

LAWTON, ANNA. *Kinoglasnost: Soviet Cinema in Our Time.* Cambridge, England, 1992.

LEDKOVSKAIA-ASTMAN, MARINA. *Russia According to Women: Literary Anthology.* Tenafly, N.J., 1991.

MARSH, ROSALIND. *History and Literature in Contemporary Russia.* Washington Square, N.Y., 1995.

MATTHEWS, MERVYN. *Education in the Soviet Union: Policies and Institutions since Stalin.* London, 1982.

MILOJKOVIC-DJURIC, JELENA. *Aspects of Soviet Culture: Voices of Glasnost', 1960–1990.* Boulder, 1991.

MISKIEWICZ, ELLEN. *Split Signals: Television and Politics in the Soviet Union.* New York, 1988.

PARTHÉ, KATHLEEN F. *Russian Village Prose: The Radiant Past.* Princeton, 1992.

POLUKHINA, VALENTINA. *Joseph Brodsky: A Poet for Our Time.* Cambridge, England, 1989.

POSPIELOVSKY, DIMITRY. *A History of Soviet Atheism in Theory and Practice, and the Believer.* 3 vols. New York, 1988.

———. *The Russian Church under the Soviet Regime, 1917–1982.* 2 vols. Crestwood, N.Y., 1984.

PROFFER, CARL, and ELLENDEA PROFFER, eds. *Contemporary Russian Prose.* Ann Arbor, 1982.

* Many of the literary works and films mentioned in this chapter are available in English translations and versions.

REAVEY, GEORGE, ed. *The New Russian Poets, 1953–1968: An Anthology.* London, 1981.

RIORDAN, JAMES. *Soviet Youth Culture.* Bloomington, 1989.

SCHWARZ, BORIS. *Music and Musical Life in Soviet Russia, 1917–1981.* Rev. ed. Bloomington, 1983.

SCAMMELL, MICHAEL. *Solzhenitsyn: A Biography.* New York, 1984.

SHNEIDMAN, N. N. *Russian Literature, 1988–1994: The End of an Era.* Toronto, 1995.

———. *Soviet Literature in the 1980s: Decade of Transition.* Toronto, 1989.

SINYAVSKY, ANDREI. *Soviet Civilization: A Cultural History.* New York, 1990.

SOLOMON, ANDREW. *The Irony Tower: Soviet Artists in a Time of Glasnost.* New York, 1991.

STARR, S. FREDERICK. *Red and Hot: The Fate of Jazz in the Soviet Union, 1917–1980.* New York, 1983.

STITES, RICHARD. *Russian Popular Culture: Entertainment and Society since 1900.* Cambridge, England, 1992. Chs. 5–7.

THOMPSON, TERRY L., and RICHARD SHELDON, eds. *Soviet Society and Culture: Essays in Honor of Vera S. Dunham.* Boulder, 1988.

Vladimir Vysotsky: Hamlet with a Guitar. Moscow, 1990.

VOINOVICH, VLADIMIR. *The Anti-Soviet Soviet Union.* San Diego, 1986.

WILSON, ELIZABETH. *Shostakovich: A Life Remembered.* Princeton, 1994.

CHAPTER 22

Post-Soviet Russia

In late December 1991, with three-fourths of the former USSR's territory and just over half of its population, Russia (more formally the Russian Federation) started down the unpaved road of its post-Soviet existence. Under Boris Yeltsin's leadership, it confronted three difficult challenges: (1) establishing a market economy; (2) creating a democratic, law-based political system; and (3) constructing a new, unified Russian state. Any one of these transitional tasks by itself was difficult enough, but facing all three simultaneously made Yeltsin's job that much more difficult. After his initial reforming efforts created additional hardships, discontentment with his policies increased. This unhappiness was evidenced in the results of legislative elections in December 1993 and again in December 1995.

In an apparent effort to increase his declining popularity, Yeltsin moved in a more conservative and nationalistic direction. This movement was evident in Russian foreign as well as domestic policy. Russia gradually became less accommodating to Western desires and more insistent on defending what it considered its own national interests.

During a presidential campaign in 1996, Yeltsin also attempted to appeal to those frightened of the election of his main rival, Communist party candidate Gennadi Ziuganov. In a two-stage election in June–July 1996, the fear that Ziuganov's election would mean the restoration of certain aspects of the Soviet past or would lead to chaos helped propel Yeltsin to victory and a new four-year term as president.

ECONOMY IN TRANSITION

Under Yeltsin, Russia accelerated its transition from the old command economy toward a market-driven one. By mid-1996, the government could point to several positive accomplishments. Most of the Russian economy was by then under private control, with more than 70 percent of Russia's gross domestic product (GDP) coming from the private sector. Many new private businesses had come into existence, especially in the long neglected area of goods and services for the consumer. The conversion of tens of thousands of state enterprises, which often passed into the hands of their managers and workers, also contributed to the increasing privatization of the economy. In late 1992, the government issued free vouchers available to all, which could be used to buy a small amount of shares of former state enterprises. These vouchers could be sold or traded to other people, and millions of Russians eventually became shareholders in the enterprises in which they worked or in other newly privatized businesses.

Another positive sign by mid-1996 was the slowing of inflation and stabilization of the Russian ruble as compared to foreign currencies. After Yeltsin's government adopted a "shock therapy" approach and decontrolled most prices in January 1992, inflation shot up 300 percent that month. After that, although prices kept increasing, the rate of growth decreased, although it still rose more than 2,000 percent for all of 1992. In each succeeding year, however, the inflation growth rate decreased: According to 1996 official figures, in 1993, the rate was about 840 percent; in 1994, about 215 percent, and in 1995, about 131 percent and from January to June 1996, about 50 percent. After plunging considerably from 1992 to 1994, the rates of industrial output and the GDP also began to level off. According to official figures, the former fell by 3 percent in 1995, compared with a 21 percent decline in 1994, and the GDP fell by 4 percent in 1995, compared with a 12.6 percent decline in 1994.[1] Finally, the Russians were gradually gaining the skills necessary to operate in a market economy.

Yet while positive signs existed, so too did more troubling ones. By 1996, the pace of privatization had slowed considerably, and many of the privatized large-scale industrial enterprises continued to be run by the same managers. These individuals often resisted economic modernization and were primarily interested in making quick profits for themselves. The privatization of agriculture proceeded slowly, and agricultural production was unsatisfactory. In both 1993 and 1994, the grain crop was lower than the preceding year, and a drought in 1995 helped account for the lowest yearly total in three decades—only about 55 percent as much grain as the Russian republic produced in 1990.

Although foreign businesses and investment increased during the early 1990s, they remained below what the Yeltsin government desired. Russia's poorly developed legal system, especially in regard to commercial and contract law, and its tax policies prevented more investment, whether from Russian or foreign citizens. So too did uncertainty about Russia's economic and political stability and the government's inability to destroy organized crime's demands on many businesses. Yeltsin's appointment of retired General Alexander Lebed, a constant advocate of harsh measures against crime, as his national-security chief in June 1996 elicited some hope of more progress in

---

[1] Exact economic figures are almost impossible to calculate, partly because of the unrecorded "black" economy and the underreporting of income to evade taxes.

fighting crime. And Yeltsin's victory in the 1996 presidential election reassured many who were cautious about investing in Russia while the possibility still existed that the anti-Western Ziuganov might be elected.

The 1996 presidential campaign, however, also produced a new economic problem. During the campaign, Yeltsin made various promises that if fulfilled would cost the government billions of additional dollars and threaten to reignite inflation.

Finally, by mid-1996, most Russians still did not believe they were benefiting from the government's economic policies. Even the government admitted that real income declined in 1995 (by a reported 13 percent) after having recovered some lost ground in 1994. Yeltsin's policies had contributed to the growth of retail trade, banking, telecommunications, construction, and service industries such as hotels and restaurants. Many employees involved in these areas became part of a new middle class, but they were outnumbered by less fortunate Russians. Furthermore, the gap between a small upper class and a much larger lower class increased during the early 1990s, although the government claimed that the differentials were beginning to stabilize by the end of 1995.

SOCIAL TENSIONS AND PROBLEMS

Although some free-market enthusiasts declared that wide income differentials were necessary for Russian capitalism to develop, the conspicuous consumption of the rich increased the envy and political dissatisfaction of many poorer Russians.

Years of official anticapitalistic propaganda, followed by the later attacks of Yeltsin and others against Communist elite privileges, made it harder for poorer people to overlook the expensive Western cars, jewels, furs, cellular telephones, and bodyguards of the rich. Some of the affluent spent more for lunch or a bottle of wine at a fancy restaurant or gambled more in one night at a casino than the average Russian earned in a month. Following the collapse of the USSR, many Russians perceived most of the new rich as crooks or members of the old Communist elite who had used their positions, connections, and know-how to benefit economically as government enterprises passed from state to private hands. This perception was partially correct, although honest, hard-working entrepreneurs were also among the new rich.

Casualties of Change

The elderly, women, children, and rural inhabitants suffered disproportionately during the early 1990s. So too did those dependent on state salaries or their savings.

Approximately one-fourth of Russia's population was over the minimum retirement age, which was 55 for women and 60 for men. This group was most hurt when inflation ravaged savings, often making a lifetime of accumulated rubles insignificant. In addition, the elderly's meager pensions often arrived

FIGURE 22.1. By 1995, advertisements had replaced Soviet slogans on Russian streets. This one on a St. Petersburg street says "GSM in Petersburg: Mobile communication of a new generation."

late, and it was more difficult for them than for younger people to take advantage of new economic opportunities.

As crime increased, older people were also victimized more. Impoverished pensioners made up a large share of Russia's growing number of homeless people, which by late 1995 was estimated to number more than 200,000 in Moscow alone. Contributing further to the suffering of the elderly was the feeling that society no longer valued them. Although such is the fate of retired people in many societies, it was made worse in Russia by the transitional nature of the times, when old values were being discarded in favor of new ones.

Among women, unemployment, which continued to rise in the early 1990s, was higher than among men. (Although registered unemployment at the end of 1995 was stated to be only 3 percent of the work force, by international standards it was actually much higher.) That a greater percentage of these unemployed were women was partly due to sexual discrimination, which Russian courts did little to prevent. One Moscow employer in 1994 noted that "if a woman working for me gets married, I fire her." In general, women earned less than men, and single women with children often found life especially difficult. In 1994, it was estimated that single-parent families comprised close to one-fifth of all Russian families and that in 94 percent of the cases, the single parent was a woman. Although these single mothers came from all economic levels of society, they generally received no financial help from the fathers of their children. Still another indication of women's status was the fact that only 10 percent of those elected in the December 1995 Duma elections were women, down from 13 percent in the previous Duma.

The condition of many children also worsened in the early 1990s. More than nine-tenths of the children in government orphanages in 1993 were abandoned children or children taken from their parents because of neglect or abuse. By late 1994, officials estimated that more than 100,000 children in Moscow and St. Petersburg were homeless. Youth drug rates and crime were also on the rise.

While social problems increased, the state cut back on social expenditures, such as subsidies for children under eighteen months of age. This was part of the effort to restrain government spending, an effort required by such outside lending agencies as the International Monetary Fund (IMF). Government and defense workers, military personnel, educators, and scientists were also hurt by cutbacks. The low pay of many government workers, including police personnel, not only demoralized them, but also inadvertently encouraged the taking of payoffs and bribes.

Among the areas hard hit by spending reductions was health care. In 1995, Russia budgeted about 1 percent of government spending for health, a percentage much lower than a decade before or than that spent by other industrial nations. This was at a time when the death rate was increasing and health problems were becoming more acute.

From 1992 to the end of 1995, the death rate exceeded Russia's birth rate, and the population declined slightly to around 148 million people. In this period, official figures indicated more than a 20 percent increase in the death rate, although the ratio of 15 deaths per 1,000 people recorded for the first nine months of 1995 was slightly lower than the 1994 rate. In these years, the birth rate decreased more than 15 percent, down to 9.5 per 1,000 people for 1995. (A World Bank survey of the birth rates of 123 countries in 1990 indicated that none of them had as low a birth rate as Russia did in each of the three years from 1993 to 1995.) Russian life expectancy, especially for men, also dropped sharply; by the end of 1995, Russian expectancy estimates for men had dropped to about 58 years of age.

Besides inadequate government allocations for health care, the reasons for the high death rates included sharp rises in infant mortality, industrial accidents, and suicides as well as an increase in infectious diseases such as cholera, diphtheria, dysentery, tuberculosis, and sexually transmitted diseases. Alcoholism; a polluted environment; stress; inadequate diets; and poor medical care, supplies, and sanitation also continued to shorten people's lives. As one indication of Russia's poor health care system, Russian officials confirmed in 1995 that ten times as many Russian women were dying in childbirth as were women in the advanced Western countries.

Crime

Along with deteriorating health conditions, increasing crime was another serious social concern. Although organized crime (often working in cooperation

Life in 1992 through the Eyes of a Young Woman

The following reflections are by a twenty-year-old office worker named Olya, as excerpted from Deborah Adelman, The *"Children of Perestroika" Come of Age: Young People of Moscow Talk about Life in the New Russia* (Armonk, N.Y., 1994), pp. 50–53. Ellipses are mine.

I want to have a child if I have a husband with a decent salary and my child will have enough to eat. But as it is now, I can just barely make ends meet myself. And if I had to live on my own, and then a child appeared, well, we'd just die. A child in these circumstances? Never! . . .

Life was simpler and easier three years ago. Everything was cheaper, and you didn't have to knock yourself out trying to find things. . . .

This is why young people are trying to go into commercial things, to do something on their own, some kind of "business" as they like to say around here. But you need some sort of a foundation for that, first. Money. Connections. Some kind of experience, so you have some idea what you're doing. And how are you supposed to do that? . . .

For me all these changes mean is that I have to worry about money all the time. Things have not gotten any better for me. Only worse. Not many people here would say that things have changed for the better! I suppose there are people who now have the opportunity to make a lot of money, that's true. But I certainly don't. . . .

I think a lot of time will go by before things get better around here.

with corrupt Communist officials) existed earlier, it continued to grow in the early 1990s, directed by thousands of "mafias." According to the head of one government agency in 1994, up to four-fifths of the country's banks and businesses and an even higher percentage of retail outlets paid protection money to such mafias. The mafias also assassinated selected individuals who refused to go along with them, who attempted to expose them, or who became involved in gangland competition with them. Among those assassinated were journalists, members of Parliament and the child of a leading stockbroker. According to Russia's interior minister, in 1993 there were 250 contract murders as a result of protection disputes.

Russia's mafias increasingly worked with foreign criminal elements and "laundered" and stockpiled profits abroad. Billions of dollars worth of illegal gains as well as valuable Russian resources were thus leaving Russia at a time that money was desperately needed for capital investments inside the country.

Despite periodic Yeltsin campaigns against organized crime, the government made little headway. Two reasons were the continuing corrupt involvement of many officials and police with mafia elements and the inadequacy of government funding, resources, and the legal system to deal with such powerful criminal elements. The transition to a market economy opened up the possibility of all sorts of new criminal scams. The government, law, and police, even when reflecting honorable intentions, were not able to match organized crime in its ability to adjust to this new world. Whether new government anticrime plans announced in July 1996, with Security Council chief Lebed spear-heading the attack, will be more successful than past efforts remains to be seen.

At times in the early 1990s, Russia seemed much more lawless than other industrialized societies. Daylight gangland shootings, signs in expensive clubs indicating that guns must be checked at the door, and newspaper columns highlighting gory killings all contributed to this perception. So too did the more than doubling of murders and attempted murders in Russia between 1990 and 1994. Despite its greater population, however, Moscow in 1994 still had many fewer reported assaults and rapes, though more murders, than New York. And overall, throughout Russia, the 1995 rate of major violent crimes was slightly lower than in 1994.

TOWARD A DEMOCRATIC AND LAW-BASED SOCIETY?

In moving toward its government's announced intention of becoming a democratic and law-based state, Russia faced several major obstacles. It had to work out a reasonably stable relationship between its president and its parliament as well as between Moscow and local governments. It had to originate and refine laws so that they were capable of being applied to the wide variety of differences that occur in a democratic society. It had to develop a stable system of political parties. Finally, more people had to become convinced that despite its many imperfections, a democratic, law-based state was preferable to any other alternative.

Yeltsin and the Russian Parliament, 1991–1993

In the early Yeltsin years, his relationship with the Russian parliament was full of conflicts. As he and economic minister Egor Gaidar pushed forward their radical economic "shock therapy" in early 1992, the Russian Congress of People's Deputies and the smaller Russian Supreme Soviet selected by it to meet more frequently became increasingly critical of the Yeltsin–Gaidar program. There was little doubt that at least in the short term it was causing much economic misery, and parliamentary opposition was not limited to those still holding on to Communist sympathies.

The Communist party itself had been banned by Yeltsin in 1991. It was not relegalized until December 1992 by one of the first major decisions of Russia's Constitutional Court, which had been created in mid-1991. Throughout 1992 and early 1993, other political parties remained insignificant. Yeltsin himself did not represent any party, and parliamentary deputies grouped themselves into ever-changing factions, which sometimes united into larger blocs.

In the face of parliamentary opposition, Yeltsin modified his economic policies in the spring of 1992, but economic decline continued, as did parliamentary resistance. Besides the executive-legislative differences over economic policy, there were disputes over the respective powers of the two branches of government. The 1978 Russian constitution as later amended by more than 300 amendments was unclear on some points, and the Constitutional Court had not acquired sufficient strength to act as a final arbitrator.

Yet the court's chairman, Valeri Zorkin, helped the two branches strike a compromise in December 1992. In exchange for the Congress's agreeing to an April 1993 referendum on a new constitution, Yeltsin replaced Gaidar, who had become acting prime minister in June 1992. His successor was the more conservative deputy prime minister in charge of energy, Viktor Chernomyrdin. The new prime minister was a former industrial manager who in the 1970s and early 1980s had presided over the development of the Soviet natural gas industry.

By March 1993, however, the temporary truce between Yeltsin and the legislators had broken down, and mutual animosity again began rising. In that month, the Congress voted against going ahead with the April referendum on a new constitution, and, after the Congress had adjourned, Yeltsin responded by declaring emergency presidential rule.

His move was condemned by most political factions, by Constitutional Court Chairman Zorkin, and by Yeltsin's vice-president, Alexander Rutskoi. The Supreme Soviet decided to reconvene the Congress so as to hold a vote on impeaching Yeltsin. Although more than half of the Congress's delegates voted to impeach him, the vote failed to gain the necessary two-thirds majority. Finally, the Congress and Yeltsin agreed to a four-question April referendum relating to Yeltsin, his policies, and the timing of presidential and parliamentary elections.

Although the referendum results indicated a little more support for Yeltsin than for the Soviet parliament, the vote settled little. Therefore, in June, Yeltsin called together a constitutional convention to write a new constitution, which he hoped would strengthen his powers. The convention agreed on a draft constitution, but the Supreme Soviet and Russia's local governments failed to support it and political gridlock worsened.

Finally, on September 21, Yeltsin issued a decree dissolving both the Supreme Soviet and its parent body, the Congress of People's Deputies. He realized that the existing Soviet-era constitution did not allow him to do so but argued that it was necessary under the circumstances. His decree also called for December elections to a differently constituted parliament and for a vote on his draft constitution.

Unsurprisingly, some parliamentary deputies refused to comply. They gathered in the parliamentary building (the White House), voted to depose Yeltsin, and declared Vice-President Rutskoi, a former air force commander, to be the acting president. Meanwhile, the Constitutional Court declared Yeltsin's decree unconstitutional.

After attempts at mediation failed, Yeltsin attempted to force the rebellious deputies out of the White House. He cut off their water, electricity, and telephone lines and surrounded the building with riot police. The opposition was led by Rutskoi and parliamentary leader Ruslan Khasbulatov and backed by Communist and extreme right-wing forces both inside and outside the White House. The standoff continued for two weeks. On October 3 and 4, it finally ended. After several thousand parliamentary supporters encouraged by Rutskoi and Khasbulatov had taken over the mayor's office and mounted an attack on the main television center, Yeltsin persuaded loyal military forces to fire on the White House and secure it. They did so at the cost of more than 100 lives and arrested Rutskoi, Khasbulatov, and others.

Yeltsin followed up this victory by suspending the Constitutional Court and outlawing some extremist organizations and publications. His supporters also strengthened presidential powers in the proposed constitution that was to be voted on in December. Although the constitution was subsequently approved by 58 percent of those who voted, only 55 percent of eligible voters participated. And the number of antireform candidates elected to the new parliament was clearly a disappointment to Yeltsin and his supporters.

The reconstituted parliament consisted of a lower-house State Duma and an upper-house Federation Council. The delegates elected to the 450-seat Duma were selected by a complex system under which half of them were chosen based on party lists. This election procedure contributed to the formation of political parties or at least quasiparties or blocs formed primarily for electoral purposes. The other half of the Duma delegates came from single-constituency districts, where some candidates ran under a party label, but others did not. Delegates to the Federation Council were to be chosen on the basis of two deputies for each of Russia's 89 territorial units, and in it regional considerations far outweighed any party affiliations. Because Chechnia refused to participate in elections to the Council, it contained only 176 deputies.

To the surprise and shock of many, the party that gained the greatest percentage vote (23 percent) in party-list elections to the Duma was the Liberal Democratic party (LDP) led by Vladimir Zhirinovsky, a man who was neither liberal nor democratic. Although his extreme imperialistic and neofascist rhetoric alarmed many Western observers, not all those who voted for him shared his extremism. Voting for him was partly a protest against developments that had hurt many people financially, increased crime, and eroded Russia's international stature.

The leading reform party, Gaidar's Russia's Choice, gained only 15 percent of the vote, partly because the proreform vote was split among several parties. Coming in third with 12 percent of the party-list vote was the Communist party. Behind the Communists were five other parties, which gained delegates as a result of obtaining at least 5 percent of the vote.

Yeltsin and the Duma, 1994–1996

Because many Duma deputies originally had no party affiliation and because some of the parties or electoral blocs that did exist were unstable, the political makeup of the Duma was fluid. Yet in 1994, four major groupings emerged: (1) the democratic reformers, led primarily by Gaidar and the economist Grigori Yavlinsky, who headed his own bloc; (2) the Communists and delegates from the Agrarian party; (3) the nationalists, whose largest party was Zhirinovsky's

LDP; and (4) a centrist group, whose leading bloc was called New Regional Politics. In addition, the Women of Russia party, which gained 8 percent of the party-list vote, had about two dozen delegates.

Although the Communists and nationalists (who together made up about 40 percent of the delegates) voted together on some issues, Yeltsin's dealings with the parliament were more stable in 1994 and early 1995 than in the previous two years. This was partly because the 1993 constitution had strengthened the president's powers. But it was also because Yeltsin's policies became less radical as Prime Minister Chernomyrdin gained increasing influence and because Duma Speaker Ivan Rybkin was more adept at compromise than Khasbulatov had been.

The Duma's two most glaring challenges to Yeltsin came in February 1994 and in June 1995. On the first occasion, it voted to grant amnesty to the anti-Yeltsin leaders arrested after the attack on parliament in October 1993. On the second occasion (after a bungled Russian attack on Chechen hostage-takers in the southern Russian city of Budenovsk), the Duma passed a no-confidence vote in the government. Although angered at the release of his enemies in 1994, Yeltsin eventually reconciled himself to it. After the no confidence vote of June 21, 1995, however, he threatened to disband the Duma if they passed another such vote. The 1993 constitution allowed him to do so, provided that he arranged for new elections within four months; otherwise, he would have to form a new government subject to parliamentary approval. A second Duma vote failed to gain the necessary backing.

In late October 1995, a heart attack incapacitated Yeltsin for several months; and in December, elections to the 450-member Duma took place. The results reflected widespread unhappiness with the Yeltsin-Chernomyrdin policies. About 64 percent of all eligible voters voted in the election, and the party that received the most votes on the party-list vote was the Communist party, gaining 22 percent of the vote. This vote, plus the Communist gains in single-constituency districts, gave them about 33 percent of all Duma seats. Zhironovsky's Liberal Democratic party of Russia came in second with 11 percent of the vote, but it won only one single-constituency district and ended up with 51 seats. The party formed by Chernomyrdin, with Yeltsin's blessing, Our Home Is Russia, came in third on the party-list vote but gained 55 seats overall. The only other party to gain more than the necessary 5 percent of the party-list vote was the proreform Yabloko party, headed by Yavlinsky. It obtained 7 percent of the vote and a total of 46 seats. Delegates representing twenty-four other parties won one or more single-constituency districts and therefore also gained Duma seats. Many of them formed themselves into three other factions, which collectively represented 114 deputies in mid-January 1996.

Yeltsin's initial reaction to the elections was to make several ministerial and staff changes, which indicated he was retreating further from earlier reform policies. For example, he removed Anatoli Chubais, who had overseen economic reform, from his position as first deputy prime minister. Despite the pressures on Yeltsin to change, however, the Communists and nationalists taken together still lacked a Duma majority, and the Duma's powers remained weak compared to those of the president.

1996 Presidential Campaign and Election

Despite Yeltsin's abysmal public approval ratings and the greater popularity of Communist leader Ziuganov at the beginning of 1996, Yeltsin overcame his liabilities and in July was elected to a new four-year presidential term. In a preliminary vote in June, Yeltsin bested Ziuganov by receiving 35 percent of the total vote to Ziuganov's 32 percent. Retired general Alexander Lebed ran third, receiving 15 percent of the vote, and Yavlinsky and Zhirinovsky were fourth and fifth in the voting. The once-powerful Mikhail Gorbachev finished seventh, receiving less than 1 percent of all votes.

Between this first vote and the runoff election in early July, Yeltsin broadened his support. He did this partly by appointing third-place finisher Lebed as his new Security Council executive secretary with expanded responsibilities for overseeing matters related to security, defense, and fighting crime and corruption. The council itself was composed primarily of important ministers and officials connected with security and had been created by presidential degree in 1992. In related moves, Yeltsin removed several hard-line advisers and ministers, including Defense Minister Pavel Grachev and the heads of the President's Security Service and the Federal Security Service.

In the runoff vote on July 3, Yeltsin won 54 percent of the vote to Ziuganov's 40 percent, with 5 percent of the ballots being cast against both men; 69 percent of the electorate voted in the runoff election. Following his victory, Yeltsin indicated that he intended Chernomyrdin to serve as prime minister in his new administration, a step requiring, and later receiving, Duma approval. Yeltsin also appointed the reform-minded Chubais as his chief of staff. After being removed as first deputy prime minister early in 1996, he had played an important part in the Yeltsin campaign.

Early in the campaign, when Yeltsin's chances still seemed bleak to some of his hard-line advisers, he apparently gave serious thought to canceling the election. He also reportedly said that he would not turn power over to the Communists. During the campaign, the media, part of which was controlled by the government, was baised toward Yeltsin; for example, they gave little coverage to his health problems when he seemed to be ailing in the days leading up to the runoff vote. Moreover, there were unsubstantiated charges of some vote tampering. The increased prominence in mid-1996 of Lebed, who at times made authoritarian or nationalistic pronouncements, did not please some Western advocates of democracy and reform in Russia. Moreover, the Security Council of which he became executive secretary was earlier criticized by some prodemocracy advocates for being too powerful for an advisory body; it had, for example, approved of military operations in Chechnia.

Yet, despite these developments and criticisms, the successful completion of a presidential election and Yeltsin's substantial victory over Ziuganov represented continued progress in Russia's attempt to establish a truly democratic political order. Although Yeltsin was far from a perfect representatitve of democratic principles, he was more open to them than Ziuganov and his fellow Communists, and there is no doubt that a majority of voters preferred Yeltsin to Ziuganov. Yelstin's appointment of Chubais as his chief of staff in July 1996 also seemed a sign that the president intended to renew some of his earlier reforming efforts.

Federal and Local Governments, Regionalism, and the War in Chechnia

Another positive sign of expanding democracy in Russia during the mid-1990s was the election of local officials. Although Yeltsin originally appointed most regional governors, they as well as mayors had to face election before the end of 1996. By mid-1996, a number of regions had already held their elections for governor, including the Nizhnii Novgorod region, where the popular reformer Boris Nemtsov was returned as governor. Another popular local politician who won an impressive victory (in June 1996) was the mayor of Moscow, Yuri Luzhkov, who received about 90 percent of the vote.

Despite these steps toward democracy, many difficulties continued to exist regarding the central government's relations with local regions and their governments. During the USSR's final months and following its collapse, a danger existed that within Russia itself territorial disintegration would continue. Smaller units of government proclaimed their sovereignty, and Yeltsin himself bore some responsibility for this by his tactics in his battle with Gorbachev in 1990–1991. In the late summer of 1990, for example, he encouraged autonomous republics in Russia's central Volga–Urals region to "take all the sovereignty you can swallow."

By March 1992, however, as president of an independent state, Yeltsin was attempting to prevent further disintegration. That month, the Russian government signed a series of agreements, collectively known as the Federation Treaty, with almost all of its administrative-territorial units—eighty-nine such units existed as of 1995, including forty-nine provinces and thirty-two ethnically autonomous areas, which included republics as well as smaller units (see Map 22.1). Two ethnic republics refused to sign the treaty, Chechno-Ingushetia and Tatarstan. In the latter, Tatars (Russia's largest minority population at about 4 percent) slightly outnumbered ethnic Russians.

Throughout 1992 and most of 1993, both Yeltsin and the parliament made concessions to local governmental leaders in the hope of gaining political support. Relations were complicated by the resentment of Russian provinces over what they perceived was the special treatment afforded Russia's ethnic republics. After disbanding parliament in October 1993, Yeltsin strengthened not only the provisions of his proposed constitution relating to presidential powers, but also those relating to Moscow's powers in dealing with the republics and other local governments. Yet in this constitution, local governments retained some powers (in actual practice, they maintained even more by often ignoring Moscow directives), and jurisdiction on some points remained vague.

The favorable vote on the constitution in December 1993 left many center-periphery problems unresolved. Among them were ones relating to rights over resources, property, and taxes as well as ethnic rights—in most of the twenty-one ethnic republics, Russians outnumbered the native nationality. (Overall, throughout the country, about 82 percent of the population was ethnic Russian in 1994–1995). In February 1994, Tatarstan signed a special treaty with the Russian government in which the latter recognized the former's right to conduct foreign and economic relations with other countries. Russia also recognized Tatarstan's right to control its own natural resources and enterprises.

Although other ethnic republics received less far-reaching rights, by January 1996 the central government had signed accords with nine more of them. It also had begun to sign agreements with a few of its forty-nine provinces such as Orenburg and Sverdlovsk. Yet Moscow still had not developed a coherent regional policy, and regional resistance to Moscow's demands remained strong.

Nowhere was this resistance more evident than in Chechnia. This area was the largest part of the former Chechno-Ingush Republic, which Russia formally divided into two republics in mid-1992. In the formerly united republic, the Chechens and Ingushi together numbered about 900,000 people, as compared to almost 300,000 Russians (1989 figures), and these Moslem peoples of the North Caucasus had long-standing grievances against Russia. They were subdued only after long and bloody fighting in the nineteenth century, and Stalin's deportation of them from their homeland in 1943 caused great suffering and many deaths before Khrushchev allowed their return in the late 1950s. In 1991, the Chechens under Dzhokar Dudaev, a former Soviet Air Force general, proclaimed an independent Chechen Republic.

After briefly sending and then withdrawing Russian airborne troops from the region in late 1991, Yeltsin for three years attempted less dramatic methods (such as giving covert aid to Dudaev opponents) to end the Chechen's attempt at secession. Then in December 1994, without the consent of parliament, he ordered an invasion of Chechnia. By late February 1995, after extensive Russian bombing and shelling of the Chechen capital of Grozny, the United Nations Human Rights Commission indicated that 24,000 civilians had been killed and that numerous violations of human rights had occurred. Yet, despite growing opposition at home and abroad, Yeltsin continued the war.

In June 1995, Chechen fighters bribed police officials to make their way to the southern city of Budenovsk. Once there, the Chechens captured more than 1,000 hostages. As part of the settlement of that crisis, the Russian government agreed to an armistice and the beginning of new peace talks.

But the agreement failed to produce lasting peace. In December 1995, violence again escalated. In January 1996, another hostage crisis developed, this time leading to a bloody Russian response, after Chechen militants seized hostages in the Dagestan city of Kizliar. Despite the death of Dudaev, killed in April 1996 in a Russian rocket attack, and a cease-fire accord, signed in late

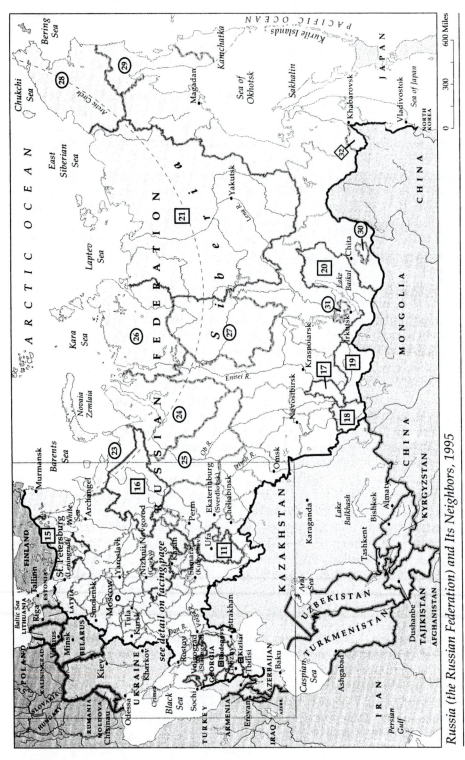

Russia (the Russian Federation) and Its Neighbors, 1995

MAP 22.1A

ETHNICALLY AUTONOMOUS AREAS OF THE RUSSIAN REPUBLIC

Autonomous Republics (21)

1 Adygeia
2 Karachai-Cherkes
3 Kabardin-Balkar
4 North Ossetian
5 Ingushetia
6 Chechnia
7 Dagestan
8 Kalmyk
9 Tatarstan
10 Udmurt
11 Bashkir
12 Mordovia
13 Chuvash
14 Marii-El
15 Karelia
16 Komi
17 Khakass
18 Gorno-Altai
19 Tuva
20 Buriat
21 Sakha (Yakut)

Autonomous Areas—*Okrugs* (10)

22 Komi-Permiak
23 Nenets
24 Yamalo-Nenets
25 Khanty-Mansi
26 Taimyr
27 Evenki
28 Chukot
29 Koriak
30 Agin-Buriat
31 Ust-Orda Buriat

Autonomus Region—*Oblast* (1)

32 Jewish

FORMER REPUBLICS OF THE U.S.S.R.

Armenia
Azerbaijan
Belarus
Estonia
Georgia
Kazakhstan
Kyrgyzstan
Latvia
Lithuania
Moldova
Russia
Tajikstan
Turkmenistan
Ukraine
Uzbekistan

MEMBERS OF THE COMMONWEALTH OF INDEPENDENT STATES

Armenia
Azerbaijan
Belarus
Georgia
Kazakhstan
Kyrgyzstan
Moldova
Russia
Tajikstan
Turkmenistan
Ukraine
Uzbekistan

▣ City where Chechens took hostages in June 1995 or January 1996

MAP 22.1B

May (intended to help Yeltsin's elections prospects), the fighting continued. Although before becoming Yeltsin's security adviser in June 1996, Lebed had long criticized the war in Chechnia, it was uncertain how much of an impact his appointment might have on bringing the war to an end.

Rule of Law and the Search for a New Identity

Following Yeltsin's suspension of the Constitutional Court in the fall of 1993, a new Constitutional Court did not begin operations until February 1995. Although by law it was to have many powers similar to the U.S. Supreme Court, especially deciding on the constitutionality of government actions, it remained unclear whether Yeltsin or any other future president would abide by all its decisions.

Another important question was whether Russian security organizations would be restrained by legal oversight. Chief among these organizations were the President's Security Service, the Federal Security Service, and the Foreign Intelligence Service, the last two having inherited many of the functions of the old KGB. Lebed's appointment as Security Council secretary suggested he would exercise more oversight, but how long he would remain in this position and whether he himself would be amenable to legal restraints remained open questions.

Although the 1993 constitution was developed in a hasty and authoritarian manner, Russia made major advances in respecting human rights and developing new laws and judicial procedures during the early 1990s. In January 1996, the Council of Europe (established in 1949 to further European unity) recognized some of these gains but still declared that Russia was not yet a rule-of-law state. The council specifically cited human rights violations in Chechnia and within Russia's criminal justice system. The problems of organized crime and official and police corruption also continued to hinder the development of a law-governing state.

Another detriment was the lack of consensus about the importance of the rule of law. In the early 1990s, Russian popular opinion was in a state of confusion and discord. The collapse of the Communist system and the USSR after more than seven decades created a major identity crisis for Russian citizens. No consensus existed on what Russia any longer stood for and how it should define itself in the future. Debates reminiscent of those of the nineteenth-century Slavophiles and Westernizers flared up, although now more complex and involving more people. Should Russia become a democratic, law-governed, and capitalistic power similar to the major Western powers and Japan, or would a unique Russian way be more appropriate? (Although opposing each other politically, both Ziuganov and Lebed often mentioned Russia's uniqueness and were indebted to some strands of Slavophile nationalism.) And what was Russia?[2] Was it only the territory of the present state, or should it include

---

[2] Jeffrey Brooks in *When Russian Learned to Read: Literacy and Popular Literature, 1861–1914* (Princeton, 1985), p. 214, noted a similar questioning spirit in Late Imperial Russia: "A quest for the definition of Russianness was shared by Russians of all cultural levels."

some of the territories from neighboring states, much of which had been dominated by Russia for centuries? Yeltsin's victory in the 1996 presidential election
did not end these debates.

RELIGION, EDUCATION, AND CULTURE

Religion

Amidst the spiritual and moral confusion of the early 1990s, the Russian Orthodox Church and religion in general continued to gain new adherents, and
religious charitable endeavors and publications increased. A 1993 survey reported that about two-fifths of surveyed adults and two-thirds of those aged
sixteen and seventeen considered themselves "believers," both proportions
being much higher than those who classified themselves as "non-believers."

In 1995, the Orthodox Church claimed to be baptizing millions of Russians
each year. Old churches continued to be restored and new ones constructed.
Most notably, in 1994, Moscow began constructing a replica of the massive
Cathedral of Christ the Savior, which had been destroyed by Stalin (see Figure
7.1 and Chapter 16). Completion of the project is scheduled for 1997, the 850th
anniversary of Moscow's founding. Meanwhile, in already existing churches,
attendance at church services was impressive. In 1995, for example, Sunday
services at the cathedral of St. Petersburg's Alexander Nevsky Monastery regularly attracted more than 5,000 people.

Among other religions, progress was also noticeable. Russia's millions of
Moslems succeeded in opening up new mosques, educational establishments,
and other centers, and Russia's government helped restore not only Orthodox,
but also Moslem places of cultural and historical significance. In 1991, Russia's
much smaller Catholic community had gained an archbishop to look out for
its interests, and in the post-Soviet period, the Yeltsin government established full diplomatic ties with the Vatican. Various Protestant denominations
stepped up their religious activities in Russia or began missionary work there
for the first time—in 1995, Baptists had the largest number of religious associations among the Russian Protestants. The emigration of Russian Jews leveled
off, and in late 1995 Russia's Jewish population was estimated at about 1.6
million people, with 200,000 to 300,000 of them living in Moscow. A growing
number of Russian Jews were becoming interested in Judaism, and the number of synagogues, Jewish schools, publications, and charitable programs was
also rising.

The attitude of the Russian Orthodox hierarchy and laity to such religious
pluralism varied, with Patriarch Alexei II displaying a more tolerant spirit than
many of those he led—for example, he criticized antisemitism and displayed
some ecumenical sympathies. Yet even he attempted to restrict the rights of denominations he believed were harmful to Russia. Some other church leaders
went much further. Before his death in 1995, St. Petersburg's Metropolitan
Ioann was a leading voice among those who thought Russian was being weakened by a Western conspiracy involving, among others, Catholics and Jews. At

a minimum, most Orthodox believers, and even some Russian non-believers, thought that Orthodoxy's historical connection with Russia had earned it a special role in Russian society.

Although the Orthodox hierarchy refused to endorse any specific political party or faction, many politicians attempted to gain nationalist support by displaying Orthodox sympathies. In 1995, Zhirinovsky declared that Orthodoxy should serve as the basis of Russia's spiritual revival and that it should be the only government-recognized religion. In December 1995, Alexander Yakovlev, who had led Gorbachev's push for *glasnost,* lashed out at the Communist party under Ziuganov for courting Orthodox favor without expressing repentance for the Soviet Communists' killing of 200,000 religious figures and destroying 40,000 churches as well as more than half of the USSR's total of Muslim and Jewish places of worship. In January 1996, Yeltsin himself, along with Patriarch Alexei, laid the final stone in the outer wall of Moscow's Cathedral of Christ the Savior.

The Yeltsin government's relationship to the Russian Orthodox Church produced occasional criticism that the government was violating the constitutional principle of the separation of church and state. The outspoken Orthodox priest and Duma deputy Gleb Yakunin, who had defied church authorities by running for a Duma seat in 1993, made such a charge in October 1995. This was occasioned by an earlier joint government-church declaration indicating that a government agency and the Orthodox Church would cooperate in the patriotic and moral education of servicemen.

Education

In education and research, the trends begun under Gorbachev continued, both of a positive and negative nature. More freedom, flexibility, and variety contributed new insights and approaches to teaching and learning, but lack of funding continued to harm education and research. In the spring of 1995, two of Russia's leading scientists claimed that less than one-fifth of Russia's scientists and scholars earned more than the minimum necessary for survival. Like many other Russians, most of these highly educated individuals were forced to supplement their salaries by other money-making activities or to find some other type of occupation. In mid-1995, the average pay of a teacher was below the poverty level and less than half of the national average. In December, teachers in many regions of Russia staged a two-day strike demanding higher salaries and the payment of back-pay—some of them had not been paid since the beginning of the school year. Besides lack of funding, power struggles between Moscow and the provinces and between educational reformers and conservatives also retarded educational progress.

Culture

Russian cultural life was even more pluralistic and diverse than the religious realm and as troubled by economic pressures as was education and research. Solzhenitsyn seemed no longer relevant to many Russians, even after he returned to his native country in 1994. Most literary critics believed that the day of the writer as a great moral authority had passed, at least for the time being. In contrast, Solzhenitsyn criticized most of the new literary trends. He believed that many writers were too concerned with self-expression and experimentation while lacking concern for Russia's problems and respect for traditional pre-Soviet culture. He tended to look upon literary and artistic *avant-gardism* and postmodernism (see Glossary) as symptoms of twentieth-century spiritual malaise.

Although some works like Evgeni Popov's *On the Eve of the Eve* (a parody of Turgenev's *On the Eve*) were labeled postmodernist, most of the best new fiction—by writers such as Liudmila Petrushevskaia (see Chapter 21), Mark Kharitonov, Vladimir Makanin, and Viktor Pelevin—was neither postmodernist nor in the Solzhenitsyn tradition. As in the late 1980s, émigré writers such as the poet Joseph Brodsky (who died in 1996) and novelists Vasily Aksyonov and Georgi Vladimov also contributed notable works.

Many writers complained that "financial censorship" had replaced the previous Communist censorship, that good literature, especially poetry, was increasingly being replaced by lower-quality works that would make greater profits for their publishers. As examples of such works, some critics pointed to the rash of "sequels" to famous works. Usually written by little-known or anonymous writers, they attempted to profit from the fame of earlier Russian or foreign classics. In 1996, for example, an anonymously written two-volume "sequel" to *War and Peace* appeared. It was entitled *Pierre and Natasha* and contained considerably more sex and melodrama than Tolstoy's classic.

Culture generally continued to suffer from low levels of government financial support. Yet some quality works continued to appear, and not just in literature. For example, Nikita Mikhalkov's film *Burnt by the Sun* won numerous awards in 1995.

FOREIGN POLICY

Russian foreign policy from 1991 to mid-1996 was marked by an early period of continuing close relations with the West, followed by increasing disillusionment with Western policies. This disillusionment was accompanied by a heightened emphasis on Russia's need to be the predominant outside influence over the other former successor states of the USSR (referred to by Russia as its "Near Abroad").

Early Hopes and Disillusionments

Following the collapse of the USSR, Yeltsin and his foreign minister, Andrei Kozyrev, attempted to build upon the foundations established by Gorbachev for improved ties with the West. Russia desired Western aid and credits and wished to integrate itself into the international structures dominated by the major powers.

In April 1992, Russia was admitted into the International Monetary Fund (IMF) and the European Bank of Reconstruction and Development. It was less successful, however, in its drive to obtain NATO membership and in its desire to transform the G-7 organization of leading economic powers into a G-8 that would include Russia. NATO all but ignored a letter of December 1991 from the Yeltsin government expressing Russia's goal of becoming a member; and although Yeltsin began attending G-7 summits, Russia was denied full membership in this elite group.

Yet, in January 1993, relations remained warm enough for Yeltsin and U.S. President Bush to sign a START-2 Treaty in Moscow. By it, both sides agreed to further drastic reductions during the next decade in their long-range nuclear arsenals and to eliminate completely nuclear multi-warhead land-based missiles.

Closer to home, Yeltsin hoped to convince the other former Soviet member republics that had joined the Commonwealth of Independent States (CIS) to maintain a common military force and close economic ties. Yeltsin, like most other Russian leaders, assumed that Russia, as the largest, most powerful state in the CIS, would naturally play the leading role within it.

But some of the other member states, especially Ukraine, desired to stake out a much more independent existence. Along with Moldova and Azerbaijan, it soon proclaimed its intention to form its own national army. By late 1992, it was increasingly clear that most CIS member states wished to stress their independence more than any unifying policies. Not only were separate national armies formed, but also trade between CIS members declined in 1992–1993.

In this same period, with Russian living standards still declining, Western economic aid turned out to be much less than promised. This fact contributed to heightened criticism of Yeltsin and Kozyrev for placing too much reliance on the West. A public opinion survey conducted by U.S. scholars in November–December 1993 found that by almost two to one, a majority of Russians believed the West was attempting to weaken Russia by means of its economic advice. The success of Zhirinovsky and other nationalists in the December 1993 parliamentary elections further strengthened nationalist critics.

Partly in response to such criticism, Russian foreign policy gradually became less cooperative with the West. Although still insisting that Russia desired close relations with the other major powers of the world, Yeltsin and Kozyrev began placing more emphasis on Russian "national interests," both in the Near Abroad and beyond.

Russian–Western Relations, 1994 to Mid-1996

As relations with the West gradually became less cordial, the earlier momentum in signing arms agreements was not completely lost, but it certainly slowed. In addition, the breakup of the USSR and the development of separate national military forces complicated the fulfillment of arms treaties that Gorbachev had signed with Western powers. The breakup, for example, left nuclear weapons not only in Russia, but also in Ukraine, Belarus, and Kazakhstan. Ukraine was especially reluctant to give them up. In late 1994, however, Ukraine followed the example of Belarus and Kazakhstan and agreed to allow their destruction. In exchange, Russia, the United States, and

FIGURE 22.2. General Kutuzov, whose statue stands here in front of St. Petersburg's Kazan Cathedral, drove the French out of Russia in 1812. By 1995, some Russians were concerned about a different type of invasion, that of Western businesses and influences.

Great Britain pledged to respect Ukrainian territorial integrity and to abstain from any economic coercion.

This agreement of December 1994 cleared the way for going forward with the nuclear reductions of long-range missiles that had been agreed to by the United States and USSR in the START Treaty of 1991.

By mid-1996, however, the 1993 START-2 Treaty had still not been ratified by the Russian Duma, and the U.S. Senate ratified it only in January 1996. The main impediment to Russian parliamentary ratification was the West's intention to expand NATO membership eastward. To become a NATO member, countries first would be required to fulfill a whole list of conditions, and Russian leaders feared that countries such as Poland and Ukraine might meet these conditions but Russia would not. Unless NATO changed its rules, once a country became a NATO member, it could veto Russian membership.

In December 1994, Yeltsin complained that NATO's planned expansion threatened to split Europe anew and that Europe was in danger of "plunging into a cold peace." He insisted that fears of "undesirable developments in Russia" were an inadequate justification for any eventual expansion of NATO up to Russia's borders.

Earlier in 1994, NATO had adopted a program called "Partnership for Peace." It provided for closer military cooperation between NATO and central and eastern European countries and encouraged these countries to undertake political, economic, and military reforms as steps toward eventual NATO membership. Although Russia agreed to join this "partnership," it did so only in May 1995 and even then warned that it would immediately suspend its participation if NATO expanded eastward to Russia's borders.

In the meantime, Russia insisted that the Conference for Security and Cooperation in Europe, later renamed the Organization for Security and Cooperation in Europe (OSCE), provided a better forum for addressing European security concerns. This organization included all European states and had provided the setting for arriving at such agreements as the Helsinki Accords of 1975 and the Conventional Forces in Europe (CFE) Treaty of 1990.

To help alleviate Russian fears and persuade Russia to join the Partnership for Peace, NATO agreed in the spring of 1995 to recognize Russia's major-power status and to consult it about—although not allow it to veto—any eastern expansion. (The feeling inside Russia that the West had ceased to treat it with the respect due to it had been one reason for Russia's anger about NATO's planned expansion.)

Russia's relationship with Western powers in the mid-1990s was also affected by Russian–Western financial dealings; concerns over the sale of arms and dispersion of nuclear materials from Russia; the war in Bosnia–Herzegovina; Russia's military campaign in Chechnia; and Russia's policies relating to other countries that had been part of the USSR, especially the Baltic nations and Ukraine.

Russian financial dealings with the West occurred directly between Western countries and between Russia and Western organizations or Western-dominated ones, such as the IMF. The general pattern was for the West to insist on economic reforms as a condition for substantial aid, primarily in the form of loans and credits. The IMF, for example, demanded less governmental spending and subsidies, reduction of the government deficit, and rapid privatization of state enterprises.

Despite billions of dollars in aid from Western governments, Western banks, and international organizations, the general Russian perception was that Western countries and the international bodies they dominated not only delivered less than promised, but also were unreasonably demanding. In May 1995, for example, after the IMF had agreed to provide more than $6 billion in monthly installments, Russia's finance minister blamed Russia's budgetary shortage on the lateness and insufficiency of IMF aid. Such criticism did not, however, prevent the IMF from approving a new $10.2 billion loan to Russia in March 1996.

Following the breakup of the Soviet Union, one of the West's primary concerns was to prevent the dispersion of Soviet nuclear materials. The United States, for example, feared that such materials might end up in the hands of anti-American countries or terrorists. When U.S. President Clinton met with Yeltsin in May 1995 in Moscow, one of his chief objectives was to talk Yeltsin out of a planned sale of nuclear technology to Iran. Clinton, however, was unsuccessful, one reason being Russia's need for increased revenue. At a Moscow nuclear summit of Yeltsin with G-7 leaders in April 1996, Yeltsin again resisted Clinton's effort to prevent the Russian deal with Iran, but the eight leaders did agree to other steps to increase nuclear safety and lessen the chances of nuclear smuggling (both major dangers within Russia). The leaders also agreed to work toward a treaty banning nuclear testing.

In the civil war in Bosnia–Herzegovina, Russia was more sympathetic to the Bosnian Serbs than were Western leaders, who saw them as the chief culprits in the war. Russia's traditional sympathy with the Slavic and Orthodox Serbs was one reason for the differences between Russia and the NATO countries. Arriving at a common approach to the war was difficult even among the Western allies themselves, however, and after a Bonsian peace accord was finally signed in late 1995, Russian troops under their own commander participated along with NATO troops in policing the peace.

Russia's war in Chechnia was still another hindrance to better Russian–Western relations. In the spring of 1995, for example, the European Union stated that Russian actions in Chechnia prevented the organization from doing more to aid Russia. At international meetings such as the G-7 meeting attended by Yeltsin in Halifax in June 1995, Western leaders complained that Russia was resorting to excessive force and violating human rights. At that time and on many other occasions, the Western leaders urged Yeltsin to seek a negotiated settlement.

In January 1996, less than a month after Communist successes in the 1995 Duma elections, Yeltsin finally replaced Kozyrev as foreign minister. Despite Kozyrev's gradually becoming more critical of Western actions, Duma critics had continued to attack him for being pro-Western. His successor was Evgeni Primakov, who had earlier served as the head of Russia's Foreign Intelligence Service. Although Primakov was considered a pragmatist and had worked under Gorbachev to improve USSR–U.S. relations, he was much more acceptable to the Duma's Communists and nationalists.

Other Soviet Successor States

Among chief Western concerns about Russia's dealings with its "Near Abroad" was the continuing presence of Soviet troops in the former Baltic republics. Russian resentment over citizenship requirements and other matters affecting ethnic Russians in Latvia and Estonia was also cause for concern. These worries lessened somewhat after Russia pulled the last of its troops from Estonia in August 1994, thereby completing its troop withdrawal from the three Baltic republics. A year earlier, the last Russian troops had left Lithuania but retained transit rights through Lithuania to Kaliningrad, which remained part of Russia.

In April 1995, Foreign Minister Kozyrev stated that Russia reserved the right to use military force to protect Russians living abroad—about 25 million of them were still living in other parts of the former USSR. In Latvia and Estonia, where ethnic Russians made up about one-third of the population (slightly more in Latvia, slightly less in Estonia), Kozyrev's statement created considerable anxiety. The decision of a majority of Estonian Orthodox believers to switch allegiance from the Moscow Patriarchate to that of Constantinople (now located in Istanbul) led to further tension in early 1996, including Yeltsin's criticism of the transfer of allegiance.

After a rocky start, Russia's relations with Ukraine improved after the election in mid–1994 of President Leonid Kuchma, an ethnic Russian from eastern Ukraine. He was in office when Ukraine finally agreed later that year to abandon its nuclear weapons. But two other major issues continued to threaten improved Russian–Ukrainian relations. One was the division of the former Soviet Black Sea fleet; the other was the status of the Crimea.

On June 9, 1995, after earlier understandings failed to resolve the first issue, Yeltsin and Kuchma arrived at an agreement that Yeltsin declared "finally put an end" to their disagreement on the Black Sea fleet. By its terms, the two countries agreed to split the fleet, after which Russia was to purchase most of Ukraine's share, thereby ending up with a little over four-fifths of the original fleet. In exchange for payment, Russia was to be allowed to continue using the naval base at Sevastopol. Dependent on Russia for energy supplies and in debt to Russia, the financial aspects of the arrangement were especially important to Ukraine. In 1995, Russia remained Ukraine's largest trading partner, accounting for more than two-fifths of its exports and more than half of its imports.

The issue of the fleet was intertwined with the Crimean peninsula, where Sevastopol was located. In 1954, at a time when it seemed to make little practical difference, the Soviet government transferred Crimea from Russian to Ukrainian control. But ethnic Russians outnumbered Ukrainians on the peninsula, and Kuchma was confronted by a separatist Crimean government that wished closer ties with Russia. The Black Sea agreement of June 1995 seemed, however, to indicate Yeltsin's willingness, at least temporarily, to accept continuing Ukrainian sovereignty over Crimea.

Relations with other CIS states varied. In a May 1995 referendum, Belarussians overwhelmingly signaled their desire for closer ties with Russia; in April 1996, the two countries signed an agreement to form a closer economic and political union. In Moldova, separatists in the Transdniesterian "Republic" received Russian support, and the "peacekeeping" force of the Russian 14th Army (under future presidential candidate General Alexander Lebed until June 1995) sympathized with the separatists. Three-fifths of the Transdniesteria's population was ethnic Russian or Ukrainian, and this majority opposed the Moldovans, who, although a minority in Transdniesteria, made up about two-thirds of the population of Moldova as a whole. Although Yeltsin in 1994 agreed to withdraw Russian troops from Moldova within three years, the Russian Duma indicated in the spring of 1995 that it would not ratify the accord until a political agreement was reached on the future of the Transdniesterian region.

Russian policies in the Transcaucasian states of Georgia, Armenia, and Azerbaijan aimed at propping up its strategic position, maintaining a major Russian role in controlling Caspian Sea oil, and preventing other foreign countries from exercising much influence in the area. Iran and Turkey had historically been major competitors in the region, and new Caspian oil finds stimulated heightened Western interests in striking deals to help extract oil and transport it.

After first assisting Abkhazian rebels against Georgia, Russia then changed its policy and supported Georgia in putting down the rebellion. In exchange, in late 1993–early 1994, Georgia joined the CIS and allowed Russian troops to be stationed in Georgia. In the Nagorno–Karabakh region fought over by Armenia and Azerbaijan, Russia deployed its troops as peacekeepers and resisted suggestions that a more international peacekeeping force be dispatched to the area.

In the five Central Asian successor states, three major Russian concerns were the ethnic Russians living there, the area's natural resources, and border security. In 1995, more than 6 million ethnic Russians still lived in Kazakhstan, about 37 percent of that country's population. Russia was also interested in Kazakhstan's oil supplies and maintaining a central role in shipping it through Russian pipelines. The Russian minority of the other four Central Asian successor states, though significant, together totaled slightly less than that of Kazakhstan.

In Tajikistan, where civil war erupted in 1992, Russian troops supported old-line authoritarian political forces against a more democratic Islamic coalition. The security of the Tajik–Afghan border and the fear of militant Islamic forces in Tajikistan and Central Asia were two reasons for the Russian involvement. In July 1996, a Duma committee stated that Russia's troops (numbering about 25,000) should remain there to safeguard regional security. In general, Russia believed its security (including that against imported drugs) necessitated maintaining CIS "external" borders, which except in the Baltic area were similar to the well-protected Soviet borders. If this was done, Russia would not have to worry as much about its "internal" borders, like the long and porous Russian–Kazakh border.

At his first press conference after becoming foreign minister in January 1996, Primakov stressed the importance he placed upon Russia's "Near Abroad." After insisting that Russia's foreign policy should reflect its great-power status, he outlined four goals. The first three were to strengthen Russian territorial integrity; to foster CIS integration; and to stabilize regional conflicts, especially in the former USSR and ex-Yugoslavia (the fourth goal was to prevent nuclear proliferation). He also announced that his first foreign trips would be to CIS countries, and within a few months, he visited Tajikistan, Kazakhstan, Belarus, and Ukraine.

Russia and the Far East

In September 1994, despite continued Chinese criticism of Gorbachev and Yeltsin for abandoning communism, Russia and China signed a series of agreements. In them, the two sides promised to reduce troops along their long common border, to cease targeting nuclear missiles at each other, and to increase trade. Already in the three preceding years, trade between the two countries had almost doubled, and by 1994, China followed only Germany in its trading volume with Russia. In January, 1996, Russia announced that it intended to sign an agreement with China that would help the latter speed up its development of nuclear energy. In April, Yeltsin visited China for three days and signed a border treaty.

Despite some attempts to improve Russian–Japanese relations, closer economic cooperation, which could be beneficial to both countries, proceeded slowly. The chief impediment was Japan's continuing demand for the return of the four Kurile islands that Russia took over at the end of World War II.

CONCLUSION

During Yeltsin's first term as Russian president, Russia continued the difficult transition it began under Gorbachev. It made considerable progress toward three main goals: (1) establishing a market economy; (2) creating a democratic and law-based political system; and (3) constructing a new, unified Russian state. As Yeltsin was about to begin a second term, there were both optimists and pessimists among those who wished to see Russia continue such progress.

Optimists pointed to the considerable advances made after 1991. They sometimes argued that the economic hardships suffered by many Russians were regrettable but almost inevitable occurrences in the transition from a command to market economy and that matters were slowly improving. Further, they maintained that the structural changes to the economy and political system, the pressures of the global economy and outside democratic forces, and the experience of increased freedom and democracy made it highly unlikely that Russia would retreat back to a pre-1985 type of Communist order.

The optimists also argued that Russia would not resort to force in an attempt to reunite the nations of the former USSR. For one thing, the Russian military was much weaker than the old Soviet military, and for another there was little support for such a policy among Russia's people. If some voices in parliament, the military, and the media advocated a more aggressive policy in and beyond the "Near Abroad," others urged a more isolationistic approach and were hesitant about any use of Russian troops beyond Russian borders. The Afghan war had been a bitter lesson. Even the use of Russian troops within Russian borders in Chechnia was opposed by many. And the idea of reuniting at least certain parts of the former USSR under Russian hegemony had its enemies as well as advocates. Many Russians believed that absorbing other Soviet successor states would be more of an economic liability than a gain.

Yet even if there was no going back to a Soviet Union, others argued there were still numerous reasons for pessimism. Although Yeltsin's presidential victory ended for the moment the threat of a Communist government, the Communists were still the largest party in the Duma. The Duma itself, although not powerful, was less progressive than Yeltsin, and unless he called for new elections, the present Duma members still had three more years to serve. There were also the continuing economic hardships and the possibility that government attempts to ease them could once again drive up inflation. Crime and corruption were still deeply embedded throughout Russia. Ample imperialistic rhetoric still rang out in various quarters, especially regarding portions of the "Near Abroad." There was also the renewed fighting in Chechnia and the possibility it would further weaken Russia's efforts to build a strong, unified political order.

Finally, there remained numerous questions about Yelstin himself, such as his health and his rumored fondness for alcohol. Having earlier suffered at least two heart attacks, he was clearly ill for an extended period surrounding the July 1996 election—although exactly with what remained a mystery. The few times he appeared in public were very brief, and his advisors announced that he would take a long vacation following his inauguration in early August as independent Russia's first democratically elected president.

Any prolonged absence from his duties might engender increased rivalries among already competing officials such as Prime Minister Chernomyrdin, Security Council head Lebed, and Yeltsin's chief of staff Chubais. If Yeltsin dies in office, the constitution stipulates that the prime minister is to schedule a presidential election within three months. Even if Yeltsin lives out his term, it is debatable how vigorously he will work toward further reform. As in his first term, it will depend in part on his advisers and ministers and their commitment toward a market economy, democracy, and a law-based state.

Although it remains impossible to predict Russia's future with any exactitude, it is certain that its past will continue to affect its future. At the beginning of this volume, we saw that Russia's long, porous, and poorly defined borders; its many non-Russian peoples; and its Eurasian location had affected its history. By 1855, it was a major European power but less prosperous and technologically advanced than its main rivals. Its people exercised less freedom and social autonomy than existed in the West, and its commercial and civil law was less developed. Today, many of these geographic, economic, and social features still exist and are liable to continue existing for some time. In 1855, Russia also still had serfdom, autocracy, and a nobility, and although all three came to an end in succeeding decades, they left behind their legacy. The Communists established their own authoritarian political system, new elite, and "second serfdom"—as the peasants perceived Stalin's collectivization and as forced labor could be construed.

Just as the Russian government attempted to hold its empire together not only by force, but also by emphasizing autocracy, Russian Orthodoxy, and the Russian nationality, so too the Communists relied on their own ideas and symbols to help keep the USSR together for almost seven decades. Besides force, other important instruments included Marxism-Leninism and the cults of Lenin and the Great Patriotic War (World War II). And just as Imperial Russia left its legacy to Soviet Russia, so too Soviet Russia has left its legacy to post-Soviet Russia. It includes not only a more technologically developed Russia and better educated population than Soviet Russia inherited, but also an authoritarian political tradition and six decades of a command economy, plus all the habits engendered by these systems. Furthermore, post-Soviet Russia has inherited not only a land of great resources, but also a polluted and scarred environment that will be costly to restore.

In post-Soviet Russia, all of these legacies have jostled together, and new combinations have emerged, such as a Communist party that has refashioned its message hoping to appeal to Orthodox Christian and Slavophile sentiments. Politicians have scrambled about attempting to discern what forces and loyalties from the past, whether tsarist or Soviet, are still relevant. Although the past can never be fully restored, materials from its collapsed edifices can be refashioned to help create new structures. What seems most likely in the future is that Russia's development, although influenced by outside forces, will continue building primarily upon its own unique past. At present, it remains in a state of transition from the old Soviet Russia to a new, still-evolving post-Soviet order.

*SUGGESTED SOURCES**

ADELMAN, JONATHAN R. *Torrents of Spring: Soviet and Post-Soviet Politics.* New York, 1995.

ASLUND, ANDERS. *How Russia Became a Market Economy.* Washington, D.C., 1995.

BERRY, ELLEN E., and ANESA MILLER-POGACAR, eds. *Re-Entering the Sign: Articulating New Russian Culture.* Ann Arbor, 1995.

BLACKWILL, ROBERT D., RODRIC BRAITHWAITE, and AKIHIKO TANAKA. *Engaging Russia: A Report to the Trilateral Commission.* New York, 1995.

BLANEY, JOHN W., ed. *The Successor States to the USSR.* Washington, D.C., 1995.

BRIDGER, SUE, REBECCA KAY, and KATHRYN PINNICK. *No More Heroines?: Russia, Women and the Market.* London, 1996.

BUCKLEY, MARY. *Redefining Russian Society and Polity.* Boulder, 1993.

COLTON, TIMOTHY J., and ROBERT C. TUCKER, ed. *Patterns in Post-Soviet Leadership.* Boulder, 1995.

CONNOR, WALTER D. *Tattered Banners: Labor, Conflict, and Corporatism in Postcommunist Russia.* Boulder, 1996.

CUSHMAN, THOMAS. *Notes from Underground: Rock Music Counterculture in Russia.* Albany, 1995.

CURH 93 (October 1994); 94 (October 1995). The entire issues are devoted to Russia and Eurasia.

DAWISHA, KAREN, and BRUCE PARROTT. *Russia and the New States of Eurasia: The Politics of Upheaval.* Cambridge England, 1994.

———, general eds. *The International Politics of Eurasia.* 8 vols. to date. Armonk, N.Y., 1994–1996. These volumes, edited by different scholars, deal with a wide variety of topics, including religion and the legacy of history.

DROBIZHEVA, LEOKADIA, et al., eds. *Ethnic Conflict in the Post-Soviet World: Case Studies and Analysis.* Armonk, N.Y., 1996.

EPSHTEIN, MIKHAIL. *After the Future: The Paradoxes of Postmodernism and Contemporary Russian Culture.* Amherst, Mass., 1995.

ERNST, MAURICE, MICHAEL ALEXEEV, and PAUL MARER. *Transforming the Core: Restructuring Industrial Enterprises in Russia and Central Europe.* Boulder, 1996.

EROFEYEV, VICTOR, and ANDREW REYNOLDS, eds. *The Penguin Book of New Russian Writing.* London, 1995.

---

*Students who do not read Russian can keep up with current developments by reading weeklies such as *The Current Digest of the Post-Soviet Press, Moscow News US Edition,* or *The Moscow Times.* See also the General Bibliography at the back of the text for a brief treatment of electronic sources available on the Internet and World Wide Web, especially the publications of the Open Media Research Institute.

FESHBACH, MURRAY. *Ecological Disaster: Cleaning Up the Hidden Legacy of the Soviet Regime.* New York, 1995.

FISH, STEVEN M. *Democracy from Scratch: Opposition and Regime in the New Russian Revolution.* Princeton, 1995.

GALEOTTI, MARK. *The Age of Anxiety: Security and Politics in Soviet and Post-Soviet Russia.* London, 1995.

Glas: New Russian Writing. A 1990s periodical published at England's University of Birmingham.

GOLDMAN, MARSHALL I. *Lost Opportunity: Why Economic Reforms in Russia Have Not Worked.* New ed. New York, 1996.

HAHN, JEFFREY W., ed. *Democratization in Russia: The Development of Legislative Institutions.* Armonk, N.Y., 1996.

HANDELMAN, STEPHEN. *Comrade Criminal: Russia's New Mafiya.* New Haven, 1995.

HOLMES, BRIAN, GERALD H. READ, and NATALYA VOSKRESENSKAYA. *Russian Education: Tradition and Transition.* New York, 1995.

ISHAM, HEYWARD, ed. *Remaking Russia: Voices from Within.* Armonk, N.Y., 1995.

JOHNSON, TERESA PELTON, and STEVEN E. MILLER, eds. *Russian Security after the Cold War: Seven Views from Moscow.* Washington, D.C., 1994.

KAGARLITSKY, BORIS. *Restoration in Russia: Why Capitalism Failed.* London, 1995.

KAMPFNER, JOHN. *Inside Yeltsin's Russia: Corruption, Conflict, and Capitalism.* London, 1994.

KARTSEV, VLADIMIR. *!Zhirinovsky!.* New York, 1995.

KNIGHT AMY. *Spies without Cloaks: The KGB's Successors.* Princeton, 1996.

KOLSTOE, PAUL. *Russians in the Former Soviet Republics.* Bloomington, 1995.

KOTKIN, STEPHEN and DAVID WOLFF, eds. *Rediscovering Russia in Asia: Siberia and the Russian Far East.* Armonk, N.Y., 1995.

KRAMER, MARK. *Travels with a Hungary Bear: A Journey to the Russian Heartland.* Boston, 1996.

LAPIDUS, GAIL W., ed. *The New Russia: Troubled Transformation.* Boulder, 1995.

LOWENHARDT, JOHN. *The Reincarnation of Russia: Struggling with the Legacy of Communism, 1990–1994.* Durham, 1995.

MARSH, ROSALIND. *History and Literature in Contemporary Russia.* Washington Square, N.Y., 1995. Ch. 12.

MICHEDLOV, M. P., et al. "Religion in the Mirror of Public Opinion," *RES* 37 (January 1995): 76-84.

MILLAR, JAMES R., and SHARON L. WOLCHIK, eds. *The Social Legacy of Communism.* Washington, D.C., 1994.

MURRAY, DON. *A Democracy of Despots.* Boulder, 1996.

NELSON, LYNN D. and IRINA Y. KUZES. *Radical Reform in Yeltsin's Russia: Political, Economic, and Social Dimensions.* Armonk, N.Y., 1995.

ODOM, WILLIAM E., and ROBERT DUJARRIC. *Commonwealth or Empire?: Russia, Central Asia and the Transcaucasus.* Indianapolis, 1995.

POPOV, NIKOLAI. *The Russian People Speak: Democracy at the Crossroads.* Syracuse, 1995.

Problems of Post-Communism. A bimonthly publication that began in fall 1994 and contains useful articles.

RA'ANAN URI, and KATE MARTIN, eds. *Russia: A Return to Imperialism?* New York, 1996.

RANDOLPH, ELEANOR. *Waking the Tempests: Ordinary Life in the New Russia.* New York, 1996.

REMNICK, DAVID. "Letter from Moscow: Exit the Saints," *The New Yorker* 70 (July 18, 1994): 50–60.

————. "The War for the Kremlin," *The New Yorker* 72 (July 22, 1996): 40–59.

RUBINSTEIN, ALVIN Z., and OLES M. SMOLANSKY, eds. *Regional Power Rivalries in the New Eurasia: Russia, Turkey, and Iran.* Armonk, N.Y., 1995.

RUBLE, BLAIR A. *Money Sings: The Changing Politics of Urban Space in Post-Soviet Yaroslavl.* Washington, D.C., 1995.

RYWKIN, MICHAEL. *Moscow's Lost Empire.* Armonk, N.Y., 1994.

SAIKAL, AMIN, and WILLIAM MALEY, eds. *Russia in Search of Its Future.* Cambridge, England, 1995.

SCANLAN, JAMES P., ed. *Russian Thought after Communism: The Recovery of a Philosophical Heritage.* Armonk, N.Y., 1994.

SHALIN, DMITRI N., ed. *Russian Culture at the Crossroads: Paradoxes of Postcommunist Consciousness.* Boulder, 1996.

SHEARMAN, PETER, ed. *Russian Foreign Policy since 1990.* Boulder, 1995.

SHNEIDMAN, N. N. *Russian Literature, 1988–1994: The End of an Era.* Toronto, 1995.

SMITH, ALAN, ed. *Challenges for Russian Economic Reform.* Washington, D.C., 1995.

SMITH, GRAHAM, ed. *The Nationalities Question in the Post-Soviet States.* London, 1996.

SOLZHENITSYN, ALEKSANDR. *The Russian Question at the End of the Twentieth Century.* New York, 1995.

STAAR, RICHARD F. *The New Military in Russia: Ten Myths that Shaped the Image.* Annapolis, 1996.

STEELE, JONATHAN. *Eternal Russia: Yeltsin, Gorbachev, and the Mirage of Democracy.* Cambridge, Mass., 1994.

"Storm Clouds over Russian Science," *Science* 264 (May 27, 1994): 1259–1282.

WALLANDER, CELESTE A., ed. *The Sources of Russian Foreign Policy after the Cold War.* Boulder, 1996.

WARHOLA, JAMES W. *Politicized Ethnicity in the Russian Federation: Dilemmas of State Formation.* Lewiston, N.Y., 1996.

YAKOVLEV, ALEXANDER M. *Striving for Law in a Lawless Land: Memoirs of a Russian Reformer.* Armonk, N.Y., 1996.

YELTSIN, BORIS. *The Struggle for Russia.* New York, 1994.

YERGIN, DANIEL, and THANE GUSTAFSON. *Russia 2010—And What It Means for the World.* New York, 1995.

Appendix A
Chronology

SOME SIGNIFICANT DATES BEFORE 1855

862	Legendary establishment of Riurikid Dynasty in Novgorod.
988	Conversion of Prince Vladimir to Christianity.
1237–1241	Mongol conquest of Rus.
1240–1242	Alexander Nevsky defeats Swedes and Germanic Knights.
1380	Dmitri Donskoi defeats Mongols, but Mongol control over Russia not completely overthrown until fifteenth century.
1462–1505	Reign of Ivan III, the Great.
1533–1584	Reign of Ivan IV, the Terrible.
1598–1613	Time of Troubles.
1613	Beginning of Romanov Dynasty.
1649	Law Code finalizes serfdom in Russia.
1666–1667	Schism in Russian Orthodox Church.
1669–1671	Rebellion of Stenka Razin.
1689–1725	Reign of Peter I, the Great.
1762–1796	Reign of Catherine II, the Great.
1773–1774	Pugachev's rebellion.
1801–1725	Reign of Alexander I.
1825	Decembrist revolt.
1825–1855	Reign of Nicholas I.
1853–1856	Crimean War.

1855–1996

1855–1917	LATE IMPERIAL RUSSIA.
1855–1881	Reign of Alexander II; Golden Age of the Russian Novel.
1856	Treaty of Paris ends Crimean War.
1857–1867	Herzen publishes *The Bell* (*Kolokol*).

515

1858	Russia and China sign treaties of Aigun and Tientsin.
1859	Russia defeats Chechens.
1860	China recognizes Russian expansion in Treaty of Peking.
1861	Emancipation of serfs; unrest among peasants and students; establishment of St. Petersburg Conservatory.
1862	Publication of Turgenev's *Fathers and Sons.*
1863–1864	Rebellion in Poland, Lithuania, and Belorussia.
1863	University Statute increases faculty rights; government changes liquor laws.
1864	Zemstvo (local government) Reform; Judicial Reform; Russia completes conquest of most of the Caucasus.
1864–1885	Russia conquers much of Central Asia.
1866	Karakozov's attempted assassination of Alexander II; P. Shuvalov becomes head of Third Section until 1874; Dostoevsky's *Crime and Punishment* published.
1867	Sale of Alaska and Aleutian Islands to the United States.
1869	Nechaev murder of student Ivanov.
1870	Birth of Vladimir Ulianov (Lenin); formation of the Wanderers (group of painters).
1871	London Convention agrees to abolition of the Black Sea clauses of the Treaty of Paris.
1873	Formation of Three Emperors' League.
1874	Universal Military Service Statute becomes law; thousands of radicals "go to the people."
1875	Japan recognizes Sakhalin as Russian possession in Treaty of St. Petersburg.
1876	Foundation of Land and Liberty party.
1877	Tolstoy's *Anna Karenina* completed.
1877–1878	Russo-Turkish War.
1878	Treaty of San Stefano; Congress of Berlin.
1879	Land and Liberty divides into People's Will and Black Repartition.
1879–1880	Unsuccessful attempts on life of Alexander II.
1880	Death of Empress Maria and remarriage of Alexander II; Dostoevsky's *Brothers Karamazov* completed.
1880–1881	General Loris-Melikov oversees dealing with terrorists.
1880–1905	Pobedonostsev serves as procurator of Holy Synod.
1881	Members of the People's Will assassinate Alexander II.
1881–1894	Reign of Alexander III.
1881	Government decrees "temporary regulations"; anti-Jewish pogroms in Ukraine; Three Emperors' Alliance signed; renewed for three years in 1884.
1882	Law prohibits factories from hiring children under twelve or from employing those aged twelve to fifteen more than eight hours a day.
1883	Death of Karl Marx; establishment of first Russian Marxist organization, the Emancipation of Labor, in Geneva.

1884	University Statutes curtail university autonomy.
1885	Russia and Britain agree on Russo-Afghan frontier; Nobles' Land Bank established.
1887	"Reinsurance Treaty" between Russia and Germany; Alexander Ulianov (brother of Lenin) hanged.
1889	Land captains established.
1890	Decree on zemstvos strengthens government's power over them.
1891	Construction of Trans-Siberian Railway begins.
1891–1892	Famine in European Russia.
1892–1903	S. Witte serves as finance minister.
1894	Final ratification of Franco-Russian Alliance (1893 O.S.).
1894–1917	Reign of Nicholas II; Silver Age of Russian culture.
1896	Coronation ceremonies of Nicholas II in Moscow.
1897	First All-Russian Census.
1898	First Congress of the Russian Social Democratic Labor party (RSDLP).
1899–1904	Russification in Finland.
1901	Party of Socialist Revolutionaries (SRs) founded.
1903	Second Congress of RSDLP in Brussels and London; Union of Liberation formed; anti-Jewish pogrom in Kishinev.
1904–1905	Russo-Japanese War.
1905	
Jan. 9	Bloody Sunday.
Feb.	All-Russian Union for Women's Equality founded.
Apr.	Government edict permits Orthodox believers to convert to other faiths.
May	Japan defeats Russia in battle of Tsushima Straits.
June	Revolt on the Battleship Potemkin.
Aug.	Publication of draft law for a consultative Duma.
Sept.	Peace of Portsmouth ends Russo-Japanese War.
Oct.	All-Russian general strike; formation of a Soviet of Workers' Deputies in St. Petersburg; Constitutional Democratic party (Kadets) formed.
Oct. 17	October Manifesto of Nicholas II promises formation of an elected legislative Duma.
Oct.–Dec.	Pogroms in Odessa and other cities; soviets established in other Russian towns.
1905–1907	Peasant disturbances.
1906	
Mar.	Government grants unions the right to gain legal status.
Apr.	Publication of Fundamental Laws; convening of First Duma.
July	Nicholas II dissolves First Duma; appointment of P. Stolypin as prime minister; Vyborg Manifesto.
1906–1911	Stolypin land reform.
1907	
Feb.–June	Second Duma in existence.

June	New electoral law promulgated.
Aug.	Anglo-Russian Entente relating to Persia.
Nov.	Third ("Masters'") Duma convenes, lasts until 1912.
1909	Publication of *Vekhi* essays.
1911	Assassination of Stolypin.
1912	Troops fire on Workers at Lena goldfields; Fourth Duma convenes, lasts until 1917.
1913	Stravinsky's *The Rite of Spring* creates an uproar in Paris.
1914–1918	First World War.
1914	Germany declares war on Russia; prohibition decreed.
1915	Formation of War Industries Committee and of Duma's Progressive Bloc; Nicholas goes to Mogilev to command troops personally.
1916	Murder of Rasputin.

(Gregorian dates below)
1917

Mar. 8	Petrograd women demonstrate on International Women's Day; crowds demand bread.
Mar. 11	Tsar Nicholas orders Duma dissolved; demonstrators fired on.
Mar. 11–12	Petrograd soldiers join rebellion.
Mar. 12	Formation of Petrograd Soviet of Worker's Deputies; State Duma members form Provisional Committee.
Mar. 14	Order No. 1 issued by Petrograd Soviet.
Mar. 15	Abdication of Tsar Nicholas I; formation of Provisional Government by committee of Duma.
Mar.–Nov. 1917–	PROVISIONAL GOVERNMENT PERIOD.
Apr. 16	Lenin returns from exile in Switzerland.
Apr. 17	Lenin proclaims his "April Theses."
May 3	Miliukov message reaffirming common goals of Allies published, sparking demonstrations.
May 15	Resignation of Miliukov.
May 17	Trotsky returns from exile in United States.
May 18	Provisional Government forms first Coalition Government; Kerensky becomes minister of war.
June 16	First All-Russian Congress of Soviets convenes.
July 1	Provisional Government launches military offensive in Galicia.
July 15	Policy toward Ukraine causes four Kadet ministers to resign.
July 16–18	"July Days" demonstrations and unrest.
July 24	Kerensky becomes prime minister.
July 29	General Kornilov appointed commander of army.
Aug. 5	Arrest of Trotsky.
Aug. 6	Kerensky forms new cabinet.
Aug. 25–28	Moscow State Conference meets.
Sept. 7–12	Kornilov heads failed counterrevolutionary movement.
Oct.	Trotsky becomes head of Petrograd Soviet; Military Revolutionary Committee created by Petrograd Soviet.

Nov. 6	Provisional Government orders closing of Bolshevik press.
Nov. 7	Forces loyal to Military Revolutionary Committee seize important positions in Petrograd; Second All-Russian Congress of Soviets meets.

1917–1991	SOVIET PERIOD
Nov. 8	Soviet troops take over Winter Palace; Congress of Soviets approves Lenin's decrees on peace and land and forms new Bolshevik-dominated government headed by Lenin.
Nov. 15	Soviet government issues a Declaration of the Rights of the Peoples of Russia.
Nov. 25–27	Constituent Assembly elections.
Dec. 15	Armistice agreed upon by Russia and the Central Powers.
Dec. 20	Cheka established.
1918–1921	Civil War.
1918	
Jan.	Constituent Assembly meets briefly before Bolsheviks dissolve it.
Feb.	Patriarch Tikhon criticizes Bolsheviks; division of church from state and schools.
Mar.	Brest-Litovsk Treaty; beginning of Allied intervention; Trotsky becomes head of the Red Army.
July	First Soviet constitution adopted; execution of Nicholas II and his family. German ambassador assassinated.
Aug.	Lenin wounded in an assassination attempt.
Nov.	End of World War I.
1919	
Mar.	Comintern (Communist International) is formed; establishment of Politburo and Orgburo; Eighth Party Congress meets.
Spring	Communist governments briefly in power in Hungary and Bavaria.
Oct.	White armies pose greatest threat as General Denikin captures Orel and General Yudenich threatens Petrograd.
1920	Russia signs peace treaties with Estonia, Lithuania, and Latvia.
Jan.	Lifting of Allied blockade.
Feb.	Admiral Kolchak executed.
Apr.–Oct.	War with Poland.
Sept.	Comintern organizes a Congress of Peoples of the East, which meets in Baku.
Nov.	Abortion legalized; Wrangel defeated and evacuates Crimea; Czechoslovak Corps completes evacuation of Russian Far East.
1921	
Feb.	Tiflis (Tbilisi) captured by Red Army.

Feb.–Mar.	Friendship treaties with Persia, Afghanistan, and Turkey.
Mar.	Kronstadt Revolt smashed; Tenth Party Congress bans factionalism; NEP is begun; Anglo-Soviet Trade Agreement; Treaty of Riga determines Russian-Polish border.
1921–1922	Famine along the Volga and in southern Ukraine.
1922	New Criminal Code drawn up and promulgated.
Mar.–Apr.	Eleventh Party Congress meets; Stalin assumes the party post of general secretary.
Apr.	Russia signs Treaty of Rapallo with Germany.
May	Lenin suffers first stroke.
Oct.	Japan evacuates Vladivostok.
Dec.	Lenin has second stroke; Union of Soviet Socialist Republics (USSR) formed.
1923	Lenin suffers third stroke; Comintern encourages uprising by German Communists.
1924	Lenin dies and USSR Constitution approved (both in January). USSR recognized officially by Great Britain, Italy, and France; "Zinoviev letter" harms British-Soviet relations.
1925	Trotsky is removed as war commissar.
1926	Zinoviev and Kamenev form a leftist alliance with Trotsky; all three men are dismissed from Politburo. New Russian Family Code makes divorce easier to obtain. Treaty of Berlin between USSR and Germany.
1927	Britain breaks diplomatic relations with the USSR; war-scare in Russia. Russia breaks diplomatic relations with China.
1928–1932	First Five-Year Plan.
1928	Trotsky exiled to Kazakhstan; Shakhty trial.
1929	Trotsky forced to leave USSR. Right Opposition squelched and Bukharin kicked off of Politburo; beginning of forced collectivization. Diplomatic relations with Britain resumed.
1930	Pravda article "Dizzy with Success" written by Stalin; Industrial-party trial.
1931	Trial of Mensheviks; neutrality treaty renewed with Lithuania (first signed in 1926); Manchuria invaded by Japan.
1932	Riutin "plot"; government introduces mandatory internal passports for urban dwellers; diplomatic relations resumed with China; non-aggression pacts signed with China, Finland, Latvia, Estonia, Poland, and France.
1932–1933	Widespread famine in Ukraine and elsewhere.
1933–1937	Second Five-Year Plan.
1933	Hitler assumes the post of German chancellor; USSR officially recognized by USA.
1934	
Jan.–Feb.	Seventeenth Party Congress meets.
Aug.	Formation of the First Congress of Union of Soviet Writers.
Sept.	League of Nations admits Soviet Union.

Dec.	Kirov is assassinated.
1935	Stakhanovite movement begins. Chinese Eastern Railway sold to Manchukuo. Russia signs alliance treaties with France and Czechoslovakia.
1936–1938	Great Terror's most intense phase.
1936	
June	Divorce made more difficult by new family law; abortions outlawed except when a mother's health endangered.
July	Start of the Spanish Civil War.
Aug.	Kamenev, Zinoviev, and other members of "Left Opposition" put on trial.
Dec.	New constitution adopted.
1937	
Jan.	Piatakov, Radek, and others put on trial.
June	Marshal Tukhachevsky tried and executed.
Aug.	Major purge of Ukrainian leaders begins.
1938	Third Five-Year Plan begun; publication of Stalin's *History of the All-Union Communist Party: Short Course*; Soviet and Japanese border clashes in Far East.
Mar.	Bukharin, Rykov, Yagoda, and others put on trial.
Sept.	Munich Conference opens the door to the dismemberment of Czechoslovakia.
Dec.	Yezhov succeeded by Beria as head of the NKVD.
1939	
Summer	Soviet-Japanese troops clash along Mongolian frontier.
Aug.	Nazi-Soviet Pact.
Sept.	World War II in Europe begins with German invasion of western Poland; Russia takes over eastern Polish territory.
1939–1940	Russo-Finnish "Winter War."
1940	Russia annexes Baltic states, as well as Bessarabia and Bukovina (from Rumania); Trotsky assassinated in Mexico.
1941	
June	USSR is invaded by Germany.
Sept.	Kiev falls; Leningrad blockade is initiated.
Oct.	Moscow is threatened; some of the city is evacuated.
Dec.	Battle of Moscow; U.S. enters WWII.
1942–1943	Battle of Stalingrad.
1943	
May	Comintern abolished.
July	Battle of Kursk; Allied invasion of Sicily.
Sept.	Patriarchate is reestablished.
Nov.–Dec.	Teheran Conference.
1944	
Jan.	Siege of Leningrad ended.
June	Allied landing at Normandy Beach (D-Day) establishes "Second Front."

1945

Feb.	Yalta Conference.
May 8	German surrender to Soviet forces.
July–Aug.	Potsdam Conference.
Aug.	USSR enters war against Japan.
Sept.	Japan surrenders.
1946–1950	Fourth Five-Year Plan.

1946

Feb.	Stalin's remobilization speech to Supreme Soviet.
Mar.	Churchill's "Iron Curtain" speech in Missouri.
Aug.	Zhdanov begins attach on Zoshchenko, Akhmatova, and other cultural figures.
1947	"Reform" of currency in USSR; Truman Doctrine and Marshall Plan announced in U.S.; Cominform founded.

1948

Feb.	Czechoslovakian Communist takeover.
June	Cominform ejects Yugoslavia; Berlin Blockade begins (lasting until May 1949).
Aug.	Zhdanov dies.
1949	Chinese Communists defeat Nationalist China.
1950	Sino-Soviet mutual assistance treaty signed.
1950–1953	Korean War.
1951–1955	Fifth Five-Year Plan.
1952	Nineteenth Party Congress meets.

1953

Jan.	"Doctors plot" alleged.
Mar.	Stalin dies; Malenkov appointed prime minister.
June	Beria is arrested and executed later in the year.
Sept.	Khrushchev officially named first secretary of the Communist party.
1954	Khrushchev begins virgin-lands campaign; Khrushchev and Bulganin visit China.
1955	Abortion legalized.
Feb.	Malenkov replaced by Bulganin as prime minister.
May	West Germany joins NATO; Warsaw Pact established; agreement signed to end Four-Power occupation of Austria; Bulganin and Khrushchev visit Yugoslavia.
July	Geneva Summit.
Sept.	USSR and West Germany establish diplomatic relations.

1956

Feb.	Khrushchev's "secret speech" at Twentieth Party Congress.
Oct.–Nov.	Soviet troops crush Hungarian revolt and support Kádár as new Hungarian leader.

1957

June	Khrushchev defeats attempt of "anti-party group" to remove him as party first secretary.

Sept.	Nuclear accident near Cheliabinsk.
Oct.	Sputnik I launched; Defense Minister Zhukov is dismissed.
1958	
Feb.	Khrushchev begins antireligious crusade.
Mar.	Khrushchev becomes prime minister, replacing Bulganin.
Oct.	Nobel Prize for literature awarded to Pasternak.
Dec.	Promulgation of school reforms and new criminal code.
1959–1965	Seven-Year Plan.
1959	Khrushchev visits United States.
1960	U.S. U-2 spy plane shot down over USSR; Sino-Soviet split begins to emerge.
1961	
Apr.	Yuri Gagarin becomes first cosmonaut in space.
June	Khrushchev and Kennedy hold summit in Geneva.
Aug.	Berlin Wall constructed.
Oct.	Twenty-Second Party Congress meets; removal of Stalin's body from mausoleum.
1962	
June	Demonstrators killed in Novocherkassk.
Oct.	Cuban missile crisis.
Nov.	Solzhenitsyn's *One Day in the Life of Ivan Denisovich* is published.
1963	Nuclear Test Ban Treaty signed; bad harvest.
1964	Khrushchev is replaced by Brezhnev as first secretary of the Communist party (Oct.).
1966–1970	Eighth Five-Year Plan.
1966	Siniavsky-Daniel trial.
1967	Andropov becomes KGB head.
1968	
Apr.	First appearance of *A Chronicle of Current Events*.
July	Nuclear Nonproliferation Treaty signed by USA and USSR.
Aug.	Soviet and other Warsaw Pact troops invade Czechoslovakia.
1969	Soviet-Chinese border skirmishes.
1970	Nobel Prize for literature awarded to Solzhenitsyn.
1971–1975	Ninth Five-Year Plan.
1972	U.S. President Nixon goes to Moscow and signs SALT treaties.
1973	Brezhnev-Nixon summit in USA.
1974	
Feb.	Solzhenitsyn is deported from USSR.
June–July	Nixon-Brezhnev hold Moscow summit.
Nov.	Brezhnev-Ford summit at Vladivostok.
1975	
Aug. 1	Helsinki Accords signed.
Dec.	Elena Bonner receives Nobel Peace Prize in Oslo in behalf of her husband, Andrei Sakharov.
1976–1980	Tenth Five-Year Plan.

1976	Helsinki Watch Groups formed in Russian Republic, Armenia, Georgia, Lithuania, and Ukraine.
1977	
June	General Secretary Brezhnev also becomes president of USSR.
Oct.	New Soviet Constitution adopted.
1978	Caucasian demonstrations over Kremlin attempts to weaken the use of native languages.
1979	
June	Brezhnev-Carter summit in Vienna, SALT II signed (though not later ratified).
Dec.	Beginning of Soviet military operations in Afghanistan.
1980	
Jan.	Politburo exiles Sakharov to Gorky.
July–Aug.	Summer Olympic Games in Moscow.
1981–1985	Eleventh Five-Year Plan.
1981	Martial law declared in Poland and Solidarity trade union banned.
1982	Brezhnev dies (Nov.); Andropov becomes Communist party general secretary.
1983	Soviet plane shoots down Korean jetliner carrying 269 passengers.
1984	Andropov dies (Feb.); Chernenko becomes Communist party general secretary.
1985	
Mar.	Chernenko dies; Gorbachev becomes party general secretary.
Nov.	Gorbachev-Reagan summit in Geneva.
1986–1990	Twelfth Five-Year Plan.
1986	
Apr.	Accident at the Chernobyl nuclear power plant.
Oct.	Gorbachev-Reagan summit in Reykjavik, Iceland.
Dec.	Demonstrations in Kazakhstan; Sakharov released from exile in Gorky.
1987	
June	A new Enterprise Law is adopted, effective as of Jan. 1, 1988.
Oct.	Nobel Prize for literature awarded to émigré poet Joseph Brodsky.
Dec.	Gorbachev-Reagan summit and signing of INF Treaty in Washington, D.C.
1988	
Feb.	Armenian demonstrations over Nagorno-Karabakh; anti-Armenian pogrom in Sumgait, Azerbaijan.
May–June	Gorbachev-Reagan summit in Moscow.
June	Millennium of Christianity coming to Kievan Rus observed; Nineteenth Party Conference opens in Moscow.
Dec.	Earthquake hits Armenia; Gorbachev and Reagan meet in New York.

1989

Feb.	Final Soviet troops withdraw from Afghanistan.
Mar.	Elections for Congress of People's Deputies.
May–June	Congress of People's Deputies and the reformed Supreme Soviet hold meetings; Gorbachev elected chairman of new Supreme Soviet (USSR president).
Aug.–Dec.	Collapse of East European Communist governments.
Dec.	Death of Sakharov.

1990

Feb.	Massive pro-democracy rally in Moscow; Central Committee votes to allow a multiparty system.
Mar–Aug.	Various republics declare their independence and/or sovereignty.
May	Yeltsin elected president of Russian Republic by its Congress of People's Deputies.
May–June	Gorbachev-Bush summit in Washington, D.C.
Oct.	Reunification of East and West Germany.
Nov.	CFE Treaty signed in Paris.
Dec.	Shevardnadze resigns as foreign minister warning that dictatorship is approaching.

1991

Jan.	Soviet troops storm a government building in Vilnius, killing fourteen people.
Mar.	Major strike of miners begins.
June	Yeltsin elected by popular vote as president of Russian Republic.
July	Gorbachev-Bush summit and signing of START Treaty in Moscow.
Aug.	Defeat of attempted Moscow coup.
Sept.	Soviet government recognizes independence of three Baltic republics.
Dec.	Russia, Ukraine, and Belorussia establish the Commonwealth of Independent States (CIS) and declare the USSR disbanded; Gorbachev resigns.
Dec. 1991–	POST-SOVIET PERIOD.
1992	Yeltsin's "shock therapy" stimulates inflation; Federation Treaty signed between Russia's central government and most of its administrative-territorial units.

1993

Jan.	START-2 Treaty signed in Moscow.
Mar.	Yeltsin declares emergency presidential rule.
Apr.	Yeltsin-Clinton summit in Vancouver.
Sept.	Yeltsin decrees dissolution of Russian parliament.
Oct.	Troops loyal to Yeltsin fire on the Russian parliamentary building.
Dec.	New Russian constitution approved and new parliament

elected; LDP, led by right-wing extremist V. Zhirinovsky, becomes largest party in Duma.

1994

Feb.   Moscow signs treaty with Tatarstan granting it considerable autonomy.

Dec.   Russian invasion of secessionist Chechnia begins.

1995

May   Yeltsin-Clinton summit in Moscow.

June   Russian-Ukrainian agreement on Black Sea fleet.

Oct.   Yeltsin-Clinton summit in Hyde Park, N.Y.

Dec.   Communist party becomes largest party in Duma as a result of new Duma elections.

1996

Jan.   E. Primakov replaces A. Kozyrev as Russian foreign minister.

Apr.   G-7 leaders and Yeltsin meet in Moscow; Yeltsin visits China.

June–July   Yeltsin wins two-stage presidential election.

Aug.   Yeltsin inaugurated as first elected president of independent Russia.

Appendix B
Glossary

Article 87 of the Fundamental Laws of 1906 by this article the tsar between Duma sessions could decree emergency laws that could continue in force for up to sixty days after a new session convened.

Black Hundreds early twentieth-century extreme right-wing organizations, especially their more activist, violent followers; often characterized by strong antisemitism.

Black Sea (or Turkish) Straits two straits, the Bosphorus (or Bosporus) and Dardanelles, necessary for ships to pass through to get from the Black Sea to the Mediterranean Sea.

Bolsheviks a Marxist group led by Lenin that emerged in 1903 during the second congress of the Russian Social Democratic Labor party (RSDLP). This faction eventually became a separate party.

Brezhnev Doctrine the name applied to Soviet justification for intervention in Soviet bloc countries. The doctrine was enunciated in 1968 and stated that "the sovereignty of each socialist country cannot be set up in opposition to the interests of the socialist world."

CMEA (or COMECON) Council for Mutual Economic Assistance, an International Communist economic alliance, founded in 1949.

Central Committee (CC) of the Communist party the most powerful and prestigious group of its size throughout most of the Soviet era. Its powers diminished, however, as it became larger—in 1923 it contained 57 full and candidate members, but by the late 1980s, almost 500 such members, who met together only a few times a year.

Cheka Soviet security police, 1917–1922, its functions were subsequently assumed by the GPU, OGPU, NKVD, MVD, MGB, and KGB.

CIS Commonwealth of Independent States, formed in December 1991 by all of the former Soviet republics except Estonia, Latvia, Lithuania, and Georgia. Georgia subsequently joined in 1994.

civil society a social sphere standing between the government and the family or individual, in which people can freely interact and create their own independent organizations.

collectivization the process begun in 1929 of forcing peasants onto collective farms and, to a lesser extent, state farms (kolkhozes and sovkhozes).

Cominform Communist Information Bureau, an organization of European Communist parties founded in 1947 under Soviet leadership; ended in 1956.

527

Comintern Communist International, the international organization of Communist parties, 1919–1943.

command economy a term frequently used to describe the centrally planned economy that began developing in Soviet Russia with the introduction of the First Five-Year Plan in 1928.

commissar the title of a high-ranking official. Although the Provisional Government appointed some commissars, the term was popularized by its Soviet use. In military units, political commissars were party representatives given sweeping powers.

Constructivism a movement in art and architecture, primarily in the 1920s. The Constructivist (or Functionalist) architects believed that modern technology and materials and the utilitarian purpose of a building should determine its form.

Cossack originally a free frontiersman. The two largest concentrations of Cossacks were in the lower Dnieper and Don river regions.

Council of State (also Imperial State Council) an advisory body created by Alexander I in 1810; in 1906, it was transformed into the upper house of the new Russian legislature.

cultural revolution an attack encouraged by Stalin from 1928 to 1931 against bourgeois cultural influences and NEP's relative cultural tolerance. It aimed to weaken existing cultural authorities and tendencies and produce a new cultural elite more representative of the masses and susceptible to party control.

dekulakization the expropriation of kulak (see below) property, often accompanied by other repressive measures such as exile.

destalinization the policy begun under Khrushchev of selectively criticizing Stalin and attempting to rectify some of his harmful measures.

détente the relaxation of Cold War tensions, especially between the USSR and the USA in the early and mid 1970s.

duma a council.

Duma lower house of legislature which met from 1906 to early 1917; the 1993 Russian constitution also established a 450-seat Duma as the lower house of a new parliament.

Federation Council established as the upper house of a new parliament by the 1993 Russian constitution. Each Russian territorial unit has two representatives on the council.

FYP Five-Year Plan.

general (or first) secretary of the Communist party the highest executive officer in the party and the most important leadership position from the death of Lenin until the late 1980s (*see* Secretariat).

glasnost openness, especially Gorbachev's policy of more freedom of expression and less censorship and government secrecy.

GPU security police, 1922–1923.

Great Purge *see* Great Terror.

great retreat a phenomenon of the mid 1930s that also has been variously labeled "the revolution betrayed" (Trotsky) and "internal détente" (Tucker). Stalin's "retreat" diluted some strands of revolutionary Marxism-Leninism by placing more emphasis on stability, social hierarchy, Russian nationalism, and motherhood and family.

Great Terror Stalin's campaign of mass arrests and executions in the late 1930s, especially between 1936 and 1938.

Gulag initials for Labor-Camp Administration, more generally the Soviet penal system, especially under Stalin.

Holy Synod chief administrative body of the Russian Orthodox Church in Imperial Russia, created by Peter I in 1721 and in 1722 placed under the supervision of a procurator.

ICBM intercontinental ballistic missile.

Imperial State Council *see* Council of State.

intelligentsia intellectuals; in Late Imperial Russia, often used more narrowly for those thinking people who maintained that Russia's sociopolitical order was unjust, especially to the lower classes. During the Soviet period, Soviet authorities used the term very broadly as a synonym for "mental-workers." In 1984, more than 42 million Soviet citizens were classified in this category.

Kadet (or Constitutional Democratic) party a liberal party founded in 1905 and later suppressed by the Communists.

KGB initials for the security police from 1954 to 1991.

Kingdom of Poland (also known as Congress Poland) a term used from 1815 to 1864 to designate a western portion of Poland gained by Russia in the Napoleonic Wars. It was originally granted some autonomy, but revolts in 1830 and 1863–1864 led to the loss of most of its special status.

kolkhoz collective farm.

kolkhoznik a worker on a kolkhoz.

Komsomol Young Communist League; an organization founded in 1918 for individuals ages 14–28.

kulak by definition a rich peasant, though Stalin applied the term to many peasants who were not wealthy but opposed his policies.

mafias organized crime organizations.

Mensheviks a Marxist group that emerged in 1903 during the second congress of the Russian Social Democratic Labor party (RSDLP). This faction was critical of Lenin's authoritarian plans for the party. The Mensheviks eventually became a separate party and were suppressed during the early Soviet period.

metropolitan a high-ranking bishop in the Orthodox Church; the chief Orthodox religious leader in Kievan Rus and Russia until Russia received its first patriarch in 1589.

mir the peasant commune; the Russian word also means *universe* and *peace*.

Molotov cocktail a home-made bomb, often a bottle filled with gasoline and fitted with a rag or wick that was lit before hurling.

MTS Machine-Tractor Station(s), in existence from 1929 to 1958.

MVD Russian initials for Ministry of Internal Affairs.

narod nation, people, especially the common people.

narodnik *see* populist.

Near Abroad a post-Soviet Russian term for neighboring countries that had formerly been part of the USSR.

NEP New Economic Policy; the government's economic policy from 1921 until Stalin ended it in 1928–1929.

Nepmen private businessmen during the NEP era.

nihilist a radical of the 1860s who was critical of traditional authorities and thought that nothing (*nihil*), including family, society, or religion, should be accepted that was not based on reason.

NKVD Russian initials for the People's Commissariat of Internal Affairs. From 1934 until 1946 it handled security-police operations earlier performed by OGPU.

nomenklatura a system and lists by which the Communist party appointed people to important positions; also the people on these lists.

obshchestvo   society, often used to designate educated society, as contrasted to the *narod* (common people).

obshchina   peasant commune.

Octobrists   members of the "Union of October 17," a moderate liberal political party active in the 1905–1917 period; they wished to implement the promises of Nicholas II's October Manifesto of 1905.

OGPU   security police, 1923–1934.

Old Believers (Old Ritualists)   a name applied to those who refused to go along with Patriarch Nikon's changes in the Russian Orthodox Church. They were excommunicated in 1667, and formed their own religious communities, some of which continue to the present day.

Orgburo   Organizational Bureau of the Central Committee of the Communist party. Originally charged with directing the organizational work of the party, including that of the Secretariat. Stalin abolished it in 1952. Its powers were assumed by the Secretariat and new party Presidium (basically the old Politburo).

patriarch   the title of the heads of the chief Orthodox Churches. Until 1589, when the Russian Orthodox Church received its own patriarch, this church was under the jurisdiction of the patriarch of Constantinople.

perestroika   restructuring, especially Gorbachev's policy of economic and, to a lesser extent, political and social, restructuring.

Politburo (Presidium, 1952–1966)   Political Bureau of the Central Committee of the Communist party. Throughout most of the Soviet post-Stalin era, this supreme policy-making body possessed ten to sixteen full members, plus candidate members.

populist (*narodnik*)   a socialist of the 1870–1890s period who emphasized the welfare of the common people, expecially the peasants.

postmodernism   in the context of Russian literature during the late 1980s and 1990s, the term implies the rejection of traditional values and styles, whether those advocated by Soviet authorities or by traditionalists such as Solzhenitsyn. Postmodernist writings reflect more of a concern with literary experimentation and "art for art's sake" than with appealing to any large readership.

Presidium of the Supreme Soviet   the executive committee of the Supreme Soviet.

raznochintsy   a term applied to those who had abandoned the sociolegal estate (*soslovie*) of their parents but had not officially joined another estate.

revtribunal   revolutionary tribunal, a type of court created in 1917, but ended during the NEP period.

RSFSR   Russian Soviet Federated Socialist Republic.

ruble   a basic Russian monetary unit; worth about one-half of a U.S. dollar before World War I.

SALT   Strategic Arms Limitation Talks between the USA and USSR.

samizdat   underground self-published literature, usually circulating in typed or mimeographed copies.

samogon   moonshine; home-brewed vodka.

Secretariat (of the Central Committee of the Communist party)   originally created to assist the Orgburo and Politburo in carrying out party work, Stalin strengthened its functions after becoming party general secretary in 1922. In 1978, it was headed by General Secretary Brezhnev and also consisted of ten other secretaries (including Suslov and Chernenko), each in charge of at least one department.

Senate   an administrative and judicial body of Imperial Russia, created by Peter I in 1711 and in 1722 placed under the supervision of a procurator general.

serf   a peasant bound to a master's estate (unless permitted to work elsewhere in exchange for compensation).

socialist realism   a doctrine the party attempted to impose on literature and other arts from 1932 until the late 1980s. By its dictates writers and other artists were to portray life in such a way as to help foster the creation of the socialist order, and they were to do so in a "realistic" manner that could be understood by the people. The doctrine opposed "bourgeois formalism, experimentalism, and aestheticism."

soslovie   sociolegal estate in Imperial Russia, for example, that of the nobility.

soviet   council; in 1905, many soviets, primarily of workers' deputies, sprang up during the turbulence of that year; during 1917, they again sprang up and eventually the term became associated with the new Communist government.

sovkhoz   state farm.

sputnik   a Soviet-produced space satellite.

SR   Socialist Revolutionary (party).

START (Strategic Arms Reduction Talks) Treaty   signed by Bush and Gorbachev in July 1991. It promised approximately a 30 percent cut in long-range nuclear weapons over the next seven years. Delayed by the breakup of the USSR, it went into effect in December 1994.

START-2 Treaty   signed in Moscow, January 1993; by it the U.S. and Russia agreed to further drastic reductions during the next decade in their nuclear arsenals and to completely eliminate nuclear multiwarhead land-based missiles. But by the beginning of August 1996, it had not been ratified by the Russian parliament.

Supreme Soviet   according to Soviet constitutions of 1936 and 1977, the USSR's highest legislative body. It replaced the All-Union Congress of Soviets. It continued in existence until 1991, though its makeup and powers were changed under Gorbachev. A Russian Supreme Soviet continued to exist until 1993.

Table of Ranks   fourteen parallel ranks for officers and officials in each branch of state service: the military, civil service, and at court; established by Peter I and continued, with a few minor modifications, until 1917.

tamizdat   foreign-published forbidden works of Soviet authors.

Third Section   political police agency from 1826 to 1880.

Uniate (or Greek Catholic) Church   created by Union of Brest (1596). It allowed converted Orthodox to maintain their Orthodox rites and customs in exchange for recognizing the supremacy of the pope.

virgin land's policy   Khrushchev's policy of opening up to agricultural production millions of acres, primarily in northern Kazakhstan and southwestern Siberia.

volost   township, canton, or district.

War Communism   term for Soviet authoritarian economic policies during the Civil War.

zemstvo   local government body at the district and provincial levels in Late Imperial Russia.

General Bibliography*

1. JOURNALS AND ANTHOLOGIES CITED IN SUGGESTED SOURCES: A LIST OF ABBREVIATIONS

AHR *American Historical Review*
BCWIHP *Bulletin of the Cold War International History Project*, 1992–. Published by the Wilson International Center for Scholars, Washington, D.C.
CH *Church History*
CMR *Cahiers du Monde Russe*
CURH *Current History*
CPER *Current Politics and Economics of Russia*
EER Raleigh, Donald J., ed., and A. A. Iskenderov, comp. *The Emperors and Empresses of Russia: Rediscovering the Romanovs.* Armonk, N.Y., 1996.
JMH *Journal of Modern History*
JSH *Journal of Social History*
MERSH Wieczynski, Joseph L., ed. *Modern Encyclopedia of Russian and Soviet History.* 58 vols. Gulf Breeze, Fla., 1976–1994. A source of great value.
PC *Problems of Communism*
RES *Russian Education and Society*
RH *Russian History*
RR *Russian Review*
RSH *Russian Studies in History*
RSSR *Russian Social Science Review*
SSH *Soviet Studies in History*
SR *Slavic Review*

---

*See Suggested Sources at the end of each chapter for more specific works. Some works dealing with Russia before 1855 can be found at the end of Chapter 1; for more complete listings, see Volume I of this text.

2. BIBLIOGRAPHICAL WORKS

American Bibliography of Slavic and East European Studies. (also available electronically by subscription from University of Illinois at Urbana–Champaign.) Published annually since 1957 at various locations. Originally published as the *American Bibliography of Russian and East European Studies*.

Black, J. L. *Origins, Evolution, and Nature of the Cold War: An Annotated Bibliographic Guide*. Santa Barbara, Calif., 1986.

Bloomberg, Marty, and Buckley Barry Barrett. *Stalin: An Annotated Guide to Books in English*. San Bernardino, Calif., 1993 (1995 printing).

Croucher, Murlin. *Slavic Studies: A Guide to Bibliographies, Encyclopedias, and Handbooks*. Wilmington, Del., 1993.

Edelheit, Abraham J., and Hershel Edelheit. *The Rise and Fall of the Soviet Union: A Selected Bibliography of Sources in English*. Westport, Conn., 1992.

Egan, David R., and Melinda A. Egan. *Russian Autocrats from Ivan the Great to the Fall of the Romanov Dynasty: An Annotated Bibliography of English Language Sources to 1985*. Metuchen, N.J., 1987. Especially good for journal and anthology articles.

European Bibliography of Soviet, East European, and Slavonic Studies. Birmingham, England. Annually since 1975.

Fitzpatrick, Sheila, and Lynne Viola. *A Researcher's Guide to Sources on Soviet Social History in the 1930s*. Armonk, N.Y., 1990.

Hammond, Thomas Taylor. *Soviet Foreign Relations and World Communism: A Selected, Annotated Bibliography of 7,000 Books in 30 Languages*. Princeton, 1965.

Heleniak, Timothy E. *Bibliography of Soviet/Russian Statistical Handbooks* (with a 1990 Update). Newtonville, Mass., 1992.

Johnston, Robert H. *Soviet Foreign Policy, 1918–1945: A Guide to Research and Research Materials*. Wilmington, Del., 1991.

Kavass, Igor I. *Demise of the Soviet Union: A Bibliographic Survey of English Writings on the Soviet Legal System, 1990–1991*. Buffalo, 1992.

———. *Gorbachev's Law: A Bibliographic Survey of English Writings on Soviet Legal Developments, 1987–1990*. Buffalo, 1991.

———. *Soviet Law in English: Research Guide and Bibliography, 1970–1987*. Buffalo, 1988.

Martianov, N. N. *Books Available in English by Russians and on Russia, Published in the United States*. New York, 1960.

Nerhood, Harry W., comp. *To Russia and Return: An Annotated Bibliography of Travelers' English-Language Accounts of Russia from the Ninth Century to the Present*. Columbus, Ohio, 1968.

Pearson, Raymond. *Russia and Eastern Europe, 1789–1985: A Bibliographic Guide*. Manchester, England, 1989.

Pierce, Richard. *Soviet Central Asia: A Bibliography*. 3 vols. Berkeley, 1966.

Proffer, Carl R., and Ronald Meyer. *Nineteenth-Century Russian Literature in English: A Bibliography of Criticism and Translations*. Ann Arbor, 1990.

Ruthchild, Rochelle Goldberg. *Women in Russia and the Soviet Union: An Annotated Bibliography*. New York, 1993.

Schaffner, Bradley L. *Bibliography of the Soviet Union*. Metuchen, N.J., 1995. Over 3,000 references, including other bibliographies.

Schultheiss, Thomas, ed. *Russian Studies, 1941–1958: A Cumulation of the Annual Bibliographies from the Russian Review*. Ann Arbor, 1972.

Shapiro, David M. *A Select Bibliography of Works in English on Russian History, 1801–1917*. Oxford, 1962.

Sullivan, Helen F., and Robert H. Burger. *Russia and the Former Soviet Union: A Bibliographic Guide to English Language Publications, 1986–1991.* Englewood, Colo., 1994. An annotated list of over 1400 entries.

Walker, Gregory, ed. *Official Publications of the Soviet Union and Eastern Europe, 1945–1980: A Select Annotated Bibliography.* London, 1982.

3. DICTIONARIES, ENCYCLOPEDIAS, HANDBOOKS, AND STATISTICS

Arms, Thomas S., ed. *Encyclopedia of the Cold War.* New York, 1994.

Batalden, Stephen K., and Sandra L. Batalden. *The Newly Independent States of Eurasia: Handbook of Former Soviet Republics.* Phoenix, 1993.

Boer, S. P. de, E. J. Driessen, and H. L. Verhaar. *Biographical Dictionary of Dissidents in the Soviet Union, 1956–1975.* The Hague, 1982.

Brown, Archie, ed. *The Soviet Union: A Biographical Dictionary.* London, 1990.

Brown, Archie, et al., eds. *The Cambridge Encyclopedia of Russia and the Former Soviet Union.* 2d ed. Cambridge, England, 1994.

Cichero, Romolo, comp. *The Tauris Soviet Directory: The Elite of the USSR Today.* London, 1989.

Clarke, Roger A., and Dubravko J. I. Matko. *Soviet Economic Facts, 1917–81.* New York, 1983.

Conte, Francis, ed. *Great Dates in Russian and Soviet History.* New York, 1994.

Dobroszycki, Lucjan, and Jeffrey S. Gurock, eds. *The Holocaust in the Soviet Union: Studies and Sources on the Destruction of the Jews in the Nazi-Occupied Territories of the USSR, 1941–1945.* Armonk, N.Y., 1993.

Feldbrugge, F. J. M., G. P. Van den Berg, and William B. Simons, eds. *Encyclopedia of Soviet Law.* Dordrecht, Neth., 1985.

Florinsky, Michael T., ed. *McGraw-Hill Encyclopedia of Russia and the Soviet Union.* New York, 1961.

Geron, Leonard, ed. *Who's Who in Russia and the New States.* London, 1993.

Great Soviet Encyclopedia. 3d ed. 32 vols. New York, 1973–1983.

Green, William C., and W. Robert Reeves, eds. *Soviet Military Encyclopedia.* 4 vols. Boulder, 1993.

Ho, Allan, and Dmitry Feofanov, eds. *Biographical Dictionary of Russian/Soviet Composers.* New York, 1989.

Jones, David R., ed. *The Military Encyclopedia of Russia and Eurasia.* 6 vols. up through 1995. Gulf Breeze, Fla., 1994–.

Karasik, Theodore W., ed. *Russia and Eurasia: Facts and Figures Annual.* (Formerly *USSR: Facts and Figures Annual*). 20 vols. up through 1995. Gulf Breeze, Fla., 1977–.

Kasack, Wolfgang, ed. *Dictionary of Russian Literature since 1917.* New York, 1988.

Kernig, C. D., ed. *Marxism, Communism, and Western Society: A Comparative Encyclopedia.* 8 vols. New York, 1972–1973.

Konn, Tania, ed. *Soviet Studies Guide.* London, 1992.

Kubiiovych, Volodymyr, and Danylo Husar Struk, eds. *Encyclopedia of Ukraine.* 5 vols. Toronto, 1984.

Laird, Roy D., and Betty A. Laird. *A Soviet Lexicon: Important Concepts, Terms, and Phrases.* Lexington, Mass., 1988.

McCrea, Barbara, Jack C. Plano, and George Klein. *The Soviet and East European Political Dictionary.* Santa Barbara, Calif., 1984.

MERSH. See Section 1.

Mihailovich, Vasa D., comp. *Modern Slavic Literatures*. Vol. 1: *Russian Literature*. New York, 1972.

Mitchell, B. R. *International Historical Statistics: Africa, Asia, & Oceania, 1750–1988*. 2d rev. ed. New York, 1995.

———. *International Historical Statistics: Europe 1750–1988*. 3d ed. New York, 1992.

Morozov, Vladimir, ed. *Who's Who in Russia and the CIS Republics*. New York, 1995.

Olson, James Stuart, Lee Brigance Pappas, and Nicholas Charles Pappas, eds. *An Ethno-historical Dictionary of the Russian and Soviet Empires*. Westport, Conn., 1994.

Orlovsky, Daniel, ed. *Beyond Soviet Studies*. Washington, D.C., 1995.

Paxton, John. *Encyclopedia of Russian History: From the Christianization of Kiev to the Break-Up of the U.S.S.R.* Santa Barbara, Calif., 1993.

Pockney, B. P. *Soviet Statistics since 1950*. New York, 1991.

Pushkarev, Sergei G., comp. *Dictionary of Russian Historical Terms from the Eleventh Century to 1917*. New Haven, 1970.

Rhyne, George N., ed. *The Supplement to the Modern Encyclopedia of Russian, Soviet, and Eurasian History*. Gulf Breeze, Fla., 1995–.

Rollberg, Peter, ed. *The Modern Encyclopedia of East Slavic, Baltic and Central Asian Literatures* (formerly *The Modern Encyclopedia of Russian and Soviet Literatures*). 10 vols. to date. Gulf Breeze, Fla., 1977–.

Shaw, Warren, and David Pryce. *Encyclopedia of the USSR: From 1905 to the Present*. London, 1990.

Steeves, Paul D., ed. *The Modern Encyclopedia of Religions in Russia and the Soviet Union*. 6 vols. to date. Gulf Breeze, Fla., 1988–.

Terras, Victor, ed. *Handbook of Russian Literature*. New Haven, 1985. A comprehensive and useful work.

Twining, David T. *The New Eurasia: A Guide to the Republics of the Former Soviet Union*. Westport, Conn., 1993.

Wieczynski, Joseph L., ed. *The Gorbachev Encyclopedia: Gorbachev, the Man and His Times, March 11, 1985–December 25, 1991*. Salt Lake City, 1993.

4. NATIONALITIES AND PEOPLES

(See also appropriate books mentioned in Sections 2 and 3 and Davies in Section 7.)*

Adshead, Samuel Adrian M. *Central Asia in World History*. New York, 1993.

Akiner, Shirin. *Islamic Peoples of the Soviet Union (With an Appendix on the Non-Muslim Turkic Peoples of the Soviet Union)*. London, 1983.

Alapuro, Risto. *State and Revolution in Finland*. Berkeley, 1988.

Allworth, Edward. *The Modern Uzbeks: From the Fourteenth Century to the Present, A Cultural History*. Stanford, 1990.

———, ed. *Central Asia, 120 Years of Russian Rule*. Durham, N.C., 1989.

———, ed. *The Nationality Question in Soviet Central Asia*. New York, 1973.

Altstadt, Audrey L. *The Azerbaijani Turks: Power and Identity under Russian Rule*. Stanford, 1992.

Banuazizi, Ali, and Myron Weiner, eds. *New Geopolitics of Central Asia and Its Borderlands*. Bloomington, 1995.

---

*Includes nationalities and peoples who at least for some period were part of the Russian Empire or USSR. See also Suggested Sources on Geography and Peoples at the end of Chapter 1.

Bennigsen, Alexandre, and S. Wimbush. *Muslims of the Soviet Empire: A Guide*. Bloomington, 1986.

Crowe, David M. *A History of the Gypsies of Eastern Europe and Russia*. Bloomington, 1995.

Curtis, Glenn E., ed. *Armenia, Azerbaijan, and Georgia: Country Studies*. Washington, D.C., 1995.

Dima, Nicholas. *From Moldavia to Moldova: The Soviet-Romanian Territorial Dispute*. Boulder, 1991.

Fierman, William, ed. *Soviet Central Asia: The Failed Transformation*. Boulder, 1991.

Fisher, Alan W. *The Crimean Tatars*. Stanford, 1978.

Gerutis, Albertas, ed. *Lithuania 700 Years*. 6th ed. New York, 1984.

Gitelman, Zvi Y. *A Century of Ambivalence: The Jews of Russia and the Soviet Union, 1881 to the Present*. New York, 1988.

Hostler, Charles Warren. *The Turks of Central Asia*. Westport, Conn., 1993.

Hovannisian, Richard G., ed. *The Armenian People: From Ancient to Modern Times*. 2 vols. New York, 1996.

Kangas, Roger D. *Uzbekistan in the Twentieth Century: Political Development and the Evolution of Power*. New York, 1995.

Kirby, D. G., ed. *Finland and Russia, 1808–1920: From Autonomy to Independence: A Selection of Documents*. London, 1975.

Kolarz, Walter. *Russia and Her Colonies*. London, 1952.

Krawchenko, Bohdan. *Social Change and National Consciousness in Twentieth-Century Ukraine*. New York, 1985.

——, ed. *Ukrainian Past, Ukrainian Present: Selected Papers from the Fourth World Congress for Soviet and East European Studies, Harrogate, 1990*. New York, 1993.

Lang, David M. *A Modern History of Georgia*. London, 1962.

Lapidus, Gail W., ed. *The "Nationality" Question in the Soviet Union*. New York, 1992.

Leskov, Nikolai S. *The Jews in Russia: Some Notes on the Jewish Question*. Princeton, 1986.

Lewis, Robert A., Richard H. Rowland, and Ralph S. Clem. *Nationality and Population Change in Russia and the USSR: An Evaluation of Census Data, 1897–1970*. New York, 1976.

Long, James W. *From Privileged to Dispossessed: The Volga Germans, 1860–1917*. Lincoln, 1988.

Longworth, Philip. *The Cossacks*. London, 1969.

Lowe, Heinz-Dietrich. *The Tsar and the Jews: Reform, Reaction, and Anti-Semitism in Imperial Russia, 1772–1917*. New York, 1992.

Magocsi, Paul Robert. *The Shaping of a National Identity: Subcarpathian Rus, 1848–1948*. Cambridge, Mass., 1978.

——. *Ukraine: A Historical Atlas*. Toronto, 1985.

Meurs, Wim P. Van. *The Bessarabian Question in Communist Historiography: Nationalist and Communist Politics and History-Writing*. New York, 1994.

Miller, Wright. *Russians as People*. New York, 1961.

Olcott, Martha B. *The Kazakhs*. Stanford, 1987.

Pinkus, Benjamin. *The Jews of the Soviet Union: The History of a National Minority*. Cambridge, England, 1988.

Plakans, Andrevs. *The Latvians*. Stanford, 1995.

Raun, Toivo U. *Estonia and the Estonians*. Stanford, 1991.

Rorlich, Azade-Ayse. *The Volga Tatars: A Profile in National Resilience*. Stanford, 1986.

Rubel, Paula G. *The Kalmyk Mongols: A Study in Continuity and Change*. Bloomington, 1967.

Senn, Alfred Erich. *Lithuania Awakening*. Berkeley, 1990.

Smith, Graham, ed. *The Nationalities Question in the Post-Soviet States*. 2d ed. London, 1996.

Subtelny, Orest. *Ukraine: A History*. 2d ed. Toronto, 1994.

Suny, Ronald. *Looking toward Ararat: Armenia in Modern History.* Bloomington, 1994.
———. *The Making of the Georgian Nation.* 2d ed. Bloomington, 1994.
Swietochowski, Tadeusz. *Russian and Azerbaijan: A Borderland in Transition.* New York, 1995.
Szporluk, Roman, ed. *National Identity and Ethnicity in Russia and the New States of Eurasia.* Armonk, N.Y., 1994.
Vakar, Nicholas P. *Belorussia: The Making of a Nation, a Case Study.* Cambridge, Mass., 1956.
Wheeler, Geoffrey. *The Modern History of Soviet Central Asia.* Westport, Conn., 1975.
———. *The Peoples of Soviet Central Asia: A Background Book.* London, 1966.
Zaprudnik, Ia. *Belarus: At a Crossroads in History.* Boulder, 1993.
Zickel, Raymond E., ed. *Soviet Union: A Country Study.* Washington, D.C., 1991.

5. SELECTED READINGS, ANTHOLOGIES, AND DOCUMENTS

(See Section 7 for Foreign Policy Documents not listed in chapters.)

Black, Cyril E., ed. *The Transformation of Russian Society: Aspects of Social Change since 1861.* Cambridge, Mass., 1960.
Black, J. L., ed. *Russia and Eurasia Documents Annual* (formerly *USSR Documents Annual*). One or more volumes published annually with varied titles since 1988. Gulf Breeze, Fla., 1995.
Butler, William E., ed. *Basic Legal Documents of the Soviet Legal System.* New York, 1992.
Cracraft, James, ed. *Major Problems in the History of Imperial Russia.* Lexington, Mass., 1994.
Crummey, Robert O., ed. *Reform in Russia and the U.S.S.R.: Past and Prospects.* Urbana, 1989.
Dallin, Alexander, ed. *Between Totalitarianism and Pluralism.* New York, 1992.
———, ed. *The Khrushchev and Brezhnev Years.* New York, 1992.
———, ed. *The Nature of the Soviet System.* New York, 1992.
Daniels, Robert V., ed. *A Documentary History of Communism and the World: From Revolution to Collapse.* Hanover, N.H., 1994.
———, ed. *A Documentary History of Communism in Russia: From Lenin to Gorbachev.* Hanover, N.H., 1993.
Dmytryshyn, Basil, ed. *Imperial Russia: A Source Book, 1700–1917.* 3d ed. Fort Worth, 1990.
Freeze, Gregory L. *From Supplication to Revolution: A Documentary Social History of Imperial Russia.* New York, 1988.
Hamburg, Gary M., ed. *Imperial Russian History II, 1861–1917.* New York, 1992.
Harcave, Sidney, ed. *Readings in Russian History.* Vol. 2. New York, 1962.
Hendel, Samuel, ed. *The Soviet Crucible: The Soviet System in Theory and Practice.* 5th ed. North Scituate, Mass., 1980.
Inkeles, Alex, and Kent Geiger, eds. *Soviet Society: A Book of Readings.* Boston, 1961.
Mendelsohn, Ezra, and Marshall S. Shatz, eds. *Imperial Russia, 1700–1917: State, Society, Opposition, Essays in Honor of Marc Raeff.* DeKalb, Ill., 1988.
Orlovsky, Daniel T., ed. *Social and Economic History of Prerevolutionary Russia.* New York, 1992.
Pintner, Walter M., and Don K. Rowney, eds. *Russian Officialdom: The Bureaucratization of Russian Society from the Seventeenth to the Twentieth Century.* London, 1980.
Pipes, Richard, ed. *The Russian Intelligentsia.* New York, 1961.
Pushkarev, Sergei, comp. *A Source Book for Russian History from Early Times to 1917.* Vol. 3. New Haven, 1972.
Raeff, Marc, ed. *Russian Intellectual History: An Anthology.* New York, 1966.

Riasanovsky, Alexander V., and William E. Watson. *Readings in Russian History.* Vols. 2 and 3. Dubuque, 1992.

Riha, Thomas, ed. *Readings in Russian Civilization.* Vols. 2 and 3. Chicago, 1964.

Rzheshevsky, Oleg A., ed. *War and Diplomacy: The Making of the Grand Alliance: Documents from Stalin's Archives.* Amsterdam, 1996.

Senn, Alfred Erich, ed. *Readings in Russian Political and Diplomatic History.* 2 vols. Homewood, Ill., 1966.

Simmons, Ernest J., ed. *Continuity and Change in Russian and Soviet Thought.* Cambridge, Mass. 1955.

Taranovski, Theodore, ed. *Reform in Modern Russian History: Progress or Cycle?* Cambridge, England, 1995.

Treadgold, Donald W., ed. *The Development of the USSR: An Exchange of Views.* Seattle, 1964.

Wade, Rex A., ed. *Documents of Soviet History.* 4 vols. to date. Gulf Breeze, Fla., 1991–.

Walsh, Warren B., ed. *Readings in Russian History, from Ancient Times to the Post-Stalin Era.* Syracuse, N.Y., 1963.

Zile, Zigurds L., ed. *Ideas and Forces in Soviet Legal History: A Reader on the Soviet State and Law.* New York, 1992.

6. GENERAL HISTORIES AND HISTORIOGRAPHY

Acton, Edward. *Russia: The Tsarist and Soviet Legacy.* 2d ed. London, 1995.

Black, Cyril E. *Understanding Soviet Politics: The Perspective of Russian History.* Boulder, 1986.

———, ed. *Rewriting Russian History: Soviet Interpretations of Russia's Past.* New York, 1962.

Byrnes, Robert F. *V. O. Kliuchevskii, Historian of Russia.* Bloomington, 1995.

Carmichael, Joel. *A History of Russia.* New York, 1990.

Carr, E. H. *A History of Soviet Russia.* 14 vols. London, 1952–1978.

Daniels, Robert V. *Russia: The Roots of Confrontation.* Cambridge, Mass., 1985.

Danilov, A. A., et al. *Essays on the Motherland: A Brief History of Modern Russia.* Conway, Ark., 1994.

Davies, R. W. *Soviet History in the Gorbachev Revolution.* Bloomington, 1989.

Dmytryshyn, Basil. *A History of Russia.* Englewood Cliffs, N.J., 1977.

———. *USSR: A Concise History.* 4th ed. New York, 1984.

Dukes, Paul. *A History of Russia: Medieval, Modern, Contemporary.* 2d ed. Durham, 1990.

Dziewanowski, M. K. *A History of Soviet Russia.* 4th ed. Englewood Cliffs, N.J., 1993.

Florinsky, Michael T. *Russia: A History and an Interpretation.* Vol. 2. New York, 1947–1953.

———. *Russia: A Short History.* New York, 1969.

Geller, Mikhail, and Aleksandr M. Nekrich. *Utopia in Power: The History of the Soviet Union from 1917 to the Present.* New York, 1986.

Grey, Ian. *The Horizon History of Russia.* New York, 1970.

Hingley, Ronald. *Russia: A Concise History.* Rev. ed. London, 1991.

Hosking, Geoffrey. *The First Socialist Society: A History of the Soviet Union from Within.* 2d ed. Cambridge, Mass., 1993.

Ito, Takayuki, ed. *Facing up to the Past: Soviet Historiography under Perestroika.* Sapporo, Japan, 1989.

Keep, John L. H. *Last Of The Empires: A History of the Soviet Union, 1945–1991.* Oxford, 1995.

Kochan, Lionel. *The Making of Modern Russia.* Harmondsworth, England, 1962.

Kort, Michael. *The Soviet Colossus: History and Aftermath.* 4th ed. Armonk, N.Y., 1996.

Lourie, Richard. *Russia Speaks: An Oral History from the Revolution to the Present*. New York, 1991.

MacKenzie, David, and Michael W. Curran. *A History of Russia, the Soviet Union, and Beyond*. 4th ed. Belmont, Calif., 1993.

Mazour, Anatole G. *Modern Russian Historiography*. Westport, Conn., 1975.

McCauley Martin. *The Soviet Union, 1917–1991*. 2d ed. London, 1993.

McClellan, Woodford. *Russia: The Soviet Period and After*. 3d ed. Englewood Cliffs, N.J., 1994.

Pares, Bernard. *A History of Russia*. New York, 1926.

Prymak, Thomas M. *Mykola Kostmarov: A Biography*. Toronto, 1996.

Pushkarev, Sergei. *The Emergence of Modern Russia, 1801–1917*. New York, 1963.

Ragsdale, Hugh. *The Russian Tragedy: The Burden of History*. Armonk, N.Y., 1996.

Raleigh, Donald J., ed. *Soviet Historians and Perestroika: The First Phase*. Armonk, N.Y., 1989.

Rauch, Georg von. *A History of Soviet Russia*. New York, 1972.

Riasanovsky, Nicholas V. *A History of Russia*. 5th ed. New York, 1993.

Seton-Watson, Hugh. *The Russian Empire, 1801–1917*. Oxford, 1967.

Shteppa, Konstantin F. *Russian Historians and the Soviet State*. New Brunswick, N.J., 1962.

Thaden, Edward. *Russia since 1801: The Making of a New Society*. New York, 1971.

Thompson, John M. *Russia and the Soviet Union: An Historical Introduction from the Kievan State to the Present*. 3d ed. Boulder, 1994.

———. *A Vision Unfulfilled: Russia and the Soviet Union in the Twentieth Century*. Lexington, Mass., 1996.

Treadgold, Donald W. *Twentieth Century Russia*. 8th ed., Boulder, 1995.

Ulam, Adam B. *A History of Soviet Russia*. New York, 1976.

Vernadsky, George. *A History of Russia*. 5th ed. New Haven, 1961.

———. *Russian Historiography: A History*. Belmont, Mass., 1978.

Westwood, J. N. *Endurance and Endeavour: Russian History, 1812–1992*. 4th ed. Oxford, 1993.

Wren, Melvin C., and Taylor Stults. *The Course of Russian History*. 5th ed. Prospect Heights, Ill., 1994.

7. MILITARY, FOREIGN AFFAIRS, AND INTERNATIONAL RELATIONS

Allen, Robert V. *Russia Looks at America: The View to 1917*. Washington, 1988.

Allin, Dana H. *Cold War Illusions: America, Europe, and Soviet Power, 1969–1989*. New York, 1995.

Anderson, M. S. *The Eastern Question, 1774–1923: A Study in International Relations*. London, 1966.

Bialer, Seweryn, ed. *The Domestic Context of Soviet Foreign Policy*. Boulder, 1981.

Boyle, Peter G. *American-Soviet Relations: From the Russian Revolution to the Fall of Communism*. New York, 1993.

Bradley, John F. N. *War and Peace since 1945: A History of Soviet-Western Relations*. Boulder, 1989.

Colton, Timothy J. *Soldiers and the Soviet State: Civil-Military Relations from Brezhnev to Gorbachev*. Princeton, 1990.

Dallin, Alexander, ed. *Soviet Foreign Policy, 1917–1990*. New York, 1992.

———, ed. *Civil-Military Relations in the Soviet Union*. New York, 1992.

Davies, Norman. *God's Playground: A History of Poland*. 2 vols. Oxford, 1981.

Dmytryshyn, Basil, and Frederick J. Cox, eds. *The Soviet Union and the Middle East: A Documentary Record of Afghanistan, Iran, and Turkey, 1917–1985*. Princeton, 1987.

Dmytryshyn, Basil, and Frederick J. Cox, eds. *The Soviet Union and the Middle East: A Documentary Record of the Fertile Crescent Arabs, 1917–1985*. Gulf Breeze, Fla., 1995.

Erickson, John. *The Soviet High Command: A Military-Political History, 1918–1941*. London, 1962.

————, ed. *Soviet Military Power and Performance*. London, 1979.

Fleron, Frederic J., Jr., Erik P. Hoffmann, and Robin F. Laird, eds. *Soviet Foreign Policy: Classic and Contemporary Issues*. New York, 1991.

Fuller, William C. *Strategy and Power in Russia, 1600–1914*. New York, 1992.

Gaddis, John Lewis. *Russia, the Soviet Union, and the United States: An Interpretive History*. New York, 1990.

Galeotti, Mark. *Afghanistan, the Soviet Union's Last War*. London, 1995.

Golan, Galia. *Soviet Policies in the Middle East: From World War Two to Gorbachev*. Cambridge, England, 1990.

Goodby, James E., Vladimir I. Ivanov, and Nubuo Shimotamai, eds. *"Northern Territories" and Beyond: Russian, Japanese, and American Perspectives*. Westport, Conn., 1995.

Gorodetsky, G., ed. *Soviet Foreign Policy, 1917–1991*. London, 1994.

Korbonski, Andrzej, and Francis Fukuyama, eds. *The Soviet Union and the Third World: The Last Three Decades*. Ithaca, 1987.

Hiden, J., and P. Salmon. *The Baltic Nations and Europe: Estonia, Latvia, and Lithuania in the Twentieth Century*. London, 1991.

Hough, Jerry F. *The Struggle for the Third World: Soviet Debates and American Options*. Washington, D.C., 1986.

Hyland, William G. *The Cold War: Fifty Years of Conflict*. New York, 1991.

Jelavich, Barbara. *St. Petersburg and Moscow: Tsarist and Soviet Foreign Policy, 1814–1974*. Bloomington, 1974.

Jones, Ellen. *Red Army and Society: A Sociology of the Soviet Military*. Boston, 1985.

Jones, Robert A. *The Soviet Concept of "Limited Sovereignty" from Lenin to Gorbachev: The Brezhnev Doctrine*. New York, 1990.

Katz, Mark N. *Russia and Arabia: Soviet Foreign Policy toward the Arabian Peninsula*. Baltimore, 1986.

Keeble, Curtis. *Britain and the Soviet Union, 1917–89*. New York, 1990.

LaFeber, Walter. *America, Russia, and the Cold War, 1945–1990*. 6th ed. New York, 1991.

Laidi, Zaki. *The Superpowers and Africa: The Constraints of a Rivalry, 1960–1990*. Chicago, 1990.

Laird, Robbin F., and Erik P. Hoffman, eds. *Soviet Foreign Policy in a Changing World*. New York, 1986.

Lebow, Richard Ned, and Janice Gross Stein. *We All Lost the Cold War*. Princeton, 1994.

Lederer, Ivo J., ed. *Russian Foreign Policy: Essays in Historical Perspective*. New Haven, 1962.

Lynn-Jones, Sean M., Steven E. Miller, and Stephen Van Evera, eds. *Soviet Military Policy: An International Security Reader*. Cambridge, Mass., 1989.

Menning, Bruce W. *Bayonets before Bullets: The Imperial Russian Army, 1855–1914*. Bloomington, 1992.

Miller, Nicola. *Soviet Relations with Latin America, 1959–1987*. Cambridge, England, 1989.

Nation, R. Craig. *Black Earth, Red Star: A History of Soviet Security Policy, 1917–1991*. Ithaca, N.Y., 1992.

Nogee, Joseph L., and Robert H. Donaldson. *Soviet Foreign Policy since World War II*. 3d ed. New York, 1988.

Odom, William E. *On Internal War: American and Soviet Approaches to Third World Clients and Insurgents*. Durham, 1992.

Pravda, Alex, ed. *The End of the Outer Empire: Soviet-East European Relations in Transition, 1985–90*. London, 1992.

————, ed. *Yearbook of Soviet Foreign Relations*. London, 1991.

Rauch, Georg von. *The Baltic States: The Years of Independence: Estonia, Latvia, Lithuania, 1917–1940*. London, 1974.

Rubinstein, Alvin Z. *Moscow's Third World Strategy*. Princeton, 1988.

————. *Soviet Foreign Policy since World War II: Imperial and Global*. 3d ed. Boston, 1985.

————, ed. *The Foreign Policy of the Soviet Union*. 3d ed. New York, 1972.

Shulman, Marshall D. *Stalin's Foreign Policy Reappraised*. Cambridge, Mass., 1963.

Sodaro, Michael J. *Moscow, Germany, and the West from Khrushchev to Gorbachev*. Ithaca, 1990.

Stone, Randall W. *Satellites and Commissars: Strategy and Conflict in the Politics of Soviet-Bloc Trade*. Princeton, 1996.

Ulam, Adam B. *The Communists: The Story of Power and Lost Illusions, 1948–1991*. New York, 1992.

————. *Dangerous Relations: The Soviet Union in World Politics, 1970–1982*. New York, 1983.

————. *Expansion and Coexistence: Soviet Foreign Policy, 1917–73*. New York, 1974.

Van Oudenaren, John. *Detente in Europe: The Soviet Union and the West since 1953*. Durham, 1991.

Walker, Martin. *The Cold War: A History*. New York, 1995.

Wozniuk, Vladimir, ed. *Understanding Soviet Foreign Policy: Readings and Documents*. New York, 1990.

Zubok, V. Vladislav, and Constantine Pleshakov. *Inside the Kremlin's Cold War: From Stalin to Khrushchev*. Cambridge, Mass., 1996.

Zwick, Peter. *Soviet Foreign Relations: Process and Policy*. Englewood Cliffs, N.J., 1990.

8. THE SOCIAL AND ECONOMIC SPHERES

Andrle, Vladimir. *A Social History of Twentieth-Century Russia*. London, 1994.

Atkinson, Dorothy, Alexander Dallin, and Gail Warshofsky Lapidus, eds. *Women in Russia*. Stanford, 1977.

Balzer, Harley, ed. *Russia's Missing Middle Class: The Professions in Russian History*. Armonk, N.Y., 1995.

Barchatova, Y., et al. *A Portrait of Tsarist Russia: Unknown Photographs from the Soviet Archives*. New York, 1989.

Boym, Svetlana. *Common Places: Mythologies of Everyday Life in Russia*. Cambridge, Mass., 1994.

Bridger, Susan. *Women in the Soviet Countryside: Women's Roles in Rural Development in the Soviet Union*. Cambridge, England, 1987.

Buckley, Mary. *Women and Ideology in the Soviet Union*. Ann Arbor, 1989.

Dodge, Norton T. *Women in the Soviet Economy: Their Role in Economic, Scientific, and Technical Development*. Baltimore, 1966.

Edmondson, Linda, ed. *Women and Society in Russia and the Soviet Union*. Cambridge, England, 1992.

Ellman, Michael, and Vladimir Kontorovich, eds. *The Disintegration of the Soviet Economic System*. London, 1992.

Gregory, Paul R., and Robert C. Stuart. *Soviet Economic Structure and Performance*. 4th ed. New York, 1990.

Gustafson, Thane. *Crisis Amid Plenty: The Politics of Soviet Energy Under Brezhnev and Gorbachev*. Princeton, 1989.

Hamm, Michael F. *Kiev: A Portrait, 1800–1917*. Princeton, 1993.

Herlihy, Patricia. *Odessa: A History, 1794–1914*. Cambridge, Mass., 1987.

Lane, David. *Soviet Economy and Society*. New York, 1985.

Liashchenko, P. I. *History of the National Economy of Russia, to the 1917 Revolution*. New York, 1949.

Madison, Bernice Q. *Social Welfare in the Soviet Union*. Stanford, 1968.

Mandel, William. *Soviet Women*. Garden City, N.Y., 1975.

Marsh, Rosalind, ed. *Women in Russia and Ukraine*. Cambridge, England, 1996.

Matthews, Mervyn. *Class and Society in Soviet Russia*. New York, 1972.

——. *Patterns of Deprivation in the Soviet Union under Brezhnev and Gorbachev*. Stanford, 1989.

——. *Poverty in the Soviet Union*. Cambridge, England, 1986.

McAuley, Alastair. *Economic Welfare in the Soviet Union: Poverty, Living Standards, and Inequality*. Madison, 1979.

——. *Women's Work and Wages in the Soviet Union*. London, 1981.

Nove, Alec. *An Economic History of the U.S.S.R., 1917–1991*. New and final ed. London, 1992.

Obolensky, Chloe. *The Russian Empire: A Portrait in Photographs*. New York, 1979.

Rutland, Peter. *The Politics of Economic Stagnation in the Soviet Union: The Role of Local Party Organs in Economic Management*. Cambridge, England, 1993.

Ryan, Michael. *The Organization of Soviet Medical Care*. Oxford, 1978.

Ryan, Michael, and Richard Prentice. *Social Trends in the Soviet Union from 1950*. London, 1987.

Sacks, Michael Paul. *Women's Work in Soviet Russia: Continuity in the Midst of Change*. New York, 1976.

Sacks, Michael, and Jerry Pankhurst, eds. *Understanding Soviet Society*. Boston, 1988.

Sutton, Antony C. *Western Technology and Soviet Economic Development*. 3 vols. Stanford, 1968–1973.

Whitefield, Stephen. *Industrial Power and the Soviet State*. Oxford, 1993.

9. CULTURE, RELIGION, SCIENCE, AND EDUCATION

A. Literature (See also Proffer in section 2 and Kasack, Mihailovich, Rollberg, and Terras in Section 3.)*

Andrew, Joe. *Russian Writers and Society in the Second Half of the Nineteenth Century*. London, 1982.

Baring, Maurice, and D. P. Costello, eds. *The Oxford Book of Russian Verse*. Oxford, 1958.

Bristol, Evelyn. *A History of Russian Poetry*. New York, 1991.

Brown, Clarence, ed. *The Portable Twentieth Century Russian Reader*. New York, 1985.

Brown, Edward J. *Russian Literature since the Revolution*. Cambridge, Mass., 1982.

Čiževskij, Dmitrij. *History of Nineteenth-Century Russian Literature*. 2 vols. Nashville, 1974.

Clark, Katerina. *The Soviet Novel: History as Ritual*. Chicago, 1981.

*Most of Russia's great and significant prose has been translated into English. Students can consult bibliographies and guidebooks such as the book by Proffer and Meyer mentioned in Section 2 and that of Terras mentioned in Section 3 for further guidance to translations of such writers as Dostoevsky, Tolstoy, Pasternak, and Solzhenitsyn, as well as to biographies and critical works about them.

Erlich, Victor. *Modernism and Revolution: Russian Literature in Transition.* Cambridge, Mass., 1994.

———, ed. *Twentieth-Century Russian Literary Criticism.* New Haven, 1975.

Guerney, Bernard Guilbert, ed. *A Treasury of Russian Literature.* New York, 1943.

Hayward, Max. *Writers in Russia, 1917–1978.* San Diego, 1983.

Hingley, Ronald. *Nightingale Fever: Russian Poets in Revolution.* London, 1982.

———. *Russian Writers and Society, 1825–1904.* New York, 1967.

———. *Russian Writers and Soviet Society, 1917–1978.* New York, 1979.

Karlinsky, Simon, and Alfred Appel, eds. *The Bitter Air of Exile: Russian Writers in the West, 1922–1972.* Berkeley, 1977.

Kelly, Catriona. *A History of Russian Women's Writing, 1820–1992.* Oxford, 1994.

Markov, Vladimir, and Merrill Sparks, eds. *Modern Russian Poetry: An Anthology with Verse Translations.* Indianapolis, 1967.

Mathewson, Rufus W. *The Positive Hero in Russian Literature.* Stanford, 1975.

Mirsky, D. S. *A History of Russian Literature, Comprising a History of Russian Literature and Contemporary Russian Literature.* New York, 1969.

Moser, Charles A., ed. *The Cambridge History of Russian Literature.* 2d enlarged ed. Cambridge, England, 1992.

Obolensky, Dimitri, ed. *The Heritage of Russian Verse.* Bloomington, 1976.

———, ed. *The Penguin Book of Russian Verse.* Harmondsworth, England, 1962.

Pachmuss, Temira, ed. *Women Writers in Russian Modernism: An Anthology.* Urbana, 1978.

Reeder, Roberta, ed. *Russian Folk Lyrics.* Bloomington, 1993.

Russell, Robert, and Andrew Barratt, eds. *Russian Theatre in the Age of Modernism.* New York, 1990.

Rzhevsky, Nicholas, ed. *An Anthology of Russian Literature from Earliest Writings to Modern Fiction: Introduction to a Culture.* Armonk, N.Y., 1996.

Segel, Harold B. *Twentieth-Century Russian Drama: From Gorky to the Present.* Updated ed. Baltimore, 1993.

Slonim, Marc. *The Epic of Russian Literature from Its Origins through Tolstoy.* New York, 1964.

———. *Soviet Russian Literature: Writers and Problems, 1917–1977.* London, 1977.

Smith, Gerald S. *Songs to Seven Strings: Russian Guitar Poetry and Soviet "Mass Song."* Bloomington, 1985.

———, ed. *Contemporary Russian Poetry: A Bilingual Anthology.* Bloomington, 1993.

Sokolov, Yu. M. *Russian Folklore.* Hatboro, Penn., 1966.

Terras, Victor. *A History of Russian Literature.* New Haven, 1992.

Todd, Albert C., and Max Hayward, with Daniel Weissbort. *Twentieth Century Russian Poetry: Silver and Steel, an Anthology.* New York, 1993.

Yarmolinsky, Avrahm, ed. *Soviet Short Stories.* Garden City, N.Y., 1960.

———, ed. *A Treasury of Great Russian Short Stories, Pushkin to Gorky.* New York, 1955.

B. General Culture, Music, Art, Architecture, Philosophy, and Religion (See also Ho and Feofanov, and Steeves in Section 3.)

Balzer, Marjorie Mandelstam, ed. *Culture Incarnate: Native Anthropology from Russia.* Armonk, N.Y., 1995.

Billington, James H. *The Icon and the Axe: An Interpretive History of Russian Culture.* New York, 1970.

Brumfield, William Craft. *The Origins of Modernism in Russian Architecture.* Berkeley, 1991.

Bushnell, John. *Moscow Graffiti: Language and Subculture*. Boston, 1990.

Campbell, Stuart, ed. *Russians and Russian Music, 1830–1880*. New York, 1994.

Clowes, Edith W. *The Revolution of Moral Consciousness: Nietzsche in Russian Literature, 1890–1914*. DeKalb, Ill., 1988.

Condee, Nancy, ed. *Soviet Hieroglyphics: Visual Culture in Late Twentieth-Century Russia*. Bloomington, 1995.

Edie, James M., James P. Scanlan, and Mary-Barbara Zeldin, eds. *Russian Philosophy*. 3 vols. Chicago, 1965.

Ellis, Jane. *The Russian Orthodox Church: A Contemporary History*. Bloomington, 1986.

Emerson, Caryl, and Robert Oldani. *Modest Musorgsky and Boris Godunov: Myths, Realities, Reconsiderations*. Cambridge, England, 1994.

Gibian, George, and H. W. Tjalsma, eds. *Russian Modernism: Culture and the Avant-Garde, 1900–1930*. Ithaca, N.Y., 1976.

Golomshtok, Igor. *Totalitarian Art: In the Soviet Union, the Third Reich, Fascist Italy and the People's Republic of China*. New York, 1990.

Goscilo, Helena, and Beth Holmgren, eds. *Russia, Women, Culture*. Bloomington, 1996.

Graffy, Julian, and Geoffrey Hosking, eds. *Culture and the Media in the USSR Today*. New York, 1989.

Hamilton, George Heard. *The Art and Architecture of Russia*. Baltimore, 1975.

Hilton, Alison. *Russian Folk Art*. Bloomington, 1995.

Holden, Anthony. *Tchaikovsky: A Biography*. New York, 1995.

Hubbs, Joanna. *Mother Russia: The Feminine Myth in Russian Culture*. Bloomington, 1988.

Iablonskaia, M. *Women Artists of Russia's New Age, 1900–1935*. New York, 1990.

Ivanits, Linda J. *Russian Folk Belief*. Armonk, N.Y., 1989.

Kagarlitsky, Boris. *The Thinking Reed: Intellectuals and the Soviet State, 1917 to the Present*. London, 1988.

Krebs, Stanley D. *Soviet Composers and the Development of Soviet Music*. New York, 1970.

Kuvakin, Valery A., ed. *A History of Russian Philosophy: From the Tenth through the Twentieth Centuries*. Buffalo, N.Y., 1994.

Leyda, Jay. *Kino: A History of the Russian and Soviet Film*. New York, 1960.

Lossky, Nicholas O. *History of Russian Philosophy*. London, 1951.

Masaryk, T. G. *The Spirit of Russia: Studies in History, Literature and Philosophy*. 3 vols. New York, 1955–1967.

Meehan-Waters, Brenda. *Holy Women of Russia: The Lives of Five Orthodox Women Offer Spiritual Guidance for Today*. San Francisco, 1993.

Milner-Gulland, Robin, with Nikolai J. Dejevsky. *Cultural Atlas of Russia and the Soviet Union*. New York, 1989.

Norman, John O., ed. *New Perspectives on Russian and Soviet Artistic Culture: Selected Papers from the Fourth World Congress for Soviet and East European Studies, 1990*. New York, 1994.

Rimsky-Korsakov, Nikolay. *My Musical Life*. New York, 1942.

Robson, Roy R. *Old Believers in Modern Russia*. Dekalb, Ill., 1995.

Rosenthal, Bernice Glatzer, ed. *Nietzsche and Soviet Culture: Ally and Adversary*. Cambridge, England, 1994.

Sarabianov, Dmtrii V. *Russian Art: From Neoclassicism to the Avant Garde: Painting, Sculpture, Architecture*. New York, 1990.

Schwarz, Boris. *Music and Musical Life in Soviet Russia, 1917–1970*. New York, 1972.

Stavrou, Theofanis George, ed. *Art and Culture in Nineteenth-Century Russia*. Bloomington, 1983.

Talbot Rice, David. *Russian Icons*. London, 1947.

Talbot Rice, Tamara. *A Concise History of Russian Art.* New York, 1963.
Volkov, Solomon. *St. Petersburg: A Cultural History.* New York, 1995.
Walicki, Andrzej. *A History of Russian Thought from the Enlightenment to Marxism.* Stanford, 1979.
Ware, Timothy. *The Orthodox Church.* New ed. London, 1993.
White, Stephen. *The Bolshevik Poster.* New Haven, 1988.
Zenkovsky, V. V. *A History of Russian Philosophy.* 2 vols. London, 1953.

C. Science, Technology, and Education

Balzer, Harley D. *Soviet Science on the Edge of Reform.* Boulder, 1989.
Berry, Michael J., ed. *Science and Technology in the USSR.* London, 1988.
Fortescue, Stephen. *Science Policy in the Soviet Union.* London, 1990.
Graham, Loren R. *The Ghost of the Executed Engineer: Technology and the Fall of the Soviet Union.* Cambridge, Mass., 1993.
———. *Science and the Soviet Social Order.* Cambridge, Mass., 1990.
———, ed. *Science in Russia and the Soviet Union: A Short History.* Cambridge, England, 1993.
Grant, Nigel. *Soviet Education.* 4th ed. Harmondsworth, England, 1979.
Hans, Nicholas A. *The Russian Tradition in Education.* London, 1963.
Joravsky, David. *Russian Psychology: A Critical History.* Oxford, 1989.
Medvedev, Zhores A. *Soviet Science.* New York, 1978.
Vucinich, Alexander. *Empire of Knowledge: The Academy of Sciences of the USSR (1917–1970).* Berkeley, 1984.
———. *Science in Russian Culture: 1861–1917.* Stanford, Calif., 1970.
Weiner, Douglas R. *Models of Nature: Ecology, Conservation, and Cultural Revolution in Soviet Russia.* Bloomington, 1988.

10. MISCELLANEOUS WORKS

Berdyaev, Nicholas. *The Russian Idea.* Boston, 1962.
Berezhkov, Valentin, M. *At Stalin's Side: His Interpreter's Memoirs from the October Revolution to the Fall of the Dictator's Empire.* New York, 1994.
Berlin, Isaiah. *Russian Thinkers.* New York, 1978.
Berman, Harold J. *Justice in the U.S.S.R.: An Interpretation of Soviet Law.* Rev. ed. New York, 1963. Pt. 2 deals with pre-Soviet law.
Carter, Stephen. *Russian Nationalism: Yesterday, Today, Tomorrow.* New York, 1990.
Cliff, Tony. *Trotsky.* 4 vols. London, 1989–1993.
Coleman, Fred. *The Decline and Fall of the Soviet Empire: Forty Years that Shook the World, from Stalin to Yeltsin.* New York, 1996.
Conquest, Robert. *Kolyma: The Arctic Death Camps.* New York, 1978.
Crankshaw, Edward. *The Shadow of the Winter Palace: Russia's Drift to Revolution, 1825–1917.* New York, 1976.
Fainsod, Merle. *How Russia is Ruled.* Rev. ed., Cambridge, Mass., 1965.
———. *Smolensk under Soviet Rule.* Cambridge, Mass., 1958; reprint, Boston, 1989.
Goldman, Minton F. *Russia, the Eurasian Republics, and Central/Eastern Europe.* 6th ed. Guilford, Conn., 1996.
Gooding, John. *Rulers and Subjects: Government and People in Russia, 1801–1991.* London, 1996.

Hammer, Darrell P. *The USSR: The Politics of Oligarchy.* Boulder, 1990.

Heller, Agnes, and Ferenc Feher. *From Yalta to Glasnost: The Dismantling of Stalin's Empire.* Cambridge, Mass., 1991.

Huskey, Eugene. *Executive Power and Soviet Politics: The Rise and Decline of the Soviet State.* Armonk, N.Y., 1992.

Keep, John L. H. *Power and the People: Essays on Russian History.* Boulder, 1995.

Lane, David. *State and Politics in the USSR.* New York, 1985.

Laqueur, Walter. *Soviet Realities: Culture and Politics from Stalin to Gorbachev.* New Brunswick, N.J., 1990.

Maxwell, Margaret. *Narodniki Women: Russian Women Who Sacrificed Themselves for the Dream of Freedom.* New York, 1990.

McAuley, Mary. *Soviet Politics 1917–1991.* Oxford, 1992.

McDaniel, Tim. *The Agony of the Russian Idea.* Princeton, 1996.

McNeal, Robert H. *Stalin: Man and Ruler.* New York, 1988.

Moynahan, Brian. *The Russian Century: A Photographic History of Russia's 100 years.* New York, 1994.

Nahirny, Vladimir C. *The Russian Intelligentsia: From Torment to Silence.* New Brunswick, N.J., 1983.

Neumann, Iver B. *Russia and the Idea of Europe: A Study in Identity and International Relations.* London, 1996.

Pallot, Judith, and Denis J. Shaw. *Landscape and Settlement in Romanov Russia, 1613–1917.* Oxford, 1990.

Pipes, Richard. *Russia Observed: Collected Essays on Russian and Soviet History.* Boulder, 1989.

Pokrovskii, M. N. *Russia in World History: Selected Essays.* Ann Arbor, 1970.

Pomper, Philip. *Lenin, Trotsky, and Stalin: The Intelligentsia and Power.* New York, 1990.

Rancour-Laferriere, Daniel. *The Slave Soul of Russia.* New York, 1995.

Rigby, T. H. *Communist Party Membership in the U.S.S.R., 1917–1967.* Princeton, 1968.

———. *Political Elites in the USSR: Central Leaders and Local Cadres from Lenin to Gorbachev.* Brookfield, Vt., 1990.

Rowney, Don K. *Transition to Technocracy: The Structural Origins of the Soviet Administrative State.* Ithaca, N.Y., 1989.

Rummel, R. J. *Lethal Politics: Soviet Genocide and Mass Murder since 1917.* New Brunswick, N.J., 1996.

Sparks, John. *Realms of the Russian Bear: A Natural History of Russia and the Central Asian Republics.* Boston, 1992.

Shlapentokh, Vladimir. *Soviet Intellectuals and Political Power: The Post-Stalin Era.* Princeton, 1990.

Szamuely, Tibor. *The Russian Tradition.* New York, 1974.

Timberlake, Charles E., ed. *Essays on Russian Liberalism.* Columbia, Mo., 1972.

Tõkés, Rudolf L., ed. *Dissent in the USSR: Politics, Ideology, and People.* Baltimore, 1976.

Tucker, Robert C. *Political Culture and Leadership in Soviet Russia: From Lenin to Gorbachev.* New York, 1987.

Ulam, Adam B. *Russia's Failed Revolutions: From the Decembrists to the Dissidents.* New York, 1981.

Utechin, S. V. *Russian Political Thought: A Concise History.* New York, 1964.

Vasilieva, Larissa. *Kremlin Wives.* New York, 1994.

Von Laue, Theodore H. *Why Lenin? Why Stalin? Why Gorbachev?: The Rise and Fall of the Soviet System.* 3d ed. New York, 1993.

Weidle, Wladimir. *Russia: Absent and Present.* New York, 1961.

Wittram, Reinhard. *Russia and Europe.* New York, 1973.

11. ELECTRONIC SOURCES

In recent years, the electronic sources and aids that have become available for the study of Russian history and area studies have multiplied rapidly, and many of them are without cost. Articles in journals such as the *Slavic Review* and *The Russian Review* are indexed in the electronic periodical indexes available in many libraries. Students with access to a computer and modem can download numerous other materials, for example, articles from the *Slavic Review* and the latest news from English-language papers such as *The St. Petersburg Press* and *Vladivostok News*.

Students can also participate in electronic discussion groups about various Russian historical topics, check publishers' electronic lists of publications, and communicate with various sources inside Russia. Better equipped computers can make use of an Interactive Russian-English Dictionary and download examples of Russian music and art, as well as Russian language materials.

A useful resource for current history and developments regarding Russia and other parts of the former Soviet Union is the *Daily Digest* of the Open Media Research Institute (OMRI), which has continued the tradition of earlier *Radio Free Europe/Radio Liberty Reports*. The *Daily Digest* and its predecessor (back to 1991) can be searched by keyword at: http://solar.rtd.utk.edu/friends/news/rferl/master.html. Access to and more information about the *Daily Digest* and other OMRI publications can be found using the OMRI Web site at http://www.omri.cz.

Another useful source of information is the Center for Civil Society International (CCSI), which publishes a monthly newsletter, *Civil Society . . . East and West*, as well as other specialized resources on nonprofit and grassroots organizations in Russia and other Newly Independent States (NIS) of the former USSR. The newsletter includes a section, "Net Talk," which provides a monthly review of Internet resources, developments, and e-mail contacts. Other publications of the CCSI include *Internet Resources in the NIS* and *The Post-Soviet Handbook* (1996), which includes a section on Internet resources. Many of CCSI's information resources are available at its World Wide Web site at http://solar.rtd.utk.edu/~ccsi/ccsihome.html. More information can also be gained from CCSI (2929 NE Blakeley Street, Seattle, WA 98105), E-mail ccsi@u.washington.edu.

The most comprehensive Internet access to information regarding Russian and East European Areas Studies can be found at the REES Web site of the University of Pittsburgh (http://www.pitt.edu./~cjp/rees.html). The number of "doors" opened by this gateway is almost countless. Casey Palowitch provides background information on this source in "Russian and East European Information via the WWW: the REES Home Pages," *Database* 18 (Feb/Mar 1995): 46–53.

Several convenient general indexes for Web pages are available, for example, at http://altavista.digital.com and at http://www.hotbot.com. Using such indexes students can rapidly find information (of varying worth) on many Russian subjects. A convenient gateway to general history and humanities information is http://humanities.ucsb.edu.shuttle/history/html. The NetNews column (begun in September 1995) of *NewsNet: The Newsletter of the AAASS* (American Association for the Advancement of Slavic Studies) provides the latest information on electronic resources of concern to AAASS members. Additional print information relevant to Russian studies (and the Internet generally) can be found in Cathy Zeljack's "Introduction to the Internet," *Problems of Post-Communism* 43 (July-August 1996): 70–71.

Electronic information availability and processing continues to change rapidly. But Slavic librarians at major universities have given every indication that they are equal to the challenge of continuing to provide professors, students, and other librarians with up-to-date knowledge of such changes.

Acknowledgments

Chapters 8 and 10, pages 172, 217: V. I. Lenin, *Collected Works*. Reprinted by permission of Progress Publishing Group, Moscow.

Chapter 11, page 224: J. V. Stalin, *Works*, Vol. 13. Moscow: Foreign Languages Publishing, 1955.

Chapter 12, page 261: J. V. Stalin, *Leninism: Selected Writings*. New York: International Publishers, 1942. Reprinted by permission; *page 256:* J. V. Stalin, *Stalin's Letters to Molotov, 1925–1936*, ed. Oleg V. Naumov et al. Copyright 1995. Reprinted by permission of Yale University Press.

Chapter 13, page 273: Vasili Grossman, *The Years of War: 1941–1945*. Moscow: Foreign Languages Publishing, 1946.

Chapter 14, page 294: A Zhdanov, *The International Situation*. Moscow: Foreign Languages Publishing, 1947.

Chapter 15, page 320: Vasili Grossman, *The Years of War: 1941–1945*. Moscow: Foreign Languages Publishing, 1946.

Chapter 16, page 341: F. V. Gladkov, *Cement*, trans. A. S. Arthur and G. Ashleigh. New York: International Publishers, 1929. Reprinted by permission.

Chapter 17, page 355: Nikita Khrushchov, *Socialism and Communism: Selected Passages, 1956–1963*. Moscow: Foreign Languages Publishing, 1963.

Chapter 18, page 392: Natalia Gorbanevskaia, *A Chronicle of Current Events, No. 3 (August 30, 1968)*, ed. and trans. by Peter Reddaway in *Uncensored Russia: Protest and Dissent in the Soviet Union: The Unofficial Moscow Journal*. American Heritage Press, 1972. Reprinted by permission of Peter Reddaway, McLean, Virginia.

Chapter 19, page 418: Boris Yeltsin, *Against the Grain*. Copyright © 1990 by Boris Yeltsin. English translation copyright 1990 by Summit Books. Reprinted by permission of Simon & Schuster.

Chapter 20, page 454: Natalia Gorbanevskaia, *A Chronicle of Current Events, No. 3 (August 30, 1968)*, ed. and trans. by Peter Reddaway in *Uncensored Russia: Protest and Dissent in the Soviet Union: The Unofficial Moscow Journal*. American Heritage Press, 1972. Reprinted by permission of Peter Reddaway, McLean, Virginia.

Chapter 21: page 472: Vasili Belov, *That's How It Is*. Translated by Eve Manning in *Soviet Literature*, No. 1 (1969): 131. Published by Aktsionernoe Obshchestvo "Lepta Interneshnl." Moscow.

Chapter 22, page 490: Deborah Adelman, *The Children of Perestroika Come of Age: Young People of Moscow Talk about Life in the New Russia*. Reprinted by permission of M. E. Sharpe, Inc., Armonk, New York 10504.

Index

551